Women Writing Africa
THE EASTERN REGION

5-08

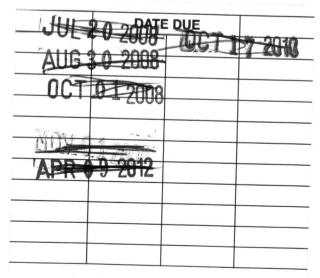

The Women Writing Africa Project

A Project of The Feminist Press at the City University of New York
Funded by the Ford Foundation and the Rockefeller Foundation

Women Writing Africa, a project of cultural reconstruction, aims to restore African women's voices to the public sphere. Through the publication of a series of regional anthologies, each collecting oral and written narratives as well as a variety of historical and literary texts, the project will make visible the oral and written literary expression of African women. The definition of "writing" has been broadened to include songs, praise poems, and significant oral texts, as well as fiction, poetry, letters, journals, journalism, and historical and legal documents. The project has been undertaken with the expectation that the publication of these texts will allow for new readings of African women's history.

PROJECT CO-DIRECTORS AND SERIES EDITORS

Tuzyline Jita Allan, Department of English, Baruch College, CUNY
Abena P. A. Busia, Department of Literatures in English, Rutgers University
Florence Howe, emerita, Department of English, The Graduate Center, CUNY, and publisher, The Feminist Press at CUNY

EXECUTIVE COMMITTEE

Anne Adams, Cornell University
Diedre L. Badejo, Kent State University
Ann Biersteker, Yale University
Debra Boyd, Winston-Salem State College
Judith Byfield, Dartmouth College
Frieda Ekotto, University of Michigan
Thomas A. Hale, Pennsylvania State University
Peter Hitchcock, Baruch College, CUNY

Nancy Rose Hunt, University of Michigan
Marjolijn de Jager, New York University
Eileen Julien, Indiana University
Judith Miller, New York University
Angelita D. Reyes, University of Minnesota
Joyce Hope Scott, Wheelock College
Marcia Wright, Columbia University
Louise Allen Zak, Marlboro College

BOARD OF ADVISORS

Jacqui Alexander, Barbados
Belinda Bozzoli, South Africa
Boutheina Cheriet, Algeria
Johnnetta B. Cole, United States
Carolyn Cooper, Jamaica
Fatoumata Sire Diakite, Mali
Nawal El Saadawi, Egypt
Aminata Sow Fall, Senegal
Wanguiwa Goro, Kenya
Asma Abdel Halim, Sudan
Charlayne Hunter-Gault, United States
Adama Ba Konaré, Mali
Joy Kwesiga, Uganda
Françoise Lionnet, United States
Marjorie Oludhe Macgoye, Kenya

Fatma Moussa, Egypt
Mbulelo Mzamane, South Africa
Lauretta Ngcobo, South Africa
Kimani Njogu, Kenya
Asenath Bole Odaga, Kenya
Mamphela Ramphele, South Africa
Sandra Richards, United States
Fatou Sow, Senegal
Filomena Steady, Sierra Leone
Margaret Strobel, United States
Susie Tharu, India
Nahid Toubia, Sudan
Ngugi wa Thiong'o, Kenya
Aminata Traore, Mali

◆

Volume 1: The Southern Region (Botswana, Lesotho, Namibia, South Africa, Swaziland, Zimbabwe)

Volume 2: West Africa and the Sahel (Benin, Burkina Faso, Côte d'Ivoire, Gambia, Ghana, Guinea-Conakry, Liberia, Mali, Niger, Nigeria, Senegal, Sierra Leone)

Volume 3: The Eastern Region (Kenya, Malawi, Tanzania, Uganda, Zambia)

Women Writing Africa

THE EASTERN REGION

The Women Writing Africa Project, Volume 3

Edited by Amandina Lihamba, Fulata L. Moyo,
M.M. Mulokozi, Naomi L. Shitemi, and Saïda Yahya-Othman

ASSOCIATE EDITORS: Austin Bukenya, Florence Ebila, Susan Kiguli
Edrinnie Lora-Kayambazinthu, Marjorie Oludhe Macgoye, Nalishebo N.
Meebelo, and Sheila Ali Ryanga

CONTRIBUTING EDITORS: Tuzyline Jita Allan and Ann Biersteker

TEXT EDITOR: Florence Howe

The Feminist Press at the City University of New York
New York

5-08 Amazon 22-

Published by The Feminist Press at the City University of New York
The Graduate Center, 365 Fifth Avenue, New York, NY 10016
www.feministpress.org

First edition, 2007

14 13 12 11 10 09 08 07   5 4 3 2 1

Library of Congress Cataloging-in-Publication Data

Women writing Africa. The eastern region (Kenya, Malawi, Tanzania, Uganda, Zambia) / edited by Amandina Lihamba ... [et al.]. -- 1st ed.
    p. cm. -- (The women writing Africa project ; v. 3)
   Includes bibliographical references and index.
   ISBN-13: 978-1-55861-534-2 (pbk. : alk. paper)
   ISBN-10: 1-55861-534-2 (pbk. : alk. paper)
   ISBN-13: 978-1-55861-535-9 (hard cover : alk. paper)
   ISBN-10: 1-55861-535-0 (hard cover : alk. paper)
  1. East African literature--Women authors. 2. East African literature--Women authors--Translations into English. 3. East African literature (English)--Women authors. 4. Folk literature, African. 5. Oral tradition--Africa, East. 6. Women--Africa, East--Literary collections. 7. Women--Africa, East--History--Sources. 8. Africa, East--Literary collections. 9. Africa, East--History--Sources. I. Lihamba, Amandina.
  PL8014.E22W66 2004
  809'.89287--dc22
                            2006036534

Publication of this volume is made possible, in part, by funds from the Ford Foundation and the Rockefeller Foundation.

Cover art: by Poni Yengi, Tanzania
Printed in Canada on acid-free paper by Transcontinental Printing

CONTENTS

The Mid-Twentieth Century (1936–1969)

LATE TWENTIETH CENTURY (1970–1995)

INTO THE TWENTY-FIRST CENTURY (1996–2004)

A NOTE ON THE WOMEN WRITING AFRICA PROJECT

The first conversation about this project took place when Tuzyline Jita Allan spoke with Florence Howe at the 1990 meeting of the Modern Language Association. Allan was responding to the recent publication by The Feminist Press of the first volume of *Women Writing in India: 600 B.C. to the Present*, edited by Susie Tharu and K. Lalita. Referring to this landmark publication as a striking example of the untapped potential of international feminist scholarship, Allan pointed to the need for a similar intervention in Africa. Both Allan and Howe knew that a project for Africa like one that the Press had begun for India could testify to the literary presence and historical activity of Africa nwomen. While Howe did not want to assume responsibility for such a project, she agreed to discuss it at a meeting of the Publications and Policies Committee of The Feminist Press held in February 1991. All present understood that so massive a project would need funding. Howe expected that the Africans interested in such a volume would prepare a grant application, organize the work, and, when it was ready for publication, offer it to The Feminist Press.

Later that year, when Howe was delivering the volume of *Women Writing in India* to the Ford Foundation to thank it for its small grant in support of that project, Alison Bernstein said, "Africa has to be next." A small group— Abena P. A. Busia, Chikwenye Ogunyemi, Peter Hitchcock, Allan, and Howe—met with Bernstein to discuss the possibility of and support for a planning meeting to follow the meeting of the African Literature Association (ALA) in Accra, Ghana, in April 1994. We are grateful to Johnnetta B. Cole, then president of Spelman College, who opened that meeting and testified to the need for such a project and to the commitment of The Feminist Press to publishing women's lost voices. Susie Tharu, who grew up in Uganda, Abena P. A. Busia, and Florence Howe also spoke with enthusiasm about the importance of such a project. They were joined by Margaret Busby and Bella Brodsky, who shared their experiences of editing individual volumes on women in Africa and around the world. In addition, some forty members of the ALA attended these two-day meetings, including Judith Miller, who has been an important member of the committtee for the West/Sahel region ever since.

Three primary considerations guided the preliminary discussions of the project. First, in spite of their overlapping agendas, Women Writing Africa could not be an exact replication of *Women Writing in India*. Africa's entrenched oral traditions called for a different response to the discursive modes of expression on the continent. To this end, reconceiving the notion of "writing" marked a conceptual breakthrough in determining how to name a project aimed at capturing African women's creative landscape. "Writing" in *Women Writing Africa* metonymically suggests a blend of verbal and written forms of expression embodying the experience of African women in envisioning their lives in relation to their societies. The project's matrix of spoken and scripted words represents the creative interaction between living women in the actual world and the flux of history: in short, African women "making" a world.

Women Writing Africa, therefore, became a project of cultural restoration that aims to restore African women's voices to the public sphere. We are publishing several volumes documenting the history of self-conscious expression by African women throughout the continent. This expression is both oral and written, ritual and quotidian, sacred and profane. We are as interested in dance songs and private letters as in legal depositions and public declamations. We hope to foster new readings of African history by shedding light on the dailiness of women's lives as well as their rich contributions to culture. In the end, seeing through women's eyes, we expect to locate the fault lines of memory and so change assumptions about the shaping of African knowledge, culture, and history.

A second consideration focused on the establishment of a framework for conducting research on the continent, and here two hard questions presented themselves: how to think of Africa regionally rather than nationally, and how to set up working groups in those regions and also in the United States. We originally projected five volumes, but conditions in the countries of central Africa led to the decision to produce four representative, rather than all-inclusive, volumes—from Southern Africa, from West Africa and the Sahel, from Eastern Africa, and from North Africa.

Following the Ghanaian planning conference, Abena P. A. Busia joined Allan and Howe as co-directors of the project. Together we formed an Executive Committee of U.S.-based Africanist scholars to serve as a resource and review board for the project's articulated goals, and an Advisory Committee of prominent scholars and writers in the field. Together we planned how to organize both regionally and nationally in the field: Allan would find the scholars in the Southern region; Busia would do the same in the West/Sahel region. For their help with this phase of the project, thanks are due to Debra Boyd and Joyce Hope Scott, who attended the Accra meeting and have continued to make contributions to the project. Then, with Africa-based colleagues, both Allan and Busia began the work of developing research teams in their assigned regions, first by locating national coordinators who would work as a team with their regional counterparts. Later, we proceeded in a somewhat similar manner in the East and the North.

The third consideration essential to realizing the project's promise was funding. The three co-directors wrote the first grant proposal to the Ford Foundation, and within two years, another to the Rockefeller Foundation. At Ford, we wish to acknowledge specifically the instigating interest of Alison Bernstein and the support of our several program officers—Janice Petrovitch, Margaret Wilkerson, Geraldine Fraser, and Irma McLauren. At Rockefeller, we wish to acknowledge the interest and support of Lynn Szwaja, our program officer.

We would like to thank both Lynn Szwaja and Morris Vogel for their support of the French editions of the Western/Sahel, the Southern, and the Eastern volumes. We are also grateful to the Rockefeller Foundation for five Team Awards to its Bellagio Study and Conference Center, where we worked with the editorial teams of the Western/Sahel and the Eastern volumes, and where we wrote drafts for this Note. We want to thank especially Susan Garfield for her administrative support, and Gianna Celli, the director of the Bellagio Center, for her continued interest in our work. The time spent in Bellagio was invaluable for editors and consultants, all of whom live in different countries and would not ordinarily have had an opportunity to work together on their volumes for an extended period of from two to four weeks.

Without the commitment of the staff and Board of Directors of The Feminist Press, we could not have done this work. Florence Howe wants to acknowledge the whole staff during the years 1997 to 2000, when she was the publisher/director of The Feminist Press, especially for their support during the weeks when she was holding meetings in Africa. In addition, she wants to acknowledge similar support during the years when she was again, publisher/director (2005) and then publisher (2006–2007).

In particular, and with respect to this volume, we want to acknowledge Cary Webb for her painstaking work seeking permissions; Jenny Kline for her detailed work on the bibliography; Jean Casella for her careful editorial work; and Hadassah Gold for her proofreading. In addition, we want to acknowledge assistant editor Anjoli Roy for her trafficking and detail work on the manuscript; and Cary Webb and Andrea Swalec for the Index. While Dayna Navaro designed the volume's cover and the series' interior, Lisa Force has creatively revised the design to suit the particular needs of this volume. We are grateful too for the work of publicist Franklin Dennis and the marketing strategies of Jeannette Petras, as well as Paul Pombo's careful attention to the myriad financial details of this project. We appreciate the continuing faith in this project of the Board of Directors of The Feminist Press, our new executive director, Gloria Jacobs, and, finally, we wish to express our thanks to friends and colleagues in the African Studies Association and the African Literature Association for their continuing interest and support.

Tuzyline Jita Allan would like to thank the friends, acquaintances, and strangers throughout Southern and Eastern Africa who became part of a great wave of kindness and support during her travels. Malcolm Hacksley, Paulette Coetzee, and other members of the National English Literary Museum (NELM) in Grahamstown were at once generous and efficient. She sincerely thanks the following individuals for dispensing generously the famed African hospitality: Nobantu Ratsebotsa, Leloba Molema, Austin Bukenya, Susan Kiguli, Sheila Meinjies, Fulata Moyo, Saïda Yahya-Othman, Naomi L. Shitemi, Sheila Ali Ryanga, Amandina Lihamba, Nalishebo N. Meebelo, and Jane Bennett, former director of the Gender Institute at Cape Town University. Allan also acknowledges the important contributions of Carol Sicherman, who traveled with her to East Africa in 1999 to set up the project and to help recruit scholars in the region, and Adam Ashforth, whose intimate knowledge of South Africa proved invaluable. She is also grateful for the expertise of Nobantu Rasebotsa, the former regional coordinator of the Southern volume, who traveled with her to Nairobi in January 2001, for another round of strategy sessions with the Eastern team. She thanks Chikwenye Okonjo Ogunyemi,

Jane Marcus, and Rashida Ismaili for their intellectual and moral support, and she is especially grateful to Hawa Allan, who used the periods of her mother's absence to develop her own intellect and creativity. Allan and Busia wish to thank Irene Asseba D'Almeida, Carol Boyce Davies, Peter Hitchcock, Nancy Rose Hunt, Brenda Berrian, Ketu Katrak, Angelita Reyes, and Mete Shayne for their wisdom and sincere interest in the project. Both Allan and Howe would like to thank the Zimbabwe Women Writers and the organizers of the Zimbabwe Book Fair for their enthusiastic embrace of the project. And all three owe a debt of gratitude to Delia Friedman for her diligence and professionalism in handling travel plans for scores of women from all corners of the globe to attend our regional meetings through the years.

Abena Busia wishes to acknowledge the support of the Department of English at Rutgers University, especially chairpersons Barry Qualls, Cheryl A. Wall, and Richard Miller for flexible teaching schedules that allowed for extensive travel in Africa. In addition, she is grateful for the support of several Rutgers University graduate students, past and present: Carol Allen, Ronald Tyson, Kimberly Banks, Shalene Moodie, and Nia Tuckson, for assistance of various kinds through the years, including teaching and monitoring classes during her absences for editorial board meetings, some of which they also helped plan. Special thanks also go to Krista Johnson and Jessica Fredston-Herman for their particular and timely contributions, their planning and research assistance. Finally, a debt of gratitude is owed to Anita Ake, her personal assistant since 2003, for her exemplary equanimity in the face of chaos.

Florence Howe would like to thank Feminist Press Board members, Helene D. Goldfarb, Mariam K. Chamberlain, Judith Miller, and Shirley L. Mow for their extraordinary support of her work. She would also like to thank Marcia Wright, Marjorie Oludhe Macgoye, and Emilia Ilieva, for their special contributions to the Eastern volume.

And the entire project will be grateful forever for the exemplary translations into French of each of these volumes by Christiane Owusu-Sarpong. The French versions of these volumes are being published by Éditions Karthala Press in Paris. Finally, a brief word about the final volume to come: The Northern volume, focused on Algeria, Egypt, Mauritania, Morocco, the Sudan, and Tunisia, will be published in mid-2008.

We are aware that Women Writing Africa represents the largest undertaking of our lives, a responsibility to set the reality of African women's lives in history and in the present before a world that is only just waking up to their importance. It is our continuing hope that these volumes will give birth to hundreds of others.

Tuzyline Jita Allan
Abena P. A. Busia
Florence Howe
Series Editors and Project Co-Directors

PREFACE

This volume, the third in the Women Writing Africa series, contains a selection of works created by women in Eastern Africa during the last three hundred years. The earliest written piece dates from 1711, and the latest from 2003.(2004!) Obviously women's creativity goes still further back in time, though much of the creativity before 1711 must have been oral, perhaps absorbed into later creative productions, as usually happens with oral arts. The editors of this volume believe that the texts offered here represent fairly if not exhaustively both oral and written genres: songs, poetry, tales, anecdotes, speeches, letters, biographies, and reminiscences.

The texts in the collection come from five countries, namely, Kenya, Malawi, Uganda, Tanzania, and Zambia. This designation of an Eastern Region is an ad hoc identification of the countries, determined by the editorial team, as a cooperative community rather than a geopolitical entity. Granted that the five countries, Kenya, Malawi, Tanzania, Uganda, and Zambia, are contiguous with one another, two of them having littoral eastern boundaries on the Indian Ocean, the five can claim neither a monopoly of being East African nor of being exclusively and unchallengeably "eastern."

While Kenya, Tanzania, and Uganda are traditionally recognized as East Africa, Eastern Africa may, according to the context, include countries as far apart as Burundi, Eritrea, Ethiopia, Mauritius, and Mozambique. At one stage in the development of the present volume, the editors seriously considered including writings from Mozambique, a good intention eventually abandoned for logistic reasons. On the other hand, any of the countries represented here may, on occasion, identify itself differently from the Eastern African entity. Thus, Malawi, Tanzania, and Zambia are members of the Southern African Development Community (SADC), along with most of the countries in the recognizably southern geographical section of the continent. In our case, our self-definition was based mainly on our readiness and willingness to work together on the enterprise when it was introduced to us by Tuzyline Jita Allan and Carol Sicherman in 1999.

Nevertheless, the grouping is not arbitrary. Indeed, one of the joys of working together on the project was the discovery of the numerous similarities among our communities. All the five countries, for example, had shared the same colonial experience of British rule, and had become independent in the early 1960s. British colonialism had bequeathed to us, perhaps inadvertently, the common transnational language, English, in which some of the texts in the volume were originally written, and into which texts from other languages were translated. Up north, in Kenya, Tanzania, and, to a certain extent, Uganda, we had another common language, Kiswahili, which was also a rich source of texts for our work, and served as a major tool of both socialization and discussion during our meetings.

But even in the multilingualism beneath the lingua franca, we discovered a reassuring element of manageability across the region. While it might be bewildering to find that our region claims a richness of over 300 languages, the project became clearer when we began to see these in clear family groups across the countries. The widest variety of languages appeared in Kenya, Tanzania, and Uganda, where the groups ranged from the Sudanic through the Nilotic to the Cushitic and Bantu. The Bantu group is the most widespread in the region and covers all of Malawi and Zambia, and most of Tanzania, except for a few areas in the central and northern regions. It comprises such languages as Luluhya from Kenya; Chichewa from Malawi and Zambia; Chibemba also from Zambia; Luganda from Uganda; and of course, Kiswahili.

What struck us even more deeply were the similarities and comparabilities of women's experiences as captured by the voices collected for the volume. Such similarities may be heard not only in the period after the imposition of colonial hegemony, but also long before the colonial period, probably because of the similar structures of the societies in our communities. Economically, for example, all our societies seemed to be divided into four main categories: the agriculturalists, the pastoralists, the fishers, and, along the coast, the traders. The uttered word in all its forms dominated day-to-day interactions. In political and administrative organization, most societies observed strict hierarchies based either on hereditary dynasties or on age-group gradations.

Most relevant to our project, nearly all the societies in the region were, and remain, manifestly patriarchal. It is true that some communities, including several in Malawi, southern Tanzania, and along the east African coast, including some of the Waswahili (Mnyampala and Chiragdin), are nominally matrilineal. But even in such societies, the dominance of male ideologies, practices, and attitudes, inherently disadvantage women. Indeed, this ubiquitous dominance of male supremacy and women's determined struggle against it became the guiding principle in the choice of the texts in this collection.

The reader will note from the texts themselves, the accompanying headnotes, and several comments in the Introduction, that almost every text in the collection contains an element of Eastern African women's fight for survival: the power to be, to do, and to grow in the face of a hostile environment created mainly by patriarchal impositions. The search for empowerment may be expressed in different ways, such as woman-to-woman solidarity and advice, self-criticism, storytelling, questioning, petitions, protests, confrontation, or outright rebellion. But the underlying essence is still strategizing, mobilizing, and, eventually, liberating action. Many of the authors herein may not be self-proclaimed feminists. But their objective experiences as women battling with the realities of existence in prescribed and "proscribed" or prohibitive communities often engender their desire and determination to transform their lives and those of other women and ultimately of all humanity. The creation of the expressive texts, like the samples presented here, is itself part of that empowering action. For, indeed, silence has been one of the most powerful tools of subjugation of African women.

Women's emancipatory struggle can also be seen in a wider sociohistorical context. Women's creativity is informed, regulated, and nurtured by economic and sociohistorical factors. Communities exist and operate in specific social formations, be they peasant, pastoral, hunter-gatherer, or capitalist. Culture and the functions of production and reproduction tend to conform to such basic structures. Depending on their needs, communities tend to relegate certain tasks—economic, biological, artistic—either to men or women. The social institutions that have evolved over time, including the institution of marriage in its various forms, the extended family, and the rites of passage pertaining to the various stages of a person's life—i.e., birth, initiation, marriage, menopause, death—also tend to reinforce such arrangements.

Using the two criteria of women's emancipation and sociohistorical significance, the editors selected texts rich in fine aesthetic qualities. While the texts cut across a host of genres, linguistic and literary traditions, geographical areas, historical periods, and thematic concerns, the editors admit that they often felt they were tightrope walking through the selection process. In the end, apart from ensuring a fair representation of the participating countries, which itself depended on the materials received from the field, the final selection of the pieces was as intuitive as it was interpretative.

As we attempt to describe briefly the procedure we followed in putting this volume together, we must remark that we are ourselves a little surprised that the work on this volume has lasted considerably more than the proverbial seven years! Indeed, by the time this volume reaches the reader it will have been a little more than ten years since we embarked on the project.

The process began in 1996, with exploratory contacts between two of the directors of the project, Tuzyline Jita Allan and Florence Howe, and several scholars from Eastern African countries. The meeting held in Cape Town that year marked an important breakthrough for both the Southern and Eastern Volumes. Tuzyline Jita Allan and Abena Busia discussed the projects goals and benchmarks with leading scholars in the field, including Amandina Lihamba, who was representing the Eastern region. In 1999, Tuzyline Jita Allan and Carol Sicherman led a full-scale effort to organize national committees in Kampala, Dar es Salaam, and Nairobi to begin the critical work of collecting texts. To the meeting in Nairobi, Allan and Sicherman also invited scholars from Malawi and Zambia. From this group of historical meetings grew the national working committees, which undertook the bulk of the work.

The various National Committees and volunteers comprised the following members:

Kenya: J.W. Arthur, Fran Etemese, Wangari Gibenye, Emilia Ilieva, Marjorie Oludhe Macgoye, Clara Momanyi, Barrack O. Muluka, Murende Mutari, Milton Obote, Sheila Ali Ryanga, Naomi L. Shitemi, Fugich Wako, and Ali Wasi.

Malawi: L. Binauli, D. Chirwa, Vera Chirwa, H. Chunga, M. Gulule, Edrinnie Lora-Kayambazinthu, Bright Molande, Fulata L. Moyo, Hendrina Msosa, Anthony Nazonche, Desmond D. Phiri, and Boston Soko.

Tanzania: Fatma Alloo, Daudi Kweba, Amandina Lihamba, M.M. Mulokozi, Rehema J. Nchimbi, Martha Qorro, Edda Sanga, Kapepwa A. Tambila, and Saïda Yahya-Othman.

Uganda: Syed A.H. Abidi, Robina Asiimwe, Jackee Batanda, Okot Benge, Austin Bukenya, Florence Ebila, Charlotte Karungi, Jane Kawalya, Mildred Kiconco, Susan Kiguli, Abasi Kiyimba, Beatrice Lamwaka, David Rubadiri Mbowa, Hilda Ntege Mukisa, Beverley Nambozo, Sarah Namulondo, Monica Arach de Nyeko, Ernest Okello Ogwang, Celestino Orikiriza, Eunice N.N. Sendikadiwa, Sylvia Tamale, and Ayeta Anne Wangusa.

Zambia: Nalishebo N. Meebelo, Mbuyu Nalumango, Mondo Sifuniso, and Maseko E. Boston.

A characteristic feature of our national-working committees was that they included men. In consonance with our philosophy of gender empowerment, it was agreed from the start that our brothers who believed in and were committed to feminist causes and to the enabling of African women's voices would be invited and encouraged to participate in the venture. Thus it was that several brothers, including Abasi Kiyimba, Austin Bukenya, and David Rubadiri Mbowa from Uganda, and M.M. Mulokozi and Kapepwa Tambila from Tanzania, were involved in the project from the development of the idea through the collection and selection of materials to the final editorial work. All of them not only appreciated the generous invitation of their sisters to join the project, but also hailed it as a uniquely enlightening learning experience and enhancement of their insight into African women's concerns.

The committees themselves were supervised by two coordinators in most countries. Naomi L. Shitemi and Sheila Ali Ryanga oversaw the Kenyan committee, Susan Kiguli and Florence Ebila the Ugandan committee, while Saïda Yahya-Othman and Amandina Lihamba took charge in Tanzania. Malawi was led by Fulata L. Moyo and Edrinnie Lora-Kayambazinthu, and Nalishebo N. Mebeelo chaired Zambia. The coordinators eventually worked also as the countries' chief representatives at various selection and editorial meetings, although other members of committees were frequently asked to contribute to these activities.

This was often a necessity. Even the idea of having two national coordinators, which we had taken for granted at the inception of the exercise, turned out to be a particularly prudent step, primarily because of the extremely taxing schedules of most of the participants in the project. The Kenyan, Tanzanian, and Malawian coordinators, for example, were all senior academics with heavy teaching and administrative commitments in their universities as well as a host of international obligations. The Ugandans were also academics and in established teaching positions. But the main demand on these two women was either to complete or to embark on their doctoral programs. In the end, the operation depended largely on an endless juggling of schedules and negotiating with colleagues to ensure that work on the project continued while our family, career, and professional demands were also met.

Thus Susan Kiguli, working on her PhD in Leeds, England, had to leave the Ugandan coordination to Florence Ebila, who patiently waited for her to come home before embarking on her own program at Madison, Wisconsin. Nalishebo N. Meebelo, too, set out on her doctoral research, in Australia, about halfway through the project. But the Malawian coordinating team faced the greatest operational challenge when Edrinnie Lora-Kayambazinthu, who had remained on the ground while Fulata L. Moyo was on a study program in South Africa, was involved in a tragic road accident that not only robbed her of a sister but also left her incapacitated for a very long time. Our entire editorial team wishes to salute and acknowledge Edrinnie not only for her sisterly company and her vigorous contribution to the project but also, and especially, for the heroic courage with which she faced her tribulations. An enduring inspiration to all of us, Edrinnie is an icon of the unbending bravery of Eastern African women.

Once the national committees had been set up, the task of collecting material for the project began. The search took the participants to all areas of the region, including remote villages and towns in the depths of the countryside; refugee and displaced persons' camps, like those in northern Uganda; personal, institutional, and governmental archives; and the libraries of several universities. The collectors paid particular attention to oral texts, as reflected in the corpus presented in this collection. The collectors were impressed with both the richness and variety of texts available in the field and by the generosity of people willing to share them. To all our field and archival informants, including our many students, and in Tanzania, Shani A. Kitogo, Joshua Madumulla, and The Tanzania Writers Association (UWAVITA), we are deeply grateful.

Even as we proceeded with collecting, the national committees met periodically to review and assess the variety and quality of texts collected. Provisional and preliminary selections of publishable texts were made at these meetings, using the general guidelines suggested by the project directors for The Feminist Press, but also refining and adapting these to the specific evaluation of the texts in hand. Meantime, Florence Howe and Tuzyline Jita Allan advised and facilitated a series of regional meetings at which the participants shared experiences and jointly assessed the texts collected from each country.

The first text selection meeting was held in Nairobi in May 2000; the second meeting, at the Sun 'n' Sand Holiday Resort at Mangochi in Malawi in September 2000. The third meeting took place at Entebbe, Uganda, in April 2001; and the final regional meeting was held in Dar es Salaam in April 2002. Tuzyline Jita Allan and Florence Howe participated in the Nairobi, Entebbe, and

Dar es Salaam meetings. They brought with them their experience from the Southern and Western volumes, and generally guided the meetings to fruitful results. Allan was particularly helpful in elaborating the vision and goals of the whole project, guiding and grounding the discussions in an Afro-feminist theoretical and ideological framework in line with the vision. The Malawi meeting, though not attended by the two directors, benefited from the attendance of the venerable Malawian human rights activist, Vera Chirwa.

An indication of the deep interest that the texts in the collection might arouse was given in July 2002, in Kampala, Uganda, when four members from the national teams made presentations at the Women's World Congress.

Indeed, almost imperceptibly, we were making steady progress from merely looking at what had been collected to determining its suitability and to considering the emerging patterns among all the texts from the various countries and finally to determining the best candidates for inclusion in the volume and considering the editorial work to be done on them. Thus, by the time we met in Dar es Salaam in April 2002, we were ready for the advice of a literary and linguistic expert, Ann Biersteker, from Yale University.

Regional meetings were followed by residential retreats at Bellagio in Italy, generously funded by the Rockefeller Foundation. The first retreat took place from 12 August to 4 September 2003, the second from 1 to 14 June 2004. These meetings enabled the editors to complete the selection of the texts, edit the headnotes, and draft the Introduction. Tuzyline Jita Allan, Florence Howe, and Ann Biersteker were always available during these meetings, critiquing the writing and deliberations of the team, and assisting with translations.

Late in 2004, the editors held one final residential session, this time back home in Eastern Africa, to review all and to edit, harmonize, expand, and complete the headnotes and to work further on the Introduction. This meeting was arranged by Saïda Yahya-Othman on the famed Zanzibar Island in late November 2004, thus incidentally ensuring that we had enjoyed a physical experience on the land of each cultural source of our texts, except Zambia. After Zanzibar, we turned the manuscript over to The Feminist Press for editing, design, and production, although it was understood that intensive consultations would continue both among ourselves and with the publishers.

The publishers did very well on this part of the understanding, especially Florence Howe, despite the extra responsibilities placed on her by her recall to head the Press. The volume editors and their associates, however, did not find it easy to meet the deadlines. Returning to our usual work and study places had the usual effect of lessening our concentration on the work of the volume and some of the crucial parts of the material, like this Preface, took much longer than we had expected to put in final form. Only the patience and diligence of our publisher have ensured that this work will appear as scheduled. For this we are profoundly grateful.

This brings us to the debts of gratitude that we owe to a host of individuals and institutions that have contributed to the realization of this volume.

Production was a long, elaborate, complex, and expensive process which could never have succeeded without the devotion, cooperation, and generosity of whole communities of well-wishers who believed in its potential value. We are deeply grateful to all of them, and we regret that we cannot mention all of them by name. Let the ones we single out here be regarded as representatives of all those who contributed in one way or another. Though formally acknowledged at appropriate points in the text, the sisters who contributed the texts in the volume take pride of place. As the project's directors, Florence Howe, Abena P.A. Busia, and Tuzyline Jita Allan initiated the Women Writing Africa project, fundraised for it, and created the theoretical framework that brought it into full flowering. Over and above that, Florence Howe and Tuzyline Jita Allan showered us with truly sisterly love, taking valuable time off their schedules to be and to work with us at every important stage of the undertaking.

We cannot overstate the importance of The Feminist Press for its administration of this project as well as its editing, designing, and production of the volumes. We are grateful to the invaluable work of particular staff and consultants: Jean Casella for her editorial work on the manuscript; Hadassah Gold for proofreading; Anjoli Roy for trafficking work; Andrea Swalec for indexing; Cary Webb for permissions and indexing; Lisa Force for design, typesetting, and production; Franklin Dennis for publicity; and Jeannette Petras for marketing. The cumulative force of talent and passion at The Feminist Press helped to sustain us throughout this project.

The sponsors and funders of the project, the Ford Foundation and especially the Rockefeller Foundation, deserve our profound thanks. We reiterate our appreciation of the hospitality of the staff of the Rockefeller Study and Conference Center in Bellagio, Italy, among whom we must mention Gianna Celli. Most important, our colleagues on the national committees did the initial work of identifying, collecting, translating, and annotating the huge bulk of texts from which the selections published here were made. Their research was often also the basis for headnotes to the selections. Finally, we acknowledge the inspiration we received from our sisters in the Southern and Western African and Sahel regions, whose volumes appeared before ours.

For us, working on these texts has been a tremendously moving and satisfying learning experience. We gained not only insight into the challenges, struggles, trials, and triumphs of our sisters over the centuries but also a deep respect for their courage, resilience, and human pride. If the readers of this volume can share some of these with us, our labors will have been richly rewarded.

Austin Bukenya

INTRODUCTION

In the written history of Eastern Africa, produced mostly by men, we read about a great many male leaders. We learn of the clan headmen who led their people into the areas they occupy today: for example, the warlords, headed by Zwangendaba, who led the Ngoni from South Africa to Malawi and Tanzania. We encounter the great male empire builders of the nineteenth century: the Mirambos and the Tippu Tips of Tanzania, the Mutesas of Uganda and the Kalonga of Malawi (Maravi). We are reminded of the heroic fighters who resisted colonialism: Abushiri, Mukwawa, Meli, and Kinjikitile in Tanzania; Mwanga and Kabarega in Uganda; Waiyaki wa Hinga and Mbaruk bin Rashid in Kenya; Maluma and John Chilembwe in Malawi.

In contrast, we rarely hear about the women resistance fighters who led the grassroots movements against the colonialists: Nehanda in Zimbabwe, Mekatilili wa Menza and Siotune in Kenya, and Muhumusa of the Nyabingi cult in Rwanda and Uganda. In fact, the movements led by such women were more successful and more abiding than the largely military and short-lived struggles waged by men. We know, for instance, that the Maji Maji uprising in Tanzania (1905–1907) against German rule would not have spread so quickly and with so much strength without the participation of women, who fed the men and cared for the children, the wounded, and the elderly while the men were working on German plantations or out fighting in the bush. Indeed, Mkomanire, a Ngoni woman who was influential in the Maji Maji war, was greatly feared by the Germans. Mobilizing the Ngoni people to participate in that war, she was instrumental in extending its duration to 1907, and she was hanged by the Germans along with the male Maji Maji leaders (Bates 1957: 11).

On the other hand, the oral traditions, the myths, and legends told by women themselves often place women where they belong: at the center of the historical and legendary origins of their civilizations, and at the heart of their peoples' struggles. It is impossible to conceive of Baganda origins without mentioning Nambi, the mythical founding mother and partner of Kintu, the founding father. The Gikuyu of Kenya find their origins in Mumbi (literally, "Creator" or "Molder"), from whom come the nine Gikuyu matrilineal clans (Kenyatta 1938). In the language of the Maasai people, the words for all the most important things in life are female.

This anthology attempts to correct distortions characteristic of Eastern African historiography and anthologizing. More than corrective, however, the anthology also celebrates women's achievements, voices, and concerns. Our focus is on women's work and thought, through which women may be seen not as passive or barely visible entities, but as articulate and talented producers of art and knowledge, and as heroic makers of history.

Not surprisingly, the project must be viewed as complexly heterogeneous, containing as it does a myriad of women's voices spanning historical time, geographical space, and a variety of literary genres, and drawn from 29 different languages, all from five countries. The heterogeneity of the anthology, in fact, contributes greatly to its wealth and its uniqueness. Chronologically, the texts traverse more than three centuries. Geographically, they have been harvested from an area covering nearly 9 percent of the continent, with a population of almost 114 million. The ideas, views, and creative techniques of eighteenth-century Swahili women are bound to be different from those of early-twentieth-century Malawi women or late-twentieth-century Ugandan women. The traditional Muslim advice offered by Mwana Kupona binti Msham (1858), urging her daughter to observe Islamic etiquette and not to associate with slaves, contrasts powerfully with the slave narratives of Bwanikwa (1895) and Mama Meli (1950s), as well as with the resolute feminism of Miria Matembe of Uganda (2002) and Wangari Maathai of Kenya (2004). Yet all these texts represent some aspect of the evolution of women's consciousness—we would argue, feminist consciousness—in Eastern Africa.

These multicultural and multilingual texts are also distinguished by their modes of expression and delivery. From the coast, we have written texts dating from the eighteenth and nineteenth centuries and employing the literary resources and genres already well-established in Swahili culture by that time. Both Sultan Fatima (1711) and Mwana Kupona (1858) are working within a tradition that evolved partly from the oral tradition, but in time established itself as a written Islamic tradition. On the other hand, we also have many texts that are purely oral and have been passed on, probably for centuries, by word of mouth. Often, however, we find links among these apparently distinct forms. Twentieth-century writers, speakers, and singers, in the various African languages and in English, draw on both oral traditions and classical Swahili traditions, even while they address more current issues. Thus, the power of speeches by Malawi's Chauwa Banda (1936) and Tanzania's Bibi Titi Mohamed (1965) derives from oral diction. Pelagia Aloyse Katunzi of Tanzania, though writing in the year 2000, employs Swahili poetics of the nineteenth century, as do such taarab singers as Siti binti Saad (1920s).

While different modes of expression and delivery dictate the nature and techniques of composition, most of the texts in this collection are united by their concern for the welfare of women. This feminist strand—sometimes appearing in a subtle, tactful, or subversive manner, sometimes more open, forceful, and unapologetically militant—unites the authors and texts in this volume. The writers and speakers address most of the important issues relating to the condition of women in Eastern Africa and in the world generally. Prominent among these is the question of gender relations within the home and within the community, culture, and nation. The subject of Mwana Kupona binti Msham's "A Mother's Advice and Prayer" (1858) is essentially marital gender relations in a nineteenth-century Islamic society: how a woman can survive, have her way, and even control her husband, while appearing to be subservient to him. The same issues come up again almost seventy years later in Zeina binti

Mwinyipembe Sekinyaga's "Civilized Motherhood" (1926), in which equality in marriage is more candidly demanded. Many years later, Monde Sifuniso's clever story "Beijing, Beijing" (1997) deals with domestic gender relations in a contemporary and explicitly feminist context.

Women are also concerned about how girl-children may be educated to fit into—or resist—their societies, and to succeed in life. Many of the volume's folktales, such as "When Ogres Lived" (1936) as well as songs such as "Birds Will Mourn Her" (1956), are cautionary, intended to guide girl-children to escape the dangers lurking in their way. At the same time, many personal testimonies, such as "I Want School, Not Marriage" (2001), along with numerous political speeches and statements, attest to the importance women have placed on more formal education for girl-children.

Beyond the conventional "women's issues" of home and family, many of the authors in this volume argue for the economic empowerment of women. They deplore the exploitation of women by men in the homestead ("Fighting for a Widow's Rights," 1947) and in the workplace ("Elizabeth," 1966, and "A Bar-Maid's Life," 1980), as well as by colonial settlers ("Song of the Coffee Girls," 1922). They also offer success stories from women who became economically independent by organizing projects with and for other women ("A Courageous Woman," 2000).

The women in this volume address large social, national, and international issues, including religion, race and racism, national identity, slavery, colonialism and the anticolonial struggles, nation-building after independence, pan-Africanism, HIV/AIDS, the environment, and globalization. They view these issues through prisms of time and place, of culture and race, offering a rich array of perspectives. The traditional religious perspective found in Ester Nakate's "Nakayima and the Wonder Tree" (1995) and many of the oral texts stand in contrast to the Islamic perspective of Mwana Kupona and others, and also to the Christian devotion found in Martha Thabi's "My God, Why Have You Forsaken Me?" (1890) and in the works of various missionaries and missionary converts. At times, the conflict between the various perspectives serves as the subject of a piece, as in "Letter Opposing Female Circumcision" (1931), which questions, from a Christian point of view, a well-established traditional custom among the Gikuyu of Kenya.

These conflicting and contradictory perspectives live side-by-side in the volume, complementing and enriching one another, just as they do in the life of the region.

The Eastern African coast was, from ancient times, a melting pot for people of many cultures and races, who arrived on the coast from the Middle East, the Far East, Europe, and the African hinterland. Some of these peoples came as visitors, others as conquerors. The inevitable result was an intermingling of cultures, languages, and races, and also the emergence of a racial divide and often outright racism.

Some of the earliest texts in the volume, including "A Royal Childhood in

Zanzibar" (1886), view the enslavement of black Africans from the perspective of the Arab ruling class of the time, while Bwanikwa's "Ten Times a Slave" (1895) tells the other side of the story. The racial dynamics arising from modern European colonialism—which in Eastern Africa involved the British and Germans—are captured in many of the texts, including several by British missionaries like Jane Elizabeth Chadwick and Eva Chadwick (1920, 1935) and settler women like Nellie Grant (1939–1963). African women, along with men, resisted colonialism in various ways. This resistance is captured in Hannah Tsuma's account of Mekatilili (2000), the coastal Kenyan woman who led the Giriama resistance against the British for several years. The anticolonial resistance waged in Tanzania, Uganda, and Malawi yielded no similar written texts, though we know that women did participate fully and heroically in those struggles, as well.

Early resistance efforts would evolve into struggles for African identity and political rights, which in turn would merge into the main nationalist movements—the battles for independence. After independence, the major political theme was nation-building, and women such as Bibi Titi Mohamed (1965) and Babro Johannsen (1964, 1965) in Tanzania, Sarah Nyendohwa Ntiro (1999) in Uganda, and Rose Chibambo (1964) in Malawi made contributions—both in and outside of Parliament. The vision of these women moved toward pan-African liberation and unity. Thus Bibi Titi Mohamed was concerned not only about Tanzania, but also about South Africa, then under apartheid, and about Vietnam, then the site of a U.S. war of imperialism.

In the last three decades, Eastern African women have written, spoken, and sung about the scourge of HIV/AIDS, which has devastated their families and communities; this volume includes speeches, stories, poems, and orature on the effects of the pandemic. Globalization and environmental destruction have also demanded attention from such concerned women thinkers and leaders as Wangari Maathai, who links environmental issues to struggles for good governance, democracy, social justice, and human rights, and insists that they disproportionately burden Africa's women.

This Introduction is organized into three roughly chronological sections. The first section focuses on the pre-colonial period, and addresses issues of women's creativity, both oral and written, in the contexts of education, religion, and slavery. The second section considers the colonial period, from the time of early occupation and resistance, to the period of foreign consolidation in the thirties and forties, and then to the nationalist awakening that led to independence. Included in this section are developments in the production of orature and written literature, including the rise of book publishing and the media. The final section treats the post-independence period, its dominant themes and preoccupations: nation-building, cultural struggles and the search for identity, civil wars and other conflicts, parliamentary struggles, and pan-Africanism. The section ends by focusing on globalization, governance, and the environment, and the future of women in the twenty-first century.

THE PRECOLONIAL PERIOD

Women Teaching Women: The Power of the Living Word

With the coming of independence in the 1960s, most African governments declared, as one of their main objectives, the elimination of "ignorance" from among their peoples. By this, they meant teaching their people to read and write, which in turn meant establishing schools of the Western type. Written literacy was in itself a highly worthy goal. By posing their objective in this way, however, the new African governments echoed their former colonial rulers in dismissing the oral literacy that had long existed in Africa, and was practiced with particular richness, variety, and sophistication by the continent's women.

Through the centuries, beginning long before the advent of missionaries and colonialism, women in Eastern Africa created, adapted, and transmitted oral literature. In large part, this literature was a tool for learning, remembering, and passing on a large body of community wisdom. Such wisdom, passed down through generations, has helped women meet the challenges threatening their communities and resist onslaughts from outsiders. Even under that most invasive of all attacks, slavery, they held their ground and persevered until freedom came. It has also helped them resist, subvert, or endure oppression within their communities, although at times the patriarchal social order forced them to incorporate practices that maintained the subjugation of other women (Chieni and Spencer 1993: 161; Phiri 2000a: 40). The fact that knowledge was passed on orally did not mean that it lacked depth or complexity. Within the clan or village, there were those who specialized in specific areas of what is now referred to as "indigenous knowledge." Knowledge about methods of farming, hunting, and preserving food; of producing cloth, leather, and iron tools; of preparing medicines, treating various diseases, and helping women through childbirth—all were transmitted through practice and observation, within an apprenticeship system (Shorter 1974: 78), and many were reflected in orature. Thus there emerged families within each clan that, through generations, trained other family members in specific skills and crafts, so that the community never lacked artisans and craftspeople of various kinds. In precolonial times, most education in Eastern Africa was home- or work-based, and depended on the resources that the family could muster.[1] It related directly to the daily activities of the young people, equipping them with the skills and knowledge to deal with their environment. Women were not solely responsible for education; they were assisted, in a seamless process, by others in the community—fathers, uncles, brothers, and elders. Each occupied a unique niche, preparing children for different facets of adulthood. Knowledge was imparted on a daily basis, as children confronted new situations. They learned both informally through observation and doing, but also formally through instruction, ritual, and stories (Shorter 1974: 77). Nonetheless, the gender-based divisions of labor placed women as central especially to the education of female children.

In "When We Say" (2001) women's singing uses proverbs to teach children basic rules of proper and ethical behavior:

When we say
A person who heeds not
Goes with feces into her mother-in-law's hut,
We mean
You need to hear others and they need to hear you.

When we say
Being near the anthill
Made the fox turn brown,
We mean
You reap what you sow.

These "socialization" processes—which like all such processes hold survival as their ultimate goal—have sometimes been romanticized. Nonetheless, it is a fact that there are still self-sustaining communities in Africa that have never seen a formal classroom, and yet their members have been "trained" to deal adequately with their environment (Shorter 1974: 75). Because much social interaction took place within ethnic groups, education was naturally conducted in the language or dialect of the group. Bilingualism was common where different ethnic groups shared borders, and among certain groups such as women who were traders.

In this context, orality was of overwhelming importance, and those who became deeply versed in a language became composers of the community's songs, dirges, poems, and jokes. Even as they address practical matters, women's oral works are important social and cultural documents. Lessons in ethnic or family history were conducted through story- and myth-telling. From them, a young girl learned the traditions and taboos of her society; as a mother, she passed these on to her children; and as an elder, she continued to instruct younger women, and became a source for the history of her people. At the same time, these oral works express individual and collective feeling, finding much of their inspiration in the joys and sorrows of a woman's life. Through song, poetry, and dance, women express jubilation, desire, and tenderness, and give vent to anger and anguish through defiant satires and mournful laments.

The creative aspect of women's orature is largely inseparable from its instructional function, but no less rich for that fact. Women have created songs, sayings, stories, and legends, which they have shared with other women and passed down to future generations. These oral works are also dynamic, changing significantly in form and content over time in an ongoing creative process.

Orature is *performed* rather than simply *spoken*, the message contained in the music, the tone, the gestures, and the actions as well as in the words. Women sing lullabies while cuddling and soothing babies, and they sing work songs while pounding grain. Reducing such creations to paper obviously flattens them somewhat. Yet even as written text, women's orature reveals power, beauty, and intelligence as well as useful advice and information.

A great deal of women's orature, including several of the pieces collected in this book, concerned initiation—in Kiswahili, *unyago*. Initiations provided an opportunity for children to learn about the tasks and challenges they would face in the future, when they became responsible for their communities, and ensured culture's passage from one generation to another. The educational rituals that made up the initiation depended entirely on oral, visual, and theatrical modes.

The initiation ceremony is generally a major event for a young girl, involving seclusion, instruction, singing, dancing, and pampering. For instance, the Taveta in Kenya undertake an elaborate process of beautifying the girl initiate, bedecking her in ornate bead jewelry and a decorated goatskin wrapper. The Maasai initiate in Tanzania and Kenya is secluded and regaled with meat and other rich foods (Makumbusho ya Taifa 1998: 62). Among the Chagga of Tanzania, parents go to great lengths to ensure that their daughter has all the necessary ornaments and decorations. She is also fed with the choicest food for up to six months following the initiation. The ceremony is preceded by all day dancing of the *kipora*.

This momentous event for a girl often includes not only pampering but also great physical pain, when it culminates in circumcision. Among the Chagga, for example, circumcision is carried out in the open, with the girl's betrothed, prospective in-laws, and other relatives in attendance (Marealle 2002: 23). Among the Chewa in Malawi, the initiation includes ritual sexual intercourse (Phiri 2000a: 35). Now a subject of mounting protest all over Eastern Africa from government authorities and women activists, female circumcision is still fiercely defended by some women elders and men. Activists' efforts have led some traditional circumcisers to declare that they will no longer perform the rites, but the practice continues clandestinely.

In those communities where it is practiced, circumcision has regrettably endowed initiation with a stigmatic stamp that threatens to obliterate any educational value it may have. Initiation rituals were primarily intended to instill in the initiates a sense of their responsibilities and loyalties as full members of the community, and to give them a greater consciousness about their identity (Bendera 1996: 16; Shorter 1974: 77).[2] Women had to be prepared for the challenges that were certain to face them in their future, both painful and pleasurable, and one of these was giving pleasure to their future husbands. Hence, female genital mutilation (FGM), if included as essential to the initiation of young girls, may be viewed as a lesson in submission to male will (Bendera 1996: 18; Phiri 2000a: 40). (Even here, however, women may resist the subjugation, for instance, by abstaining from the marital bed [Moyo 2005],[3] or returning home to parents.)

Some have argued that, in the absence of sex education in most school curricula in the region, initiation practices fill a dearth that has become especially dangerous as HIV/AIDS stalks the continent. The challenge at present is how to integrate the positive aspects of initiation ceremonies into modern training, and to separate the ritual of circumcision from the social and economic education that provides cultural continuity and arms the initiate with some vital survival skills. A primary function of initiation rituals has been to prepare the girl for "service" to her husband. The communal song from the Iraqw of Tanzania, "Gidmay: Farewell to a Bride" (1950s), outlines the kinds of wisdom and stamina required of a woman if she is to survive and sustain herself in marriage. The bride is made aware of male dominance and the possible physical and psychological assaults, literal and symbolic, that are likely to come her way:

> . . . you will face those sticks long stored on the roof,
> The sticks full of dust; you'll think they are for herding calves,
> But alas! They are for teaching you a lesson!

At the same time, however, "Gidmay" satirizes the patriarchal marriage system with a series of insults leveled against the groom.

> Why did you accept him, this one with heels as rough as roof tiles?
> This one with rough heels, like those of salt lake warthogs.
>
> He is inclined to live on stale local beer,
> To live on stale beer made from scum.

Women's orature from Eastern Africa includes a wealth of songs meant to protest against and sanction wayward men who are not responsible husbands. In "Songs Complaining about Husbands and Lovers" (1996–2001), women from various ethnic groups sing to shame men who are impotent and yet presume they can still woo a woman; men who are greedy and gobble up all the food in the house; and men who migrate and forget those they leave behind. In one song from the Rumphi District of Malawi, women chastise a man who has gone to work in South Africa and forgotten his wife and mother at home.

> You who go to Johannesburg,
> Please please tell him,
> I am naked and so is his mother.

The Borana women of northern Kenya, who generally occupy a subservient position in their society, have license to sing about male failings during traditional naming ceremonies, as they do in "Alisoo Is an Insult" (2001).

> The market is tomorrow; he sells his cattle;
> He receives the money; he asks for the beer hall.
> One liter of alcohol is one sip for you.

The price of one bull is one day's expense for you.

In the first of the "*Vimbuza* Songs" from northern Malawi (1997), women go so far as to rejoice that a promiscuous man has earned his just desserts by being infected with syphilis and rendered sterile by the disease.

Songs protesting or satirizing women's predicament in an unequal society concern not only men and marriage, but a broad range of subjects. Even lullaby texts can contain defiant messages, as in this Kiswahili lullaby from Tanzania (2002):

> When my mother brought me into the world, she called me *Kukuwa*.
> All the Prophet's people recognize me as such.
> He who is not my creator cannot uncreate me

Another lullaby from the same group transmits its subversive message through metaphor.

> A snake lies on the path, let's crush its head
> To let by hewers of wood, and fetchers of water.

And in another, the singer adopts the point of view of the baby, who, as a grown woman, would rather share her secrets and her valued possessions with her mother than with her husband.

> That canoe approaching, no doubt has something for me.
> It has beads for me to string, the size of my neck.
> I will not string them, nor give them to my mate.
> I will give them to my mother, who shares my secrets.

Many oral works describe—and accompany—work performed by women. One early-twentieth-century text by a settler woman, E. May Crawford's "Face to Face with Wangu wa Makeri" (1913), describes in detail some of the activities of Gikuyu women and girls in a typical day, and the process through which they learn to do such work. She notes that at a very young age, girls learned to look after their siblings, collect firewood, and fetch water from the river. To these burdens would later be added many others, including day-long digging and weeding, cooking, basket-weaving, and the ubiquitous pounding of grain—an activity that inspired an especially large number of songs. This volume's collection of "Pounding Songs" (2001) captures the rhythm of this communal work. Once again, they also include expressions of social protest—in this case referring to the unequal distribution of labor between the sexes. One of the songs, for example, mocks the man who does nothing but consume what is produced by others.

I am pounding for Mr. John.
He is lying there in idleness, Mr. John,
With his big stomach, Mr. John,
Like a toad, Mr. John.
Look at the chunks he takes off, Mr. John.
Look at the way he swallows, Mr. John.

Women's work has long included caring for the health of others within the community. Ways of healing were passed on through the family structure, and women became "specialists" in midwifery, in bone setting, and in treating other maladies. In "Hush, My Child, Hush" (1983), there are numerous references to the traditional herbs, beverages, and cleansing practices that eased the tribulations of a difficult pregnancy. Although written in the 1980s, the poem pays tribute, in form and content, to women's traditional knowledge.

These customs of old
Were full of wisdom,
Replete with value.
Give them deep thought.

Taken together, in the orature and other traditional texts in this volume women present the collective wisdom of their societies to other women. While advising them to conform in ways necessary to their survival, many of the texts also offer examples of women's resistance, through explicit protest, through subversion and satire, or simply through a sense of solidarity with other women. It was very rare for women to overturn the social order entirely. But in one text, a retelling of the Gikuyu folktale "The Story of Wacu" (2004), a young woman who "lived the life of a humiliated wife" breaks the taboo of women not eating meat in public, after she receives a providential gift of sausage dropped by an eagle. "This reminds us," the tale declares, "that our God loves even those who are held in contempt by others."[4]

Patti Duncan wisely comments that women's oral creativity above all reflects "creative responses to oppressive situations" (2004: 160). What is especially inspiring is the fact that women often respond in ways that are vital, joyful, and uplifting.

The Sacredness of Mother Earth: African Traditional Religion
From time immemorial, African women were perceived in terms of their pro-creative power, often described using the metaphor of garden or soil.[5] In African Traditional Religion,[6] women were perceived as both unofficial caretakers of the land, the iconic symbol of African existence, and as guardians of the spirits.

The Gikuyu of Kenya provide a representative explanation for such conceptions: "The Gikuyu consider the earth as the 'mother' of the tribe, for the reason that the mother bears her burden for . . . nine moons while the child is in her womb, and then a . . . time of suckling" (Kenyatta 1938: 13). The soil then takes over, feeding this child for a lifetime, and after death the soil continues nursing the Living Dead for eternity. Most African ethnic groups still bury the umbilical cord in the soil after it falls from a newborn's navel. This practice has deep religious connotations for them. It connects them not only with the land as a nurturing mother, but to their ancestors who are nurtured by the same soil (Mpassou 1998). Among the Bahaya in Tanzania, the link between woman and land was captured by the Goddess Nyakalembe, who determined when and how the tilling of the land should take place (Mulokozi 2002: 570).

Women's relationship with the land was linked also to the perception that women were custodians of the well-being of the community. They were responsible for both "reproduction and production, ensuring that there was adequate food for the family and extra for the various functions on which the status of the homestead depended" (Kenyatta 1938: 37–38). Men assisted in clearing land, but left women to plant, weed, harvest, and oversee the disposal of all food crops. "To cope, women evolved the *ngwato* system under which members' farms were worked in rotation. An *ngwato* was comprised of women married to men of the same lineage" (cf. Kenyatta 1938: 35). The *ngwato* would also serve as a safe space in which women might share their stories of powerlessness as land custodians, not owners. Ironically, women could not own the land, in spite of the fact that they were its main caretakers. Nevertheless, whatever the patriarchal realities, the religio-cultural connection of land with motherhood alludes to the inherent power of women in this region.

Ontologically, women have been regarded as more important in African Traditional Religion than in Islam or Christianity. In many African societies, women are viewed as the source of life and the spirits of love and fertility. Childlessness, in this scheme of things, is a disgrace. In some cultures, women have served as high priests and mediums, on a par with men. They have likewise been deeply involved in healing rituals, and they were usually the best traditional doctors and midwives.

Among the Bahaya of Tanzania, for example, the goddess Muhaya determines matters of love and marriage, while the Gikuyu consider Mumbi the mother of their people. In the Maasai oral tradition, the founder of the Maasai nation was a woman called Maa-Sinta, who was married to Leeyo. God ordered Maa-Sinta to bear children and fill the world with Maa people. In response to God's bidding, Maa-Sinta bore seven boys, who became the founders of the seven Maasai clans. Not surprisingly, the Maasai believe that women are closer to God than men; hence they have usually been in charge of important religious prayers and rituals (Makumbusho n.d.: 122). In the Maa language, all words for things of fundamental importance to Maasai existence are feminine in gender. These include such concepts as *e'nkai* (God), *e'nkop* (earth), *e´nkare* (water), *e´nkiteng* (cow/bull), *e´nkerai* (child), and *e´ndaa* (food) (Makumbusho n.d.: 32).

Unfortunately, however, this ostensibly high status was often marred by other considerations and practices that disadvantaged women. Maleness remained the gauge of status even in traditional priesthoods, so that in some cases a woman priest or medium was, in ordinary life, symbolically regarded as a man, and was usually addressed as such. Paradoxically, both male and female priests in the Great Lakes region (Burundi, Rwanda, Uganda, and portions of Congo-Kinshasa, Kenya, and Tanzania) were also, during rituals or séances, symbolically considered to be women in relation to the spirits they represented. Thus, when carrying out religious rituals they were not allowed to wear male attire.

Despite the religio-cultural belief in the continuity of life after death, disease and death were not usually considered natural. The general view was that one dies because of some evil eye or witchcraft unleashed by one's enemies. Hence, during an extended illness or misfortune, or after a death, the witch had to be sought and punished. This belief, which still persists, has caused much suffering to innocent people, particularly old women, who were often the butt of such accusations.

Death, dying, and the accompanying burial and funeral rites were usually gendered. While both men and women became spirits after death, male spirits were usually viewed as more powerful and permanent than female spirits, at least in patrilineal societies, where men were the ancestors of the clan or lineage, and thus receive offerings from their offspring. In many societies, women's funerals were shorter and less elaborate than men's, reflecting the difference in status (Marealle 2002: 63–66). Only in special cases did female spirits acquire a similar status, thereby turning into deities, as in the case of the legendary Makewana ("mother of the children") of the Chewa in central Malawi and of Nakayima, the Baganda priestess immortalized in "Nakayima and the Wonder Tree" (1995).

Ultimately, women's status under African Traditional Religion depended on fertility. Even in death and in conceptions of the afterlife, a woman without children had no status; in some societies, such women were not buried in the common graveyard. Moreover, various communities carried out burial rituals to ensure that barren women's spirits would vanish completely from their communities because they would have left behind no descendants to sustain their names. In "Birds Will Mourn Her" (1956) the Sukuma women of Tanzania lament the loneliness of a childless woman who, when she dies, will have no child to grieve for her. For her, there will be no immortality.

Other manifestations of the culture, such as art and literature, were also influenced by beliefs and practices. For instance, sculptures and masks served as religious and ritual items (cf. Mulokozi 2001; Ott 2000). Religious beliefs and myths inspired numerous songs, stories, and epics, depicting the worlds of humans and spirits, and the concerns of humans in this life and the next one. In many of these, female symbolism and images predominate—for instance, in the Mwanahiti sculptures made by the Wazaramo and other related peoples in Tanzania. The Mwanahiti sculptures served as ritual objects during women's initiations, and as symbolic spirits at women's grave sites (Jahns 1994). Objects of material culture, such as housing, dress, food, and tools, also had a religious and ideological dimension. In many cases these objects symbolized women's procreative power. Traditional homes, for example, were most often round in shape, mimicking the shape of women's breasts and pregnant bellies and thus serving as symbols of fertility. These and many other expressions in traditional life point to that all-pervading connection between women as procreators and the land as life-giver and sustainer.

The nonindigenous religions that began filtering into Eastern Africa around 800 C.E. were already becoming well-entrenched in some parts by the 1850s, thanks to the tolerant attitude of African traditional religions on the one hand and the might of the sword on the other. In addition to suppressing existing religious beliefs, these religions also introduced new practices and taboos. Nevertheless, in spite of the spread of Islam and Christianity, indigenous African beliefs, taboos, and customs still persist, though often stripped of their traditional religious meaning.

African traditional religions were organically intertwined with the origins, culture, and social structures and aspirations of the entire society. Religion was so central to the being of the African people that it even influenced their basic worldview. For Eastern African women religion was not Marx's opium of the people; it was the source of supernatural empowerment, which exalted them beyond their presumed powerlessness within patriarchal structures toward positions of "divine" and even social authority. It situated women in a place that was beyond the reproach of worldly authority, where they might seek to alter the otherwise unalterable, and seek more just and inclusive communities (Moyo 2004). Since these communities comprised African peoples whose religious beliefs permeated all realms of life (Mbiti 1979), whatever these women denounced or upheld was taken as divine commandment—the voice of the spirit, speaking through the body of women (Berger 1976). To resist them, therefore, would be to resist the will of God.

In the "*Vimbuza* Protest Songs" (1997), for example, spirit-possessed Tumbuka women from Northern Malawi were (and still are) empowered to denounce their experiences of oppression within the patrilineal family system. *Vimbuza* spirit possession cults are said to date from the time of the migration of the Ngoni to Malawi, in the 1840s. Through spirit possession, women could express their innermost thoughts against male misbehavior without fear of reprisals. One recent *Vimbuza* protest song, "Mr. Nyirongo I," illustrates how women have used this medium. This song publicly chastises a husband who has contracted and transmitted syphilis from his extramarital sexual adventures. Such a denunciation of unfaithfulness among husbands would not be accepted in normal circumstances. The double-standard that allows men to stray while demanding unwavering obedience from women would also expect women to be more understanding and more forgiving of men's intransigencies. Furthermore, the sterility that, according to the song, resulted from untreated syphilis would be a terrible blow to an African man. Masculinity is conceived mainly in terms of sexual virility, without which a man would be viewed as being "as good as a woman." Men's sexual potency is so central to their identity that a public declaration of its absence deprives a man of the very basis of his patriarchal powers. Women could speak out in such an "outrageous" manner only because of the "divine authority" they wielded when possessed by the spirits of the *vimbuza*.

Ten Times a Slave: Women and Slavery in Eastern Africa
This volume's texts on slavery clearly indicate that African slavery, whether traditional or commercial, was neither humane nor identical everywhere. Its form and practice differed from place to place. For instance, there are indications that the enslavement was sometimes a temporary state, and sometimes hard to define. Slaves could sometimes own slaves in their own right. In Swahili and many other Eastern African societies, a woman slave who married her master or married into his family often became a free woman upon producing a child, and the children born of slave women (*vizalia* in Kiswahili) automatically became free persons. Emily Ruete's "A Royal Childhood in Zanzibar" (1886), for example, describes many children of the sultan born to slave mothers. Furthermore, slavery was not confined to a particular social category of women, but affected all classes. Even a royal or ruling-class woman could overnight be turned into a slave. Mama Meli, who relates her story in "From Slavery to Freedom" (1950s), belonged originally to a chief's family, but was captured in a raid and enslaved while still a child.

Prior to the nineteenth-century slave trade, and in the absence of economic demands for intensive, plantation-type slave labor, most slaves in many Eastern African societies were women. Men, who were generally unskilled in household labors, could in fact pose a real danger to the masters. Thus male slaves were rare and temporary. Male war captives were soon either redeemed, after paying a ransom, or killed. In some languages, such as Luhaya in northwestern Tanzania, the word for slave (*omuzana*) refers only to women. That a low premium was often placed on women is evident from the way Bwanikwa was taken into slavery. She was surrendered by her father as payment for a fine. Had she been a boy, she would probably not have been so treated.

In traditional slavery—until about 1800, and in some places even later—one became a slave through birth, capture in war or raids, indebtedness, kidnapping, purchase, destitution, or through a legal or royal decision. Whatever the mode of enslavement, in most cases the end result, for women slaves, was the same: domestic slavery.

Two nineteenth-century texts, by Mwana Kupona and Emily Ruete (the name assumed by Princess Salma Said of Zanzibar after she married a German merchant), portray domestic slavery among the Swahili in Kenya and Tanzania. Mwana Kupona, writing a lengthy poem to her daughter in 1858, is very conscious of the divide between her family and the slaves. She advises her daughter not to associate too closely with slaves, lest they lead her astray. Emily Ruete, writing in 1886 about her childhood in Zanzibar's royal family several decades earlier, describes the relations between African slave women and their young Arab masters in the Zanzibar palace, and criticizes the enslaved nursemaids' "bad habit" of recounting what Ruete calls "dreadful and absurd stories"—obviously, African folktales—to their young charges. Yet the line between slaves and free persons appears to have been very slim. Ruete herself, with the sultan of Zanzibar as her father and a Circassian slave woman as her mother, would have been a slave had she been born in the American South at the time. That she was a free princess was due to the fact that Eastern African domestic slavery allowed certain shifts in status for slaves and their children through marriage to free men. The text also offers us a glimpse of the mixed origins of the slave population, especially among the women. While Ruete's own mother was a Circassian (from the northern Caucusus); the other slave women in the palace included Ethiopians, Europeans, Asians, and local Africans.

Another account of traditional semi-slavery is provided by Genda, a member of the semi-pastoral Iraqw people of Tanzania. While her text, "An Unusual Girlhood," dates from 1964, the autobiographical story she narrates took place many decades earlier, in the late 1880s. Kidnapped and sold while still a small child, Genda was later married off by her master into a family where she was treated even more harshly. Hers was a life of toil without respite, as she handled unaided all the domestic chores in the homestead, including milling the grain, cooking, cleaning, and tending to the livestock. Her working day began very early in the morning and ended very late at night. Eventually, she managed to run away and return to her people.

In "Ten Times a Slave" an autobiographical account first recorded by missionaries in 1895, the young Bwanikwa is given away by her father and later her master, probably in the 1870s, as payment for customary debts. Thereafter she was sold and resold by her successive masters in exchange for Western items, including gunpowder and pieces of cloth, until she was finally bought by and married to the servant of a European traveler. Bwanikwa's treatment was an abuse of the traditional system of domestic slavery, and indeed represented a transition from traditional modes of enslavement to the commercial enslavement of Africans by Arabs and Westerners in the nineteenth century. The fact that fathers would give away their female (not male) children as slaves to pay for debts is evidence of the thin line that existed, for women, between freedom and slavery.

In "From Slavery to Freedom," recorded in the 1950s but set in the late nineteenth century, Mama Meli tells a story similar to Bwanikwa's. Captured in a war raid while still a small girl, she became a slave in the household of one of the conquering warriors, and was later sold or married to a succession of

Swahili slave traders. In Mama Meli's case, marriage to free men did not bring her emancipation, because her husbands were not averse to selling her to the highest bidder. She was finally rescued by Europeans and married to a Christian convert, probably in the year 1900.

In royal courts in centralized states such as Buganda, and along the Arab-dominated coast, domestic slavery existed side by side with institutional and plantation slavery. The former sometimes took the form of harem slavery, in which a king's or nobleman's concubines were kept in seclusion and virtual imprisonment for life. In Zanzibar such women, known as *masuria* if they were not proper wives according to Islamic law, lived under the watchful eye of stern eunuchs. Sultan Barghash of Zanzibar (1870–1888) had one wife and ninety-nine *masuria* at his Maruhubi palace. In Buganda, there was no limit to the number of wives and concubines a nobleman could have. *Kabaka* (King) Suuna (1832–1856) is reported to have had 148 wives and more than twenty thousand concubines and slave women (Nsobya 2000: 222). Both Mwana Kupona and Emily Ruete offer glimpses of domestic and harem slavery in coastal ruling houses.

A more entrenched form of institutional slavery affecting women had to do with religious beliefs and rituals. In some societies, certain individuals were dedicated to certain spirits, gods, or shrines for life. In Buganda, each shrine of a dead *kabaka* had several "wives" ministering to it for life. These were drawn from the clans of the former *kabaka's* wives. Such women—who exist to this day at many shrines—were not and are still not allowed to marry and have children.[7] This system was duplicated in most of the kingdoms in the Great Lakes region. There, too, women, including priestesses, were sometimes dedicated to certain spirit shrines for life; they had to remain virgins. The high social status seemingly enjoyed by such women cannot mask their bondage, though, for ideological reasons, such arrangements were not usually labeled as slavery. This kind of bondage is mirrored in the celibate, sometimes cloistered Christian religious orders introduced in the colonies by the missionaries.

The nineteenth-century empire builders (Milambo, Tippu Tip, and even the *kabakas* of Buganda) intensified the institutionalization of slavery in the societies affected by their campaigns and rule. Thus the Ngoni, who moved from South Africa during the Mfecane and arrived in this region in the 1840s, are said to have reduced to slaves some of the conquered peoples in their path as they moved northward. Such slaves were expected to do all the farm work and hard labor while the Ngoni men engaged in warfare. Women slaves among the Ngoni were also buried alive with the kings' bodies when the latter died. A similar practice was observed in some of the Great Lakes kingdoms, such as Karagwe (Katoke 1975).

Between the late-eighteenth and early-nineteenth centuries, commercial slavery in Eastern Africa acquired great importance and a more sinister character, fueled by a greater demand for slaves to work in the French-ruled islands of the Indian Ocean or in the United States, to which they were transported via the Cape to the south and the (then Belgian) Congo to the west. The inland areas around Lakes Nyasa and Tanganyika, the homelands of Bwanikwa and Mama Meli, and beyond into the Congo, became the major source of slaves, with bands of Swahili, Arabs, Yaos, Nyamwezi, and local warlords marauding the area looking for souls to enslave and sell, usually in exchange for Indian cloth and beads, guns and gunpowder (cf. Tippu Tip 1974; Sheriff 44). The inland trading depots of Tabora and Ujiji in Tanzania, Nkhotahota, and Karonga in Malawi, and Kazembe in Zambia, thrived on the slave trade. The ports of Bagamoyo, Zanzibar, Kilwa, Mombasa, and Dar es Salaam became export points for slaves destined for the Indian Ocean islands, the Cape Verde islands off the West African coast, the Arabian peninsula, Asia, and the Americas. Indeed the name "Bagamoyo" which derives from the Kiswahili *bwaga moyo*, meaning "lay down the heart," alludes to the town's role as the main embarkation point for slaves from the hinterland: here, in total despair, they embarked on boats for unknown lands, never to return.

The texts by Bwanikwa (1895) and Mama Meli (1950s) point toward the increasing commercialization of slavery in the nineteenth century. Bwanikwa's story, for example, illustrates the deadly interface between traditional slavery and commercial slavery. Originally enslaved for customary reasons, Bwanikwa is ultimately sold to coastal slave traders, and would conceivably have been transported to the coast had it not been for European intervention. A comparison between these texts and the nineteenth-century slave narratives of African Americans reveals some interesting parallels. African slave narratives usually begin with the subject's enslavement through capture or purchase, proceed to describe hardships in captivity, followed by repeated attempts to escape, and culminate in escape or liberation through the assistance of white abolitionists or missionaries. The final escape is often followed by conversion to Christianity (cf. Equiano 1789 and Mbotela 1934). In some of the African American narratives, the tales begin with a description of the narrator's suffering and hardships under slavery, followed by repeated attempts at escape, and finally the escape, also often assisted by white abolitionists or Quakers.[8] These similarities may be explained partially by the fact that the narratives included in this volume were recorded in mission stations and come from women who had converted to Christianity and settled at the missions. Stories of the slave women who were not linked to European missions are far less likely to have been written down, and are yet to be discovered.

The perspective of the slaves themselves toward slavery, and hence their strategies for resistance and emancipation, were bound by the surrounding circumstances. While slavery was abhorred by most of the enslaved, as evidenced by the many attempts to escape made by Genda, Bwanikwa, and Mama Meli, sometimes slaves were afraid to be freed, unsure about what lay "in freedom." This was not so much a result of their having been brainwashed or psychologically traumatized as of practical considerations about their personal security and survival (Wright 1993). These same fears may have influenced their decisions to remain attached to European mission stations once they had been emancipated, as did Mama Meli and Bwanikwa, and as did the Freretown freed slaves at Kisauni in Mombasa, Kenya (Mbotela 1934).

In domestic slavery, slave women had no opportunity to organize in groups that might have created effective resistance. Resistance in these cases was often subdued, in individual acts such as malingering at work or repudiation of sexual advances, and, once again, occurred mainly in songs and other forms of expression, including the autobiographical storytelling found in this volume's texts. At best, the slaves could resist with their feet—by running away.

Colonialism for the most part ended traditional slavery, and the abolition of slavery, in Europe and its colonies and then in the United States, effectively closed the slave trade. At the same time, colonialism ushered in new forms of enslavement, conforming to the new economic demands of the colonizers. For women, these new forms of slavery, many still prevalent today, included serving as cheap labor in homes, plantations, and factories, along with prostitution and sex trafficking.

Islam: Conversion and Conversation

The earliest invaders of Eastern Africa, well before Christian missionaries and European colonizers, were Arab traders. The arrival of the Arabs preceded the migration to Eastern Africa of the Ngoni (Malawi, Tanzania, and Zambia), Nyanja/Chewa (Malawi and Zambia), Tumbuka (Malawi and Zambia), Acoli (Uganda), and other ethnic groups from other parts of the continent. Apart from mercantile goods such as guns and cloth, the Arabs brought with them a plethora of new cultural practices. They also brought one of the world's great religions, Islam.

Since religion has always been central to the lives of Africans—and especially African women—Africans found themselves in what Jean and John Comaroff (1991) call the processes of conversion and conversation, during different periods, with Muslim (Arab) traders, conquerors, and Christian (European) missionaries and colonizers.

In its early centuries, the history of Islam in Africa was dynamic and turbulent, with various dynasties and reform movements clashing with and succeeding one another. Gaining power depended on securing trade routes into gold-producing areas in sub-Saharan Africa. Islamic rulers expanded north and west as well as south, dominating the Mediterranean world in the last quarter of the eleventh century, and placing much of the Maghreb under Ottoman rule between the sixteenth and the nineteenth centuries. By the 1880s, Islam had taken root on one-third of the continent.

The Muslim traders' acceptance of polygamy and certain other religio-cultural practices that prevailed in most Eastern African communities might have contributed to the positive response Islam received in this period, despite the fact that many of these traders were involved in the slave trade. Unlike the Christian missionaries of a later period, who, according to Etherington, wanted the Africans' souls, the Arabs had other interests (quoted in Camaroff 1991: 6). De Vere Allen suggests that, although the Arabs began visiting the Eastern African coast as early as the eighth century, proselytizing was not one of their priorities then (1993: 179). It is more likely that the earliest conversions were carried out by the Shirazis from Persia, and these would have been widespread by the twelfth century (De Vere Allen 1993: 183). Thus, Muslim women in the coastal communities would have begun to achieve written literacy at that time, using the Arabic script. (With the advent of Western colonialism, literacy in the Arabic script would be dismissed, and not included in calculating literacy rates.)

Although the existence of powerful Muslim women in medieval times is well documented (Dunbar 2000: 409; Pouwels 1987: 28), the presence of a text from one of those women is a rarity. In the 1711 text we have called "Peace and Security," Sultan Fatima binti Muhammad Mkubwa, the ruler of the city-state of Kilwa Island, writes to invite all peace-loving people (except Europeans) to come to Kilwa, "where God's peace prevails." It is not clear why Sultan Fatima dictates the letter, whether because of her high status or because she is illiterate. What is clear is her power, along with her desire to bring her people home. In the letter, Sultan Fatima expresses her authority not only as a ruler of her people but also as a ruler of equal stature to the male ruler to whom she writes. She speaks of a peaceful sultanate unified with other sultanates under a Muslim religious leader. But she cautions against the potential danger of dealing with the Portugese. She extends her invitation to all except the Portugese, whom she saw as enemies of both her state and her religion.

Another of the earliest texts in the volume, also written in Arabic script by a Muslim woman, addresses women directly. In "A Mother's Advice and Prayer" (1858), Mwana Kupona binti Msham offers her daughter instruction on how a Muslim woman should behave in matters of the household and marriage. When Mwana Kupona asks her daughter to listen to her with "pen and ink," we understand that the daughter is literate. Islamic education for boys and girls probably began before the tenth century.

In her poem, her last will and testament to her daughter, Mwana Kupona finds strength and solace in her faith in God. She wants to offer her daughter detailed, practical advice, and at the same time she wants the girl to remain true to the dictates of Islam.

> If you remember my advice,
> My child, you will never suffer.
> You will walk across this world
> And, later, you will enter paradise.

Mwana Kupona instructs her daughter to be subservient, but at the same time aware of the power she does have. A husband is to be elevated to the highest possible level, not only by the things his wife does for him, but by the way she cares for herself—maintaining her absolute cleanliness, bedecking herself with jewelry and henna, perfuming her body, and generally cultivating her sensuality for the pleasure of the man. Mwana Kupona also presents social relations as a reflection of a woman's respect and dignity. In giving advice to her daughter, she draws closely on Islamic teachings regarding how a woman should behave in a marital relationship. These teachings would have been imparted partly in the *madrassa*, the Qur'anic school, and partly within the household. It is interesting to note contrasts between Mwana Kupona, writing within the Islamic reality where she had always lived, and Emily Ruete, writing of her royal childhood in Zanzibar from the perspective of a convert to Christianity and to Western ways. Ruete describes dispassionately the rote learning practiced in the madrassa, designed to teach children to recite the Qur'an in prayer, though not necessarily to understand it. But children also learned to read and write Arabic script, which, Mwana Kupona, for one, used to remarkable effect.[9] While Mwana Kupona urges her daughter to heed the Muslim directive to make no distinction between religion and daily life, between the secular and the spiritual, Emily Ruete clearly rebels against what she has been taught, rejecting both her religious and social obligations and choosing to marry a foreigner and a Christian man.

Even limited education may have helped some Muslim women find a voice with which to express their own points of view, and to protest practices that were unjust. As early as 1926, a Muslim woman, Zeina binti Mwinyipembe Sekinyaga, penned such a protest, in the very public form of a letter to a Kiswahili newspaper in Tanzania. In "Civilized Motherhood," she outspokenly argues for gender equity and advocates the elimination of certain cultural practices, such as bride price and polygamy. Whether monogamous or polygamous, the Islamic concept of marriage strongly opposes divorce, yet Zeina binti Mwinyipembe Sekinyaga goes so far as to allude to the possibility of divorce on grounds of the gender inequalities that she raises. If she was a Muslim, as her name would suggest, then her courage in presenting these arguments challenges the generally held views regarding the position of women in African Islamic societies.

While the Swahili on the Eastern African coast had their differences with the Arab rulers, Qur'anic education itself, at least on the coast, did not meet with the kind of opposition that greeted Christianity and Western education in the interior.[10] Several reasons may be posited for this contrast. First, Islamic education was offered only to those who were already converts to the religion. Secondly, the instruction provided was purely religious, without many incursions into worldly matters (although for devout Muslims the line between the two is hardly distinct). Finally, once they were outside the madrassa, African students could continue their usual religious practices without much sanction.

For women, "conversion" to Islam or to Christianity sometimes provided a measure of empowerment through education, as well as an escape from some aspects of traditional African patriarchal oppression, expressed, for example, in forced child-marriages, bride price, and FGM. The fact that they offered an alternative to such practices may have aided both Islam and Christianity in expanding their influence. In the process of this "liberation," however, women may have acquired different forms of oppression.

THE COLONIAL PERIOD

Colonialism: The Beginnings

The history of African women is in part a history of migration. African women have traversed many mountains, valleys, deserts, and rivers, sometimes with their men, sometimes alone, more in suffering than in pleasure. While most of the movements would have been within the continent, some, as during the time of slavery, hurled women into places and cultures that were alien and hostile.[11] The history of Africa is also a history of migration to the continent from other lands. Thus African women encountered men and women who had come from the Middle East and then, more sweepingly, from Europe, bringing tremendous changes to African communities, identities, social relations, and development. Colonialism, like the international slave trade, was ideologically premised on the myth of European supremacy. The alleged cultural inferiority and irrationality of the Africans signaled their need to be "civilized" by their colonizers.

In the 1880s, the prevalent European view was that local societies were at worst less than human and at best devoid of knowledge, cultural institutions, and history. These ideas provided the moral justification for economic exploitation and cultural oppression, for plunder as well as race-based subjugation. The "civilizing" mission also propelled European missionary and settler women to work in the region as evangelists, educators, and health workers, as well as economic opportunists and partners of administrators. These migrations into Africa thus defined not only the relationships between indigenous women and migrant men but also between indigenous and migrant women. Under colonialism, the relationships between European migrant women who settled in Africa and African women were defined in terms of rulers and the ruled, colonizers and the colonized. African women's responses to colonialism ranged from accommodation to resistance, from adaptation to war.

Up to the early 1880s, European incursion into east Africa had been gradual, with attempts at economic penetration and the establishment of monopolies through trade, as well as the founding of missionary posts by various Christian sects. The Portuguese had followed the Arabs, Persians, and Chinese, who had been in contact with the peoples of east Africa before the advent of Christianity. During the sixteenth and seventeenth centuries the Portuguese competed with the French and the indigenous Yao (the latter acting as brokers) for the East African trade in ivory and slaves (Curtin et al. 1978). The conquest of Africa, which had begun in earnest with the rapid annexation of African lands by competing European nations, culminated in the Berlin Conference of 1884–1885. In Eastern Africa, the British and the Germans managed to divide the territory between themselves.

"Praised Be Jesus Christ": Christianity and Women

For women in Eastern Africa, Christianity was an agent of great change. Christianity first came to parts of the coast in the fifteenth century, although in the interior, most people continued to practice African traditional religions undisturbed until the middle of the nineteenth century. At that time, Christian missions to Africa increased, driven by both the antislavery crusade and the European drive to colonize Africa.[12]

In the coastal areas of Kenya and Tanzania, as well as some pockets of the hinterland, Christianity met its greatest challenge not only from African religions but also from Islam, to which some Africans had already converted. We know through Sultan Fatima's letter that by 1711, Islam was the predominant foreign religion not only in her own realm but also in most of the coastal areas of Eastern Africa and along some inland trade routes. Christianity had also grown in these areas with the gradual European incursion, but some local rulers and their subjects preferred Islam over Christianity. At the end of the nineteenth century, however, Christianity became the religion of colonialism, and provided a strong challenge to both Islam and African Traditional Religion. Commenting on how women in northwestern Tanzania embraced Christianity, Spear has noted:

> Women were attracted to the mission from an early stage as it provided protection (*busirika*) to royal "slaves," girls escaping unwanted or unhappy marriages and women fleeing widowhood. Many subsequently entered an unofficial sisterhood (*Bashomesa*) whose members took annual vows and served as teachers, nurses, evangelists in the community. (1999:18)

For the women who embraced Christianity, the religion provided both a sense of new identity and an alienation from the old. Many women converts became fervent adherents of Christianity, profoundly taken with its symbols and images. Perhaps the greatest symbol of Christianity, the cross, spoke to women who knew about suffering and about making sacrifices for others. Martha Thabi, in a hymn written in Malawi in 1890, quotes the words Jesus is supposed to have said as he was dying on the cross, " My God, Why Have You Forsaken Me?" These words indicate a recognition of one's dependence on God as one calls for His help in times of need, thus turning humility into strength.

Christianity destabilized the status quo, sometimes undermining the traditional patriarchal powers of African men while bringing new opportunities to some female converts. From the Christian missions came the teaching of a loving God who brought hope for disadvantaged women reeling under slavery, early and arranged marriages, and other forms of oppression. The establishment of mission centers provided refuge for some disadvantaged girls and women. In "Praised Be Jesus Christ" (1963), a girl writes to her father from a Roman Catholic mission, refusing an arranged marriage. Usually, elders from two families negotiated marriage terms and even fixed a wedding date without seeking the affected couple's consent. The couple was not expected to object to the arrangement, since marriage was regarded not as an individual matter but as a community concern. As the letter indicates, the writer, who found her way to a Roman Catholic mission in Tanzania and converted, could now choose to become a nun in the convent instead of getting married. She clearly draws on her sense of power to overrule her father's authority, replacing it with the Christian God she now worships. This otherwise "powerless" young woman may also have been empowered through solidarity with other women; she mentions the leader of the convent in her letter.

Along with the contentious issue of arranged marriages, especially for very young women, the Christian missionaries opposed FGM, as argued in the "Letter Opposing Female Circumcision" (1931). From 1927 to 1929, prior to the writing of the letter, female circumcision was hotly debated in Kenya, splitting Gikuyu communities in two. Songs were composed to air the views of each side, and it must have been in such an environment that the women wrote their letter.[13] The women who wrote the letter belonged to a group called, Ngo ya Tuiritu, the Shield of the Young Girls, formed at a Presbyterian mission station. As Christians, they invoked the church's stand on female circumcision, and appealed to the government to do the same. However, they were also advocating for choice, insisting that women should not be forced to be circumcised. Written at a time when resisting female circumcision was not popular in most African communities, this letter stands as one of the early African women's appeals for personal choice over one's body. From the content of the letter, it is clear that not even all Christian women advocated choice or supported the church's position.

Another major point of contention between early Christian missionaries and the local people was a perception that the missionaries recruited converts from the margins of society, including slaves and outcasts. Many of the early women converts along the east African coast were indeed from such groups, a fact that challenged the authority of the local rulers who had often brought the groups into existence. In other parts of the region, notably Uganda, conversion was attempted from the top down through the ruling group or family which would then deliver the whole community to the new religion. Depending on the area and circumstances, missionaries followed both or either of the approaches.

African women brought to Christianity traditional ways of organizing and mobilizing for action. According to Oduyoye (2000: ix), most African cultures provide for the creation of a women's "platform" from which to influence the community and stimulate change. Women's solidarity with other women and their impact on society as a whole is made most visible through their organizations and their regular consultations with one another (Oduyoye 2000: ix). Such safe spaces act as shields of resistance to oppressive practices and structures. In a 1934 "Letter to the Bishop," members of the Mothers Union in Buganda urged the Bishop of the Native Anglican Church (NAC) of Uganda to denounce injustice in the wider social and political sphere. Their letter testifies to their knowledge of these issues and of the church's power over its members, including the *Kabaka*, King of the Baganda, who had promoted a local chief whose record the women found despicable. Determined to fight against injustice, the mothers say they are prepared to appeal even to the colonial powers should the church authorities not produce the desired results. Referring to themselves as "mothers of the nation," the women wrote as mothers, wives, nationalists, and Christians, positions that the church had variously extolled. These women felt empowered enough to challenge the Bishop to come up with any argument that could contradict theirs, asking quite simply, "Your Lordship, what reason is there for the promotion of an administrator who was publicly found at fault . . . ?"

Individual Christian women, empowered by education and their conception of God as their creator and image-giver, have also protested against patriarchal church leaders who abuse their leadership positions to dehumanize women. Kanyoro (2002) acknowledges the powerful ways in which women have found liberation through their own conceptions of God's revelation. In "Every Woman a Child of God," Janet Karim draws heavily from what has been conceived as the word of God in both the Old and New Testaments to advance the idea that women are children of God on an equal footing with men. Reacting to a particular incident in the life of the church in Malawi, Karim quotes specific biblical texts to support her argument for equality between women and men in the church.

But Christianity was not always liberating for women; it carried its own Western forms of patriarchal oppression.[14] For example, the biblical teaching in Genesis 2:20–24, where woman is created from man's rib and marriage is conceived as a union in which the woman loses her own identity by becoming one with her husband, has encouraged and justified marital inequality. In the name of such teachings, abusive husbands have demanded unwavering submission from their wives as their "help." In some African cultures, such things were clearly conceived differently before the arrival of Christianity. According to Phiri, the Chewa matrilineal system accorded women some value and status through initiation rites. But the coming of patriarchal Christian missionaries contributed to the destruction of even such limited dignity (1997: 45). To reclaim this dignity, some women converts, helped by missionary women, pioneered the Christianization of initiation rites as well as the founding of women's organizations as safe spaces within the old and newly established patriarchal structures. As early as 1901, Donald Fraser, working among the Ngoni in northern Malawi, was already instituting a more inclusive church leadership by the creation of *balalakazi* (women elders) in the Presbyterian Mission of Livingstonia. However, such steps were far from universally accepted.

> Though the eligibility of women as deacons was accepted by presbytery in 1922, it was not until 1935, and after a strong appeal by Fraser's widow, Dr. Agnes Fraser, that the presbytery agreed to recognize women elders

on the same basis as men. And it was not until 1966—thirty years after the Church in Livingstonia had taken the step, and more than sixty years after Fraser had first introduced *balalakazi* in uNgoni—that women became eligible for election as elders in the Church of Scotland. (Thompson 2002: 15–16)

According to Lattinga (2000), the spread of Christianity in its original rigid European form denied African people pride in their culture and ceremonies. The mission centers were good at "brainwashing" the African converts, "diverting" them from their Africanness, and converting them to a Christianity clad in Western clothing. Yet, blinded by racism and class bias, the missionaries would not provide these African converts with a Western education of the same quality they provided to their own children. In *From Slavery to School* (2001), Charlotte Poda, who was educated in a mission school in Mombasa in the late 1940s, describes how she was driven by the poverty of Western education for Africans to start her own independent black school in the 1950s. The segregation of Africans from whites became an issue within the churches themselves, which in some places developed separate white and African "wings."

The spread of missionary education was not uniform across the region. Missionaries arrived earlier in the coastal zones, but there had to contend with the already well-established Muslim communities. Some cooler areas devoid of pestilent diseases were also more attractive to missionaries, and these reflect a better-developed educational network even today. In all cases, however, women were in the forefront in the literacy campaigns, in providing voluntary labor for building schools, and in starting women's clubs to develop "suitable" skills for women, such as knitting, sewing, pot-making, and hygiene (Kimambo 1991: 130). Our early texts by women educated under foreign missionaries provide examples of attempts to train women in European (mostly English and German) household practices and forms of dress. "Should Women Be Educated?" (1933) and "Women's Education" (1936, 1937), espouse the virtues of Western education to their communities, their nations, and to the women themselves. Undoubtedly, the missionaries used education as the carrot they could dangle before those they planned to recruit into the Christian world.[15]

While they held strong appeal for many individual Africans, especially girls and women, missionary schools were often greeted with alarm by the chiefs. Shorter points out that the schools threatened the traditional structures of initiation and consequently the power of the chiefs, who fought bitterly against them, refusing to enroll their children and punishing those who did (1974: 78–79). A glimpse of such opposition is provided in the notebooks of Jane Elizabeth Chadwick, included in the text "My Students" (1920). Chadwick describes a missionary-educated girl named Kitandi who is shunned by her community because she refuses to wail in mourning with the traditional flourishes when her mother dies; they understand her to be abandoning the ways of her people because of her Christian education. Hay talks of Luo women educated by the missionaries in Maseno, Kenya, being scorned and sometimes stoned by their in-laws (1976: 100), and Larsson describes similar actions against women in Bukoba, Tanzania (1991: 184–85). Various protests against missionary education expressed fear of the changes heralded by both Christianity and colonialism. In such an atmosphere, some women saw themselves as guardians of the community's traditions and rituals, oppressive as some of them were for women.

Parents were often torn between conflicting desires: While many wanted the new education for their children, in part so that they might know the ways of the conquerors, they wanted also to sustain African beliefs, and African realities, to which they were accustomed. Missionaries sometimes began by co-opting some of the influential members of the community, such as chiefs' sons, who then recruited their mothers and friends (Hay 1976: 101). With education so closely linked to religion, those who were taught to read and write were expected to become religious teachers, and of course, the Bible generally served as the teaching text.

Soon the hunger for the new education became overwhelming.[16] Some Muslims even changed their names to gain admission into missionary schools. Missionaries encouraged the admission of girls, and in later years many schools came to be run by women. Women viewed the new education as emancipatory, allowing them to explore new horizons and break through the limits that had confined their mothers. They could now travel to new areas, as described in the "Women's Education" (1936, 1937); say no to arranged marriages, like the author of "Praised Be Jesus Christ" (1963); and become successful teachers of the very boys who had once scoffed at them, like Kitandi in "My Students" (1920, 1935).Their status and well-being within the society were enhanced, their differences from other women marked.

Thus, the tension between knowledge transmitted through informal socialization and that imparted through formal teaching continues today as community elders still insist on locating girls and their major activities within the family "compound," within what Michelle Rosaldo has called the domestic realm (1974: 23). Formal education, on the other hand, attempts to wrench her out of this compound, into public space. Both provide refuge and a degree of self-confidence for the girl. The former cradles the girl within a warm, safe, known, and largely predictable environment, where actions are conducted according to tradition and long-held customs, and where the support of others is largely assured. Susan Wood, in "What We Have in Common" (1964), notes the same need of European women settlers to cling to the past.

In the early days, colonial education for women was extremely paternalistic, conceived as what Gaitskell has called "education for domesticity" (1983: 241). In Eastern Africa, for example, a Commission on Higher Education, presuming to know the "needs of women," recommended "home-making" courses for women entering Uganda's Makerere University, the region's most prestigious institution (Tamale and Oloka-Onyango 2000). The women themselves were nevertheless very eager to take up this training as an avenue to other possibilities. At the very least, such education gave them a better understanding of hygiene and nutrition, thus reducing mortality among their children.

While missionary schools spread far and wide, and continued to outstrip government schools in the years ahead, such colonial education, in a sense, bore the seeds of its own destruction. The Germans in what would become Tanzania taught prospective clerks and administrators (among whom there was not a single girl) in their own schools (Larsson 1991: 171, 173). The British across the region had the specific objective of producing "good citizens" for the colonial government. As they conceived it, African men, after basic primary education, would provide support services in their administration, while African women, for whom education was provided much later, would provide comfortable homes for their husbands. The prescription for both was servitude. The aim, according to the colonialists, was to "lift" Africans from the quagmire of ignorance and depravity in which the colonialists thought they had found them, while at the same time keeping them "in their place." The colonized, however, used the education acquired for their own ends, including fighting and getting rid of the very people who provided that education.

Early Writing and Publishing

The interface between orality and writing reflects the historical fact of the co-existence of the two media for more than a millennium. Written literature in Eastern Africa dates from around the eighth century, when the Arabic script was introduced along with Islam. Some of the earliest extant manuscripts, such as *Siri l'asirari* (Secret of Secrets), from Kenya and dated 1663, are believed to have been written by women. Both the Arabic and Roman scripts were introduced within the process of evangelization. Hence, most of the early writings by women, both Muslim and Christian, are religious. The volume also includes early examples of letter writing.

With writing in Roman script came modern publishing. Religious texts were published for church use, and soon secular books and translations for use in schools were published and widely distributed. In 1948 the British government set up local literature bureaus, namely the East African Literature Bureau (EALB) to cater to Kenya, Tanganyika, Uganda, and Zanzibar, and the Northern Rhodesia and Nyasaland Publication Bureau to serve what are now Zambia and Malawi. These bureaus were entrusted with the task of publishing books, mostly in local languages, for schools and the public. From the 1950s onward, some British publishing houses, including Oxford University Press and Longman, opened local offices in the region.

Even today, when book publishing is fairly well-established, it does not meet the needs of all, or even most, women writers. Historically, the resources have been even more inadequate. Hence, many women have published in other forms, including newspapers and magazines, and have written for radio and television as well as for the stage and other types of performance. In Tanzania in 1926, for example, Zeina binti Mwinyipembe Sekinyaga wrote her essay on

"Civilized Motherhood," setting forth a kind of agenda for women's liberation, as a letter to the editor of *Mambo Leo*, a colonial government-sponsored monthly newspaper. In Uganda in 1932, Lusi Kyebakutika addressed the then-nascent problem of prostitution in a letter to a Luganda newspaper, the piece we call "The Word *Prostitute* Has Confused Us." And in Malawi in 1933, Emily Mkandawire, in the readers' forum of a local periodical, boldly addressed the question, "Should Women Be Educated?"

Whereas between 1890 and 1950 Eastern African women's writing (in this volume and in general) consisted mostly of short pieces such as songs, hymns, and poetry, personal letters, letters to the editor, petitions and complaints, short stories, and essays, after 1950, full-length books, dramas, monographs, and other academic writing by women began to appear in both local languages and English.

Settler and Colonial Women

While fewer European women than men came to the region as colonialists and settlers, their numbers increased as the colonial economy developed and demanded their services. Settler women accompanied men as spouses, daughters, and home caretakers, and also worked in the colonial economy. Some were evangelists, educators, and health workers; others ran plantations and involved themselves in colonial commerce. Settler women also collected and documented local cultural artifacts, activities, rituals, oral literatures, and languages.

Some of the texts in this volume were written by settler and colonial women who variously tried to come to grips with Africa—the Africa of their own experience, and the Africa of European myth. Through these texts, we glimpse not only their prevailing views of African women and men, activities and culture, but also some of their ideas about Eastern African politics, economics, and development. In "Letters from Africa to a Daughter in England" (1939–1963), Nellie Grant describes the frequent movements of women between the colonies and their home country. As daughters they were educated in Europe and visited there during holidays; as mothers they sent their children to school there or visited to conduct business for themselves or their spouses. Nellie Grant's letters cover the period from 1939, when colonial and settler domination in Kenya was institutionalized, to 1963, when the first elections, the forerunner to independence, were held. The letters detail the settlers' comfort and security of the late 1930s, despite a worldwide depression and a plague of locusts, as well as the threat of World War II. By the 1950s, the letters reveal growing anxiety and the fear of economic ruin as African labor became unreliable due to Mau Mau resistance. In her letter of 16 March 1953, Grant writes:

> On the Hodges' farm in Sabukia the labour all went overnight, leaving their maize, turkeys, clothes and every single thing; the Hodges will be practically bust this year as all their maize and pyrethrum is lying out unpicked; no one has been kinder or better to their labour than they have.

Colonialists, like slavers before them, could never understand why their "kindness" was not reciprocated by those they dominated. Grant, who like her neighbors tried to treat her African servants better than most whites did, is clearly distressed, even angry, that the Africans were not more discriminating in their rebellion against the settlers.

Many settler women, Nellie Grant included, were not blind to the contradictions and conflicts engendered by colonialism. Grant's letters nonetheless indicate that the Mau Mau resistance largely defined her own ambiguous relationship with African workers. On the one hand, colonialists and settlers found it convenient not to understand Africans and their reality; on the other, they harbored great fears and constructed myths and speculations about their capabilities and weaknesses. Nowhere is this more evident than in the Europeans' fear of African sexuality, which led them not to tolerate sexual contact and relations between the races, especially between European women and African men. Nellie Grant's letters allude to these fears and intolerance, but her attitude is restrained when compared to the mainstream of white settlers.

By the early 1960s, colonialism and thus settler ambitions were in retreat. The dwindling colonial influence is captured in Nellie Grant's letter of 13 June 1960, when she writes about closing her school.

> I have decided to say the school must go away. The teachers' houses want renewing and the school buildings are very dicky. I started the school thirty two years ago as a tiny thing, when I had a thousand acres and quite a labor force. I have now fifty acres and there are a hundred and fifty-three children in the school of whom twenty come from this farm, three teachers, and everything expanding, and lots of other schools around.

Throughout, Grant's letters underscore some of the settler notions of alleged African unpredictability and cunning. While Grant expresses, in various ways, the prevailing view of European cultural superiority, she also reveals the fear that, if a colonial woman were too friendly with Africans, she could face negative consequences from her own people.

In E. May Crawford's "Face to Face with Wangu wa Makeri" (1913), a settler woman strikes an unusual balance in her attitude toward the Africans she encounters. The text carries the characteristic zeal of European missionaries in documenting local cultural events to inform those at home, but differs from many conventional European accounts of its time. Colonialist writers needed to justify the colonial and Christian mission of civilizing and ruling the local population, and often did so by putting emphasis on what they thought was "backward" or "barbaric" in the African societies they observed. Such writings often critiqued local cultural, economic, and political practices and beliefs. Crawford's text, based on her encounters with Gikuyu women, is such a critique, at times dismissive and typically racist. Yet it also contains a measure of admiration and awe for some of the practices and personalities. She is impressed by the women's creativity, their endurance and resilience, and their manual skills and aptitude at "buying and selling." She also sees them confined within a strenuous life ruled by cruel cultural norms: "Though practically slaves from childhood they bear life's burdens very philosophically and are generally ready with a laugh and a jest." While she affirms their cleverness in some areas, Crawford was not an admirer of African women's intelligence; she found them "dull and torpid," an observation claimed by other settler women and men throughout colonialism. And even as she tries to describe her observations accurately, her narrative never loses its tone of superiority or exoticism, as when she depicts the warm welcome she receives when she arrives to meet the woman chief, Wangu wa Makeri.

> They ascended the hill in hundreds to perform a dance in my honour. Nothing would content them but that I must be dragged into the centre of the ring, to endure with as cheerful a countenance as I could muster the din of their savage song and the smother of dust raised by their feet.

In the collection called "Letters on Race and Politics," written in 1942 by Elspeth Huxley and Margery Perham, two white British women with experience in Africa debate the rights and privileges of the settlers and colonialists in Kenya. Elspeth Huxley, daughter of Nellie Grant, expresses the prevailing position of the settlers in relation to native Kenyans, the direction of the country, and the settlers' status in the colony. She refutes the notion that the settlers did not have the interest of the Kenyans at heart.

> Africans are being taught skills and trades of all kinds. . . .Therefore to suggest, as you seem to, that the Europeans want to sit on the Africans' heads and prevent advances seems to me to give an entirely false impression.

Huxley's frustration, like that of other settlers, was directed at their home government, which seemed to waver in their support for settlers' aspirations. Writing from her authoritative post in Oxford, however, Margery Perham suggests that the settlers should stop being selfish and moderate their ambitions:

> Any settlers who cannot accept this check to their attempt to dominate, which will do no injury at all to their personal security and prosperity, should move to a country where conditions allow them the full citizenship to which their traditions have accustomed them.

While describing the intimate link between race relations and colonial politics, the correspondence touches on the uncertainty of colonialism's future in Eastern Africa. Developments in South Africa, where settlers set the agenda for the colony's autonomy and exercised power over the local population, cautioned Britain against allowing similar excesses in the Eastern Africa region.[17] The correspondence between the two Europeans points to differences of opinion among settlers and administrators. But it also highlights the unequal political and economic position of, on the one hand, the privileged settlers who defended the right to occupy the colonies and treat local people as they saw fit, and on the other, the exploited local people. Huxley's paternalistic and condescending tone is symptomatic of settlers' attitudes, and her polite language does not hide her impatience with a government she saw as lacking a clear position regarding the settlers and the local population.[18]

Capitalism, Social Change, and the Proletarianization of Women

In introducing new economic demands and imposing an administration to ensure compliance, colonialism brought about sweeping social changes. The colonial period saw the reorganization of societies, the movement of peoples, and the emergence of different sociocultural relations within and among African communities. Social units, including new tribes, were invented to rationalize types of colonial governance that required such creations.[19]

The social changes effected by colonialism changed women's lives sometimes in contradictory directions. As Iliffe has put it, "the colonial world was a man's world and women probably took less part in political leadership than before, while several matrilineal societies moved towards patriliny" (Iliffe 1979: 300). The introduction of cash-crop production, for example, brought in new marital patterns or exaggerated the old ones. The growing need for cash, for taxes or personal use, and its availability in places far away from home facilitated marital estrangements and short-lived liaisons. Men traveled from their home villages for work on colonists' plantations, in mines, or in urban centers. Women were not always welcomed in such places, and went there at their own peril and risk. Marriage was still seen as a link between families and clans who knew one another, and marrying strangers was frowned upon. In "Modern Marriages" (1936), Princess Kaiko Nambayo warns men against marrying unknown women in faraway cities: "You ought to know that it is difficult to milk a cow when you have no idea which kraal it comes from." Women often found themselves either unexpected co-wives or long-distance widows. If men marrying unknown African women was seen as a problem, so too was African women marrying European, Indian, or Arab men. C.M. binti Hassan's 1946 poem, "An African Marries a White Through Mere Worldly Desires," highlights the issue of interracial and cross-cultural marriage. The poet questions the colonial situation that enabled European and Asian men to marry African women, but not vice versa. She doubts the soundness of personal and family relationships governed not by mutual respect, but by imposed ideas of racial superiority and inferiority. Such a marriage, the author suggests, could only bring social alienation to the woman, her children, and her family. The disadvantages of such unions to the women involved seem so obvious to the poet that she proclaims economic opportunism their only possible motivation.

Most white missionaries and settlers were, not surprisingly, even more strongly opposed to interracial marriages. Loise Kalondu wa Maseki, the narrator of "A Courageous Woman" (2000), tells of the resistance she faced in 1954 when her daughter chose to marry a white teacher at the local mission. Both young people were Christians, but "the missionaries said that it was not God's will that a black person should marry a white person."

Whether by choice or by necessity, some women took advantage of the change and mobility afforded by colonialism to solve some of the social and economic problems in their own lives. Their "solutions," however, sometimes brought new problems of their own. Unattached women who sought work on the plantations or in cities faced practical hardships as well as social and sometimes legal censure. Some turned to prostitution, and even those who did not were often considered to be immoral and untrustworthy. Two colonial-era texts come to the defense of such women. In "The Word *Prostitute* Has Confused Us" (1932), a Ugandan woman, Lusi Kyebakutika, objects to the fact that, "When somebody sees a woman without a husband, she is called a prostitute." She also criticizes the double standard that condemns prostitutes, but not the men who seek out and pay for their services. In a letter to a local newspaper, she asks, "When a woman is called a prostitute, what shall a man be called?"—and then she answers her own question.

> You know, a man is the real prostitute. Sometimes, you are walking on the road, when you see a man coming from a house. Then he calls you, "Madam, come and have some tea and rest. I will take you later where you are going." Yet the resting he is talking of is not good. Therefore, was it the woman who called the man?

Kyebakutika's protest seems not to have been an isolated incident. Eighteen years later, a group of women in Uganda protested not only against the label of "prostitute," but against some measures taken against independent women by the local authorities, including restrictions on their travel. Their petition, "Women Are Human Beings" (1950), echoes Kyebakutika's letter, asking, "If we are called prostitutes, can a woman make herself a prostitute on her own? First of all, is not a prostitute the man who gave us the money?" The writers condemn the colonial administration for approving the restrictions, which they see as an example of the unequal justice afforded to women.

> When the men instituted the laws to forbid us to go abroad to find work to help ourselves and our parents, the law was brought to you and to our rulers to be accepted. But we were not called to any meeting to be asked why we go abroad rather than staying at home, and what problems sent us there. . . . We are sorry when we see that women do not get the protection of our sacred government.

Several other texts show African women challenging the colonialists for being inconsistent and, by their own standards, unjust in their treatment of colonized peoples. In "A Petition" (1930), Mwana Hashima binti Sheikh pleads with the colonial government in Kenya to recognize that she resolved a local conflict, and to reward her fairly for her service: "As far as I know if anyone serves the Government, he is usually given something as reward or pension, and I did a great work for the Government and I hope that the Government will not cast me aside."

Another woman who took advantage of the changes wrought by colonialism appears in the text called "I Want a Divorce" (1922), taken from court records. In spite of her youth, Luiza defies tradition and challenges male authority by publicly pleading her case against the husband who has abandoned her. Because of her age and sex, she would likely not have been given such an opportunity in a traditional setting. The colonial system is also used to personal advantage by Nyense Namwandu, author of "Fighting for Widow's Property" (1947). As a Christian and an educated woman, Namwandu must have been aware of the colonial administration's position on the two issues of widow inheritance and the status of girl-children. In her appeal, she highlights the conflict between traditional African practices and the new beliefs, daring the colonial administration to back its own beliefs by acting in her favor.

Some of the new social changes were evidenced in the breaking down of social etiquette and cultural norms. In "Domestic Violence" (1939), Erusa Kibanda complains about her brother's behavior in her home. Had the extended family all been living together, as had earlier been the custom, the brother would probably have not dared to behave as he did for fear of immediate social sanction from relatives around him.

Some of the effects of colonialism, however, were acutely felt in those areas where land was expropriated and new colonial economic demands were put in place—for example, with the cultivation of such cash crops as coffee, tea, and sisal. The work on these plantations was characterized by exploitive wages, intolerable and inhuman working and living conditions, and all manner of cruel treatment. Reactions against such situations were inevitable.

"Song of the Coffee Girls" (1922) exemplifies women's collective resistance and protest in Kenya in the early part of the twentieth century. This resistance was directed toward an economic system that enabled settlers and the colonial administration to conscript men and women for cheap plantation labor. Although the recruitment of men from far away was encouraged and even enforced, women and girls working in the plantations were usually nonmigrants and came from the surrounding communities. The working conditions for these women were dismal. Using both spontaneous and organized protests to draw attention to their plight, the women responded to the leadership of Harry Thuku, an African labor leader who tried to mobilize the workers to demand their rights. "Song of the Coffee Girls" paid tribute to Thuku, calling him "chief of the coffee girls," and denounced not only the colonists but the Gikuyu chiefs they had appointed, who had supported Thuku's imprisonment in 1922. Many women were among the many unarmed Africans killed by colonial police and settlers during a demonstration demanding Thuku's release, including Mary Muthoni Nyanjiru, who had challenged the timid men to take action to free Thuku. The song could have been part of the repertoire on that fateful day.[20]

During the late 1930s and early 1940s, the effects of World War II were felt in the warring Europeans' Eastern African colonies. While African men fought with British forces, African women bore the brunt of war's impact on the home front. In the second of the letters included in "War Time in Zanzibar" (1943), Zeyana Ali Muh'd describes the shortages and other hardships women endured, as well as their resourcefulness and solidarity with other women during troubled times—a departure from the severely hierarchical nature of Zanzibari society in that era. On a larger scale, the additional hardships faced by Africans during a war whose outcome was unlikely to benefit them only served to accelerate growing demands for liberation.

Anticolonial Resistance and Liberation Struggles

The oppression, exploitation, and contradictions engendered by colonialism made resistance against it inevitable. Women's resistance took a variety of forms, both individual and collective. Unfortunately, few texts from that period reflect the experiences of women during struggles against colonialism. We do have texts written or recorded much later in the twentieth century, including some first-hand accounts, describing women's active participation in liberation movements.

One of the earliest women freedom fighters in Eastern Africa was Mekatilili wa Menza, who has achieved legendary status in Kenya. In a text written in 2000, Hannah Tsuma describes Mekatilili's leadership of her people, the Giriyama of coastal Kenya, in a rebellion against their British colonizers in 1913 and 1914. Mekatilili saw forced and unpaid labor and lack of respect for local cultures as a form of slavery. She showed fearlessness in the face of physical danger and imprisonment, denouncing the local chiefs who cooperated with the colonizers and focusing much of her effort on mobilizing women to refuse to send their sons to fight for the British in World War I.

Mekatilili's story shows how she was able to use all the talents and draw on the resources of her position as woman, mother, community leader, orator, and performer. Traditional systems of beliefs and protection through medicines, social equilibrium, trust, and commitment, demonstrated by oath-taking, became vital factors in her campaign. In this, Mekatilili was not alone. Before and after Mekatilili, ritual and belief systems were important to the resistance movements in the region, including the Nyabingi revolts in Uganda and Rwanda during the early years of the twentieth century;[21] the Nehanda resistance of 1897–1898 in Zimbabwe; Mkomanire's Maji Maji wars of 1905–1907 in southern Tanzania (Iliffe 1979); the 1915 John Chilembwe revolt in Malawi (Rotberg 1965; Rotberg and Mazrui 1970); and the *mbiru* protest against colonialism in northeastern Tanzania, where women participated fully (Kimambo 1971: 1991; Spear et al. 1999).

Later, in the second half of the twentieth century, other women would also draw inspiration and strength from rituals and belief systems. Warrior priest-esses Alice Lenshina of Zambia and Alice Lakwena of Uganda built their polit-ical bases, using their spiritual and ritual gifts and positions. Both became charismatic leaders by harnessing both African and Christian beliefs, thus demonstrating not only women's spirituality but also their quick adaptation to elements they find useful, materially or spiritually (Roberts 1970; Berger 1976).

While Mekatilili, Lenshina, and Lakwena were self-made women, arising from among their people to become leaders, others inherited their positions as rulers. Such were Mwami Tereza Ntare of Tanzania, Princess Nakatindi of Zambia, and Chauwa Banda of Malawi. Both groups were united in perceiving colonialism as an intrusion and a threat politically and culturally. In a 1936 proclamation, published in this volume as "Fighting for My Chieftaincy," Chauwa Banda posits colonialism as a threat to the political and economic organization of her society, as well as to the individual and collective identity of her people, the Banda. Mamdani (2002) points out that the colonial project created political identities that were vertically based on race and horizontally based on ethnicity, legitimizing both new hierarchies and ethnic differences at the same time. Chauwa Banda was thus protesting the imposed political sys-tem, which the colonizers created by handpicking local individuals and giving them power, against the wishes of authentic traditional rulers like herself. The newly appointed chiefs, however, were not secure in their power: They feared conspiracies by their own people and worried about falling out of favor with the colonials. The appointment of a male chief to replace Chauwa Banda was also symptomatic of the colonial administration's preference for male rather than female political leaders in Africa. In the colonial era, spaces where women tra-ditionally exercised political power became less important or disappeared alto-gether. Chauwa Banda harnessed her strength as both ruler and woman by tap-ping her people's beliefs in their cosmology: "I am the descendant of Chauwa, the founder of the Abanda clan," she proclaims. She also appeals, "If you acknowledge that I am your mother, please attend the meeting." In reminding her people that she is their mother-ruler, she was contesting the redefinition of her identity and potency.

Walter Rodney describes the effect on African women of colonialism's imposition of new values and identities.

What happened to African women under colonialism is that the social, religious, constitutional, and political privileges and rights disappeared, while the economic exploitation continued and was often intensified. It was intensified because the division of labor according to sex was fre-quently disrupted. (1972: 227)

Rodney argues that the colonial mentality preferred men, who entered more easily and in greater numbers into the all-important cash economy (226–27). Because women's work was devalued and made inferior, women's status also deteriorated. Colonialism thus intensified the marginalization of women by reinforcing and extending some of the worst elements of African patriarchy.

Of the five countries represented in this volume, only Kenya waged a fierce anticolonial armed struggle, in which women not only participated but also distinguished themselves as military leaders. The Kenyan struggle was typical of colonies with strong settler communities, for whom defending their own interests meant opposing Africans' movements toward independence. In "Warrior Woman" (1993), Field Marshal Muthoni highlights the heroism of women leaders in the Mau Mau uprising. Writing of her own experiences in the 1950s, Muthoni describes women's courage under fire and through painful material hardships, negating any notion that women in the Mau Mau movement were the tools of men. Just as they did in Mekatilili's struggle, spiritual energies and ritual strengthened the Mau Mau warriors' commitment, discipline, and hope for the future.

In Kenya, the years of "the Emergency"—a period of martial law declared by the British in response to the Mau Mau resistance—affected both the women who fought in the bush and those who remained behind in their homes. African communities—in particular the Gikuyu, who were the main constituents of the Mau Mau—faced severe hardships, including forced internal exile. Hannah Kahiga's "A Model Day during the Emergency" (1966) provides a firsthand account of women's day-to-day lives in one of the British concentration camps. These camps—rationalized by the British, according to Nellie Grant (1939–1963), as "villagization" schemes—were designed to monitor and contain the Africans' movements. Facilities were overcrowded, meager, and often unsanitary, and residents were overworked, underfed, brutalized, and encouraged to betray those at home and in the forest. Besides the people in the "villages," reports show that by 1954 there were fifty thousand detainees and seventeen thousand convicts scattered in camps and prisons (Rosberg and Nottingham 1966). While the strategies of war on both sides included terror and fear, the ratio of African to British deaths was likely more than one hundred to one (Elkins 2005). In the camps and in the forest, death was always close, whether brought by attacks, starvation, or disease. Women such as Wanjiru Nyamarutu, Gakonyo Ndungi, and Wambui Kamuirigo were relied on for their crucial and loyal services in the provision of food, intelligence, organization, logistics, legal counseling, and health.[22]

Both "Warrior Woman" and "A Model Day during the Emergency" present women not as victims but as wartime fighters, overtly or subversively. They depict women bearing the suffering of war, which exacerbated daily deprivations, oppressions, and marginalization. But they also show women's commitment, resilience, resourcefulness, and courage in rising to the challenges of a war in which they themselves had a vital stake. Women's texts about their experiences during the Mau Mau uprising remain rare, but the ones presented in this volume, as well as Wambui Otieno's *Mau Mau Daughter: A Life History*, give us a sense of their valor in a war against colonialism.

Anticolonial struggles drew to a close in the 1960s, not only in Kenya but throughout the region. Nationalists had organized major anticolonial opposition in their countries, culminating in the formation of political parties to mobilize for independence. At this stage, women became, more clearly than ever before, indispensable to the struggle for African liberation.

INDEPENDENCE AND AFTER

"Take a Look at Our Joy": Women Celebrate Independence
The years between 1960 and 1965 were momentous ones for the women of Eastern Africa. The end of colonialism and the coming of independence brought not only the joys of liberation but also new struggles and the challenges of development. Women, along with men, had to untangle colonialism's legacy of contradictions. Having suffered some of the worst effects of colonialism, women embraced independence with vigor and hopeful anticipation, but they also remained cautious and concerned about the future.

The five countries in the region became independent in succession—Tanganyika in 1961, Uganda 1962, Kenya and Zanzibar 1963, Malawi and Zambia 1964. In 1964, Tanganyika united with independent Zanzibar to form Tanzania. The British flag that had flown over the five countries was replaced by five national flags, representing governments that were led by prime ministers and/or presidents as well as parliaments. Independence, as a political milestone, at first brought tremendous euphoria, captured in the "Independence Song" sung by girls from Zambia's Roma Girls Secondary School at independence celebrations in 1964. The feelings expressed by the lyrics link the political to the spiritual.

> Our God, take a look at our joy
> In this our land
> Which you have given us,
> That it may be ours
> With all that is in it.

Such words were echoed throughout the region as women sang and danced while asking God's blessing on the five countries—in all of their various languages.

In "Independence 1962," a recollection composed in 1998, Winnie Munyarugerero tries to remember the excitement and energy she felt thirty-six years earlier, on Uganda's independence day: "What characterized the occasion, however, was the excitement that permeated the atmosphere. The excitement was so heavy and real that you could almost touch it, you felt it in your blood stream, right through your entire body."

Independence was as fresh as the young girls who sang the independence songs, promising development, prosperity, and new opportunities. Because the idea of independence was so intense, the often difficult realities that unfolded in subsequent decades provoked equally strong reactions: In 1998, Munyarugerero—along with many of her generation—asks, simply but heartbreakingly, "What went wrong?" What, she wonders, happened to the dreams and hopes of independence? While Munyarugerero attributes her reaction to the disillusionment engendered by the politics and economics of the post-independence era, the text by Field Marshall Muthoni, also speaking years later, in 1993, expresses the sense of betrayal she felt because she was not accorded the recognition she deserved and had been promised for her contributions to the anticolonial struggle. Returning, after independence, from the Mau Mau struggle, Muthoni, and many others like her, was treated as a stranger in a country she had helped liberate. She remained a nonentity, while some—those who belonged to more privileged or dominant groups, or had more shrewdly positioned themselves for the post-independence era—reaped the rewards of the battles she and her comrades had fought.

Some of Muthoni's sentiments are shared by Princess Nakatindi in "The Princess of Politics" (1963, 1971). She attributes the ills of post-independence Zambia to tribalism and lack of economic independence, proclaiming, "We have political power but without economic power we cannot really be free." For these women, the problem resides in the conflict between the promise of independence and the failures of execution. Through their texts, the women project a sense that the independence aspired to by most people had been hijacked by a group for its own ends. This has remained a major concern and several texts in the volume repeat this post-independence dismay.

Visionaries and Mothers of the Nation: Women in Parliament

For the women who were selected, nominated, and voted into or appointed to seats in post-independence parliaments, these legislative bodies would serve as platforms from which they could bring women's points of view to the coming battles over the development of independent Eastern Africa.[23]

In "Let us Praise Phoebe, Our MP," the singer posits women's entry into parliamentary politics as an act of subversion and a challenge to the traditional status quo, shifting the fly whisk, a symbol of power, from the men's hands to the women's. Grace Awach, who sang this song in 1994, underscores the fact that, in Kenya, women were rather late in entering parliamentary politics, becoming significantly involved only in the 1990s. In Malawi, Tanzania, Uganda, and Zambia, however, women were active parliamentarians from the early days of independence. In spite of tremendous odds, the creeping betrayal and disillusionment, women, though few in number, worked hard to claim a place in formal post-independence politics. Their voices, some of which are included in this volume, have been at times quite radical.

Unlike the other women parliamentarians whose texts are published here, such as Bibi Titi Mohamed (1965) and Lucy Lameck (1965) in Tanzania, Rose Chibambo (1964) in Malawi, or Joyce Mpanga (1961, 1989) in Uganda, Barbro Johansson, author of the speeches published in this volume as "The Advancement of Women" (1964, 1965), came to Africa as a missionary and educator.

She was inspired and engulfed by the political atmosphere in Tanzania in the days following independence, took up the causes of her adopted country, and became an active political figure inside and outside parliament. Like the others, she chose a public political career that gave her a platform on which to resist and challenge the male hegemony that expressed itself in the family, the society, the political parties, and the parliament.

In addition to such women as Bibi Titi Mohamed, Lucy Lameck, and Rose Chibambo, who were in politics as a continuation of their pre-independence struggles, others, including Joyce Mpanga and Phoebe Asiyo (the subject of "Let Us Praise Phoebe, Our MP"), came from the ranks of women's organizations formed after independence. They entered or continued in politics not only as a means of attaining personal advancement, but more importantly, because they hoped to use their positions to fight for the liberation and advancement of women. Princess Nakatindi (1963, 1971), for example, declares: "Politics is in my blood. I simply want to serve my people and the nation."

The few women who managed to enter parliament immediately after independence, along with many who later joined them, used their seats to confront national as well as women's issues. Those whose voices are included in this volume display not only individual styles of oratory but also intense passion for the subjects they expose and address. Florence Lubega's 1959 speech, "Debate on Higher Education," brings up many of the issues surrounding women and education at that time. While she strongly believes that secondary and university education for both men and women is essential to development in Uganda, and indeed all of Eastern Africa, she insists on the need for proper planning, policies, management, and government oversight, lest both scarce resources and irretrievable opportunities be squandered.

One of the most powerful voices of this period was that of Bibi Titi Mohamed of Tanzania. In "Sacrifices for Change" (1965), she expresses an awareness of her young nation's vulnerability to being defined by the interests and relations of the Cold War superpowers. Galvanized by the support of African women who attended the All African Women's Constitutional Congress in 1962 in Dar es Salaam, which she chaired, Bibi Titi Mohamed became a great champion of Pan Africanism, campaigning for the cause not only in Tanzania but also in Kenya. In parliament, she spoke of the need for a united anti-imperialist stance and for the liberation of the whole of Africa. She castigated the superpowers, and especially the United States, for using developing nations from the Congo to Vietnam as pawns in the Cold War. The United States president, she declares, "wants to prevent Communism. Why doesn't he go to fight Communism in Russia where it all started?"

In her speech, Bibi Titi Mohamed also criticizes the postcolonial economic agenda, under which developed countries continue to build their own wealth while exploiting and weakening newly-independent states. She points out that "the whole economy of this country has built Britain," and argues that Tanzania's problems are compounded by the fact that in spite of independence, "many of us are still mentally controlled by our former colonial masters." She urges her colleagues in parliament to "let the people know that the colonialists have really left this country." She advocates social, cultural, political, and economic revolutions for her country and for all of Africa, turning to universally understandable metaphors to make her point:

> We want to revolutionize, although some people from other places misunderstand the meaning of revolution. Our revolution is an economic revolution for a better life and we should be able to reproduce a lot. Some generations die due to sick stomachs. When a child wants to develop inside one, one develops stomach problems, and you abort—is this how we are going to increase the population here? We want a revolution. We want to procreate. I too would like to have a baby and hold a child one day.

In "Africans Are Not Poor," also drawn from a speech made in the Tanzanian parliament in 1965, Lucy Lameck tackles many of the same issues, though she expresses them differently. Lameck speaks of self-reliance in its totality as the relevant direction for national development: "We have a great responsibility . . . that of laying the foundations that conform to the needs and experience of Tanzanians themselves." She saw this foundation as politically and economically "homegrown," and in harmony "with the people's experience." This idea was tied to the notion of an African form of socialism, which she saw as the best model for development. Both Lucy Lameck and Barbro Johansson (1964, 1965) advocated this model some years before the Arusha Declaration of 1967, which was a blueprint for Tanzania's program of African socialism, called Ujamaa, and which became a pivotal document in Tanzania's contemporary history. Tanzanian women supported the Arusha Declaration overwhelmingly because it promised structural changes that would benefit them.

One of the overriding concerns of the women leaders inside and outside of parliament has been the contradiction contained in Lucy Lameck's cry, "Africans are not poor." Africa suffers from more extreme poverty than any other continent, which in turn undermines its ability to develop and improve the well-being of its citizens through better education, health care, and other services. Yet its poverty is based upon geopolitical power structures, and not upon any lack of natural resources, which Africa has in abundance (Gioseffi 2003). As Lameck argues, Africa faces great developmental challenges because it cannot follow the model set by the developed countries, which achieved their development through exploitation. Princess Nakatindi, Lucy Lameck, and Bibi Titi Mohamed all point to the need for Africa to develop its own economic power base in order to gain economic independence. It was this impulse that in part fueled support for the idea of African socialism as exemplified by the Arusha Declaration in Tanzania—which, in the end, failed to put in place an alternative to the capitalist system of development.

These texts also examine the functions of institutions such as the World Bank, the International Monetary Fund, and various government and non-governmental organizations. Several of the writers in this volume find that these institutions, though garbed in development coats, in fact serve as instruments for the oppression and subjugation of women. They use their power to set conditions for African states and people, often without regard to the realities on the ground, and without considering true grassroots needs. The solutions they offer are often both constricting and unsustainable, because at the grassroots level, people can neither identify with them nor own them. The programs they impose are sometimes especially insensitive to the needs of women, failing to include them in the development process and seeking to institute alien values and practices while relegating traditional sociocultural values and practices to the periphery.

Development efforts have particularly left unaddressed many issues pertinent to women's specific needs. Sarah Nyendohwa Ntiro's autobiographical text "Fighting for Women's Rights" (1999) underscores struggles for women's legal rights generally, and interventions against arranged marriages for Hindu and Muslim women specifically. The failure to address problems such as forced early marriage, female circumcision, widow inheritance, and other traditional customs that impinge upon women's rights is also noted in Lucy Lameck's speech. The societal changes required to promote women's welfare became major rallying points for Lameck, Rose Chibambo, Bibi Titi Mohamed, Barbro Johansson, and others. "I want major revolution. I want major changes in the entire structure of our society," Johansson proclaimed in 1965. "Girls and women must have the same opportunities as men."

Women's commitment to national development and their political parties, however, provided them with neither security nor peace. When they fell out of favor with their heads of state, Bibi Titi Mohamed was jailed for many years, while Rose Chibambo and Sarah Nyendohwa Ntiro were forced into long-term exile. What befell these three women, in Tanzania, Malawi, and Uganda, was symptomatic of the crisis in governance and the intensification of conflicts among different groups vying for political and economic dominance after independence. Rose Chibambo's 1964 parliamentary speech, published here as "The Truth Will Always Speak," details her attempts to defend herself from accusations of treason for allegedly failing to support Prime Minister Hastings Kamuzu Banda. Her position, and that of other women like her, rested on the whims of ruling men, who did not usually countenance criticism or dissent. Knowing this, however, did not deter the women from expressing contrary views on economic policies, international politics, and the behavior of (male) leaders. Despite political persecution, which in some cases meant they could no longer serve in government, these women also remained politically active, in one form or another, throughout their lives, dedicated to bringing about improvements in the lives of women through their political work

Thorns, Ghosts, and Wandering Spirits: Conflicts and Civil Wars

In the years immediately following independence, there was already deep dissatisfaction among some groups in Eastern Africa. In 1964, the armies of Tanzania, Kenya, and Uganda mutinied. In the same year, there was a cabinet crisis in Malawi when a group of ministers revolted, and some were forced into exile. And 1964 was also the year of the Zanzibar revolution, which ousted the ruling sultanate and paved the way for the island nation to join with Tanganyika to form the current United Republic of Tanzania.

Throughout the region, conflicts intensified as the ruling groups struggled to give their societies political, cultural, and economic direction, while at the same time curtailing political freedoms and limiting political participation through establishing one-party states. Some of these conflicts developed into civil wars, which have had a great impact on the lives of women in the region, and several texts in the volume expose women's suffering in these wars.

Uganda has seen one of the most protracted internal conflicts in post-independence Africa. The existence of civil war in some parts of the country has been virtually continuous since 1966. Political strain within the ruling group in Uganda exploded in 1971, when President Milton Obote was ousted by Idi Amin, his army chief of staff. Amin's regime, which was generally hostile to women's rights, as well as the regimes that followed, failed to resolve Uganda's political and economic problems, instead exacerbating conflicts as different political cliques vied for power.[24] The impact of these conflicts was felt outside of Uganda, as hundreds of thousands of women and men took refuge in all the countries of the region. Some of the neighboring countries felt threatened by these conflicts, and indeed were drawn into them, as was the case with Tanzania, which went to war with Idi Amin. Tanzanian forces joined with Ugandan exiles in overthrowing Amin in 1979 and reinstalling Obote.

Another coup, in 1986, installed Uganda's current president, Yoweri Museveni, ushering in a new and brutal period of civil war in the northern provinces of Uganda. Resistance against the Museveni government in the north was greatly influenced by a woman named Alice Auma, often called Alice Lakwena because, as a spirit medium, she was believed to be representing the spirit Lakwena. During the 1980s, she employed her spiritual and ritual resources to mobilize one of the most enduring and controversial resistance movements in the post-independence period. The fighting continued even more viciously after Auma went into exile and a new leadership emerged in the form of the Lord's Resistance Army, led by Joseph Kony, who also proclaimed himself a spirit medium. Arac de Nyeko's 2003 narrative, "In the Stars," laments the brutal effects of this conflict. The author condemns both the brutal rebel group and the corrupt and ineffectual government forces for the immense suffering on the ground. As is so often the case, this suffering has been borne largely by women, who are subject to rape as well as massacres, and by children, thousands of whom have been forced to become child soldiers. Even where women's sympathies lie with one side or another in civil war, they have often voiced resistance to the destruction war wreaks on their lives, families, identity, and dignity. Monica Arac de Nyeko refers to the war survivors as "a generation of thorns," living for almost two decades with "images of ghosts of dead friends and relatives." She also illuminates the cosmological and spiritual consequences of war. Africans are known for their reverence of the dead and for the rituals performed on burial grounds, which connect the living to the dead. Not knowing where the body of a relative lies is thus a major spiritual and psychological torment. Arac de Nyeko's family was devastated by the fact that they were unable to recover the body of an uncle, who died in the conflict. Arac de Nyeko attributes her mother's death not only to meningitis but to the spiritual and psychological effects of the war:

> Worry had drained Ma's spirit. She carried memories. She suffered pain of knowing the past and future. . . . She had died knowing we would never go to school because it was always bullets and bombs. Our virginity would fall prey to wicked savagery. We would be abducted and forced to fight. Our bodies would rot in the wild.

Because armed conflict exacerbates the already existing inequalities that women experience, violence in various forms becomes a manifestation of the unequal power relations (Gardam and Jarvis 2001). Arac de Nyeko points to the psychological and physical trauma, the savagery of sexual violence, the brutal deaths, the fear, the helplessness and hopelessness, the distrust and perception of betrayal from national and international bodies, expected to intervene but failing to do so. "We know nothing of treaties. . . . But we know that we are going to die."

Similar sentiments find expression in an earlier poem from Uganda, "Pray No Revenge" (1979) by Grace Akello, who fled the brutal regime of Idi Amin. Akello's text resonates with the displacement and loss of identity and peace that is the lot of refugees and exiles. Her poem conveys not only the physical displacement of the living, but also the fate of the spirit that wanders aimlessly, finding solace only in death.

Some of the greatest conflicts, yielding the largest number of refugees, have taken place in the Great Lakes region. Uganda, Congo-Kinshasa, Rwanda, and Burundi have produced millions of internal and external refugees, and the rest of the countries of Eastern Africa, especially Tanzania, Kenya, and Uganda, have served as sanctuaries. Malawi and Zambia have not been spared the refugee exodus either, since victims have tried to flee as far as possible from the atrocities of war.

One of the most horrendous chapters in the history of this region's conflicts has been the Rwandan genocide of 1994, in which estimates of those killed have ranged between 500,000 and 1 million people. In her text "In the Shadow of God" (2000), Ugandan writer Goretti Kyomuhendo asks, as many others have done, "Who killed them? Why were they killed?" Kyomuhendo asks the questions in the self-contradictory setting of a church—a place where one expects to find both physical and spiritual peace and refuge—which has served as the site of a massacre, in effect a racial pogrom. Women in Rwanda were subject to rape and torture as well as mass death. Agathe Uwilingiyimana, the first woman prime minister in Rwanda—in fact, in the whole eastern and central African region—was killed, as were many other women who were Tutsi or moderate Hutus. Women were targets not only in their own right, but for their affiliations as wives and relations of the intended victims. Many women also participated in the killings and the violence.

Mamdani (2002) attributes the genocide to several factors, primary among them the colonial legacy that endowed certain groups with a racial identity perceived to be superior to others. Colonialism, he argues, advocated what has come to be known as the Hamitic factor, which identified any advances in the region as foreign, brought by what were considered superior races. While the actual ethnic distinctions between the Tutsis and the Hutus were slight, the Tutsis were designated a race with origins outside the region, and thus a superior one. The identities of the two groups were differentiated in part through supposed contrasts in their physical features, which were much remarked by the colonialists. These differences became the "original sin" that Kyomuhendo alludes to in her narrative. The failure of the postcolonial governments to dismantle this system of differentiation, instead assigning either privilege or persecution on the basis of ethnicity, created fertile ground for the genocide. The roots of the genocide, however, also need to be understood within a regional context, where issues of citizenship, indigenousness, and ethnic identity extend beyond the borders of Rwanda (Mamdani 2002).

One of the greatest tragedies of Rwanda was the fact that the world hesitated and turned away while the killings went on. Amid the horrors of war, however, women mourned the dead and provided solace to the victims left behind, through their presence and their voices. In Kyomuhendo's text, however, even these merciful images are overshadowed by images of destruction and contradiction—the haunting image of a church whose outside is surrounded by "green hills wrapped in fertile volcanic soils," while "inside skulls and bones recline."

Losses and Gains: The Late Twentieth Century

Well into the postcolonial era, activists and educators were still emphasizing the importance of education for girls and women, signaling continued imbalances in its availability. All governments and civil society groups have paid lip service to the cliché, "If you educate a woman, you educate the family/the world," while in practice providing education disproportionately to boys and men. Access to education has been skewed over the centuries, although with Western education the inequalities appear more pronounced. Even today, as George Malekela writes, "The psychological resistance to girls' education may be in recession, but the structural obstacles are still intimidating. Girls have a harder time attending school because of their other responsibilities at home" (Malekela 1983). Several of our texts reveal the extent to which young mothers, themselves children, have to be responsible for others of similar ages—for example, Mama Meli's "From Slavery to Freedom" (1950s) and Anna Chipaka's "A Bar-Maid's Life" (1980s). Special facilities for girls in school are almost totally lacking, including even such basic amenities as toilets (Nkamba and Kanyika 1998). Girls are inhibited or discouraged from pursuing career paths that teachers consider too "challenging" for them, such as those involving the sciences. They often experience sexual harassment from teachers and fellow students (Yahya-Othman 2000: 41–42). Girls who become pregnant while in school are barred from continuing with their education. Those who perform well are accused of offering sexual favors in exchange for good grades. Just as the title character of the story "Binti Ali the Clever" (1914) and Kitandi in "My Students" (1920, 1935) surprised even their own parents and mentors with their intelligence and foresight, so too do teachers and male classmates today still marvel that girls can outperform boys. Adult women wanting to achieve literacy find their household chores obliterating all else (Nyoni 1994). It is clear that those who have managed to overcome these hurdles possessed deep reservoirs of courage, diligence, and tolerance.

Two texts in this volume, Florence Lubega's "Debate on Higher Education" (1959) and Martha Qorro's "Language in Tanzania" (2003) question whether pupils' cognitive development is being stunted because they are taught in a language in which they clearly lack proficiency. The fact that these texts are separated by nearly half a century shows how deeply the problem persists. Ogot cites research indicating that the high failure rates in African schools is partly a function of the use of a foreign language such as English (1995: 222).

The quality of education in the region has long been the subject of intense debate. Parents and educators, activists and politicians, have all expressed concern about the curriculum and instructional methods, questioning everything from the admissions process for students and the content of examinations, to the quality of the teachers. The decline in educational quality and accessibility, unsurprisingly, affects girls more than it does boys. Modern education comes at a price. Although governments in the region espouse free universal primary education (UPE), in effect contributions are demanded for various school projects. When fees are due, parents with several children are sometimes forced to make choices on who can go to school and who cannot (Sumra and Katunzi 1991; Graham-Brown 1991). In most cases it is the girl-child who suffers, on the assumption that she will be looked after by her future husband. If she does go to school, she is unlikely to perform as well as a boy, because she faces a heavier workload at home.

Throughout the region, the universality of UPE (where it exists at all) ends at class one of primary school. The numbers begin to dwindle as girls proceed to the upper classes, through failure of parents to buy uniforms and pay the various fees demanded by schools; through pregnancies; and through parents pulling girls out either to marry them off or to assign them household work (Hyde 1993: 114). The numbers drop even lower at the juncture of admission into secondary school, since girls have to compete with boys for very limited places. Efforts by some governments to operate a quota system that favors girls and children from underdeveloped regions have recently come under attack, and in the case of Tanzania for example, were forced to cease (TGNP 1993: 84). In her 1959 speech, Florence Lubega makes a rousing call for an increase in the admission of girls to higher education, as well as for more support for universities. The same call might be made, with even greater fervor, today.

In 1965, Bibi Titi Mohamed lamented the control of African governments by foreign powers, and its negative impact on African people. Her words ring equally if not more true in the present millennium. The international financial institutions dictate policies that affect African educational systems in a number of ways. Their structural adjustment programs sometimes demand that Africans cut social spending, including spending on education. They also weigh in on where remaining funds should go, urging governments to focus on primary and secondary education while effectively depriving most Africans of higher education. Cuts in funding lead to cuts in admissions and in government subsidies for school expenses, and with fewer places and less support to go around, girls and women are, once again, most likely to suffer the consequences.[25]

Apart from barriers to admission, women at universities face a harsh learning and working environment. Sexual harassment from both fellow students and male lecturers is rife. Phiri describes not only the sexual harassment of students at Chancellor College in Malawi, but also the harassment of those who dare discuss the issue (2000b). At the University of Dar es Salaam in Tanzania, the notorious practice of "Punch," wall literature attacking women, led to the suicide of Revina Mukasa in 1990, after she was harassed because she had rebuffed the sexual advances of a fellow student (Mkude 1990). At Makerere University in Uganda, there have been several recent cases of murders of women students. Generally, women feel insecure and threatened, and the security precautions in place are not sufficient to give them the confidence and freedom they need in order to maintain matriculation at these higher-education institutions.

Opportunities for career advancement and further training are curtailed by patriarchal assumptions that women need to "raise their families," and that they will not be able to cope with children and a demanding job. Because the pool of women at the lower levels is small, attempts even by well-meaning administrators to recruit women meet with little success. The sciences, mathematics, engineering, and related disciplines present a particularly daunting challenge. Significant work has been undertaken by the Pan-African Forum for African Women Educationalists (FAWE), headquartered in Nairobi, whose objective is to improve the access to and quality of education for girls and women throughout Africa. FAWE has at least thirty-three chapters, and has mounted various programs to increase and improve the participation of girls in education, with a special focus on math and science. The Female Education in Mathematics and Science project (FEMSA) runs in ten countries in southern, western, and eastern Africa. The science project has also been boosted by the provision of pre-entry training for prospective university students who have not done well in the sciences. The University of Dar es Salaam conducts such courses.

FAWE also runs centers of excellence (CoEs), in which they provide an intervention package of effective strategies to address concerns in girls' education. The CoEs are expected to produce girls who are high achievers, self-confident, potential leaders and widely read. Sarah Ntiro, author of "Fighting for Women's Rights" (1999) has been extensively involved in FAWE's work, she herself having been a victim of discrimination in her early school years.

As a positive result of the struggle to provide girls with equal access to education, all five countries in the region are now providing free primary education. Additionally, in Kenya, Malawi, and Zanzibar, girls who become pregnant while in school can now return to school after giving birth. In Malawi, the GABLE project provided fee waivers for girls in primary and secondary schools, and set an admission target for girls of 33 percent (Dorsey 1996: 78). Other affirmative actions common in the region include the use of a lower cut-off point for qualified women university entrants, the offer of certain scholarships to women only, and the running, in ten countries, of the TUSEME project, which aims at empowering girls to overcome obstacles they face during the educational process.

One feature of both colonial and postcolonial education is the "black skin, white masks" effect that Franz Fanon talked about more than fifty years ago—the ways in which colonialism transforms the psyche of the colonized, so that they dance to the colonizer's tune. This phenomenon is now being reincarnated under independent governments, except that now the piper calling the tune is Western education and the International Financial Institutions (IFIs). The curricula make little effort to address issues of African identity and social justice. Instead, individualism and competition are justified in the name of globalization. Identity crisis and cultural alienation are issues rapidly emerging in the cities and towns of the region, where many young people not only do not know, but do not *want* to know, the languages, music, dances, and traditions of their communities. As Paul Zeleza argues, among the trends established by globalization are the commercialization of learning and the commodification of knowledge (2002: 66). Everything is being privatized, and knowledge is a commodity for sale to the highest bidder. All this deeply counters the spirit of the texts in this volume, most of which emphasize collectivism and community participation.

In the new millennium, the interface between socialization and education has become both more complex and more tenuous. On the one hand, parents have more and more to assume the work of schoolteacher, as pupils and students receive reduced attention in the classroom. Doing homework together, or arranging extra tutoring for children, has become the norm. On the other hand, if teachers cannot cover even the "syllabus," they are not likely to teach children about the finer points of social behavior and survival in a harsh world, much less to help them develop inquisitive and creative habits of mind. The girl-child emerging from the public school system is unlikely to have garnered the leadership qualities, confidence, independence, and sense of responsibility that Joyce Mpanga describes in "On Education" (1961, 1989) as benefits of her own schooling. And yet girl-children are not short of these qualities. Are parents shouldering a heavier burden now in the socialization of their children, or, as the Kiswahili proverb "*asiyefunzwa na mamaye hufunzwa na ulimwengu*"—"one who is not taught by one's mother will be taught by the world"—would have it, is the "world" now socializing African children? Graham-Brown (1991) notes that the increase in female-headed households also has grave consequences for education. Not only do single mothers tend to be poorer, but they also have less time to give children the support they need. Anna Chipaka's movement of her children from her home to her mother's and back again, described in "A Bar-Maid's Life" (1980s), testifies to the difficulties of such a situation. An often-asked question is the extent to which formal education empowers women and advances their development. Most of the texts here would seem to speak in favor. Nevertheless, empowerment does not necessarily mean liberation. Often, Western-oriented education offered by the school system leads to mental and cultural enslavement for both women and men, even as it offers them some "skills." Thus graduates of the school system are not always aware of the *African* situation and *Africa's* needs, and are ill-prepared to help their countries deal with their predicaments. When it comes to the needs of African *women*, education is still less capable of clearly dealing with their needs. Only a sweeping transformation—a contemporary re-Africanization—of the whole educational system in organization, content, and language would address this entrenched problem.

Unfortunately in some instances education has served to sustain commonly held views about what is "befitting" for females in social relations and in the workplace (Graham-Brown 1991). Still, as Mama Loise Kalondu said in 2000 in "A Courageous Woman," "Those who did not educate their girls in those days now regret it. They realize there is wealth in education."

New Enslavements, New Plagues

New forms of slavery in Africa, which are becoming more widespread each day, include the sexual trafficking of women and forced prostitution. Recent studies have revealed cases of girls as young as ten being forced into prostitution as a means of eking out a living. This new enslavement of women reverberates in the texts on women in urban slums. Urbanization, the growth of the African townships, and the accompanying migration from village to city, provide the backdrop for some of the writings by women in the post-independence period. Marjorie Oludhe Macgoye's text "Learning the Sex Trade," an excerpt from her 1993 novella *Victoria*, examines in vivid detail the plight of rural women in an urban setting who turn to prostitution for survival. Such village women are forced by circumstances beyond their control to break out of the rural *boma* that shuts them in both mentally and economically, but they are as yet ill-equipped for the demands of the townships.

While Macgoye's character Victoria manages to achieve some success in her life through prostitution, the young woman in Elieshi Lema's 1994 story "Tryst with Peril" only *thinks* she has made it because of a first rendezvous with a man of substance, while the "Slave Girl" of Vuyo Ophelia Wagi's 1999 poem experiences, as a houseworker and virtual sex slave, nothing but drudgery, rape, and an unwanted pregnancy.

> Cook, clean, wash, babysit, and the boss
> Wants more besides.
> More, sir?
> Skincrawl groping hard breathing
> And furtive looks, suggestions, plans:
> "I will be at the chicken shed at dawn."
> He gathers eggs too?

In the last few decades, women have faced harsher economic conditions, and many have been driven to the cities to seek employment. Uneducated, but supposedly in a free market of unlimited opportunities, they find only backbreaking, hazardous labor on construction sites or stone quarries, or long hours in sweatshops or cleaning streets, or domestic servitude in the homes of the rich. Usually, these women are left without any of the protection that they may have enjoyed in their village environment.

In some villages, however, some traditional cultural practices may brutalize, suppress, or humiliate women. Within the institution of *nyumba-ntobo* in the Mara region of Tanzania, poor women "marry" wealthy women who need labor for their farms and children for their homesteads. The "female husbands" select male partners for their "wives" and the children born of the union belong to the "female husband." Ruth Meena describes this system in her 2003 text, and calls for an alternative culture in which women have a free choice of partners, and are not brutalized. Recent interviews with *nyumba-ntobo* "wives" aired on Tanzanian television, however, indicate that women choose this mode of marriage because it is more humane and less demanding of them than the usual patriarchal marriage. In the *nyumba-ntobo* system, both the "female husbands" and the "wives" actualize their womanhood through other women, thereby keeping males on the periphery of their lives rather than at the center. *Nyumba-ntobo* is thus a mechanism that enables women to associate mostly with other women in the context of traditional power relations, although, even then, the women still have few real choices. *Nyumba-ntobo* is thus a form of protest as well as a means of escape from sexual and patriarchal bondage, but it remains highly imperfect and controversial.

In the early 1980s, the scourge of HIV/AIDS emerged as yet another devastating obstacle in the way of women's advancement in Eastern Africa. For cultural and biological reasons, women are the most vulnerable victims of this pandemic. Some of the voices in this volume are those of HIV/AIDS sufferers who decided to reveal publicly their HIV status. In the first of her "Two Riddle Poems" (2000), entitled "What Sugar Is This That Contains Poison?" Pelagia Katunzi of Tanzania employs the traditional Swahili dialogue poetry genre to raise awareness about the risk of HIV/AIDS, urging people to think carefully about the consequences of their behavior, as they consume the "sugar"—sex—that contains the poison of HIV/AIDS. Katunzi, who is herself HIV-positive, refuses, however, to accept the official church stand regarding AIDS prevention—that people must abstain from promiscuity or unsafe sex. She argues that such a view is based on morality rather than reality, and will not work for everyone.

In her 1999 poem "AIDS Orphan," Vuyo Wagi captures the plight of the millions of children who have lost their parents to AIDS, and are left to take on adult tasks and responsibilities even before they have grown up. For these children, the AIDS pandemic becomes a chilling rite of passage to nowhere. In "The Wasting Disease," excerpted from Marjorie Macgoye's 1997 novel *Chira*, the pandemic becomes symbolic of the moral and social decay within the wider society, in this case Kenyan society. As the twenty-first century unfolds, the HIV/AIDS pandemic is still growing and still as lethal as ever. Women's voices are vital to the struggle to publicize and combat the disease, especially for other women.

The Barrel of the Pen: Writing by Women

Some African writers have pointed out that European languages provided an opportunity to consolidate colonial domination. This was very obvious in education. While some of the colonialists, such as the Germans, preferred to use the local languages in the schools they operated, the British made few concessions. Local languages were allowed in the very early grades, but thereafter it became important to establish English as the primary language of education, used to consolidate British rule through the teaching of British culture and the importation of British books (Pennycook 1994). In the entire region, English came to represent education, and those who did not or would not speak it were considered uncouth and backward. Parents were convinced that English would open doors to myriad opportunities for their children. Since formal education was not accessible to all, English became a gatekeeper for the educated elite, allowing a few to enjoy further education, good jobs, and political power (Pennycook 1994; Phillipson 1994). By the same token, the few writers who had mastered English enjoyed access to the few, mostly British, publishing outlets in the region.

Here, too, women were affected by the inequities in access to education. Girls admitted to secondary and higher education were in the minority. Women in the region were exposed to Western education much later than those in southern Africa or northern Africa, for example. Hence the number of women writers in the prestigious English medium was extremely small. Even in the local languages, there were proportionally few women writers. But it is no accident that most of the texts in this volume—more than 60 percent—were written in African languages. African writers continue to debate the question of language. Although writers in the region have been writing in local languages for centuries, Kenyan writer Ngugi wa Thiong'o recently raised the intensity of the debate: After writing several acclaimed works in English and winning an international audience, Ngugi announced in *Decolonising the Mind: The Politics of Language in African Literature* (1986) that he would henceforth write only in African languages. Writers who have not yet gained wide recognition, however, face the choice of either writing in their local language and reaching an African audience (of varying size, depending on the language), or writing in English and gaining access to an "international readership." Penina Muhando Mlama takes up this question in "Creating in the Mother-Tongue" (1990). While Mlama concedes that that there are various obstacles to writers using African languages, including ethnic tensions, limited proficiency, and a limited readership, the society in which they create demands that they grapple with their people's problems in a way that is most accessible to them. Using African languages also defies European superiority, and insists upon the viability of African culture and identity:

> Writing for the African people today is writing for a people who have largely lost their perception of what constitutes "African," their ability to determine or influence their own way of life, their indigenous values and attitudes, and their identity as a people. . . . [I]f the writer has a genuine interest in saving the African cultural identity from this chaos (indeed, this humiliation), he or she will find many roles to play in the struggle.

Beginning in the 1960s, the establishment of regional or national publishing houses enabled several women writers to be published locally. The East African Publishing House (EAPH), the East African Literature Bureau, the Tanzania Publishing House, and the Jomo Kenyatta Foundation provided extremely valuable avenues for writers in the region. More recently, publishing firms have emerged that are either partly or wholly owned by women. These include E & D, based in Dar es Salaam, Tanzania (established in 1989); FEMRITE, in Kampala, Uganda (1997); and Focus Publications, in Nairobi, Kenya (1991). The first two are owned wholly by women, emerging in response to the realities that have constrained women's endeavors generally, and especially women's writing.[26]

FEMRITE is an association of women writers that also engages in publishing. One of the founders was Goretti Kyomuhendo (whose work appears in this volume). The publication of Kyomuhendo's first book brought her to the attention of seven other women, who then founded a women writers' organization. Their aim was to "inspire, encourage and assist women writers to have their manuscripts published." Having set up the collective, they had to organize staffing, marketing, and distribution, as well as funding. With no shortage of manuscripts, they have published an average of five books a year—still only a fraction of the work their writers produce. Their refusal to borrow money from banks or microfinance institutions has kept them short of cash, but has also aroused the antagonism of rival publishers, who accuse them of ruining the competition because they get "free money" through donations (Jay and Kelly). These challenges aside, FEMRITE is one of the most successful publishing projects in the region.

Another success story of feminist publishing is that of E & D in Tanzania, owned by two remarkable women writers and gender activists with extensive experience in publishing and development. Their mission is "bringing a more gender balanced view of social development into literature and publishing." To achieve this mission, E & D has structured their activities into three divisions: commercial publishing, which takes care of the trade, children's, and textbook publishing that are gender sensitive, transformative, and socially relevant; package publishing, meeting specialized needs of users who may not have publishing capacities; and publishing and development, handling specially designed projects that are then funded by donors. Since its inception, E & D has published numerous children's books, textbooks, serious political and social treatises, Kiswahili novels, and the first serious English novel by a Tanzanian woman writer, Elieshi Lema, one of the publishers (whose work also appears in this volume). They have overcome many challenges with foresight and creative approaches to running their business.

Two writers published in this volume demand special mention in this discussion of identity, language, and culture in Eastern Africa. As writers and as people, they both identify themselves as African, although they are not of African descent. Neera Kapur-Dromson, author of "Seeking My Husband in Kenya" (2000), is a fourth-generation Kenyan of Indian descent. Thousands of Indians were brought to east Africa by the British, many of them to work on railway construction, and they form a small but significant minority in Kenya and Tanzania today. (Far fewer remain in Uganda, where they were forcibly expelled under Idi Amin.) Kapur-Dromson's story, an excerpt from a recently published novel, is told from the perspective of a young Indian woman at the turn of the twentieth century, who makes an arduous journey by sea and rail to Nairobi, searching for the husband who disappeared after he traveled to Africa on business. In a different context, the activities of the ruling class, the British, could not but generate their own share of women writers who produced both memoirs and works of fiction. One of those included in this volume, whose work has had a significant impact both in the region and worldwide, is Marjorie Oludhe Macgoye. Arriving in Kenya as a British missionary, Macgoye adopted Kenya as her home, married locally, and has produced many works that address African themes, and especially the travails of Kenyan women. Her books have been adopted as school required readings, a rare achievement for any author. Overall, works like those of Macgoye and Kapur-Dromson introduce us to the concerns, despairs, and hopes of migrant women who have found a home on

African soil. These writers reveal that Africa, like the United States, is a melting pot that, at its best, accepts and respects those who accept and respect it.

Into the Twenty-First Century: Still Fighting for Women's Rights
In "I Must Call Myself a Feminist" (2002), Miria Matembe of Uganda writes:

> . . . I had refused to be called a feminist. The reason was basically that the word *feminist* did not augur well . . . at the time. According to public perceptions of the period, "a feminist" was dangerous, a terrible woman. . . . people would distance themselves from you. . . . I came to understand that a feminist is a person who is struggling to uplift women . . . challenging systems and structures that oppress women. . . . if that is the proper designation, then I must call myself a feminist.

As the end of the twentieth century approached, women in Eastern African forcefully addressed the global issues of gender, environment, human rights, and democratization, while continuing to grapple with their conditions of existence and the political realities within their specific societies. As the issue of gender became central to women's sociopolitical activism and discourse, many women began asking the question, "What kind of feminism?" How were African women to be part of the global feminist movement, while retaining their cultural specificity and autonomy? Was it possible to speak of an African feminism?

The Mexico City Conference for Women in 1975, in which Eastern Africa was represented by such militants as Wangari Maathai and others, and the subsequent United Nations Decade for Women (1975–1985) have had major impacts on the Eastern African women's movement. This impact was to be reflected in the offer by Kenya to host the Nairobi Conference on Women held in July 1985, which was attended by more than 13,000 international delegates. The Nairobi conference served to bring the ideas of feminism and women's struggles closer to home. In time, discourse on gender relations and equity, and gender sensitivity generally, began to influence local cultural behavior. Indeed the word *Mbeijing* (with the plural form *Wabeijing*) entered the Kiswahili language as a common referent to women, especially those engaged in the struggle for gender equity.

These struggles in the international and national arena were no doubt assisted by a strong belief among east African women that change is possible through the creation or transformation of social systems. The story told in "Binti Ali the Clever" (1914), which posits the issue of gender role-playing, is a familiar tale along the east African coast. What defines Binti Ali as male or female are the clothes and ornaments she wears, and not her wit, intelligence, or boldness. Here is a notion of gender as created and sustained by custom and social practice. As such, gender roles can be deconstructed and altered, just as Binti Ali's clothes were changed. Part of the optimism in many African women's struggles arises from this belief.

Women in Eastern Africa have planned for change in the region by organizing at the community, national, and international levels. They organize as associations, NGOs, clubs, parties, and in many other forms, but they also identify themselves with issues that galvanize movements at the civic levels. Central to this dual goal is a recognition of the need to eliminate oppression and violence in whatever forms they take. The greatest oppression for African women is poverty, which works together with a variety of other factors to place them in a highly disadvantaged position. In seeking to combat this oppression, African women have become eminently resourceful, operating on multiple levels in their societies, through different types of projects and processes, always searching for those that can best effect systemic structural change.

Eastern African women have exercised their leadership not only within their families but also in churches and mosques, in community groups and national, regional, and international organizations. There are Christian and Muslim women's guilds, councils, and associations all over the region that have general and specific religious and social objectives. They are known to be the keepers of community opinion and views, as demonstrated by the wide influence of the Mother's Union. They may or may not use religion to mobilize for social action. Church leadership and that of leading Muslim women have enhanced the social position of some women.

Such activities and engagements by women in social and economic struggles appear to offer one answer to the question, "What kind of feminism?" Through their actions, they suggest that African feminism should be a movement for change; that it should address the fundamental issues of gender and economic exploitation and oppression in a practical down-to-earth manner. Three Eastern African women, whose voices are present in this volume, may be seen as spokeswomen for the cause of gender justice, representatives of feminism for change.

Miria Obote's "Speech on International Women's Day" (1984) addresses the factors that expose women's relegation to poverty and second-class citizenry. Produced twenty years after Uganda's independence, the text calls urgently for "more attention being given to women's issues . . . to achieve equality." Obote describes the social, economic, and cultural disequilibrium caused by historical oppression. At the same time, she outlines the means to achieve social and political balance and eliminate oppression.

One of these ways is through solidarity and partnership with other women "As we recognize the efforts of all the women of the world in the struggle for social justice and equality." When Miria Obote proclaims, "We resolve henceforth to be a part of the International Women's Movement," she is speaking for many women in the region who hope that the internationalization of their concerns propels more rapid change. But Obote's text points to the slow pace of development for women and the intensification of contradictions between women as national economic producers, and their economic and social marginalization—this in spite of the UN Decade for Women, expected to end in 1985, a year after Miria Obote's text was composed. For those who expected that international solidarity would "lead to total elimination of all discrimination against women," the reality must still be discouraging.

Nonetheless, the will and energy for feminist change have endured on the continent. During the 1990s, the women's movement was focused by the 1995 United Nations Women's Conference in Beijing, and the adoption of the Beijing Platform of Action, a rallying cry for gender and feminist activism. Gertrude Mongella, the secretary general of the conference and a Tanzanian, and the other women who made Beijing possible, became role models, and symbols of the promise of Beijing. Many changes in gender relations have been attributed to women's participation in the Beijing conference. The 1997 story "Beijing Beijing," by Zambian Monde Sifuniso, captures this spirit of change, embraced by the women but viewed with apprehension and dismay by the men left behind to deal with child care and other domestic duties (and who humorously fail to fulfill them). The main male protagonist is especially disturbed to find that not only his wife but also his mistress has gone to Beijing. Beijing is thus presented as both a catalyst and a subversive element in the social status quo. Relationships—between men and women, but also between women and other women—are redefined and the "received" reality challenged. The lighthearted text manages to draw attention to the serious objectives of the women's movements and struggles—the realization of new social realignments in which women partake of their fair share, and the reconstruction of gender roles.

Local or international, Miria Matembe sees women's struggles as feminist struggles that incorporate not only issues of gender identity, class, race, and ethnicity, but also all other struggles against sources of oppression. "I came to understand that a feminist is a person who is struggling to uplift women, someone who is challenging systems and structures that oppress women," as Matembe explains in her text. African women have not always identified their struggles as "feminist," and the label has not always been acceptable in certain circles of the African women's movements. Labels aside, as Chandra Mohanty points out, and as numerous texts in this book demonstrate, women's struggles against oppression are indeed feminist in their objectives and even in their stated agendas (Mohanty et al. 1991).

Matembe exposes the dilemma of most "educated" African women, who for a long time could not associate their work with feminism for fear of being socially rejected. It is Matembe's recognition that the definition comes from the work, however, that makes her comfortable to name herself a feminist. Matembe's text indicates that African women have strategically avoided the label of feminism in order to avoid undermining their struggles. She writes, "It was a good strategy to vehemently deny you were a feminist and call your activism something else." This strategy has been used to counter perceptions that feminism is an imported Western concept that threatens African traditions and culture. In such situations, feminism has been seen as un-African, a contention that Miria Matembe's text refutes. Whatever labels they may use, however, African women are busy chipping away at oppression, individually and in groups that traverse the boundaries of community and nation.

Until recently, the work of Kenyan activist Wangari Maathai in building a sustainable environment led to her isolation, harassment, and imprisonment. It took major political changes to bring her recognition, which culminated in her being awarded the Nobel Prize for Peace in 2004.

Maathai started the Green Belt Movement in 1977, partly in recognition of the dwindling sources of support and sustenance for women in terms of their access to water, food, shelter, and income. Maathai realized that the environmental degradation then taking place was in part due to poor governance and irresponsible profit seeking. Her movement, which began as a struggle to protect the environment, soon expanded to encompass democracy, good governance, economic justice, and human rights. In her 2004 Nobel Prize acceptance speech, Wangari Maathai connects women's struggles against poverty and oppression to global concerns: HIV/AIDS, the environment, and democratization, among others.

Deeply steeped in the African tradition that views the tree as a symbol of peace, Maathai remarks: "[T]he elders of the Kikuyu carried a staff from the thigi tree that, when placed between two disputing sides, caused them to stop fighting and seek reconciliation. Many communities in Africa have these traditions."[27]

Awareness of such traditions convinced Maathai that the struggle to preserve the environment is inseparable from wider struggles:

> Although this prize comes to me, it acknowledges the work of countless individuals and groups across the globe. They work quietly and often without recognition to protect the environment, promote democracy, defend human rights and ensure equality between women and men. By so doing, they plant seeds of peace.

In her address, Maathai emerges as a pan-Africanist and internationalist, who speaks not only for Kenyan women and society, but also for the whole of Africa:

> I know that African people everywhere are encouraged by this news. My fellow Africans, as we embrace this recognition, let us use it to intensify our commitment to our people, to reduce conflicts and poverty and thereby improve their quality of life. Let us embrace democratic governance, protect human rights and protect our environment. I am confident that we shall rise to the occasion. I have always believed that solutions to most of our problems must come from us.

The current manifestation of globalization continues to make borders porous and national boundaries irrelevant. However, the "global village" has its owners, and they are not African women. For the women of Eastern Africa, globalization has meant an intensification of poverty and greater threats to livelihoods, the environment, and cultures, as well as to peace and security in the region. Technological advances in communication, however, have enabled women to create networks from the grassroots to the global levels. These networks assist women to organize political action to meet the challenges of globalization. Even as they continue to work individually, their collective action through groups and social movements provides essential energy and strength. In the process, such leading women activists as Maathai and Matembe help to unite the various strands of women's and men's struggles to create invincible civic movements, which address many of the national, regional, and global concerns of the twenty-first century.

Amandina Lihamba
Fulata L. Moyo
M.M. Mulokozi
Naomi L. Shitemi
Saïda Yahya-Othman

NOTES

1. In some communities, such as that of the Wahaya with their Omuteko schools, education was offered in traditional schools for several months. Traditional priests were also trained in isolated locations, as were some initiates.

2. Community elders have insisted that the circumcision ritual is intimately intertwined with the training that imparts social and economic knowledge for the initiate's survival in her environment. This partly explains the resistance to the abolition of FGM, which is likely to continue unless alternatives for the ritual are found.

3. Moyo (2005) describes how Yao women in Malawi use red beads to signal their menstrual periods, and therefore their unavailability for sexual intercourse, even when they are not menstruating.

4. Food taboos mean that women are forced to subsist on a diet that is in many ways deficient, and may actually harm women's health. In many societies, women are not allowed to eat certain traditional delicacies, including meat, chicken, eggs, certain types of fish, and edible grasshoppers. The Maasai actually starve expectant mothers in the belief that this will bring them easier births, but this practice often results in the mothers being too weak at the time of delivery (Chieni and Spencer 170).

5. In discussing the African concept of time, Ocaya argues that time has a foundation in the reality of events that become points of reference. Otherwise it does not exist merely in the mind, nor can it be seen in absolute terms. For example, some periods in history are marked by the events that dominated them so you may find people talking about the time of the plague to indicate the years when there was a pandemic of bubonic plague. Failure to trace any event as far back as possible from the discussed event is what leads one to speak of "from time immemorial" (Ocaya 1989: 77).

6. The African Traditional Religion may be defined as African people's beliefs and opinions concerning the existence, nature, and worship of the Supreme Being through

the Spirits of their Ancestors, and the divine's involvement in the universe and the created order, including human life. In this section, we choose to use the singular version of African Traditional Religion (ATR). We are aware of the current thinking on the need to speak of African Traditional Religions in plural, in acknowledgment of the diversity of religio-cultural beliefs and practices among the different African ethnic groups, clans, and communities. While acknowledging the validity of such thinking, we find ourselves questioning the choice to emphasize the differences rather than the similarities, which are even more basic, especially when no such choice is made concerning Christianity and Islam, which encompass similar diversity. As long as we still speak of "Christianity" rather than "Christianities," and of "Islam" rather than "Islams," we will continue to refer to "ATR" rather than "ATRs." We might further argue for the use of "African Religion"or "AR," forgoing the "Traditional," with the understanding that every religion has its own traditions. When it appears in ATR, it seems to contain hidden connotations, suggestions that it is backward or uncivilized. While not aligning ourselves with any such judgmental connotations, we choose to use ATR, so as to retain the emphasis on these influential traditions in the lives of Eastern African women, including those who are adherents of Islam and Christianity.

7. A member of the editorial team of this volume visited some of the *kabaka* burial shrines in Uganda to survey the condition of the shrine "wives." He discovered that they have been virtually abandoned to their own devices and are no longer cared for by the royal authorities; hence many, who are now quite old, are leading a very uncertain existence.

8. Examples of U.S. slave narratives that follow this pattern, or a close variation, include those of Frederick Douglass (1845) William Wells Brown (1848), Solomon Northrop (1853), and Harriet Jacob (1861), to name only a few. The same pattern appears in the one and only comprehensive Kiswahili slave narrative, *Uhuru wa Watumwa* (Freedom for the Slaves) by James Mbotela (1934), and in many West African narratives, including *The Interesting Narrative of the Life of Olaudah Equiano, or Gustavus Vassa, the African* (1789).

9. In fact, Nimitz maintains that some leaders in the interior, for instance those of the Yao in southern Tanganyika, welcomed Islam and the literacy it offered as a means of countering the challenge of colonization (1980: 8). Additionally, within the households or the neighborhoods, there was likely to be someone who understood Arabic, and could offer elementary interpretation of the Qur'an, the hadith (collections of traditions relating to the words and deeds of the prophet Muhammed), and the principles of social relations according to religious teachings.

10. Nimitz notes that the Shirazi civilization in the hinterland came under attack from both the Portuguese and the African people in the sixteenth and seventeenth centuries, leading to its eventual decline. But these attacks appear to have been motivated more by the desire to control trade routes than by opposition to Islam (1980: 4–5).

11. The great migrations of the Bantu people from the west and center to other parts of the continent, and the resulting intermarriages with the communities they displaced, must have had a shattering impact on the women of the time. But the intercultural contacts after that time have been no less devastating.

12. The many missionary groups arriving in the region included the British Universities Mission to Central Africa (UMCA), Church Missionary Society (CMS), Africa Inland Mission (AIM), United Methodist Mission (UMM), and Gospel Missionary Society (GMS), as well as the Church of Scotland (CSM); the French Roman Catholic White Fathers, and the German Lutheran Leipzig Mission. Their doctrines and practices varied from very strict to more liberal.

13. Rosberg and Nottingham cite CSM *Memorandom* V (122, 365) for the following lyrics:

"Little knives
In their sheaths,
That they may fight with the Church
The time has come."

"I'm going to break all friendships,
The only friendship I shall retain
Is between me and Jehovah!"
The DC_____
Is bribed with uncircumcised girls
So that the land may go."

"When Johnstone [Kenyatta in England] shall return
With the King of the Kikuyu [Thuku in restriction]
Phillip and Koinange
Will wear women' robes."

According to Rosberg and Nottingham, "Phillip James Karanja and Koinange, Secretary and Chairman respectively of the Kikuyu Association, were at this time outstanding in their support of the Government and missions" and for this reason were compared to women in the final verse.

14. In 1995, female employees in the Church of Central Africa Presbyterian (CCAP) Blantyre Synod wrote a petition demanding gender justice in conditions of service. They cited a salary structure and pension scheme that unfairly favored male employees. In reaction to the petition, the Synod, represented by the acting general secretary, punished these women with sanctions, and even threatened to dismiss them if they did not comply. For details, see Phiri 1996.

15. In some communities, such as the Baganda, the link between education and religion was so close that the expression "omusomi" (literally, a student or learner) was taken also to mean a religious adherent.

16. Kimambo observes that an adult-literacy campaign among the Pare in northern Tanzania, begun in 1949, had attracted fifteen hundred learners by 1951, most of them women (1991: 121). After World War II, the plan for Tanga province, in which Upare was located, aimed at enrolling 50 percent of children in primary school, against the national average of 36 percent. However, by 1952, Upare had reached 90 percent enrollment (127).

17. Settlers in South Africa not only gained their independence from Britain, but themselves became the ruling group of other colonies, and developed the notorious apartheid system which, like colonialism, engendered a fierce war of liberation. See Daymond, et al. 2003.

18. Kanogo (1987) has argued that the settlers' seizure of the most fertile lands not only disinherited the local Africans, but opened the door for them to become squatters. At first, the Africans found opportunities to utilize areas that the Europeans could not put under production; their situation deteriorated, however, as settlers, through the colonial state, initiated laws that disillusioned and impoverished these squatters. Kanogo argues that the squatters became an important factor in the Mau Mau resistance as hostilities and conflicts intensified during the 1930s and 1940s.

19. In his history of Tanganyika, Iliffe has discussed the creation of tribes in Africa as a colonial initiative (1979: 318–41).

20. The massacre of 1922 was thus reported: "Mary Muthoni Nyanjiru (from Waithaga in location 10 of Fort Hall District) leapt to her feet, pulled her dress right up over her shoulders and shouted to the men: 'You take my dress and give me your trousers. You men are cowards. What are you waiting for? Our leader is in there. Let's get him'" (Rosberg and Nottingham 1966: 51–52). Harry Thuku was detained from 1922 to 1931.

21. At the beginning of the twentieth century, Muhumusa and her Nyabingi cult served as an example of an African woman in the region who led her people not only to revolt against the local leadership, but also to resist an imposed foreign rule. Muhumusa was involved in a power struggle in Rwanda after the death of her husband, Mwami Kigeri Rwabugiri, in 1885. Commanding great power as leader of the Nyabingi cult, she was also credited with an outstanding personality, organizational powers, and great intelligence. She operated not only in Rwanda but also in Uganda, where she was captured in 1911 after waging a war of liberation against both local and foreign aggression. See Hopkins (1970).

22. According to Kanogo (1987: 143–48), even though women were only 5 percent of the total guerrilla army, there was a large civilian "army" as well. Kanogo describes Wanjiru Nyamarutu as a political activist who became the general in charge of food, with her own large subordinate staff. She mobilized various resources for the Mau Mau movement. After successfully evading the colonialists for many years, she was eventually arrested. Gakonyo Ndungi was known for her skills in the treatment of ailments and healing powers. She was popularly known as one of the "forest doctors." Wambui Kamuirigo was an ardent guerrilla fighter who was also a trusted executioner of traitors of the Mau Mau cause. See also Likimani (1985) and Presley (1986).

23. Throughout the region, the number of women's voices in parliament, though still small, has increased, and a few more women have been appointed full or junior ministers. Ministries responsible for women and gender issues in Uganda and Tanzania have also been established. In 1999 women made up 4 percent of parliament in Kenya, 16 percent in Tanzania, 10 percent in Zambia, 6 percent in both the lower and upper houses in Malawi, and 18 percent and 10 percent in the two houses in Uganda. While there were still no women holding ministerial positions in Kenya, they held 9 percent of such positions in Malawi, 13 percent in Tanzania, 10 percent in Uganda, and 6 percent in Zambia (Tripp 2000).

24. Mamdani has argued that the regime of Idi Amin in Uganda tried to use the mantle of morality to mask policies and practices that were destructive to women physically and psychologically. It created an atmosphere that caused women to be perceived as the enemy of national morality, and this paved the way for groups and individuals to inflict violence on women (1983: 54–55).

25. In addition, the numbers of female university admissions are low. Uganda's Makerere University is doing best, with 47 percent of its places going to women. In Kenya, women's admissions are at 36 percent. In Tanzania, of the total students enrolled in primary school in a particular year, only 0.4 percent gain university admission. Of those, between 20 and 30 percent are women (29 percent at the University of Dar es Salaam in 2004, for example). Women's admissions are at 20 percent in Malawi, and at similar levels in Zambia. While these percentages have been reached only through affirmative action, there is ample evidence that once admitted, the women do just as well, and sometimes better, than the men.

26. On how some of these publishers came into being and the hurdles they had to overcome, see Jay and Kelly (2002).

27. Indeed, the thigi tree used by the Gikuyu was also used for the same purpose by the Wachagga of Tanzania, who called it *lisale*. It was also used for the purpose of demarcating individual plots, so as to maintain peace among neighbors, by the Bahaya of Tanzania, who called it *omulamula* (literally, "tree that settles disputes"), and by the Baganda of Uganda.

Works Cited and Select Bibliography

African Gender Institute, University of Cape Town. 2002. "Intellectual Politics." *Feminist Africa* 1.

Ake, Claude. 1996. *Democracy and Development in Africa*. Washington, D.C.: Brookings Institution.

Bates, Margaret. 1957. "Introduction," *The Maji Maji War Epic*. Shani A. Kitogo and M.M. Mulokozi, eds. East African Swahili Committee, Kampala (new edition published by the Institute of Kiswahili Research, the University of Dar es Salaam in 2006).

Baur, John. 1994. *2000 Years of Christianity in Africa*. Nairobi: Paulines. 233–44.

Bendera, Stella. 1998. "Girls' Primary Schooling and Puberty in Tanzania," in Stella Bendera and Mary Mboya, eds. *Gender and Education in Tanzanian Schools*. Dar es Salaam: Dar es Salaam University Press.

Berger, Iris. 1976. "Rebels or Status Seekers? Women as Spirit Mediums in East Africa," in Nancy J. Hafkin and Edna G. Bay, eds. *Women in Africa: Studies in Social Economic Change*. Palo Alto, CA: Stanford University Press. 157–82.

Besha, Ruth M., ed. 1994. *African Women: Our Burdens and Struggles*. Papers from an IFAA Residential Course. Johannesburg: Institute for African Alternatives (IFAA).

Bone, David S. 2000. *Malawi's Muslims: Historical Perspectives*. Blantyre: Christian Literature Association in Malawi (CLAIM).

Brock-Utne, Birgit. 2000. *Whose Education for All? The Recolonization of the African Mind*. New York and London: Falmer Press.

Brown, William Wells. 1848. *Narrative of William Wells Brown, a Fugitive Slave. Written by Himself*. Boston: Anti-Slavery Office.

Campbell, Horace. 2003. "The Redefinition of African Politics," in Isaria N Kimambo, ed. *Humanities and Social Sciences in East and Central Africa: Theory and Practice*. Dar es Salaam: Dar es Salaam University Press. 150–85.

Chachage, Chachage S. L. and Marjorie Mbilinyi. 2003. "Introduction: TGNP and Struggles for Gender Equality, Development and Democracy," in Chachage S. L. Chachage and Marjorie Mbilinyi, eds. *Against Neo Liberalism: Gender, Democracy and Development*. Dar es Salaam: Tanzanian Gender Networking Program (TGNP) and E & D: Ltd.

Chieni, Telelia and Paul Spencer. 1993. "The World of Telelia: Reflections of a Maasai Woman in Matapato," in Thomas Spear and Richard Waller, eds. *Being Maasai: Ethnicity and Identity in East Africa*. Oxford: James Currey; Dar es Salaam: Mkuki na Nyota; Nairobi: East African Educational Publishers; Athens: Ohio University Press.

Comaroff, Jean and John L. 1991. *Of Revelation and Revolution: Christianity, Colonialism and Consciousness in South Africa*. Vol.1. Chicago: University of Chicago Press.

Curtin, Philip, Steven Feierman, Leonard Thompson, and Jan Vansina. 1978. *African History*. Toronto: Little Brown and Company.

Daymond, M.J., Dorothy Driver, Sheila Meintjes, Leloba Molema, Chiedza Musengezi, Margie Orford, and Nobantu Rasebotsa, eds. 2003. *Women Writing Africa. Vol. 1: The Southern Region*. New York: The Feminist Press at the City University of New York.

De Vere Allen, James. 1993. *Swahili Origins: Swahili Culture and the Shungwaya Phenomenon*. Oxford: James Currey; Nairobi: East African Educational Publishers; Athens: Ohio University Press.

Dorsey, Betty Jo. 1996. *Gender Inequalities in Education in the Southern Africa Region: An Analysis of Intervention Strategies*. Harare: UNESCO.

Douglass, Frederick. 1845. *Narrative of the Life of Frederick Douglass, an American Slave. Written by Himself*. Boston: Anti-Slavery Office.

Dunbar, Roberta Ann. 2000. "Muslim Women in African History," in Nehemia Levtzion and Randall Pouwels, eds. *The History of Islam in Africa*. Athens: Ohio University Press; Oxford: James Currey; Cape Town: David Philip. 397–417.

Duncan, Patti. 2004. *Tell this Silence: Asian American Women Writers and the Politics of Speech*. Iowa City: University of Iowa Press.

Elkins, Caroline. 2005. *Imperial Reckoning: The Last Days of British Rule in Kenya*. New York: Henry Holt; London: Jonathan Cape.

Emecheta, Buchi. 1986. *Feminism with a Small "f!"* in Kristen Holst Petersen, ed. *Criticism and Ideology: Second African Writers' Conference*. Uppsala: Scandinavian Institute of African Studies. 173–85.

Equiano, Olaudah. 1789. *The Interesting Narrative of the Life of Olaudah Equiano, or Gustavus Vassa, the African*. London: Printed for the Author.

Friedman, Susan S. 1998. *Mappings: Feminism and the Cultural Geographies of Encounter*. Princeton University Press.

Gaitskell, Deborah. 1983. "Housewives, Maids or Mothers: Some Contradictions of Domesticity for Christian Women in Johannesburg, 1903–39." *Journal of African History* 24: 241–256.

Gardam, Judith G. and Michele J. Jarvis. 2001. *Women, Armed Conflict and International Law*. The Hague, London, Boston: Kluver Law International.

Gioseffi, Daniela, ed. 2003. *Women on War: An International Anthology of Writings from Antiquity to the Present*. New York: The Feminist Press at the City University of New York.

Graham-Brown, Sarah. 1991. *Education in the Developing World*. London: Longman.

Greeley, Andrew M. 1995. *Sociology and Religion*. Chicago: Harper Collins College Publishers.

Hafkin, Nancy J. and Edna G. Bay, eds. 1976. *Women in Africa: Studies in Social and Economic Change*. Palo Alto, CA: Stanford University Press.

Hastings, Adrian. 1994. *The Church in Africa: 1450–1950*. Oxford: Clarendon Press, 371–384

Hay, Margaret Jean. 1976. "Luo Women and Economic Change during the Colonial Period," in Nancy J. Hafkin and Edna G. Bay, eds. *Women in Africa: Studies in Social and Economic Change*. Palo Alto, CA: Stanford University Press.

Heinrich Böll Foundation in cooperation with Mazingira Institute, African Academy of Sciences (AAS), and Africa Peace Forum. 2001. *Sustainable Development, Governance and Globalization: African Forum on Strategic Thinking Towards the 2002 Earth Summit and Beyond*. Proceedings and recommendations of forum, Nairobi, 17–20 September. Online: http://www.worldsummit2002.org/index.htm?http://www.worldsummit2002.org/activities/nepadforum.htm. Accessed 30 September 2006.

Himmelstrand, Ulf, Kabiru Kinyanjui, and Edward Mburugu, eds. 1994. *African Perspectives on Development: Controversies, Dilemmas and Openings*. Nairobi: East African Educational Publishers; Dar es Salaam: Mkuki na Nyota; Harare: Baobab; Kampala: Fountain Publishers; Oxford: James Currey; New York: St. Martin's Press.

Hopkins, Elizabeth. 1970. "The Nyabingi Cult of Southwest Uganda," in Robert I. Rotberg and Ali Mazrui, eds. *Protest and Power in Black Africa*. Oxford and New York: Oxford University Press. 258–336.

Hrbek, I. ed. 1999. *Historia Kuu ya Afrika: Afrika Kuanzia Karne ya Saba hadi ya Kumi na Moja [General History of Africa Vol. 3: Africa from the Seventh to the Eleventh Century]*. UNESCO/Taasisi ya Uchunguzi wa Kiswahili (TUKI). 340–42.

Hyde, Karin A. L. 1993. "Sub-Saharan Africa," in Elizabeth M. King and M. Anne Hill, eds. *Women's Education in Developing Countries: Barriers, Benefits and Policies*. A World Bank Book. Baltimore: John Hopkins University Press.

Iliffe, John, 1979. *A Modern History of Tanganyika*. Cambridge: University Press.

Isichei, Elizabeth A. 1995. *A History of Christianity in Africa: From Antiquity to the Present*. London: Society for Promoting Christian Knowledge (SPCK). 145–50.

Jacob, Harriet A. 1861. *Incidents in the Life of a Slave Girl. Written by Herself*. Lydia Maria Child, ed. Boston: Published for the author.

Jahns, Jens, ed. 1994. *Tanzania Meisterwerke Afrikanischer Skulptur*. Berlin: Haus der Kulturen der Welt and Kunstbav Lenbachhaus.

Jay, Mary and Susan Kelly. 2002. *Courage and Consequence. Women Publishing in Africa*. Oxford: African Books Collective.

Kaggwa, Apollo. 1971. *Bassekabaka ba Buganda* [The Kings of Buganda]. Nairobi: East African Publishing House.

Kanogo, Tabitha. 1987. *Squatters and the Roots of Mau Mau, 1905–1963*. London: James Currey; Athens: Ohio University Press.

Kanyoro, Musimbi. 2000. "Where Are the African Women Theologians in Theological Debate?" *Journal of Constructive Theology* 6(2).

———. 2001. "Engendered Communal Theology: African Women's Contribution to Theology in the 21st Century," in Nyambura Njoroge and Musa Dube, eds. *Talitha Cumi! Theologies of African Women*. Pietermaritzburg: Cluster Publications. 158–80.

———. 2002. "Beads and Strands: Threading Beads to her Story in the Circle," in Isabel A. Phiri, Devakarsham B. Govinden, and Sarojini Nadar, eds. *Her-Stories: Hidden Histories of Women of Faith in Africa*. Pietermaritzburg: Cluster Publications. 12–32.

———. 2002. *Introducing Feminist Cultural Hermeneutics: An African Perspective*. Cleveland: Pilgrim Press.

Katoke, I.K. 1975. *The Karagwe Kingdom: A History of the Abanyambo of North-Western Tanzania c. 1400–1915*. Nairobi: East African Publishing House.

Kenyatta, Jomo. 1938. *Facing Mount Kenya: The Tribal Life of the Gikuyu*. J.M. Kariuki, ed. Nairobi: Heinemann Kenya; London: Secker and Warburg.

Kimambo, Isaria N. 1971. *Mbiru: Popular Protest in Colonial Tanzania*. Historical Association of Tanzania Paper 9. Nairobi: East African Publishing House.

———. 1991. *Penetration and Protest in Tanzania: The Impact of World Economy on the Pare*. Oxford: James Currey; Dar es Salaam: Tanzania Publishing House; Nairobi: Heinemann Kenya; Athens: Ohio University Press.

Larsson, Birgitta. 1991. *Conversion to Greater Freedom? Women, Church and Social Change in North-Western Tanzania under Colonial Rule*. Unpublished doctoral dissertation, University of Uppsala.

Lettinga, Neil. 2000. *African Christianity: A History of the Christian Church in Africa.* http://www.bethel.edu/%7Eletnie/AfricanChristianity/index.html. Accessed 30 September 2006.

Likimani, Muthoni. 1985. *Passbook Number F.47927: Women and Mau Mau in Kenya.* London: Macmillan Education.

Lodhi, Abdulaziz. 1973. *The Institution of Slavery in Zanzibar and Pemba.* Research Report 16. Uppsala: Scandinavian Institute of African Studies.

Makumbusho ya Taifa. 1998. *History and Some Traditions of the Maasai.* Dar es Salaam: National Museum.

Malekela, George A. 1983. *Access to Secondary Education in Sub-Saharan Africa: The Tanzanian Experiment.* Unpublished doctoral dissertation, University of Chicago.

Mamdani, Mahmood. 1983. *Imperialism and Fascism in Uganda.* Nairobi: Ibadan; London: Heinemann Educational Books.

————. 2002. *When Victims Become Killers: Colonialism, Nativism, and the Genocide in Rwanda.* Kampala: Fountain Publishers; Dar es Salaam: E & D .

Marealle, Petro Itosi. 2002. *Maisha ya Mchagga hapa Duniani na Ahera.* Dar es Salaam: Mkuki na Nyota.

Maxon, Robert M. 1995. "Social and Cultural Changes," in Bethwell A. Ogot and William Robert Ochieng, eds. *Decolonization and Independence in Kenya: 1940–93.* Oxford: James Currey; Nairobi: East African Educational Publishers; Athens: Ohio University Press.

Mbiti, John S. 1970. *African Religions and Philosophy.* Garden City, NY: Doubleday.

Mbotela, James. 1934. *Uhuru wa Watumwa* [Freedom for the Slaves]. Nairobi: Nelson.

Mies, Maria. 1986. *Patriarchy and Accumulation on a World Scale: Women in the International Division of Labour.* London: Zed Books.

Mies, Maria and Vandana Shiva. 1993. *Ecofeminism.* London: Zed Books.

Mikell, Gwendolyn, ed. 1997. *African Feminism: The Politics of Survival in Sub-Saharan Africa.* Philadelphia: University of Pennsylvania Press.

Miller, Charles. 1971. *The Lunatic Express: An Entertainment in Imperialism.* London and New York: MacMillan. 130–71.

Mohanty, Chandra Talpade. 1991. "Cartographies of the Struggle: Third World Women and the Politics of Feminism," in Chandra Talpade Mohanty, Ann Russo, and Lourdes Torres, eds. *Third World Women and the Politics of Feminism.* Bloomington: Indiana University Press. 1–47.

Moyo, Fulata L. 2004. "Religion, Spirituality and Being a Woman in Africa: Gender Construction within the African Religio-Cultural Experiences." *Agenda* 61: 72–78.

————. 2005. "The Red Beads and White Beads: Malawian Women's Sexual Empowerment in the HIV and AIDS Era." *Journal of Constructive Theology* (July) 11(1): 53–66.

Mpassou, Denis. 1998. "The Continuing Tension Between Christianity and Rites of Passage in Swaziland," in James Cox, ed. *Rites of Passage in Contemporary Africa.* Cardiff: Cardiff Academic Press. 15–33.

Mugabe, John. 1999. *Intellectual Property Protection and Traditional Knowledge: An Exploration in International Policy Discourse.* Nairobi: ACTS Press.

Mullings, Leith. 1976. "Women and Economic Change in Africa," in Nancy J. Hafkin and Edna G. Bay, eds. *Women in Africa: Studies in Social and Economic Change.* Palo Alto, CA: Stanford University Press. 239–64.

Mulokozi, M.M. 1982 "Protest and Resistance in *Kiswahili* Poetry 1660–1900." Kiswahili 49(1): 25–51.

———. 2001. "Some Thoughts on African Traditional Religion and Sculpture," in Manfred Ewel and Anne Outwater, eds. *From Ritual to Modern Art.* Dar es Salaam: Mkuki na Nyota. 29–42.

———. 2002. *The African Epic Controversy.* Dar es Salaam: Mkuki na Nyota.

Ngugi wa Thiong'o. 1986. *Decolonising the Mind: The Politics of Language in African Literature.* London: J. Currey.

Nimitz August H., Jr. 1980. *Islam and Politics in East Africa: The Sufi Order in Tanzania.* Minneapolis: University of Minnesota Press.

Njinya-Mujinya, Leuben, ed. 1989. *The African Mind: A Journal of Religion and Philosophy in Africa* 1(1).

Nkamba, Manasseh and Joe Kanyika. 1998. *Zambia: The Quality of Education: Some Policy Suggestions Based on a Survey of Schools.* SACMEQ Policy Research Report 5. Paris: International Institute for Educational Planning.

Northup, Solomon. 1853. *Twelve Years a Slave: Narrative of Solomon Northup, a Citizen of New-York, Kidnapped in Washington City in 1841, and Rescued in 1853.* Auburn, N.Y.: Derby and Miller.

Nsobya, A. T. Bro. 2000. *Ennono n'Enkulaakulana ya Buganda.* Kisubi: Marianum Publications.

Nyoni, Generosa. 1994. "Factors Affecting Women's Participation in Adult Literacy Education." Unpublished independent study for B.Ed., University of Dar es Salaam.

Nzomo, Maria. 1993. "Engendering Democratization in Kenya: A Political Perspective," in Wanjiku M. Kabira, Jacqueline A. Oduol, and Maria Nzomo, eds. *Democratic Change in Africa: Women's Perspective.* Nairobi: Association of African Women for Research and Development (AAWORD), ACTS Gender Institute, African Center for Technology Studies.

Oduyoye, Mercy Amba. 2000. Foreword to Nyambura Njoroge. *Kiama Kia Ngo: An African Christian Feminist ethic of Resistance and Transformation.* Legon: Legon Theological Studies Series.

Ocaya, Victor. 1989. "Philosophy and Philosophers," in Leuben Njinya-Mujinya, ed. *The African Mind: A Journal of Religion and Philosophy in Africa* 1(1).

Ogot, Bethwell A. 1995. "The Construction of a National Culture," in Bethwell A. Ogot and William Robert Ochieng, eds. *Decolonization and Independence in Kenya: 1940–93.* Oxford: James Currey; Nairobi: East African Educational Publishers; Athens: Ohio University Press.

———. and William Robert Ochieng, eds. 1995. *Decolonization and Independence in Kenya: 1940–93.* Oxford: James Currey; Nairobi: East African Educational Publishers; Athens: Ohio University Press.

Okeke, Philomina. 1996. "Postmodern Feminism and Knowledge Production: The African Context." *Africa Today* 43(3):223–33.

Ott, Martin. 2000. *African Theology in Images.* Blantyre: Christian Literature Association in Malawi (CLAIM).

Oyewumi, Oyeronke, ed. 2003. *African Women and Feminism: Reflecting on the Politics of Sisterhood.* Lawrenceville, NJ: Africa World Press.

Pennycook, Alastair. 1994. *Cultural Politics of English as an International Language.* London and New York: Longman.

Phillipson, Robert. 1994. "English Language Spread Policy," in *International Journal of the Sociology of Language* 107: 7–24.

Phiri, Isabel Apawo. 1996. "Marching, Suspended and Stoned: Christian Women in Malawi 1995" in Kenneth R. Ross, ed. *God, People and Power in Malawi: Democratization in Theological Perspective*. Blantyre: Christian Literature Association in Malawi. 63–105.

———. 1997. *Women, Presbyterianism and Patriarchy: Religious Experiences of Chewa Women in Central Malawi*. Blantyre: Christian Literature Association in Malawi (CLAIM).

———. 2000a. *Women, Presbyterianism and Patriarchy*. Kachere Monograph 4. Blantyre: Christian Literature Association in Malawi.

———. 2000b. "Gender and Academic Freedom in Malawi," in Ebrima Sall, ed. *Women in Academia: Gender and Academic Freedom in Africa*. Dakar: Council for the Development of Social Science Research in Africa (CODESRIA).

Pouwels, Randall L. 1987. *Horn and Crescent: Cultural Change and Traditional Islam on the East African Coast, 800–1900*. Cambridge: Cambridge University Press.

Presley, Cora. 1986. *The Transformation of Kikuyu Women and their Nationalism*. PhD thesis, Stanford University, California.

Probyn, Elspeth. 1993. *Sexing the Self: Gendered Positions in Cultural Studies*. New York: Routledge.

Puja, Grace and T. Kassimoto. 1994. "Girls in Education and Pregnancy at School," in Zubeda Tumbo-Masabo and R. Llijestroin, eds. *Chelewa Chelea: The Dilemma of Teenage Girls*. Uppsala: Scandinavian Institute of African Studies. 54–75.

Ruete, Emily. 1886; tr. 1993. *An Arabian Princess Between Two Worlds: Memoirs, Letters Home, Sequels to the Memoirs*. Leiden; New York: E.J. Brill.

Roberts, Andrew D. 1970. "The Lumpa Church of Alice Lenshina," in Robert I. Rotberg and Ali Mazrui, eds. *Protest and Power in Black Africa*. New York: Oxford University Press. 513–88.

Rodney, Walter. 1972. *How Europe Underdeveloped Africa*. Dar es Salaam: Tanzania Publishing House.

Rosaldo, Michelle Z. 1974. "Woman, Culture and Society: A Theoretical Overview," in Michelle Z. Rosaldo and Louise Lamphere, eds. *Woman, Culture and Society*. Palo Alto, CA: Stanford University Press.

Rosberg, Carl and John Nottingham. 1966. *The Myth of Mau Mau: Nationalism in Kenya*. Nairobi: East African Publishing House; New York: Frederick A. Praeger.

Ross, Kenneth R., ed. 1996. *God, People and Power in Malawi: Democratization in Theological Perspective*. Blantyre: Christian Literature Association in Malawi (CLAIM).

Rotberg, Robert I. ed. 1965. *The Rise of Nationalism in Central Africa: The Making of Malawi and Zambia, 1873–1964*. Cambridge, MA: Harvard University Press.

——— and Ali Mazrui, eds. 1970. *Protest and Power in Black Africa*. New York: Oxford University Press.

Sall, Ebrima, ed. 2000. *Women in Academia: Gender and Academic Freedom in Africa*. The State of Academic Freedom in Africa Series.Dakar: Council for the Development of Social Science Research in Africa; East Lansing: Michigan State University Press.

Shahari, Riziki. 2003. "Inheritance in Islam," in Chachage S. L. Chachage and Marjorie Mbilinyi, eds. *Against Neo Liberalism: Gender, Democracy and Development*. Dar es Salaam: Tanzanian Gender Networking Program.

Sheriff, Abdul. 1987. *Slaves, Spices and Ivory in Zanzibar*. Dar es Salaam: Tanzania Publishing House; Oxford: James Currey.

Shorter, Aylward. 1974. *East African Societies*. London and Boston: Routledge and Kegan Paul.

Spear, Thomas T. and Isaria N. Kimambo, eds. 1999. *East African Expressions of Christianity.* Oxford: James Currey; Dar es Salaam: Mkuki na Nyota; Nairobi: East African Educational Publishers; Athens: Ohio University Press.

Stichter, Sharon B. and Jane L. Parpart, eds. 1988. *Patriarchy and Class: African Women in the Home and the Workforce.* Boulder and London: Westview Press.

Strobel, Margaret. 1976. "From Lelemama to Lobbying: Women's Associations in Mombasa, Kenya," in Nancy J. Hafkin and Edna G. Bay, eds. *Women in Africa: Studies in Social and Economic Change.* Palo Alto: Stanford University Press. 184–211.

Sumra, Suleman and Naomi Katunzi. 1991. *The Struggle for Education: School Fees and Girls' Education in Tanzania.* WED Report 5. Dar es Salaam: University of Dar es Salaam.

Swantz, Marja-Liisa. 1985. *Women in Development: A Creative Role Denied?* London: C. Hurst; New York, St. Martin's Press.

Tamale, Sylvia and Joe Oloka-Onyango. 2000. "Bitches at the Academy: Gender and Academic Freedom in Africa," in Ebrima Sall, ed. *Women in Academia: Gender and Academic Freedom in Africa.* Dakar: Council for the Development of Social Science Research in Africa.

TGNP (Tanzania Gender Networking Programme). 1993. *Gender Profile of Tanzania.* Dar es Salaam: TGNP.

Thompson, Jack T., 2002. "Donald Fraser and the Ngoni Church." Lecture delivered on the occasion of the Centenary of Loudon Station. University of Edinburgh, November. http://embangweni.com/FraserNgoni.htm. Accessed 30 September 2006.

Tippu Tip (Hamed bin Muhammed el-Murjebi). 1974 *Maisha ya Hamed bin Muhammed el Murjebi kwa maneno yake Mwenyewe* [Autobiography of Hamed bin Muhammed el-Murjebi]. Nairobi: East African Literature Bureau.

Tripp, Aili Mari. 2000. *Women and Politics in Uganda.* Madison: University of Wisconsin Press.

Van Breugel, J.W.M. 2002. *Chewa Traditional Religion.* Kachere Monograph 13. Balaka: Montfort Media; East Lansing: Michigan State University Press.

Vaughan, Megan. 1991. *Curing Their Ills: Colonial Power and African Illness.* Palo Alto: Stanford University Press.

Veney, Cassandra Rachel and Paul Tiyambe Zeleza. 2001. *Women in African Studies: Scholarly Publishing.* Lawrenceville, NJ: Africa World Press, Inc.

White, Seodi Venekai Rudo, Tinyade Kachika, Asiyati Lorraine Chiweza, Dorothy nyaKaunda Kamanga, and F. Gomile-Chidyaonga. 2002. *Dispossessing the Widow: Gender Based Violence in Malawi.* Blantyre: Christian Literature Association of Malawi (CLAIM).

Wipper, Audrey. 1989. "Kikuyu Women and the Harry Thuku Disturbances: Some Uniformities of Female Militancy." *Africa* 59(3).

Wood, Susan. 1964. *A Fly in Amber.* London: Collins Harvill.

Wright, Marcia. 1993. *Strategies of Slaves and Women: Life Stories from East and Central Africa.* New York: Lilian Barber Press; Oxford: James Currey.

Yahya-Othman, Saïda. 2000. "Engendering Academic Freedom," in Ebrima Sall, ed. *Women in Academia: Gender and Academic Freedom in Africa.* Dakar: Council for the Development of Social Science Research in Africa (CODESRIA).

Zeleza, Paul Tiyambe. 2002. "African Universities and Globalization." *Feminist Africa* 1: "Intellectual Politics." Cape Town: African Gender Institute.

THE EIGHTEENTH AND NINETEENTH CENTURIES

Sultan Fatima binti Muhammad Mkubwa
PEACE AND SECURITY

Tanzania   1711   Kiswahili

Sultan Fatima binti Muhammad Mkubwa was the ruler of the city-state of Kilwa Island, off the coast of present-day Tanzania. Little is known about her life or her reign other than that her father and her brother ruled before her and her brother's son succeeded her. She may have become the ruler of Kilwa as the eldest surviving child of Sultan Muhammad Mkubwa, or she may have been serving as a regent for her brother's son until he was old enough to assume leadership of the sultanate. In some other city-states, rule was passed from mother to daughter: In the early 1800s, for example, Queen Mwanzuani succeeded her mother as ruler of Kua on Mafia Island, and in the late 1800s Sabani binti Ngumi, the ruler of Mikindani, was succeeded by her daughter.

Scholars have documented twenty-six women rulers of the city-states along the East African coast during the seventeenth, eighteenth, and nineteenth centuries, and there may well have been more, since the historical record in this area remains incomplete. The names of earlier women rulers became praise names for individual city-states, and these praise names were used in poetry to comment on the communities and their inhabitants. For example, as explained by Mohamed H. Abdulaziz in his book *Muyaka: Nineteenth-Century Swahili Popular Poetry*, the Mombasa poet Muyaka bin Haji referred to Mombasa as "Gongwa of Mwana Mkisi." "Gongwa" is an earlier name for Mombasa and "Mwana Mkisi" is the name of the legendary female ruler of Mombasa. Similarly, Muyaka referred to the people of Zanzibar as "the descendants of Mwana Aziza" after the island's legendary female ruler. Abdulaziz also finds references in poetry to "Mwana Mize of Lamu," "Mwana Musura of Pate," and "Mwana Shamba Shale of Vumba."

In 1711, Sultan Fatima composed a letter to Mwinyi Jumaa, whose father seems to have been from Mombasa. The scribe, whose name is not legible in the manuscript, wrote the letter in Swahili in Arabic script. Both Swahili and Arabic were used by the elites of the Swahili city-states during this period, and it is likely that Sultan Fatima was literate in both languages. While Arabic was used for communication with Omani officials and merchants and was also used, along with Portuguese, for communication with Portuguese officials and merchants, it appears that Swahili written in Arabic script may often have been used for communications between Swahili city-states. Messengers who traveled by dhow transmitted letters from one city-state to another.

At the time Sultan Fatima wrote her letter, Portuguese control of the East African coast was waning and Omani Arab dominance of the region was being established. In the letter, Sultan Fatima seems to indicate that she has established an alliance with or accepted the protection of the ruler of Oman. Presumably, Portuguese officials intercepted the messenger, confiscated the letter before it reached Mwinyi Jumaa, and had it translated into Portuguese in their Goa headquarters by Bwana Ndau ibn al-Sayyid Mbwana Shaka, who identifies himself in his translation as a prince of Faza Island. Faza Island is located off the northern coast of Kenya and was another Swahili city-state.

Ann Biersteker

In the name of God, the Merciful, the Compassionate,

I, the ruler of Kilwa, Sultan Fatima, daughter of Sultan and former ruler Muhammad Mkubwa, dictate this letter to our friend Mwinyi Jumaa, son of the late Sayyid Mwinyi Kaje:

My greetings. This letter is to inform you that I have seen the governor of the Imam and the emissaries of the Imam, Sheikh Ali ibn Muhammad and Muhammad ibn Mubarak al-Bukhayt. They told me that we should be given a letter from our Lord the Imam saying that we should write to all of our subjects who are in the Kerimba region and tell them that they should come to Kilwa where God's peace prevails.

Anyone who wants to should come, and if she or he come with their possessions, no one will rob them. Those who want to sell Islamic foods should come. There is nothing to worry about. If a person intends to come to his or her home, he or she should come. There is peace, and no one will seize that person's property. Tell this to all the people who are there, except the Europeans. They are the enemies of the Imam. Anyone who is a Swahili person will not be ill-treated by an Arab.

The end, in peace.

Translated by Ann Biersteker

Mwana Kupona binti Msham
FROM A MOTHER'S ADVICE AND PRAYER: AN EPIC POEM

Kenya 1858   Kiswahili

Mwana Kupona binti Msham was born in 1810 on Lamu Island, off the Northern coast of Kenya, and spent much of her life on nearby Siyu Island. Her husband, Mohammad Is-Haq bin Mbarak bin Muhammad bin Umar L'Famau, also known as Bwana Mataka, ruled the city-state of Siyu and defended it against the conquest of Sayyid Said of Zanzibar. After his death and the conquest of Siyu, Mwana Kupona returned to Lamu.

Mwana Kupona was a devout Muslim throughout her life. When she composed this poem in 1858, she was terminally ill and had been bedridden for about a year. Knowing that her death was near, she wrote this poem for her seventeen-year-old daughter (Mwana Hashima binti Sheikh, author of another text in this volume). The poem was to serve the daughter—and, by extension, all young women of her station—as an initiation into puberty and the life of a woman. Mwana Kupona died two years later, in 1860.

This epic poem attracted scholars in the early twentieth century, who translated and edited it into various written forms, thus creating variations, especially in the numbering of stanzas and the overall length of the poem. Near the end of the poem, the author mentions that she has composed 102 stanzas. Although Mwana Kupona, in the opening stanzas, asks her daughter to "Come with paper and ink," no manuscripts survive in the hand of either mother or daughter.

Rather than lecturing, the author threads together, stanza by stanza, the "beads" of her advice, which she aptly portrays as precious and protective ornaments, into a poem she variously describes as a pendant, a charm, a necklace, and a beautiful garland of fragrant flowers. In the absence of an authoritative original text, we have chosen stanzas to provide a flavor of the whole. These focus on admonitions to the daughter and a passionate prayer to God to care for her family and community, revealing a consciousness of her own failing health.

The poem is of the *utendi* narrative genre of Kiswahili poetry in quatrains: Each line contains eight syllables; the first three lines rhyme; and the fourth line of every stanza rhymes with the fourth line of every other stanza. The language is the Kiamu dialect of Kiswahili, spoken on Lamu Island and its environs even now. The prosody has been sacrificed in order to provide a new modern translation.

Naomi L. Shitemi

✦

1. Come near, my dear daughter,
You, a young inexperienced woman,
Listen to my advice
That I hope you will remember.

2. I have been ill
The entire past year,
So ill that I could not speak
Even a word of advice to you.

3. Come to me and hear me,
Come with paper and ink,
For I have a story
That I want to tell you.

4. Now that you are near me,
Say *Bismillahi*, In the Name of God.
Pray for the Holy Prophet
And also his companions.

5. After you pronounce the name
Of God Almighty,
We will pray for a future
That God may grant us.

6. The human being is nothing
And the world is not ours,
For certainly, there is no one
Who will ever be immortal.

7. Take my advice, my child,
And my blessings also,
For God will protect you
And keep you from evil.

8. Take this charm that I give to you,
Tie it securely with a cord,
Honor and treasure it.
May you care for it always.

9. I will string for you a precious amulet
Of pearls and coral beads
To adorn you elegantly.
May it glow upon your neck.

10. I would like to give you a pendant,
One precious, perfect, without fault,
To wear around your neck.
You shall see its benefits.

11. If you remember my advice,
My child, you will never suffer.
You will walk across this world,
And later you will enter paradise.

12. First, remain loyal to your religion:
Fulfill the *Faradhi* that is required,
Follow the *Sunna* that is advised.
This is your obligation.

13. Second, be virtuous:
Have a sweet tongue
That you may be respected
Wherever you may go.

14. Be trustworthy.
Hold firm to your beliefs.
Avoid those who are unjust;
Shun their company.

15. My daughter, take special care
When you meet the powerful:
Wherever you may meet them,
Quickly show them respect.

16. As they approach,
Rise to meet them cheerfully,
And when they depart,
Escort them as they leave.

17. Be amusing when you speak,
Without being malicious.
Do not argue needlessly,
Lest people despise you.

18. Speak jokingly with people;
Use pleasant and joyous words.
Better to be quiet
Than to use words that spite.

19. Avoid those matters
You do not understand;
Even aimless talk and grumbling—
Avoid these, I beg of you.

20. Stay away from the slaves
Except when doing chores,
For they may harm your reputation.
Perhaps I have said this before.

21. Avoid the company of the ignorant,
Who do not behave properly,
Showing no generosity toward others.
Keep away; do not approach them.

22. Darling, listen to what I'm saying:
A woman requires five approvals
If she is to rest
In paradise and on earth.

23. These are of God and the Prophet,
And of one's father and mother.
The fifth is of one's husband,
As you have heard many times.

24. You should have your husband's approval
As long as you are together,
So that when you are separated,
His approval will have been given.

25. Should you die before him,
His approval should be with you.
You will carry it with you.
It will show you the way.

26. On the day of resurrection,
Your husband's wish will be granted.
He will be asked what he wills,
And all will be as he wishes.

27. If he wills paradise for you,
Certainly, you will enter.
If he wills that you perish in hell,
Certainly, there you shall go.

28. Live with him courteously.
Do not drive him to anger.
Should he be angry, do not respond;
Make every effort to remain silent.

29. Be in harmony with him;
Deny him not what he desires.
Do not quarrel with him;
If you do, you will be the loser.

30. If he leaves, bid him farewell.
When he returns, welcome and honor him,
Then prepare a comfortable place
Where he may rest.

31. When he sleeps, do not stir about,
But lean towards him, and stroke him.
He should not lack
The enjoyment of a cool breeze.

32. If he dozes while leaning on you,
Move not, nor raise your voice.
Sit still, stir not,
Lest he be startled awake.

33. When he awakens, care for him.
Offer him a fine meal.
Also care for his body:
Massage him and wash him.

34. Shave him, caress him,
Trim his beard,
Burn incense around him
From morning until evening.

35. Care for him as though
He were a very young child,
Who could not yet speak;
Anticipate his needs and desires.

36. Amuse him until he's entranced.
Do not reject his command.
If he behaves disgracefully,
Surely God will take revenge for you.

37. My child, do not be slovenly.
Act as you see best,
But never ignore, not even once,
Matters of cleanliness.

38. Bathe often and carefully.
Braid your hair,
Adorning it with jasmine blossoms;
Also put them on your bedclothes.

39. Dress yourself beautifully
As though you were still a bride.
Wear ankle bracelets
And bangles on your wrists.

40. Hang amulets and pendants
Always around your neck.
Smooth your body with fragrance
Of perfumes and sweet oils.

41. Wear rings on your fingers
And henna on your palms.
Put kohl around your eyes
And also on your eyebrows.

42. Keep your house neat
To lift your husband's status,
And when company enters,
Praise him to them.

43. Whatever he desires,
Follow that same desire.
What he disapproves,
Be not the person who brings it to him.

44. If you must go out,
Seek his permission.
If he does not give it,
Stay at home; do not argue with him.

45. Follow his guidance
To ensure his approval.
Do not stay outside,
Especially after ten at night.

46. Do not engage in idle chatter.
Do not unveil yourself.
Cast your eyes down in humility.
Your expression should be shy.

47. Quickly return to your home
To keep your husband company.
Prepare a place of comfort
Where both of you may sleep.

48. Praise your husband.
Make his reputation known.
You should not compel him
To undertake what he is not able to do.

49. Receive whatever he gives you
With joy in your heart.
What he does not willingly do,
It is not for you to tell him.

50. When you encounter his face,
Smile and laugh.
Do what he tells you
Unless it is against God.

51. My darling, do not be quick to speak.
Ask me, your mother.
I was married for ten years;
Not once did we disagree

52. Your father married me
In joy and in bliss.
We never embarrassed each other
All the days we were together.

65. Listen to my words, beloved daughter;
I beseech you not to ignore them.
You surely will see their benefits
In heaven and here on earth.

66. That is the end of my words
Of advice to you, my daughter.
Now I will pray to God
To grant my prayer.

67. However much we talk,
Human beings are worthless.
God is the one who is able
To destroy and to save.

68. I pray to You, Almighty,
To aid me
In what I say
And in what I have not said.

69. All that I have said,
God, accept from me;
And I pray to you again,
Dear God, provide for me.

70. Look after my children
And my younger brother.
May their names become renowned
And known in other places.

71. God, take care of my family,
And the children of my family members.
May they extend throughout the world
In goodness and prosperity.

72. Those of the Islamic faith,
God, please bless them.
Fulfill their desires
And make them happy.

Translated by Ann Biersteker and Naomi L. Shitemi

Emily Ruete, also known as Princess Salma of Zanzibar
A ROYAL CHILDHOOD IN ZANZIBAR

Tanzania 1886 German

This extract is taken from the autobiography of Princess Salma (sometimes spelled Salme) Said, later known as Emily Ruete. Princess Salma was born in 1844 according to her own statements, or 1840 according to other sources, in the house of Seyyid Said, who was Sultan of Oman and Zanzibar from 1804 to 1856. Princess Salma was one of Seyyid Said's more than thirty children. She grew up in her father's various palaces until she was about sixteen. After her father's death, she eloped with a German businessman, Heinrich Ruete, went to live in Germany, and converted to Christianity, adopting the name Emily Ruete. Her husband died in an accident a few years later, leaving her with three small children. She lived and raised her children on her own with very meager resources. Her attempts to recover the inheritance she would have been due as a member of the royal family of Zanzibar were not successful. She died in 1924 and was buried in Hamburg.

Princess Salma's autobiography, *Memoiren eine arabischen Prinzessin*, was completed in 1886 and first published in Germany in 1888. It was soon followed by an English translation. In her preface, the author says she wrote the book for her children, since she feared she might not live long enough to tell them her story when they grew up—a concern that turned out to be unfounded.

Princess Salma's is the first full length autobiography written by a Tanzanian. It provides a unique insider's glimpse of life in Zanzibar, and especially in the royal palaces, in the middle of the nineteenth century. Even more remarkable is the fact that the story is told from a woman's perspective, casting light on the rights, duties, and predicaments of upper-class women, in the midst of incessant palace intrigue; the relations between Arab rulers and African servants in the palace; and the general court culture and manners. Princess Salma's depiction of her life in German culture, as a lonely Arab-African widow in an alien—and cold—land makes sad and engaging reading. In her memoir as a whole, she emerges as a courageous and single-minded rebel and provides what is probably the first record of a Tanzanian woman of her stature defying the strict social norms of her time, place, and position.

In the Zanzibar of Princess Salma's time, it was quite unthinkable for an upper-class Muslim woman to marry a non-Muslim, let alone a foreigner.

Upper-class women in Zanzibar were usually secluded from the prying eyes of all males other than their very close relatives. They were required to hide themselves whenever visitors entered the house, and to be fully shrouded, and escorted by armed eunuchs and servant women, whenever they went out. It is thus difficult to know how the young German businessman managed even to meet Salma, let alone come to an agreement to elope with her. In any case, had their love affair been discovered in Zanzibar, Princess Salma would probably have faced death, and the German would have been expelled from the islands.

At the same time, Princess Salma's writing reflects the prejudices and limitations inherent in her position as a member of the Arab ruling class in a slave society; these attitudes may explain her negative sentiments regarding Africans. Zanzibar in the middle of the nineteenth century was an Arab feudal sultanate reigning over a commercial and plantation empire inhabited largely by Africans, whose dominant culture was Swahili. The island of Zanzibar became a province of Oman following the ouster of the Portuguese around 1700, and in 1840, Sultan Seyyid Said, Princess Salma's father, decided to move his capital to Zanzibar. In the nineteenth century, Zanzibar was at the center of European gunboat diplomacy and was eventually ceded to the British in 1890. The Arab sultanate nonetheless remained in place, in some form, until the month after Zanzibar's independence in 1963, when it was overthrown by a violent revolution and Zanzibar united with Tanganyika to form Tanzania. Of late there has been a revival of interest in the Arab period; currently, a whole room in Zanzibar's Palace Museum is devoted to Princess Salma.

M.M. Mulokozi

✦

As long as the child does not have enough strength to wear sandals (the wooden ones for girls and women are called *kubkâb*, the leather ones for boys and men are called *watje*), it runs about barefooted. Because the *watje* are considerably lighter to wear than the *kubkâb*, very small girls initially are made to walk on the former until they have acquired the necessary skill to wear the *kubkâb* forever. Neither children nor adults of both sexes wear stockings; only more aristocratic ladies use them now and then when riding, as custom requires one to cover the ankles.

Already at the age of two to four months, two or three slaves, besides the wet nurses, were allotted to the child by our father. From then on they remained its property. The older it grew, the more slaves it received for its personal attendance. If one of them died, our father replaced him, or gave an appropriate sum of money. Up to a certain age, little girls wear boys' caps in the house.

Until his seventh year each prince at home stays among the women. At this age the mosaic rite [circumcision] is performed on him. Ceremonies of course play an important role on this occasion, the closing of which, after the child's recovery, forms a peculiar festivity, in which all dignitaries and high officials are allowed to take part. This deed, if in any way possible, was enacted in the country and in the presence of our father. A public entertainment, usually lasting for three days, also accompanied this.

From this time onwards, every boy received a quiet mare of his own. His escort could take their mounts from the stables, where a couple of hundred Arabian horses were standing. In this way the boy, at a very early age, learns to ride well and acquires a very outstanding skill and nimbleness, which only a trained circus rider is otherwise credited with. Since we had neither a true saddle nor stirrup, it required of course much more dexterity to gain a firm seat than in this country. Our father followed a characteristic custom when his sons ran into some mishap while out riding. In that case not only they themselves but also their escort could expect punishment. For our father assumed that the latter, with the tight warrants and instructions which he had conferred on them, must have behaved much too indulgently towards the princes.

Not one of us was spoiled in any way. My father's high sense of justice and unparalleled generosity was combined with an equally firm consistency which did not know any weakness. All of us had to obey our teachers and educators on the strength of their word [be they Arabs, Abyssinians or simple negroes]. If occasionally we complained to our father, we certainly left his presence in tears or shame for our behaviour. This severity taught us the reverence due to such people, and with increasing age the appreciation of how deep our moral indebtedness to them was also grew.

The nurses, even if they had served as such for a very short time, were particularly honoured and enjoyed special esteem for the remainder of their life. By birth they were always slaves, but as a rule they were freed in reward of their fidelity and devotion. The black wet nurses especially distinguished themselves by extraordinary fidelity and attachment. Even the most cautious mother might in all confidence leave her child with the wet nurse, who usually considered herself as its second mother and acted accordingly. How the lack of interest and the heartlessness of the wet nurses in these parts stand out in stark contrast with this! Often enough have I felt myself forced to give, on a public walkway, a good talking to such a character, totally unknown to me, for her brutal treatment of the little thing entrusted to her. This contrast between the wet nurses of these parts and our Arab ones may possibly be explained by the fact that the former are forced by their poverty alone to entrust their own beloved child to complete strangers under much sacrifice. Only for money's sake they serve masters; whether the child to nurse is called Tom or Dick is indifferent to them; their thoughts and feelings naturally linger with their own child. And which mother would hold this against her!

How very different is a black nurse's attitude towards her mistress's child entrusted to her. For years she is in the latter's service, she may even have been born in her house; it then is understandable that she does not have many private interests, that she makes those of her masters her own. Moreover, there is the most important fact that a black wet nurse only very rarely, if ever, is required to part with her child, but may quietly retain it. The wet nurse's child then receives the same nourishment as its little master or mistress, the same milk soup, part of the same fowl, etc.; the same goes for the bath, and the used dresses fall no less to its lot. When its mother stops serving as a wet nurse, her child continues to be the playmate of her second foster-child. Though remaining a slave, it is always preferred to the rest of the slaves, and only bad people offend against this attachment to the foster-brother.

The black wet nurses, however, have one very bad habit. They know how to tell the little children of three to five years old very dreadful stories and fairy-tales. Partly to amuse them, partly also to keep them quiet. The lion (*simba*), the leopard (*tshui*), the elephant (*tembo*), and the numerous witches (*watchawi*) occupy of course the first place in these often also for adults horrifying fables.

On the whole, rearing a child in the south is unquestionably much easier than here in the north: above all, the everlasting colds and everything they usually entail are rare. Notwithstanding all indolence, children there are very independent and adroit, for they are allowed to play and jump freer and more unconstrained (both in space and in dress) to their heart's content. Though gymnastic exercises are completely unknown, it is no rarity that a boy of ten to twelve in playing takes a stiff run and leaps over one or even two horses. High jumping in general plays an important role, and everybody strives as much as he can to surpass the other.

Swimming in the sea was practised no less eagerly, and everybody taught himself without any guidance. Shooting too began early and was pursued with great passion. Mock-fights were extraordinarily favoured; from youth onward many an hour was devoted to them. Though the boys went about armed to the teeth and carried as much powder and lead as grown-ups, one hardly ever heard of an accident caused by imprudence.

Up to a certain age only, the young princes, as already mentioned above, lived in their father's house. Then a house of their own was assigned to each to keep independently, as a rule with their mother if she was still alive. As maintenance he was granted by our father a certain monthly allowance, and then he had to "cut his coat according to his cloth," which was certainly matching the needs. At marriage, at an increase to the family, or also for exceptional conduct, he might count on an extra allowance, but in no other case. Only when our father's ships arrived annually with the new purchases, did all my brothers and sisters living outside the paternal house come with their families to receive each the share belonging to him, whether he needed it or not. If any one of them had the great misfortune of spending more than what his allowance brought in, it was never made easy for him to pay his debts; nothing was more hateful to our father, and the one who had brought this disgrace to himself was very much on his guard not to incur the same a second time.

If a war broke out, as unfortunately was so often the case in Oman, all the princes, the half-grown included, had to take the field too and to take part in the fight like any common man. On the whole, discipline was strict, but it only raised the respect and reverence of the sons for their father. As a child I often saw with astonishment how my elder brother, anticipating the slaves, hurried to put in readiness the sandals my father had left at the door of his room. The elder brothers appeared also in the paternal house several times a day, as soon as our father was present, and then took part in the meals.

There is but very little to say about the education of a princess; the first years it is the same as that of her brothers, with the exception that the latter at their seventh year obtain a much greater freedom outside the house. The only thing deserving mention at a princess's birth is that, in accordance with the hairdress in our country, a broad comb, generally of silver, is placed under the back of the newborn to give it a flat shape for later age. When a Princess is married to one of her cousins, who to be sure are more numerous in Oman than in Zanzibar, she of course leaves the paternal house in exchange for that of her husband. The former, however, the sole and real bulwark against all hardships of life, remains always open as a place to live. But if she prefers, she can also go and live with a brother. Every sister has her favourite brother, and vice versa; in joy and sorrow these two stick together and support each other by word and deed. As praise-worthy and, for those concerned, as much a blessing as this habit was in such a numerous family circle as ours, it understandably created many jealousies among brothers and sisters, and it often required a strong character to overcome all these.

Often such a loving sister had to intercede with our father for some impru-dence of her favourite brother, for he liked to favour his daughters and rarely left their requests unheard. To his elder daughters in particular he was extraor-dinarily obliging; he usually went to meet them from afar and had them seated by his side on the sofa, while the grown-up sons and we little people stood respectfully before him.

Schooling (*mdarse*) is of very little importance for the Oriental in general and consequently for us too. In Europe school is at the center of State and Church, without distinction for prince and citizen; for both the formation of his character and his prospects for the future, the individual depends essentially upon it for his success. But in the Orient the *mdarse* is altogether a matter of secondary importance; for a good many people it does not exist at all. But before engaging in further discussions, I wish to say something about what we called school in our house.

At the age of six to seven, all my brothers and sisters, boys as well as girls, had to enter the *mdarse*. We girls were only required to learn to read, the boys to read and write. For teaching there was at both Bet il Mtoni and Bet il Sahel only one lady teacher, whom our father had sent for from Oman. When the teacher fell ill and was confined to her bed, there was always great joy among us; no replacement could be procured for her, and so we had holidays.

There was no specific schoolroom, lessons took place in an open gallery, to which pigeons, parrots, peacocks and ricebirds found free entrance. From there we also had a free view of the courtyard and were able to amuse ourselves with watching its busy life down there. The furniture of the schoolroom consisted of a single, immense mat only. Our school equipment was equally simple: we only needed a Kurân with its stand (*marfà*), a small inkstand with ink, a bamboo quill, and a well-bleached shoulder-blade of a camel. The latter is the substitute for the slate; writing with ink on this is quite easy, and the nerves are certainly less assailed than at the scratching on the slate. Our slaves usually took care of wiping off the blades.

The first thing we had to learn, exactly as is done here, was the very complicated Arabic alphabet. Then, for want of any other school-book, we started reading the Kurân with which, as mentioned above, writing lessons were connected for the boys. When one was able to read a little, one joined the others who all read in a chorus and mostly very loudly. But that was all, for what is read and learned is never explained. Hence there was at most only one among thousands who understood word by word all the meanings and precepts of the Holy Script of the Muslims and who was able to explain them, though probably eighty out of one hundred had learned half of it by heart. Reflecting upon the Holy Script was even considered irreligious and unauthorized; people should simply believe what they were taught, and this maxim was rigorously carried out.

Having enjoyed some fruit, we had to assemble at seven o'clock in the morning on our mat, which had been rolled up during the night and was now swept clean, and had to await the arrival of our severe lady teacher. Until she arrived, we whiled away the time to our heart's content with wrestling, boxing, jumping, climbing the railings which was life endangering, and other favourite amusements of the children's world. We set a watch at the bend of the gallery, who by simulated coughing announced the teacher's arrival from afar. In no time we were all sitting on the mat, an image of the greatest innocence, and only when her steps came near, did we rebound like India rubber balls, to shake hands respectfully with the dreaded one and to wish her good morning. She always carried the detested bamboo cane in one hand and a large brass inkstand in the other. We stood in file before her until she had taken her seat; only then were we permitted to follow this example. All of us sat cross-legged on the mat, flocked together in a circle around the teacher.

She now would begin to recite the first *sura* of the Kurân, the Muslim Lord's prayer as it were. We prayed in chorus after her and concluded with the well-known *Amin* (*not Amen*). Then we repeated what we had learned the day before, and after that we were given a new piece for reading or writing. Lessons regularly lasted until about nine o'clock, and then, after breakfast, again till about noon, the time of the second prayer.

Each of us was allowed to bring some of his slaves to school to take part in the lessons; they sat at some distance behind us, while we grouped ourselves as we pleased, for there were neither fixed places for us or division in different forms. People had not the faintest notion of school reports, which a few times every year occasion feverish excitement in this country. If someone made particularly good or bad progress, distinguished himself particularly through good or bad behaviour, this usually was reported orally to the respective mothers and to our father. From the latter the lady teacher had the explicit order to punish us severely, if there was any cause. And our great wildness obliged her to use the evil bamboo cane.

Besides reading and writing, we were taught a little arithmetic, numbering up to one hundred in writing and up to one thousand orally; what is beyond that is believed to be from the evil one. With grammar and orthography not much pain was taken, and the rather complicated *Ilnahû* [grammar, from Arabic *al-nahw*] was only acquired by much reading over the years. At home I never heard of such sciences as history, geography, physics, mathematics or how they are all named let alone that I learned them. It was only in this country [i.e., Germany] that I had the pleasure to become acquainted with all these fields of knowledge. But it will remain an open question to me whether, with the little wisdom laboriously acquired here, I am now better off than the others over there. That I have never been more deceived and swindled than in the time of my greatest knowledge, this is certain. Oh you happy people at home! Not even in your dreams do you surmise all that is connected with holy civilization!

Translated by E. van Donzel

Martha Thabi
MY GOD, WHY HAVE YOU FORSAKEN ME?

Malawi   1890   Ngoni (Zulu)

Martha Thabi was born about 1870 and was educated in Njuya, in what was then called Ngoniland, now the Mzimba District in northern Malawi. The region's name reflects the area's settlement, earlier in the nineteenth century, by the Ngoni people, who had migrated north from the kwaZulu-Natal area. Thabi was one of the first women to attend a mission school opened by the Scots at Njuyu in 1886, and she became a teacher before she was twenty years old. While Njuyu was a primary school, as early as 1894, Scottish missionaries opened a high school and technical college at Khondowe called Overtoun Institute. Thabi did not enter Overtoun Institute because of her early marriage to Reverend Andrew C. Mkochi of Engalaweni.

In addition to her teaching, Thabi took a prominent part in church affairs as the pastor's wife. She also cultivated gardens, harvested and pounded maize, and bore eight children, four female and four male, all of whom went to school. A highly respected citizen of her community, she died some time after 1912. Thabi begins this poem, which takes the form of a prayer, with Jesus's famous appeal to God from the cross.

Desmond D. Phiri and Fulata L. Moyo

✦

1. My God, my God,
Why have you forsaken me, my Lord?
Behold, you are far away from me.
Help me, my Lord.

2. My God, I cry
Day and night,
But you do not answer me.

3. I am but a worm.
I am not a righteous person.
I am unworthy of you, my Lord.

4. Do not move away from me
Since troubles are very near.
But you are my strength, my Lord.

5. My God, come
back to me, my Lord.
Help me.

6. Hear my cry.
I cry to you, Father,

Answer my prayer.

Translated by Desmond D. Phiri

Jessie Nyagondwe
LET NOT YOUR HEART BE TROUBLED

Malawi 1890s   Chitumbuka

Jessie Nyagondwe, the composer of this hymn, is the only woman composer whose name appears in a collection of hymns published in the Tumbuka language (Chitumbuka) in 1961. It is quite possible that many other hymns, credited to "Anonymous," were also composed by women, who were such a primary force in church life.

While the hymn was not published until 1961, evidence suggests that it was composed in the 1890s. Jessie Nyagondwe was one of the earliest Christian converts among the Ngoni and Tumbuka in northern Malawi in the 1890s. She must have been born in the area sometime in the 1880s, and she was among a group of enslaved girls rescued from slave traders by Dr. Robert Laws on the northern shores of Lake Malawi. She was kept at the Livingstonia Mission in Khondowe, where she became one of the first girls to be educated at Overtoun Institute. Like other talented composers, she began to express her new faith, Christianity, in the form of hymns.

Her song and others were introduced and practiced at great choir festivals organized by the Scottish Missionary Donald Fraser in the first quarter of the twentieth century. During this period, Fraser organized large revival meetings throughout the Mzimba District in the northern part of Malawi, and he converted many to Christianity. Nyagondwe's composition proved so popular that it spread rapidly and became part a body of locally composed hymnology in use throughout northern Malawi.

Fulata L. Moyo

✦

Let not your heart be troubled
By all earthly things.
Instead rejoice
That we shall sing to Jesus.

Refrain:
We will sing
To Jesus, our Redeemer.
We will sing to Jesus.
We will all rejoice in Him.

Do not pile up
Treasures on earth.
They perish while you hoard them.
Weevils and rust destroy them all.

Refrain

Instead, you should store
The enduring treasure in heaven,
Where Christ, Our Leader,
is gone.

Refrain

Around us and within us
Are foes who would destroy us.
Protect us from them, Jesus,
And we will gladly praise you.

Refrain

On earth many sorrows
Press upon us daily.
Lord, free us in your mercy
From all these foes.

Refrain

Translated by Desmond D. Phiri

Bwanikwa
TEN TIMES A SLAVE

Zambia 1895   Chiluba

The survivor of many crises and dislocations, Bwanikwa told her story of having been "ten times a slave" shortly after the turn of the twentieth century, while living in the relative quiet of a mission-sponsored community in northeastern Rhodesia, the present-day Luapula Province of Zambia. The experiences she narrates took place mainly in what is today the southeastern Congo province of Katanga (formerly Shaba), first in a time when the stamp of colonial boundaries was still to be impressed and then as the colonial conquest took place.

In the late pre-colonial decades, the commercial hegemony established by Msiri, a Nyamwezi trader, was buttressed by state-building. By the 1880s, Msiri ruled a large kingdom and received tribute from neighboring areas. At Msiri's capital, hundreds of slaves contributed to the maintenance of services and provisions for the caravans that arrived and departed, both to the Atlantic port of Banguela in Angola and to the Indian Ocean coasts dominated by the Sultanate of Zanzibar. Msiri's origins were in Unyamwezi, in west-central Tanzania, and his control of the Katanga area, in the years after 1890, faced crises of insurrections by the indigenous people and of famine, both dislocating people even before the coming of the Belgians.

Bwanikwa's origins in the Luba-speaking society meant that from birth she spoke Chiluba, part of a language family widespread in eastern Congo and northern Zambia. In that language she recounted her narrative of slavery to missionary Dugald Campbell, who in turn translated it into English. The tale of her successive owners and alliances provides, from a rare female point of view, a picture of dislocation, insecurity, and opportunism, up to a kind of stabilization within the early colonial situation. The English translation of Bwanikwa's story was published during World War I as part of an appeal to British women for material support of missionary endeavors on the part of Campbell's society, the Plymouth Brethren. A book subsequently written by Campbell supplies information about Bwanikwa's later life as a successful petty trader and practitioner of herbal medicine and also tells of her self-redemption: She eventually repaid her husband the amount he had given her last slave-master. Following this act, as Campbell tells it, the pair lived as equals to a degree exceptional in local African society, sharing tasks, eating together, and addressing one another in highly respectful terms. In old age, Bwanikwa returned to Luba country in Congo, residing there in a Christian community.

Marcia Wright

✦

I, Bwanikwa, was born on the banks of the Dindie, a small river in our Luba-land.

Our part of the country was thickly populated, and our principal chief was Goi-Mani. My father's name was Kankolwe. My mother was called Mikomba. I was one of a family of five. Our only brother had died; four girls remained, of whom I was the second oldest.

My father had a dozen wives. His head-wife was the daughter of chief Katumba. She was an important woman. At the time I refer to, the head-wife had just died. According to Luban custom [my father] was mulcted for death dues. He was ordered to pay three slaves, as compensation for his wife's death, and to ensure inheritance by the dead wife's sister. They did not produce a sister to take the dead woman's place till the death had been paid for to the relatives. Three slaves were demanded, and my father could only raise two.

One of his four daughters had to be handed over to make a third, and I was chosen. I was the second oldest, as I said, and my father loved me. When he handed me over to my master, he said to him as we parted: "Be kind to my little daughter; do not sell her to anyone else, and I will come and redeem her." As my father was unable to redeem me, I was left in slavery.

My father did not come to redeem me, and my master sold me to some of Msidi's people who were out man-hunting. I was sold for a packet of gunpowder, worth two shillings and sixpence, and was taken to Chifuntwe's village in the Balomotwa country. At that time I was small, unable to walk.

It appears that my master had, at this time, offended the principal chief, and was ordered to pay up several slaves. Amongst those slaves given to pay for my master's crimes, I was handed over. Thus I was sold again. The chief to whom I was given in payment of a fine handed me to one of his warriors as wife, saying, "Take her as your wife, she's young." After a while he said "She's only a young girl, and I don't want her." He sold me to a man named Mukoka for a gun. Mukoka bought me, with another woman and child, intending to sell us later to the Biheans. He took me as his wife. I bore him a child which only lived three days. His other wives were kind to me. Though he sold many other slaves to Biheans, he never sold me, nor did he threaten to do so.

I lived with Mukoka till Msidi's death and the break up of his power by the Europeans. At this some of us slaves saw our chance and fled. We scattered. Men, tired of Msidi's despotic rule, would take some or other woman slave, and both would head north, south, east, or west, in search of freedom and a new start in life. When possible, each headed for the old homestead.

A well-known elephant hunter and fellow-slave in the same village, whose name was Kabongo, took me, and we ran off east. Our old master set out in search of a new home and village site. We crossed the Luapula River to Kazembe's to try and begin life anew. Chief Kazembe cast his eye upon me and asked Kabongo to give me to him for a wife. Kabongo refused. We left Kazembe's capital, came back west, and settled in Sakungami village. We lived and cultivated there for two years. Some slaves heard of our old master having built at the Luisi River and suggested our returning together. My husband refused at first but afterwards agreed to join the party.

When Chief Mukoka saw me come back, he said, "My wife's come back." On hearing this, Kabongo was angry, and said, "No, I won't let you take her from me; she's my wife." Thus the altercation grew, and they almost came to blows.

Kabongo had killed a bull elephant and intended to give the tusks to the chief. However, owing to Mukoka taking me from him, he hid his ivory in the forest and threatened to kill some of Mukoka's people in revenge. Mukoka was afraid of Kabongo's threats and sold me to a band of West Coast slavers who had just turned up. Said he, "If I'm not going to have her, neither shall he." He sold me to the Biheans, and I started, a slave bound for the West Coast. Immediately after I left, Mukoka caught Kabongo and killed him.

On the road west I took refuge with Inansala, Msidi's sister, who hid me in one of her houses. Shortly after, she was caught and eaten by a lion. On account of her death I was afraid, came out of hiding, and traveled to the mission station. At this time I had never heard the Gospel and was very ignorant.

I met a man named Wafwilwa, who, seeing me alone, asked me to be his wife. I refused at first, but he persisted and would not leave me. I had need of a protector, so I finally gave in and became his wife. We lived near to the mission at Lufoi. Wafwilwa, with two others, was sent to build a mission house on Lake Mweru. We women accompanied them there. On arrival he was sent to the Government Post Office with mission letters, and Wafwilwa insisted on my going with him. His reason for my going soon appeared.

On arrival at Kalunguisi, in British territory, he sold me secretly to some Arabs for calico. I overheard whispered conversation among the Arab traders. Said one of them, "She's very pretty" (*Mzuri sana*). I became suspicious and said to them "Who is pretty?" "Oh," they said, "we're just talking." Then I heard someone say, "She's the slave they're buying." I became afraid and began to cry. Shortly afterwards the Arabs came to me and said, "You're our slave now. Go into the house and sleep; it's night." Then I knew I had been sold again. I refused to enter the house, but my refusals were met by force.

I was pushed inside the house, and a woman kept guard over me. Wooden bars were put across the doors to prevent my escape. The woman was soon fast asleep, while I kept awake. I got up in the middle of the night, removed the bars, and, getting out, ran to the soldiers' headquarters in the government location. I hid there. In the morning the Arabs, finding their slave had escaped, went to Wafwilwa and made him disgorge his ill-gotten gains.

The soldiers threatened to report the matter to the magistrate, but Wafwilwa paid them up and begged them to say nothing. They then handed me back to him; we recrossed the lake and rejoined our friends. Mishi-Mishi was then a Christian, and on hearing my story was angry with Wafwilwa. I refused to live longer with him.

Mr. Campbell then came from the West Coast, via Lufoi. A man in his caravan named Kawimbe, nephew of Chief Mwemmena, asked me to be his wife. I married him. Wafwilwa, seeing this, sent in his account for my keep while I was with him, and Kawimbe paid him a gun. Thus I was enslaved for the tenth and last time.

Translated by Dugald Campbell

THE EARLY TWENTIETH CENTURY
(1900–1935)

E. May Crawford
FACE TO FACE WITH WANGU WA MAKERI

Kenya 1913   English .

The title of May Crawford's 1913 book, from which this excerpt is taken, is *By the Equator's Snowy Peak: A Record of Medical Missionary Work and Travel in British East Africa*. What Crawford describes as a "record," factually accurate as it is, is by no means dry, detached, and neutral, but reflective, interpretive, and engaged.

May Crawford and her husband, Dr. T.W.W. Crawford, were Canadians working with the British Church Missionary Society in what was then the Kenya Province of British East Africa. The Crawfords first lived among the Gikuyu (Kikuyu) people of the Fort Hall District from 1904 to 1910. When they arrived, the missionary presence in Gikuyu country was less than five years old. The East Africa Protectorate had been set up in 1895, and the first foreign trading post in the area dates from 1890, while Gikuyu expansion to the south was still proceeding. Therefore, unlike workers at the coast, the missionaries arrived with virtually no prior briefing about Gikuyu language, customs, social institutions, or cultural phenomena such as the pentatonic scale, which May Crawford could not at first recognize as music. The couple had to learn as they went along. "What strenuous lives they led . . . I found out by degrees," says May Crawford, presenting the overseas reader with a remarkably close analysis of women's routine. Dismayed by such traditions as the chewing of fibers to make string and the cosmetic stretching of earlobes, she may soon have found out that her own long hair and boots were repulsive to some.

From 1910 to 1912 the Crawford served in Embu District, where, amid privations and hardships, the couple worked with great devotion. The medical treatment and education they offered were largely appreciated by the communities they served. As far as the "transforming touch" of Christian divine love was concerned, the couple looked thankfully at the "first fruits of the coming harvest," yet, confronted with "the greatness of the need" had to conclude that "what ha[d] already been done s[a]nk into absolute insignificance."

The most extraordinary aspect of the passage below is the meeting between the missionary and the first female chief to serve the British Protectorate government, Wangu wa Makeri. Wangu has attained an almost mythical status in Kenyan culture. She is referred to in poetry and drama, although the first book-length study of her life and achievements appeared in *Wangu wa Makeri* by Mary W. Wanyoike only in 2002.

In May Crawford's book we see Wangu through contemporary European eyes as a handsome and energetic physical presence. She immediately takes charge of proceedings, being probably more familiar with intercommunal protocol than anyone else present. At the time she had been in office for two years. By conferring her friendship on the missionary she enables the meeting of cultures to proceed. On the other hand, May Crawford failed to see Wangu's position and example as an extension of the trading activity that she recognized as important to women, though in sadly dismissive terms.

Wangu reputedly took her duties seriously and applied traditional punishments with gusto. Her downfall came though failure to observe social limits. She usurped male prerogatives in several ways, most dramatically when she joined male dancers in the *Kibaata* dance, which is performed virtually naked. This was a breach of taboo that society could not tolerate, and she had to resign from office. The circumstances are ambiguous, since her mentor, District Chief Karuri wa Gakure, was also defying tradition by dancing with younger men. Wangu nonetheless continued to be greatly respected until her death in 1936. Her son, Jacob Muchiri, occupied her old post as headman of Weithaga Location from 1915 to 1936. Her administrative camp is today the site of an orphanage, and a sublocation has been named after her.

Marjorie Oludhe Macgoye and Emilia Ilieva

✦

The most interesting event after our arrival at Weithaga was the welcome extended to me by the Kikuyu women. Led by their chieftainess, Wangu [wa Makeri], they ascended the hill in hundreds to perform a dance in my honour. Nothing would content them but that I must be dragged into the center of the ring, to endure with as cheerful a countenance as I could muster the din of their savage song and the smother of dust raised by their feet. A presentation of a sheep followed, and after this Wangu seemed to claim me as her particular friend! She is quite a remarkable person in her way, and is the only female chief we have ever known. Probably she would never have been recognized by the Government in this capacity had not her husband, to whom the authority of sub-chief was originally given, proved incapable, while Wangu demonstrated herself to be "the better man of the two"! With well-oiled body, draped with skins, smeared with red clay and grease and ornamented with an amazing quantity of beads, Wangu is well able to hold her own as the "leading lady" of the country!

Every Kikuyu woman wears a "tailor-made" costume, the goatskin clothing being shaped and sewn by the men; and she is very particular about the cut, although the fashion is unvarying from year to year! Her skirt hangs long behind, terminating in two points or tails, and is folded across a short leather apron in front. A goatskin cape, suspended by a string from one shoulder, covers the upper part of the body but is usually laid aside during manual work. The women have their own methods of dressing the skins, which are rubbed with fat until quite soft and pliable, when they are frequently smeared over with red clay. White or coloured beads are sometimes sewn into the seams and round the edges of these garments, thus rendering them ultra-stylish!

It is strange how dearly an African loves a decoration of beads! The Kikuyu women are sometimes quite heavily laden with them. Large hoops of beaded wire hang from their ears; and bead necklaces, varying in number according to the estimation in which they are held by husbands or lovers, are strung around their necks. Young girls are decorated with a frontlet of beadwork over their foreheads and a kind of corset to blue and white beads just below the waist.

Beads are not, however, the only ornament. Coils of brass wire, kept brightly shining, are worn on the arms and above the ankles, if the woman be a person of any importance. If she has attained the rank of *mutumia* (a married woman with grown-up children), she must keep her head entirely shaved and also insert huge brass rings in the distended lobes of her ears. The younger women shave the front and back of the head, leaving only a circle of hair on the crown. As soon as a girl is able to take a part in the general work of the village, her hair is cut in this curious way, and the wretched custom of distorting the ears begins. Three punctures are made in the upper edge, into which small sticks of equal size are inserted. A much larger hole is made in the lobe, which is continually stretched by the introduction of chunks of wood. These are again and again replaced by wedges of a larger size until the lobe is so extended that it will sometimes reach to the shoulder. Necklaces are often threaded through the ears, making it somewhat difficult and painful to turn the head. Little girls seldom wear anything but a small leather apron, and a string of beads round the neck.

As I sat in the center of the ring of merry women and girls dancing in my honour, I could scarcely realize what strenuous lives they led, but this I found out by degrees, as we watched them come and go day by day and visited them in their villages. Though practically slaves from childhood they bear life's burdens very philosophically and are generally ready with a laugh and a jest. See the tiny girl of four or five years trotting bravely along with a baby almost as big as herself on her back! Look at her again as she follows her mother with a bundle of sticks poised on her slender shoulders or a little gourd filled with water from the river! As she grows year by year the burdens will become gradually heavier and heavier, but her muscles will be so strong that she will usually carry them cheerfully. We have seen women carrying loads of firewoods that weighed quite 180 lbs.! The small Kikuyu maiden is early taught to handle her little cultivating knife in the gardens, digging and weeding all day long beside her mother; then after assisting to carry home the produce of the fields, she must help to cook the food for the lazy men folk at sundown! If not engaged in the fields, the women may be seen busily employed at home, pounding maize in a large wooden mortar or grinding the corn on a smooth slab of stone, by means of a smaller stone which they work to and fro with their hands. This latter process, being accomplished in a kneeling position, must be very fatiguing.

Sometimes when taking a walk in the cool of the day, we have come upon a number of women pounding sugar-cane for the brewing of native beer. For this a large log of timber is felled, and as it lies on the ground a long row of holes resembling mortars is carved on its surface. Pestles of hard wood are prepared, about six feet in length and each weighing seven or eight pounds avoirdupois; with these the cane is pounded to a pulp, which is then carried to a group of men sitting near, whose duty is to wring out the juice. This is poured into large gourds and allowed to ferment. A still more intoxicating drink is made from honey. Pottery is an important industry which is entirely in the hands of the women. They will travel many miles to procure the right kind of sand, and it is really remarkable with what skill they will fashion the large cooking-pots which are so much in demand.

A Kikuyu woman scarcely knows what idleness means. Her leisure moments are occupied with the manufacture of string bags which are used for carrying the garden produce or the ripe corn from the fields. Even when she has become habituated to attending the mission service on Sunday, she may be seen in her place in church busily plying her fingers as she pulls the threads in and out, while a half-finished bag lies on her lap. The twine for these bags is made by a method which would hardly commend itself to friends at home, namely, by chewing strips of wild ramie fiber in the mouth before twisting them into string.

Although the women have no share in the discussion of public affairs, yet in buying and selling they are experts. Were it not for the native markets which are held every fourth day at recognized places all over the country, there would be indeed be little to sharpen their wits. But the constant bargaining over the exchange and sale of their wares and garden produce tends to somewhat develop their otherwise dull and torpid minds. The market is a place of social reunion, and between the hours of eleven and twelve in the morning, when the fair is at its height, it presents a seething mass of black humanity.

Of recreation the women and girls have little, but on moonlight nights they come out to dance on the open spaces outside the homesteads, and the hillsides echo with the shrill trilling of their peculiar song. It is only as a woman advances in years that she may hope to meet with much respect from the other sex. Young men are expected to step out of the path to allow an old dame to pass, if it be a very narrow one. The head wife of a member of the *Kiama* (council of elders) is permitted to be present at the tribal councils; of this privilege, however, the women seldom avail themselves. During a woman's existence she passes through the following stages: (1) *Karegu* (little girl); (2) *kiregu* (big girl); (3) *muiretu* (marriageable girl); (4) *muhiki* (bride or young married woman); (5) *wabai* (mother of young children); (6) *mutimia* (mother of children who have attained their majority); (7) *kiheti* (old woman).

Anonymous
BINTI ALI THE CLEVER

Kenya 1914   Kiswahili

The story "Binti Ali the Clever" is taken from a children's book *Black Tales for White Children*, compiled by Captain and Mrs. C.H. Stigand and published in London in 1914. The book contains a brief account of the Swahili people and of the circumstances of oral narrative, as well as drawings of African musical instruments and other cultural objects. Unlike other stories in the book, which are simply presented as traditional communal tales and end with a formula in the Swahili idiom, this one is attributed. The authors indicate that this "tale comes from the Wazir and his daughter, the last born, who was called Binti Ali the Clever"—the latter also the heroine of the story. (The wazir was the chief administrative officer under the ruling sultan.) This tale, written during the period of the British East Africa Protectorate, invites comparison with earlier and later versions of the woman-outwits-man theme.

Captain Chauncy Hugh Stigand gives himself the title of "Swahili interpreter." A British army officer, colonial administrator, geographer, explorer, naturalist, and big game hunter as well as a linguist and writer, he traveled through East Africa and the Sudan in the early years of the twentieth century, writing about wildlife, language, administrative methods, and local history. His best-known books are *The Land of Zinj* and *Hunting the Elephant in Africa and Other Recollections of Thirteen Years' Wanderings*. He later became governor of the Upper Nile Province (Sudan), where he was killed in a revolt in 1919.

Marjorie Oludhe Macgoye

✦

Once upon a time there was a Sultan and his Wazir, and that Sultan had seven children, all sons, and that Wazir had seven children, all daughters.

Those daughters of the Wazir had no mother; their mother had died, and they were very poor.

The sons of the Sultan used to laugh at the daughters of the Wazir, saying, "You poor people, what do you eat? It is our father who pays your father his wages, and how do they suffice for you seven people who are in one house? You poor creatures, you have not even a brother to help you."

Now those girls used to plait baskets and sell them. They lived for many days like that, their work being to cry every day, and when they came out of school they used to plait and sell their baskets. Till one day the youngest daughter, who was called Binti Ali, was sitting with her father, and she said to him, "What advice have you to give us, father?"

Her father asked her, "Why, my child?"

She said to him, "We are only seven girls; we have neither husbands nor brothers. Should anything happen to you, who will be our headman? Father, you must arrange to have a ship built for me, and it must be ready in the space of three years."

Her father said, "All this wealth, where shall I get it from, that I may build a ship?"

She answered him, "God, the merciful, will provide."

In the morning the Wazir arose and went to the Sultan and said to him, "Give me help, for my youngest child wants a vessel built for her."

The Sultan brought out nine lakhs of rupees and gave them to his Wazir. Then the Wazir sought for workmen and told them to build a ship and have it ready in three years' time.

Now that child, Binti Ali, was very beautiful, more beautiful than all her sisters. Many men had come to seek her in marriage, but she had refused them, saying, "I am poor; my father has not wealth to suffice for my wedding."

At the end of three years the ship was ready, and her father called her, "Eh, my child, Binti Ali." And she answered him, "Lebeka, father," which means "Here I am" in the language of today; but long, long ago, Lebek was the name of the god worshipped by the Phoenicians at the temple of Baal-lebek (Bal bek).

Her father said to her, "Your ship is finished and ready for you."

So she went to see it and found that it was built in a wondrously fine way. When she returned she said to her father, "Now you must find me a captain and sailors, and you must put on the vessel enough food to last three years."

So he found a crew for her and provisioned the ship and returned. Then she said, "Father, now you must buy for me fine raiment, a sultan's turban, a shirt and coat, and a sword and dagger. Also you must get for me sandals of gold braid and two men's gold rings."

So her father searched for one hour and half a second and then returned and said, "My child, the things you want are ready."

Then he asked her, "My child, where are you going? Tell me."

She said, "Father, have you no understanding? I am going to the country of the Sultan Makami."

Her father said to her, "My child, you are already lost. Do you not know that a woman may not go to the country of Sultan Makami? Any other than a male who enters the country is put to death."

Binti Ali said to him, "Father, have you no wits, you, a full-grown man, who rules all this land? Do you not see that all these clothes which you have brought for me are men's clothes? I want to go and see Makami's country."

Her father said, "I do not approve of this journey you are setting out upon."

His daughter replied, "What comes to me is in the hands of God."

Then she entered the bathroom and washed herself, and when she came out she was dressed as a man. Now that girl had wisdom more than all her sisters, and she was well read in the Qur'an.

She took her dog, whose name was Atakalo, and she entered the ship and set sail.

She travelled day and night for three years, and there in the midst of the ocean she taught her dog till it attained great learning.

At the end of the third year she drew near to the country of Sultan Makami, and she ordered a salute to be fired, and the people on land replied also with a salute.

When her vessel drew near, the Sultan's son rowed out to meet her. He climbed on board, and there he saw a handsome Arab youth sitting on the deck.

Binti Ali arose, and they greeted one another after the fashion of men: "Peace be with you," "And with you peace."

She went ashore with that son of the Sultan, and they came to the palace.

When they came to the palace he said to his father, the Sultan, "How shall we see that this is a man and not a woman? Let us give him very hot gruel, and if it is a woman she will not be able to drink it, and then we will kill her."

So they ordered food to be brought, and slaves were told: "Take matting and platters and very big trays and cups of gold, and place them ready for the feast."

When the food was ready they brought gruel for that foreign youth to drink, and it was very hot.

Binti Ali took it and threw it away, saying, "Am I a woman, that you bring me cold gruel like that?"

So they prepared fresh gruel, steaming hot, and gave it to her, and she said, "Ah, that is more fit for a Sultan's son to drink."

So she put it beside her, and her dog Atakalo blew on it, so that it quickly cooled, and she drank it.

Very good food was then brought, and they fed, and she returned to her ship.

The Sultan then said, "To-morrow we must take this foreigner to my store of jewels and ornaments, and if it be a woman we will surely see, for she will take delight in women's jewellery."

All night long Binti Ali taught Atakalo what he should do, and in the morning the Sultan's son came to fetch her.

He said, "My father says that I am to take you to his store and show you his treasures."

So they went to the Sultan's treasure-house, where they showed her neck chains and nose pendants, anklets and bracelets, women's gold rings and ear ornaments.

She said, "Have you in this country no men's ornaments, that you should show me nothing but women's jewellery?"

So they brought her to the next store, wherein were gold-hilted daggers and all manner of arms, swords, and pistols, guns, and muskets. These she admired, and meanwhile Atakalo went and swallowed all the gold ornaments he could find and took them to the ship, till he had brought much wealth aboard.

Then the Sultan's son said to his father, "Now what shall we do so that we may kill her if she is a woman?"

So the Sultan said, "Make him take off his turban, and then we will surely see by the manner in which he ties it whether it is a woman or not."

So the Sultan's son said, "Now will you not wash?"

Binti Ali said, "Thank you, I have already bathed on board."

So he said, "If it is only your face, I beseech you to wash."

So she said, "Certainly; but first you and your father must wash."

So they took off their turbans and began to wash, when suddenly there was a shout from outside: "The Sultan's house is on fire."

Behold, that dog Atakalo had brought a brand and set fire to the palace. Then the Sultan and his son and all the people in his house rushed out, with their turbans in their hands, to see what was the matter and help put out the flames.

Binti Ali went down swiftly to her ship and got on board, and meanwhile Atakalo had run round and bored a hole in the bottom of every boat and ship in the Sultan's harbour. Then Atakalo came back to her vessel and said, "Mistress, I have finished."

So she weighed anchor and changed into her woman's clothes. The Sultan and his son and all the people, when they saw that she was sailing off, rushed down to the beach and tried to row out and stop her, but every boat they launched sunk; and so they were not able to get to her.

Then they saw her come up on the deck.

Then, changing her clothes as a woman, she sang—

"Makami, behold my bracelets and rings.
See my anklets, Makami. Aha, behold!
See the chain for my neck of beautiful gold.
Behold now my ear-rings and nose-stud see.
Lola, Makami, lola, look well at me.
I'm Binti Ali, the Wazir's daughter;
I came, Makami, from over the water.
We are seven in all, the last born am I.
Farewell, Makami, for I bid you good-bye.
Lola, Makami, lola, farewell."

Then she said to the captain, "Set sail, and let us return home."

When she arrived home there in her town her father and sisters were holding a great mourning for her, for they said, "Our youngest one has now been away many years; surely she must be dead."

When they saw her their hearts were very glad, and a feast was made for her for the space of three days. And the riches she brought with her, which her dog Atakalo had taken from the Sultan's treasure house, were brought to land; and when he saw them her father rejoiced greatly.

After a space of ten days she said to her father, "I know that Sultan Makami's son is making a plan to get me. If he comes here and asks for me in marriage, do not refuse him, but agree. My cleverness, which I have in my heart, is that which will save me."

One day the Sultan of Makami's son arrived and came to the Wazir and said, "I want your daughter, Binti Ali, in marriage."

So the Wazir agreed.

Binti Ali took a large pumpkin and filled it with honey and placed it on her bed, and she herself got under the bed.

That night the Sultan of Makami's son came into her room and said, "Ee, woman," and she replied, "Lebeka, master."

Then he said, "You, woman, you think that you can come to our country and cheat us, pretending that you are a man. Behold, to-day is your last, so make profession of faith quickly, so that you may be prepared for death."

Binti Ali said, "I testify there is no God but one God, and Muhammad is the prophet of God."

So he drew his sword and struck a blow which cut the pumpkin in two, and then he went out quickly and got on his ship and sailed away. When he came to look at his sword, to wipe the blood off, he found no blood but only honey stuck all over it.

This is the end of the story. The tale comes from the Wazir and his daughter, the last born, who was called Binti Ali the Clever.

Translated by Captain and Mrs. C.H. Stigand

Jane Elizabeth Chadwick and Eva Chadwick
MY STUDENTS

Kenya   circa 1920; 1935   English

Jane Elizabeth Chadwick arrived in Africa in 1895 as part of the first group of female missionaries sent to Uganda by the Church Missionary Society for Africa and the East, founded in 1799 in London by the Evangelical clergy of the Church of England. She held various posts, eventually joining her brother Walter Chadwick, whose job it was to set up a station in Butere, in the present-day Western Province of Kenya. Arriving in 1916, she committed herself to pastoral and educational services among the women of the area. She served for almost ten years until her retirement in 1925, when she returned home to Ireland.

By 1918, Jane Elizabeth Chadwick—who went by the name Lissette—had attracted a large number of girls to the school she founded, which grew into Butere Girls High School. Chadwick's involvement in and perceptions of pioneer education for girls are captured in an undated, handwritten manuscript and in the almost one hundred letters written to her friend Ethel Magowan of Belfast.

Students at Chadwick's school might awake at three or four in the morning, do their field chores, and then walk miles from surrounding villages to school. The school day began with prayers, and then music and some recitation, before the arrival of older students who had morning chores to do before they could come to school. Students learned to read and write, to draw and to sew. They were expected to read and own a Bible before being baptized, a significant outcome of the educational process. (Chadwick refers to the "catechumen's class," meaning those preparing for Christian baptism.)

Students were also expected to arrive at school properly clothed, and when a family owned but one dress, girls had to take turns at school. According to Lissette Chadwick's manuscript, the most severe punishment one could mete out to girls was to keep them at home. Schoolgirls were expected to return to their village and tell others what they had learned.

This excerpt from Lissette Chadwick's manuscript focuses mainly on a student named Kitandi. The additional text, written in 1935 by Lissette's sister Eva Chadwick, appears on a page inserted into the manuscript and is included here because it continues the story of Kitandi.

Fran Etemesi and Naomi L. Shitemi

By Jane Elizabeth Chadwick
Amongst my first school girls at Butere were two, Kitandi and Mapesa, who came together a walk of over two miles. I noticed that whenever one was absent the other did not appear. On asking the reason I heard that both girls had been partly betrothed by their fathers to heathen men with several wives already; i.e. a couple of cows had been offered and accepted as part payment for the maidens; who however wished to be single wives of Christian husbands. But if either came the long walk to school without a friend to raise alarm, she fully expected to be seized and carried off to the undesired husband, as the Bahanga custom was.

Kitandi was a strapping big lass and often came carrying on her shoulder a devoted four-year-old cousin, who would cry if left behind, but could not walk too far; and as time went on a group of young girls from all along that road attached themselves to the first two so that they made quite an addition to my flock. Both Kitandi and Mapesa advanced quickly and were admitted to the catechumen's class, and Kitandi, always the leader, became a pupil teacher. Early in the days of the great war, I had seven of these bigger girls helping to teach besides the two Baganda women who had answered my appeal for help from the center.

As thousands of Kavirondo boys were month by month drafted to the war, a few as recruits in the army but most of them as carriers, and after my brother had followed them down to "German East [Africa]," the girls, with fewer to cook and work for at home, came in increasing numbers to learn; especially on Sundays we often had more than three hundred in the girls Sunday-school alone so that when the drum sounded for service I could only send the senior class on to church with the adults and the boys, while with the juniors we carried on a little service of our own, with a great deal of singing. These Bahanga, unlike the Baganda, were naturally a very musical people and loved to sing in parts. During this time of crowded school my friend Kitandi disappeared for a fortnight, and I was told that her mother was very ill and Kitandi was nursing her day and night, the two other daughters, heathen, leaving all the work to her. Then one day they told me that the mother was dead and Kitandi dying. I had seen her a few days before, tired but well. So immediately after school I called my car-boys and set out to their hill where I found the heathen funeral customs being carried on in even unusual wildness. Wailing was loud and continuous; men would from time to time climb up the poles of the little grain stores and fling themselves down yelling; one would rush into the cook-house, seize a water pot or cooking-pot, and fling it into the midst of the circle in the court-yards, smashing it to atoms; another caught a fowl and wrung its neck; yet another tore a cloth from a woman's back and tore it to shreds. All these hysterical doings supposed to propitiate the spirit of the departed as being done in her honour. My inquiries as to Kitandi only elicited, "She isn't here." At least I persuaded a young boy to guide me a quarter of an hour's walk on a track over the hill to the house where she had been deposited. They told me that when the mother died her relations started the wailing and called the girl to join in; she refused and knelt down to pray in a corner. Again they called her to help wrap up the body and found that, worn out with sorrow and watching, she had fainted. Imagining that the spirit had struck her down because she refused to wail, some of them lifted her up, carried her unconscious to the nearest Christian house, and flung her in the doorway saying, "Take your Christian." She had a severe illness after that, tended only by one little brother who would come to fetch soup and medicine for her and by the Christian young man into whose hut she had been so unceremoniously thrown.

After the war was over, when our boys, diminished in numbers, returned, I soon became distinctly anxious over my pupil teachers, who came late instead of punctually, dull instead of cheery, shrugging their shoulders when asked to put out the reading sheets or slates, cross or falling asleep in their classes. I began to wonder whether we were to have an outbreak of sleeping sickness, and whether the government doctor would come and examine them! Then one day a man catechist came and asked me, "Do you think that it is wise what these girls of yours are doing?" and I begged him to tell me what it was. So it came out that the boys during the campaign had been much laughed at by the more civilized coast boys both because their faces showed the old tribal marks, or scars, of heathen days, and because most of them could not read. And on their return they found that their sisters had got ahead of them. So as many of them had acquired lamps or lanterns each held one of my pupil-teachers and made them start night classes, fifteen or twenty youths to each lamp, and some of these carried on up to 3.00 a.m., the lassitude of the girls thoroughly accounted for. The help of the men catechists made some other arrangements, and the girls were told only to teach by daylight in the kraals, say for an hour before sunset. Kitandi, a few months later had got together a village gathering of sixty under a big tree, some old women and little children who could not so far as Butere to learn. She was later married to a teacher of the Luo tribe who at this time of writing (1935) is in the divinity school preparing for ordination, and she is the mother of five children. When her probation time was over and she asked me to select a name for her in baptism, I chose Lydia, remembering the women in faraway Philippi who gathered by the riverside for prayer.

Note added by Eva Chadwick

When my sister, after her retirement, told me the story of Lydia, she told also of the following episode, which I eventually add, because it seemed to me to be the climax of the whole.

Shortly after my mother's death my sister was visited one evening by a group of those wild young men on their way home from the war, of whom she has written in another place. This group came from a village on the foot-hills of Mount Elgon, and they told her their needs bluntly enough: "We just learnt one thing at the war, that is that we must have the whole men's learning so give us a missionary." My sister had to tell them sadly that it must be a long time before that could be. The Archdeacon, who had been in charge of the whole district, was dead. The mission was depleted, few young recruits arriving. They must be patient, but they were anything but patient; after a few minutes debate among themselves they turned to her again. "Then we will take you."

But again she must refuse. She tried to explain to them that she was in a position of trust, left alone to try and keep her brother's work together until it should be possible to fill his place. Greatly as she was touched by their even thinking it possible that a woman should teach them, she could not go.

"Give us one of your girls."

But it was unthinkable that she should send one of her young, newly taught Christian maidens away in the hands of men like this. They must be patient— they must indeed. Yet she thought of them and their crying need for a long time that night. She would see them again in the morning and assure them that she would do all she could to help them. But in the morning they had vanished— and they had taken Lydia with them.

There was nothing she could do at the moment. Her work must go on. But when, a few days later, one of the nearest clergy cycled over to see her, hopeful of a pleasant visit and refreshing cup of tea after his long hot ride, he found himself, instead, promptly dispatched on a longer and hotter journey in search of Lydia.

He had considerable difficulty in finding the village, but once there no difficulty at all in locating Lydia. She was established in all honour in the largest hut in the place, surrounded by most of the children and as many of the women as could possibly be spared from digging, intent on the rudiments of that most difficult art of reading.

The education of the young men had not yet begun; they were still fully occupied in running up at all speed a good sized school house in which all sections of the community might take their turn of instruction, and where perhaps, some day they might all meet in worship. When they had learned what worship meant. Lydia was entirely mistress of the situation. She was a born teacher and here was a whole village hungering to be taught. What could be happier?

The missionary only mounted his bicycle and rode wearily homewards. There was nothing he could do, except indeed to resolve very earnestly that he would second all Miss Chadwick's efforts to secure a teacher as quickly as possible for a village among the foothills of Mount Elgon.

I wonder whether, in after days, Lydia even introduced her Luo Padre to her own first parish.

Siti binti Saad
FOUR SONGS

Tanzania 1920s   Kiswahili

The renowned singer Siti binti Saad was born in Fumba village in Zanzibar in 1880. Her family was quite poor, and she followed her mother's practice of making and selling pots and mats. The extraordinary voice that would later win her fame was first heard as she walked through Zanzibar town, singing to call attention to her pots.

Siti moved to Zanzibar town, as the popular story goes, after her pottery business came to ruin when she fell one day and broke all of her wares. She soon became the only woman in a small musical group. In the beginning, the group was poorly equipped, and Siti faced some resistance as a singer both because she was a woman and because of her poor rural background. She nonetheless quickly gained popularity, reaching her peak in 1928, when she traveled to India to record under the Gramaphone Company's His Master's Voice label. During that trip and another in 1929, her group recorded a total of 126 songs. These were probably the first gramophone records ever made by East African artists.

Siti binti Saad sang in the *taarab* musical tradition, which blends Swahili music with Arabic and Indian. Prior to Siti, *taarab* singers were most often well-off, cultured, and male and sang in Arabic. Siti, who was illiterate but had a gift for memorizing songs, began the now well-established practice of singing in Kiswahili. Her career served to give the language prestige and bring it to audiences outside of East Africa. She performed in the sultan's court and for many events hosted by the wealthy residents of Zanzibar's Stone Town, thus gaining considerable financial rewards.

Although she eventually earned an international reputation, Siti's songs were most popular along the East African coast, the listeners in the interior finding her lyrics too closely tied to the context of Zanzibar and thus too opaque. Siti had the gift of transforming various important social and cultural issues of Zanzibar into songs offering critical commentary. She sang on love, on class and gender inequalities, on the injustices of the court system, and more generally on the various sagas of Zanzibar town. Her lyrics are usually allegorical, filled with allusions, often touching on the political and moral implications of behavior.

Siti's achievements prepared the way for other women singers to join previously all-male *taarab* groups, and her recordings came to be heard internationally as the voice of East Africa. When she died in 1950, she had become not only a musical legend but an icon of Tanzanian women's struggle for equity and recognition. The Tanzania Media Women's Association, for example, acknowledged her by naming their magazine *Sauti ya Siti*, or "Voice of Siti." ("Siti" translates to "woman" or "lady.") Siti was also the subject of a biography written by Tanzania's most prominent male poet, Shaaban Robert, in 1958.

In "Kijiti," Siti recounts the true story of a man who killed a woman visitor from Dar es Salaam. He took the woman out, along with her friends, then raped and killed her. Siti questions the system of justice that jailed the woman's friends but allowed the murderer to escape to the mainland. "There Is No Damage" also recalls a real incident in which a wealthy Arab landowner and government clerk was arrested by the British government for embezzling public funds and sentenced to work in a quarry. The man had also been in the habit of defrauding poor people by taking advantage of their illiteracy. "With Missive I Am Sending You" is a prayer for good health and true friendship, perhaps referring to Fatuma binti Baraka, known as Bi Kidude, a protégé of Siti who also became a renowned *taarab* singer. "Do Not Expose a Secret" is a medley of allegory and allusions to love, sex, and infidelity, with a hint about promiscuity in the last verse. In typical *taarab* tradition, these verses allow listeners to hear what they will, depending on the context in which they are sung.

Saïda Yahya-Othman and M.M. Mulokozi

✦

KIJITI

Look, look you all, what Kijiti has done,
To take a guest and give her the runaround.
He took her into the bushes and brought her back dead.
We left home without permission;
We had our gin in our basket.
The dance was in Chukwani; death awaited us in Sharifumsa.

Kijiti said to me, let us go woman.
If only I had known, I would not have gone.
Kijiti you will kill me for one peg of gin.
The judge, presiding, was angry.
He said "Bloody fools!" to Kijiti's witnesses,
And sentenced Sumaili and Binti Subeti to prison.

These matters are strange, however you look at them.
Kijiti killed someone who was pregnant.
He crossed the river but the witnesses drowned.

Kijiti, I advise you not to go to Dar es Salaam;
You will encounter there a man with a razor.
Everyone is cursing you that you may get elephantiasis.

THERE IS NO DAMAGE

There is no relationship; I am so and so.
The word, like a sin, is branded on the chest.
The name is yours, old man, and the stone is on your head;
    The stone is on your head.

Stop your meanness and robbing of the poor,
Especially those who speak not, the ignorant of the ignorant.
Their pen always is ink on their thumbs,
Is ink on their thumbs.

Pilfering is wrong; stealing from the government.
Their books are open, with all signatures,
A matter of long ago, comes under scrutiny,
        Comes under scrutiny.

Friends, don't be duped; hark my words.
Maintain caution; don't let it leave your hearts.
Let little satisfy you; that which is your right, clerks;
That which is your right, clerks.

WITH MISSIVE I AM SENDING YOU

Oh, missive, I am sending you, to my confidant,
To my generous Lord, who has no compare.
The stones have turned well, with speedy peace.
I pray respectfully, with my hands beseeching:
Rid us of enmity and secret envy.
Prayers I have read; may they reach the heavens,
        May they reach the heavens.

Your compassion, oh, Lord, let it be with you.
Every time I look at them, I discover them in my heart.
I pray for health and freedom from suffering,
        And freedom from suffering.

Oh, Prophet, stand up with the angels in heaven,
Together with Bi Fatuma and Hussein her grandson.
Oh, Prophet, it behooves you, since God mandated you
To pray for the human race in heaven and earth,
        In heaven and earth.

DO NOT EXPOSE A SECRET

Do not expose a secret
With colored ink.
You have to understand:
If you have many problems,
You self-destruct
Through your own ignorance.

Give the poison to the cat
Who has many lives,
Not the goat;
You will kill it,
For every lecher
Dies deprived.

Poor stars
In the clouds,
I never imagined
That you would be unfaithful.
Come back, my love,
And end my grief.

Show me.
I swear I can't sleep;
Quench my desire by action.
Being apart from him
Makes me crazy.

A ripe fruit must be picked.
A dry leaf is withered by the sun.
The one with a scar may still be hurting.
My love, don't agitate me.
Love does not last without tolerance.
Understand, speed is not progress.

The sweetness of sugar
Does not surpass that of sugarcane.
Sugarcane has juice
Dripping down on you.
With sudden sweetness,
The soul melts.

A decorated cup
Is good for tea;
Add some milk
And sugar aplenty.
When you depart,
Another is waiting.

Translated by Saïda Yahya-Othman

Communal
SONG OF THE COFFEE GIRLS

Kenya 1922   Gikuyu

In colonial Kenya, many young women worked on privately owned coffee estates in order to earn money and get away from uncongenial home conditions. Labor on the plantations was not compulsory, though no doubt there were violations of the law. On 15 March 1922, Harry Thuku, a government-employed clerk and telephone operator and a leader of the East Africa Association, one of the earliest groups formed to oppose the injustices of the colonial system, was arrested. He had particularly objected to women doing forced roadwork and had communicated directly with the Colonial Office in London.

The government charged Harry Thuku with subversion and placed him in detention in Kismayu. On 17 November 1922, the Presbyterian missionary Dr. J. W. Arthur sent the text of a song with his translation to the Chief Native Commissioner as evidence of the strength of feeling in the community about the abuse of women's labor. His letter provides documentation of the exact date and group authorship of the song. For the rest of his life, Thuku would often be addressed in the Gikuyu language as "Chief of the coffee girls." His protest is also a landmark event in nation-building in that Thuku, who came from Kiambu, received a warmer reception in the Nyeri and Murang'a sections of Gikuyuland than in his home area, where he was seen as a threat to the authority of the Gikuyu chiefs appointed by the British government.

As sung, the song contained four verses, all identical except for the names of the four Gikuyu chiefs, whom the coffee girls blamed for allowing the detention of their champion, Harry Thuku. We know that there were other versions of the song that were forbidden by the government. Thuku is quoted in supplements to the *East African Chronicle* of 17 February and 8 March 1922 as having called Koinange wa Mbiu, Josia Njonjo, Philip Karanja, and Waruhiyu (his spellings) "Judases."

Marjorie Oludhe Macgoye

✦

Filipu let him be cursed.
It is they who have caused to be taken away
the Chief of the girls
who live in the coffee.

Koinange let him be cursed.
It is they who have caused to be taken away
the Chief of the girls
who live in the coffee.

Josiah let him be cursed.
It is they who have caused to be taken away
the Chief of the girls
who live in the coffee.

Kinyanjui let him be cursed.
It is they who have caused to be taken away
the Chief of the girls
who live in the coffee.

Translated by J. W. Arthur

Luiza
I WANT A DIVORCE
Zambia 1922 English

"I Want a Divorce" is taken from the record of a February 1922 civil court cases in what was then Northern Rhodesia. A young woman named Luiza, of Luangwa district in the Eastern Province of the country, is suing her husband, Luka. She wants the legal process to free her from her absent husband. As her testimony reveals, she had tried once before to obtain a divorce but was denied, and she has come back again determined to state her case. Her complaint is recorded more or less verbatim by the court.

In general, it was taboo for a woman publicly to question the actions of her husband. Such matters as wife-abuse were considered the private domain of family elders. Wives were to bear whatever befell them, and certainly they were not supposed to move their private lives into courts of law. It was also common in those days for husbands to leave their wives and children in order to find work in the mines of Zimbabwe (then Southern Rhodesia) or South Africa, as was the case with Luka. In his absence, he was represented by his brother.

In her testimony, Luiza explains her reasons for wanting the divorce, and objects to her husband's demand for 30 shillings as reimbursement for cloth he allegedly bought her. In other testimony from the case, her brother-in-law claims that she has "refused" to sleep with her husband. The divisional headman, Ambisia, then testifies that "defendant is impotent" and that the cloths were purchased prior to the marriage, and the headman of the village, Tensiako, confirms that testimony. The verdict of the court is "divorce granted," without any reimbursement for Luka because "these cloths were supplied during the time defendant and plaintiff were betrothed."

Nalishebo N. Meebelo

✦

Luiza states: I am the wife of defendant Luka. I married him two years ago. He paid one shilling as earnest of dowry. I have married him according to our custom. I now want to divorce defendant because he has beaten me three times and I don't like him and also because he hasn't yet paid dowry. I co-habited with defendant for two months after we were first married, and last June I came with defendant before the M.C. Feira and claimed a divorce, but the M.C. refused my application and ordered defendant and I to live together for six months because there was no sufficient grounds for divorce. I still refused to live with defendant and ran away.

Shortly afterwards defendant went away to S[outh] A[frica] to work. He is still away but has written a letter to his brother Gutinyu who is appearing for him offering to divorce me if I pay 30 [shillings] being the cost of clothing he has provided me with during the time since we first married. Defendant has only provided me with one large cloth and one small one of [one] yard only. These cloths would not cost 30 [shillings]. I refuse to pay 30 [shillings] for this because he co-habited with me for two months. . . . I cooked and worked for defendant all the time until he went away to work. I have not got 30 [shillings]. Both my mother and father are very sick and cannot appear. They have heard about the letter and refuse to pay 30 [shillings] to defendant.

Zeina binti Mwinyipembe Sekinyaga
CIVILIZED MOTHERHOOD

Tanzania 1926   Kiswahili

Nothing is known about Zeina binti Mwinyipembe Sekinyaga, other than the fact that she wrote a letter to a local publication in 1926, when literate Tanzanians were few, literate women fewer still. The publication, *Mambo Leo*, was a colonial government monthly paper in Kiswahili that began publication in 1923. In 1926, the British had dominated the colony they called Tanganyka Territory for less than a decade, having obtained control of this part of German East Africa after World War I.

The sophistication and smooth style of presentation in Sekinyaga's arguments give an impression of formal education. Depending upon her age, she may have been educated in a British missionary school or more likely attended classes run by the Germans. However, while names are not always sure indicators of religion, it is worth noting that Zeina is a Muslim name, and it would not have been easy for her to attend a missionary school as a Muslim. If this was indeed the case, it is an added credit to Sekinyaga's character as a radical woman of her time, who either disregarded religious differences or was so eager to learn that she could risk being submerged in an alien religious environment.

Sekinyaga's letter indicates that she was a keen reader of *Mambo Leo* and an activist for gender equity, who was dismayed by the deep-rooted male chauvinism around her. One could call her an early African feminist, since she strongly advocated the elimination of certain cultural practices, such as bride price or dowry and polygamy. A further interesting feature of this letter has to do with the Kiswahili language, since she wrote at a time when Kiswahili orthography had not been standardized, and this is clearly reflected in her letter, in the spelling of words and in nominal concord. To strengthen her final point, the author uses a variety of words in Kiswahili, Kihehe, and Chigogo for bride price, a custom she strongly opposes.

Joshua Madumulla

◆

Please allow me to join the community of your readers, in your esteemed "council," and permit me to exchange a few ideas with the gentlemen who are your readers and get some answers to my questions.

1. In all the things that are being said, intended to enable Africa to prosper in future, I have yet to hear of a black African man who endeavors to speak for women and defend us so that we may be treated justly and well in our present state of oppression. I read Mr. Peter Kiobia of Bukoba, who has a reputation for despising women, and by following up his endeavors to the end, I realize that he wrote because he knows how to write not because he intended to. If this is indeed the situation, will men alone really manage to make Africa of the future prosper? I beg all of you who desire to see your countries succeed in the light of this civilization to read my words as a favor to me, Oh blessed ones.

2. Many traditions of black people in the world were not codified into law, hence I feel they were in the dark. Among the many savage practices that existed, the most enduring was to despise women, deprive them of their rights and enslave them. All men demand many wives, so that they will not have to work in the fields or on construction sites. When a man has slaves, such tasks are done by the slave and the man's wife. Now, judge for yourselves whether it is a mark of respect for the wife to toil with the slaves. At home we black women have no rights, except by chance. The man goes wherever he wants without informing his wife. Sometimes he has his dinner there and comes home and says: "Today I do not want to eat!" Or maybe because of his wanderings, he returns later than his usual time and when he finds the food cold, raises hell more terrifying than the thunderbolt. Nor is justice observed in such cases, for if the wife tries to defend herself by claiming that it is not her fault that the food has gone cold, the man retorts: "Shut up, after all you are my property, I can do anything I want with you!" For these and other reasons, we women are whipped worse than stubborn donkeys. I won't tell you of the insults and bad words that we receive from our husbands. Anyone who is kind at heart can realize the bitterness we black women carry in our bosoms: trembling every hour, worried every minute, forever steeped in sadness. These afflictions, which have hounded us for many centuries of savagery, have forced us not to trust men, so that very often we meet to denounce and speak evil of them. These problems, which are like a cancer, have come into existence because, when we marry, the man has to pay something to our parents. Indeed this custom is no different from slavery. For whoever buys a slave must pay, and likewise whoever wants a

woman to be his wife must pay, and sometimes the value of the slave is higher than that of the wife. This shows that, to her husband, the black woman is at the same level as the slave and is equal to a chattel, such as a cow, a goat, or a chicken.

3. Being sold by our parents lands us in slavery, deprives us of our dignity, and renders us devoid of any rights before our husbands. For does a chattel have rights vis-à-vis its purchaser? That is why when men are beating their wives, they often speak to them the words I have cited above! Know ye that we women are bereaved without a death, are hungry in the midst of plenty, and are dead while still living.

4. Had these things been mere primitive acts, i.e., [customary] law, we would ignore them if the men who have converted to any of the religions would treat us justly as ordained by their religions. Yet, the worst offenders in doing bad things to women are these converted husbands! Now, didn't these religions create laws to help us and ensure that we have dignity and are justly treated? I would like this to be clearly explained to me.

5. In anticipation of that dawn of Africa of the future, I request you, our parents, to abolish this custom which is worse than a cancerous sore—this custom of selling your daughters to whichever man you choose! Why should the parents' permission be necessary for marrying off the daughter? Why do you demand "wealth" before the marriage of your daughter? Isn't the love of the betrothed enough to cement their union permanently? Or does it mean that without money your daughter has no valid marriage? Understand that this custom is primitive and whoever follows it, even if he or she sleeps on learned books, is primitive too.

6. To my fellow women, I say this: Shall we not be obedient daughters to our parents if we refuse to be sold? Shall we not earn the title of "wife" if we are not auctioned to wooers as they are used to auction us? Whether it is *mahari* or *kilemba*, *mafungu* (*Wahehe*), *vigumo* (*Wagogo*), it is a traditional custom not a law. Can't it be abolished by a new law? Why was a man allowed to become "master" of many wives, but a woman not allowed to become "mistress" of many husbands? And who indeed invented this custom? Mr. Cock and Ms. Hen claim that the custom emanated from them. Without our contribution, would the world be as full [of people] as it is today? Women, let us not devalue ourselves, let us understand that we are precious, superior beings of great value, for through us the Almighty God creates human beings whom we bring out [into the world] imbued with life. So from now on let us know that we are the "mothers" of the civilized who will teach the Africans of tomorrow. Let us always keep our eyes open, force ourselves to go to school, even if our elders won't like it. Let us turn a deaf ear to them, let us go to school, and let us learn civilized motherhood. And you men, allow your wives [to study], even if it is only once a day, for it is better to get [a little], even if it is an "a," than to miss everything. The greatness and dignity of our country will not be manifest unless we women acquire what the schools can

offer. And you men, if you want civilization, you have first to educate your wives and daughters, the mothers of the civilized, so that they may be on the same level with you, even if you are still the bosses. If you do that, the noise and wrangling at home will cease, and the words "divorce me" as used at present will no longer be heard. You husbands will be happy to see your wives, and you wives will be joyous to see your husbands. Certificates of divorce, which are stacked up in all government offices, will be returned to where they came from.

I hope I will be excused and will receive an answer to these questions that I have posed today.

Translated by M.M. Mulokozi

Mwana Hashima binti Sheikh
A PETITION

Kenya 1930   English [Kiswahili]

The author of this letter is writing, at the age of ninety, to protest the breach of an agreement between herself and the government that took place perhaps half a lifetime earlier. At that time, the British colonial government had asked Mwana Hashima to help resolve an issue of local warfare by negotiating a peace with her stepbrother, who had run off to the mainland and whose sons had been arrested. The government sought Mwana Hashima's assistance, believing she could probably get her brother's attention in this matter. She was promised a reward in return for her help. Mwana Hashima made known the demands of each group to the other, and the fighting was resolved amicably.

While Mwana Hashima successfully fulfilled her obligation, her mediation was never acknowledged, and she never got her reward. In a time of severe need, she wrote a new petition letter asking for the compensation she was due. At an advanced age but with a clear mind, she is bold enough to hold the government to its word and ask them to keep their early promise.

The letter testifies not only to aspects of resistance to colonial rule but also to the colonist's clear need for the assistance of influential members of society in order to secure their control. Mwana Hashima's plight in her old age propels her to reveal history that might have been irretrievably lost. The letter, written on 30 September 1930, was collected by Alice Werner and William Hichens and published in 1934 as an appendix to the poem of the mother of Binti Sheikh (Mwana Hashima), "A Mother's Advice and Prayer" (see page 72 in this volume). The account notes that, according to Mr. Whitton, the local justice of the peace mentioned by Mwana Hashima died before the case was resolved. Werner also comments that, though published in English and probably translated by an unknown Arab clerk, Binti Sheikh's letter was originally written in Kiswahili, most likely in the Kiamu dialect spoken on Lamu Island, off the Kenyan coast.

Naomi L. Shitemi

I have already informed Mr. Whitton, Justice of the Peace, to send my news to the great officers of the Government regarding my work, which I did with my clear heart in the Government, when I was in great hope that the Government would recognise my work which I offered to them. My work I did as under:

Two young men were imprisoned, and they were the sons of Sheikh Omar bin Mataka; their names were Muhammad bin Omar and Sheikh Mataka bin Omar. Mr. Rogers imprisoned them in Lamu Fort. Their father, Sheikh Mataka bin Omar, had run away to the mainland with a great number of people, and he had made trouble at the mainland to the inhabitants, as same as the Siu people; the Liwali of Siu, Omar bin Isa, could not stay at Siu, and he came to Lamu, and one Akida Abdulla bin Selim was sent to Siu. The late Provincial commissioner, Mr. Rogers, had sent people to the mainland several times to Sheikh Omar bin Mataka in order to make peace with him. Afterwards he instructed the late Liwali of Lamu, Abdulla bin Hemed, to go owing to great hostility. Mr. Rogers came to my house and said that he came in order to send me in purpose of the Government's work.

He said that he knew that I could not afford this as I was a woman, but there was no help but to send me, and as Sheikh Omar bin Mataka is my brother, there was no one who could talk with him as well as I. He had prepared a boat to take me to Siu and from there to send some men to the mainland with my letter to my brother asking him to come and make peace. And he said that if peace was made and guns were returned to Government and he (Omar) came to Siu, the Government would be glad because they did not want trouble to be made on the mainland— "so if this is done and the Government becomes grateful, you will be given a reward." I followed Mr. Rogers' requests, and I left with my son and husband for Siu, and from there I sent my husband and son and my nephews to the mainland with my letter to my brother Sheikh Omar bin Mataka who wanted his sons to be released from prison and I sent a letter to Mr. Rogers asking him to release the sons of Sheikh Omar from prison, and let them stay at Lamu until Omar returned to Siu and to take away Akida Abdullah bin Salim from Siu because *fitina* [intrigue] increased when he was at Siu, and many people had moved from Siu to the mainland owing to his *fitina*. Mr. Rogers released the sons of Sheikh Omar b. Mataka and allowed them to stay at Lamu, and he took away Akida Abdullah b. Salim from Siu. I informed my brother that his sons were released and that they would stay at Lamu till he came back to Siu and gave up all the guns; that was the Government's request. He agreed with my advice. . . . So I came back to Lamu, and he sent me all the guns, and I handed them over to Mr. Rogers who had them broken and put them all in the sea in front of the Customs House, and Sheikh Omar bin Mataka came back to Siu. Mr. Rogers gave me a certificate for my work which was taken by the Interpreter to Mr. Harding, Salim bin Azan, to show to Mr. Harding. Afterwards Mr. Rogers called me to go to take my certificate as it had been returned by Mr. Harding, and he informed me that he would start soon from Lamu for Zanzibar.

But at that time I was ill . . . and my son was away, and when Mr. Rogers went away I kept quiet because I had means. My husband was alive, and my son was employed. But now I am an old woman, I am ninety years of age and ill; my husband has died, and my son lost the Government's work owing to illness, and he cannot do any other work; so I became poor. For this reason I have communicated to the Government my request, and I hope that the Government will remember me and give me something.

The above mentioned information was known to all the people of Siu and others who have served the Government since they were young men till they become old men and retired. Also I made peace at Jongeni but failed to complete it because the inhabitants were bad people. As far as I know if anyone serves the Government, he is usually given something as reward or pension, and I did a great work for the Government and I hope that the Government will not cast me aside, for I am an old woman now, of old age and poor.

Nyambura wa Kihurani, Raheli Warigia wa Johanna, and Alice Murigo wa Meshak
LETTER OPPOSING FEMALE CIRCUMCISION

Kenya 1931   Gikuyu

In 1928, Protestant missionaries in central Kenya began requiring church members to adjure the practice of female circumcision. For Gikuyu parents at that time, circumcision was part of the ritual process by which socially and bodily immature children were made into responsible adults. Pubescent girls and boys from a given locality were circumcised on a public initiation ground; afterward, they went through a weeks-long education on proper social and sexual conduct. The missionaries, who had begun work in central Kenya in the late nineteenth century, made no objection to male circumcision, and male adolescents were being circumcised by mission hospital attendants as early as 1912. Female circumcision could not so easily be medicalized: After attending a 1915 circumcision, a Dr. Philp declared himself appalled at the "cruelty shown by the old woman" performing the procedure. Missionaries argued that the cutting the girls experienced at adolescence inhibited childbirth by blocking the birth passage with fibrous scar tissue. By September 1929, Presbyterian missionary Dr. Arthur was touring Gikuyu churches, requiring members to sign a pledge against circumcision.

Many Gikuyu people were horrified by the church ruling. In their view, the churches' anticircumcision campaign attacked the basis of gendered order. They were led in argument by the Kikuyu Central Association, a party of men educated at Protestant mission schools. Writing from the city of Nairobi, KCA leader

Jessie Kariuki argued that "those who are protected [from circumcision] are the first to join prostitution." The anticircumcision rules were thought to undermine sexual morality, inhibit biological reproduction, and make girls beastly. Besides, the churches' critics argued, circumcision was no hindrance to childbirth. "Circumcision has been practiced since long ago among us," went an anonymous 1929 letter to Dr. Arthur, "and you do not produce more children than we do."

The song *Muthirigu*, the "Song of the Big Uncut Girl," elaborated on these arguments: "I cannot marry an uncircumcised girl," went one of its many verses: "She tells her husband she will make the baby sleep, then beats him." *Muthirigu* was first sung in the southern Gikuyu district of Kiambu late in 1929. One elder, James Miti-ini Weru, remembers that people in his village in northern Gikuyu-land sang it on Christmas Day. Instead of going to church to sing "The Savior has been born," he recalled, people gathered on a public ground to sing "I swear by Mount Kenya I would rather rear a monkey than rear a *kirigu* [uncircumcised girl]." Some Gikuyu women and men, however, did support the missions' ban on circumcision. Women at the Presbyterian mission station at Tumutumu formed Ngo ya Tuiritu, the Shield of the Young Girls, in 1930. They vowed to protect girls who wished to avoid circumcision. Most of the members were wives or daughters of church teachers or evangelists. Cecilia Muthoni Mugaki, daughter of a teacher, remembered living with adolescent girls in the mission's dormitory and locking the door when their fathers came to take them away for circumcision. It was fearful work. Daniel Muriithi, son of an early member, remembered that crowds gathered around his mother's door, singing *Muthirigu* and ridiculing her as a servant of the whites.

In October 1931, Wairimu wa Nguyo, a Tumutumu boarding school student, was forcibly circumcised while returning home to collect her school fees. Her mother held a hand over her mouth while other women performed the circumcision. With this and other forcible circumcisions in view, incensed members of Ngo ya Tuiritu wrote this letter to the government's Local Native Council for legal redress. It is hard to ignore the Christmas-day date on the church women's missive. Was this their reply to the singers of *Muthirigu*, who had on an earlier Christmas ridiculed uncircumcised women as willful, wayward, and barren? Were these women casting themselves in the model of Mary, reminding their critics that even unlikely vessels could bear children?

The "female circumcision controversy," as it has been named, was a pivotal moment in Kenya's political and ecclesiastical history. Thousands of men and women left mission churches, forming "independent," Gikuyu-run church organizations. A later generation of historians would see in this early controversy evidence of a nationalist consciousness among Gikuyu people. But as this letter, found in the archives Presbyterian Church of East Africa, shows, there was no united Gikuyu perspective on female circumcision. Both critics and supporters of the circumcision ban thought themselves defenders of Gikuyu womanhood. Both sides argued that outsiders should not intervene in matters best left for mothers and fathers to decide. And both sides cast themselves in the light of the nativity, as fruitful, productive, and responsible to Gikuyu motherhood.

Derek R. Peterson

To Local Native Council South Nyeri District, 25 December 1931

1. The Council of the Ngo ya Tuiritu met here at Tumutumu because we've heard that the people in the country have prayed for female circumcision to be allowed by the government.

2. And we of the Ngo ya Tuiritu heard that there are men who talk of female circumcision, and we get astonished because they (men) do not give birth and feel the pain and even some die and even others become infertile, and the main cause is circumcision.

3. Because of that the issue of circumcision should not be forced. People are caught like sheep; one should be allowed to cut her own way of either agreeing to be circumcised or not without being dictated on one's body.

4. Because Agikuyu say women cannot give birth without being circumcised, and because Gikuyu girls have given birth to children even having not been circumcised, what then is the reason for circumcision? We cannot see any reason.

5. Because among the Agikuyu, if a girl fails to give birth, she can be returned to her father even if she is circumcised, where then is the profit for circumcision? It can only be given by one who advocates circumcision.

6. Now, what we ask from the government, because Gikuyu men have more power than women, is that women be assisted in their complaints by the government to avoid further suppression.

Translated by Joseph Kariuki Muriithi

Lusi Kyebakutika
THE WORD *PROSTITUTE* HAS CONFUSED US

Uganda 1932   Luganda

This letter appeared in *Matalisi*, a colonial-controlled newspaper in Kampala, the capital of Uganda, in June 1932. Nothing is known about the author, Lusi Kyebakutika, other than the fact that she was one of a handful of women then literate. Probably she had attended a mission school, since her first name, Lusi, is the Lugandan version of the Christian name Ruth. Since writing, even in the nation's capital, was the province of men, it is not surprising to see her opening plea that her letter be published.

As a very early feminist text, the letter is striking. Kyebakutika's prose is politely logical. She doesn't need to raise her voice. She poses a real question about a commonly used word, *prostitute,* and asks for a word that might describe the men who, in fact, partner with the women in their immoral act by soliciting and buying sex from them. Her ultimate weapon is humor. Hers is a rare voice that stands out uniquely amid the silence of gender-related oppression. (A note on the place names to which Kyebakutika refer in her letter: Bwayise is a suburb north of Kampala, and Bulemezi is a county that was regarded at the time as backward.)

Jane Kawalya

✦

Sir,

I am humbly trusting that you will be able to publish my letter to the readers.

Sir, I am asking why a woman is called a prostitute. For what reason? When a woman is called a prostitute, what should a man be called? The woman who is called a prostitute, with whom does she go? Does she just go to the streets and get men to go with her? Yes, it is a man who tells a woman to sit on his bicycle that they may go to his home. If you refuse and say that a woman is not to be picked from the streets, the man says, "Aren't you a prostitute?" Then he drives away hooting, to go to Kampala, where there are many women who are beautiful and smart, and he will show off his car, and they will all come, and he will choose which women to take. When he starts the car, he tells them how he has met a backward woman, maybe she was not from town, "I found her at Bwayise, she is from Bulemezi." Then they would all laugh.

You know, a man is the real prostitute. Sometimes, you are walking on the road, when you see a man coming from a house. Then he calls you, "Madam, come and have some tea and rest. I will take you later where you are going." Yet the resting he is talking of is not good. Therefore, was it the woman who called the man? It is a pity!

Sir, the man also needs to be called a name. The word *prostitute* is too much in use for women alone. When somebody sees a woman without a husband, she is called a prostitute. Perhaps one should consider the proverb: "*Gwe busulako avuma gwe bukyalira,*" meaning a person who is more of a fool blames the one who is less foolish. Therefore, a person who is more of a prostitute blames another. It reminds me of a man who divorced his wife for being a prostitute, and yet in his own house women are his pillows because they are too many and there is nowhere for them to sleep, but he lays his head on some of them.

Yours, sir,
Lusi K. Kyebakutika
Makerere Kyadondo, 17 June 1932

Translated by Jane Kawalya

Emily Mkandawire
SHOULD WOMEN BE EDUCATED?

Malawi 1933 Chitumbuka

Apart from what is found in her published letter, no information exists about the life of Emily Mkandawire. Mkandawire—which may be either the writer's maiden name or her husband's name—is a very common name in northern Malawi. We know she was one of a handful of women then literate and that she lived in Mzimba, in the north central part of the country.

Mkandawire was probably educated at one of the mission schools run by Livingstonia Mission in the north. Though Livingstonia encouraged both women and men to develop independent minds through education, women's education even in more recent times emphasized domesticity and child care. Emily Mkandawire seems to be thinking of this kind of education for girls. She suggests that education benefits young women both as an alternative to early or hasty marriages and as a means to acquiring the judgment they need to choose a husband wisely when the proper time comes.

Vyaro na Vyaro was a mission newspaper that Livingstonia Mission began publishing in 1932. It accepted articles in Chitumbuka as well as in English. Emily's letter was written in Chitumbuka. Unlike the common practice of women contributors using initials to protect themselves, especially when writing about unpopular issues, Emily Mkandawire chose to sign her full name.

Fulata L. Moyo

✦

Friends, listen to me now! Some elderly women, girls, elderly men, and drunkards say discouraging and painful things about educating girls. They say, "Why should you girls go to school? Where will school lead you? If you fail, what can school profit you?" "Just get married! All your friends are married, and some even have children! You are just wasting your time." "Do you really believe school would make you useful?" "Do you really think that women should be educated?"

Sometimes you answer them, "We are not supposed to rush into marriage. We are supposed to get a formal education first and then later, after much thought, get married."

One day I was reading an article by Maria Gondwe in *Vyaro na Vyaro* where she argued that waiting patiently is important so that God can choose someone who is suitable with whom we can share our lives in a Christian marriage and family. "Yes, waiting is good and yields sweet results! My friend, do not be attracted by clothes on the body, hats on the head, and shoes on the feet. Such appearances might deceive you, and yet on the inside, a man may be like a bitter fruit! Before you say 'yes' to any man, discover whether he is well-behaved, trustworthy, and educated. To such a man, were he even an orphan, you could still say 'yes.'"

All of us know friends who married drunkards. These women are forced to brew beer. You can see smoke coming from their houses, the women dark with soot from the beer pots, their eyes as red as fire because of the smoke! See the crowds gathering at their houses and hear the noises! Some of the noise comes from the singing and dancing of those who are drunk, some of them covered in beer residue. Others actually fall asleep naked. Some beat each other to death with sticks, producing more chaos, as if these houses were filthy dens of hyenas or pigs.

Would any of you, friends, recommend such a life? Please try to accept marriage proposals only from those who are trustworthy and respectable. Take time to know the man before making a decision. Let those who are happily married be your examples. Well, certainly you have heard my opinion!

Translated by Fulata L. Moyo

Mothers Union Members
A LETTER TO THE BISHOP

Uganda 1934   Luganda

Members of the Mothers Union, sometimes referred to as the Married Ladies Association, in Buganda, wrote this letter to the Right Reverend Jaimeson J. Willis, the Bishop of the Native Anglican Church (N.A.C.) of Uganda, in 1934. The Mothers Union, founded in the late nineteenth century, is an influential association of women in the Anglican faith, which stretches across the Commonwealth. In the Ugandan Church in the 1930s, the Mothers Union was finding new power and voice through the leadership of educated women graduates of Gayaza High School, Lady Irene College, Ndejje and King's College, Budo. Although the Mothers Union was and is traditionally regarded as an instrument for the promotion of spiritual and domestic values, such as the maintenance of marital harmony and the proper upbringing of children, the women strategists of Buganda quickly realized that it could take on wider social and political advocacy.

In this letter the women protest not only the patent immorality of the nominated chief, but also, and even more vehemently, the political and judicial wisdom of keeping such a person within the administrative system. Their activism may also be seen in the keenness with which they followed the divorce suit against Mr. Senkonyo. The letter testifies to the women's understanding not only of the social and political system but of the levers of influence that can help them achieve their objectives. Aware that they had no sanctioned traditional channel for presenting their case to the Bugandan king, or *kabaka*, they decide to go through the Native Anglican Church, of which the *kabaka* and most of the aristocracy were, at least nominally, members. But they are prepared to go even further and plead their case before the superior colonial powers, represented by the provincial commissioner and the colonial governor.

The British governor was the local head of the government in the Uganda Protectorate, dividing Uganda into four provinces, each headed by a British provincial commissioner. The Buganda Kingdom, one of the provinces, stood in a special, semi-autonomous relationship to the colonial administration, formalized by the Buganda Agreement in 1900. While confirming his recognition of the protectorate's authority, the *kabaka* continued to rule over his territory in much the same way as his ancestors had done before the advent of colonialism. His hierarchy, all male, comprised a network of administrators ranging from village and parish headmen through subcounty and county chiefs to a regional assembly and cabinet headed by a prime minister. The king personally appointed all county and subcounty chiefs, who acted as both administrative and judicial heads of their districts. This would explain the concern of the Mothers Union about the administration of justice if Mr. Senkonyo became the head of an important sub-county. Each county and subcounty had its designation, like the "Mumyuka" and "Sabawali" mentioned in the letter, and had its own status, based on its traditional links and duties to the monarchy.

Lusi Kafero, a ripe nonogenarian at the time of this volume's publication, confirmed that the king rejected their petition and appointed Mr. Senkonyo despite such significant opposition.

Austin Bukenya and Florence Ebila

✦

N.A.C. Mengo
August 29, 1934
Your Lordship,
We members of the Mothers Union of Buganda are writing this letter to you with humility to put before you these matters of painful and serious concern to us. We have received with serious note the news that His Majesty the Kabaka of Buganda has chosen his man, Mr. N. Senkonyo, the Mumyuka of Singo County, and promoted him to head the bigger and more important subcounty of Sabawali in Kyagwe County. This gentleman, however, does not deserve any more promotion; rather, he should be gradually phased out for the reasons given below.

That gentleman was sued by his wife in the High Court at Kampala on grounds of adultery, mistreatment, and cruelty when he took to his home two other women, Naomi and Wanyana, with whom he ganged up to subject his wife to extreme abuse: The judge upheld the wife's complaints and granted a divorce and maintenance of twenty shillings per month, on these grounds. Truly, Your Lordship, we know these things well because we sent twelve of our members to closely observe the proceedings in this case. So, Your Lordship, what reason is there for the promotion of an administrator who was publicly found at fault in a case of that nature? How can an administrator of that kind fairly judge people who indulge in actions like those? If that man is not promoted, is there any great loss to the Buganda government?

But if he has been selected just like any other person, we, as the mothers of the nation, demand, Your Lordship, that you convey to the government these complaints of ours. For, Your Lordship, if such matters are not given serious consideration, it will be a matter of great disgrace. The nation will simply perish and all the hopes of Buganda will be dashed, never to be realized.

We, as the mothers of the nation, who are deeply concerned about our nation, humbly beg you, if you are unable to handle this matter, Your Lordship, to introduce us to the Provincial Commissioner, [of the] Buganda, or the Governor himself, before this gentleman is confirmed, so that, through our chosen representatives, we can further explain our feelings of pain and shame as a nation and as Christians. We are, Your Lordship, your respectful members of the Mothers Union, Buganda.

Lusi Kafero	Secretary of the Union at Natete
Everini Segobe	Secretary of the Union at Kibuye
Tabisa Sonko	Secretary of the Union at Kungu
Naomi M. Binaisa	Secretary of the Union at Namirembe

Translated by Hilda Ntege Mukisa and Austin Bukenya

THE MID-TWENTIETH CENTURY
(1936–1969)

Chauwa Banda
FIGHTING FOR MY CHIEFTAINCY

Malawi 1936 English [Chichewa]

According to oral traditions, in pre-colonial times, women of the Banda clan served as priestesses in various parts of Chewaland. The main rain shrine was under Makewana at Msinja in Lilongwe district, now the capital of Malawi. Other minor rain shrines were under rain priestesses such as Mwali in Dedza District, Matsakamula in Ntchisi, Salima in Salima District and Chauwa Banda at Chilenje (Nkhoma) in Lilongwe District. Chauwa Banda was a renowned priestess in her time. Members of the Banda clan, one of the two major clans of the Chewa people, referred to Chauwa as "Mother of the Banda." Birth dates were not recorded in pre-colonial times, but from extant texts, it can be deduced that she was probably born in the late 1800s. Chauwa Banda held both religious and political power, but delegated most of her political responsibilities to her brother, Mdzinga. When, in the late nineteenth century, the Ngoni invasions combined with the teaching of Christian missionaries to destroy Chauwa's rain cult, she continued to retain her religious office, even through the early years of the British, who established the Nyasaland Protectorate in 1891.

In the 1930s, when the British began to appoint Native Authorities (NAs), Chauwa Banda attempted to use her precolonial identity to assume power in colonial society. In 1933, however, the British recognized Justino Mazengera—a member of the other major Chewa clan, the Phiri—as Native Authority (NA) for Section Five of Lilongwe district, an area settled by various clans, including the Banda. Chauwa and her Banda sympathizers called for a separate Banda chieftaincy in the area because they claimed that, although the area had apparently been characterized in the past by the harmonious intermixing of various Chewa clans, historically the Phiri and the Banda had never ruled each other.

She was the first woman in Lilongwe to take advantage of the fluid nature of indirect rule, in which the traditional local power structure was incorporated into the British colonial administrative structure—to advance her interests. In 1929, Chauwa had contested Justino Mazengera's chieftaincy but had failed in her quest to be appointed principal headwoman. Though defeated in 1929, Chauwa did not give up. She revised her strategy and made another effort to become NA in 1936.

When formulating her strategy, Chauwa Banda must have been aware of two important points. First, that the colonial state used "history" to verify some Chewa ruling families' territorial claims in Lilongwe district. Second, that the support of village headmen and women was crucial if one was to be elected NA. When the Banda demanded the colonial state's recognition of Chauwa as ruler of all the Banda of Nyasaland, they had been convinced that her history would support their claims. Further, she appealed to members of her clan for support by emphasizing the importance of women, especially mothers, in the economic and social organization of Chewa society.

In order to accomplish this, she invited a number of Banda NAs and village headmen and headwomen in Lilongwe to a meeting. From the invitation letter, it is quite clear that Chauwa wanted all the Banda in Lilongwe to recognize her as their "mother" and matriarchal ruler. It is also apparent that she wanted all members of her clan to see NA Mazengera as their enemy. In order to persuade the Banda elders to act, she addressed them as "her children," thus evoking the important religious and political positions she had held through her life.

Following Chauwa Banda's letter is a portion of the speech she made at the gathering. In the archival records from which these texts were retrieved, it is noted that after this powerful speech, the chiefs, headmen, and men decided to send a petition to the Nyasaland government supporting her claim. Chauwa Banda spoke in Chichewa but the archival document is the work of a translator, probably a clerk of the period.

Hendrina Msosa and Edrinnie Lora-Kayambazinthu

✦

To Chiefs: Casaba, Chamita, Chitukula, Masula, Kamgunda and Njewa
I am inviting you to a meeting to be held on Monday, August 18, 1936. The main agenda of the meeting is to bid farewell to you my children because Native Authority Mazengera is threatening to have me deported from this area. He intends to do this because I attended the Abanda meeting at Nathenje though I sent prior notification to both the Native Authority and the District Commissioner at the *Boma* [district administrative center]. Also, he maintains that he does not want my children, [who are] other Abanda chiefs, to visit me. Mazengera further informed me that, as Native Authority of this area, he has the right to appoint *Mdzinga* [chiefs]. This remark surprised me because, even during the time of our ancestors, it was unheard of for a Phiri to get involved in matters concerning a Banda chieftaincy. In addition, Mazengera stated that I should not have gone to the *Boma* when the D.C. [District Commissioner] called Abanda elders to give an account of our history. He feels that I went there to back bite him. This is why he is expelling me from Chilenje, the land of my ancestors. As such, make plans to attend this important meeting so that you can appoint a *Mdzinga*, your uncle, before I leave this area. If you acknowledge that I am your mother, please attend the meeting.

Your mother,
Chauwa

Native Authority Mazengera sent for me on Sunday, the 9th of August 1936. His messenger found me unwell. I was suffering from headache and aching of feet. I told the messenger that I was unfit to travel any distance and asked him to spend a night at my village so that we could set out for Mazengera's the next day. The messenger said, "The order that I have been given by N.A. Mazengera is that it does not matter you are sick. I must take you away from your village." While discussing this the sun set and the messenger mercilessly took me away from my village and made me sleep at Kunthole village, a village that is about 800 to 1000 yards from mine. We arrived there after dark. The next day,

Monday, we set out for Mazengera's. Certain men of my clan followed me, some found me on my way, others just after I arrived at Mazengera's.

I entered his court where a great number of people were sitting. N.A. Mazengera said, "This is the very woman whom I want to see mostly. She is the woman who intends to take away my *nkhanju* [garment of chieftainship]. I warn you that you and your Abanda men should be aware. If you don't know me, you will know me now. You went to Nathenje and held a meeting of the Abanda, and again you went to the D.C. when the Abanda were called. What were you telling the D.C.? I know you meant to hold a secret detraction against me, therefore, prepare you and your men. I will make you eat hot chillies. I hear that your Abanda men are often visiting your village, such as Chimutu of Chiwamba, Kalumba of Chitsime and many others. I don't want these men to come to your village at all. If they continue coming, know that I will collect Abanda of all sexes that are in my land and get them exiled to an unknown country.

I tried to explain the subject of the meeting at Nathenje. . . . My simple explanation was like to kindle a flame of fire in his heart, and he scolded me heavily. Being a woman, I feared greatly because when he was speaking he kept hitting the book on the table. One or two of my men tried to explain in the same manner but in vain. . . . He continued threats of doing away with the Abanda in his country. I am the descendant of Chauwa, the founder of the Abanda clan, and the order of Mazengera is rather hard for one living to observe, unless in a grave where a person is buried alone.

Princess Kaiko Nambayo
MODERN MARRIAGES

Zambia   1936   Silozi

Princess Kaiko Nambayo is a descendant of King Lewanika of Barotseland, today part of the Western Province of Zambia, bordering Namibia and Angola. He was the person who, in 1890, signed an agreement with Cecil Rhodes of the British South Africa Company that allowed Rhodes to exploit Barotseland's resources, and later made it part of the colony of Northern Rhodesia. While guaranteeing the people of Barotseland protection from local enemies, the relationship also facilitated their use as a pool of cheap labor for domestic copper mines and for mines in Southern Rhodesia and South Africa, while contributing little to the region's own development. British control did, however, offer some new educational opportunities to women. These were extended early to members of the royal family, including the Princess Nambayo, who had moved out of the rural area to live in Mazubuka, a city along the railroad line.

In October 1936 Princess Nambayo wrote a letter to *Mutende*, a multilingual African newspaper circulated through Northern Rhodesia. Her letter addresses problems arising from the widespread migration of men to copper mining towns to seek work and to live in urban areas. Not surprisingly, especially if they were going to stay on where they were, they married women they met in the towns. Hence, marriage between people of different tribes was apparently not uncommon.

In her letter, Princess Nambayo is displeased with what she calls "modern marriages" and especially intermarriage. She encourages young men to return to their villages to choose brides from their own tribes—hence, the analogy of the cow, the kraal, and the reference to a woman's pounding. (Pounding grain into meal was a major component of women's work.) She is equally critical of young women from Barotse villages who go to the city seeking wealthier husbands, and the men who are foolish enough to marry them.

Nalishebo N. Meebelo and Elizabeth Mfune

✦

Modern marriages are surely very disgraceful. There are many women who have come [to the city] on their own, without their husbands, from the Barotse Kingdom, and it is apparently impossible that a woman who has come alone from her home village could remain married only to one man. When she sees people who are richer than her husband, she divorces her husband. Any man who marries such a woman, knowing perfectly that she came on her own from her village, should not be amazed when she divorces him too.

Have you men already forgotten these incidents? Why don't you go to your villages to marry women who are better than those that you marry here in the city?

You ought to know that it is difficult to milk a cow when you have no idea which kraal it comes from. It is more or less the same as marrying a woman whose origins you do not know, as well as where she used to pound from.

Similarly, my fellow women and I should not disgrace our parents by practicing bad habits. We should not always seek to be married to rich people. Do not rush for riches only; do not place money above the value of a good human being.

Mukwae Kaiko Nambayo, Mazabuka

Translated by Nalishebo N. Meebelo

Martha Kapanga and Mrs. E. Akapelwa Inambwae
LETTERS ON WOMEN'S EDUCATION

Zambia 1936, 1937   Silozi

Prior to missionary settlement in Zambia, young boys and girls in the village were educated under close supervision by their parents, with input from the entire community. Children were taught the responsibilities of adulthood, including how to care for the young, and most girls were offered for marriage quite early. Men of the village taught educational programs for boys, generally comprising skills in farming, hunting, fishing, and firewood gathering.

When Christian missionaries established schools in Zambia in the nineteenth and early twentieth centuries, they initially focused on educating boys in large numbers, due to social norms that subjected girls and women to performing household chores. Gradually, some women began to receive formal education as well.

Martha Kapanga, a teacher from Kasenga in northern Zambia, and Mrs. E. Akapelwa Inambwae, a citizen of Barotseland in the west, wrote to the *Mutende*, an African newspaper for what was at that time the British colony of Northern Rhodesia, in 1936 and 1937 respectively. The *Mutende* was published monthly in English, Chibemba, Silozi, Cinyanja, and Chitonga, to provide news to all people. Women were encouraged to write to the editor.

Revealed in the two letters to the editor is the fact that some people of that period regarded areas where people spoke different languages, dressed differently, and had dissimilar cultural practices as separate countries. Teaching was viewed not only as an important career but as a gateway to these other lands and cultures. Both of the letter writers seem to view this broadening of horizons, along with modernization in general and perhaps even Westernization, as positive, important to their country's future as well as their own personal enrichment. Kapanga seems awed by the idea that she has had the chance to "tread in a country where my great grandfather had never been." Inambwae extols the virtue of modern education for girls and of English as a common language for the land's various peoples (as well as admiring the lighter *chitenge* or *ichikwembe* wrapper that women from other provinces of Zambia wore, over the heavy skirts of Barotseland, which she desribes as "many skirts at once"). One intriguing aspect of these letters is their relationship to current ideas and debates about globalization.

Nalishebo N. Meebelo

✦

1936

I am telling you fathers who can read *Mutende* to send your daughters to school to become teachers. In this way they can travel to other tribes. My father will never come to where I am now teaching at Kasenga. I did not know that I would tread in a country where my great grandfather had never been. But through education I have done so. Never let your daughters stay in one place. Girls also have their work to do for poor little Northern Rhodesia.

Martha Kapanga

1937

On reading *Ling'usa la Bulozi*, I was delighted to see that girls who had been educated at Mabumbu School had had a meeting in May.

I see that a ray of light is shining on the girls of Barotse, because in meetings like this they gain strength, though I do not know for what reason they met; unless it was because boys are taught well but there is no progress in the education of girls; there should not simply be education for boys, but girls should be taught exactly like them; for women are the light of the village and the bringers-up of children. So they should be educated like men so that they may become lights to lighten the darkness, and the Chief's country may grow up in new ways.

To convince you, my friends, we old Mabumbu girls when we go to other countries differ from local girls in two ways: (1) Clothes. They dress better than we do by not wearing many skirts at once. (2) They speak English better than we do; I do not pine to know English myself but can see clearly that English is the thing which binds all the British Empire together. If one knows English one can converse with Nyanja, Tebele, or Kalanga people, with Europeans and other nationalities which I cannot tell you of, in this very English.

Mrs. E. Akapelwa Inambwae

Translated by Nalishebo N. Meebelo

Erusa Kibanda
DOMESTIC VIOLENCE

Uganda 1939   Luganda

There is no information about the author of this letter other than what can be gleaned from the text itself. The sender's address on the letter suggests that Erusa Kibanda lived in her marital home in Mutundwe, a southern suburb of Kampala City. The pattern of Kiganda names in the letter further suggests that Erusa Kibanda and her violent brother, Masembe, like their father, Mr. Kabali, belonged to the Nseenene (grasshopper) clan. This group was particularly influential in Baganda society in the early decades of the twentieth century, one of their members being the long-serving regent and prime minister, Sir Apollo Kaggwa. Erusa's surname, Kibanda, is not from the Nseenene clan, and it is most likely her spouse's.

The Western practice of women calling themselves by their fathers' or husbands' names instead of their personal, clan names was introduced into Kiganda society through mission schools, especially those of the Anglican Church. The family's Anglican affiliation may also be seen in the English and Hebrew biblical names, Erusa (the Kiganda version of Jerusha), Zerida (Jeridah), Jeni (Jane), and Mary. As was the practice at this time, Erusa Kibanda would have received a basic education at one of the mission schools. This accounts not only for her literacy but also for the quiet but firm confidence with which she denounces her brother's boorish conduct. A close relationship apparently existed between Erusha Kibanda and her parents, despite the rather stiff formality with which she addresses them. She does not ask them explicitly to do anything about the incident. She informs them and expresses her abhorrence, apparently in the confidence that they will know how to treat her brother.

The wording about the transfer of the child from Erusa Kibanda's home suggests that Masembe's home was close to that of his sister. Of the two other places mentioned, Buwaya is near Entebbe on the shores of Lake Victoria, about twenty-five kilometers from Kampala, and Hoima is in the Bunyoro region, some two hundred kilometers west of Kampala. It was unusual that Zerida, Masembe's wife, should have undertaken what in those days would have been such a long journey. It is possible that Zerida was a native of Hoima or that she had relatives living there. It is also interesting to note that Erusa Kibanda had expected a written message from Masembe about his wife's visit to his sister's home, indicating that they were accustomed to communicating in writing.

This letter, found in the Church of Uganda archives at Namirembe in Kampala, is written in a rather informal style, with little punctuation and lengthy uninterrupted sequences. For ease of comprehension, some of these have been broken into sentences in the translation.

Austin Bukenya and Hilda Ntege Mukisa

◆

Mutundwe
7.12.1939
To my parents, Mr. And Mrs. E. Kabali
I hope you are well, dear Father and Mother. We, too, are here but not doing very well, falling sick from time to time and losing some of our people. How are my sisters?

I am writing to you, Mother and Father, to tell you about a terrible incident at my home yesterday when my younger brother, Masembe, insolently stormed into my house and started a fight, beating up his wife and accusing me of wronging him by allowing his wife to go on visits to Buwaya and Hoima while she had a child nursing serious burns. Masembe just barged into the house and stood there without any consideration for or reference to us, the owners of the house at home. He would not even acknowledge that there was a man in this house to which Zerida, his wife, had come. Instead, he just started barking at us in the house in the middle of the night, treating all of us like rubbish.

1. When his wife was coming here, Masembe did not write me any letter to show how many days he expected her to stay. Even when he came here, he did not tell me anything about his wife's movements.

2. I never sent for his wife to come and visit me. The visiting plans were made entirely between the two of them.

3. Namyenya, the child, was not badly burned, and anyway, it wasn't me but her mother who burned her with a lamp. Even by the time we lost our aunt, the child's burns were drying up, and she did not have any other illness or injury. In any case, I could not have abandoned a seriously sick child and just walked off. But I left even all my children, including little Jeni, at home. But when Masembe came over, he ordered Mary to bring Namyenya over, leaving Jeni and the other children all alone.

4. From all this—Masembe invaded my house as if he was walking into abandoned ruins, treating us with utter disrespect and beating his wife while we looked on helpless and dumbfounded—I think he treated me with such contempt because I am a woman. He wanted to humiliate and embarrass me, with everyone saying that my brother had staged a fight inside my house. If

I had been an elder brother of his, I think there would have been no peace between us. His wife has now left my home.

Well, that is it, my dears. Peace.

Your daughter,
Erusa Kibanda

Translated by Hilda Ntege Mukisa

Nellie Grant
LETTERS FROM AFRICA TO A DAUGHTER IN ENGLAND

Kenya 1939–1963   English

Nellie Grosvenor was born in 1885 into an aristocratic and adventurous English family that was unable to manage money intelligently. The family sent her to Cheltenham Ladies College, which she left in 1901, with examination results that could have earned her admission into university, if anyone had thought of it. Soon after coming out formally into English society, she married Josceline Grant, also adventurous and imprudent. He had invested in a Portuguese East African diamond mine, which seems only to have ever produced three diamonds, all small enough to be set in Nellie's engagement ring. He then invented a type of motor car that earned the title "grunt and dawdle." Not surprisingly, it became necessary to leave the scene of disaster, and so in 1913, the couple sailed for British East Africa where they used their remaining capital to buy five hundred acres at Chania Bridge (now Thika) at four British pounds an acre—a steep price in 1913—from a friend who had been at Eton with Josceline.

As described by their daughter, Elspeth Huxley, in *The Flame Trees of Thika* and its sequels, the venture did not prosper. After Josceline Grant's diplomatic service in Europe during the war years and Nellie Grant's year-long course in agriculture at Cambridge, they returned to Thika but had to sell out. In 1922, a friend of Nellie provided them with a thousand acres at Njoro, where they lived until 1963, when Nellie, then a widow, sold the fifty acres that remained at a low price to a cooperative of her former employees. She left the country and died in Portugal in 1977.

Nellie Grant was seen by her neighbors as somewhat eccentric. She was a member of the Makerere College Board of Governors and would invite students to spend a vacation on the farm. She spotted the talent of Tanzanian painter Sam Ntiru when he was a student and provided materials so that she could be "the first person to have an Ntiru in my collection." She would go to the cinema with her cook after they had finished their marketing. She was always trying her hand at a new crop or a new handicraft project for the local women. Both Nellie and daughter Elspeth spoke Gikuyu.

The following extracts from her letters come from a volume compiled by

Huxley and published under the title *Nellie: Letters from Africa* in 1980. They testify to the preoccupations of a farmer with weather and crop prices, recipes, and a round of committee meetings, together with the real dangers and frustrations of the Emergency period of revolt against British rule. Nellie, who had founded a school on her land and treated her "labour" well by colonial standards, exhibits a sense of betrayal at the Africans "defection to Mau Mau." But in her last entry, written after the first democratic elections and shortly before Kenyan achieved independence, she relates how she returned the "cock-a-doodle-do" of some passing youths, the cock being the symbol of the Kenya African National Union (KANU).

Marjorie Oludhe Macgoye

◆

15 September 1939
Had about a hundred Kikuyu in the sitting room today to listen to the weekly broadcast. They certainly enjoy it. Govt. is starting a Swahili paper from tomorrow called Baraza. . . . The Secretariat burnt itself to ashes Tuesday night, and all the early records were lost.

17 October 1939
We're in the throes of the worst drought since '18, and some say worse than '18. Production is sinking like a stone, we shall presumably have to import food to feed the swarms of militaires, and not a whisper of any plan to keep production going at all, let alone increase it. Truly a strange, strange war.

16 March 1953
The "villagization'" scheme has been suddenly and violently put into force to the utter disruption of all Kikuyu labour. The govt. made one scheme for farms of whatever size, which couldn't have been sillier. The result here was that all Kikuyu labour would have been squashed up like sardines. . . . My chaps all said that they would be photographed and finger printed but that they would *not* live like sardines. . . . Personally I think the Kikuyus are so pushed about and harried and worried that they just listen to the last chap who comes along. . . . If only it would rain I believe they would settle down, as they would literally dig themselves in and couldn't bear to leave the sprouting maize if they could see it sprouting. . . . On the Hodges' farm in Sabukia the labour all went overnight, leaving their maize, turkeys, clothes, and every single thing; the Hodges will be practically bust this year as all their maize and pyrethrum is lying out unpicked; no one has been kinder or better to their labour than they have.

7 October 1953
Would you believe it? Njoro settlers Asscn. are asking Bishop Beecher to address a meeting and bring an educated African with him. This was my suggestion. I pointed out that we had really better know a bit more about the

modern African than we do and that the best way would be to meet a real one. Fixing the time of the meeting led to much talk—it couldn't be in the club house at 6 p.m. as usual because it wouldn't do for the educated African to see European ladies in the bar (really because one of the members thought he might get landed in the position of having to offer a "bloody nigger" a drink). I longed to ask why an educated African couldn't see this, as a long succession of uneducated African bartenders had survived the spectacle, but thought the company had had about as much as they could take for one day, so sweetly said what about an afternoon meeting and that was agreed. Leonard Beecher is very good value indeed.

19 January 1954
Sunday was a great day on the farm as there was a circumcision for two girls, old Nganga (gardener)'s debutante and a very much younger sister of Mbugwa's. Nganga had repeatedly asked me to ask Dick Prettejohn for the loan of a skilled operator in his employment. I was naturally reluctant to countenance the ceremony, but in fact one has no legal right to prohibit it, and Dick agreed that it would be a very bad plan to drive it underground just now, especially as it has so often lately been used as a cloak to oath-taking . . .

12 December 1954
Mr. Humble came up yesterday with Bethel his no. 1 screener and coped with Mbugwa all over again. Humble says they have got the blackest things against Mbugwa through cross-checking—it seems till right into 1953 he was allowing [Mau-Mau] ceremonies to be held *in his hut* here and was deep in it, he *won't* come clean . . .

26 December 1954
I have withdrawn from any attempt to foster friendship, understanding etc. with the Africans after their defection to Mau Mau but must say came very near to it again when, on Xmas morning, Mbugwa staggered in with my morning cuppa and laid a huge box of potatoes on my bed tied up in (my) brilliant violet crepe paper. This is a very special sort of spud called *Mweri Umwe* [one month] which he knows I love and have looked for in vain for a long time now; he had got some and grown it specially for me. Disarming? Especially as this year I didn't give anyone a single thing for Christmas . . .

There was one continuous bombing on Kipipiri for two days before Xmas, making the dogs bark here and shaking the windows in Nakuru; nothing was said as to whether any of the gangs were inconvenienced on Kipipiri itself or not.

9 November 1958
Had twenty-two African ladies to see the veg. and have tea on Thursday, and it did actually drizzle and spoil the garden trip, and we had to have tea indoors. Mbugwa was superb. A Kipsigis lady said to me "How old are you?" I felt too

weak to go into the matter of manners, leading questions, etc., so said simply "Three hundred." Mbugwa came in at that moment, so I said to him: "You have known me for two hundred years, haven't you?" Without batting an eyelid he replied: "I think slightly more, madam." To my horror the lady took out a pen and started writing it all down.

22 May 1960

The drought has got simply terrific, grass all brown, people wilting and maize going at the rate of knots. Friday morning woke up to very low cloud, quite a fog, and bone dry like dry ice. Never seen it before. Then at 4 p.m. two thunderstorms met over this house. Torrents of rain and lots of hail which we could have done without. I was paying wages outside the kitchen door when a flash and a bang went off absolutely overhead and a horrid rending noise; don't know what was struck—something. Muchoka took to his hands and knees and fled round the corner—a new technique to avoid being struck by lightning, but anyway someone was as frightened as I was. We got 2.7 inches in about an hour—just a flash in the pan. No rain since.

13 June 1960

I have decided to say the school must go away. The teachers' houses want renewing, and the school buildings are very dicky. I started the school thirty-two years ago as a tiny thing, when I had a thousand acres and quite a labour force. I have now fifty acres, and there are a hundred and fifty-three children in the school of whom twenty come from this farm, three teachers, and everything expanding, and lots of other schools around.

20 May 1963

Well, the first elections are over, and only one DO [District Officer] coshed on the head. I went down to Njoro on Sat. with a few chosen ones, others having gone at daybreak. About a thousand people there, representing about three thousand voters. Everything was very well done. I've never seen anyone better at his job than the little African in charge of my booth—so good-natured and unflustered—and a very tricky job checking up on everyone for hours on end. We all had to dip a forefinger into a bottle of indelible red ink; at the next election, another finger, and so on, so you can't vote twice, and we'll all have bloody finger tips for weeks. On the way some KANU youths made KANU noises at me, so I said "Cock-a-doodle-do" back at them, which left them guessing.

Zeyana Ali Muh'd
WARTIME IN ZANZIBAR

Tanzania 1940, 1943   Kiswahili

Zeyana Ali Muh'd was a primary school teacher in Zanzibar during World War II. One of the few women teachers at the time, she was a frequent contributor to the monthly journal *Mazungumzo ya Walimu* (Teachers' Conversations), which was run and published by Zanzibari teachers themselves. Most of the contributions were from native Zanzibari teachers, although there were also many British teachers in the profession. The teaching profession then carried very high prestige; the teachers would have been considered the cream of the educated elite in their society.

Women contributors to the publication were, however, rare, partly because there were still very few women teachers, and partly because women were a bit wary about publishing under their own names. Several of them wrote under assumed names. The name of the journal truly reflected the contents. It was informal in style, and contributors discussed a wide variety of topics, including their travels, cooking recipes, noteworthy developments in their schools, upcoming events, cultural practices and their seeming erosion, proper behavior, and the like.

In the 1940 text, Zeyana Ali Muh'd discusses her "travels" in other parts of Unguja, the main island of Zanzibar. Jambiani, the village she visited, is located on the southeast coast and is now a major tourist attraction, its whole coast dotted with tourist hotels. At the time this text was written, however, it would have been occupied almost entirely by the local community, with a few houses owned by town dwellers who would come on occasional visits. The distance from the city of Zanzibar to Jambiani is no more than forty kilometers, but the road was so bad that it took several hours to get there, which explains the writer's fatigue.

The Wahadimu mentioned in the text are indigenous inhabitants of the south and east of Zanzibar. They are thought to be descendants of both the Shirazi from Persia and immigrants from the mainland. Remnants of Shirazi culture are still visible in the area, including a restored mosque nearly nine hundred years old.

The southeast is rather infertile, consisting of rocky terrain that supports only hardy crops. Apart from growing the crops mentioned in the text, the men occupy themselves with fishing, and the production of coir, which is mentioned, is also a major preoccupation of the women. The life of backbreaking work described in the text—and especially the daily hardship of finding and hauling water—is common to most women in rural Africa. The writer, although a middle-class Arab woman who would not be directly familiar with any of these tribulations, nevertheless empathizes with the Jambiani women. She attests to their cheerfulness, although it remains unclear whether their affect reflects their nature or their fortitude. In recent years, women of the area have had a more lucrative source of income in the cultivation of seaweed.

To the credit of the teachers, they managed to produce the journal even in wartime, when most goods were scarce. Unlike World War I, World War II saw no combat in East Africa (south of Ethiopia and the Sudan), but Zanzibar, like other British colonies, was a source of soldiers for the empire and subject to the hardships of the wartime economy. The 1943 text is, in fact, precisely about wartime shortages, particularly relating to food rationing. The staple Zanzibar diet was (and still is) rice and foods made from wheat, and Zanzibaris used to consider maize meal as an inferior food, associated with migrant laborers from the mainland. Even the universal *ugali* (the thick African porridge which forms a staple in most African countries) was in Zanzibar made from cassava flour, and not maize flour. During the war, however, the food shortages were so acute that even cakes and "pudding" had to be made from maize flour. People in rural areas would have felt this shortage more acutely, because the rationing was based on racial lines, with rations being meted out to the Asians, Arabs, and Africans, in descending order, using color-coded cards. The struggle over food rations was so fierce that many people of African origin attempted to be ethnically reclassified as Arabs, so that they could get full rations. One writer notes that the best recognised name of the war for Zanzibaris of that time was *"wakati wa mchele wa kadi,"* or "the time of rationed rice."

The enthusiasm with which the program of cooking lessons was greeted also points to the effort to find new interesting ways of cooking "boring" maize meal. Cooking cakes and puddings on cooking stones could not have been an easy task, but for most Zanzibaris at the time it was commonplace. It is interesting that these culinary adventures came to be repeated in the 1960s after the revolution, when food became equally scarce, and residents could only make use of that which was locally produced.

Saïda Yahya-Othman

✦

TRAVEL AND LEARN

On Tuesday 21st March, I went to Jambiani on a visit. I very much wanted to see the village. I arrived late in the evening, and was so tired that I could not manage to go round. The following morning I spent visiting the sights. I found the village very fascinating, full of charming and jolly people. Eggs and milk were in plenty; big fish were available; and certain goods sold cheaply in shops. But the most harrowing thing was the scarcity of that important commodity, water. The water obtainable here was, more often than not, brackish, and if one needed nice drinkable water, untainted with salt, one had to go into immeasurable difficulties to get it. So I asked some of the villagers, "Where can one get nice water which is not brackish?" And they replied, "It is obtainable far from here in a hole in the rocks. Would you like to go there and have a look?" I replied, "Yes I would." So in the afternoon we paid a visit to the place. The road leading to the place is bad, very rocky. One had to move slowly and carefully to avoid hurting oneself from the sharp stones or by tripping over.

Also, one needed to wear shoes. Without shoes it was impossible. We walked for nearly an hour, and we finally arrived at the scene. We rested a while before descending into the cave.

Surprisingly, lianas [woody vines] grow in abundance there, and they assisted people to make the descent into the cave. And the descent is quite treacherous, sloping down 30 feet into the cave. At the mouth of the cave there are huge trees, and the overhanging branches form a sort of canopy over the entrance. As a result it is rather dark and very damp inside the cave, and if one remains inside for long one tends to become short of breath. I think it is because there is a poor circulation of air inside the cave, and sunlight does not freely penetrate through. And it is for this reason, I think, that the cave is named The Shadow.

In the recesses of the cave there is a small inner cave. That is where the water is found. The water does not seem to originate from a spring; it is very still, and the level neither rises nor falls. But during the long *masika* rains the level increases and sometimes the water overflows. This is the water used by the villagers for drinking and for cooking sweet dishes and brewing tea. But for savory dishes the villagers use the brackish water from the wells in their vicinity. They use this water also for washing and for other household needs. In Jambiani the houses do not have corrugated iron roofs (as is the case in Chwaka) so it is not possible to harvest rain water and preserve it in tanks for emergency uses. So we can imagine the plight of the people resulting from the scarcity of water.

Fetching water is done exclusively by women. In fact, the women there have numerous arduous tasks to perform, especially in the Hadim farmsteads. These tasks include fetching water, cutting firewood, cultivating the fields, and thrashing coconut husks. This in addition to the housework, the rearing of children, and other chores. In my view, cultivation is the most difficult of these tasks, because the women have to walk a fairly long distance to the fields, where they have to break the rocky soil in order to plant seeds. The crops which flourish in these areas are pigeon peas, maize, green gram, pumpkins, yams, sorghum, bulrush millet, beans, and cow peas. When harvesting draws near the peasant farmers and their families have to move from the village and set up camp in the cultivated fields to guard their crops from forages of monkeys in the day-time and wild pigs at night.

To conclude, I would say that the women in Jambiani work harder than the men. And yet if you happen to come across them on their way to their daily chores, they appear bright and cheerful, not spiteful and grumpy.

COOKING LESSONS IN THE VILLAGES

I think that many readers will be surprised that the 1942 issues of *Mazungumzo ya Walimu* have a few articles on cooking. Possibly many of us do not know the purpose behind the inclusion of these articles in the journal, and what is being done in this regard in the villages.

In mid-1942 when there was scarcity of rice and there was need for eating maize meal instead, it behoved the women in G.G. School [Government Girls'] to go round in the villages to instruct village women on the various ways of cooking maize meal.

The administration, and that includes district officers, were receptive to the idea and therefore the undertaking was fruitful. Each district administrative officer came to know the day when he would be visited by the cooking instruction group. He would then inform the various Ward Executive Officers under his jurisdiction.

It was programmed as follows: At two in the afternoon on Wednesday the women teachers would leave for the nearby villages. And at 9:30 in the morning on Saturday they would visit distant villages where they would remain till evening. The programme formally started at Mangapwani on Wednesday 17th June.

Instructions were given on the cooking of the following five dishes:

1. bread made from fresh corn
2. millet bread
3. meat balls made from meat and cassava
4. bread made from corn flour
5. pudding made from corn meal and dates.

When the teachers, including Ms. Purnell and Ms. Knowles, arrived they were met by 80 women students who had cooking stones on the ready in an open air place. One of the teachers came forward and addressed the gathering. After the preliminary introduction she went on to talk on the difficult conditions occasioned by the war and the scarcity of rice and other imported commodities. And we have been sent here by the government, she went on to say, to assist you and show you how you can cope with the situation, now and in the days to come. Thanks to our glorious British government we get food. Food is necessary to life. Without food we cannot sustain life and living. Had it not been for the government keeping a watchful eye on shopkeepers, prices of goods would be deadly.

After the address, instructions began on the cooking of one of the dishes. The pot was placed on the fire; instructions were repeated again and again interspersed with questions and answers. Then another teacher followed with instructions on the cooking of another dish, just as the first one did. This went on until all the dishes were cooked, while the women were looking on with glee. Afterwards the food was distributed so that each of them could have a taste. Also distributed were buns we had brought with us from town.

Eventually, the teacher who had initially addressed the gathering gave a farewell address, thanking them all for their attendance. The women in turn also thanked us profusely. The gathering dispersed with joy and ululation.

These visits to the villages went on till the end of the month of Shaaban.

There were in all 10 visits. Some other villages, on hearing about our visits, asked us to visit them as well and we responded accordingly.

Translated by Abdulhakim Yahya

Elspeth Huxley and Margery Perham
LETTERS ON RACE AND POLITICS

Kenya   1942   English

Elspeth Grant Huxley was born in 1907 in London, the only child of Nellie and Josceline Grant. Her parents left her behind briefly when they went to East Africa to repair their failing fortunes. Despite other separations, Huxley recalls a generally happy childhood in her series of autobiographical books, beginning with *The Flame Trees of Thika*, published in 1959.

After university studies in Britain and the United States, she married Gervas Huxley in 1930 and thereafter lived mostly in Britain. She was commissioned to write the life of the famous Kenya colonialist Lord Delamere, and in the preindependence years produced a number of potboilers which, though not individually distinguished, gave interesting and sometimes surprising insights into the mindset of the time. She and her mother, Nellie Grant, received official permission to live for some weeks in the Gikuyu "reserve," where white settlers were forbidden to occupy land, while Huxley gathered material for her novel *Red Strangers*, published in 1939. In the preface to that novel, she wrote, "The story of the coming of the white man is related as it was told to me by a number of people who were grown up at the time. But I am well aware that no person of any race and culture can truly interpret events from the point of view of individuals belonging to a totally different race and culture. It was the consideration that, within a few years none will survive of those who remember the way of life that existed before the white man came, that led me to make the experiment of this book." After the World War II, Huxley traveled widely in Africa, producing such thoughtful books as *The Sorcerer's Apprentice* (1948), *Four Guineas* (1954), and *The New Earth* (1960).

Margery Perham was also widely traveled in Africa. She was a British scholar, a reader on colonial administration at Oxford, and the first fellow of Oxford's newly founded Nuffield College in 1939. In the course of investigative trips, she would sometimes visit a sister and brother-in-law in the colonial administration in Tanganyika and elsewhere. In 1941, she published *Africans and the British Rule*, and later became well known for her two-volume *Life of Lord Lugard* (1956 and 1960), *Colonial Reckoning* (1963), and the two volumes of *Colonial Sequence* (1967 and 1970). She also wrote the foreword to the East African edition of J.M. Kariuki's *Mau Mau Detainee*. In 1960 she was awarded the CBE, though all of her work suggests that she would not have liked to think of herself as a Dame Commander of the British Empire. Though twelve years older than Huxley, she came from the world of the British intellectual left, and was clearly more sympathetic to the position of the native African majority in the colonies.

The single-minded correspondence between these two women, in letters dated 1942 and 1943, was prompted by Perham and intended for publication. Their letters were published in London in 1944 as *Race and Politics in Kenya: A Correspondence Between Elspeth Huxley and Margery Perham*. It is extraordinary that the future of Kenya should have been thought of sufficient importance to allow the book's publication in that year, when wartime rationing of paper restricted publishers' output.

Marjorie Oludhe Macgoye

Elspeth Huxley: Should the settlers be expropriated?
22nd March 1942
Dear Miss Perham,

Thank you for answering my letter, and for explaining your point of view so clearly. To begin with, you suggest that a healthy state can't be built on a basis of rigid racial discrimination. I agree with that. But I don't agree that Kenya's feet are necessarily set on this path. For one thing, I don't see how such a state—a little South Africa, you might say, in a political sense—could possibly arise within the framework of the British colonial empire. The general principles and laws on which that empire is based simply wouldn't allow it. For another, I think Kenya has already passed far beyond the stage where such a rigidly repressive state *could* be organized, even if the most reactionary elements were given a chance to try.

You imply that settlers in Kenya wish to deny to Africans "the gradual advance in economic and political status to which they are successfully rising in those other parts of Africa where they have not a white colony sitting on their heads." The facts don't seem to me to support this. Does native education in Kenya, for instance, lag behind that in other African dependencies? Surely not. Africans are being taught skills and trades of all kinds, and as a matter of fact the settlers have frequently prodded the Government in this respect. In politics Africans have their Local Native Councils which raise and spend their own taxes, they have a record of slow but steady advance. So far as I know the settlers have opposed none of this. On the contrary, they have often supported it. Therefore to suggest, as you seem to, that the Europeans want to sit on the Africans' heads and prevent advances seems to me to give an entirely false impression.

You say that you sympathize with those who distrust and fear the settlers' influence, and you explain why. I certainly can't agree with you that these critics are always on the defensive; on the contrary, they are always attacking the settlers' position, and the Kenya Government. One has only got to read the Parliamentary questions, for instance, to see that. But that's a minor detail. The main question, granting your fears and misgivings, is—what do you want to do about it?

It seems to me that there are only two alternatives. One is that the white population of Kenya, settlers and traders and everyone but Government officials and perhaps missionaries, should go, leaving the country in the undisputed possession of the native and immigrant Indian peoples. The other is that the whites should stay where they are. And if they stay, they must somehow or other be fitted into the economic and political structure of a future East African state.

They go, or they stay. Look at the first possibility. They won't go voluntarily. But we live in an age of vast upheavals, of the tearing up of roots, of revolution and change. The settlers could be forced to go. They were, as you know, invited to Kenya in the first place by the Imperial Government, which spent time, thought and even money, from 1903 to 1923, in attracting Europeans to the Kenya highlands and persuading them to take up land. The Imperial Government is responsible for the presence of these settlers. It wouldn't be impossible for the Imperial Government to announce that it had changed its mind, to withdraw its invitation, and to turn them out again. There would be difficulties, of course. There would be breaches of faith. But it would not be beyond the bounds of the feasible to compensate the owners of land and to arrange, perhaps, for them to take up new farms, if they so wished, in one of the Dominions.

I don't suggest that this would be a popular or an easy move. The Imperial Government would have to provide the money, and would probably have to use force to carry through the eviction. I only suggest that it isn't physically impossible, given the resolve. And it is, surely, the logical goal at which those who condemn the experiment of white settlement in Kenya should aim. If white settlement is wrong, let it be liquidated: that is the honest viewpoint, or so it seems to me.

But if, on the other hand, such a liquidation is found to be impossible, then only the second alternative remains. If the settlers are not to be turned out, they must stay; and if they stay, a place must be found for them in the design of an East African future. The question at issue then becomes: what sort of place can, and should, be found for them, and what sort of attitude towards East Africa's future development would you wish them to adopt?

Now we've come to the fundamental point on which it seems to me that we disagree. If the settlers are there to stay, is it wise, is it even moderately sensible, to regard them always with this mixture of hostility and distrust? And to offer them no hopeful goal for their own future? You reject the goal that they worked towards in the past—self-government. But you don't suggest any other. Is this negative approach likely to make them more amenable to reason, to encourage them to show moderation and liberality, to persuade them (if necessary) to mend their ways?

No, I can't help but feel that this attitude is both defeatist and sterile. It takes as self-evident things which are not necessarily true: that the interests of the settlers are at all points antagonistic to those of the natives; that, broadly speaking, all settlers have the same interests and ideas; that they can survive only by clinging to an island of privilege protected by a reef of racial discrimination; and that there's nothing to be done about it except to offer this blank wall of resistance and opposition to any move on the settlers' part.

I venture to doubt whether this attitude will lead to a fair or lasting solution to any of Kenya's problems. An entirely new approach is, I think, needed.

Now I've aired my opinion, and perhaps you'll tell me where I'm wrong. The burden of my complaint is this: that the critics of Kenya affairs are often both defeatist and unrealistic. They believe that the evils of Kenya are due to the presence there of European settlers, but they don't propose any honest and practical steps to get rid of the element they deplore. And if they believe it can't be got rid of, then I think they are more defeatist still: for by their unremitting attacks on the white population, by their constant opposition to any and all of the Europeans' aspirations, they drive the settlers more and more into a corner, they trample underfoot the shoots of co-operation, they scorch the chances of peaceful persuasion—in short, they do everything to antagonize and embitter the settlers, to force them on to the defensive, but nothing to understand, guide or persuade.

For myself, I believe that the ills of Kenya (and Heaven knows they exist) are due, in the main, to other causes altogether, causes which this attitude of blaming everything on the settlers tends to obscure.

But before we go into that, will you let me know what you think? Would you like to get rid of the settlers and start again? Do you believe this could be done? And if you don't, what do you hope may be gained by this constant opposition and active hostility towards the settlers and all their works which, as I am sure you'll agree, is so often displayed by those who are planning from London and Oxford the design of a new African world?

Yours sincerely,
Elspeth Huxley

Margery Perham: Expropriation impracticable, but expansion undesirable
30th March 1942
Dear Mrs. Huxley,
You ask me if I think it would be better to buy out and repatriate the settlers. I think in view of the policy followed by the small number of settlers of trying to obtain domination over the three million Africans, and the repercussions this policy, if pursued, is likely to have upon the even larger surrounding African populations, that it might have been better. But if it were possible at any time, that time has gone. It may sound very practicable in a study but it is the sort of thing no Government—or, since 1939, I should say, no British Government—is ever likely to attempt against the settlers' will. Especially as the Europeans in South Africa would almost certainly oppose it on general principles and as a weakening of their continental strength.

Also I fully agree with you that the settlers came upon the invitation of the British Government. Moreover, only a few years ago, a government, and that a Labour government, made a promise to the colonists upon this point. In their White Paper of 1930 they repeated the words of the White Paper issued in 1923 by the then Conservative Secretary of State for the Colonies, the Duke of Devonshire, on behalf of the Imperial Government.

"Primarily Kenya is an African territory, and His Majesty's Government think it necessary definitely to record their considered opinion that the interests of the African natives must be paramount and that if, and when those interests and the interests of the immigrant races should conflict, the former should prevail." That is clear enough and surely unquestionable. But the statement goes on to say that the interests of the other communities must be safeguarded. "Whatever the circumstances in which members of these communities have entered Kenya, there will be no drastic action or reversal of measures already introduced . . . the result of which might be to destroy or impair the existing interests of those already settled in Kenya." With this, which, of course, covers Indians as well as Europeans, the Labour government concurs and it seems to me to rule out completely the compulsory, wholesale repatriation of the Colonists.

But is the alternative, as you seem to suggest, for the government to give way to the settlers' demands? This is where we must face our quite different views of the settlers. You write of the settlers as if they were unfortunate victims, who had been badly treated and were likely to be victimized further. As I see it, the settlers have suffered nothing but occasional criticism—for the criticism is by no means a ceaseless chorus—which has had little effect except to encourage the government to maintain certain fundamental defences in the interests of the African majority. The settlers have, indeed, carried most of the outworks and are now the dominant party in the country. It is not the British government or people who have been the aggressors. They have been rather sluggish defenders. The settlers whom you see as a rather pathetic group under attack, I see as a highly organized, ceaselessly alert group of shock troops, ready at any moment, when the defences are weak, by assault or by stratagem to seize the last inner stronghold of the constitutional citadel. The government therefore is right in its policy I would say, of no *more* surrenders, no *more* constitutional privileges, and, I would add, no more land or immigration for the settlers until a proper survey has been made of the native economy and the native labour which must serve them.

It is for the settlers to call off the assault; for them to say if they will accept the system as defined by the Imperial Government. In recent years the government has in some ways consolidated and improved the positions it has put up in defence of the other races. But I am not sure whether these defences are yet strong enough.

So when you ask me what the government should do about the settlers, I would rather say they should continue their policy of "thus far and no farther" to their advance, and go on righting the balance in favour of the other races, and especially, of course, of the three million Africans. Any settlers who cannot accept this check to their attempt to dominate, which will do no injury at all to their personal security and prosperity, should move to a country where the conditions allow them the full citizenship to which their tradition have accustomed them, but which Kenya conditions make impossible. No pledge was ever made—it could not constitutionally have been made—to them that they should have domination over the other races. They have already won, by their abilities, great influence. The onus, it seems to me, is now upon them, to show how their special position can be adjusted to the right of the other less privileged, less vocal groups, to advance in their turn.

To sum up, then, I can't accept the drastic "either-or" that runs through your letter. These uncompromising alternatives are effective in argument but man's political life is not like that. There is a middle road for the settlers between domination and ruin. When you say "a place must be found for them in the design of an East African future," I reply that a place *has* been found for them, a very privileged, favourable and influential place, even if it falls short of their large and determined political ambitions. I do not understand you when you suggest in forcible terms that there is something oppressive or unnatural about the settlers continuing to occupy this place and it appears that in this I am sharing the view of the Government and people of this country.

Yours sincerely,
Margery Perham

Miriam Wandai
WHEN OGRES LIVED

Kenya 1946   English [Luluhya]

Miriam Wandai was born at Butere in western Kenya in about 1913, into the family of a well-known, polygamous medicine man. She was already teaching in the part-time school for women and girls on the Church Missionary Society Mission Station at Butere when Miss Lee Appleby (who would later become deaconess) arrived there in 1931. Wandai became one of the first young women in the area to receive teacher training. She remained a devout Christian, close to the mainstream Anglican Church, for the rest of her life. Wandai chose never to marry—not because she felt a particular vocation to remain single, but because none of the proposals brought to her family came up to her standards. She repeatedly had to pay dowry for her brothers to avoid being married off. In later life, she would say, "I praise the Lord for my old age and for my virginity."

By contemporary standards, Miriam Wandai was not highly trained, but many professional people remember the patience with which she taught them to read Oluluyia and Kiswahili. She worked in Butere, Kisumu, Nairobi, and Kericho. She was also in great demand as a speaker in Christian women's meetings far from her home. She built a house and shop in Butere for her retirement and died there in 1969. One of her brothers offered a burial site at his homestead, since members of the clan on whose land the Butere Church was constructed would not allow the churchyard burial she had desired.

The story of Shilikhaya and Nabwende comes from a volume of folk stories Wandai compiled for the Church Missionary Society's Highway Press, later translated into English and published as *When Ogres Lived* by East Africa Educational Publishers.

Marjorie Oludhe Macgoye

✦

Ogres had eaten up all human beings in the land. There were, however, two people who had survived the onslaught. They were brother and sister, who had successfully stayed in hiding. The boy was called Shilikhaya and the girl Nabwende.

One day, as they sat by the fire in the evening, they talked about their future. Shilikhaya, now an energetic young man, said to his sister, "My dear sister. I am getting on in age. Should I want to get married, whom shall I marry, now that beasts have eaten up all the young women in the land?"

Nabwende thought about this for a while before saying, "Yes, my dear brother, I have also been thinking about this matter. It is quite clear to me that I too cannot get someone to marry me, since all the young men have been eaten up."

For many days, they thought about this question. At last they decided that the only way out was for them to wed each other. "We have no choice in this matter," they said. "We just have to wed each other."

They started to make wedding arrangements. Although there would be no other people to witness their marriage ceremony, they still wanted to have a proper wedding. Finally all the plans were in place.

But on the eve of their planned wedding, their house caught a mysterious fire while they slept. Shilikhaya was the first to wake up. The house was alight with bright flames and full of suffocating smoke. Quickly, he shook his sister into wakefulness. They tried to run out of the burning house but failed. The fire had already engulfed the whole place, including the only exit from the house.

Sister and brother were eventually overcome and they collapsed in the hungry flames, as they struggled for breath. Soon the roof of the house caved in and covered them in a painful death.

Not long afterwards the rains came. Soon the whole place was full of fresh tendrils and other plants, pleasant to the eye. In the midst of this, a strange thing happened. Nabwende and Shilikhaya who had been killed in a house fire now sprouted into good to behold vegetables! Shilikhaya grew into *olusaaka* while Nabwende grew into *libokoyi*.

Unknown to Shilikhaya and Nabwende, there was another part of the country where some other people had survived the Ogres' onslaught. Among these people, there lived a man called Omuliebi. Omuliebi was a polygamous man. Among his many wives was one by the name Omukumba. Now Omukumba was barren. She had visited medicineman after medicineman and diviner after diviner, but none of their prescriptions gave her a child. At last Omukumba gave up on child-bearing.

One day, Omukumba went out to look for vegetables to eat with her *obusuma* in the evening. It so happened that the rains had failed and the whole country was now dry and dusty. The only edible vegetable one could occasionally come across was a white shrub called *eshilietso*. Omukumba walked from place to place with her vegetable basket but found nothing, not even *eshilietso*.

She soon realized that she had wandered too far. She was about to turn back when she discovered that she was in a deserted homestead. She noticed the leftovers of a house which must have been burnt down by fire.

Walking towards the remnants of the house, she was pleasantly surprised to see two stalks of vegetables dancing to the tune of the evening wind. It was a truly strange sight to behold in those dry days. "Oh my God!" Omukumba marvelled. "Am I not in for a truly satisfying meal! Who would have thought that such healthy *okusaaka* and *libokoyi* existed anywhere?"

She uprooted everything and carried it home in her basket. When she got home, she showed her vegetables to the other women in the homestead. They were all surprised to see such healthy looking vegetables in those lean days.

"Where did you get such good vegetables?" one of them asked.

"Oh, out there, where I went searching," Omukumba said.

"I wonder whether someone could have grown such healthy vegetables!" another one ventured.

"I found them in the leftovers of a burnt house," replied Omukumba.

"They are too healthy," said another one. "They must have grown on the heads of the dead."

When Omukumba had finished cooking her vegetables, she tasted a little to see whether they were ready. She found that they were extremely bitter. She added a bit of water to them and boiled them a little longer. But when she tasted them again, she was surprised that they were even more bitter than before.

"I wonder what could be happening to my vegetables!" she said to herself.

Omukumba called in two of her co-wives and related to them the strange story of the bitter vegetables. They advised her to remove them from the fire and keep them in her granary overnight. This, they said, would make the vegetables less bitter the following day.

The following day, Omukumba went to her granary, very early in the morning, anxious to see whether her vegetables tasted less bitter. When she uncovered the pot, she was shocked to see not her vegetables but two strange creatures, closely cuddled together.

She broke into strange sweat, wondering what was happening. "Oh my God! Have my ancestors cursed me? Or else, what are these strange happenings?" she marvelled. Afterwards, her co-wives came to her and enquired about the vegetables. "How come you haven't given us any of your vegetables?" they asked.

"Oh well, they're all finished," Omukumba said rather quickly. "Besides, you would not have liked them. They were extremely bitter."

"Still, you should have let us give them a try. Aren't you just mean and selfish?"

"No, I'm telling you the truth. None of you would have liked those bitter vegetables," she said, becoming slightly annoyed.

"How can we be choosers of what we should eat in these difficult times? Do we have vegetable gardens of our own?" said one of the co-wives.

The following day, Omukumba visited the granary once again. She was shocked to see that the strange creatures had now become two tiny babies—a boy and a girl. "This must be the work of the spirits of the dead," she said to herself.

All this while, Omukumba did not say a word to anybody about these strange things. She feared that if anyone should get to know about these things, they would laugh at her and make mockery of her for having found little goblins in her cooking pot.

Once again Omukumba visited the granary. She saw that the children had grown bigger. They could hardly fit in the small vegetable pot! She also saw that the children were very good looking. "Perhaps it's the sun and our God, Wele, who have given me these children. Perhaps they would like to take the shame of childlessness from my face. Or maybe these characters are just the spirits of the dead sent to me by my dead ancestors to torment me."

While she reflected on this, the children smiled at her. Once again she saw how pleasant they looked. "Surely they have been sent to me by Wele and the sun."

She fetched two giant calabashes and put one child into each.

On another occasion, she found that the children were now too big to fit in the calabashes. She saw how big and good looking they were. She desired to carry them in her arms and hug them. But she feared what people would say, should they see the children. What she feared most was the question, "Where did you get these children?"

She could hardly sleep at night. She spent the whole night turning and tossing, wondering what she would do. She longed to carry and bathe her two children.

The following day she secretly moved them from the granary into her house, where she lived alone. She put them in a huge pot in one of the innermost chambers of her house. She made a daily programme which allowed her enough time to attend to her children. She would always wait until there was nobody else about the place, then she would bring out her lovely children, bathe them, feed them, hug them and play with them to her satisfaction.

And so the years rolled on. Omukumba had found a perfect way of dealing with her lovely children without anyone else getting to know about their existence. This way, Shilikhaya developed into a handsome young man while his sister, Nabwende, grew into a bouncing beautiful maiden.

One day, as an Ogre was passing close by Omukumba's house, he saw Nabwende taking a bath behind her mother's house. "My goodness!" he said to himself. "Who would have thought that such a beautiful girl lived in this home? I must come back, some day, to ask for her hand in marriage."

Not long afterwards the Ogre turned himself into a handsome young man and came visiting Nabwende's home. He was warmly received by the young men in the home, who welcomed him into their huts, *tsisimba*, and chatted with him over this and that.

After talking on many issues and eating and drinking, the Ogre eventually came to the point that had brought him. "Good people, I wish to relate to you what has brought me here," he said.

"We are listening," his hosts answered.

"I wish to ask for the hand in marriage to one of the girls in this home," he went on.

Since the young visitor had so far impressed his hosts, they were pleased at these tidings. They thought it would be good for him to marry one of the girls.

In those days, girls did not have much say on whom they married. They simply married whoever their parents approved of. And so all the girls in Omuliebi's homestead were summoned together so that the visitor could say who among them he wished to marry.

After carefully looking at each of the girls in turn, the Ogre reported with disappointment that the girl he desired was not among those gathered.

"Oh, well," said his hosts, "These are all the daughters of this home. Perhaps you saw the girl you wish to marry elsewhere."

The Ogre went away a very disappointed person. But he came back after a few days to report that he had once again seen the girl he wished to marry. Everyone was perplexed. They did their best to convince the young suitor that he was mistaken, but he would not listen to them. Eventually, fed up with him, they asked him to show them the house behind which he had seen the girl bathing.

"That one," he said, pointing at Omukumba's house.

Now everyone was convinced that this suitor was thoroughly mistaken. Or, perhaps, he was mad. "There is no child in that house," the owner of the homestead said. "You must have seen a visitor."

But the Ogre insisted, "There is a boy and a girl who live in that house. I have seen them with my own eyes, more than once."

"My friend," said Omuliebi. "I think you are out of your mind. Ever since I married the woman who lives in that house, many years ago, she has never had a single child. Quite honestly, I don't understand what you are talking about. I think you need help. You must be sick."

Meanwhile Omukumba was getting worried. She moved closer to the Ogre and rebuked him saying, "Young man, why have you come here to make mockery of me? Am I the only barren woman on earth? Please, stop there. Enough is enough."

For several nights thereafter, Omukumba could not sleep. She kept on turning and tossing, lamenting at her ill fortune. "Oh my God!" she said. "After many agonizing years of childlessness our God, Wele, remembered me. But now comes this troublesome young man. What does he want of me!"

But the Ogre didn't give up his quest for the beautiful Nabwende. Every few days he would come over and renew his request. But he always met the same answer. Finally the owners of the home decided to ignore him altogether. This saddened and angered him greatly. He started thinking of the best way to punish them so that they may at last give in to his request.

"If I should hide under the sea and dry up all the water bodies in the land and cause a terrible drought, it may just happen that mankind will suffer heavily that they will finally force this man to give me the girl I want?" he said to himself.

And so he got into the sea and settled at the very bottom. Soon, the sea started disappearing and the sun became increasingly oppressive and unbearable. Rivers and lakes started drying up too. Even the smallest streams and ponds dried up. The sun became increasingly scorching and unbearable. All the grass dried up. Man and animal alike had nothing to drink. There was hardly anything to eat. Animals started dying in large numbers. The smell of death filled the air.

People got very worried. They could see death staring them in the eye. They decided to do something about it. They went to the greatest diviner in the land, Akamanya, to find out what they must do to overcome this catastrophe.

After consulting and communing with the mysterious world, Akamanya announced that the suffering in the land had been caused by an irate Ogre who had gone to stay at the bottom of the sea after failing to marry the girl he desired. The diviner reported further that the Ogre had once seen the girl bathing behind her mother's house and that although he had made repeated visits to her home, her father had insisted that he had no such daughter. And so the entire human race must perish because of the Ogre's wrath. When it became known who this man was, it was decided that a delegation should be sent to persuade him to give the Ogre the girl he wanted. Much as Omuliebi tried to convince them that he had no such daughter, they kept on coming back to him to plead with him to take pity on them and their emaciated animals.

At last, fed up with the tragedy that had befallen his homestead, Omuliebi took one of his daughters and went with her to what had once been the sea shore. When he got there he sang in a tremulous voice

> *Shili mwalo, shili mwalo*
> *Hamba, omukhana ngwuno*
> *Hamba, omukhana ngwuno*
> *Umbe khumatsi ing'ombe yinywe.*

which means

> You who lives under water, you who lives under water,
> Come, here is a girl
> Come, here is a girl
> Please give me some water for my cow.

But the Ogre replied:

> *Oyo ni mulamwa*
> *Oyo ni mulamwa*
> *Nanga nabwende ing'ombe yinywe.*

which means

> That one is my sister in-law
> That one is my sister in-law
> Give me Nabwende and the cow shall have water to drink.

The man brought all his daughters to the Ogre, but he achieved nothing. With no more daughters left, he even brought his sons but the result was the same. Finally he decided to offer the Ogre his wives. Again the Ogre turned them all down. He even brought all his animals to the sea but he still achieved nothing.

Meanwhile it was getting drier and drier. People and animals were now dying in even larger numbers. Everyday was a burial day. Everyone was very unhappy with Omuliebi.

"What is wrong with this man?" they asked. "Doesn't he have a single grain of sympathy in his veins? Why does he let our people and animals die in hundreds everyday? Why can't he take his daughter to the Ogre and save us all?"

Some suggested that they should threaten him with death. "Let us go to him and tell him that we shall put him to death if he continues being stubborn. Maybe that way, he will give in and bring out this girl," they said.

Once again they visited his homestead early the next morning. After much argument, during which Omuliebi tried to assure them that he had no children besides the ones he had already taken to the Ogre, it was agreed that all his houses should be ransacked without further delay.

The assembled people divided themselves into several search parties and soon the search was on. It did not take long for a team which had been assigned Omukumba's house to come out with a young man and a very beautiful girl. The children looked as if they were duplicates. Never before had the people of this land seen such dazzling beauty.

Everyone was dumbfounded. They confronted Omukumba's husband, seeking an explanation to all this. "Tell us," the leader to the delegation said. "Why have you been cheating us all this time, while knowing very well that you were hiding these two there?"

Omuliebi was completely lost for words. He did not know whether to marvel at the beauty of the two children, or at the fact that they had always lived in his home without the slightest knowledge on his part. He simply stared at Omukumba, wondering what she could have been up to all this while.

Eventually the people decided that the girl should instantly be taken to the Ogre. But her brother intervened saying, "No! She shall be taken to the Ogre tomorrow and not today."

He told them to take word to the Ogre that his new bride would be given to him in marriage the following day. "But tell him that the girl shall not be taken to him in the sea bed where he lives. He should instead come to the Eshikulu cliff where he will find his girl waiting for him."

Having waited for many long and dry months, they did not see why they should not wait for one more day. "What difference will it make anyway?" they said.

A messenger was immediately dispatched to the Ogre with the good news about his impending meeting with Nabwende the following morning. So pleased was he to receive the news that he decided to give people a little water. Soon clouds began gathering. Everywhere lightning started flashing and thunder rolling.

In no time the place was awash with floods. It rained so heavily that even the oldest man in the land said he could not remember ever having seen such rain and so much water.

Early the following morning, Nabwende was led to the cliff where she would meet her new husband, the Ogre. She wept frantically, but her brother tried to console her saying, "Do not cry, my dear sister. Whatever eats you must eat me first."

And they walked on in the midst of the escort party to the cliff. Shilikhaya had fashioned a bow and made hooked, double-pronged arrows which he carried with him.

Meanwhile Omuliebi walked to the sea where he called out to the Ogre.

You who lives under water
You who lives under water
Come, here is Nabwende
Please give me some water for my cow.

The Ogre was overjoyed to hear that they had brought him Nabwende, at last. He hurriedly rushed out of the sea, dancing and running about the place as if he was possessed. He did a little dance and threw his staff skyward. Immediately, the heavens opened up and it was soon raining, more than the day before. The Ogre took no notice of the rain. He ran on up to the cliff to meet the girl he so much desired.

When the Ogre was only a few metres away from Nabwende, Shilikhaya, who was hiding in an opening in the cliff unleashed the first arrow at him. It struck him in the back. As he slipped down the cliff he asked in surprise, "What has stung me? Where could it be hiding?"

All this time Nabwende was weeping uncontrollably. For the third time, the Ogre tried to climb up the cliff. This time round, the arrow got him squarely in the chest. He completely lost his grip and came tumbling down the cliff. Shilikhaya shot more arrows into him. The Ogre was now unable to rise up. Eventually, he collapsed and died from his wounds.

Shilikhaya helped his sister down the cliff and led her back home. There, they found their mother almost dying of a broken heart. That same day, Omukumba moved away from Omuliebi's homestead with her children and set up a new home far away.

Translated by Barrack O. Muluka

C.M. binti Hassan
AN AFRICAN MARRIES A WHITE THROUGH MERE WORLDLY DESIRES

Tanzania 1946   Kiswahili

This Kiswahili poem discusses one of the major social issues of the colonial period in East Africa, that of interracial marriages.

Racial socialization or intermixing during colonialism was not acceptable-hence intermarriage often led to the alienation of the couple from social contacts or tension with in-laws and relatives. Interracial marriages were also, inevitably, shaped by colonial-era racism. To begin with, the terms were one sided: foreign men, including not only Europeans but Indians and Arabs, married black African women, but African men could not marry foreign women. And as the author makes clear in her poem, African women and their relatives were likely to be treated as inferior beings.

The poem appeared in a Kiswahili newspaper, *Mambo Leo*, a colonial periodical established by the British government in 1923. The periodical did much to promote writing in Kiswahili. Like most Kiswahili papers then and now, *Mambo Leo* had a poets' page on which poets could publish their poems, usually debating pertinent issues of the day in true Kiswahili dialogic tradition. C. M. binti Hassan's poem appeared in the September 1946 issue. When she writes, in the first stanza, "Today I wish you to consider this matter," she is inviting fellow poets to respond, and several did, supporting or opposing her point of view.

There is no available information about the author of the poem, nor have any other poems by her been located. Her full name is not given; we only have the initials C.M., followed by her father's name. But her address appears after her signature: "N.A. School, Nyonga, Tabora." She may well have been a teacher at a primary school in Tabora. The poem is written in traditional tarbia quatrains, still the most popular Kiswahili verse form. This type of rhyming verse has sixteen syllables per line, divided into eight-syllable hemistiches (called *vipande*), and four lines per stanza.

This poem may be viewed in the context of black African awakening in the 1940s, exhibiting an increasing distrust and cynicism toward white colonists, and chastising those Africans who allow themselves to be coopted or mistreated by whites for the sake of material gain, or "mere worldly desires."

M.M. Mulokozi

✦

1. Lots of greetings to you, Africans,
Christians and Muslims, all those in the city.
Today I wish you to consider this matter:
An African marries a white through mere worldly desires.

2. I have read in the gazette, I have seen the arguments
Of these foreign people marrying Africans.

I thought it was curious that such acts should make sense:
An African marries a white through mere worldly desires.

3. The African women should never marry a foreigner.
You pretend to be ticks with no brains in your heads.
Better to eat jack-fruit, which is beneficial to the body.
An African marries a white through mere worldly desires.

4. To claim that the African cares little for his wife at home,
That things go wrong because of wrangling in the households:
I am writing these things for you to keep in your minds.
An African marries a white through mere worldly desires.

5. You will see these shameful things in towns,
Especially acts by Arabs—they are unspeakable!
When the grandfather comes, he is invited only onto the veranda.
An African marries a white through mere worldly desires.

6. You never see the father, the siblings, and the relatives.
You stay indoors silent, gazing through the window.
This happens to us because of greed; we place ourselves in slavery.
An African marries a white through mere worldly desires.

7. You say it is proper to get married; I do not oppose that.
One never questions what God advises.
Now, and even before, separation was never ordained.
An African marries a white through mere worldly desires.

8. Try and go to India, there is no daughter of so-and-so.
On the Asian continent, no daughter of so-and-so.
Even in Russia, no daughter of so-and-so.
An African marries a white through mere worldly desires.

9. You turn God, our Creator, into a fool
For having created different groups in the world.
Comrades, if you are lost, you are shaming us.
An African marries a white through mere worldly desires.

10. To marry an African is twenty times better.
He would bury your elders—that is what is important.
When you prosper, you may forget your native culture.
An African marries a white through mere worldly desires.

11. Let's say you are married to that foreign man
And tea and coffee are not available
When your relatives come from home to visit you.
An African marries a white through mere worldly desires.

12. In your mother's home it is an honor to invite guests into the store room:
Can we say it is a good thing to be isolated like a baboon?
Such occurrences are not hearsay—I have witnessed them myself.
An African marries a white through mere worldly desires.

13. Visitors are made to sleep on mats in the shop,
While the host sleeps on the bed and the master in the bedroom.
The visitor's toilet is the bush—morning and evening.
An African marries a white through mere worldly desires.

14. Neither your father nor your uncle is allowed in the sitting room.
That's the sitting arrangement you wanted.
As a result you never see relatives coming to visit you.
An African marries a white through mere worldly desires.

15. I want a learned person to respond to me in public.
Let him or her not speculate but speak honestly with certainty.
Say that you are after the goods in the shop.
An African marries a white through mere worldly desires.

16. I have yet to see an African marry an Arab girl
Or a young African an Indian.
Do not merely argue; weigh the issues carefully in your minds.
An African marries a white through mere worldly desires.

17. The fault, you know, lies among parents in the homes:
Filled with greed, they place us in bondage.
When you bear a child—to which country will it belong?
An African marries a white through mere worldly desires.

18. If it comes to Africa, we say it is an Indian;
When it reaches India, they say it is an African.
Which tribe should it belong to, in which tribe be named?
An African marries a white through mere worldly desires.

19. Greetings to all in Ujiji, all the youth in the town.
I am not squandering my words—do weigh them carefully.
I am expecting you to tell me the real truth.
An African marries a white through mere worldly desires.

20. Two numbers, twenty stanzas, I stop here in print.
I am not a newcomer, though I am a visitor.
If I am attacked on the head, I will strike facial blows.
An African marries a white through mere worldly desires.

Translated by Martha Qorro and M.M. Mulokozi

Nyense Namwandu
FIGHTING FOR WIDOWS' PROPERTY AND THE RIGHT TO REFUSE MARRIAGE

Uganda 1947   Luganda

Nyense Namwandu was a subsistence farmer resident in Kalama Village, in the Kyamuliibwa area of Kalungu County in Masaka District. Though a widow, Nyense Namwandu was still of childbearing age when she wrote her letter of complaint in 1947. She admits in her letter that she is younger than some of her late husband's children, including his son Ntonio, who wanted to take her as his own wife "on behalf of the clan." Clearly, then, she had been married to Ntonio's father in his later years as a second, third, or even fourth wife.

The widow's two names are revealing. Namwandu is more of a title, a formalization of the widowed status of the woman, than it is a personal name, although it is often used as such. Nyense Namwandu probably used it deliberately to indicate acceptance of her widowed status and her refusal of Ntonio or any other man. Nyense, on the other hand, is a Lugandan form of Agnes as pronounced in French (just as Ntonio is the Lugandan form of Anthony). Nyense Namwandu had been baptized at a Catholic mission, run by the French-speaking White Fathers. Since literacy was a necessary requirement for baptism, Nyense must also have received a mission education.

Nyense Namwandu's strategy of bypassing the conspiring local chiefs, to make her appeal to a higher authority and to put her complaint on the public record, testifies to the new awareness modern education had aroused in Baganda women. She knew that it would be difficult for the authorities to ignore or snub her plea, especially as she had put it on record, and kept a copy to boot. Her appeal to the subcounty chief, a kind of medium-range administrator, signals that she is prepared to take her case to the highest levels of the administration if necessary. As it turned out, the case was decided in Nyense Namwandu's favor. She was neither evicted from her land nor required to marry Ntonio.

Though not frequently discussed, the practice of widow inheritance by a brother or a cousin of the deceased was, apparently, widespread in Kiganda society, as in many other African communities. The unusual twist in Nyense Namwandu's case is that the person seeking to inherit her was her stepson. Apparently, because of the polygamous nature of the society, sons of the deceased were sometimes allowed to inherit young widows who might not yet have had children. In Nyense Namwandu's case, however, she had had children with Nto-nio's father, so any intimate relationship with him would be clearly incestuous. Nyense Namwandu's analysis of the situation rightly identifies Ntonio's intentions as manifestly sexist and oppressive. He concludes that she has not had children with his father because her offspring are girls, whom the patriarchy does not regard as "real children." Threatening to evict her from her home is obviously a ploy to force her into the liaison.

The officials whom Nyense Namwandu mentions as conspiring with Ntonio against her reside in the lowest echelons of the Baganda administrative hierarchy, preserved through most of the colonial period and beyond. They range from the village through the parish and subcounty to the county and ultimately to the regional supreme ruler, the *kabaka* or king. Above the *kabaka* was of course the colonial administration, replaced in the post-independence era by the central government.

Austin Bukenya and Abasi Kiyimba

✦

Kalama, Kyamuliibwa
Kalungu, Buddu
19th March 1947
To the Sub-County Chief
Dear Honoured One,
I am writing to you to make an appeal on the matter of my son, my late husband's son, Ntonio Zebalaba, who wants to evict me from the land which my late husband left me, because I have refused to marry him.

Ntonio says that since I had not produced a male child when my husband died, he should inherit me and I produce a male child for the clan. Although this practice was used among the Baganda of long ago, it is now not proper because female children are also people. Ntonio may be older than me, but my children are his true sisters, because they are his father's children.

Ntonio says that if I do not marry him, I should leave the land where my husband left me. Where should I go with my children?

We have sat through this matter at the court of the village and the parish chiefs, but they seem to be in support of him because he is their friend. That is why I have decided to appeal to you.

I am,
Nyense Namwandu

Translated by Abasi Kiyimba

Z and G
WOMEN ARE HUMAN BEINGS

Tanzania 1950   Kiswahili

This is a petition written by two prostitutes on behalf of a larger group, protesting the measures taken by local authorities in Bukoba, Tanzania, in the late 1940s, attempting to stop them from traveling outside the district. The petition, addressed to the District Commissioner in November 1950, was a response to a two-year smear campaign against the Bahaya women, who had been traveling regularly to the urban centers of Kampala, Nairobi, Mombasa, and Dar es Salaam allegedly to serve as sex workers. These trips angered the conservative male establishment, including the Bakama Council (the council of chiefs), who claimed that the women were harming the good reputation of the Bahaya community.

Prostitution on a large scale began in the region at the turn of the nineteenth century, following the establishment of colonial rule and its accompanying commercialization. Colonial *bomas*, or homesteads, had numerous single men who served as *askaris* (soldiers and police), porters, or casual workers, and these provided a ready market for enterprising women prostitutes. White officials and traders, and even some missionaries, were also known to enjoy their services. The rapid rise of prostitution was facilitated by customs and laws that prohibited women from inheriting or owning clan land. Thus widowed or divorced women found themselves destitute, many resorting to prostitution as the only alternative left short of taking church vows.

By the 1940s, Bahaya women could be found in all large cities of East Africa. Many of these women returned annually to Bukoba laden with presents for their parents and relatives, and some with enough money to buy banana *shambas* (plots of land), build houses, and even pay for the education of siblings and their own children. Such economic success stories were seen as bad examples for other women, some of whom left marriages to work in prostitution.

The hostility of the male establishment toward these women prompted the measures taken against them. One such measure prohibited women to travel by steamer—the major means of travel across Lake Victoria. Those who broke this rule were stopped and sometimes abused at the port. The women reacted by mobilizing their vast East African network to oppose the measures. Women in Nairobi, Mwanza, Dar es Salaam, and elsewhere hired lawyers to defend their rights. Initially the District Commissioner supported the restrictions on women, but the Provincial Commissioner eventually ordered the district to withdraw its support because the actions were illegal. The women's protests succeeded, and the illegal order was rescinded in 1951.

M.M. Mulokozi

✦

Sir,

We women are human beings like the men. God created us all to assist each other, men and women. Now for about 2 years we see that we women are returning to slavery. You Europeans came to help us to completely finish slavery so everybody should get freedom.

When the men instituted the laws to forbid us to go abroad to find work to help ourselves and our parents, the law was brought to you and to our rulers to be accepted. But we were not called to any meeting to be asked why we go abroad rather than staying at home, and what problems sent us there. We hear our opponents saying that we go because of prostitution (*Umalaya*). This word is an insult to us. If we are called prostitutes, can a woman make herself a prostitute on her own? First of all, is not a prostitute the man who gave us the money? . . . They do not think of that.

It would be better to forbid the men to travel, because they let their coffee plantations fall into decay or they sell the plantations which they have been entrusted by their fathers and go and make mischief. When we return home we buy the plantations of those scoundrels. The drunkards do not know how to take care of the plantations they have gotten from their fathers. The men do not know how to treat their wives well. When a man sells coffee he divides up the shilling in two parts—to get drunk and to give to someone who has done nothing for the money he gives away for fornication. Perhaps he sends you, his wife, to bring him his money order; if you refuse you will be beaten and chased away, because you do not follow orders. It is difficult to talk about our lives together with our men. We endure for the sake of our children.

Now we ask you, sir, to give the order to our council that we may discuss with our husbands and parents. The person whom it is necessary to forbid to travel may be stopped. The one who has the right to go may be allowed, but do not despise us because we are women. Even if we are women, our fathers and our husbands ought to thank us, because the plantations we have bought would have been taken otherwise by foreigners like the Rwandese and tribes outside Bukoba.

We ask for your mercy to meet with you, since we are beaten and chased away at the harbour, as if we are animals. We are sorry when we see that women do not get the protection of our sacred government.

We are the humble and obedient Z and G, your children from Kiziba.

Translated by Birgitta Larsson

Bibi Pirira Athumani
TWO POEMS

Tanzania 1950s   Kiswahili

Pirira Athumani was born at a fishing village near Tanga in 1920, and passed away in 2002. Tanga is a Swahili town with a largely Islamic culture and a long tradition of literacy (in Arabic script) and literature. Many distinguished Tanzanian writers of the nineteenth and twentieth centuries (including Hemed Abdallah and Shaaban Robert) lived and worked there. The German colonialists turned it into a center of the sisal industry. Tanga's now waning prosperity was based on this industry.

Athumani grew up in Tanga, but had no opportunity to go to school. She thus acquired literacy as an adult. She married several times, but did not have children. Like many other African women, however, she had ample opportunity to raise several generations of her relatives' and probably co-wives' children. Her poem "The Stepmother" is thus based on her own experience.

In many traditional tales, the stepmother is usually depicted as a demon, a tyrannical, cruel, and greedy woman. Hence the Kiswahili saying "*Mama wa kambo si mama*"—"The stepmother is no mother." Yet many children are brought up by stepmothers, and many have only fond memories of them. Athumani, herself brought up by a stepmother, was to become a stepmother in turn. In this poem, Athumani directly addresses her listeners, and especially her fellow poets, arguing against the traditional stereotype of the stepmother. The poem—in the traditional tarbia or quatrain form—falls within the Swahili sung poetry tradition. Athumani might have sung it at public occasions or dance events, and other interested poets would have replied in the same mode.

In "Love Has No Cure," Athumani compares love to juju, or magic. The content of the poem derives from the common belief in Africa that love can be induced, controlled, or maintained through the use of the occult. This widespread belief has often been a source of suffering, especially for women. Seeking to ensure that they do not lose the affection of their lovers or husbands, especially in polygamous households, women sometimes squander their meager resources on the *waganga* (witch doctor, or traditional healer), who claim to have the love potions or medicine they need. Quite often, such women lose their husbands or lovers as soon as their dealings with the *waganga* are discovered. Likewise, some men also go to such doctors for similar reasons.

In this cynical and humorous song, Pirira castigates such beliefs and practices, claiming that there is no love medicine save the language one speaks to a partner. Athumani's view is, in her context, quite unorthodox and very progressive.

Athumani herself was married into a polygamous household, and for a time suffered utter neglect from her last husband, who favored his younger wife. She later left him, and by the time he realized his loss, it was too late; she was unwilling to return to him. Her experience may have inspired this poem.

The poem is in song measure; the lines are uneven and depend on the melody of the song. The short lines, comprising the solo and chorus, have eight syllables each.

Athumani has long been a renowned dance singer and storyteller with a very large repertoire. Her recorded songs are preserved in the archives of the Institute of Kiswahili Research at the University of Dar es Salaam. While these songs were recorded in 1991, they were composed earlier; "The Stepmother" is known to have been composed in the 1950s.

M.M. Mulokozi

◆

THE STEPMOTHER

I begin in the name of Allah, I want to join the dance
Nor have I any hindrance; please bear with me, you poets
It is rice and coconut it pains me, chew on it:
Not all stepmothers are bad; the heart of each is different.

The heart of each is different; all stepmothers are not the same.
Not all grab the income so that it goes nowhere.
That is only a practice of some—as of Mashaka and Kilokote:
Not all stepmothers are bad; the heart of each is different.

I tell you, experts, leave jokes aside
Of the left and on the right, explore all.
It only happens with some people; it is not the case with all women:
Not all stepmothers are bad; the heart of each is different.

I saw Wadia; she loved all the children,
Cooking for them, tea, meat, and bread,
And when a child cried, she would say, "Bring it here."
Not all stepmothers are bad; the heart of each is different.

For instance, this Sofia, she should love all the children,
Yet she slaps the child on the head, the arms, and everywhere.
By every means, reducing the child to a mere reed.
Not all stepmothers are bad; the heart of each is different.

Now let us turn to this Amina—she loves the whole group.
She pours her treasures into all the shops
Of the Banianis and the Chinese, so as to dress and adorn the kids fully.
Not all stepmothers are bad; the heart of each is different.

Bye-bye, I tell you, let us not quarrel or dispute.
Now I put down the pen, for all the ink has dried up.
Don't accuse me of fleeing; I am always here.
Not all stepmothers are bad; the heart of each is different.

Love has no cure, except on your tongue.
I warn you, end your arrogance or you will sleep alone.

Solo: If you are a healer,
           Heal your uncle.

Chorus: If you are a witch,
           Bewitch your aunt.

You will use up all the herbs in destroying others.
We know you, we let you make a habit of it, and we let you squander your
    money.

Love has no cure, except on your tongue.
I warn you, end your arrogance or you will sleep alone.

Solo: If you are a healer,
           Heal your uncle.

Chorus: If you can do magic,
           Spin it on your aunt.

You will use up all the herbs in destroying others.
We know you, we let you make a habit of it, and we let you squander your
    money.

Translated by M.M. Mulokozi

Communal
GIDMAY: FAREWELL TO A BRIDE

Tanzania 1950s   Iraqw

The Iraqw people, thought to have originally migrated south from Ethiopia, are
concentrated in north central Tanzania. Gidmay is a traditional song that is sung
to a bride by age mates from her village on the day they bid her farewell as she
departs for her groom's home.

In the Iraqw community, a wedding ceremony lasts a whole week, and sometimes longer. Preparations for the ceremony normally include painting and drawing on the walls of both the groom's and bride's homes with different colors,
mostly white, black, and red. (White is obtained from ashes, black from soot or

charcoal, and red from ochre.) For several days and nights, various groups sing in praise or reproach of the bride or the groom, depending on which side the singers come from. On the groom's side, age mates and relatives, mostly young men, sing praise songs for the groom, such as, "You're a lion who has brought home a buffalo," or, "You're a kite [or an eagle] and have brought home a chick [or dove]." On the bride's side, age mates and relatives, mostly young girls, sing songs like this one. They lament the bride's departure, provide some words of warning for the bride, and make a few sneering comments about the groom. The singers' insults are meant to be taken in good humor, and are sung with the knowledge that the groom will have praise poured on him when he gets back home with the bride beside him. The reference to the spider invokes the wish for the couple to bear many children. The Iraqw believe the spider is the insect which produces the highest number of offspring.

Gidmay is the generic name of the song. Gidmay and Lanta stand for the bridegroom and the bride. In actual singing, these names are replaced by those of the couple.

Martha Qorro

✦

1. Gidmay son of Da/ati, Gidmay the bulls are fighting.
Gidmay the bulls are fighting, in the land of *Masabeda*,
In *Masabeda* at the house of Tekwi Yawari.

2. Lanta, my dear, when I saw decorated walls, When I saw the decoration,
I thought this was done for mere beauty,
Thought it was for mere beauty, but I realize it's because you are leaving.

3. Be strong; that you have to leave is your parents' decision.
Be strong, even though you've been sprained while very young.
You've been given away very young, the spider of true color.

4. Had I been your parents you wouldn't go there.
I'm not your parents, what can we do?
My dear Lanta, be strong.

5. This distant stranger, why did you accept him?
Why did you accept him, this one with heels as rough as roof tiles?
This one with rough heels, like those of salt lake warthogs.

6. You have accepted a stranger; you've already accepted him.
You've accepted a stranger, whose back is covered with dirt scales,
Whose back is covered with dirt scales, like that of a hyena from Gorowa land.

7. The man you have accepted,
The man you have accepted has a back covered with dirt scales.

His back is covered with dirt scales, like the earth-roofed house of the cold
   uplands.

8. This stranger, what does he like best?
He is inclined to live on stale local beer,
To live on stale beer made from scum.

9. The spider of true color, my heart has sunk.
My heart has sunk, until my sweat dried
If my heart has sunk so much, what about those of your parents?

10. Daughter of our father, cry in your heart,
For the stranger of that family has no brothers.
He has no brothers in our midst, as he comes from the Hadza tribe.

11. My dear girl, cry in your heart.
Tell your father to give you a cow,
To give you a pregnant cow to keep.

12. Life is to be lived carefully, not in a hurry.
Living in the home of other people requires calm.
Life is not to be hurried, it is one step at a time.

13. If you take life with lust, you will face those sticks long stored on the roof,
The sticks full of dust; you'll think they are for herding calves,
But alas! They are for teaching you a lesson!

14. My dear Lanta, I am going back home.
I am going back home; I leave you in peace.
I leave you in peace; be strong.

Collected by Matle Akonaay
Translated by Martha Qorro and Yusuf Lawi

Mama Meli
FROM SLAVERY TO FREEDOM

Zambia 1950s   Chimambwe

Mama Meli's story was taken down by her grandson, H.E. Silanda, in the early
1950s, when he was a university student. He viewed his grandmother's account as
a family history that could also serve a cultural purpose. In publishing it in the

original Chimambwe, Silanda sought to enlarge the corpus of literature in Chimambwe, a language he feared would be lost owing to the adoption of Chibemba as the vernacular language of schooling throughout the Northern Province of Zambia—then still Northern Rhodesia. Mambwe country, which straddles the Tanzania-Zambia border, was in the nineteenth century hard-pressed by the aggressive Bemba from the south and itinerant long distance traders, both the Nyamwezi from west central Tanzania and the Muslim Arab-Swahili from the Zanzibar-dominated Indian Ocean coast.

Meli's story begins in a part of Mambwe country subordinated by Bemba chiefs, with her seizure as part of a penalty for a sexual transgression, adultery with a wife of the local Bemba chief, by her male relative. Her narrative of successive transfers and experiences at the hands of various owners is marked by a sense of her family's notability. Mwenya, as she was known before her baptism as Meli (Mary), let her owners know that she was a "princess" likely to be retrieved once her important relatives knew where she was. This consciousness counters the generalization that slaves became completely estranged from their kin. The combination of her good fortune in not being taken away from her own dialect zone and her eventual return to Mambwe country and recognition by her family must both be taken into consideration when assessing the construction of the narrative. It is also important to recognize that her account of her slavery and liberation would have become practiced early in her life after slavery, as a protégé in the mission community.

The later part of the autobiography provides an extremely unusual portrait of a Zambian woman in the context of the progressive elite in the colonial situation. She became first socialized into a Western way of life within a missionary household at the London Missionary Society's principal station in the region, Kawimbe. Then, upon her marriage to a Christian carpenter, she became subject to more traditionalist values. Following her husband's premature death during the influenza pandemic of 1918, she lost control over herself, her children, and the conjugal property that was inherited by her husband's family. Finally, she trained as a community welfare auxiliary in a new program inaugurated in the mid-1930s. Upon returning to Kawimbe, where her son was a teacher, she became one of the first female elders in the church. She survived a quarter of a century beyond the closure of this autobiography.

After its translation into English in the 1970s, her narrative became accessible to a much wider audience of Zambian women, who have sometimes spoken of their shock of recognition, in particular upon reading of Mama Meli's experience of being stripped of everything by her deceased husband's heirs.

Marcia Wright

✦

When we were at Nkulumwe I was only a small girl. Whenever the elders were seated together they talked about Ponde's warriors. Men at the *insaka* (the village meeting place) and women in small groups, near their homes, used to say, "Friends, can we not flee and seek refuge with the white people at Kawimbe? There we can live in real safety."

One day early in the morning people scattered, some going to get *masuku* in the bush because it was the period when *masuku* are ripe and fall from trees. Others had simply fled. Father had accompanied Mulama to Ndaela. My mother and I were still in bed because mother had a bad sore on her lower back. At dawn, mother sent me to ask for water from the house of Museo, Namwezi's grandmother. I took a cup. When I entered the house I found it empty and in disarray. *Masuku* fruit was scattered about, the bed mats were torn up and flies were buzzing all around. Then I thought to myself, where would the people of this house have gone? I searched the place and then ran back to tell mother all I had seen. She said to me, maybe they have gone to pick *masuku*. But I said it seemed strange that they would have destroyed their bed mats and scattered the *masuku* they had gathered only the morning before. Mother could not imagine where they had gone. As we were speaking, my elder brother's wife, Mulenga, came and beckoned to me. I went out and she whispered to me, "Tell my mother-in-law I would like to go into the bush to pick *masuku*." Mother agreed on condition that she first drew some water from the stream for us. Mulenga refused by shaking her shoulders and head, for it was not customary to speak to one's mother-in-law. Mother said, "Well, you may go, but come back early. Mwenya will fetch the water when the sun comes up."

Later I picked up a gourd and went to Melu and said to her, "Let us go to the stream to fetch water." Because her house was nearer to the river, my friend poured the water into an *nsembo* (water pot) and returned to the river without me. By the time I came out of our gateway I saw my friend returning from the river. I told her, "My friend, why did you leave me behind?" Without answering my question, she said, "Hurry up, go and fetch your water, you will find me here." I ran quickly and drew some water. When I had partly filled my gourd, I heard shots. I lifted the gourd and ran up the bank. I heard my friend shout, "Mwenya, hurry up! Be quick, let's go!" I thought perhaps she had seen a python. I became frightened and thought it might catch me. I had gone a little way when Melu said, "Mwenya, hurry up! It's an army, run lest we die." We fled following the little stream until we reached the place where it joins the Nku-lumwe River. We went into an abandoned village. As we were about to hide in thick elephant grass we saw three warriors running after us. My friend said, "Let us run." We heard these people shout, "Halt! Halt! Or else we will shoot you down." We stopped and they captured us. When they saw people fleeing from the village they stood and watched. I thought these men were only scaring us. I did not know who they really were. Among the people fleeing the village, because they were at a distance, I only recognized Kazata who once lived at Mpanda Lyapa, and one woman, the wife of Nkunkulusya. This woman surren-dered herself to the warriors because they had already killed her child. When she reached them she said, "Go ahead, kill me too! I want to follow my child." But they only pushed her forward saying, "Move! You dog!" They then took us to the village where my mother was detained.

When we came to where they had left my mother we found she had escaped. For this they said to thesmelves, "Let her go, with such a terrible wound she cannot walk far." When I heard that, I realized that they were talking about mother. I became very upset and put my hand over my mouth. We reached the gate. When I looked around I saw that the wife of my uncle Swata had been struck in her neck and killed. Her lameness must have been the reason. That is when I fully realized that these men were our enemies! When I looked over my shoulder I saw the severed head of uncle Kasinte, nearby. I shouted, "Ow! That is my uncle's head!"

Captured as Slaves

Just then they rushed, herding us together. They were wearing quivers at sides. Some were wearing skins. They took pots and chickens from the village as loot and tied them up with bark string. The adults among us had to carry them. We went as far as the village where Namuzewo the wife of Kasengele lived. It was deserted. We crossed the Sambwe stream and reached Simutowe's village at Cimbili where Mpande, now the village headman at Chipundu, lived.

When we reached the foot of a small hill, mothers became completely exhausted because they were carrying very heavy loads and at the same time had babies on their backs. Our captors then separated babies from their mothers, tied them into bundles like maize and hung them up on trees. Babies remained crying hysterically while their mothers were led away. We then climbed another hill and came to the place chosen for our overnight rest. Hunger said, "(I'll be) wherever you go!" Our captors wondered how to feed such a large crowd. Their leader said, "Roast maize for them to chew." They roasted the maize and beans but gave us only beans. You should have heard the sounds that we made: *kukutu, kukutu, kukutu*. We sounded like goats chewing maize. After we finished eating our beans, thirst also said, "(I'll be) wherever you go!" We asked for water from our captors. They said, "Where have you seen water? You may as well drink your own urine." We spent the night with dry throats.

Next day with the sun almost above our heads, we reached chief Ponde's village. That was when hunger nearly devoured us. The only food they gave us was made of boiled leaves of beans. One night, three days later, the older ones amongst us started to plan an escape. I started to cry and appealed, "You are not going to leave me behind, are you?" Ntawa said, "I will carry you on my back." Before cockcrow, Ntawa tied me to her back, and we slipped away. When day broke one of our captors found the house empty. He shouted, "The people have escaped!" They followed our trail and no sooner had we reached the thick bush than they caught up with us and threatened, "If you try to run we will shoot you!" We stopped still with nothing to say. Ntawa put me down. At this point they put all the older ones in yokes, with the exception of Zongoli and me, because we were young. They took us back to the village.

Two days later we were taken from the house where we had been held and put in a big house which had no verandah. It was very dirty, untidy and infested with bugs. It was horrible! All those confined in yokes were forced to sleep with them attached to their necks. Since two persons were held by a single yoke it was very hard for them to turn at night. Whenever one needed to go outside, the other had to go as well, even if he did not want to.

During the next two days the adults planned another escape, and we children wanted to go with them. They disapproved saying that it was our presence that had caused them to be recaptured. When we heard them say this we cried uncontrollably. I begged Ntawa, "My older sister, are you going to leave me behind?" She sadly told me, "Yes, I wouldn't have the energy to carry you and the grass is very tall." My friend Zongoli was slightly bigger, but she was ill and could not travel with them.

They then realised how difficult it was to move with yokes around their necks, and began to ask each other what to do. Ntawa said, "It is not difficult, I will show you what to do." Just as the cock crowed, they left. Ntawa helped them put the poles of the yokes on their shoulders and they formed a single line. (With Ntawa carrying the yoke of the last person, they left, walking on their toes like thieves fearing detection in the night.) When we tried to follow, they chased us back and we went into the house sobbing helplessly.

Three of us were left behind: Zongoli, Ntawa, and me. At daybreak, our captors came and asked us where our people were. We simply told them, "They have left." The command was given to go after them. The Chief said, "If you find them, kill them all!" The men picked up their spears, bows and arrows and started to run. As they were leaving, they talked among themselves about the possible places where our people might be found. But in the evening they returned empty-handed.

Early the next day they divided us up among their people. We were absolutely famished. Unable to withstand the hunger, Zongoli picked up someone's excrement to eat. From that point on, I do not know what became of Zongoli.

I Burn a Hut

When *katila* (a type of early millet) ripened, the man looking after me, with his wife, three children and myself as the sixth person, moved to the gardens where we lived in huts. My job was to frighten away monkeys. During that time of year it rained continuously. One day one of the children gave me the task of drying *katila* near the fireplace. Because of the severe cold brought on by the constant rain, I put more wood on the fire to warm myself. The hut was small and it suddenly caught fire. I shouted, "Help! The hut is on fire!" The woman and the husband were furious and they scolded me very strongly. The husband, mad with rage, seized me and almost threw me into the fire. But, thank God, the woman objected strongly saying, "Do not bring evil upon us. Don't you know that this person belongs to a Chief's family?" The man said, "You have been saved. But from now on you will eat only wild things you find for yourself." Soon after that, I became very sick. When I became worse they took me and threw me into a pit, leaving me to die. After I had been there for two days a little boy brought me bits of pumpkin to eat. When I recovered they came and took me out of the pit.

After reaping the millet, the villagers started harvesting peanuts. I was left home to fetch water because I was not strong enough to go to the distant gardens. Every day I went to the stream, I saw a leopard, although I did not know what it was. I thought it was just an ordinary animal. I admired it and said to myself, "What a beautiful animal, if only one could get the skin for wearing." Then one day the woman who looked after me went to the stream with a small dog which the leopard caught. When the dog yelped, the people went and chased the leopard away. That is when I told the elders, "I always find an animal at this same place and it has very beautiful spots." They said, "You are lucky to be alive, you could have been attacked." We finally stored all the harvest and went back to the village.

I Am Sold to the Arabs

One day there came a large crowd of people from Chona Maluti's place. This Chona Maluti was a Lungwana (a Swahili trader) settled in Bembaland. He used to kill elephants and buy slaves. People called him Chona Maluti (Spender of Gunpowder) because he used a gun which made an exploding sound whenever he shot elephants.

He sent his people to look for slaves. When they came to where we were they inquired in the village if there were any slaves for sale. My keeper told them, "I have a small slave girl, if you like her, you may buy her." I was kept totally in the dark about this. Only later did I see them bring *mpande* (conus shells) in a basket. Although I am uncertain how many *mpande* there were, there were not more than four. They bought many other slaves and early the next morning they took us to Chona Maluti. It was during the dry season, soon after the grass had been burnt.

One day Chona Maluti and his people went out hunting and found and shot an elephant. But the elephant seized Chona, threw him down and trampled him to death. His men fled for their lives and then ran to tell the villagers. The people went to retrieve the body. The elephant, when trampling over him, had torn off one of his arms; it was found a little way from the rest of the body.

After a few days some people came and reported the death of my father. I cried very much but those who owned me stopped me, saying, "Did you think he was still your father?"

At the end of the dry season, they took us to the *Lungwanas* (Swahili settlement) in Chief Nkula's area. We stayed for the whole rainy season. The *Lungwanas* pierced my nose and renamed me "Naumesyatu."

During the rainy season I became very sickly and skinny. My owners complained, "She has cost us money for nothing. This little person will not benefit us at all." That same rainy season the Yeke (Nyamwezi) came with ivory looking for slaves to buy. One of them bought me. After buying me he cut a piece of cloth for me to wear, because when he bought me, I was clothed only in a small *mwele* (a strip of cloth suspended from a string tied around the waist, covering one's private parts). This man showed some kindness; he fed me well. I noticed an improvement in my health as I put on weight. Mulama, my cousin, was also in this village. When he recognised me he told me, "One day I shall escape with you and take you back home." Upon hearing this I was overwhelmed with joy. Each time we went to fetch firewood from the forest I would ask him, "When, if ever, shall we escape?" He would say in answer, "Patience! We will have to wait for the end of the rainy season. At the moment rivers are very full and we could drown." Yet whenever he found any food he shared it with me. Those were days of hunger.

Before we could make an escape my owners took me away into unfamiliar country, eastward, until we eventually reached a very big river. I thought that it was the Luangwa River because the people we found there spoke a strange language that I did not understand. Also the people used the word *akencembele* as a word for maize, rather than the word *cisaka* as it is in my language. They were cultivating *nkona* (sorghum). At harvest time we went back to the village in Nkula's country. The white men had about then established a Boma (government post) at Kawa (Fife).

The Whites Save Us from the Arabs

Upon our return at harvest time, we heard of the order issued by the whites that there must be no more buying of slaves. But even then some people called Nyanyembe (Nyamwezi), from Tabora, had come from their home and resolved, "Whatever the problems, we shall find our way unnoticed past the white man until we reach Bembaland to buy slaves." These Nyanyembe were accompanied by two Arabs and had a little boy called Nasolo with them. One of the Arabs had along a pregnant wife. They went to the Chief Chitimbwa's area and bought some slaves, and eventually came to Chief Nkula's where we were. Chief Nkula himself took his own child and sold it instead of a slave. We too were sold, for cloth. Because I had been ill for some time, they were pleased to get rid of me, saying, "Let her go and die elsewhere." After being bought I was given a new piece of cloth to cover myself and they gave me a new name, Mauwa, and I was never again called Naumesyatu.

After the sale, we spent the night in their grass shelters. Early the next day, just as the sun was about to rise, we left and walked until it was time to sleep. On the third day one Arab killed a buffalo. We spent a day there (to cut up and dry the meat or to skin and stretch the hide). That day, a man whose child they had bought when they left Nkula told the Arabs, "I will show you the safe way to go because the white people have forbidden the buying of slaves. Otherwise you may pass near them and be caught." This man then went on to say, "Remain here drying meat. Let me go and spy because we are about to reach the white men's place." He got up and went to the white people at Ikomba and informed them that the Arabs had come with slaves bought in Bemba and Lungu country.

Upon hearing this, the white men were pleased and sent word to Kawa where the white commander of the *askaris* (soldiers), Mr. Bell, lived. Our guide, the brave man, said, "I shall come with the caravan. You make your preparations."

As we relaxed in the evening we saw him come back and start to lie to the Arabs about what he had seen. He lied, "I have spotted a very safe path which we shall use."

Meanwhile Mr. Bell with his *askaris* approached Ikomba and his fellow whites told him everything the man had said. Mr. Bell was very delighted and the *askaris* began to take their positions.

We left and went past the road from Ikomba to Ikawa This same man told the Arabs, "This is the road from Ikomba. Now that we have gone past this road we are out of danger. We are heading for Mwenzo." When the whites realized we were near, they went to Chitete ahead of us to lay a trap. When the evening came this man said, "Let me go and scout the way again." He went and found the whites and the *askaris* had reached Chitete. The man came back late in the evening. We left. We reached the village and the Arabs decided that we would pitch camp outside the village because it was crowded with people. One of the Arabs went to the village gate, but no one told him his enemies were inside. The villagers came to see us, and even asked the Arabs if they were willing to buy slaves. The Arabs agreed, not knowing that they were being deceived.

On that journey we had been divided into six groups. My group was in the lead. We crossed a stream called Chitete and heard the signal to make camp. We started to prepare shelters. We, the younger ones, carried branches of trees cut by the elders. Our shelter was near an anthill. The Arabs had donkeys which brayed every night, but not this particular one.

Early the next morning, the horn sounded, telling us to tie up our bundles. The second horn was sounded, signifying departure time. One Arab took a child from its mother, telling her to dress so that we could leave. After a short while we heard gun shots. Everybody was scared and jumped and scattered into the bush. What confusion! The Arab holding the child had nowhere to put it and he kept jumping to and fro with it. I went to the ant-hill where I found a little boy hidden. He said, "Hide your head in the elephant grass. Get down. Don't let them see us." As I was stopping, another child joined us.

Then gunfire shattered the silence. The shooting was continuous. Armed men were running towards the ant-hill where we were. We thought perhaps they had spotted us. We were already running when we saw that the child had been shot in one leg and was crying out in pain. A woman too had been shot in the back. She asked for help. In response I showed her my leg where *nkololwe* (a thorny plant) had scratched me and blood was oozing. I lied and answered, "Look, I have also been shot." Then I ran away to an ant-hill with the two little boys following me. The gunfire ceased and all was quiet. We whispered to each other saying, "Perhaps they have now gone." There were a few more shots. When one of the boys climbed to the top of an ant-hill to spy he saw no one. Then everything became silent.

Because we had been running to and fro, we lost our sense of direction. When we asked one another where we had come from, one of us suggested that we should surrender ourselves to the people firing guns because otherwise we would be lost. I did not know where the Arabs and the rest of the people had gone. When the sun was over our heads, we began to feel very hungry. We forgot all about the soldiers and were concerned only about what we might eat. When we looked about, we saw only trees and because we were all children, we invoked our fathers, "What shall we do?" We asked each other, "Have you been shot?" The other boy said, "No." I said, "I was only scratched by a thorn." One of my companions said, "When I was coming here I found they had killed an Arab's wife." At that point, I told my friends "Let us find a place to go, or are we going to spend the night here?" We then left the ant-hill, moving furtively.

After a short while we then heard the drums summoning the soldiers back to their camp. The sound of drums came from where we had camped. We followed the sound which stopped after a short time. We found a small path and hoped it would lead us to the place. It only led us into gardens. Since we were so hungry we plucked and ate the millet like goats. We went on into a field of sorghum and ate that too. One boy noticed peanuts and called us to that place. We ran there and began eating. Thirst also overcame us. When we were full we followed a path and after going a little distance found soldiers' tracks and then a village where people were sitting on an ant-hill. They saw us and said, "Look, there are some children coming." When we got near we realized that they were in fact the people on the white man's side. An order had been made forbidding any person to leave the village: that is why they were standing, keeping watch on the ant-hills. They came and led us to where the whites were.

The White Men Send Us to Kawimbe

Thereafter, they took us into the village. I noticed that the donkey used by the Arabs was tied to a stake: its foreleg was broken. They gave us food. Early next day they took us to Ikomba. All of us who had been caught were sent to Kawa and on the way we met an *askari* who was coming from there. He had been sent to announce that we were free again, and all those who knew where they came from were free to return to their homes.

Everyone who knew, went, but we went on to Ikomba, where I saw people from Chitimbwa. These were the people the whites said we should live with.

After some days a letter came from Kawimbe inquiring about the girls who had been rescued from the Arabs. The white man at Ikomba told the Chitimbwa people, "Take these girls with you and leave them at Kawimbe because they are small children and cannot go alone." The girls with me were Maci (Maggie) the daughter of Musindo, Zini (Jean), the wife of Malombola and others whose names I cannot remember. We spent four days on the way and on the fifth we reached Lombe, Nzika's village. Nzika was the younger brother of Chief Fwambo. Chief Fwambo was building a village at Mulanda in 1899. Early the next day we reached Kawimbe and found people roofing the church.

As we arrived, we saw Mama Purvis sitting, sewing something. She was reclining with her legs crossed. We went up to her, greeted her and sat nearby. She asked, "Have you come from Bwana Bell?" We said we had. She said, "That is fine, we are very happy that you have arrived safely." As she talked to us I noticed that she had no toes. I drew Maci's attention and said, "Oh look, she has no toes! Her foot is all smooth and round." My friend said, "Yes! Even those who sent us here had similar feet." Shortly after the husband came and greeted us: he too had no toes! We then wondered how these people were made. Of course we realized later that they wore shoes. After a short while they took us to a house. They put my friends in one room, and I was put among the boys. The next morning they named me Jim. Later I told them that I was not a boy and they exclaimed, "Oh, all along we did not know that you were a girl!" They decided to rename me Mary (Meli) and put me with my girlfriends. The people I stayed with were Maci from Yendwe, Nele, Kasulambeka's daughter, Mutawa and the wife of Mulanda. All together there were seven of us, although I have forgotten some names.

I Am Identified by My Relatives
We settled at Kawimbe where people had built their houses surrounding the white men. The whites' village was fenced. One day I happened to stroll with my friends around the village. When I looked around, I saw my uncle Kapempe and the sister-in-law of Museo who was the grandmother of David Namwezi, and many other relatives of mine. When I first saw them, I thought that they were other people whom I had just mistaken for my relatives because our home was far away and there was no reason for them to come here.

One day I went out and as I was leaving the white man's gate, I met Chinyanje. She looked at me closely and asked, "Young girl, who are you?" I answered, "I am Mwenya." She then replied, "Mwenya the daughter of Mumemba?" I agreed. She left, apparently satisfied with her inquiry and told Uncle Kapempe, "Do you know, I have seen Mwenya." My uncle replied, "Where have you seen her? The child was lost a long time ago! Is she likely to reappear now? No, you have only seen some other person who resembles her." But she insisted, "No! It must be she. I have even asked for her name and she told me she was Mwenya the daughter of Mumembe. She passes near here every day." Then one day they came to the gate and saw me walking. Chinyanje said to my uncle, "Here she comes!" When I arrived where they were, they embraced me and began to cry. My uncle also cried and before long we were all crying. The next morning they sent word to Chief Changala in Bembaland. They sent for my elder sister, the mother of Mulenga Chisani, to come and identify me conclusively. When she came my uncle fetched me. When Mulenga's mother saw me she said, "Yes, she is definitely the one." She then asked me about how I had been captured, sold, moved about, and suffered. I told her everything. She was very amazed but at the same time rejoiced at seeing me. For the two days she spent with me, we sat looking at each other. The following day she went back to Bembaland.

When she got there all my relatives heard that I was alive and Chief Changala was told the story. The Chief then sent three of my elder brothers,

Mupemba, Ntindi Lubanda, and Chiluwa Mulendo, to verify the story. He told them that, if they found that it was truly I, they should tell the white men to allow me to return with them to Bembaland.

Indeed they found I was the one. They asked the white men for permission from them to take me. The whites said, "This person was brought to us. We therefore cannot let you take her. If you really recognize her as one of your family, go and tell Chief Changala himself to come and bring a cow with him to redeem her." My brothers were very sad to hear that they refused to let me go. They then went back and told Chief Changala who said, "Oh dear, what a difficult condition. Where shall we find a cow? In Bembaland too the situation is the same. There are no cows!"

After a long time the Chief sent my brothers to the white men with the message that as he had no cow with which to redeem the child, would they not just let the girl go without seeking payment? The Chief had continued, "Other people are identifying and freely taking their relatives, why shouldn't I?" The whites said, "True enough you have identified your relative, but you may not take her now because she is very hard-working in the house and at school. Perhaps the best you can do is to come and visit her here occasionally and when she marries she will then come to your home with her husband." They agreed. One of them decided to remain at Kawimbe saying, "I will stay and keep an eye on this child." He stayed a year but because he was used to *citemene* as opposed to digging the soil, he gave up and went back to Bembaland. Despite his absence Kawimbe village was still crowded with my relatives.

I Become Engaged

When my brother returned to Bembaland, I remained with the whites, doing domestic work and learning in school. In 1900 Bwana Purvis went to Mbereshi, leaving me in the care of Mama May. He went to Mbereshi with a young carpenter called Jones Changolo, the son of Mutota Simusokwe. In 1901 he sent word to Bwana Govan Robertson to say that he intended to become engaged to me and sent a *nsalamu* (token payment to indicate interest in marrying a girl). Bwana Robertson called the elders and asked them how engagement ceremonies are conducted under Mambwe custom. The elders then told him how it was done. They then asked him, "Who is the young man who wants to become engaged to Meli?" He replied, "It is Jones Changolo." They answered, "Oh, is that so? We know him well. He is the nephew of Chileya Sichikandawa." The whites said, "Well, we shall hear what his uncle has to say because the girl has already agreed." They then called and asked him. He refused and said, "I cannot agree because the girl is lazy and does not even know how to cook and prepare *nsima* (stiff porridge)."

The white man informed Jones that I had agreed but that his uncle Chileya had refused, saying the girl was lazy and did not know how to cook relish or prepare *nsima*. Upon hearing this Jones was very upset and sent word that he would marry the girl even if she did not know how to cook. She would learn when she grew older. He further said, "I do not like small women. I want one with a big body."

The white men sent for the elders a second time and informed them that the young man still wanted to become engaged to the same plump girl. The elders agreed. The white men then asked, "What do you pay in order to seal an engagement, *nsambo* (bracelets) or beads?" They answered, "If the girl agrees and the father has given his blessing, one also pays *icumalui* (a token payment to request admission to the girl's home, literally meaning a knocking fee), a hoe striped with lines drawn out of white lime. After all these tokens are accepted the boy makes *nsambo* (bangles) for the girl to wear on her legs. Finally, a bridewealth of ten sheep (an installment) is paid."

The whites, upon hearing all this, sent word to Jones saying that the girl had agreed and the elders had explained the traditional things to be carried out and the dowry that he would deliver. He should therefore come back in the month that the rain finishes. When he came, Chileya discouraged him and said, "The girl you want is not a good one. Many people do not like her because she is hopelessly lazy. She does not know how to prepare *nsima*, she is a useless woman. We want you to become engaged to Nele who is hard-working." But Jones Changolo, whose other name was Silanda, refused. The elders also discouraged him and said, "If you want a girl that is big in size you can choose Mpatame." Nevertheless, he objected strongly. They then said, "Well, you go ahead and marry her on your own but we do not like her." He replied, "Yes, that is all right, she is the one I want." These words were exchanged in the evening of the day he arrived from Mbereshi. His father, Mufota, did not know anything about all this. That same evening the whites, having heard that Jones had come, summoned Chileya and his relatives and asked them, "The young man has come. What is your stand? We want to hear from you in his presence." Silanda told the boy they sent, "Go and tell the whites that I shall come early tomorrow." The whites came and told me, "Your fiance will come early tomorrow, so wash your body well and dress properly." As I was dressing, Mama May came to see how I was doing and she gave me some oil to rub on my body. After a short while we saw the young man had arrived holding a lovely walking stick in his hand. He was very handsome. He waited outside. As she turned her head, Mama May saw him standing there. She ran to me and said, "Meli, hurry up! Your fiance is here." I went and greeted him and all my friends too greeted him. They whispered to each other saying, "What a tall handsome man, so dark—as dark as *lufungo* (a dark plumlike wild fruit)." Mama May led us into the house and called Robertson. They asked the young man if his intention to marry me was serious. He said, "Yes." He went home. The next day they came with *icumalui* and the ten sheep. He spent only two weeks at home and then went back to his job.

The Wedding

In the year 1902 the whites sent word to my man asking him to come back to wed me. Mama May particularly told him, "It would be a good idea for you to return and have the wedding, for I am going back to England. I want to marry off my 'daughter' before I leave." Silanda, not one to refuse, came at harvest time and the preparations got under way. Mama May told my Uncle Kapempe and my father-in-law Chileya, "I do not want this wedding to be organised by you. I shall do everything and I will not do it in a European way. I shall not even insist on going to church at all. I want to learn the Mambwe customs. I shall do everything properly; I shall buy the oil, perfume, and flour to anoint her during the wedding." She did everything and bought all the things required for any wedding. She even bought a black cloth. "But," she said, "I will not brew beer."

The wedding day came. Mama May invited many people, men and women, my relatives and my bridegroom's relatives. All came on the arranged day in the late afternoon when it was cooler. The women went into Robertson's room and began to dance to the *nsimba* (finger piano), while also playing *vingwengwe* (clay pots rubbed upside down against another object to produce a rhythmic sound). They ululated (made a high trilling sound). Yes, there was great rejoicing. I was hidden away in a dark corner and covered with cloth. After some time the women told Mama May, the bride's "mother," "Mother of the girl, why don't you come and take up the *nsimba* and let it be heard?" but she replied, "Fellow women, you must show me how." They forced her and she joined in the dance. When the people saw how she danced they went wild dancing. She got them to stop ululating and it became quieter. They danced on. The house was filled with excitement.

The bridegroom's party was sitting outside. He was ushered there. In his left hand, he held a bow, arrow, and a spear and in his right hand, the tail of a Zebra. A lot of youths had come and many people were beating drums and dancing *kaonje* (a type of dance). Men would form a line on one side and women another line on the opposite side and then choose partners. They danced *kaonje* for only a short time and began to sing around the bridegroom. He raised the tail in his right hand and then lifted the left hand holding the bow and spear and then spread out both his hands to either side. Nearby a girl was carrying water in a clay pot resting inside a *civo* (a basket). The bridegroom dipped the tail in the water and then splashed it over people. The girls ululated. The youths then encircled the bridegroom and his best man, singing:

Siwinga Mwanche
wazana twakwima inkolongo
tusiule cisiu ciondo
tusiule cisiu ciondo

They continued dancing. The bridegroom and his best man outdanced everyone. The girl carrying water put some of the water into her mouth and sprayed it on to the face of the bridegroom and the best man in order to make the oil in their skin shine.

When the bridegroom danced outside, I was inside being anointed with oils, perfumes, and talc. As they anointed me they also sang many wedding songs. One went:

Chilende ndulole . . .
Vino akauzo kaya onga!

After they had finished anointing me, the best man took *usule* (small objects equivalent to confetti placed on the bride's head) and patted the bridegroom on the face with it. Then they gave me *luwazi* (a cooking spoon). I took it and shyly bent my head. They then led me out of the house and sat me at the entrance. The bridegroom moved forward and lightly touched my head with the bow. People then shouted with joy; I was lifted shoulder high and taken to the gate near where Kawimbe school now stands.

While returning from the gate I held hands with the bridegroom and walked ceremoniously in short slow strides. During the procession, the bridegroom was brushing my bent head with the Zebra tail, wiping off the *nkula* and *usule* as we walked. He dipped the tail into water and then brushed it over my hair, as if to clean my head. When we reached the house we stopped and I quickly went into the house. The bridegroom remained standing outside and they began to give him words of advice. After they had all spoken, Mama May, as the bride's "mother" came and took the bow, the arrow, and the fez hat from the bridegroom, then she entered the house and placed them on a shelf. Thereafter, the bridegroom and his party came in. When the wedding ended the whites advised my husband, "You are now married and it is a good thing, but our 'daughter' will stay with us. She will be yours when the new leaves come (September). We want you to escort Mama May to Karonga (in Malawi) because she is going to England." Mama May gave my husband two shillings.

During the wedding people feasted a lot because the whites had slaughtered two cows for the occasion. One cow was for the bridegroom's party while the other one was for the bride's. In the evening the wedding moved over to the bridegroom's home. The next evening we were seated to receive more words of advice. The whites, including the bride's "mother," came to the village to witness the occasion. Early the next day they packed me a basket of mealie meal and I went back home.

When I reached the entrance I stood with the basket on my head, holding a walking stick in my hand. Mama May came out to welcome me, received the basket, and then gave me two shillings. From this day onwards I never went back to my husband's home. Upon noticing this my husband wondered, "Hey, what kind of marriage is this where in the beginning they 'confiscate' your wife?"

The time for the journey to Karonga arrived. It was towards the end of harvest time when we travelled to Karonga. We stayed there a whole month waiting for two white strangers, Stewart Wright and his wife. They finally came.

Mama May told them, "Look after this girl and her husband. Do not give her to her husband until September." We finally went back home and I spent three weeks working for Mama Wright. Then they finally called my husband to come and take me away.

My Second Wedding

My father-in-law, Mutota, did not know about the wedding. Apparently he did not even know that I was engaged because most of the time my husband stayed with Sichikandawa, who wanted to totally isolate my husband from his other relatives. Thus all along, when the negotiations were going on, no one bothered to inform his father.

When Mutota heard that his son was married he became furious and said, "Just how can the Sichikandawa clan marry off my son without letting me, his father, know so that I could contribute a cow? They did not even tell me about the engagement negotiations. All right, I shall also conduct a wedding, I, Simukowe from Misansansa, *Kwakwe Kungwi Muntapona*" (a saying in self praise).

Mutota began to prepare the wedding. He soaked a large quantity of millet and made plenty of beer. Then they came to take me for the second time. My father-in-law was at this time still at Yanda. When he reached the gate they gave me a billy goat as a token of welcome.

I was seated in the house. They gave me a piece of red cloth. After anointing me, they gave me six *nsambo* (bracelets). The person who anointed me was my husband's stepmother, for his real mother was dead. They allowed his stepmother to anoint me because she was born into their family.

The next morning, my sister-in-law Namukale brought me a small hoe from Lunda. It was very well decorated and beautiful. When presenting me with her gift, she advised, "My sister-in-law, look at me. In my family we are not many— we are only three, with the youngest one seated over there. Even though they are present at your wedding, we do not acknowledge the others." She then handed me a tray full of millet with some bracelets on top, ceremoniously inviting me to grind the millet. When I saw the millet I said to myself, "Oh, dear me, how shall I grind all this millet, a thing I have never done before in my life! . . . As if back home at Kawimbe we grind millet." I took the bracelets and gave them to Nyina Kangwa, asking her to grind the millet. When the wedding came to an end we went back to Kawimbe, where we found that a house had been built for us near the white people.

On moving into that house the whites gave us many household articles. Mama May and Mr. Purvis had already packed the things that were to be given to me. Dr. Morris gave us a lot of paper, other writing materials, and medicines. The whites with whom we came from Karonga gave us some plates and cups. Mr. Ndelempa (Draper) said, "For my part, I am not giving you anything today, but I will help you with anything you may need from time to time because Silanda has worked with us for a long time."

One day all the whites gathered to discuss the distribution of bridewealth my husband had paid to marry me. They then decided to give it all back to my husband. They told him to bring the rest that was still owed. They would then give back the money, the value of the ten sheep, and, in addition, a cow. He thus gave them twenty-five shillings. Then they gave him one small cow, which he gave the name *Acisi kwa mwene cili uku milimo ya Mambwe*. When interpreting this name he said it meant that white men did not care about wealth as the Mambwe do. And so we set up house. After one year we had our first child whom we named Elizabeth.

We Become Wealthy

As days went by, while we were still there, a *mzungu* (literally white person, but popularly anyone of Western culture) called Heman, a black, came from America, from the people they call Negroes. He stayed at Kawimbe only a short time before they sent him to Niamukolo, near the lake. One day he came from there to visit his friends, who welcomed him warmly at Kawimbe. I did not know he had come that day. I only heard the next day as I was to go out to the gardens to harvest millet. I then said to myself, "I shall come and greet him after work."

As we came from the gardens we met him just by the workshop. He stopped and saw me. I then greeted him, and he asked me, "Young girl, where are you coming from?" I replied, "Sir, I have come from the gardens." He said, "Why did you not come to greet me? Did you not know that I came yesterday?" I then replied, "Sir, work preoccupied my mind. In fact, I did learn that you had come only this morning as I picked up my basket to go harvesting millet. So I decided that we would meet when I came back." He then said, "Well, that is a fine young woman. I want you to visit me one day and afterward I shall come to see your baby."

When this man (*mzungu*) went back to his home, my husband bought a sheep and a goat as a gift. We started for Niamukolo, sleeping at Isoko and arriving the next day. However, while we were still in the wild bush on the slopes of mountains, the sheep broke its rope and ran away. My husband gave chase, but unsuccessfully, because there were plenty of stones. The sheep was never found. We reached our destination, found Bwana Heman, and greeted him. We told him how the sheep we were bringing had escaped into the hills. He thanked us for the goat. They accommodated us in David Musena's house. We spent five days and while there he served us with rice and fresh fish.

The days of our visit came to an end. The evening before our departure we told him, "Sir, tomorrow we are leaving." He agreed and told us, "Come and say goodbye to me in the morning." Early next day we went to bid him farewell. My husband was given a roll of calico drill cloth (*merikani*) and six shirts. The child was given little dresses and diapers. I was given a small roll of spotted cloth, fashionable for women, and a bunch of black beads (*ntundukalu*). He gave us a tin of sugar, three boxes of soap, sugarcane, a bunch of bananas, and a bag of rice. He also gave us two people to help us carry the gifts. We left and he and his wife escorted us for a short distance and blessed us, saying, "May God be with you so that you have a safe journey to Kawimbe."

At this time our poverty ended. This man is the one who helped us very much because my husband then began to sell the cloth and other things he gave to us. Finally, we were running a little shop.

We Have More Children

Our first child, born in the year 1903, was indeed a very healthy child who did not fall ill very often. When she reached the age of two, however, she caught smallpox. This disease was very serious. The child suffered a lot and soon died. By the time she died the disease has blinded her.

In 1907 we had our second child, a boy. The midwife gave him the name of Satu. They used to praise him: *Mulansa Satuka ali yayili yatize yakwane uwa-mamba.* This praise arose because Mr. Sichikandawa, my husband's uncle, often argued with his father over my husband. Both wanted to claim him. Each one would say, "He is our child," and the other one would say, "No, he belongs to us." That is why they gave the infant this name. It meant that they were giving a message to the father of the baby, to say in effect, "Poor man wake up, do not let these two people tie you down in servitude." They were really telling him to go back to his father.

After three months, we requested baptism of the child and he was given the name of Michael by Mr. Wright, who baptized him. Many people could not pronounce the name properly so he was given another name, Ernest. His spiritual name was Mfwambo. This child had many names indeed!

In the year 1910 we had another male child; this one was named Kela. He did not live long, only nine months. He died when he was able to crawl and laugh. In 1911 we had another baby girl, and she was named Lukoti, whose Christian name was Agnes. The last-born was named Henry.

How I Was Baptized

In the year 1910, all the missionaries gathered at Kawimbe. Missionaries of the Free Church of Scotland came from Mwenzo, Kondowe, Ekwendeni, and many other places in Nyasaland. Some church officials came from England. It was a very big meeting.

On Sunday there was a big religious festival and all Christians attended, but not I. When the communion ended Donald Siwale and Peter Sinkala from Mwenzo asked my husband why I was absent. He replied, "She is not yet baptized." They then came to me and asked whether I would like to be baptized and I agreed. The person who baptized me was Mr. Robertson. When the white men from England were coming for the conference, Mama May told them, "When you get to Kawimbe, look for a girl named Meli and her husband, Jones Changolo." Thus, when they arrived, they were anxious to come to my home. Mr. Robertson came and said to me, "Today white visitors are coming to your home." I replied, "But what are the dignified people going to eat in a poor man's home?" He replied, "They will eat whatever you will gave them." I then replied, "Yes, a Mambwe saying goes, '*Umwenyi wakwe siche akalya tuno siche akalya*' (A guest eats what his host eats)." I borrowed plates from him. At midday they came. Both were men. They found that I had fried a chicken and boiled Irish potatoes, cooked pumpkins, beans, and prepared tea. They settled down and I served them the food. I thought they might refuse it, but I saw them eat willingly without any hesitation. They left in the afternoon. A few days later, they returned to England.

After a long time at Kawimbe we moved to Mfundula. When the whites saw us leave they were not happy and even took from us the girls they had given to us to help us with work.

The world war in 1914 forced us to move again. The Germans looted the little wealth we had and dug up the floors of the whole house in search of money. We moved to Kela. The boma (district officer) gave my husband the job of buying mealie meal for the forces. We stayed at Kela for a very short time and then the boma sent us to Chief Nsokolo's village where we lived until 1915. We left there and went on to Mwalu. At this place my husband distributed war supplies such as mealie meal and many other things to the military carriers. We were there only two months. At the end of the dry season (November) we came to Nchengwa where the missionaries had sought refuge. Here the boma told my husband to hunt for game to feed the soldiers. They paid him twelve shillings and sixpence whenever he killed a large animal, such as a bushbuck or an antelope.

In the year 1916 we returned to Kawimbe with the missionaries. This was a year of starvation everywhere around Musia's area where the Germans were. The boma told my husband to look for food to help people. He bought plenty of millet in Chief Chakonta's area and distributed it to all people who were suffering from famine.

My Husband Dies
In November 1918 we heard that the Germans were coming to Mbala. Many people came to witness the surrender of the white man. I and my husband too went. When we were coming back my husband passed through Maswepa to collect the millet he had been buying for the Boma. On the day that he returned, his relative, Mbokosi came to talk with him. As they spoke, my husband said, "Brother, even though we are chatting like this I am a sick man. I feel pain in my back." It was Thursday, the 29th of January, 1919. That evening he became seriously ill and during the night I went to fetch medicine from Mama Ndelempa (Draper). Early next day, the 30th, he was much worse and his elder brother, Cambala came. He remained in that state on Friday and on Saturday he came close to the point of death. When the sun was about to set, [our son] Ernest was in the yard outside making a toy bicycle from reeds without knowing that inside the house his father was on his death bed. I drew him away and reprimanded him; he ran away and continued his toy-making. We suffered the whole night until, at cockcrow, he passed away.

We started mourning. When I looked at the three children he had left me I was distraught, crying until there were no more tears to be shed.

In the morning of the first day of February, a Sunday, we sent word to the whites. They sent back a person with the message that he should not be buried until they came and prayed. Such crowds of people came to this funeral that one might think the entire population of Mambweland had come to mourn. We buried him. After we came back and the house had been cleaned, Inoki Nsokolo "boiled up" and said, "Jones was my debtor, I want all my money today." People who came to mourn told him, "Young man, have you lost your senses? The custom is to restrain yourself and not seize things abruptly. Be patient. Today we have only come to mourn." But the brute refused. He beat his walking stick on the ground so they let him have it.

Two weeks later the question of inheritance arose. All my late husband's relatives gathered and began the task of choosing a person to succeed my husband. The Sichikandawa family said, "Let us take it." They had even chosen Njoni (John) Kalyonga to be the heir. The Simusokwe family, however, objected strongly. There was a heated argument until the Sichikandawa family finally gave in.

The Simusokwe family chose Chimbala, but he declined. Then Mbokosi stood up and declared, "I shall then succeed because I have the energy to go to all this (dead) man's debtors and collect all his money." I refused and said, "No, I cannot marry him because Mbokosi has a wife and I am a Christian and cannot therefore enter a polygamous marriage." On hearing this, the people dispersed and the whole matter of inheritance ended there.

After a week Mbokosi came back and told me that he had divorced his wife. I did not believe it. A month passed. Then he came back and insisted that he had truly divorced his wife. After some time I gave in. He consummated the marriage and took me to his home.

When this man succeeded my husband, he took all the wealth left by my late husband and squandered it. With some of it he paid the fine in a case in which Silanda had been involved. He also sold all the cattle, together with other things. The children were not properly supported by this man and it pained me greatly. So in 1922 I left him and went back to Kawimbe to Mama Ndelempa who gave me a domestic job.

In the year 1925 Harry Sichikandawa married me. This man said he was unmarried but he lied to me. When he took me with him to Kasama I found he had another woman from Bembaland, a Bisa of the Ngumbo clan. I stayed in the same house with this woman.

While I was still in Kasama, word came round that at the hospital they wanted some women to learn midwifery. I went and enrolled. We used to go into the villages around Kasama looking for pregnant women. In 1934, while I was working my husband died. I returned to Kawimbe.

After returning I went to stay with my sons Ernest and Henry at Mulanda. There I found Ernest had had two children, Howard and Monica. Their sister, Agnes, was then in Nyasaland.

After a short stay my son-in-law came and took me to Nyasaland. In 1935 I came back and Mama Brooks at Kawimbe wanted me to help her look after school girls. I went there and settled, not to teach but only to look after the school girls.

The Days That Followed

As I did my job of looking after the school girls I noticed that the white woman was very keen on working with me at all times. In 1936 a mishap occurred at Senga. Porrit's wife died. She was Mama May's daughter whom I used to look after, the one I used to call "my sister" because her mother had cared for me as if I were her own child. Bwana Porrit found it hard to remain alone at Senga, for it was an isolated place. Therefore he came to Kawimbe and married Mama Brooks. The school was closed!

My job too ended and I went to Nyasaland. While there I received money from Mama Baker at Kawimbe asking me to go back to help her work in a home for orphans. I returned and we worked together looking after the children. This woman truly worked very hard in this cause. I did not work alone, for I had companions, Namuzoo, Causiku, Ndumoa, and many others. We all worked together very happily because Mama Baker was a good white woman, polite and cheerful.

In 1945 this woman went to help lepers at Kabalenge near Mbereshi. She then returned and worked among lepers at Kawimbe. Many people were upset about her departure because they liked her very much and trusted her. When she left, all of us midwives scattered to our villages like sheep without a shepherd. The hospital itself closed down. I remained looking after three orphans, Jenita Chombo, Timu, and Chisambi.

While I looked after these children, the congregation chose me to become the preacher in villages surrounding Kawimbe, and in the same year ordained me as an elder of the church. Others chosen with me were Chisya Yambala, Bwana Abel, and Mama Luxon, the lady in charge of the schools, who worked hard to develop primary education at Kawimbe. She was the one who started to send children to high schools at Munali and Chalimbana. Benjamin Simpungwe and David Namwezi were the first ones she sent. The day on which we were installed as elders was a great one because it was the first day on which we welcomed the leaders of the London Missionary Society. Many people from small congregations in villages came to witness what was going on. The missionary who officiated was Reverend K. D. Francis. People were overjoyed to see this new development.

Forever after I have praised God for rescuing me from great hardship.

Translated by M. Sichiolongo and Barbara Lea

L.B.
THE IMPORTANCE OF READING

Malawi 1951   Chichewa

This letter appeared in the women's column of *Mthenga*, a newspaper of the
Nkhoma Mission in central Malawi, in 1951. It is signed only with the initials
"L.B." The writer opens her letter by referring to another rare article by a woman,
this one published in the May-June 1938 issue of *Mthenga*, and signed by Juliana
Nangondo. Nothing is known about either writer, but both would have been
among the few literate women of their time.

It is clear from the references to Nangondo's article that the debate about girls'
education had already begun as early as the mid-1930s in Nkhoma, a region where
the mission educational strategy aimed to produce obedient and industrious
women, not readers of interesting and informative books. L.B. begins by summa-
rizing Nangondo's discovery of reading and her subsequent encouragement to
other women to read books. Then L.B. elaborates on these ideas by suggesting
that mature women, including the wives of elders and (male) teachers, help local
children learn to read. The implication left by the brief article is that education,
perhaps especially education for girls, needs some assistance even from informal
sources.

Fulata L. Moyo

✦

Today I want to speak with you about gaining wisdom. I was looking at old
issues of *Mthenga* and I found the May-June 1938 issue, in which I found an
article by Juliana Nangondo of Katitima, Mvera. The following is a short sum-
mary of what she wrote:

She wanted to discuss several issues with women including their Christianity. She also wrote about her experience when she followed her husband to live
in town, where he was working. One day she became so lonely after her husband went to work that she started searching for a book to read from her husband's pile of books. She discovered very interesting small books. When her
husband came, she asked him where these books came from. She was told that
they were books from Nkhoma Printing Press in our area.

Mrs. Juliana urged women to learn how to read so that they can read these
interesting books. Now Nkhoma Printing Press produces many books at a very
low price, which would give us a lot of wisdom, especially to help us learn how
to live a good life and how to take care of our children and families in our villages. We can be the eyes of those who cannot read themselves. At most of our
mission stations there are bookstores where we can get these good books, from
which we can learn so many helpful things.

These days it is very important that children learn how to read, helped by
Christian women belonging to Chigwirizano, a women's guild. Traditional
advisors, teachers' wives, and wives of elders should help children who other-

wise might go astray. If a mother could read these books filled with advice for her children, then these children would benefit. And the women would benefit even more.

I am your friend,
L.B.

Translated by Bright Molande and Fulata L. Moyo

Ng'washi ng'wana Nzuluge
BIRDS WILL MOURN HER

Tanzania 1956   Kisukuma

Ng'washi ng'wana Nzuluge was born in the region of Mwanza and Shinyanga in Tanzania. She composed the poem in 1956, although it was not recorded until 1999.

Since childbearing occupies a very important place in Sukuma society, those who cannot conceive seek the help of herbalists. A woman without children is pitied or frowned upon, even by other women, and a marriage without children is considered a weak arrangement. Children are to be the guardians of aged parents; they are expected to take charge of their burial. Elders without children have no one to look after them.

In "Birds Will Mourn Her," Ng'washi ng'wana Nzuluge writes of a woman who cannot conceive, perhaps because she has lived frivolously ("preferred fashion"). Now she is desperate to have children, but has passed the birthing age. She considers herself a person of no value—"like bitter cucumber"—who will be mourned by no one but birds.

Ng'wanza Kamata

✦

They are seeking local water herbs
A hint to the boys
They are seeking local liquid medicine.

She is looking for local liquid medicine
A hint to the boys.
Daughter of Kisinza,
How will you give birth
Since your womb is burnt out?
Because you preferred fashion
You have failed to give birth.

Only birds will mourn you.
At his home, Kiloma is rich

Even if I sleep.
Child of Kinya,
Child of Makungu, I am a bitter cucumber.
I cannot be eaten.
Yes, I cannot be eaten.
I cannot be eaten.

I shall be mourned only by birds.
I shall be mourned by birds.
At his home, Kiloma is rich
Even if I sleep.
Child of Kinya,
Makungu's child, I am a bitter cucumber.
I cannot be eaten.
Yes mother, I cannot be eaten
I cannot be eaten.

Translated by Stanley Sabuni and Amandina Lihamba

Zaynab Himid Muhamed
LETTER ON OWNING LAND

Tanzania 1956   English

This letter was written by a Zanzibari schoolteacher, a middle-class woman of Comorian descent. (The descendants of immigrants from the Comoros, islands off the coast of Madagascar and Mozambique, were treated by the colonialists as a separate group from the indigenous Africans, and often received favors, such as bigger education quotas, or bigger rations during the war.) She was about thirty-eight years of age at the time.

There were few Zanzibari women in the British colonial administration, the author herself having been one of the first to be admitted to school. For these first admissions, education would have been available only at primary level, secondary education having started much later. Consequently, the level of English fluency gained would not have been high, and the author had to seek assistance in refining the draft of her letter.

It was also fairly unusual at the time for women to own property. They could inherit if there were no male children, and the author had the good fortune of inheriting a house from her father. Following her father's death, she undertook repair work on the house, after receiving a government loan. Loans were regularly given to civil servants with a certain salary level, and many people, including several women, took loans to build or renovate their houses.

The author recalls paying 128 shillings per month to service her loan, a process that continued up to the time of the 1964 Zanzibar Revolution, which took place a month after the island achieved independence, overthrew the sultanate, and led to unification with Tanganyika. A minister in the new government then wanted to nationalize all buildings whose owners had loans, but Zaynab made an appeal to the new president, Abeid Karume, who ordered the cancellation of her debt, which at the time stood at 12,000 shillings.

The request for a leasehold would have been necessary at the time because most of the houses in the area would have been not much more than huts, constructed on unsurveyed plots without the necessary government approval. Zaynab subsequently obtained the lease to her plot of land.

The author died in 2002, but the house remains family property. She had retired from teaching in 1967.

Saïda Yahya-Othman

✦

Zaynab Himid Muhamed
Kisiwandui Government Girls' School,
Zanzibar
9th October 1956.
Land officer
Zanzibar.
Sir,

I have the honor to apply for a lease with the Government on the Government plot of my house No. 1039 situated at Malindi for which I now pay monthly rent.

This house belonged to my parents for well over 50 years before it came to me, and we have had the right of this plot from the Government on a monthly tenancy ever since.

I have applied for a loan from the Civil Servants' Housing Loans Board for improvement on the house, and approval has already been given by the Board, but the loan cannot be granted until I produce a lease of the plot. Unfortunately, I was not aware of this condition for when I received the approval of the loan in principal, I straight-away gave the work to a Building Contractor and paid him half the amount on an agreement to pay him the remaining half on completion of the work, hoping that I shall get the money from the Board when the work is certified complete.

I attach herewith plan No. 89 of 26/4/56 for the said building. All the work is complete and I have a certificate to this effect, but I cannot get the money to pay the Contractor without having the lease of the plot, and I request you Sir, to be good enough as to approve a lease on the said land for a period of 99 years with a clause for renewal.

The Contractor is pressing for his money and to save me from falling into an outside mortgage of exorbitant interest, I shall be grateful to get your approval of the lease at your earliest convenience, for which I beg to thank you in advance.

I have the honour to be,
Sir, Your obedient servant,
Zaynab Himid Muhamed

Florence Lubega
DEBATE ON HIGHER EDUCATION

Uganda 1959   English

In 1959, Uganda was still under British colonial administration, and there were relatively few black Africans in parliament, let alone women. Of the forty-nine males in Uganda's law-making body, the Legislative Council (LEGCO), twenty-eight were whites and twenty-one blacks. There were four females in parliament, two blacks and two whites. Sarah Ntiro, a renowned scientist and academician, was one of the two black female parliamentarians. The other was Florence A. Lubega, the author of this piece on higher education.

In this speech to parliament, Florence Lubega is responding to a report on higher education in Eastern Africa, which includes recommendations for the future. In her eminently sensible and forward-thinking response to the report, Lubega anticipates the challenges that the Ugandan educational system will face in the years following independence (which would be achieved just a few years later, in 1962), and even up to the present day. Responding to plans for the creation of a second university, the Royal Technical Institute, Lubega argues that the nation should first attend to problems in secondary schools, which are failing to prepare students for higher education. She points to the fact that Uganda is not even producing enough qualified students to fill its long-established university, Makerere.

Makerere was—and continues to be—one of the most prestigious universities in Eastern Africa, and a magnet for students from Kenya, Tanzania, and elsewhere. Lubega also wants to ensure adequate support for Makerere, which is lacking in well-trained teachers and other vital resources. "If another university is opened prematurely, Makerere may become crippled," she declares.

Based on this statement, it appears that Lubega has a sophisticated understanding of such things as finance and strategic planning (more sophisticated, one suspects, than most of her male colleagues'). She argues against grand plans that do not reflect factual realities, and warns her fellow parliamentarians not to depend too much upon promises of financial support from Britain, which has evidently agreed to provide funding for the new university.

It is remarkable to note how many of Florence Lubega's points still resonate in Uganda today. At the beginning of the twenty-first century, free secondary education was still available to less than a quarter of the nation's children, prompting the government to announce an ambitious scheme for Universal Secondary Education (USE). While Uganda's progress in meeting its earlier goal of Universal Primary Education (UPE) has been widely praised, critics of USE echo the concerns expressed by Lubega nearly fifty years earlier: Its success will rely largely on funds provided by Western donor nations, which not only may prove unreliable but also come with strings attached. Already Ugandan institutions—including its educational system—have seen a dramatic move toward privatization, in part to meet growing demand, and in part to accommodate the structural adjustment policies demanded by the West. The qualifications of university staff also remains an issue in contemporary Uganda: The 1999 Mujaju Report shook up higher education by taking the position that all lecturers at Makerere University must have doctorates.

Even the question of science education for women, so prevalent today, was on Lubega's agenda in 1958: "If we are to expect to have women doctors and women science teachers," she declares, "more science laboratories should be established in girls' schools."

Florence Ebila and Austin Bukenya

◆

Mr. Speaker, listening to the honourable the Minister of Education and Labour last Friday, putting before the House in the most able way the proposals in the Report of the 1958 Working Party on Higher Education in East Africa, I could not help thinking that there was no need for fear in going ahead fast with the scheme, since the greatest obstacle has been removed; money was coming from Britain and the Minister himself had said that the Makerere College was not going to be interfered with in its development. We need more and more people to receive higher education and here is the way being opened. But Sir, looking at the report of the Working Party, and also at the White Paper on Higher Education in East Africa, and then turning to the White Paper on Education in Uganda 1958/59 by my own Government, I fail to see how the scheme could be brought into operation very soon until we have made enough provision for secondary education. And, although some territories have been able to do so, it is obvious that they are not going to get enough graduate teachers to teach in these schools. And so the scheme to improve higher education will not be a success. Therefore, Sir, I feel that the Minister's motion needs to be debated thoroughly in this House before it is noted and endorsed.

The problems should be pointed out, the difficulties and the need for careful thinking, careful timing, seriously emphasised. The proposal that there is need for additional institutions of higher education in East Africa and that the United Kingdom government is taking over the financing of these universities could not be more appreciated. And the fact that the East African Governments, in proposing this scheme, were well aware of a number of difficult academic and financial problems, makes me feel confident that there will be careful planning in the development of higher education in East Africa.

Sir, if I repeat what the Minister has already explained, I hope he will forgive me because I could not hear him clearly, because of sitting behind him. The Minister said in his speech that the Royal Technical College will be converted into a university in the next quinquennium and that will be in 1961. But he did not satisfy us as to why there is need for that urgency. Such a scheme as this requires a great deal of discussing by the public before implementing it. Great care should be taken on the question of timing, since on this will depend the future success of every university in East Africa, old and new, and of the standards of higher education.

I would have liked the Minister to have gone at length into considerable details of the scheme; giving us at least a satisfactory picture of a steady flow of students from Uganda alone, who will be going to Makerere College for the next few years, without Kenya coming into the picture, and also the financing of Makerere and the other universities, so that we know how much Britain is proposing to spend on each university in the next quinquennium. For although we have been told by the Minister that the financing of these universities will be taken over by the United Kingdom government, I still feel, Sir, even Britain could be helped and advised not to take on "premature babies" too early.

Although she is responsible and is committed to the building up of universities in East Africa and elsewhere in the Commonwealth, by doing more hard thinking on our part and not allowing political pressure to make us act in haste unless we must, we could save Britain a great deal of worry for the discontent among the Africans not only as regards higher education, but other things as well, that seems to be prevailing in East Africa today.

It is known, and the Working Party commented on it, that there is something like a state of emergency in East Africa, arising from the lack of young people with training needed to support a rapidly evolving society.

Now, one could say that here is a way of meeting that need, we are opening a new university to help these young people to be trained. But I still think that would be putting the "cart before the horse." It is impossible to build up universities before we expand secondary education. In fact our present secondary education standards cannot meet the requirements of two universities. If Makerere were filled to net capacity then we could open up a new university. Sir, the Working Party came to examine and advise on these proposals, they did not propose the scheme themselves. They were invited to come and make recommendations on the White Paper which was issued jointly by the East African Governments, and because of their great experience in the field of education and their knowledge, they warned us against falling into traps as regards developing higher education in East Africa. They made it clear from the start that secondary education and higher education are mutually beneficial and necessarily bound up together.

Sir, they warned us that, without an adequate flow of good students from senior secondary schools, the colleges would suffer great handicaps and their development would be delayed and that to flood our universities with students of low qualifications would be a serious disservice to the communities at this stage of their development and would be unduly expensive. University planning should, therefore, be related to the progress of the scheme for the development and multiplication of secondary schools in all the territories. The introduction of the sixth forms in increasing numbers should be thought of seriously as an essential condition of full university development before we open up another university in the near future. Also, Sir, we cannot hope for good secondary schools which are to feed these universities, functioning without a staff of thoroughly well-trained teachers. . . .

Makerere is still having difficulty in recruiting its staff and it had 20 senior staff vacancies last August, and I have been told there are even more vacancies now. The staff are overworking at Makerere College and they have no time for research. Now, I should like to know how many members of staff there are at the Royal Technical College, and why those people do not get transferred to Makerere College and to fill up these 20 vacancies, and some more, which I hear they have got now. If they fill up that gap they will relieve the people at Makerere from overworking, and leave them free to get on with their research.

The Working Party also stressed the point that it is of vital importance that, in spite of all the difficulties, every effort should be made to search the world over for the ablest men and women to be lecturers in these universities. I should like to know what the Royal Technical College has done about recruiting its staff?

Sir, another point is the financial problem; although we have been told that Britain is going to finance these universities, we have already heard what the Financial Secretaries in all these territories have said, that they have run out of money, and we know that the position is not to be recovered overnight. Their revenues are too small in proportion to the country's current needs. I do not think Britain can give us every single cent to use in these universities. We assume we will take part in the financing of these universities. I should like to hear from the honourable the Minister of Education as to how the governments of East Africa are going to make their contributions when we have more than one university. I should also like, with all due respect, to ask the East African governments to follow the good example of the British Parliament; of submitting, and well in advance, university programmes covering say five, six or seven years, and secondary school programmes, for the public to see, or for the House to be able to discuss.

You may say that Britain has money to help her to make plans well ahead, but I believe that, although we have limited funds, we can still give a fair picture of what it will be like in the next five or six years if we start another university. I should like therefore, Sir, to ask all the governments to draw up their university programmes stating how many students will be forthcoming during those years, with either Higher School Certificate or School Certificate first grade qualifications. How many of those will go to Makerere College and how many to the Royal Technical College and how many to the new university, if it is started during the next quinquennium?

They should also show the senior secondary school development programmes. Although Kenya has already done so to some extent, we could still have some more information on how they are going to get the teachers, and graduate teachers, to teach in their new schools.

I feel the graduate teachers are the main obstacle. Sir, these two programmes are essential to the steady development of our universities, and as responsible governments we could not do without them. I want this point to be taken seriously by the Minister of Education and Labour, for these universities must be judged, not according to the political power in each territory, but exactly judged in relation to the supply of students of good quality if we expect our universities to have success in international standing and to attract students even from outside East Africa. One college may have enough of such good students but what about another? We must work in co-operation and have higher education discussed together. Unless we do so it is likely that staff, time, energy and money will be wasted. If another university is opened prematurely, Makerere may become crippled.

Let us turn to Makerere College now. It is important to see that Makerere, as the University College of East Africa—for it does not consider itself to belong only to Uganda, since it draws students from all the territories—emerges successfully from its special relationship with the University of London not later than 1966. We should not propose new schemes to interfere with this work. Sir, if this timing is not given serious thought and careful consideration, very grave damage may be done to the cause of higher education in East Africa and the success already achieved may be in danger of coming to an end.

Makerere should be allowed to admit students from all over East Africa in the next quinquennium, then left to its own development towards academic autonomy at the end of that quinquennium. This institution is now eleven years old, but I am subject to correction here. I think it started in 1949 and, in the same year, it started degree work and it has been doing wonderful work from the reports we study; and I am sure that we could still ask for it to remain, in the future, the co-ordinating university of East Africa. It has also been stated, and I think it is correct, that it has 895 students from all over East Africa and is not yet filled to its capacity. . . .

Now, supposing we start at the beginning of the quinquennium, let us assume that the Royal Technical College is allowed to start, as suggested in the report of the Working Party, a Faculty of Arts and Science. Since I believe Makerere College draws more students from Kenya than anywhere else into these faculties, I should like the honourable the Minister of Education and Labour to show us how we are going to fill up that gap. It must be realised that the staff at Makerere are doing more work than they need, in order to coach students in the preliminary year to get to Higher School Certificate standard for their degree work. They are anxious to stop this and this means that we have to start Higher School Certificate courses in as many secondary schools as possible. Makerere College is also doing some other work and that is to improve the English of the students in order to make it better for their work as degree students. We hope that the honourable the Minister of Education and Labour is going to note these very important points and give the lecturers at Makerere time to do their proper work and research, without doing the sort of work that should be done in secondary schools.

Now, let us look at the problem in Uganda alone of secondary education. Secondary education in Uganda has to improve if Kenya and Tanganyika are going to keep their own students. It has been often stated that the best students at Makerere College do not come from Uganda. Why? It has also been often stated that the English of the students from Uganda is not as good as it should be. This is another matter that the Minister could probably look into and see how it could be improved. In the White Paper on Education in Uganda on page 9 it says: "Academic courses leading to School Certificate will continue to be provided as at present in the senior secondary schools. It is an aim of policy to transfer to the schools work at the higher school certificate level and to this end three schools will start the two-year course for higher certificate in 1959, in arts and science; while a further school will start in 1960. In the beginning these courses must be partly experimental and it is felt desirable to review the early results before expanding or increasing the courses at present contemplated. No further expansion of Higher School Certificate work will therefore take place for four years, at the end of which time the matter will be reviewed in the light of experience." Now this is the statement, Sir, which I found contradictory to the White Paper on Higher Education. We are faced with another university, and it means, if we are to do Makerere justice, that we have to start Higher School Certificate work straight away without even making experiments. But how are we going to do it? Where will the teachers come from? That is the question; Makerere should not feel that it has to depend on Kenya and Tanganyika students.

The White Paper on education in Uganda also says, Sir, that it must be repeated, that from any one group of children, no more than one-fifth are likely to be suitable for an academic course. As far as finance permits, therefore, the Government will aim at providing places in academic course in senior secondary schools for a maximum of one-fifth of the children who complete the best course; but our children fail a great deal because of their English, so we cannot rely on one-fifth coming through straight away. The report also goes on to say that to provide a good secondary education fully qualified specialist staff are required, together with the specialist facilities such as science laboratories. That is another point, Sir, I should like to look into. How many science laboratories have we in our secondary schools and if we want more where will the money come from? Makerere draws most of its students from Kenya and Tanganyika for the Science Faculty, and if we have to get students from Uganda alone to feed Makerere in the next quinquennium, how could that be done. And even if we forget the next quinquennium, I still feel that something should be started straight away on the lines of having good science laboratories in secondary schools. Science teaching in most of our schools is very poor indeed, because there are not enough teachers and not enough equipment, especially in girls' schools. If we are to expect to have women doctors and women science teachers, more science laboratories should be established in girls' schools.

I mentioned earlier on, Sir, the problem of English in our secondary schools and that the Makerere staff was doing most of the work to improve the English of the students before they start their degree work. The teaching of English needs a great deal of improving in many schools in Uganda. Very often I meet students who have failed to get into Makerere and many people will agree with me that it is not because they are not intelligent enough, but because they had a bad start learning English and they have not had good teachers to teach them the language, which is the medium of instruction. I feel sorry for these young men and women who are really very intelligent but who, because of failing in one or two subjects—and it is not altogether their fault but the fault of the bad teaching and especially in the subject of English—miss their chance and cannot achieve their ambitions.

There is another point, Sir, which I should very much like to emphasise; to see if an investigation could be made to find out if these people are really stupid and unable to manage the course in higher education. There are many people who meet these young men and women and who feel absolutely sure that, if they were given another chance, taught English by either a European or a very well-trained African in the teaching of English, they would get their degree straight away without any difficulty.

Another matter, Sir, which is in the White Paper on Education in Uganda 1958/59 and is contrary to the recommendation in the White Paper on Higher Education and the report of the 1958 Working Party, is on page 16 of that White Paper and reads as follows: "To a great extent the curricula and syllabuses of secondary schools are tied by the requirements of the Cambridge Overseas Certificate. It has been, and will continue to be, the responsibility of each school which offers a School Certificate course to plan its own work. Assistance is given in the form of conferences and refresher courses, arranged either at Makerere College for teachers from the whole of East Africa, or at training colleges for teachers in Uganda. The help which the staff of Makerere College—in particular the Faculty of Education—has given towards the improvement of the standards of teaching in secondary schools of the Protectorate has been most valuable and much appreciated. It is intended that conferences and refresher courses on specific subjects should continue to be held in the future, as they have in the past."

This is a very slow development. I feel, Sir, that there should be a definite plan and improvement on these two points. As regards Cambridge School Certificate, how can each school plan its own work? And again, unless you have got very good, and able teachers to do so, how can we go ahead quickly? This raises the question of the Working Party's recommendations on Makerere College, advising on courses being taken in secondary schools. I should like to know, Sir, if Makerere College has already started or will be starting very soon this job of trying to advise on syllabuses and courses for secondary schools.

The last point, Sir, is the teacher training colleges or the duty of training teachers. I should like the honourable the Minister of Education and Labour to look into the question of teacher training in Uganda, to see if we could not raise the standards in many of the colleges, and to see that the teachers receive extra time to study the teaching of English. They also need more help generally, such as putting the children first before anything else, so that they would be saved from failing in their examinations without any good reason. It has been expressed several times that Uganda has not a good secondary school system, designed to feed Makerere College. I have not made investigations for this statement but I think I have mentioned enough points to make me believe that we have not got a good secondary school system designed to feed Makerere without difficulty, in turning out students of good quality. I cannot see how we can start another university and leave Makerere in the standards of our secondary education, and then see that, at the end of the next quinquennium, the Royal Technical College starts its own courses. Sir, with these observations, I beg to note and endorse the report of the 1958 Working Party on Higher Education in East Africa.

Joyce Masembe Mpanga
ON EDUCATION

Uganda 1961, 1989   English

Born Joyce Masembe in 1935 in the Buganda area of central Uganda, Joyce Mpanga graduated from the two best-known Anglican-run girls' high schools in the country, the Lady Irene College in Ndejje and Gayaza High School. She went on to take a degree in history at Uganda's Makerere University before proceeding to Indiana University, where she earned a master's degree in education in 1962— probably the first graduate degree ever earned by an East African woman. Upon her return from studies abroad, she served as the first African deputy head teacher at Gayaza High School.

Joyce Mpanga's leadership qualities and her excellent education had caught the attention of British colonial administrators, who nominated her to the country's law-making body, the Legislative Council (LEGCO) in the heady days just before independence. Joining her two fellow Gayaza alumnae, Sarah Ntiro and Florence Lubega, in the LEGCO, Mpanga soon established herself as an eloquent advocate of women's rights, and especially of enlightened educational policies. She was to remain in politics, with changing fortunes, for the next forty years. At independence in 1962 she was elected to parliament, where she was part of the first coalition government of Milton Obote. But when Obote abrogated the independence constitution in 1966 and abolished the Buganda Kingdom's autonomous government, in which Mpanga's husband Fred Mpanga served as attorney general, the family had to flee to London. As Uganda experienced coups and countercoups, she returned in 1972, only to flee once more, this time to Kenya, and for a longer period still.

In 1986, under the new government of President Yoweri Museveni, Joyce Mpanga was appointed the first minister for women in development. Later she became state minister for primary education. She was elected women's member of parliament for her home district of Mubende, serving in parliament until 2001.

Among Mpanga's achievements are her distinguished service as deputy secretary to the East African Examinations Council; as chair of the Uganda Council of Women; and, alongside Janet Museveni, as chair of the founding task force of the Uganda Women's Effort to Save Orphans, a nongovernmental organization formed in response to the ravages of war and the HIV/AIDS pandemic. Joyce Mpanga was also called upon, after the 1994 genocide in Rwanda, to help set up a ministry of gender and community development there. She continues to serve on several national and international boards and committees, including the Board of Evaluation of External Support for Education in developing countries.

In Joyce Mpanga's June 1961 speech to the Legislative Council, she explains her three-pronged opposition to the motion in support of the Ministry of Education's budget. First, she deplores the meagerness of the funds allocated to educational services, anticipating, rightly, that this would require parents to pay higher school fees for their children—and knowing that whenever school fees become too heavy for parents, girls are the ones to be withdrawn from school even when their brothers stay on. Second, she notes with dismay the ministry's failure to provide the necessary resources to prepare students for real-life work, and also deplores the blatant inequalities in the admission of women to the few technical institutions available. Third, she faults the ministry's proposals for their flippancy about disabled children and other socially disadvantaged students. Nearly all the problems Mpanga finds in 1961's educational proposals still afflict Uganda's education and employment system today, some even more critically.

In 1989, Gayaza High School's *Golden Jubilee* magazine published Joyce Mpanga's essay recalling her years as a student in the late 1940s and early 1950s. She was the "head girl" at Gayaza during a crucial stage in the school's development, when it was establishing a full-fledged secondary section that prepared young women for university. In the course of her narrative, she mentions the donation of a block of classrooms by "His Highness the *Kabaka*," Edward Mutesa, the traditional ruler of the Baganda, who was later the first president of Uganda. She also mentions Joan Cox, the Englishwoman who spent all her working life at Gayaza, founded its secondary section and headed it for thirty years, and then wrote a history of the school.

These recollections provide a sense of the spirit of self-respect and confidence that Gayaza came to inspire in its graduates. Founded by Anglican missionaries in 1905 to prepare prospective wives for the educated sons of Buganda aristocrats, Gayaza later became the training ground for Uganda's women leaders in all fields—including most of the Ugandan women who appear in this volume. What Joyce Mpanga describes as the "Gayaza way of doing things" reflects the philosophy of the new Ugandan woman: spiritual, caring, articulate, self-confident, and determined, epitomizing Gayaza's motto, "Never Give Up."

Austin Bukenya

✦

SPEECH TO THE LEGISLATIVE COUNCIL

Mr. Speaker, I rise to oppose the motion and these are my reasons. Much has been said about education and I will try not to repeat what others have said, but I entirely agree with whatever has been said, especially about girl's education. Sir, our educational needs are many, our funds are limited, and I also appreciate the fact that the minister of finance was faced with the problem of funding: which project would give the quicker return. It is true, sir, that education is a very slow process, but I believe it is a very good investment and we will not lose by investing more in it. At this stage of development, Sir, we cannot afford to waste any educational chances and we must set ourselves a goal, and it should be to make education available to each and every child in Uganda.

It is their birthright to be educated, but this, I agree, cannot be done in a day but we must gradually work towards it. In this year's budget, Mr. Speaker, it is very distressing to see that instead of making education more and more available to the children, we have made it more unavailable for them by reducing the grants to schools, and as a result fees might go up and parents will find they cannot afford to send their children to school. My main worry about this, Sir, is that very often when a parent cannot afford school fees he always asks the girl to stay at home because he believes that a boy needs it more. I feel, that as we are taxing these people more we should satisfy their needs more and this we should give by giving them more education and increasing the facilities for education.

Looking at the budget again, Sir, it is very distressing to see that in spite of the almost complete lack of classroom equipment, there is not anything said about it and there is no money given towards this end. Someone said yesterday that there might be something wrong with our education system and I think this is one of those things which are wrong, especially [in] primary and junior secondary schools. The government should see that steps are taken to provide good facilities for good teaching.

While this budget caters for leper children, it completely ignores all other handicapped children. The minister of finance is aware that this is creating a problem. He says somewhere in his speech that there is a class of unemployed educated people and he admits too that they are frustrated but what has the government done towards this before it becomes acute. Children leave primary six and junior secondary two when they are too young to be employed by private companies and to be taken in training centers, and it has been the government policy in the past to see that they get jobs, but we have been told last week by the permanent secretary to the minister of education that he expects about a quarter or half of these children who could not go to senior secondary schools to return back to the land, but how much are we giving them to enable them to go back to the land and work? How much do these pupils at the age of 13 or 12 know to go back and be able to fit on the land and make it more productive? Why can't we, then, instead of sending them straight back when they are still young, give them education in scientific methods of farming and then expect to get better results from them? The minister of finance, Sir, said that he is interested in increased production. I feel we should look at our problem in a more realistic way. It is a fact, Sir, that about 50 per cent or over 50 per cent of our farming in Uganda is in the hands of women, and yet in spite of this there are only three girls at Bukalasa, and this is a course for senior secondary girls, but the majority of the girls who leave primary six and junior secondary two are those who go back to the land and actually live on the land and are not given any facilities to be taught agriculture. If we are to stop giving lip service both to increased production and girls' education, we should give girls more facilities for agriculture training and production. Let us not wait until they are too old and have gone wrong, and then give them the training. I completely deplore the fact that in spite of increased industries, there is a complete lack of industrial training.

GAYAZA HIGH SCHOOL AT THE DAWN OF MODERN TIMES, 1947–1952

My introduction to Gayaza High School was nothing very impressive. My primary school, Ndejje High School, had much better buildings, but despite all this I was still excited over the fact that I had made it to this famous school. The compound, as we were to learn later, was often overgrown and at one time we cut the grass ourselves. All classrooms were grass thatched, mud and wattle walls—white washed—and a number of such temporary buildings went up, whenever there was need. Then what was it that people made so much fuss about? It was only later as you grew up that you discovered that it was a number of so many intangible things, like living and learning, that there is a Gayaza way of doing things, like learning to share experiences and improving together. It was a spirit of togetherness that bound the whole family together. It was the pride of belonging to a school with history, a school so respected by all in society, and a school that taught pride in real values—not materialistic—but we learnt to be content with the little we had.

It did not take you long to discover that although the Chapel was tucked behind the Headmistress's house, it was the center of life at Gayaza. In the Holy Week we took all benches and chairs out and sat on the mats on that uneven floor. Each day beginning with Psalm Sunday we acted the event of the Day. On Good Friday we acted a Crucifixion play adapted by Miss Cox from *A Man Born to Be King*. Miss Patterson did the costumes; Miss Corby and later Miss Galer arranged the music. It was a team production. The parts were played by the same people every year; they were only replaced when they left school or if one's behavior did not merit being an actor in a Holy Play. It was taken as a disgrace when that happened. Some years the public and parents were invited, other times not. Yet each year that play had new meaning for you and each year many people were so emotionally involved that they cried at the Crucifixion.

The dawn of modern times started with the coming of electricity and the opening of the new classrooms built in the woods where they now stand. His Highness the Kabaka visited Gayaza just after the Art Room was condemned. He gave the school a gift of four classrooms. It took weeks to prepare for his visit, and we were all excited when it resulted into the promised gift. Talks of the new building materialized and we began to see the eucalyptus trees cleared, and materials brought in. At about the same time our dormitories were wired for electricity. Then the day came, you entered the dormitory, switched on a light, and that put an end to the whole house of seventeen to twenty people crowding around one hurricane lamp on the floor in revision time. The school programme changed too. We then did our Prep after supper, and the games period after tea was extended. It meant too that, if it was your turn to prepare breakfast for the school, you had enough time to collect the water from the pump near the Konko Valley. We took it in turns to do that and we worked in pairs. If you had no strength to bring enough water and collect firewood and there was not enough tea or porridge, the hungry eyes looked at you in accusation. This was enough incentive to do the job well. Thanks to the coming of electricity one didn't have to miss "Prep." We took the event of the coming of electricity in our stride. The only strange change for which I have never been able to find a justifiable answer was the strict rule set in connection with the main switch. This switch was [placed] very high [on a wall]. It switched off all the lights in the dormitories and dining room, for our classrooms were then grass-thatched and had no electricity yet. The members of staff decreed that the light should be switched on at 6:30 P.M. and switched off at 10 P.M. at lights out. And so it was.

The makers of the decree were the only people to touch the main switch. Finding it was too high for any of them to reach, a special stick was designed and made by the school carpenter, and with this, only the staff on duty switched on or switched off the lights at the appointed time. I was the only one who shared this privilege with members of staff—for as a head girl, for two years I was the person on duty every Thursday. Obediently I used to walk from my dormitory to Bethlehem, the staff house, to fetch the stick, and at 10 P.M. I would walk back to Bethlehem to return the stick. I have never known why I did not take a broomstick to do it and save myself the walking. At one occasion, Busoga College Mwiri [a boys' school] visited the school. They were to stay overnight. We had a concert in the dining room beyond ten. Miss Cox had allowed us to have it without the supervision of the members of staff. It was done in good faith to give the girls and boys a good time, and as we found out later it was a test to see how we could keep the good name of the school in mixed company. As head girl I had decided to extend the concert beyond lights out and my friends seconded the idea. At 10 P.M. sharp the matron switched off the main switch and the boys and girls yelled. We quickly had our conference, and decided not to let the Mwiri boys find out that they do this to us—so this time, I ran to Augustine and using a broom stick, I switched on the light. "Temporary fault" we all declared to the boys. The Matron could not forgive me for this misbehavior but Miss Cox did. . . .

This period would not be complete if I did not tell you about our class. After Junior III, there were five of us left and promoted to what we called Secondary 4. We were short of classrooms. There were two girls, pioneers of Secondary 5. These were Eseza Nsibirwa (now Eseza Kironde), who was specializing in domestic science to join a domestic science college the following year, and Beatrice Nakaweesa (now Beatrice Kuuya), specializing in fine arts at Makerere the following year. . . . We shared the same class and practically did the same lessons except in their field of specialty. Occasionally Miss Cox asked Secondary 5 and Secondary 4 to stand up after us. These were the times we remembered that we were two different classes.

The following year there were four of us left—we still had the same problem. We found ourselves sleeping in one side of the Wilberforce House, a room in the middle of the old dormitory of which one side was demolished so our classroom was on the other side of the same room. This was to be the home of the first School Certificate Class. If a teacher came too early, before we finished our drinks at break time, cups or glasses went under the desks, and we giggled as she went around in case we were discovered. In our final year, we had a doctor from India, a friend of Miss Cox, coming to Gayaza for holidays. She declared our diet insufficient for growing brains, particularly for the School Certificate Class. This was the beginning of many delicious dishes sent specially from Miss Cox's house to supplement our diet. We enjoyed milk, eggs, and other delicacies; then, when examinations were near, a pot of steaming stew, warmed daily by an officially-appointed girl. We must have been envied by other girls. . . .

To end on a personal note, I must say Gayaza prepared me well for life after school. I came to Gayaza a shy and self-conscious girl who did not like to be noticed by other people, particularly my teachers. I ended my school career as a head girl, taking prayers, giving out notices in assembly, handling girls, and mobilizing them to do community work. Gayaza gave me the moral values that have enabled me to live in Uganda. Training for leadership for me started early in life—being the eldest girl in the family, nobody allowed me to be young. Gayaza trained me for responsibility, from being a letter monitress to being a head girl. As head girl, you had to make important speeches; you had to be on duty and had to learn public relations with the staff and children to ease your work. Judgment of what is right, what to say, of people's character became your daily activity. This has assisted me in my work as a teacher, a deputy headmistress, and a lecturer, an Assistant Secretary in the East African Examinations Council, a Deputy Chairman, Public Service Commission and now as a Minister.

I have known Gayaza High School, first as a student, a head girl for two years, a Deputy Headmistress, a parent and now as a member of the Board of Governors for a long time. I feel proud to have been called to this great society where we value service above self: where nothing but the best is good enough; where we never give up. In other words, we don't accept defeat—other people should learn from us: where we learnt to be creative and use our imagination to overcome our difficulties; where there is a will there is a way.

Anonymous
PRAISED BE JESUS CHRIST: A LETTER

Tanzania 1963   Kiswahili

Mbeya, in southwestern Tanzania, occupies rich, fertile soils with enough rain to support paddy, maize, plantain, coffee, and tea cultivation, as well as livestock. The strong agricultural community has supported relatively permanent social formations, although a vacuum was created by the migration of young men to South Africa and to Northern and Southern Rhodesia seeking employment in various colonial ventures in the early 1900s. Traditionally, social arrangements were determined by elders; elders from two families negotiated marriage terms, and often fixed a wedding date without seeking the marrying couple's consent. The couple was not expected to object to the arrangement, since marriage was not an individual matter but a community concern.

At the same time, Christian missionary activities in the area had begun in the late nineteenth century. Many children were sent to mission schools, sometimes boarding there, and a few girls and boys were taken in to live at the missions. Some of these were freed slaves, who thought of the church as their savior. Life education, baptism, and other religious teaching gave these young people new norms, attitudes, beliefs, and culture—in effect, new identities, redefined to suit a new sociocultural and ideological environment.

Along with new social and cultural values, the missions brought somewhat expanded choices for women: A young woman could become a nun, stay and work for the convent or mission, or return to her family and get married. Traditional marriage allowed for polygamy as an option; Christian marriage forbade it. Tradition called for obedience to the community elders; Christianity for obedience to God and the church. Christianity thus became a springboard for cultural conflict.

Such conflict is reflected in this letter, from a young woman at the Galula Roman Catholic Mission in Mbeya to her father at home in her village. The signature on the letter is not legible and the writer's name is not known.

Rehema Nchimbi

✦

Galula Mission
P.O. Box 179
Mbeya Diocese
15-6-1963
To You
Dear Father,
Praised be Jesus Christ.
It is my hope that you are all well in your household and enjoying good health as you informed me in your letter. I am very well indeed; God Almighty has taken good care of me.

I am writing this letter dear father with the aim of beseeching you to understand me your daughter. As regards relations with men and getting married,

God has not arranged it for me. I have a calling to become a nun and my life here in the convent is a happy one and full of hope.

Regarding that Kanzaga the son of Mr. Suha from whom you claim to have already received five head of cattle as bride wealth for me, I have never talked to him about anything whatsoever. I am therefore advising you to return all their cattle and to disabuse yourselves of the idea that a day will come when I will get married.

God, the Beloved father, is the one who gives one a good husband or wife. Therefore, it is not good to receive people's property without knowing what your child says herself about the prospective husband.

Let me end my letter here today. Greetings to my mother and my young brothers and sisters. The Head of the convent sends her regards.

I am your loving child,

Translated by Kapepwa Tambila

Princess Nakatindi
THE PRINCESS OF POLITICS

Zambia 1963, 1971 English

The first Zambian woman from a royal household to participate in politics, Princess Nakatindi was the daughter and granddaughter of *litungas*, or kings, of Barotseland. She was the first member of the Barotse royal family to complete junior secondary school, and later she studied in South Africa among such future leaders as Seretse Khama, who became the first president of Botswana. In the days before Zambian independence, the Barotse royal family maintained good relations with the British, which had granted Barotseland a measure of autonomy within the colony of Northern Rhodesia. Nakatindi, however, defied her family by joining the Zambian freedom struggle in the early 1960s, at a time when the colonial government described members of the liberation movement as cannibals and murderers. Nakatindi, a mother of eleven children, would go on to become the first director of the Women's Brigade, the first woman member of the United National Independence Party's (UNIP) Central Committtee, and the first woman to be appointed permanent secretary in the Zambian Civil Service. She was a junior minister from 1965 to 1968 and later became Zambia's permanent representative to the United Nations.

The first of the following extracts comes from an informal talk Nakatindi gave at a party rally in 1963, to celebrate the departure for England of Kenneth Kaunda, who the following year became the first president of independent Zambia. In this speech she identifies herself and Zambian motherhood with the causes of political struggle. In Nakatindi's 1971 speech, she speaks as both a patriot and a feminist. After making a plea for national unity across tribal lines, she asserts that women must have the same rights and opportunities as men, so that they may make an equal contribution to building their young nation. (Some of the issues she mentions in 1971 have been acted on: The Intestate Succession Act of 1989, for example, protects widows from losing their property.) This speech was covered by the *Sunday Times of Zambia*, and published under the headline, "The Princess of Politics."

Boston E. Maseko and Nalishebo N. Meebelo

✦

Blessing the Journey of Kenneth Kaunda

It is a great honour to be given the opportunity of opening this rally. I am very grateful indeed and I am certain this pride does not fill my heart alone but also that of all women in this country. May I therefore address myself on behalf of all women to the President before he goes on this important trip to England in order to fight for independence we so long to get. Sir, we as mothers of this country are the ones who brought up all the people. We rear the young and helpless babies until they grow into manhood and womanhood. We know by heart if our children are well or unwell, whether they are small or grown up. Our children and the people of our country are always close to our hearts. In our customs at home, a mother lifts up her breasts when she gives blessings to a person spoken to. I am doing this now for all mothers of this country, blessing you and wishing you luck and success for your important task. We are saying farewell to you, sir, hoping that you may not come back empty handed, but bring with you the freedom and independence we are so anxiously waiting for. May your trip be blessed and the day of your return be crowned with success.

The Princess of Politics

Public life is in my blood. My father was the Litunga of Barotseland and from early childhood I watched him making speeches and helping people. I was reared to the idea of public service. I was the first member of the royal family to join the freedom struggle, and I had to break through traditional ways of living in order to join the fight.

In those days Barotseland stood very strongly against joining with President Kaunda and his people. But I knew it was no use for us to try to stand, alone. To be successful the nation had to stand as one family. The Colonial Government has given the Barotse people the idea that they would lose their identity and their rights if they joined with the rest of the country. I never did believe their stories. I said if we joined the freedom movement a Zambian government would listen to our needs and honour our way of living.

I used to meet and talk with the men who were detained in Barotseland. We had been told by the Colonial Government, that they were cannibals and murderers. But I found they were just men fighting for their rights and I decided to join them in the struggle. I was never gaoled. I don't think the government dared to put a woman into prison. But they issued many strong warnings and went to my uncle, the Litunga, to try to influence him that I was a bad person, mixing with equally bad people. I reminded my uncle that my father—his elder brother —who had been the Litunga before him, had always taught us that we should not segregate along tribal lines. That we were all people together.

I regret nothing about those days. I believe wholeheartedly that my stand had been justified by events. Zambia has done so much more for the Western Province than the Colonial and Federal Governments ever did in the past. I was the only woman to fight the election of 1962 and I won. Of course it was unheard of in those times for a woman to dirty her hands with politics. Some people thought I was mad. My family disapproved strongly. Not only was I going against Royal tradition, but some believed that I was selling them to the UNIP people. For me, the winning of independence was just a beginning. I still see very clear goals for myself and for Zambia. We must crush the tribalism that has grown up since independence.

During the struggle we were all united. But since then we have tended to drift back to tribal thinking. We must also fight for economic independence. We have political power but without economic power we cannot really be free. But my personal goal, the one that absorbs my personal energies is to promote the women of Zambia. In the past we women were in the kitchen. Now that is not so. We have realized that we can do the same work as the men—apart from very heavy jobs in the mines and so on. Women have the same brainpower as men. All they need is a chance to take their rightful place alongside their menfolk.

The government is giving us that chance and we are lucky to have a President who is keen to see women uplift themselves. We have been thrown the ball—it is up to us to catch it. Of course I don't expect all women to enter politics. That would be a foolish idea. I just want to see them become better educated—in fact, I think it's more important to educate a woman than a man. After all women are the mothers. What they teach their children is never lost. What we learn from the cradle is with us all our lives. And women are sincere.

There are some husbands, too, who don't like to see their wives in public life. So much depends on the family and on the beliefs of the husband. If a husband realizes that it is important for his wife to be educated and contribute to society, then he will be willing to help and encourage her. I have known husbands to look after the children while the wives go abroad to further their studies. I admire such men.

I have been very fortunate in this respect. My husband, Mr. Nganga, who is the Prince Consort, Malundwelo, is very understanding. It would be very difficult for me to enter politics if he hadn't agreed. He has always given me support and helps me in my work as a chief. Fortunately he also agrees with my ideas on women's rights—there would be a lot of arguments in our home otherwise!

There are changes I would like to see made. I would like to see widows protected by law. Tribal custom often dictates that a widow's property can be taken away by her husband's relatives. Sometimes she is even beaten by them. This must be changed. I also want to see a national board of all women's organizations set up. A body that is non-party political and where we can all be free to express our views and promote the welfare of women.

My life is very full even though I lost my Parliamentary seat in 1967. For a time, I was ill and was ordered to stop some of my activities. But I am right back into things again. If the next general election was near I'd certainly stand again. But it's too far away at the moment for me to make any decisions. Perhaps, perhaps not. I simply want to serve my people and the nation. I'm proud of what I did in the past and I don't worry about what will happen in the future. . . . I prefer to stand by what I have done already and leave the future to itself.

S. Nyakire
LETTER ON SECLUSION

Tanzania 1964   Kiswahili

This letter appeared in *Kiongozi*, a periodical owned by the Catholic Church and first published in the 1940s in Tabora, in the west of what was then Tanganyika. In the 1950s it openly took the side of the nationalists struggling for independence from Britain. It also initiated debates on such important issues as the payment of dowry, the viability of marriages between "educated" men and "non-educated" women and vice-versa, interethnic and interracial marriages, and various aspects of development. For a newspaper produced in a provincial town, it was quite progressive.

Nothing is known about Mrs. S. Nyakire, other than the fact that she wrote from Masasi, in southern Tanzania. A check on her return address reveals that the post office box was being used by the Ministry of Agriculture in 1996. Since ministries seldom change their postal addresses, it is likely that Nyakire was somehow connected with that ministry.

Nyakire writes in response to a previously published letter concerning the practice of keeping women in seclusion. This custom was and still is common in some parts of the Islamic East African coast. It was not generally enforced by African Muslims in the interior, except by those of Arab descent, many of whom were shopkeepers. Mr. Latif Tajmohamed, the person who provoked Mrs. Nyakire's letter, lived in Bukene, which used to have sizable numbers of Arabs residing in its rural areas. Many of them were married to black African women, who were more likely to rebel against the custom of secluding women. The term *Wamatumbi*, though an ethnic group in the southeast of Tanzania, was used in 1964 to connote black people generally.

Written just a year after Tanzania achieved independence, Nyakire's letter challenges the custom not only because it is oppressive to women, but because it is damaging to the welfare of the new nation. She calls for women to participate in developing the country, citing the Kiswahili term *"harambee"*—"pulling together"—which had been adopted by Jomo Kenyatta as the slogan of Tanzania's newly independent neighbor, Kenya.

Kapepwa Tambila

✦

Arabs and Tradition
Publisher of *Kiongozi*
Sir,
Allow me space in our esteemed paper so that I can enlighten Mr. Latif Tajmohamed of Bukene on the above subject, [in response to] what was published in *Kiongozi* of 1/6/1964.

Keeping women in seclusion in the house cannot be compared to wearing long beards or robes and turbans. Such practices are purely personal, intended to attract attention. It appears from your statement that to you women have no value whatsoever, that they are on a par with robes, turbans, and beards. You do not realize that women form the basis of a healthy and generally prosperous household. If you keep the woman permanently secluded, who will implement or be responsible for the five-year-plan? Or are you suggesting that we should leave this plan to our men only?

I agree with you that keeping women in seclusion is an Arab custom; however, you should not think that every custom is good. That is one of the worst customs and should be fought against. I am pretty certain that those who are thus secluded do not like it. It is like children playing by throwing stones into the water, unaware that they are thus endangering the lives of the frogs.

You say the Arabs [women] are deserting [their husbands] because of that custom. I do not think that is the case. After all most of the women are *Wamatumbi*, who are secluded against their own will, owing to Arab jealousy. Their desertion is a lesser evil than allowing them to retard their development.

Are you indeed aware of the call by Kenya's Father of the Nation? *Harambee!* [Let's pull together.] Is this *Harambee* for men only?

There! Sisters, this is the time: Time to better our lives! What do you say?

Yours,
Mrs. S. Nyakire
P.O. Box 21, Masasi

Translated by M.M. Mulokozi

Genda Mislay Lohi
AN UNUSUAL GIRLHOOD
Tanzania 1964   Iraqw

Genda Mislay Lohi's exact birth date is unknown. Her account notes that when the Germans arrived in Mbulu, in northern Tanzania, her third-born son was "at the age of paying the head tax," which was about eighteen years old. The Germans arrived in 1890, although Grandma Genda's family might have encountered them some time later. The earliest events she describes, therefore, must have taken place some time in the 1850s or 1860s. Since Grandma Genda related this story to her great-grandchildren in the early 1960s, she clearly lived a long life. This story was written down by Martha Qorro, Grandma Genda's great-grandchild, specifically for this project.

This was a period of famine, and also of epidemics of smallpox, rinderpest, plague, and other highly contagious diseases that attacked people and livestock. Grandma Genda herself used to refer to this period as "when famine and small-pox met in our land." In an effort to limit the spread of these diseases, the families of those who died were placed in a kind of quarantine, in what was known as *meetaa* or *meetimaan*. People who were away from home when a death occurred could not go back home until the period of *meetaa* was over, usually one year. Up until early 1950 the practice of *meetaa* was still part of Iraqw culture; it ended only with the introduction of Christianity and modern medicine.

When her mother died, Grandma Genda's father took her to live with his relative, Manimo, and went away to the land of a neighboring tribe to the south. Her life as a child and later as a little girl with the Manimo family was full of hardships that included going without meals, going to the stream very early in the morning to fetch water, and sitting by the doorstep in the evenings when darkness fell to scare away hyenas while the family was taking their meals. It was a time of famine and food was scarce. The geographical setting of the story is northern Tanzania between the land of Iraqw, which is the present Mama Isara Ward in Mbulu District, and the the land of Mbugwe, on the southwestern shores of Lake Manyara, between Tarangire National Park and the Rift Valley wall. Grandma Genda told her story to her great grandchildren often in the late 1950s and early 1960s. This was during the time of the nationalist struggle for independence, and Grandma Genda wanted to counter the young people's repudiation of the British colonialists with accounts of how much she and her family had suffered under the Germans.

Martha Qorro

✦

That day, I went to the stream to fetch water as usual; it was very early in the morning. I was crying and thinking what life would have been like if my mother had been alive. I was only a little girl, able to fetch water and do some household chores. As I stood by the stream crying, with gourds in my hands, a stranger came and asked:

Stranger: You little girl, what is your father's name?

Genda: Mislay Lohi.

Stranger: And your mother, whose daughter is she?

Genda: She died, long time.

Stranger: Where is your father?

Genda: He has gone to Gorowa land.

Stranger: Leave the gourds and come with me.

I followed him. It was very early in the morning; the sun had just risen. We walked until we reached his home. He asked me to sit outside while he went into the house. I heard him talking to his wife. Then he came out with an empty bag, folded and rolled on the lower end of his stick. He put his stick on his shoulder and said "Let's go." We went—he walked ahead and I followed him. We walked until we got to Kitolay slope [rift valley escarpment], then we went down Kitolay to the land of Manda [Mbugwe]. The sun was overhead and it was very hot. I was very hungry and tired. My throat felt dry. We met an old man herding his cattle. When the old man saw me he asked the stranger, "Can you please give me this child?" "No," the stranger said, "this child belongs to someone."

We left, and a few steps down the path we met with a group of [Mbugwe] youths who had just come out of their initiation ceremony. When they saw me they said:

1st youth: This little girl is going to be my wife.

2nd youth: No, she's mine.

3rd youth: No, mine.

The other youths responded: "She belongs to none of us, so let none of us get her," and they all raised their spears ready to strike. I looked up at all of them. All around me spears were raised—I was terrified. The stranger, realizing that I was in grave danger, told them, "Wait, wait young men, this child belongs to that old man, don't kill her please." He then called out to the old man: "Mzee! Mzee! Your child is being killed, come quick!"

The old man came rushing. "Young men, what's wrong, don't kill my child!" he said. Seeing the old man from their tribe, the young men lowered their spears and walked away.

The old man took my hand and said, "Come my child, let me take you home." I was greatly relieved. We all three walked to the old man's house. His wife, an elderly woman, received me with a lot of joy. She took me into the house while the old man and the stranger remained outside. I heard them murmuring and later the old man came into the house with the stranger's empty bag and filled it with white millet.

I was given some fresh milk to drink but vomited all of it. Then porridge was prepared and I took some and lay down exhausted. Then I fell sick. Having not eaten for a long time, it took time for my body to start accepting food. The elderly woman who I now called my mother fed me with *ugali* [maize porridge] cooked with *ghee* [clarified butter]. It helped soften my stomach.

I lived with the elderly couple until I grew into a big girl. They had a son, Tundu, who was big and strong. Every season the stranger would come, talk to the old man, and be given a bag of white millet. He would tell me that I was his niece and he was my maternal uncle. He had probably told the old man the same lie. On one of the visits—which turned out to be the last—he asked me if I would go back with him to Iraqw land. I didn't like the idea. My new parents did not like the idea either. In fact they were very unhappy. I thought I had to find a way of telling him off. I thought of that day when he found me near the stream and took me to his house. I was very hungry. He didn't give me food; if they had *metimani* he could have asked me to take a raw maize cob from the *shamba* [garden plot] in front of their house, or even a *migagi* [maize stem], but he didn't. What kind of man was this? Where was he going to take me? These questions went through my mind and I made up my mind not to go with him. So I confronted him with questions.

"If you really are my uncle, can you tell me my mother's name? What is her mother's name? And where does her clan and her family live?" The "uncle" could answer only the first question because he remembered it from our encounter at the stream that first day, years ago. The rest of the questions he could not answer. It then became obvious that he was not my uncle, and the old man refused his taking me. That was the last I saw of him.

Years passed and I became betrothed and married to a man called Matkayko Migengi from a rich family with big herds of cattle, goats, and sheep. My day began immediately after the first cock-crow, with grinding millet for morning *ugali* and cooking the morning meal, followed by cleaning the cow-shed, which took me to ten o'clock. Then came the grinding of millet for the afternoon meal and cooking the meal itself. And when the sun was beginning to move past overhead, I had to go back to grinding millet for the evening meal. Before the sun went down, the goats and sheep return from grazing. Anything that had not been said before that time could not be said and heard until the cries had died down. It was difficult to hear each other amid the noise of cows, goats, sheep, and their young ones. My major duty at this time was to direct each young to its mother. This activity lasted until after darkness fell. Then I started cooking the evening meal.

After the meal everyone went to bed. I stayed behind to put the dishes and utensils away. I would usually be the last to go to bed. All this work took place in the main house—my in-laws' house. My husband and I slept in our little house a few steps away from the main house. He would normally wait for me until I was about to finish, then proceed to bed and I joined him a short while later. This life went on for a month. Then one day I realized that every time one of my bead-strings broke, I had to put it away because I had no time to mend it. Slowly all my bead-strings were breaking, one after the other, and I had no time to mend them.

Then one day I thought it could not go on like that; I needed to do something about it. I decided to go back to my "parents." It was full moon and the skies were clear and bright. I decided this was the day to run away. So after everyone had retired to bed and my husband had gone ahead to our little house I put away everything and walked out. My in-laws thought I had gone to bed. My husband thought I was still in the main house. I rolled my cloth around my waist and walked away quietly, then started running. I ran all the way home, knocked, and when they saw me, they inquired what was wrong. I told them everything and said that I had run away and was not going back. The next day my father-in-law came. Traditionally the father-in-law was not allowed to talk directly to his daughter-in-law, so I was telling them to say that I was not going back. I did not go back. My father-in-law left and my parents had to return the dowry.

After some time [two seasons later] I married a man called Gitew. Our marriage was short-lived because my husband died. Then I heard that my father had returned to Iraqw land from Fyomi land where he had been since I was a child. I went back to Iraqw land to meet him. He had remarried and their child had just died. They were therefore in *metimani* and could not allow me into their house. My father took me back to my uncle's house where I had lived and had used to fetch water as a little girl. I stayed there until the period of *metimani* was over, then went to live with my father and stepmother.

I married Bea and we had six children, three boys and three girls. Gwaydumi, my eldest son, was killed by the Maasai, who burned our house and took all the cattle. Massay, my third born, was at the age of paying tax when the Germans came to our land. He worked as a messenger for the Germans and later, after the war between the Germans and the British, he was taken by the Germans to carry their baggage as they were leaving the land. After two days' travel towards the land of Irangi, Massay and another young man escaped the Germans and returned home. He settled in this area that is now called Dareda. And that is where we have lived up to now.

Translated by Martha Qorro

Rose Chibambo
THE TRUTH WILL ALWAYS SPEAK

Malawi 1964   English

Rose Chibambo was born Rose Ziba on September 8, 1928, at Kapukuni village in the Mzimba District of northern Malawi. She went to primary school in Kafukule and later on went to Ekwendeni, one of the earliest mission schools at the Mission Station of the Church of Central African Presbyterian (CCAP), where she completed grade seven. She was unable to finish her schooling because of an early marriage to Edwin Chibambo, but she continued to study privately and attained a junior school certificate. She bore nine children.

Chibambo was exposed to politics while she was at Ekwendeni, when the first political movement, the Nyasaland African Congress (NAC), now the Malawi Congress Party, was taking root in the country. However, her political career began in earnest in August 1945, when she attended a political address by a Reverend Charles Chidongo Chinula, the vice president of the Nyasaland African Congress (NAC), who urged Malawians to participate in the struggle for independence from the British. Chibambo would soon become a significant figure in the liberation movement, taking her place among the first cadre of Malawian women who managed to combine their political activism with their domestic and child-rearing responsibilities.

In 1951, Chibambo became active in resistance to the British plan to join Malawi with Northern and Southern Rhodesia into one federated colonial territory. In 1952, Chibambo became treasurer of the Blantyre District Committee of NAC, led by the militant Grant Mikeka Mkandawire, and in 1954 she joined with other women to launch the NAC's Women's League, and was elected its first chair. On March 3, 1959, the colonial government declared a state of emergency; the following day it detained Chibambo, who had given birth to a daughter just two days earlier. Mother and child remained in prison for thirteen months.

In 1964, after Malawi achieved independence, Chibambo stood for elections, representing the NUC's successor, the Malawi Congress Party. She became the first woman member of parliament in Malawi, and was appointed deputy minister of the Natural Resources, Survey and Social Department, with special responsibility for social development and community development. Later the same year, the country was plunged into a cabinet crisis generated by the introduction of hospital fees in the health system and by President Kamuzu Banda's uncritical views toward apartheid South Africa and Portuguese East Africa (now Mozambique).

Banda expelled the dissenters from the cabinet on September 7, 1964, and called an emergency session of parliament the following day. There he dismissed Rose Chibambo, accusing her of spreading the word that people should not pay the hospital fees. She responded to Banda in the speech that follows. Chibambo lived in exile in Zambia for twenty-eight years, while Malawi was under one-man, one party rule. She returned to her country in December 1993, after Malawians voted to institute a multiparty democracy and a general amnesty was declared for exiled Malawians.

Edrinnie Lora-Kayambazinthu

❖

Mr. Speaker, Sir, I am rising here as a back-bencher . . . to speak on the motion that has been moved by the Prime Minister. . . . I have come to be a back-bencher today, after hearing what has been said. I got it just as hearsay that I am no longer a member of parliament; I am no more parliamentary secretary.

Today is the 8th of September 1964, and to me it is a day when I was born, and it is a day that I am exposed to such a situation in which I am. I have always, always, in the past been with the Prime Minister. I gave all my services that I would want to give as an honest follower of the nation of Malawi, as an honest follower of the Ngwazi Kamuzu Banda . . . which I feel up to this day. Even some of the Members say I have failed. I have not failed, and I will never fail.

I must always speak only the truth and it is only the truth we will not appreciate to say. I am not even afraid to say that I am afraid, because I know what I am talking about. I am really disgusted with the statements that have been made. I know that all these things that the PM has been talking about weren't even aforementioned from outside by those people. I was appointed as a National Chairman of the League of Malawi Women and I honestly worked until the day when this State of Emergency was declared. . . . I was not doing those services because other people were doing them, but because I dedicated myself to the nation and to the leader. I did not care about my family, neither my children, whom I left, fighting for the good of the people. No matter, I was arrested. No matter, I was taken from the maternity ward, from labor, and put in prison. I did not care because I knew what I was doing. Not for the sake of myself but for the sake of the nation and the leader; we must be free and let us get what we should get.

I am very sure that I can stand here talking about these things, being put in a situation being regarded as a traitor, which I am not and have never been.

Let us face truth if we want to know the truth, and if we want the truth, the truth will always speak. Why should I do those things today, that I conspire and speak against the Prime Minister today? I am not a person who can easily be deceived, or be bought by anyone. I do not worry because I always tell the truth, and it is only the truth that I must speak of, and it is only such things that will make me say what I know is true. I have never changed my colours ever since I identified myself with the cause, for the liberation of this country. I have never.

If we want to be honest in this country, if we want to save ourselves, if we want to live to save this nation, it is better that we give the Prime Minister the true stories that we know. It is better that we must explain to our Prime Minister what the feelings of the people are.

I have sung Kamuzu No. 1. I have sung that Kamuzu is the only one in this country. I have not forgotten, even now; I still say so that he is the Prime Minister, he is the leader, because that is what I believe; he struggled and I followed him as one of the people who struggled with him, not because there was anything else but because he was fighting for the truth and he said let us save this country. I did not fight for myself. No matter what happened. I did not care. I said [I] would always be with him and, even now, I say I will be with him because it is the duty of the nation, who has taught us all to do something if we are able to do it.

It is better to be honest and I must say that I will always speak the truth, nothing but the truth, and this is what I am saying.

Susan Buxton Wood
WHAT WE HAVE IN COMMON

Kenya 1964   English

Susan Buxton was born in 1918, in what was then the Belgian Congo. Her maternal grandfather was the formidable cricketer and missionary C.T. Studd. Her mother, Edith Buxton, later wrote a memoir, *Reluctant Missionary* (1968), in which she describes some of the domestic hazards and surprises of the place and time. Her father, Alfred Buxton, later moved to work in Kenya, but their children were educated in England, where Susan studied nursing in wartime London.

In 1943, Susan Buxton married Dr. Michael Wood. They moved to Nairobi after the war partly because of Michael's asthma. He began working as a general surgeon, but then decided to pursue reconstructive surgery, an urgent need in Kenya. His interest in flying led him to pioneer the Flying Doctor Service in Kenya, associated with the African Medical and Research Foundation (AMREF). In the early days, the couple moved from the city to a farm at Limuru on the edge of the plateau, described in the first of the passages that follow, and then to one on Mount Kilimanjaro on the Tanzanian side of the border. At first, the airplane allowed them to commute to Nairobi, but as AMREF developed along with other medical initiatives, they lived in Nairobi as a base. In her retirement, after Sir Michael's death, Lady Wood has been running a jewelry craft project to open commercial opportunities for African women.

A Fly in Amber, Susan Buxton Wood's 1964 memoir, conveys aspects of the lives and thoughts of the third missionary generation, who lived through the period of Kenyan independence. The text reveals a preoccupation with home-building, community-building (almost inevitably paternalistic, considering the attitudes of the time and the high regard given to medical skills), and human needs. Around the time of independence, the Woods were associated with the short-lived Capricorn Society, which advocated racial parity rather than direct democracy. They were able to transcend this view in the new society that emerged after *A Fly in Amber* was published, but the second excerpt reveals some ambivalence and wistful regret about the changing social order in Kenya. The moving scene described in the third excerpt, which is not dated, shows some of the soul-searching that preceded the growth of that new Kenyan society.

Marjorie Oludhe Macgoye

✦

The site which we had chosen for the house was a gently sloping piece of ground which needed only a little levelling to make interesting banks and different levels of lawn for the garden. I had, however, chosen it mainly for the beauty of the view. In front of the house stood a very fine wild fig tree, a flat-topped thorn tree and a rare grey-leafed tree from Japan. The main windows were to be at the back of the house overlooking the rippling countryside stretching to the horny back of the Ngong hills, which lie like a sleeping dragon on the horizon. To the left was the farm and on that morning I could see, in place of the tangle of bush, the neat paddocks we planned and the honey-coloured Jersey cows we coveted, munching idly under the trees which would line the garden.

At the edge of the farm the land dropped suddenly into a steep valley with red eroded soil running down each side to the stream at the bottom. Each succeeding ridge was lower than the farm, so that the view down to Nairobi and the plains was uninterrupted. The air was clear and Nairobi could be seen etched against the great backcloth of wide plains and the distant sturdy blue mountains. To my mind the view combined the charm of dairy pasture with the vastness of space. The most important thing to me in the building of the house was that this sense of space, peculiar to Africa, should be felt inside as well as outside. No more small latticed windows and dark rooms, I said to myself; this house will reflect the breadth of sky and horizon.

"I see what you mean," said the little man, and together we consulted the plan. We each took one end of a long piece of sisal string and measuring the distance either way from the spot on which we stood, we firmly pegged the string to the ground. . . .

[During a flying medical safari to Marsabit in the early 1960s, the Woods encounter the husband of a woman who had been a pupil of Susan's father many years before.]

"Things are not as they were in your father's day," he replied. "Then there was life in the church. People thronged to it, and the school was flourishing too. Now the people go from bad to worse. They are turning again to witchcraft and of course when they do that they get so deep in evil that they cannot return, and they die."

I was not sure whether he was referring to spiritual or physical death so I said "Oh!" in non-committal wonder.

Our visit and the talk of old times did not seem to cheer him much, although our presence caused a considerable diversion among his children while we sipped the hot sweet tea. They returned repeatedly to the doorway each time with a new flashing smile. When we left, the old man insisted on giving us a box of oats, which he had harvested from his small plot of land. He escorted us down to the car and on the way we admired his maize and beans and a few coffee trees which he had newly planted. No doubt the man was feeling too low physically to enjoy life much; I discovered afterwards that Michael was due to operate on his lung that afternoon. He remains a sad figure in my memory. His sense of depression over the work which had been so much of my father's life left me feeling dejected. Father had been so full of life and creativity that people loved to follow him and be with him. I could not imagine him living in this atmosphere—there must have been an earlier splendour. . . .

I was awoken at three in the morning. A woman in the farm camp was in labour and in difficulty. . . . The rain fell heavily. . . . I reached the hut and went in, shaking myself like a dog in the warmth of the room. The only light came from the fire. . . . My eyes smarted and watered as I slowly made out the forms of three women, two were sitting beside the fire and the woman in labour was lying on the ground beside them.

She lay on an old sack and under her head was a wooden stool. In the firelight her face shone with sweat and her eyes were wide open with fear. The two old crones, who had been with her all night, added their lament to the woman's groans. . . . Her pulse was strong, so I gave her a sedative and took her hand and said, "This is the most important work a woman can do and you are doing it beautifully. Hold my hand tight and when the pain comes don't fight it. Let it do the work for you."

One of the old wrinkled women leant over from the fire. "You'll break Mama's hand if you hold it as tight as that," she said, giving the girl an impatient tap.

"Leave her alone," I said. "She will have to do as she's told all the days of her life, but not tonight. This is her night and she shall do as she likes . . ."

In the dim light filtering through the cracked mud wall, the baby was born. . . .

So another life has begun, I thought, and the first thing which we have in common, before all else, is pain.

African women . . . [l]ike the English memsahib . . . have been conservative, clinging to the old tribal ways which were familiar and which gave them influence and standing. . . . Perhaps all women, black or white, suffer from the same strange schizophrenia. On the one hand we create new life, and on the other we try desperately to protect, and carry on in the old familiar ways.

Barbro Johansson
THE ADVANCEMENT OF WOMEN

Tanzania 1964, 1965   Kiswahili

Barbro Johansson was one of a few European missionaries who came to Africa to propagate the Christian gospel, but identified with the African nationalist aspirations of the 1940s and 1950s, joined the struggle for independence, and eventually adopted Africa as a permanent home. In Tanzania, she was popularly known as "Mama Barbro."

Born in Sweden in 1912, Johansson came to Tanganyika as a Lutheran missionary-teacher in 1946, and was assigned to Bukoba District in the northwest. Shortly afterward, she founded the only girls' middle school in the district, Kashasha Girls Middle School, where she taught for many years. She joined and supported the independence movement in the fifties, and worked with future president Julius Nyerere to spread and strengthen the Tanganyika African National Union (TANU) party.

After the nation achieved independence in 1961, Johansson served as a member of parliament for about twenty years, until she retired in 1985. She was named Tanzania's first ambassador to Sweden in the 1960s. In addition to her parliamentary duties, beginning in 1965 she also served as headmistress of Tabora Girls School, the government's only secondary school for girls, which she had rescued from imminent closure owing to alleged lack of discipline. After her retirement, when her health deteriorated, she went to live in Sweden, where she died in 1999. The Barbro Johansson Girls' Education Trust, founded in her name in 1997, has opened a model girls secondary school near Dar es Salaam.

Tanzania's adoption of a relatively progressive policy regarding women's rights and gender equality generated heated debates in parliament, often reflecting the conflicts between official policy and social practice. In these excerpts from two of her speeches in parliament, Johansson combines a concern for the future of Tanzania's young people with a dedication to gender equality. Following the attempted coup in 1964 against the Nyerere government, National Service was begun in order to involve young people in national development and to make them more "patriotic." In the first speech excerpted here, made on February 20, 1964, Johansson expresses her concern about the place of and benefits for young women in this new scheme. In the second speech, made on June 29, 1965, Johansson supports equal rights and equal opportunities for women. As in her speech on National Service, she recognizes differences between women and men, but insists that all Tanzanians must be given "a chance to discover, develop, and nurture their natural talents."

Like many other writers in this volume, Johansson sees gender equality as integrally tied to the project of nation-building in postcolonial Africa. Soon after these debates, Tanzania launched Ujamaa (a Kiswahili word meaning "familyhood"), the socialist program that collectivized land and resources, and also promoted social, economic, and political equality, including gender equality.

Debates in Tanzanian parliament are usually carried on in Kiswahili, the national language, thus enabling people who do not speak the colonial language, English, to participate. This practice has helped make it possible for citizens who have lacked access to formal education—a group that includes disproportionate numbers of women—to become parliamentarians. In one part of her second speech, Johansson supports Kiswahili as a unifying national language, and advocates for improvement to Kiswahili instruction in higher education.

M.M. Mulokozi

✦

ON NATIONAL SERVICE

Mr. Speaker, . . . I am happy to note that in Article 5 both female and male youths are being considered [for National Service]. This is a big step forward, and I appreciate it. Today we have heard the Minister referring to this bill as the Bill on the National Service Force. The word "force" is not bad. I like it. However, it does show that weapons will be used. I would like us to think of a less dangerous future, particularly as regards the participation of women and female youths in the National Service.

I would like discipline to be emphasized. Women should also learn discipline. In the army women need discipline even more than men. Our women should acquire discipline and learn drills and sports so that they may later help their people in the villages and homes. However, remember that after the two years of national service, there will be differences between servicewomen and servicemen. Women will have a different kind of life. Hence, during training, servicewomen should take into account their future mode of life. . . .

I do like equality before the law. A traitor is a traitor, whether a she or a he. I do not want to segregate the sexes before the law with regard to punishment for crimes committed. However, in the training, we should make allowance for differences in the talents of women and men . . .

ON A NATIONAL LANGUAGE

The Minister spoke about Kiswahili. I listened carefully, and I was pleased to hear that he has tried to make a plan [for promotion of the language]. But, Mr. Speaker, the Kiswahili language is not adequately taught in higher education. Even though the Minister has appointed two people to go around and try to help, I do not think that that is enough. I would also like to ask about the amount of money allocated to the Institute of Kiswahili Research: Nine hundred pounds, Mr. Speaker, would create a mere pygmy among giants. Yet the value of the national language is such that it deserves a bigger allocation of funds. Let us have a thorough crash program to teach the language well. And it is necessary to train indigenous Kiswahili specialists; foreigners cannot be of much use in this matter.

ON OUR YOUNG PEOPLE

Now, I would also like our youth to be people who are willing to be led, so long as the leadership is right. They should be shown living examples. We should therefore take politics to the schools: I hear there are plans to do that, and to form political [party] branches in the schools. I would be happy, Mr. Speaker, if that could be done. However, as it is voluntary to join and buy a TANU party card outside the school, joining the TANU Youth League in the schools should also be voluntary. And the leaders of the school branches should also be trained to become real leaders, and their training program should be on a par with the school curriculum. And maybe in the Youth Center, which we are building in Dar es Salaam, we shall be able to train many leaders who shall be responsible for leading the TANU Youth League branches in our schools.

I also thank the Second Vice-President, who has said that these days many of our youths will join the National Service. In many countries, youths are taught to use arms and to prepare for war. Fortunately, our National Service has many branches; it will be good if our secondary school youths are given an opportunity to build the nation in various ways, such as building roads,

Translated by Saïda Yahya-Othman and M.M. Mulokozi

teaching villagers, or engaging in scientific agriculture. This matter should be implemented as early as possible. . . .

Now, I return to the word *manpower*. Here, too, Mr. Minister has mentioned the word *revolution*. I want major revolution. I want major changes in the entire structure of our society. Girls and women must have the same opportunities as men. *Manpower*, Mr. Speaker, does the word signify men only or is *manpower* to be understood to include women as well. In the capitalist and imperialist countries, they were very late in using their reserve "manpower," i.e. women. Women's advancement in those countries was delayed. Women had to go through the kitchen and the natal clinics first, before getting a chance to contribute to other community work. I am not saying that that kind of work is unimportant. In fact, I want to emphasize those areas of work very much, and I would even ask the Minister to help all the home-craft centers in the country. It is shameful, Mr. Speaker, that we don't assist those who teach in the home-craft centers.

But if we look at the socialist countries, countries such as Russia, Cuba, East Germany, China, women are equal in every way to men. Furthermore, the new developing countries, Tanzania among them, have an opportunity to avoid delay and procrastination. If we will give girls the same places as boys, then the "manpower planning unit" should budget for them as well. The world loses a great deal when many people don't get a chance to discover, develop, and nurture their natural talents; and to transform those natural talents and to become people whose creativity and expertise will function for the benefit of the communities in which they live. In this way, each post will be held by that person who is better qualified to fill it.

We will be working against this goal if men can compete for a post established only for men, while certain jobs are set aside as suitable for women. We are losing a lot of wealth in this world, truthfully. A person's abilities should be allowed to develop to advance the whole society.

There are many signs in Tanzania that women are advancing much more than in many other countries that I have seen. But it is not enough; I want to emphasize that their abilities must be allowed to blossom a lot more, and they should work together with men to build our nation, so that we don't lose this important asset. It will be a great revolution if we do that, and we will see miracles.

With that small contribution, Mr. Speaker, I support this motion.

Translated by Saïda Yahya-Othman and M.M. Mulokozi

Lucy Lameck
AFRICANS ARE NOT POOR

Tanzania 1965   Kiswahili

Lucy Lameck, whose full name was Lucy Selina Lameck Somi, was born at Moshi-Njoro, in Kilimanjaro region of Tanzania, in the 1930s. She received her primary and secondary education in the Kilimanjaro and Tanga regions, and completed her training as a nurse. However, she refused to work as a nurse in Tabora under a discriminatory colonial system, choosing instead to study stenography. Between 1955 and 1957, she worked as a secretary with the Kilimanjaro Native Cooperative Union while at the same time engaging in politics as an activist with the Tanganyika African National Union (TANU). In 1957, she accepted a two-year scholarship to Ruskin College, Oxford, where she earned a diploma in administration, sociology, psychology, and economics, and worked on nationalist politics among the East African community in Great Britain. She spent a semester in the United States, studying international relations at Western Michigan University, before returning to Tanganyika in 1960.

Lameck resumed her work with TANU, and was nominated to serve in parliament by Prime Minister Julius Nyerere. She later became a parliamentary secretary in the Ministry of Commerce and Cooperatives. She died in 1992.

Lucy Lameck belonged to the new breed of upcountry young nationalist politicians who were relatively better educated, in the Western sense, than the majority of Dar es Salaam activists. They grew up in areas with considerable missionary influence, where there were many primary and secondary schools, where the cash economy was entrenched, and where people had adopted some Western values and practices. In Kilimanjaro, Lucy Lameck had also been born into a political family: Her mother was a TANU activist who used to host Nyerere at her house whenever he was in the area on political campaigns, and she was a local leader in the women's wing of TANU.

The text that follows attests to her original and unorthodox perspective. In the speech, made in Parliament on June 15, 1965, when she was deputy undersecretary for the Ministery of Commerce and Cooperatives, Lameck emphasizes the need for community self-reliance and sacrifice to the creation of a strong and buoyant economy. She refuses to accept the common belief that Africa is "poor," noting that Africa's wealth and sweat built the economies of the rich countries of Europe and the United States. Properly utilized, this wealth could also build the local economy of Tanzania. At the time Lameck made this speech, two years before Tanzania embarked on the *ujamaa* program of African socialism in 1967— the country was still "groping in the dark," as Nyerere used to say; Lameck comments on the "confusion" reigning in politics. Lameck, like Nyerere, is struggling to find a clear vision of a modern, functional political and economic system that will be truly African, reflecting of African realities and values, rather than just mimicking the West. In this same vein, Lameck speaks about the need to preserve many "venerable and respectable" African customs, while abandoning others that "retard the development of our country," and especially the advancement of women. In addition to such customs as high dowries, early arranged marriages, and female circumcision, Lameck regrets what she sees as a resistance to change on the part of some of the Maasai people of Tanzania, who "keep on wearing skins and being photographed by Americans."

M.M. Mulokozi

✦

Mr. Speaker, we have also decided that in our efforts to develop our country, one of our major objectives is to build this country on the basis of self-reliance. For this reason I welcome very much the speech of the Honorable Minister for Finance and, especially, the new estimates, or the [proposed] new contribution, which he calls the development levy, a contribution which, truly speaking, at present is only paid by every Tanzanian who earns an income exceeding 10 pounds per month.

I am not in agreement with my fellow members that a person earning 200 shillings per month or below should not pay anything because his wants are many, he has school [costs], children, and various other costs. But Mr. Speaker, we must remember two things. The first thing is that if there is no other way of increasing national income in general, the numbers of schools cannot increase, nor can roads or hospitals. The second thing, in my opinion, is that in times of war, it is the responsibility of each citizen to tighten belts, for you can't fight for something for which you do not care, and it is the responsibility of all Tanzanians, including those with 10 cents, 20 cents, 30 cents and even 1,000, to tighten their belts and contribute something into our national coffers so that we may get enough revenue, which will enable us to consolidate our country in the coming years, and also to implement self-reliance policies. So I maintain that we all have this responsibility.

Therefore, in general, Mr. Speaker, I find that these "Estimates of Income and Expenditure" have written a new chapter in the history of our country for four major reasons.

First, they uphold our objective of self-reliance; second, they sustain a permanent basis for socialism; third, they call on each citizen to make sacrifice in the great war of revolutionizing the conditions of life of our people and, in this way, eradicating the oppression and humiliation suffered in the past at the hands of imperialist governments. Last, they also address the fundamental objective of putting the country's economy into the hands of Tanzanians as quickly as possible.

Mr. Speaker, the question of the economy is fundamental, because if we can't make use of the freedom that we have now to revolutionize the economy, our politics becomes useless, aimless, and targetless; our future children will laugh at us and reproach us for having failed to use the opportunity we had to lay the foundation for the economy of our republic. Hence, it is quite right that a self-governing country should make every effort to enable it to govern itself in all economic matters. In general, I very much welcome the estimates brought by the Minister. I am sure that, after not too long a period, we shall begin to see changes in our republic, even though some of us are complaining right now, seeing this as a great burden. But what can we do? It is our responsibility.

Honorable Mr. Speaker, I have three very brief things to say; hence I won't take a long time. There is one thing which, to say the truth, disturbs me whenever it is talked about by the various leaders in our republic. It is something that is often talked about and it bothers me and it is my responsibility to talk about it here in the House today.

Among the words we use when addressing the public, or in various councils, is the phrase that "we are poor people," that our country is still young, and that we Tanzanians are "still poor." This word has been worrying me for quite a long time because, Mr. Speaker, I don't agree at all that our country is poor and that Tanzanians are poor people. Our country today has value, it has riches, it has culture, it has people, it has agriculture, it has good land, it has animals, different types of livestock, minerals—and it is rumored that there are millions and millions of [tons of] coal, iron and other ores—which we have not yet managed to find the means to explore and exploit and process for our benefit. Hence, I don't agree at all that our country is poor and, indeed, when we use the word we only humiliate ourselves. Today, when I looked at the speech delivered by the Honorable Minister, and went over the financial figures for the period from 1960 that he was explaining to us—I can it see here, Honorable Mr. Speaker, I will read—I am sorry I don't have the Kiswahili version, I have the English one—Mr. Minister says: "When we took over the government in 1960 the total budget under the colonial regime for that year was 19,000,000 pounds for recurrent [expenditure] and 6,000,000 pounds for development, making a total of 25,000,000 pounds. Today I am happy to say that the Nationalist Government has more than doubled the size of the country's budget. The total budget which I have presented amounts to a little over 36,000,000 pounds recurrent and 31,000,000 pounds development, a total of 67,000,000 pounds in one year." Honorable Mr. Speaker, in poor countries people walk [live] on the streets, they go without food and die of hunger, they have no farms, no houses; they have nothing. One could not use the language used by Mr. Minister here in reference to such people. In a one-year period we have been able to raise 67,000,000 pounds. Therefore, Mr. Speaker, we have to be a bit careful about the word "poverty," because we will condition the thinking of the people. Our growing schoolchildren, whom we would like to grow in an independent country, should be able to enter the army of the builders of our republic; if we still tell them every day that we are poor, we will be debasing ourselves and debasing our other foundations. What we lack—and this we have to accept—is that our situation is weak because right now we don't have enough experience and our revenue is erratic. The most important resource for us is knowledge: In our present circumstances, the government is directing its efforts towards attaining expertise in different fields, so that we may disentangle ourselves from this problematic situation, and use our new knowledge to explore the minerals, exploit our resources, expand our industries, and employ many workers, so that we may extricate ourselves from this despicable situation.

Mr. Speaker, I think the other thing that makes us feel very poor is the situation of the world in which we live. The world surrounding us is developing fast in the economic and scientific spheres: rockets are being sent into space, huge buildings are being erected, the condition of life is so different, there are many industries, etc. That is why we feel that we still have a long way to go, that we have yet to arrive. But I would like us to remember, whenever we compare ourselves to others, the methods used by them to build their countries' economies. The British, the Americans, and others have built their countries from the sweat of other people. The British had many colonies in Africa and other lands; the Americans had several slaves who cultivated their cotton and other farms. The Negroes were, and are up to today, cheap labor. In these countries, the governments belonged to a few people, the rich people ran the governments. They used to get materials and other things from our countries. Yes, we are indeed far behind, it is true. We are many steps behind, but we must always remind ourselves of the basis and the means these fellows used to get where they now are. Let this be an objective and a warning to us, reminding us of our principles. Our objective in this country is to see to it that this country develops in general, right from the districts, towns, villages, and neighborhoods; that the living conditions in our country change step by step, village by village, and neighborhood by neighborhood. That being the case, we have to accept that one of our greatest responsibilities is to tighten our belts and do everything we can in order to increase the income of our country, so that our country can develop as fast as we are able to make it. At the same time, we have to remember that we have a great responsibility towards our republic, that of laying the foundations that conform to the needs and experience of Tanzanians themselves: economic, political, and developmental foundations for the people and the community which are home-grown and not stolen from foreign countries, but arise from and are in harmony with the Tanzanian people's experience and traditions.

Honorable Speaker . . . we are thankful that, when our Central Committee of TANU met recently, it authorized the Father of the Nation [Prime Minister Nyerere] to appoint a special council or commission to deliberate and advise him on how we may formulate a policy based on African socialism. I very much welcome the idea, for indeed, it will help us overcome many economic problems. It will elaborate on what should be the basis of our socialism, how we should move forward, which of the things inherited from the colonial era are right, and which things in our traditions still have great value and should be preserved.

I think this council will greatly help us because there is a lot of misunderstanding, and I often ask myself about the African Socialism that we Tanzanians want to follow. Some few years ago, the republic tried to lay down a basis without a clear system and without a guidebook, like a Bible, that elaborates what African socialism is all about. It tried, as much as it could, to use advice and the existing foundations to adjust our institutions so as to have a policy which reflects the principles of our African political democracy. However, right now there is a great need to have a clear vision of the kind of future we want.

For at times, there is confusion. There is a lot of talk. Today it is declared that big vehicles should be appropriated; tomorrow small cars are declared bad; the day after there will be this and that declaration. There is confused talk, so that we do not really know where we are going and what we want to be: Will there be motorcars or not? Will there be farms or not? And if farms will be there, on what basis will they be run? What type of economy shall our country have? Will foreigners and the common people living here go on with the same type of life or will their lives be organized differently? Hence, Honorable Speaker, I welcome the council, which will be established by the Honorable Father of the Nation so that it may expound more on our political principles and chart out a good and clear way forward, so that we do not quarrel in future, or fumble and stumble every day as humans are wont.

On the second matter, I just wanted to hint . . . to the Honorable Minister here . . . that there are some complaints . . . regarding the expenditure of [public] funds. There are various complaints as to whether government money is equitably spent. I am sure that he is a responsible person and he will investigate this and if there are any practices that he thinks lead to misuse of public funds, he will no doubt take the necessary corrective measures as soon as possible, for very often our people are ready to contribute whatever they can to the nation-building effort, but the effort should not only end at taking the money, the expenditure side should also be monitored, and the Honorable Mr. Minister himself must keep a strict eye [on the funds]. For the people who contribute the money have only a low income, and it won't be good if the complaints continue without the Minister taking the necessary steps.

Finally, the Honorable Mr. Minister will be happy to learn that my last point does not concern him directly. It is about customs, and of course it does concern him very much as a leader.

First, Honorable Mr. Speaker, I would like to take this opportunity to congratulate the leaders of the various local governments in our republic, which have helped us to tackle the problems pertaining to customs. Our country, Honorable Mr. Speaker, has many laudable and respectable customs. And as it has been said, it is the intention of the government to see to it that customs are preserved, and that some are developed, so that they may serve to sustain our successive generations and our country in general. But it is openly known that there are some customs that very much retard the development of our country. I am one of the many people who shout a lot about this matter, and I will not tire of shouting about it, because it is quite clear that such customs retard the development of our country.

These customs are well known to you, Honorable Members. I know most of you married quite a long time ago after paying a heavy bride price—you have paid many cattle: That is one of the customs which, truly speaking, don't help us now. And I thank one member who asked a question about cattle: That is, how should a person who owns many cattle be taxed? Our cattle have a high value in the country, if only they will be utilized, and the government has plans for using them in a better way. But there are still such customs of cattle hoarding; people still marry by paying many cattle.

Another custom which I know, Honorable Members, is that of marrying off our children while they are still too young, still infants. I know that there are places where young girls are removed from school, where once a girl comes of age, she is removed from school and kept indoors so that she may be married off to a man without her consent, and without her knowledge—because customs say so. Indeed there are also some customs that humiliate and reduce the beauty of women in our republic—you see women having their ears pierced; they have their arms pierced; they are pierced here, everywhere. Other people in some areas have the habit of circumcising girls; such practices aren't good at all. There are other bad and retrogressive customary practices that continue even now in several parts of the country.

Several local governments, as I have said, have made great strides. I would like to take this opportunity to congratulate especially the Rungwe District Council, Musoma Local Authority, Morogoro Local Authority, and others that I can't remember now, which in the past never thought about such customary issues. For instance . . . the day before yesterday I arrived in Rungwe in one local authority—where we recently made noise about the hefty bride price—where the bride price was twenty cattle, but I am told, the local authority has recently passed a by-law reducing it to six cattle. . . .

The Musoma Local Authority has also passed a by-law on a matter that used to exist regarding matrimony. It has been passed, in Musoma Local Authority and Morogoro Local Authority, that no father of an underage school girl shall be allowed to remove the girl from school to keep her inside or to marry her off. This is something that has been outlawed by the local governments, and these local governments deserve to be highly congratulated.

Lastly, Honorable Mr. Speaker, this problem of customs does also exist in the Maasai area and I would like to remind this house that . . . the Maasai area is a very big part of our republic; the Maasai people are citizens of this republic. We should not accept nor should we be satisfied that they should keep on wearing skins and being photographed by Americans or other people, but we should satisfy ourselves that one day the Maasai will change and that they will be just like their other fellow Tanzanians.

Honorable Mr. Speaker, with those few words, I support the motion.

Translated by Saifu Kiango and M.M. Mulokozi

Bibi Titi Mohamed
SACRIFICES FOR CHANGE

Tanzania 1965   Kiswahili

The history of Tanzania's struggle for independence is incomplete without mention of the central and decisive role of Bibi Titi Mohamed in mobilising both women and men all over the country for the struggle. She is, indeed, often known unofficially as the "Mother of the Nation."

An articulate, urban, Matumbi-Swahili woman, Bibi Titi Mohamed was a *ngoma* (traditional dance) leader before she became a platform politician; both her talents as a performer and her connection to women's dance associations would prove important tools for her political organizing. As a Mmatumbi, an ethnic group that spearheaded the Maji Maji struggle against German colonialism from1905 to1907, she viewed herself as a freedom fighter belonging to that heroic tradition. Born in 1926, she was schooled in the Qur'an , and then had four years of further education.

Bibi Titi joined the nationalist struggle for independence soon after the founding of the Tanganyika African National Union (TANU) by Julius Nyerere and his colleagues in 1954. She was soon prevailed upon to form a women's wing, and henceforth devoted herself fully to the independence struggle. A talented, fluent, and humorous Kiswahili speaker, she toured the whole country with Nyerere spreading the "good news" of *uhuru* ("freedom" in Kiswahili) and gaining converts for TANU in the process.

By the time of independence, Bibi Titi was easily the best-known and most important politician after Nyerere. She became a junior minister in the independence government, and a member of parliament until her resignation after the 1967 Arusha Declaration, which established Nyerere's *ujamaa* program of African socialism and also codified one-party rule in Tanzania. (She would later say that what she objected to most about the declaration was "the undemocratic manner in which it was being imposed upon us.") When she fell out with Nyerere in 1969, she was implicated in a plot to overthrow him and jailed for several years before being pardoned in 1972. Her spouse abandoned her because of her political activities, and most of her property was confiscated. Upon her release from prison, Bibi Titi lived quietly in retirement until the early 1990s, when her role as a national hero was once again acknowledged and her properties were returned to her. A major street in Dar es Salaam was also named for her. She died in 2000.

The following excerpts come from parliamentary speeches, the first made on June 14,1965, and the second on July 1,1967. Bibi Titi speaks as the Undersecretary for Development and Culture. She reveals her deep concern for the social and economic interests of the common people, especially women, and her sophisticated pan-Africanist vision of African liberation. She also expresses her distrust not only of the former colonizer, Great Britain, but also of the Cold War–era United States, after two CIA-backed coups in the newly independent Congo, and U.S. involvement in conflicts in Vietnam and elsewhere in the developing world.

Biti Titi's mastery of both political rhetoric and Kiswahili storytelling, along with her earthy humor, are discernible in these speeches. Other MPs often interrupt her speeches with laughter, applause, and cries of "Hear, Hear."

M.M. Mulokozi

✦

This Is the People's Country

According to the financial estimates presented by the Minister for Finance, this is a very big budget, and as we know, we Tanzanians have a very big country. In Tanzania we have places inhabited by human beings; we have a big area inhabited by animals. Tanzania is a very big country in East Africa. Our population is perhaps about ten million or even twelve million, but I might be wrong if I say twelve million for we have carried out no census since we attained independence. We are told that the whole population of our country is about nine and a half million or ten million. This is according to the British statistics, but at that time, if you came to me in a village and asked me whether I had a husband, how many children I had, I would never say that I have four, five, or six children—never. If I have four children, I might say I have two children; and I know that these two children of mine are not there, they are in Dar es Salaam—they are not in that village. And if I have a husband I hide him unless the headman is lucky enough to know how many people are in his village. So I also don't believe that we are ten million. Mr. Speaker, in this country we feared to say that we had a big family because of the problem of taxation, so husbands slept in the bush to escape taxation, children ran away from here to the bigger town of Dar es Salaam in order to hide—for this city swallows everything. When they want taxes, I don't think they can collect them through searches in a city because the city is filled with alleys where people can hide themselves. I don't believe, therefore, that we are only ten million, we might be twelve million or eleven million. I don't know, but the government should do all it can so that we know—our main aim is to first know how many people there are in our country, that's all.

And we have a very big country—poor roads, no water wells in our villages, there are no dispensaries, there aren't enough hospitals, there are no community centers for adult literacy classes, we had no equipment to use for our farms, we didn't have enough tractors nor did we have enough oxen ploughs in this country. We, therefore, took over at a very difficult time. A time of great hardship. But through the efforts of our government, our ministers, our representatives, together with the other leaders in the country, and the people themselves, today we have perhaps trebled our annual national budget.

If we look at the population of Ghana, they are now, perhaps, about seven million people but when they took over the administration they were about six and a half million by the British account; their budget was about two hundred million and their country is very small, about the size of one Tabora province before it was divided into two. The population is small and the country is small. In terms of wealth, I don't know whether Ghana is first in Africa or South Africa is first and Ghana is second, but there are fewer people because the country is small. Our population in Tanzania is big and the country is even bigger, but its income is small. Therefore, I agree with the advice given to us by the Minister for Finance, that if we want to build our nation we must sacrifice; for those who preceded us built their nation through sacrifice, and some started colonization for the benefit of their country. We used to be a British colony here and the British brought a District Administrative Officer in one place; in another a middle-ranking officer; another one with a little higher position; a Mr. D.O. of whatever type, I don't know; a top level D.C. [District Commissoner] here; a P.C. [Provincial Commissioner] and another below the P.C. He brought many of his own people to rule here and these were paid salaries from this country of ours.

Likewise, the whole economy of this country has built Britain. That is also sacrifice. They began by sacrificing, they came out, they weakened, and went to rule over other countries so as to bring money and wealth into their country. I can also give the example of China. There are no people who sacrifice as much as they do.

Although we have prepared this budget, the government also needs to look into how people spend their money in this country, for our expenditure exports money involuntarily; we should also ask our government to exert greater efforts to bring in small industries. If people like riding bicycles, why should bicycles . . . be manufactured outside this country? Why can't we make an effort to have bicycle industries in our country? Why don't we make an effort to have radio manufacturing industries? There are now many people who like radios, and if you go to my home, Rufiji, you will see a woman with her pot or tin of water on her head and a radio tucked under her armpit. And this is something that sends money outside. We should also think of those people we want to prevent from exporting the money outside. The government should use all its wisdom to prevent these people. Mr. Speaker, those industries that cause us to export our money, like the radio and bicycle industries, should become our own in Tanzania. This should have been the first issue on retaining money in our country.

When taxes are imposed upon people, such as taxes on products or salaries, we want the people to see the benefits. At the moment people see what their taxes are doing and now taxes have been increased, so we want greater government efforts to show people how their money is spent. Taxes are collected differently now than they were before. In those days we were taxed arbitrarily. Today we have our District Councils, we have City Councils, we have our own Town Councils; we have our own representatives who can collect the taxes and when ready can themselves divide them: This amount will build a hospital in some place; this amount will be for a dispensary or a well in some other place. When we get the taxes, we want the councilors to make a great effort to show people that their money has not been lost. It won't be good if people pay taxes, but the roads are poor. There are some people here in Tanzania who have no roads to transport their products to a market, and also you can't convince a rich man to establish a market at a place where the people are if there is no road to transport the crops to where he wants them. Because of this, the ordinary person experiences great problems with crops around his house. Now that he has cultivated crops, he wants clothes.

Many people living in this country live in villages. What do they depend upon to send their children to school? Their crops. What do they depend upon to marry off their children? Their crops. What do they themselves depend upon when they want to marry? Their crops. Even for those who want to get married, I can't even marry until next year; I mean, before I get a bed with which to go to a husband, what do I wait for? To cultivate [my crops so I can] get a beautiful bed to go to a husband with, for these are our customs. Now, if someone has farmed and he or she has his or her target in front of her or him, but then is delayed because buyers don't go where he or she is, we as representatives face great problems and some of us don't come back to this parliament because there is no road. "Ah! This member of parliament hasn't brought us a road at all. He or she hasn't brought us a dispensary, she or he hasn't brought us that." Many people have such goals. So, when we increase taxes we do so for the interest of the people. . . .

We want to revolutionize, although some people from other places misunderstand the meaning of revolution. Our revolution is an economic revolution for a better life and we should be able to reproduce a lot. Some generations die due to sick stomachs. When a child wants to develop inside one, one develops stomach problems, and you abort—is this how we are going to increase the population here? We want a revolution. We want to procreate. I too would like to have a baby and hold a child one day. There is nobody who doesn't want to bring another human being into the world. If we are counted, we are ten million here but we are not in Dar es Salaam town. The ten million are not in Tabora town. They are not in Mwanza town, not in Moshi town, not in Arusha town, not in Tanga town. The ten million are in the villages. The ten million are suffering from disease, the ten million are suffering from ignorance, and this is adults and small children. The ten million want development. They want adult education and to learn contemporary processes. The ten million want to increase their income, to use the land in our country. People in the villages, not us. Not here, but there. The ten million want to sleep in clean houses, drink clean water, sleep in good beds. Soft beds have not been made for townspeople only. We want everybody to enjoy themselves before they die. One's paradise is here on earth. Living in a good place is one's paradise. You can't listen to the paradise of heaven. There are God's Ten Commandments, how can you circumvent them to reach God's paradise? It is dangerous. It is as if you have been offered something across a big gulf and you can't reach there. What we are saying is that, while human beings are alive, we should make an effort to have them stay in a good place, eat well, and enjoy themselves in this country. We want everybody to realize that they have attained true independence in Tanzania We don't want an independence that benefits us only. . . . We want to change from British colonialism and let the people know that the colonialists have really left this country. And we can inform the people of this only through change. We are ready to pay taxes, but we want change. . . .

We Tanzanians believe in African unity. We believe African unity is the right of Africans and that all Africans are one. Up to now we still believe that we cannot lose heart. We cannot change our aims as regards our brothers and sisters of Kenya. They are our everlasting brothers and sisters. Our children and their children will still be brothers and sisters. But I tell you that when the topmost leaders, such as our ministers and theirs, our leaders and theirs want to say something, they should do so like adults, they should know what they are saying. They shouldn't speak *haphazardly*. The East African Federation doesn't belong to Mr. Nyerere, it is not Mr. Kenyatta's, nor is it Mr. Obote's [leaders of Kenya and Uganda]. The East African Federation belongs to the people of East Africa and the future generations of East Africa. We have been put here by the people, and our leaders have been put there by the same people. We have no right to utter words that contradict the views of our people.

Great responsibilities have been entrusted to us by our people. When you have been given responsibilities as a leader, then your trust extends all the way to God. Not everyone can be a leader, even if one has two thousand degrees. But if you are elevated and made a leader, then you have been given light by the Almighty God and you must have the wisdom to use it. We must know this. We believe that one day East Africa shall be one. We really believe so, but I tell you, we shouldn't give our enemies cause for amusement. We shouldn't give the enemies windows to infiltrate and disturb our unity, for while we speak we should also be vigilant against the dangers of tomorrow. We have attained independence peacefully; we must use our independence for building our countries; we must use our independence to develop the economy to benefit our people in this country. We must use our independence to unite our people, not to separate them. Therefore, I have faith that what we believe is what the people of Kenya believe, and that is that we in East Africa are one, as they themselves sing in a record:

The East African Federation
We are all delighted.

These are Kenyans singing. If you come to Tanzania, they sing. If you go to Kenya, they sing that this is their country. Even though we are leaders today, this is the people's country. And they are happy about the federation. Therefore, we can't say to hell with the federation, no. We will do everything to overcome the enemy so that the East African Federation is formed.

They Can Never Rule Us
Mr. Deputy Speaker, today I am very pleased, for there is in the House a fierce, wonderful, and exhilarating motion. But unfortunately, my fellow Members have already made a lot of useful contributions. I have only one or two words to support the motion presented by the Honorable MP Mr. Mbogo.

Mr. Deputy Speaker, the thoughts of all Africans who at that time were not yet independent, who were living in the countries ruled by colonialists, at the time of British elections, they all spent sleepless nights waiting to see who would win the elections. And they stayed awake because they were praying to God that the Labour Party would win the elections. We did not pray for the Labour Party's win because we love the Labour Party very much, but rather because we thought that the Labour Party Constitution favored the downtrodden, not only in their own country but also in their colonies. And their great pledge was that if they came into power, the colonies would be free. Even during these last elections, although we in this country are already free, we still stayed awake through the night to hear who would win. We stayed awake up to 5 A.M. as they were counting their votes. When we heard that Labour had won, albeit with a small margin, we were very happy. And those who could afford it held some small parties with their friends to celebrate the news. We were joyous for our comrades and sisters who were still under British colonialism; we thought that they would get out of colonialism like we did. But we were wrong.

Members have said here that the Commonwealth [meeting] this time would reflect not only the opinion of Tanzania, but of the whole world. They knew that the most important item would be about our comrades and sisters of Southern Rhodesia [Zimbabwe]. People spoke who were not used to speaking, but it is said that the British had no response. Instead of working in collaboration with the existing regime in Zimbabwe and allowing the people to elect their own government, the British have now come up with another idea of sending a delegation to Vietnam. This is very disgraceful of the British, who have ruled half of the world but have failed to fulfill their promises. We ask the British as our friends, we as members of the Commonwealth, that they reverse their decision. They should speedily convene the meeting they want and change their objectives, and they should give Zimbabweans the freedom to elect their own government as soon as possible. This will be very beneficial to them and will enhance their respect in the world. But if they simply sit and spin their British intrigues, it will be useless for them and a great injustice.

On African unity, some members have said that although we are now our own rulers, we are timid. We Africans may have flag independence, but many of us are still mentally controlled by our former colonial masters. This is where our timidity comes from. One has no freedom to decide things for oneself. This is why in our countries all we can do is talk: We talk in our meetings, in our parliaments, but we do not really put the talk into action. If we did, we would be giving our comrades and sisters in Southern Rhodesia the hope of an end to their sufferings. Perhaps as the Honorable Joseph Nyerere has said, since the Commonwealth is in London, when they go and see London and are welcomed by the Queen . . . perhaps sometimes some Africans feel overawed and think that the power of the British persists even in countries that are governing themselves.

Why should the Commonwealth, which belongs to all, always meet in London? What does this mean? If it is the Commonwealth of Nations, why shouldn't the meetings sometimes be held in our nations? And if the Commonwealth has childish notions, what is the advantage of this Commonwealth? How does it help us Africans? We must ask ourselves the question, What do we gain? We thought that in the Commonwealth there would be friendship and fraternity where people listen to each other. If the Commonwealth itself appears to be a group of mindless children, like people who have no authority, what gain does it bring us? What gain will the Commonwealth bring us? If some are mocked at the Commonwealth—our elders, our leaders in whom we trust—of what use is it?

The Americans have gained power because the United Nations is in their country. Although members meet there and complain and support each other in all ways, what can they do? The United Nations is in America. This is the time for people to consider where the United Nations can be. And if it isn't so, must it be only in America? At times even the United Nations itself will not be useful.

We therefore say that for Southern Rhodesia, the British must respond by giving it its independence. That is why I am very afraid for our President, Mwalimu Julius Nyerere; I am very, very afraid. For these people who want to penetrate people's minds, if they find they are unable to penetrate certain minds, it is difficult and dangerous. The British display their arrogant, swollen heads when Mwalimu Nyerere says anything there. And this is to let the world know that in Africa there is a dangerous man called Mwalimu Julius Nyerere. This is dangerous and, honourable members, we must protect our President. It is not a small matter; it is a very serious matter, for you can't control Mwalimu's mind, for that is his nature. How can you change one's nature? He may seem to be a very good friend of yours, and given the needs of this country, you can give him many things that are both useful and needed in Tanzania. Then you might think: Now I can control him, but he would never agree to that. And this is not only true today; the British know him very well. Since he began to lead TANU, there was no way to control him. And this is why we Tanzanians have no doubts about Mwalimu Julius Nyerere . . . because we know his true nature, we know how he is, we know his constancy, we all trust him today; all the peoples of this country trust. . . .

Today Americans are imperialists in the world, but they must remember the history of Hitler. Hitler was an imperialist in the world. Hitler's imperialism did not just worry us in Africa. We Africans had not even attained our independence, but Hitler's imperialism worried the whole of Britain and the world. . . . The powerful, the wealthy, and the authorities seem to forget that there is God, for if they knew that there is God, they would not have found it easy to create dangerous weapons and spend a lot of money to destroy people's lives. But they should remember that although Americans have rockets and atomic bombs, they will one day hunt one another the same way the Germans are hunting each other today.

The people of East and West . . . what are they vexing other countries for? God has given them a lot of wealth, international respect, mighty power, what more do they want? They want to rule the world. Have they become God? It is God who rules the whole world; it is He who rules us all and He rules paradise as well! Will they be able to rule like him? Will there be two Kingdoms in the world? It will be impossible!

That is why the Chinese are exploding atomic bombs. That is the beginning and it is very dangerous. . . . We will also be asked to learn how to make atomic bombs; that is not just a story. For when some people read in newspapers, or when they hear on the radio, they say, These are only talking nonsense, how can they do it? Who knew that China would become a great nation in the world and a fearsome one, too? Some take it as a joke. But the Swahili say: "What people talk about exists, but if it doesn't, it is on the way." If we haven't experienced it, then our children or even our grandchildren will see it. Africa will also look for a way of fighting and defending itself. Yes, it will, whatever the cost! Africa will not accept living in a perpetual state of anxiety. We have a government, but it is as if we don't; we have power, but it is as if we don't. We fear the American! That means, if an American comes here right now, we will all run. We have no flag, we have no soldiers, we have nothing and nobody! How can we live in the world like this? The almighty God can't leave us in such anxiety, for He has created us in the same way He created other people. He has given us intelligence like other people. Our anxiety must have a limit. . . .

The American [president] has made a mess in the Congo and he has killed millions of people. More than three million people have died in Congo because of him! As they have said there, he is not a citizen there. No one knows what he is fighting for there; no one knows what he wants there. He has no need of soldiers there; he has no need of the country; I don't even know why he is fighting there. He claims he wants to prevent Communism. Why doesn't he go to fight Communism in Russia where it all started? He is coming to ill-treat us, why not go to the root of Communism in Russia! If he wants to prevent Communism from entering Africa, he should stop the Russians, for if they are beaten, they won't have the strength to spread Communism in the world. But those [the Russians] are as fierce as they [the Americans] are. As the Indians would say: "He ill-treats a goat, but the bull he fears." How come? There are the Russians. Why doesn't he go to fight them, for they are the ones who are sending rockets to space all this time. . . . The Russian leader said . . . yesterday on the radio, "I will help the people of Vietnam until they win in their war and I will help anyone in the world who is oppressed." He [the American] should go to fight there [in Russia] with his equal in strength, but instead he is coming here to persecute us. He is losing millions in money to destroy our lives. . . .

Vietnam will win because Americans are fighting from monetary greed, and they will ultimately lose their lives. These Americans are mindless people; all they do is to follow what [President] Johnson and his committee decide. Don't they pity themselves and the way their children, their husbands and their comrades are dying? Aren't these human beings? Why don't they pity themselves and ask their President, Why are we fighting? and let him give his reasons. . . . Vietnam will fight until it wins, and it will win. Americans will be in great disgrace in the world. They [the Vietnamese] are fighting for their blood, they are fighting for their country, they are fighting for their lives, and they are fighting for their coming generations. The Americans will be defeated! They can persecute us. But with them, they will lose. Even here. The Americans should know this. They can never rule us, just because they have the atomic bomb; we will never accept that! We had all better die so they would rule over a desert! We cannot accept our minds to be controlled and instructions to come from Johnson to us in Tanzania. We won't agree to that, and we also won't agree for any Africans in their own country to be controlled by Johnson! We won't agree to that and we will keep on protesting and we will boycott him and spit on him! We won't agree to that! We are telling our African leaders that the words they utter are the words of their people whom they lead, and they must act on their talk. It would be useless that everyday money is lost on OAU [Organization of African Unity] transport for leaders to discuss OAU matters. Of action in the OAU there is none!

Some people have already realized the value of African unity but we, ourselves, are not aware of the benefits of African Union. We are telling our African leaders that the liberation of Africa doesn't need words but actions. We should begin with . . . Angola [along with Mozambique, still a Portuguese colony]; only then can we boast of our ability to confront South Africa. If we won't manage here, then we will never be able to do it in South Africa! We shouldn't just say empty words and be reported in newspapers or on the radio just talking. We should start passing this test. Our unity should work in Africa to bring independence to our comrades; we then enter Mozambique, Angola, and deliver their freedom to them; that is when we can have hope to let the world know that Africa can fight [in] South Africa to bring our African comrades their own government. Otherwise, we will talk, we will be laughed at and we will be seen as *hayawani*, as mindless birds or animals. But people who are intelligent human beings, must have commitment when they utter words.

Translated by Saifu Kiango, Saïda Yahya-Othman, and Amandina Lihamba

Hannah Kahiga
A MODEL DAY DURING THE EMERGENCY
Kenya 1966 English

Hannah Kahiga was born in 1944 in Tumutumu, Nyeri District, Kenya, where she completed primary school and high school. She completed her undergraduate studies in English and sociology at Uganda's Makerere University in 1968, returned briefly to Kenya, and then left again, this time for the United States. Kahiga earned graduate degrees at Columbia and Adelphi Universities in New

York, and taught at the City College of New York before returning to Africa with her family in 1981, settling in Cameroon, her husband's country. There Kahiga—who now goes by her husband's name, Tiagha—worked with the Ministry of Social and Women Affairs, developing services for disadvantaged youth, and was involved in the struggle to integrate women into the development process, helping to empower them as participants and beneficiaries. Kahiga remained in Cameroon until 1989, when she joined the United Nations Economic Commission for Africa (ECA) in Addis Ababa, Ethiopia. Since then, her work on behalf of women has been focused on Africa as a continent. Her efforts promote mainstreaming gender concerns into the policies, plans, and programs of national, subregional, and regional government institutions.

Kahiga wrote "A Model Day during the Emergency" in 1966, and it was first recorded and presented on Radio Uganda's monthly program *In Black and White* in May of that year. Conducted by Miles Lee, and with commentary by David Cook, then professor of English at Makerere, the program introduced new writers and writing from East Africa. Kahiga presents a factual account of human suffering during the 1950s, at the height of the anticolonial resistance movement. This movement included both political organizing around the Kenya Africa Union, and the violent activity known as the Mau Mau uprising. The colonial government's attempt to suppress it culminated in the imposition, in October 1952, of a State of Emergency, and with it martial law. Resistance leaders, including future president Jomo Kenyatta, were jailed, the forests where the Mau Mau had their camps were bombed, and tens of thousands of Gikuyu were herded into "protected villages." Kahiga's text deals specifically with the horrific realities of concentration camps, where many Gikuyu people were confined and forced to dig trenches (some of them literally worked to death), all in an attempt to cut off the freedom fighters in the forests from their supporters in the communities. The Gikuyu were a special target because, as the community that was most affected by the seizure of African lands for white settlers, they constituted the core of the resistance movement and the Mau Mau uprising.

As a girl, Kahiga herself lived through the experience she recounts. She vividly remembered it nearly fifty years later. "My family and everyone else around us were rounded up and put into newly constructed huts all grouped together in thousands to create artificial villages that could be more easily controlled. . . . My mother, brothers and sisters lived in one such hut along with three other large families. My father lived elsewhere along with other men. Daily life as I recall is what is described in the story," she said in an interview in July 2002.

Edward Blishen, the well-known English writer and scholar who at the time of *In Black and White*, was presenting the Writer's Club program on the BBC Africa Service every week, had referred with admiration to what he felt was the "cool tone" of much of East African writing. David Cook preferred to describe it as "controlled writing." Kahiga's prose gives us an idea of what they both meant.

Emilia Ilieva

✦

They lived in round huts, the Kikuyus, roughly and urgently built. They themselves built them under the supervision of Homeguards as instructed by the foreseeing European administrators. Within a week, a hundred huts were finished, with fairly high conic roofs, two windows each and with a circumference of about twenty-five feet. They were thatched with grass, and had mud walls. All were in rows, one hut about five yards from the next.

The rows were separated by pit latrines, about five holes under one roof.

Each hut accommodated at least five families, regardless of the number of children each family had. It did not matter, whether there was enough room or not; the Kikuyu community had to be collected together to prevent the spread of Mau Mau movement, the white administrators thought. Thus, all the Kikuyus were made to abandon their roomy houses to be crammed into these sooty holes for security purposes.

In the early hours of the evening, while the mothers boiled green maize or stirred porridge for dinner, the school children did their homework amidst the smoke and stuffy conditions. There was no room for five tables, one for each family, in this hut. Stools, boxes and things were thus made to serve that particular purpose. Tables or no tables those sums had to be finished, for who wanted to be sent back to the village by their teacher tomorrow, having failed to accomplish the set task? By and by dinner was served and the study corners were soon converted to dining rooms. It was understood in every family that once one had swallowed his or her lump, the next move was to bed. There was no need to ask for a second helping even if one felt like it, for these were treats and, as such, rarely available. Dinner over, the dining corners are then converted to bedrooms. Everything is collected and heaped in two or three corners. Sisal bags are spread on the floor and farther, mother and children line themselves up on these bags. This needed skill and care for nobody among the five families was to be left without sleeping room. Thus with *sufurias* [pots and pans], plates and stools at the bottom of the bed, boxes, bags, and other items at the upper end, the families fitted themselves in the remaining space. There they lay still, children snoring, a baby crying at that corner, a man turning at the other and some sleepless mothers staring at the roof till the break of the day.

On the stroke of four o'clock in the morning the huge gong at the Headman's camp is hit hard and loud. At the sound of this the mothers quickly shake themselves up and steal out of their bags. Hurriedly they kindle fires and boil some porridge. This they put in bottles to take with them on their long safaris and the rest leave in the pots for the sleeping children to enjoy later. The remains of supper are packed in tattered pieces of paper and put in small sisal bags. Infants that cannot be left behind are securely fixed on their mothers' backs. Elder children are woken up to be given the day's instructions—what to do after school or even instead of going to school. Within three quarters of an hour, with pangas and shovels in one hand, luncheon bags hanging from their shoulders and the other arm at the back supporting the babies, the gallant mothers hurriedly make for the Headman's camp to join the men who have already got there. They must be punctual lest something extra lies in wait for them even after the hard day's work.

At the Headman's camp the multitude lines up in twos and the homeguards check that all are present. This finished, all homeguards are distributed along the long rows and the long march begins. Kialua is fifteen miles away, their destination. They have to reach there before seven o'clock in the morning. A constant moderate pace had to be kept, therefore. A whip always accelerated the speed of those who lagged behind.

The minute they reach their destination, the day's toil begins. The digging and the shoveling go on incessantly. The ditch they worked so hard on was meant to go all round the forest. A trench fifteen feet deep and ten feet wide with sharp sticks planted at the bottom, was good enough to keep the terrorists from crossing over into the rural area. Every day, the ditch had to be advanced ten yards. Babies would cry, women would faint, men would collapse, but who cares? The target had to be hit, and that before the end of the day. Half an hour's break was given for lunch. Few carried any. For most people the precious half hour was more for resting their weary bones than for filling their stomachs. Time and again some fell into eternal sleep even during the half hour, but all passed unnoticed. The ditch had to be dug up; Mau Mau terrorists had to be kept off from the people; security had to be given to the Kikuyu tribe.

As the sun goes down, the people go down with it. Most women have already reached the end of their tether. It is therefore for the stronger men to put more effort and dig up the last foot to set their comrades free. With persistence, the last bit is done. The last grain of soil is shoveled out and backs can be turned to the cruel ditch. Limping, ill and utterly exhausted, the Kikuyus drag themselves back to the village and into their huts. Some have to answer unwelcome questions from the children at home. "Where did you leave Mother, Aunt?" or "Where is the baby, Mummy; you did not leave it behind?" Slowly shaking their heads and with tears in their eyes, the answerers tactfully explain how the missing comrades achieved eternal rest by the Kiahia Ditch.

Grace Akinyi Ogot
ELIZABETH
Kenya 1966   English

A pioneering writer of modern African fiction, Grace Akinyi Ogot was born May 15, 1930, in Kenya's Central Nyanza Province, where she has lived most of her life in the town of Gem. A child of Luo parents who had converted to the Anglican Church, she attended Ng'iya Girls' School, where her father taught, and Butere High School, and trained as a nurse and midwife in Kenya, Uganda, and England. Ogot later worked variously as a scriptwriter and journalist for the BBC

Overseas Service, a community development officer, and a public relations representative of the Air India Corporation of East Africa. In politics, she served both as an elected and nominated member of parliament, an assistant minister of culture, and in ambassadorial positions at the United Nations and UNESCO.

Ogot's reputation, however, rests mainly on her career as a writer. A founding member of the Writers' Association of Kenya, her early stories including "The Year of the Sacrifice" (1962) and "Ward Nine"(1964) appeared in *Black Orpheus*, *Transition*, and *East Africa Journal*. Ogot continued on a trailblazing path with the publication of *The Promised Land* (1966), which shares with Nigerian writer Flora Nwapa's *Efuru*, published the same year, the status of being the first modern novels written in English by African women. Ogot's literary output consists of two novels, the second being *The Island of Tears* (1980); a novella, *The Graduate* (1980); two volumes of short stories, *Land Without Thunder* (1968) and *The Other Woman* (1976); and a rewriting of the Luo myth of lost innocence first published in Dholuo as *Miaha* (1983) and republished in English as *The Strange Bride* (1989).

Ogot's fiction draws equally from the rich history and customs of the Luo people and her own multidimensional career, which spans Kenya's rural and urban experiences. "Elizabeth," the story selected for this volume, was published in 1966 in *East Africa Journal* and later incorporated into the collection *Land Without Thunder* under the title "The White Veil." Ogot presents the rape, pregnancy, and subsequent suicide of a young female secretary as a crisis in gender and class relations with dreadful emotional and psychological consequences for women seeking the validation of their communities.

Marjorie Oludhe Macgoye and Tuzyline Jita Allan

✦

It had just struck 8 o'clock when Elizabeth entered her new office. Immediately the telephone rang, and she picked it up nervously.

"Hullo, 21201."

"Hullo there, is that Mr. Jimbo's secretary?"

"Speaking, can I help you?" Elizabeth tugged the telephone under her chin and drew a pad and a pencil from the drawer.

"Oh, yes, may I speak to Mr. Jimbo please."

"Sorry, he has not come yet; he does not come till 8:30 a.m. Could you kindly ring again, please?"

"Right-o, I will do that."

"Hullo—hullo . . ." but Elizabeth heard the click the other side and then the usual buzzing sound. She replaced the receiver with a bang, annoyed that she had not got the caller's name.

The door leading to Mr. Jimbo's office stood open. The spacious office, with a huge mahogany desk and a deep green carpet covering the floor, was neatly arranged. There were no curtains on the windows; instead, light Venetian blinds were drawn up on the large windows facing the main road, suggested that the sun entered the offices in the afternoon. Everything was neatly arranged on the table and a photograph of a very attractive woman holding two little boys stood smartly at one corner, like watchmen guarding the office. Elizabeth scrutinised the photograph and then returned it to its place. She went back to her office and stood at the little window to look at the jammed traffic below. The offices of the Department of Aviation were in Manila House on the 4th floor on Heroes Lane. From there one could see a good part of the city and the stretch of empty land that extended along the Mombasa road to the airport.

Elizabeth wondered how long she would stay in the Department of Aviation. She had moved from two offices in a matter of months since she returned from the U.S. where she had taken her secretarial training. She first worked for four months in a big American motor firm as a secretary to the assistant manager; and when that failed she found employment with the Wholesalers and Distributors Limited, as secretary to the European manager. After two agonizing months, and unable to satisfy the demands of her boss, Elizabeth walked out of her job without giving any notice. Both bosses had given her the impression that she ought to be a cheap girl ready to sell her body for promotion and money. When Elizabeth turned up at the Department of Aviation for interview, the personnel officer apologetically but conclusively told her that they could only take her on at £790 per annum instead of her previous salary of £850.

Footsteps on the stairs alerted Elizabeth. She walked back to her desk and busied herself on the typewriter. Presently, the door opened and Mr. Jimbo walked in. Elizabeth got up automatically and opened the door leading to the main office after murmuring, "Good-morning." Her new boss eyed Elizabeth from foot to head and then sat heavily on a rocking chair. Elizabeth closed the door gently and continued with her work.

Before long the bell rang, and a green light flickered above the internal line. Elizabeth picked up the receiver.

"Would you come for dictation right away, please?"

"Yes, sir, right away." She picked up her shorthand notebook and pencil and entered the main office.

"Sit down, will you."

Elizabeth obeyed. At that moment the private telephone rang, and Mr. Jimbo relaxed in the rocking chair and spoke leisurely to the caller. Elizabeth examined her new boss surreptitiously. He was about 40 years or so. About 5'9", jet black, he had an oily skin, chubby face, and boldly brushed black hair. His upper teeth looked too white to be real—and his dark gums exaggerated the whiteness. His deep fatherly voice was full of confidence and authority. He did not look the mischievous type, nor did he look fierce. But Elizabeth knew that time alone could tell; she would do her best to stay on the job this time, if only to avoid being a rolling stone.

"Right, see you and madam at about 8 p.m. Bye."

He replaced the receiver and started dictating straight away.

At 11 a.m. Elizabeth had typed a heap of letters—and she placed them before Mr. Jimbo for his signature. He frowned at her. "That was quick."

Elizabeth smiled and closed the door behind her. She had been warned about the amount of work in Jimbo's office by the previous secretary, but she was confident she would manage. By 12.15 p.m. she had cleared her desk, and she walked out for lunch feeling less nervous than she had been in the morning.

The following Monday a beautiful woman walked into Elizabeth's office to see Mr. Jimbo, who was having a meeting with senior members of the department. Elizabeth wondered where she had seen the woman before. She was tall and slim, with a pale chocolate skin and a startling hair style.

"Is he busy?" she asked cautiously.

"Yes, he is having a meeting," Elizabeth told her. "What is your name please? I will tell him on the phone."

"I am his wife," the lady told her with a genuine smile.

"Now I remember where I've seen you! I have seen the beautiful photograph you took with your two sons. Please sit down, Mrs. Jimbo. I will mention to him that you are here."

Elizabeth pressed the bell and whispered, "Your wife is here—shall I tell her to wait?"

"No—I will speak to her right away."

The telephone clicked, and before Elizabeth could give the message, Mr. Jimbo stood at the door.

"Sorry, Amy dear, would you take the driver, the meeting is still going on. I will give you a ring when I finish."

"Right, will be hearing from you then." She turned to Elizabeth. "I'd better be going."

Amy Jimbo thanked Elizabeth and left with the driver. She looked a contented good wife. Elizabeth believed in a happy marriage—that was her secret dream. Now to see the Jimbos so confident and in love intensified her longing for her lover at Ohio State University in the United States, where he was finishing his post-graduate studies in engineering. She stared into space for a while, and then returned to her typewriter.

The busy weeks slipped into months, and when Easter came, Elizabeth with two girl friends took a long weekend to Mombasa where they did nothing but bathe, eat, and write the longest love letters they had ever written. For Liz, there was plenty to be thankful for. At last God had answered her prayers: she was working among people who respected her womanhood and capabilities. Mr. Jimbo had given her the respect she had longed for and other members of staff had not molested her in any way. Sometimes he had given her much work, and often she worked late in the evenings when all other secretaries had gone home. True, during the past weeks, with plenty of late hours, she had experienced moments of fear. But what had calmed her eventually was Jimbo himself: the fatherly boss. He once told Elizabeth, "I hate to leave you to walk to the hostel alone when it is so late, but I don't believe in giving lifts to young girls. Soon the town would start gossiping and you would get a bad name for nothing. You have a long future in front of you, my child. You should protect your name."

The girls arrived back in the city by night train, ready for work on Tuesday. With only a few days to go before the International Aviation conference in Nairobi, Mr. Jimbo's desk was piled with numerous draft documents for stencilling. And a pile of cards to be sent out for a cocktail party to be held on the eve of the conference still stood untouched. Elizabeth worked late each evening to reduce the pile. Mr. Jimbo gave her a spare key so that she could leave the office when she pleased. He also instructed the watchman to be around the building whenever Elizabeth was working late.

That Saturday afternoon was particularly hot. Liz glanced at her watch; it was about 1:30 p.m. As she covered her typewriter to dash out for lunch, the door flung open and there stood Mr. Jimbo beaming at the door. "You poor kid—still working! The world is not ending today, my dear."

"Thank you, sir, I have finished now. I will have plenty of time when the conference is over next week—have you forgotten something, sir?"

"No, I thought you might still be working and I came to release you."

"That is kind of you," Elizabeth answered with a smile. It was rare to have bosses who really cared about the amount of work their secretaries did, she thought.

Jimbo walked into his office, and Elizabeth took her handbag and magazines ready to leave.

"All right, sir, I am off now."

"Just a second," he fumbled with some papers and then looked up. "I have more packed lunch here than I really need—here, have a bite."

Elizabeth did not want to share Mr. Jimbo's packed lunch—he had not expected to find her in the office anyway and she knew Mr. Jimbo was just being polite.

"Thank you, sir, but I would rather not—my lunch will be waiting at the hostel."

"Go on, don't be shy. I can't eat all these, come in and sit down."

"No, sir, I really must go, I would rather have a proper lunch—I missed breakfast."

"Come on, don't argue, just one."

Out of sheer politeness, Elizabeth went in and sat on a settee. She did not want to appear rude to a man who had treated her with great respect. Yet she hated his persuasiveness. He handed her a packet, and she picked out an egg sandwich. Then out of the blue, the boss moved over and sat with a big sigh beside Elizabeth on the settee.

"I am impressed with your work, my girl. Since you came, this office looks different. One never really knows what a good and efficient secretary is until one has one." He paused and picked up another sandwich.

"Thank you, sir—pleasure is mine—you are an easy person to work for—I was not that good till I came to this establishment." She tried to dodge the rough surface of Jimbo's tweed coat that rubbed against her upper arm.

"I'm glad to hear that. The only thing that worried me is this, my child." He fingered the little diamond ring on Elizabeth's left finger.

"Oh that—sir, nothing doing for another two years or so and by that time a lot of changes will have taken place."

She almost told him the truth: that Ochola was coming back in November and they planned to get married on New Year's Day—but that was still a secret.

"Who is he—I mean this lucky chap—what does he do?"

"Still a student," Elizabeth answered nervously.

"He is lucky, a real lucky man to possess you. You are efficient, you are feminine, and you are very beautiful." And his heavy arm went round Elizabeth's slender waist and gripped her tight.

"Oh, please, sir, please—stop this—please," and she struggled to her feet.

"Listen to me, Liz—listen," Mr. Jimbo spoke sternly. "I can't hurt you, I like you like my own child, I can't hurt you—honestly. I—I just wanted to tell you that you are so enchanting, and I—I just wanted to feel your body close to mine, but I won't hurt you. I promise."

She felt the hard pounding of his heart. He looked at her warmly, with yearning. Elizabeth pulled herself together and broke loose from Jimbo's grip. The humid air stifled her.

"Please, sir—let me go, I am engaged to get married soon—please, Ochola will not understand, nor will your wife, your children, and the people. And think of my job—oh, please, let me go—" and she sobbed aloud.

"Now you are to behave like a good girl—the people will hear us—and think of the scandal. I've told you that I can't hurt you—I care too much to hurt you." He locked the door and put the key in his coat pocket. Beads of perspiration stood on his nose and his forehead, his muscles were as taut as the top of a drum, and his face was wild with excitement.

Elizabeth never suspected that beneath the firm crust of Jimbo's restrained face, a volcano simmered. Physical contact had provoked an eruption. "I just want to feel your breasts, nothing more—then we can go to lunch."

He moved over to her, but she ducked behind the desk—and then to the window, and to the door and back to the desk. But Jimbo caught up with her and dragged her to the settee. He searched for Elizabeth's mouth but the girl was too violent and buried her face in her skirt. "Please Liz." He kissed her ears and her neck, then her upper arm, while his big hands reached desperately for the young breasts. His hot breath and the masculine odour that radiated from his body made Elizabeth quite sick. She drew away from him, her face in a grimace of pain.

"No, Liz, you're so lovable," he whispered. "Your lovely skin is smooth and tender like the petals of a flower. No, no, I can't hurt—I can't, I care too much. Just let me feel the warmth of your womanhood. I won't hurt you, Liz. I promise. I do—I do—." Elizabeth fought helplessly beneath this bulky man who had posed as an angel for so many months. And it was like one of those terrible nightmares without an end.

The day was spent. Elizabeth threw blankets off from her body. Her pillow was damp, and the crumpled photograph of her fiancé which she was tightly embracing when she dozed off to sleep had fallen on the floor. She got up slowly and walked to the window facing the city centre. The pain between her legs had worsened and her whole body was aching as it did on the first day when her friend tried to teach her to ride a bicycle. The city looked peaceful except for a few cars moving homewards away from the business area. The tip of Manila building could just be seen facing Embakasi Airport which it served. Down below in the central park were hundreds of sightseers—mostly Asians—sitting in groups, men and women segregated. Their innocent children ran wildly like bees among flowers. As a child, Elizabeth had felt happy chasing grasshoppers in the open fields below her home opposite the River Nzoia. She and her little cousin had looked forward to the time when they would be adults. They wanted to discuss adult subjects and perform adult duties.

Then she thought of the day when her periods came at the age of eleven, how she ran to her grandmother's hut weeping that she was sick and how her granny comforted her and told her that she was now a woman and must behave like an adult, and stop playing with boys. She remembered how she had looked her in the eye and asked innocently: "What do you mean?" To which her granny had replied, "When a mature girl plays with boys, it is like a child playing with fire; the child can burn herself and probably burn her parent's house and cause great sadness. In the same way, when a mature girl plays with boys and becomes pregnant outside of wedlock, she destroys herself and eventually destroys the whole family."

Although she did not understand the words of her grandmother, the horror in her face indicated to her that it was a bad thing and she ran back to her mother's house reciting the words—"It is like a child playing with fire; it can cause much sadness."

Elizabeth drew up the curtains to shut out the city and its people from her. She felt out of step with the sophisticated life in towns. She wondered whether she would ever get used to it. A sudden aching longing for her home in the country, the close-knit family life she had shared there, and the security she had felt, gripped her. She took her toilet bag and walked slowly to the wash-room. She entered the incinerator room, pulled out her blood-stained nylon pants that Ochola had sent her for Easter, and wrapped them tightly in a brown paper bag. She pressed the incinerator open, and dropped the pants in the fire and let it close. She stood there sobbing quietly as the pale smoke reluctantly curled up towards the sky. Jimbo had robbed her of the treasure she had hidden away for so many years. Her whole world had fallen apart, and she felt nothing but bitterness and sorrow at the thought that she had nothing left to offer her man on the wedding day.

Elizabeth left the hostel early Monday morning with a group of friends. But instead of catching the double-decker bus that went to Heroes Street, she took a footpath across the central park towards Station Road. She walked briskly, dodging the stream of cars that poured into the city. When she reached the Labour Office at 8 a.m., hundreds of women of all ages had already arrived and were waiting for the doors to be opened. Some gray-haired women sat in a group, talking in low voices. Elizabeth's heart went out for them. Sorrow had eaten away their youth, leaving permanent lines on their foreheads.

As the number swelled, their morose faces reminded Elizabeth of the seekers of the kingdom of God who used to throng her father's church on Sunday, when she was small. But no! She felt that God must have moved to another land where people acted more justly.

A hand resting on Elizabeth's shoulders startled her, and she turned round sharply.

"Liz, what are you doing here? Come into the office." She followed the Labour Officer into the crowded office and sat down.

"Don't tell me you have left that job again." Elizabeth nodded.

"Why this time, Elizabeth, were they being naughty again?" She nodded.

Mrs. Kimani, a middle-aged motherly woman had dealt with hundreds of cases similar to Elizabeth's, and seeing that Elizabeth did not want to say much she did not press her.

"I can't press you to tell me the story, my child—my heart is full to the brim with story after story of you women who have suffered shame and cruelty in this city. You see those young women out there. They are secretaries and typists who want different jobs."

Elizabeth looked at Mrs. Kimani with keen eyes. "That is what I want—help me find a different job, even if it carries half my present salary."

"No, Liz, don't say that—you are one of our best secretaries, we can't lose you. Let us try Church Organisations this time Liz, don't give up too soon."

Elizabeth looked at Mrs. Kimani with stray eyes—she liked her motherly advice, and she had helped many girls to get good jobs, but this time it was not her fault.

"Ma, remember how you talked to me when I left the American firm and the Wholesalers? You assured me that working for a fellow African with the country's progress at heart, would be different. Ma, now that it has failed with the African, I have a strange feeling that it may not work even with Church Organisations. They all seem to be alike, inside the Church or outside. I have made up my mind."

"O.K., Liz, try these places. I will ring to tell them that you are calling this morning. Call on me if you are unsuccessful. And remember what I tell so many young people like you. Man has defied the Laws of society; God alone will deal with him, and it has to be soon." Mrs. Kimani watched Elizabeth disappear at the gate.

At the end of the week Elizabeth got a simple job with the Church Army, to care for destitute children in a small home. The work needed simplicity and patience. The woman in charge of the home asked her to shorten her nails. She had to wear a white overall, a white hairscarf and flat white shoes. One look at herself in the mirror nearly knocked her down.

"A nun? No, a nurse? No, no, no, a shop assistant? Oh no, an ayah? It looked like it. From a top grade secretary to an ayah!" Elizabeth tucked in a little flimsy hair that stuck out of the scarf near her ears. She followed Mother Hellena into a big hall where some thirty grubby-looking children were playing. Some were clay-modelling, some were painting, while the smaller ones were playing with wooden bricks. Mother Hellena turned to Elizabeth.

"All these poor things have never known anything called love. They know they were brought into this world by somebody, but they don't know who! They hear other children like themselves have mothers and fathers, brothers and sisters, but they have nothing. What you and I can give them is what they will ever remember. Their whole future is in our hands."

All these eager and pathetic eyes were fixed upon Elizabeth and tears stung her eyes, for she knew she had no future to offer them. She herself had lost her bearings. She had escaped from the sophisticated life of the city, hoping to find solace and comfort among the innocent children. Now they were all looking at her with yearning eyes, each one of them calling out to her, "Our future is in your hands, give us love and comfort which we have never known."

Elizabeth suppressed her tears and turned to Mother Hellena. "I did not know you had such a great task, mother. I will offer them the little I have."

Ochola was shocked to hear about Elizabeth's new job. Her letter sounded pessimistic, but Ochola felt too guilty to press her. It was a mistake on his part to have allowed Elizabeth to return to Africa. He could have married her in the United States and they would have returned together as man and wife. But Elizabeth had insisted that she wanted to be married among her people and he gave in to her. Now with so many miles between them, Ochola found it difficult to be tough with her. He was returning home in five months' time and he hoped to have everything under control.

Elizabeth struggled through the first week—the children were noisy, reckless, and often rude. They had looked eager on her arrival, but now they resented her presence. She thought of ringing Mrs. Kimani and telling her that she had changed her mind, but she could not bring herself to it. After one month the children started to like Elizabeth. Their pathetic gratitude made her at once humble and frustrated. The children needed so much more than she could give. She asked God to give her patience and understanding.

In the middle of June, Elizabeth felt very sick. Mother Hellena nursed her at home for two days but her position gradually deteriorated and she had to be admitted into hospital.

She spent three restless nights in hospital, but on the fourth day, Mother Hellena was allowed to talk to her. She was better and could eat. Mother Hellena pressed her hands tightly and looked away from her.

"Elizabeth, the doctor tells me that you are expecting a baby." The young woman's heart pounded painfully against her chest and she felt very hot like a person suffering from a severe fever. The words played in her ears again. Did expecting a baby mean the same thing as being pregnant? She sat upright with a jerk and faced Mother Hellena.

"Did the doctor say so, did he say I am pr—?"

She let her lips close and ran a hand over her belly under the bedclothes. The confusion, the bitterness, and the self-reproach for what she regarded as personal failure had blotted everything out from Elizabeth's mind so that she had not realised she had missed two months. She grabbed Mother Hellena's arm and did not let go—she had to hold on to some thing. Violent pain was stabbing at her throat, her chest, her belly. The look on Mother Hellena's face could only be rebuke to her: "You are going to bring another unhappy, fatherless child into the world. Another destitute."

She recollected the admonition of the grandmother: "When a mature girl plays with boys and becomes pregnant outside of wedlock she brings much sadness to herself and to her family."

Exactly one month after leaving the hospital, Elizabeth made up her mind. Sooner or later Mother Hellena was going to get rid of her. The man she loved tenderly would not understand her even if she spoke with the tongue of angels. She could not return home to face her parents and grandmother. And she knew that firms did not like to employ pregnant women. The picture of Amy Jimbo came to her mind—it was the first time she had thought of her. Happy, contented, and secure for life, when she, Elizabeth, in her tender age, had no roof above her head. No, it was not fair. While Jimbo posed as an angel in the eyes of his wife, she, Elizabeth, was suffering shame and want—how heartless! She slipped her engagement ring on her finger and when the children were resting in the afternoon she dashed into town to have her hair done. As she sat lazily on the hair-dresser's chair, the woman teased her:

"You have got a twinkle in your eyes. Are you meeting him tonight."

"Yes," Elizabeth whispered back.

"You are a beautiful woman, he is so lucky."

"Thank you—he is very handsome too, and kind."

The words resounded in her mind to mock her.

In the evening Elizabeth told Mother Hellena that she would spend the weekend with her uncle's family in town. She pulled out a notebook from her handbag and gave it to Mother Hellena. "Perhaps you may like to read about my childhood and my life in the city. I wrote it some time ago—I will take it on Monday." She pressed Mother Hellena's hand and left to catch a bus to the city.

There was nobody at Mr. Jimbo's home when Elizabeth got there—they might have taken the children for a drive, and perhaps the servants were spending their Sunday afternoon seeing friends. Elizabeth stood at the door for a while but the wind was biting around her ankles: it was going to rain. Presently she noticed the laundry-room near the garage was open. She pulled a notebook from her handbag and scribbled a message: "I have come to stay, it is chilly standing at the door, so I thought I would wait for you in the laundry-room. It is me, Elizabeth."

She tied the note on the door handle. The Jimbo family returned home just before sunset.

"Somebody has been visiting us," Amy said, opening the note. Then she read it aloud. Mr. Jimbo snatched the note from his wife's hand. He tried to say something but only smothered meaningless sounds came out. Then he walked down to the laundry-room in silence, while his wife, Amy, and the children stood dumbfounded near the door.

Jimbo flung the door open, and saw the body of a woman dangling on a red scarf. His feet gave way and he sagged to the ground.

"Quick, Amy, quick, the police please, an accident!" Dusk was gathering fast. The police were on their way to the house. They will probe, cross-examine and double-check their facts till they reach the truth, Jimbo thought. Oh my God, ending up like this!

Elizabeth Masaba's notebook was handed over to the police by Mother Hellena, and she knew she was doing the right thing. The Mother Superior thought grimly of all the other girls who were trapped in this way by those who are more powerful than they are.

Hamida Mohamedali
THE RETREAT
Kenya 1967 English

Drum Beat, the collection of poems from East Africa compiled by Lennard Okola in 1967, has a unique significance in the history of East African literature. It is one of the earliest products to reflect the concept of East Africa as a unified poetic entity. It also assembles, through careful discrimination and selection, those poets who both excel individually as practitioners of their genre, and represent collectively the emerging trends in the region.

Hamida Mohamedali, one of only two female authors in the volume, therefore, stands out as a pioneer East African poet. She was born in Nairobi in 1946. At the time of this poem's publication, she was twenty-one years old and an arts student at University College, Nairobi. The poem is full of spiritual longing, expressing the desire for retreat into a deeper, truer, but thus far still-elusive abode.

Emilia Ilieva

✦

I have lusted to flee away,
From the insane wantonness
Of a feeble mind
Teased by doubt, hate, and fear.

I have lusted to flee
Where the virile spring

Loosens the spirit from the womb,
To be left off, scampering, sheathed
By streaks of shimmering splendour
Of the sun. Set aflame by
Twin Destinies
Love and Hope.

Truth, God, my Father;
Thou, whom I discern
In the glinting dew drop
Perching, in the quiet of the morn,
On green cactus;
Thou, whom I discern
In the cold clod of mud struggling
With a young blade of grass.
My song to Thee remains unsung.

I have sought quietude in the
Lingering tender *sitar*,
The panting rhythm of the drum,
The seductive scraping of the violin.
I have yet to banish
Anguish and weariness of this aching existence.

Rose Mbowa
THREE POEMS
Uganda 1967, 1971   English

At the time of her death in 1999, Rose Mbowa was associate professor of drama at Kampala's Makerere University, the first academic and the first woman to achieve that rank. A graduate of Makerere and the Theatre School of Leeds University, England, she chaired the Music, Dance, and Drama Department at Makerere for nearly a decade. She contributed significantly to the modernization and promotion of Ugandan theater, and several of her compositions and productions, including her epic musical play *Mother Uganda*, about Uganda's postindependence experiences, were performed across Africa and Europe.

Born in Kibuye, Kampala, in 1942, Rose Mbowa attended Kibuye Primary School, Buloba Junior Secondary School, and Gayaza High School before entering Makerere University, in 1964, to take an honors degree in English. At Makerere the early- to mid-sixties are often referred to as the "golden years" of Ugandan literature. From that time forward, many of Mbowa's classmates also built distinguished literary and scholarly careers. Vital components of their education were regular public readings of young writers' work and student-edited literary periodicals. Such activities engendered the poems included here.

Two other Makerere activities that contributed significantly to Rose Mbowa's development as an artist were the weekly radio program featuring East African writers called *In Black and White*, and the Makerere Free Traveling Theater (MFTT), both run by Rose Mbowa's teacher and friend, David Cook. The MFTT was both a cocurricular training exercise in drama for undergraduates and an outreach program to take theater entertainment to upcountry and especially rural East African communities. Every year, during the university's long vacation, members of the program traversed the East African countryside performing—free of charge, as its name indicates—elaborate repertoires of plays and other entertainment.

After a brief spell in broadcasting, Mbowa entered professional theater, eventually recognized as Uganda's best actress. A winner of nearly all the top national theater awards (best actress 1973, Presidential Meritorious Award 1975, best producer 1982 and 1983), she also held several international awards, including the U.S.'s Manillow Fellowship. In 1998, shortly before her death, she received a standing ovation at the Kennedy Arts Center in Washington, D.C., for her performance as Mother Courage in *Nalukalala*, a Ugandan adaptation of Brecht's famous play. Among her many pioneering activities was the launching of theater-in-development activities in Uganda, where performance not only entertained but also sensitized and mobilized rural communities, encouraging them to discuss and deal with developmental problems and challenges.

The three poems below were written during Rose Mbowa's undergraduate years at Makerere. They exhibit obvious influences, including stylistic quirks, of the kind of English verse that Ugandan undergraduates then studied, including Shakespeare, the Metaphysical poets, the Romantics, and a smattering of T. S. Eliot, as well as the King James Bible. Beyond this, however, the reader senses the emergence of an individual and original voice, aware of the challenges facing a young person coming to maturity in the early years of Uganda's independence. In both "Light" and "Ruin," the author explores that perilous but inevitable, "unquenchable" struggle for self-knowledge that ends in ambiguous "transfiguration." Both poems have a strong metaphysical aura about them, rendering them open to various interpretations. A feminist reading of "Ruin," seizing on the striking images of the imposing, solid structure and the tenacious "she" who dares to confront it, may justifiably identify a challenge to patriarchy. Rose Mbowa confided to friends, however, that the poem was inspired by a physical reality in the neighborhood of her childhood home in Kibuye. There was a big abandoned house on a rise near her home, she said, about which she and her friends speculated as they walked by, wondering what lurked behind those imposing closed doors. "That Game," on the other hand, is more specifically grounded in Uganda's historical experience. It contains numerous allusions to the troubled political events, beginning in 1966 and culminating in 1971 with the total usurpation of the original independence mandate, first by Milton Obote's dictatorship and ultimately by Idi Amin's.

Austin Bukenya

RUIN

Up on a hill it stood immovable,
Dark and gloomy in the dusk;
A heavy silence hung in the air
Restraining her courage, her will;
But on she walked.

A cricket whistled breaking the silence,
Lighting her path and her will;
Then suddenly it stopped,
As if suppressed by a heavy hand,
Still—on she moved.

Every move drew her nearer,
Every move gravitated towards the gloom;
Giant trees, heavy and dark before her rose,
Guards on duty, erect in the dark,
Through them—she pushed.

With eyes closed, arms outstretched,
She groped in an envelope of black;
The air grew dense and doomed,
Her heart drummed faster and louder;
To the door—she stepped.

With trembling hands she pushed,
A squeal pierced the air;
Flashes blinded her sight;
And down she descended at a blow,
On the grim, rude stone.

THAT GAME

With dazzling eyes: sweet poison in teeth,
He to the core armed plays his game;
Triumphantly the fools applaud,
While the wise weigh;
With feet on edge, mouth in mid-air
He cunningly his prey surveys;
Then suddenly he aims his shot:
Fool and wise applaud,

The game is won,
In the center firmly he stands:
Luxuriously flies by that time.

The time has flown: no fruit has yet emerged:
Fool and wise their heads together bend;
Meanwhile he comfortable puffs his pipe,
Belching the while for the richness of it all;
Then suddenly—
Eyes open: ears unstop
As the crowd clamours,
Clamours for its share:
Eyes left—right—
Up and down he stares,
Starts—

Gripping the table he aims his shot:
Once sweet, bitter becomes the poison:
Edgeward blows the storm,
Persists—accelerates
Arms outstretch
Eyes madly dart;
Topples—and stares into darkness.

LIGHT

To fight reality is to open a swinging door,
the blows we aim, on us do land:
we stagger transfigured in the truth, and
victors in defeat we stand to live

as from cells prisoners burst into life.
Thus she staggered as into being she came:
she'd believed she lived life in her cell
and had cried for a veil over her newborn light
that melodiously burns unquenchable.

That flaming self answered, and
now steadily rises on the way
till caution pricks that sole to
a halt that gnaws—

O fount of joy—peak of light
let light have light, then
life will be.

Mwajjuma Nalwadda
A WIDOW'S LAND INHERITANCE

Uganda 1969 Luganda

Mwajjuma Nalwadda represents the new Muslim Ugandan woman, strategizing to fight for her rights in the face of traditional Ugandan patriarchy. Her name, Mwajjuma, an Africanized form of "Bint Juma," indicates that she is a second- or even third-generation Muslim, and she is clearly conversant in Islamic law and practices. Armed with this knowledge and with her literacy, she takes on the sheikhs who have conspired to deny her and her daughters their rightful share in the family's property. Mwajjuma Nalwadda's challenge provides intriguing insights into the predicament of the Ugandan Muslim woman, perceived by many to be doubly disadvantaged by African tradition and Islamic male supremacy. Her tactical approach is not to oppose either institution head-on, but to demand that they play fair on their own terms—and to her advantage. Nalwadda understands that the injustice being done to her and her children is essentially sexist, but ultimately she interrogates the sheikhs' distorted interpretation of even the little to which the system entitles her.

Islam was introduced into Uganda in the middle of the nineteenth century, when the Waswahili and Arabs from the East African coast established close links with the rulers of the country. It has remained a significant religious force, with a following of about 10 percent of the country's 24 million people. Several factions have developed among the believers over the years. The Nateete Bukoto African Muslim Community, of which Mwajjuma Nalwadda's husband was the leader at the time of his death, was characterized by its preference for the blending of Muslim beliefs with African customs and traditions. Apparently this positive approach could be used opportunistically, as demonstrated by the sheikhs' recourse to traditional clan structures in refusing to allocate land to Mwajjuma Nalwadda's grandchildren.

Kiganda society is structured into fifty-two clans, each characterized by a totem, subtotem, drum signal, name list, and ancestral territory. The totems are often animal symbols, hence Nalwadda's reference to her grandchildren as belonging to the Leopard clan. The clans are patrilineal, meaning that a person inherits her or his clan from the father. Since the clans are also exogamous, forbidding intermarriage among members of the same clan, women will automatically belong to a different clan from that of their mothers. As such they would not be eligible to inherit land from their mothers' clans. This is an aspect of the tradition that Mwajjuma Nalwadda challenges as contradicting the *sharia*, the Islamic legal framework. The "fire" for which she threatens to pray is of course hellfire, or *jehanam* of which, in Islamic belief, there are seven levels of increasing severity, depending on the gravity of the sinner's transgressions.

Nalwadda's appeal is addressed to the leader of the African Muslim Community Bukoto Natete in Kampala.

Austin Bukenya and Abasi Kiyimba

16 November, 1969
Sheikh Zaid Mugenyiasooka
The President General
Sir, I am writing to you on a matter that you know well, the matter of my land as the widow of the late Sheikh Abdurahman Sekimwanyi.

I explained to you that three of my deceased children were entitled to a share of [their late father's] land, according to the Islamic Sharia, because they died long after their father had died. But the people who distributed the land delayed [and the children died before the distribution]. So whose fault was this? As their mother, I am entitled to inherit their land, according to the Islamic Sharia.

My daughter, who died last, Aisa Najjuma, left three children, and these children should be given her land. This idea of saying that the children are of the Ngo clan and cannot inherit land of the Lugave clan is not valid in the Islamic Sharia.

Lastly, as a widow of the late Sheikh Sekimwanyi, I am entitled to a share of his land.

Sheikh Kayinda and his colleagues, who handled the land distribution say that I shall not get my share as Sheikh Sekimwanyi's widow, and that I shall also not get the share of my children who died after their father. My three grandchildren, who lost [their] mother, have also been denied their mother's land; so where is the justice, and how do they [these sheikhs] understand the Qur'an? Are they torturing me because I am a woman? Have they forgotten that we were created by the same God?

Now Sheikh Kayinda is ill, and may die before settling this problem [of the land]. I am appealing to you to intervene in the matter before it is too late; for if Sheikh Kayinda should die before he puts right this issue, the fire that will burn him will be constantly requested for by me.

I am,
Muwajjuma Nalwadda
Widow of the late Sheikh Abdurahman Sekimwanyi

Translated by Abasi Kiyimba

LATE TWENTIETH CENTURY
(1970–1995)

Grace Akello
PRAY, NO REVENGE

Uganda 1979   English

Grace Akello was born in 1950 in Katakwi, formerly part of Soroti district in the eastern part of Uganda. After studying at Tororo Girls' School, she attended Makerere University, graduating with a degree in social work and social administration in 1974. Akello left Uganda for Kenya during the military dictatorship of Idi Amin, and lived in exile for years. After returning to Uganda, she became a member of parliament for Katakwi in 1996, and in 1999 was made minister of state for Gender, Labor, and Social Development (Entandikwa). Currently, she is the state minister for Northern Uganda Rehabilitation.

Grace Akello has been active in political, social, and cultural issues in Africa for more than thirty years. She is a founding member of the Nile Book Service, which specializes in sending textbooks to African schools. She has served as a board member of Christian Aid, worked with the Commonwealth Secretariat and the German Agency for Technical Co-operation, and served as deputy editor of *Viva*, a Nairobi-based women's magazine.

Akello's collection of poetry, *The Barred Entry*, was written in the 1970s while she was in exile in Kenya, and published in 1979. The poems are a lament for Uganda, giving voice to both the living and the departed who suffered under war and repressive dictatorship. "Pray No Revenge" reflects the voice of a victim for whom exile was a form of death.

Florence Ebila and Beverley Nambozo

✦

I found neither time nor place
To howl my revenge
To threaten vengeance
Thick and fast
On my treacherous seed

I found neither time nor place
To curse them
To annihilate them
To annihilate their existence
To wipe out their seed

I found neither time nor place
To prowl over their exhausted sleep
With spiteful claws strangle
Their supple pulsating throats
Or spirit evil
Mangle and destroy
The seat of their reason

I found neither time nor place
To perch over my weed-smothered grave

My grass-garlanded grave
To wait and shock pregnant women
With my vanishing dissipated corpse

I found time and place
When rejected and confronted
My ancestors
Showed Creator-endowed mercy
And prisoner-like
Seeking solace and justice
My erring, rebellious breed
I paraded before their eyes
Till sick with pity
My bosom they clasped
In eternity-lasting warm embraces
Accepting without question
My deserted
Rejected
Unmourned death

Miriam K. Were
THE MISCHIEVOUS COW
Kenya 1980   English

An internationally acclaimed medical expert in public health, particularly in the
area of HIV/AIDS prevention and control, Miriam Khamadi Were is also a successful author of books for young people. Between 1970 and 1980, she published
four novels in rapid succession: *The Boy in Between* (1970), *The Eighth Wife*
(1972), *The High School Gent* (1973), and *Your Heart Is My Altar* (1980), all of
which have been standard secondary school readers. The novels capture the troubled state of adolescent life in a society in transition from the tradition-bound
world to the modern, which is embodied by the values of Western education and
the search for individual fulfillment. *The High School Gent*, for example, belongs to
a subgenre of East African writing in the 1970s aptly called "the university
novel," for it depicts conflicted school-aged characters caught between two cultures. The young female protagonist in *The Eighth Wife* faces a threat from the
power of polygamy to render her, as it did the sixth wife, "a mere showpiece," and
in *Your Heart Is My Altar*, the dilemma facing the narrator is how to forge a

sexual and cultural identity unmarred by conflicts of gender and ethnicity.

With the honest emotion typical of a young, precocious mind, Chimoli, the narrator and main character in *Your Heart Is My Altar*, provides insights into the limited ways women are perceived in the society and how this affects the personal growth of young boys and girls. The novel's implicit message is that self-worth is a gift African societies must give their youth, and that gender prejudice, as manifested in the bullying tactics of some of the male characters and in the local chief's opposition to female education, considerably narrows young women's chances for success. The novel's first chapter, titled "The Mischievous Cow," introduces readers to the narrator's world of family and friends and its impact on her budding sense of self. It blends the images of repression at home and violation in other arenas to make clear early on that coming of age is not going to be easy for the narrator. Her identification with the "mischievous cow," the family's favorite among a herd of cattle, points to both vulnerability and strength as an important dynamic in the lives of the young.

Were was born in Kakamega District of western Kenya, the sixth of ten children of devoutly Christian parents. She attended William Penn College in Iowa and studied medicine at Indiana University, completing her medical degree at the University of Nairobi. Her academic achievements also include a master's degree in education at Uganda's Makerere University and a master's and a doctorate in public health from Johns Hopkins University. Were served for several years as the Kenyan representative at the World Health Organization, and was head of the Kenyan mission in Ethiopia, where she also served as director of the United Nations Population Fund (UNFPA) and the Country Services Technical Team in Addis Ababa (CSTAA). Currently, she is chair of the board of the African Medical and Research Foundation (AMREF) and the Kenya National AIDS Control Council. Her tireless advocacy on the behalf of young people and public health has earned her numerous awards, including the first U.S.-sponsored George P. Tolbert Health Award for outstanding contributions to International Health in 1980 and the International Order of Merit in 2000.

Tuzyline Jita Allan

✦

"I'm going to kick the whole lot of you out of my home," the familiar voice of Father rang and echoed throughout our homestead.

"If your mother takes your side again," he continued, "she can take the whole lot of you back to her clan with her. I can manage this home alone much better without a lot of good-for-nothing mouths to feed."

Father was at it for a long time. And for what must have been the one thousandth time, Mushitoshi was the cause. Mushitoshi, that cow with a demon in her head, had again sneaked out of the *boma* and into the neighbour's crop. At the very sound of Father's voice we went to our usual hiding places in the small bushes in the homestead. I could see my little brother, Chimwani's head peeping out from behind the banana leaves. He was not too young to know that he, too, must hide, but not old enough to realise that too much curiosity can reveal your hide-out. I and my sister Limwenyi, just older than I, were desperately trying to find shelter behind a bush that was not big enough for one of us.

"Ssss," I hissed as I crouched down, "you stepped on my toe."

"Shut your mouth!" she hissed back.

"But you stepped on my toe!" I insisted.

"A beating with a whole bunch of sweeping sticks will hurt a whole lot more than a little pressure on your toe. Can't you hear he is close to us?"

That it hurt from a beating with a bunch of sticks wasn't a lie. We had all had our turns of it, on and off. I could very well remember the kind of feeling one got when a whole bunch of sticks descended on the legs and behind. It wasn't as if Father went to get the sticks just to wallop us. He simply picked up the bunch we used for sweeping around the outside of the homestead.

"Keep on hiding," Father's voice rang out. "I know only too well where to catch you. Lazy ones like you have pits for stomachs and your mouths will soon be watering."

"God, I am hungry," I whispered to my sister as Father's voice reminded me of food.

"When are you not ever hungry?" my sister whispered impatiently as she put her hand across my mouth.

Well, I couldn't blame my sister. Quite often I wished I was like her. She could sulk for a whole day and keep her mouth closed, closed even to food. I couldn't say that of myself. I always made up for any difference between Mother and me, often by giving in, I guess because I didn't want the sun to set while I was angry, but also because my stomach wouldn't give me peace over one missed meal.

Listening to my sister's talk, you might have thought she hated me. But in fact she always hid me in the furthest corner, away from my father's sticks. There was that time I was trying to fight her when she hit me just a little too hard and I let this be known with my strong voice. Since fighting was illegal in our home, it meant a beating for both of us. When Father entered the kitchen where we were, my sister helped me out of the house first by putting me through the window. When we got outside, it was raining and we could not go to hide in the shrubs. There was a big woven *lwichi* (tray) leaning against the house, so my sister hid me in that while she pressed herself against the wall.

Father followed us to the back of the house. He saw my sister standing against the wall.

"Where is your sister?" he asked with what was supposed to be a firm voice but which sounded full of concern. My sister did not answer back. She just changed positions, placing herself between the *lwichi* and Father. Father must have been curious that she was not trying to run away and thought she was protecting something behind the *lwichi*. He took her by the hand just as I peeped to see what he was going to do. His eyes grew wide as he saw me.

"So you're hiding your sister from me," he said in almost laughing tones. "I thought you two were fighting!" So saying he walked off amused. As soon as he left, my sister pointed an unfriendly finger at me. I held her across the waist.

"I am your friend," I told her. "You hid me from Father."

"You are not my friend," she told me but I didn't care what she said. She was not pushing my hands off her waist. Besides she was stroking my head.

Father's voice was still ringing out as he addressed the air when Mother returned from the market. We could see Mother through the spaces between the branches. Father happened to look back and his eye caught her figure.

"Where are your children?" he demanded of her.

"How can I know where *your* children are when I spent the whole day at the market?"

"No doubt you will be cooking for them," Father continued.

"What have they done wrong?" Mother asked.

"What have they done wrong?" went on Father. "They left Mushitoshi loose and drove her into the maize crop!" he told her pointing to the garden.

"We didn't drive her into the maize crop," I protested in a whisper. Father had apparently forgotten he was a Christian, and should tell only the truth.

My sister did not say anything then. She just pulled my ear.

"Mushitoshi is not a cow," Mother was saying. "She is a better thief than even Icheji." She referred to the well-known thief of the area. "The devils are on the head of that cow," she declared at last.

I could no longer keep my head under the bush. For one thing, there were goodies in my mother's basket. For another I just wanted to have a look at her when she dared stay near to Father and talk with him when he was in this mood. It was a mood that made Father a completely different man. It gave him eyes that I feared to see. No one saw my head pop up from behind the bush. Father was following Mother into the house, reminding her in quieter tones of what a useless bunch of children she had borne him, and how they had all taken after *her* clan. Mother had, over the years, reminded him that there were more useless people in *his* clan than in hers. But having noted that this did not change his opinion, she just heard him in silence.

No sooner had Father's voice died down than our ears were met by the shrill tones of the owner of the maize. Everytime I heard Nyamusi's voice I thought she must have a sharper voice than anyone.

"You wealthy plough-users will not let a poor hoe-digging woman harvest anything," she was saying in that voice of hers.

"This time I will not let it pass," she continued. "I will miss church for once and go to the witchdoctor and you will wake up one morning and find all those cows dead."

No wonder Father's countenance changed when cows went into the crop. He must have dreaded hearing that sharp voice. The memory of it could bring to mind a night of howling dogs and owls, and ghosts dancing in the nude.

Mushitoshi had caused more trouble in the home than anyone I know. She would be placed in the *boma* with the rest of the cows, but she would never be found there in the morning. She would keep nudging at the poles until they gave way and then she would sneak out alone. Father decided to tie her up with a rope. For a while, this worked beautifully. But one morning she wasn't there and only a piece of the rope was left. Our joy and jeers at her defeat were thus short-lived. It was not the piece of rope that told us she was gone. It was a man's voice one early morning.

"I am going to sell this beast and make good the destruction she has brought about in my crop," he bellowed.

Even Father was spell-bound. He couldn't wait to dress. He went to see the speaker with a blanket wrapped around him.

"Neighbour," Father answered as amicably as he dared, "I myself tied up this cow. I do not see how it could have found its way to your crop."

I guess Father was thinking what we all thought: that there had been too much quietness and some neighbour had come to untie Mushitoshi and lead her to the man's *shamba*.

"Is this not your cow?" asked the angry neighbour.

"It is," agreed Father. "Come to the house, neighbour," he continued. "Let's go on talking there."

They went in to the hot tea awaiting them. Later on they walked off together amicably; this time with Father wearing a shirt.

That evening we told Father we thought some neighbour was playing a trick on us. He dismissed it weakly. In fact he was of the same opinion but dared not be too outspoken about it.

"I'm going to catch the man in the act," declared my big brother, Ligami.

"I'll come with you," little brother Chimwani said excitedly offering to join my brother in the nightwatch.

"Yes, you can come tonight!" he said to a very delighted Chimwani.

"I'll come with you," I had also chimed, caught up in the excitement.

"This is not a woman's chore," retorted Ligami.

Well, that is the way it was. I was either too young or I was kept away because I was a woman. What was there in this world for a youngster that happened to be a woman? Someday, there must be an answer.

That night there was mad tapping on our door.

"Come and see!" Ligami called to us.

Well, I guess that is usual. First boys tell you to keep away because they do not want girls and the next minute they are calling for you.

"Come and see Mushitoshi at her tricks," he added. I stumbled after my sister, who was already up and was now standing in the doorway.

Mushitoshi was a white cow with black streaks. It was easy to see her on such a moonlit night.

Mushitoshi walked slowly towards the tree onto which she was tied, with a new rope. Then with great speed she ran back. She did this several times.

"So this is the way she weakens the rope and eventually breaks it!" someone wondered.

"Who said cows don't think?" Limwenyi exclaimed.

"You always say my brain is thick as that of a cow," I reminded her. "Cows are not so stupid after all."

Mushitoshi had the surprise of her life that night. She was just about ready to gallop off when she noticed us all round her. Ligami tied her forelegs together and her hind legs together and tied these in turn to a tree. She lay down and was so still that she seemed dead. Hence my father's shock that next morning. It was a pity, because we were sure that for once we wouldn't wake up to the voice of someone screaming at our homestead on account of that Mushitoshi. But all the same we woke up to the resonant notes of Father's voice who didn't like the idea at all. Ligami painstakingly explained to Father how Mushitoshi gets away and how this was the only way to restrain her. To our surprise and delight Father agreed that we should picket her this way.

But it was difficult to be one thought ahead of that cow. She who had been meek and manageable most of the day, keeping her tricks for the night, decided to try out all her mischievous ideas in the day-time. This made my distaste of cattle-herding even greater.

"It's easy," my sister would tell me. "That's why the men do it."

"That's true," agreed her girl friend. "You just sit under the tree and let the cows graze. When they are satisfied, you simply drive them to the stream to drink and then they walk quietly home."

As a matter of fact, girls often looked forward to the times when their brothers were away so that they could look after the cattle, and have a lazy day. I had not been lucky with cattle-watching.

The first time I took the cattle grazing I came back with less than a third of them. The next time it was Mushitoshi who saved my day. I guess she had the sense to notice how frightened I was. Whenever she saw a cow wander off, she would go with it. As soon as she stopped she would moo loudly enough for me to hear her. Then I would run and drive the wanderers back to the herd. It surprised everyone to see the complete herd coming home that day.

"How did you manage it?" someone asked.

"Mushitoshi was wonderful," I told them. "She did the watching for me."

"Don't talk so loudly," Ligami cautioned, "It will harden Father's heart." Ligami and the rest of us had been trying our best to persuade Father to sell that cow, but he just wouldn't hear of it.

There had been the time when Mushitoshi broke her legs and we all thought that now she would only be fit for someone's meal. No one in our home would eat her meat of course; she was so much one of the family. But it was odd with Mushitoshi and us. If you asked any of us what we wanted done with the cow, we always said, "get rid of her." But when it came to negotiating the deal, nothing was good enough in exchange for Mushitoshi. When she broke her legs, we were not brave enough to kill Mushitoshi ourselves. None of us would do it. I guess we wanted the excitement that came with her adventures. So we took turns nursing Mushitoshi's broken legs until she was able to walk again. As if to thank us, her adventure and misbehaviour became less.

For me Mushitoshi was wrapped up with the memories of a special day. It was the day I discovered that young boys could be nice to strange young girls.

It was the year I had started school. Ligami and Limwenyi had been at school for a long time. Now it was my turn. But I had to miss school now and then when the herds-boy was away. This particular Saturday the latter and my brothers had gone to watch the circumcision rites of a cousin. Mother insisted that Limwenyi was now too big to herd the cattle, so I was sent off with them.

There are disadvantages of not going cattle-watching regularly. I missed out on a lot of things that I should have known or I would not have been so easily fooled.

The boys of my clan were so powerful that we had no trouble with intruders from the other clans coming into our land, so we spent the time playing.

We would play *Ndaroba*. Each one of us has a stone and we sat in a circle as usual.

Ndaroba
        Nandaroba
Ndaroba
        Nandaroba
Makuli yetsa
        Makuli yetsa ne fifye na ndaroba
Majina ngako
        Majina ngako noshinda no sasakwe.

We played this for a while and booed those who were slow and were caught. Then we played *Awoyi Kongolo* followed by *Ing'ombe*. I was feeling good that afternoon and thinking that boys were not so bad after all. I guess that is why they caught me.

"Let's show Chimoli something," one of them said. It must have been their password for what followed. No one asked what.

"Yeees," they agreed in a chorus. I looked from one boy to the next, perplexed.

"It's really simple," one of the boys explained to me.

"Bring her here," one of the called out. "We'll show her here."

I was getting a bit frightened but I was also curious. After all, I reasoned, these were boys from my clan. They couldn't bring too much harm to me. So I walked on to the spot. I was really surprised by what I saw.

"What is new about cattle dung?" I asked them. For there was only a pile of dung. It must have been dropped there by a great big bull.

"Nothing really," said the boy who had called to us plucking a piece of grass as he said so. He stuck the grass right in the centre of the cow dung pile. He turned to me.

"I'll pick up this grass," he said, "and put another one there to see if you can pick it up. We'll pick up grass without teeth." As he said so, he knelt down and picked up the grass without difficulty.

"There is nothing difficult about that," I told them. "But I won't pick it up with my mouth because I hate the smell of cow dung."

"Come on," someone said. "If you don't we'll know that girls can't do such a simple thing." That did it. Did these idiotic boys think I could not pick the grass up with my mouth just because I was a girl?

I decided that I could show them. I knelt down and bent my head to the grass. I was just plucking the grass from the dung heap when someone pushed my head down. My face right to my ears sunk into the heap, a good measure of it going into my mouth. There followed a roar of laughter that deafened my ears. In the meantime, I tried to get the dung out of my eyes and mouth. I was so filled with rage I could have wrung anyone's neck. But there were no necks to be wrung. So I just wailed as loudly as I could while I made my way to the stump where I had left my gourd of drinking water. I washed off as much dung from my eyes and mouth as I could and sat down weighing out the various types of revenge that came to my mind.

Boys are funny, I thought. They make you happy and then play such a dirty trick. I said in my heart a hundred times that I would never again join in any fun games with boys however innocent they looked. Who knows how they can twist things around. I also said in my heart that I would never take up a pre-arranged challenge just because someone told me that if I didn't do so then they would conclude something about me. To hell with their conclusions!

Just the thought that the dung had gone in my mouth made me start crying again. I started to curse in the words Mechi wa Lukulu used when he came and asked for food and found that it wasn't ready.

"As you walk may you stumble on a stump and may it pierce your intestines to shreds," he would say.

Thinking of some of the curses I had heard made me cry and laugh. I was quite unaware of time and of the person who had approached me. To make things even worse he was a boy, and a strange one at that.

"Go away," I shouted at him holding up my gourd ready to strike. I hoped he'd go quickly since he was much bigger than I. He was the size of my brother, Ligami, and I didn't really want to start a fight. I also noticed another thing. Mushitoshi had plodded her way to me and was rubbing her nose on my leg. I guess she was reassuring me of her support in case I needed it. I moved to the other side of the cow so that the cow was between me and this strange boy.

"I know you," he said to me. "I go to school with your brother and sister."

"Go away," I hissed again. "I have never seen you before."

"I am not from these parts," he said amicably. "I often visit my relatives in the clan next to yours and come to your clan sometimes."

"Go away!" I screamed.

"I saw what the boys did. They are bad boys. I was sitting in the tree from over there and I had been envying your fun. Then they did that to you."

"Go a-w-a-y," I started crying all over again.

"I had made something for you while I sat in the tree. I was afraid to bring it lest your boys beat me. I was going to give it to you when you started off back home. Then they did that to you."

All he was succeeding in doing was to make me cry more and more. By this time Mushitoshi had lain down and I was sitting beside her.

He sat on the other side of the cow.

"Try it on and see if it will fit," he said, reaching across the cow and handing the grass-woven bracelet to me. It was lovely. It was even better than the ones my sisters made. It was cream in colour with red spots. A beautiful bracelet.

"Why did you make it for me?" I asked unbelievingly.

"I like you," he said shrugging his shoulders. "I like the way you were laughing as you played with those boys."

"You don't know me," I said.

"I like you," he said for the last time and stood up. "I will help you round up your cattle and drive them home."

Mushitoshi must have decided that he wasn't too bad; she was rubbing her nose against his leg while he walked off and rounded up the cattle. It had become late. We drove them to the stream where I washed my face a bit more thoroughly, and then we drove the cows towards my home.

It is no problem driving cattle home with a stranger you don't know. You don't have to talk to each other. You just make sounds for the cattle to move on. Every so often, I looked at the woven bracelet on my wrist.

"Goodbye," he said when he came close to our homestead and he ran away. And I did not even know his name!

Boys are funny, I thought. One minute one of them is being very cruel and you want to send the whole lot of them to the bottom of the lake, and the next minute one of them is being very kind. I guess if you take revenge you hurt a lot of innocent people.

Anna Chipaka
A BARMAID'S LIFE

Tanzania 1980s   Kiswahili

Anna Chipaka was born in 1955 and grew up during the early years of Tanzania's independence, when girls who wanted an education faced many obstacles, not least among them early pregnancies. In some towns there were few openings for women who dropped out of school beyond working in bars, brothels, and petty trade. Anna Chipaka dropped out of school because of pregnancy and faced a difficult life, both as a wife and later as a barmaid and trader. Yet, in spite of her lack of formal education, she exhibits a high level of awareness of how her own life experience relates to larger social and economic issues affecting all working women.

The text that follows has been excerpted from a longer narrative, recorded in Kiswahili in the mid-1980s as part of a project to document the lives of ordinary

Tanzanian women, and later published in English in a book called *Unsung Heroines*. In these selections, Anna Chipaka tells of her early life, including her relationship with a kind and loving stepmother—a contrast to the common stereotype of the "evil stepmother." The rural African communal way of life also comes into play, when young Anna goes to the village to live with relatives. Training in matrimonial matters is usually given by the aunt or the grandmother or the *somo*, the village woman responsible for initiation rites. Girls who spend their early lives in towns rarely receive this training; as a result, they are usually—as in Anna's case—very ignorant regarding sexual matters until it is too late.

After her early premarital pregnancy, described here, Anna Chipaka did marry and have more children. Later, she divorced her husband and, left on her own to support herself and her family, returned to Mbamba Bay to live with her mother. She offers a rare glimpse into the unenviable conditions of life for barmaids, who form a special caste of sexually and economically exploited women in African urban areas. In her later life, Chipaka settled in Dar es Salaam as a trader. She died in 1992, survived by five children, all of whom she managed to educate up to postsecondary school level.

M.M. Mulokozi

✦

I was born in Mtwara (where my parents had moved to, from Mbamba Bay for wage employment) in the month of February, 1955. My parents are from the Wanyasa tribe living on the shores of Lake Nyasa, in Mbinga District. I was the youngest of the three children. There were two girls and only one boy who later died. I didn't know much about my mother until I was about fourteen. My parents separated when I was about three years old, and after a divorce, my mother moved back to Mbamba Bay. We were brought up by our father and stepmother. From what I can remember we were a happy family and we lived comfortably. Both my parents were workers; my father traveled a lot. His job as a trade unionist demanded long and extensive travels; we did not see as much of my father as we would have liked. He was a good man but strict, and he provided well for us. I do not remember going hungry; we were a happy family.

My step-mother, on the other hand, was quieter. She looked after us and fed us well. She did not talk much, but she gave us all the freedom and she loved us. We got on very well. In 1958 my step-mother gave birth to a pretty baby girl and I loved my pretty little sister very much. I carried her on my back as I played. My mother worked hard; she woke up early in the morning, prepared breakfast for us and made sure we ate breakfast before she left for work. She had a full day, working from morning and coming back late in the afternoon. While she was away, we were left in the care of a young ayah. We used to play with other young girls in the neighborhood, and we had great fun together.

As I was growing up I usually played with the neighbors' children my age. Some of my playmates were slightly older, but we got on well. The older girls sometimes sent us away, but as I grew up I was accepted and played with them and the boys. When I was about thirteen I had my first menstrual period. It came as a shock to me, as I did not know what it meant. . . . From my aunt I learned about the new changes taking place in my body. . . . While staying with my aunt I was only taught the basics and a few facts of life which I did not even understand; and I went to school as usual.

I became pregnant when I was fourteen and in primary school in Dar es Salaam. I do not remember what happened. It was such a long time ago, but I know the man was much older. . . . After I was six months pregnant I realized something was wrong. . . . I was very healthy and plump and nobody noticed that I was pregnant, not even my step-mother or neighbors. A few months later my step mother did notice; and she began to ask questions. I was frightened but she was even more frightened because she did not even have the courage to tell my father. When I was in my eighth month my step-mother picked up courage and went to see my uncle and told him the "bad" news. My uncle in turn went to see his younger brother and together with my step-mother they discussed the issue and decided to tell my father. . . .

The meeting of my aunts, uncles, my grandfather, my sister, myself and my parents took place in our house one evening. . . . My father was so angry that he threatened to throw me out of the house but my aunts and uncles calmed him. I was made to reveal the name of the man who was responsible. The next day a message was sent to his home and he came with his brother. Naturally, as is usual, the man refused responsibility.

I could not believe my ears. I think I began to grow up from that day. . . .

I decided to work in the bar as a waitress or barmaid. At least they didn't ask for a certificate or high education. Some of the girls I came to know were bargirls and they made enough money to live on. It was not much, but it kept them going. It was not a decision I made on impulse. It took me weeks before I gradually accepted my situation and plucked up courage and applied for a job in a bar. I did not like the idea but the odds were against me. I was determined to bring up my children myself and support them too.

I approached one of the bar owners about a job. He wanted to know if I had any past experience as a barmaid. I said no. He said, "I wonder if you can do it. It is a tough job." I said, "I could try." So I was offered a job. I got my first orientation on how to attend customers and take their orders. Some customers were nice but others were not. It was a traumatic experience with all these men around you, each one trying to catch your eye or paw you. Eventually I got used to it. The job involved serving drinks to customers, providing a pleasant atmosphere in which customers would want to spend their money, and ensuring that they came back. Some of the customers were very pleasant, but occasionally we got customers who, after a drink or two, turned nasty or misbehaved, and as a barmaid you had to take in the whole scene silently. It was expected of you, if you wanted to keep your job. So most of us stood the test and silently accepted abuse without reacting.

I was not earning much—my salary was meager—but I got enough money from tips. Most barmaids make a lot of money from tips, for some customers are very generous, and especially the regulars. Somehow there develops some kind of bond between the bar girls and customers. I cannot explain what it is. If you are good, well behaved, and pleasant, they like you. Of course a lot of other things happen in bars, and some women earn additional income through prostitution.

In 1979, after working in Songea as a barmaid for a few years, I found myself a bigger house and bought a few more household goods, and went back to the village to collect my other children. I wanted to be near them. I was used to having children around me, and I missed their joy and laughter, even the times they were naughty and difficult. We had a long discussion with my mother about the welfare of the children and the job I had taken. My mother tried to persuade me to give up the job and stay in the village. I explained to her that she need not worry. I had made up my mind to work and support my family. I explained to her that I could not cope with *shamba* (farm) work, and since my ambition was to educate the children beyond primary education, I did not see how I could raise enough money by growing crops. There was no market, not even the co-operative authorities came to buy crops from peasants, and from what I could see, people did not produce for the market but mainly for their own consumption. Sometimes they sold rice or nuts, cassava and maize, which are staple foods through a barter system, but normally people do not sell such crops. A lot of fishing goes on, but it is on a small scale, and this is normally a male-dominated occupation. So I had a limited choice for generating cash to support my children. . . .

Towards the end of 1980 I decided to move to Dar es Salaam. I had resigned from my job on a matter of principle. You see, the owner of the bar was a very unscrupulous man. He cheated us on our salaries. For a long time we were paid less than our actual salaries. . . . This is what he used to do on payday. He would call you into his office and pretend to count eight hundred and fifty shillings, but first he made you sign the receipt for the money and then he only peeled off two hundred and fifty, which he gave to you. We used to protest but not loudly because we were afraid of losing our jobs. We knew he was exploiting us but we also knew that by signing the receipt of 850 shillings even though we did not get the money, we knew it would be very difficult to prove that he was stealing from us, no one would believe that we did not actually get our full salaries if he saw that we had actually signed the receipts ourselves.

But one day I just got fed up. I got drunk and told him off, and the next day I reported the matter to the police who came and questioned him. He denied it, but I told them to ask the other girls. He was finally told to pay me my full salary. He paid me two months salary and I left! I took all the children back to my mother except for the youngest one and I told her I was going to Dar es Salaam to look for a job.

In Dar es Salaam I lived with my sister in Tandika for a few months before I finally decided to look for a job. In 1981 I got a job at Silent Inn. It was interesting but very tiring. We worked for long hours. This was the time when Kamanyola—(Marquis du Zaire Band), one of the best bands in town used to play at Silent Inn. The weekends were full and we worked very hard serving customers. It was backbreaking. On Saturdays for example we worked from 5 p.m. to 4 a.m. in the morning. You could not go home at that time because transport was not provided. So we normally stayed on until the early morning hours. We complained to the management about our security, so he provided a room within the bar where we could stay if we were unable to get home. Sometimes, if it was your turn to prepare food for the customers (food was also served at Silent Inn), it meant you continued to work until the beans or meat was ready—so you just rushed home for a short nap and at 5 p.m. you were back again working. The management was mean. Do you know how much we got paid? Five cents per bottle! But one could sell up to 50 crates of beer during weekends. But you did not get much money still. All of us got more from tips than from our salaries, as you can see, and that is why we stayed. I had already sent for my other children by then. Two of them came. So I had three with me and my mother kept the other two.

Mlimani Park bar had by this time been opened and we heard that they were paying decent salaries, that is, the official minimum wage. Most of the girls left Silent Inn including myself and we joined Mlimani Park. For those who were not officially employed, they were paid by the bottle like at Silent Inn except that here they paid one shilling instead of five cents per bottle. I was employed and received the basic minimum wage. Because of my long experience and satisfactory work performance I was promoted to position of supervisor. My schedule of duties as a supervisor included supervising all the barmaids, to maintain discipline, settling disputes among fellow workers and generally seeing to it that everything was going smoothly, and bringing up any issues of importance to the attention of the manager. I liked my job. My salary was 650 [shillings] per month on top of money from tips I received from customers. That way we managed to lead a decent life and the children had enough to eat; my second daughter was already in class three by now. I found someone to look after the youngest child so that the others could attend school properly and regularly.

Working as a barmaid has its pros and cons. First there is no job security, you can be hired and fired at a moment's notice. Second, there are no fixed salaries, as most of the bars are owned by individuals who unilaterally decide how much to pay you. The women who opt to work in bars are in any case desperate and do it at their own risk, so they accept the arbitrary conditions and terms of services as stipulated by the owner. . . . This is very exploitative relationship. The barmaid's real money comes from tips that we get in cash or kind. On average a barmaid can make between 400 [shillings] and 800 shillings a day from tips alone. . . . Most of the women who come to work in bars are often single parents with children. They are divorcees or widows, deserted wives, and sometimes young school girl dropouts. They are not stupid, because at the back of their minds they are thinking of their children and how to support them. So if you are offered a beer, you will accept it, while you sit and chat with the customers. For the second beer and many others, you will ask the barman to keep them for you. If you happen to get "Konyagi" or any other hard drink, you deposit it with the barman. Instead, you fill your glass with either water or soda and lace it with a bit of whisky. At the end of the day you reconcile the number of bottles with the barman and either you sell them back to the bar or customers and collect your money and go back to your children. Thus life goes. Being a barmaid one has to be intelligent and sharp.

However there is no security of employment as mentioned earlier, you can be hired or fired at a moment's notice and there is no compensation. There is no Pension or Insurance either. In other organizations they have the "Akiba ya Uzeeni" (National Provident Fund) to which both worker and employer send monthly contributions in cash-form. However, there is nothing like that in our case. After termination or dismissal you leave as empty handed as you came and if you decide to terminate your services before the end of the month you don't get paid—so you stay on until the end of the month. You get leave if you ask for it but it is unpaid leave. The same applies to maternity leave. So if you get pregnant you get leave but most women come back to work a month or less later to earn money to support their families. Most women do not get financial support from their partners. No woman likes to leave a young baby in the care of another young child—but it is a risk we take—and leave everything to God. Everybody knows about our working conditions and our rigid working hours, 5.00 a.m. [to] 11 or 12 midnight or even longer on weekends. Like any other woman, we worry about our children and about ourselves as we work so late and the children are alone or with neighbors or young ayahs.

I have told you about job security. I must say something about personal security. We get all kinds of customers coming into the bar. Usually when they come in they are gentlemen but after a couple of beers, some of them begin to misbehave and mishandle you as if they own you! And all along you are expected to remain calm and not lose your temper, and keep on smiling. Some will insult you or paw your ass, shoulders, etc., and you just pretend it is okay. Sometimes you lose your temper, but often you shrug and laugh, or pretend you like them. You have to acquire the technique of diplomacy and survival.

There are times when a man will try and force himself upon you or decide to take you home against your will. We also develop defense mechanisms about how to get away from such a situation. Sometimes it works but often times it does not. You see you can always get rid of him if you don't like him. Our customers also apply different and sometimes mean techniques if they want to hurt a woman. For example he may try to hit you and accuse you of having stolen his money. Others seem to think that once they have offered you beer, then they have bought you. Although the management always intervenes, they always obey the principle of a "customer is always right." They are interested in their money and therefore it is important for them to maintain good relations with customers. They can always get another barmaid! So often they will calm the customer, and, if he says you stole his money, the management will offer to refund him. But you know it is not the end, you know at the end of the month they will get it out of your salary! So we end up paying for money we did not steal and that means hardship. It can be very humiliating.

Not all the customers who come to the bars misbehave. You see, there are different categories of people who come to the bars: there are those who come to have a good time and peacefully go home after closing, and there are those who come looking for excitement and women. Some women come to socialize and meet friends. Couples too come and go. You also have some customers who come because they are lonely and feel they can find company and a sympathetic ear. They often find a sympathetic ear in a barmaid. So you listen to their problems and sympathize. It makes them feel great. You relieve them of their tension and anxieties, and you reassure them and make them feel confident! Most barmaids are good listeners. You learn and develop these skills with time. Being a barmaid is also an art—it requires a lot of patience and tolerance, and I think you can cope with so much because you yourself have gone through a difficult time. Not every barmaid sleeps with every man, and not every drinker comes looking for women. Many people cannot understand this. I know. They think that just because you are a barmaid then automatically you became a prostitute. I am not saying that there is no prostitution. It is there; of course most barmaids do not understand that women do not do this for pleasure. It is all a question of economics! It is often not by choice that a woman becomes a prostitute. I am sure most people believe that we are all prostitutes just because we work in a bar. Some of us have one permanent boyfriend and don't just sleep with any man around.

I must say, not every woman who works in a bar is a prostitute. Some women are decent and being a barmaid should be considered a job like any other although the job carries with it a degrading social stigma. The woman bears most of the blame and the man who comes is never branded as a prostitute even though he entices and pays for sexual favors. His money and status and power give him the power to dictate the time and terms of the relationship, even when we know the sexual act is an act of equals. . . .

The man with money can use it to speak for him; and they always use your reputation as a barmaid against you. Society looks down on barmaids because most of us do not live according to conventional expectations, so they say. So you can imagine what it would be like to fight against your boss! Today some bar owners pay a regular salary to their barmaids, but I know a lot more women are exploited and are paid less. However at least you can move on to another place if the conditions become intolerable. Currently the salary of a barmaid is between 700 [shillings] and 1000 [shillings] a month. Perhaps Dar es Salaam Development Corporation barmaids get the official minimum wage—but I am not sure. Most women are thankful to get at least a job to support their families.

Translated by Alice Nkhoma-Wamunza

Fatma binti Athman
TWO SATIRICAL POEMS

Kenya 1983   Kipate/Kiswahili

Fatma binti Athman has spent most of her life on Pate Island, off the northern coast of Kenya. Her language, Kipate, is a Kiswahili dialect. She was in her early sixties in 1983 when she performed the first of these poems for Ibrahim Noor Shariff and Ahmed Sheikh Nabhany, and in her late sixties in 1989 when she performed both poems for the Swahili Poetry Video Project team led by Ann Biersteker and Richard Randall. Fatma binti Athman has been blind since birth and learned these poems, and the many others that she knows, by listening to the performances of others. She does not perform poetry professionally or publicly.

Both poems are examples of *tumbuizo*, or commiseration songs. The *tumbuizo* genre is considered to be one of the oldest forms of Swahili poetry, usually performed by women for audiences of women and children in private settings. Unlike other Swahili poetic genres, there is no set metrical pattern for *tumbuizo*, nor is a particular rhyme scheme associated with the genre, although rhyming words often are used. As is the case with other available examples of *tumbuizo*, the names of the original composers of these poems are unknown.

"My Husband Went to Pate" appears to be a parody of the first section of a poem that appears near the beginning of this volume, "A Mother's Advice and Prayer" by Mwana Kupona binti Msham. The narrator reports that she took care of her husband by performing the actions that Mwana Kupona recommended to her daughter in 1858, but the ideal marriage promised by the first poem hardly materializes here. The narrator's anger intensifies when she learns that the mother of her husband's second wife has advised her daughter to use the rind of the fruit of the *mkungu* tree to massage the husband. This rind produces an oil that is used to soften the skin. In "The Daughter, the Mother, and the Husband," a mother commiserates with her married daughter, who is being psychologically abused by her husband.

Ann Biersteker

✦

MY HUSBAND WENT TO PATE

My husband went to Pate to harvest oranges; I waited to welcome him.
I waited standing until I fell because of fatigue.
I waited for him happily until my heart became sad.
I waited and when he entered I told him, "I greet you."
I received him in a cleared space and hung away his bow.
I received his axe and hoe and I put them behind the door.
I removed his head covering and put it in front of the door.
I took him to the bathroom and washed off his dust and dirt.
I rubbed him with oil and water; I shaved him where necessary.
I removed his farming clothes and dressed him in his finest garments

I made him drink lots of water to clear his stomach.

And at night we lay down together and he told me deceitful tales.

He told me, "Dear, I'll never marry another and will not do anything to
    hurt you.

In the morning I will go to the workshop and make ornaments for you.

I will make clasps, beaded and chain necklaces to circle your neck.

I will make ankle rattles for you and ear plugs and bracelets to remove your
    fatigue."

In the morning I went to the kitchen and heard the sounds of celebration.

I asked, "What's going on in this town?" I was told, "Your husband has
    gone off.

He has married a young girl and the dowry is the sum of your efforts.

He has married a virgin today and her mother can do nothing but say,

'Give me the fruit on the mkungu tree.

Its rind should be used to rub his spine.

You should rub him on both sides but especially on his back bone.'"

Then I smashed the pots and pans on to the ground.

I threw myself down, then stood and broke the small and large beds

And I cut the bed caning; then I left the house.

Transcribed by Ibrahim Noor Shariff
Translated by Ann Biersteker

THE DAUGHTER, THE MOTHER, AND THE HUSBAND

Mother:
    Day and night his behavior grows more grievous;
    As a disgraceful husband he has no equal.

Daughter:
    There's no one like him; he has no rival.
    He has passed beyond all limits.
    He brings nothing but hostility when he enters our house.
    When he comes inside, he exudes nothing but hostility.
    His screams and shouts torment me.
    Even the walls and doors all tremble.
    Even the walls and doors shake with fear.
    Everything trembles when he enters.
    He brings war all day and I am afraid to speak.
    I am silent and fear to speak.
    I am silent when he enters shouting
    With derision and hostility.
    I have no chance to rest—none.
    Never do I have a chance to rest, not once.
    Mother, you should not see me thus.

I am drained by his hostility.
If I were plump and jolly it would be surprising.
It would be surprising were I were plump and jolly.
Mother:
What is surprising is why you have not forced him to leave.
He did not build your home.
You must respond to him.
Why have you kept him in your house?
You must respond to him. Why have you kept him in your house?
Why have you kept him in your house?
You must speak.
Daughter:
He says: "You will not depart until I bury you.
What you want is a divorce.
What you want is for me to divorce you—
That is what you want—I buried your mother
And you have no father."
There is no one he does not curse.
But no one curses him.
Who is there he does not curse?
Who dares to curse him?
It's best I be killed so I may die and rest.
Being married to him, what happiness is this?
What happiness is this? To be married to him?
He says: "What happiness is this?
All right, I'll kill you so you may die and rest.
On my part should I cry—whose loss is it?
Whose loss is it? Should I cry?"
Mother:
Whose loss is it? Your friends would
Respect you for responding.
Even if he is a *Sharif*, why have you kept him in your house?
Why have you kept him, even if he is a *Sharif*?
Why have you kept him?
Do you keep a dog if it torments you?
If it's his house, go to the coast.
Go to the coast, if it's his house.
If it's his house, then
That which is written must be.
To be married to him, I would have rejected it, my dear.
I would have rejected it, my dear.
The marriage was ordered by your father.
He commanded that you marry this man.
You wanted to stay cooking at home.
Cooking at home was where you wanted to stay.

Daughter:
    I wanted to stay cooking at home
    But I was forced into this marriage.
    I know he is not a husband. Why did I not refuse?
    Why did I not refuse? I know he is not a husband.
    Why did I not refuse and stay at home with you?
Mother:
    Your dilemma is sorrowful,
    And that father of yours, why is he silent?
    Why is he silent, that father of yours?
    Why is he silent, my child?
    And if I look after you,
    What will others say about your pain?
Daughter:
    Why do they speak, saying I've become thin?
    I've become thin as a dried fish.
    My friends say: "You are nauseous, my friend;
    You are nauseous, my friend.
    I think you are pregnant.
    You are nauseous."
    I did not become pregnant.
    My husband torments me.
Daughter and Mother together:
    They say, "Shhh—don't be like that dog.
    Don't relive her story.
    Shhh—don't be like that dog.
    Don't relive her story; be careful."
    Truly there are no husbands.
    Truly there are no husbands.
    I said I did not become pregnant.
    I am tormented.
    They say, "Shhh—Don't be like that dog.
    Don't relive her story.
    Look at her carefully."
    Husbands there are none.
    "Don't relive the story of her mother."
    She who desires;
    She who desires; don't relive her mother's story.
    Those who are troubled are like elders.
    To be married to them, what happiness is there for me?
    What happiness is there for me to be married to them?
    What happiness is there for me to be married to any man?
    What does it bring me?
    Even did I desire another to enter,

Were another to enter my desire,
For another to enter could be
Beyond this evil, and you would not have
Even a water jug and a cloth to carry it—
They would be stolen from your head.

Transcribed and translated by Ann Biersteker and Salma Hussein

Zaynab Himid Mohammed
FROM HUSH, MY CHILD, HUSH: OF ONIONS AND FRANKINCENSE

Tanzania 1983 Kiswahili

Born in 1918, Zaynab Himid Mohammed began her education at the age of five in a Qur'anic school. In 1927 she became one of the first sixteen girls to attend a government school for girls opened in Zanzibar, headed by an Englishwoman; this first group of students would go on to become the first Zanzibari women teachers. A pioneer of women's education, Zaynab Himid Mohammed herself became the head of Town Primary School, the most prominent girls' school in the islands, and the very school in which she had studied.

Much of the author's poetry was written to mark special occasions in Zanzibar, such as the tenth anniversary of the Zanzibar Revolution, and the opening of various schools in Zanzibar. She has also written an autobiography and a short history of the Wangazija people, who came to settle in Zanzibar from the Comoros. Another of her epic poems, "*Utenzi wa Mwanakukuwa*" (The Epic of Mwanakukuwa), has recently been published together with the poem excerpted here, "*Howani Mwana Howani*," or "Hush, My Child."

"Hush, My Child, Hush" is an epic poem composed of 401 stanzas, and highly reminiscent of another well-known epic excerpted in this volume, "A Mother's Advice and Prayer," by the celebrated nineteenth-century poet Mwana Kupona. The poems are similar in form: both are *Tendi*, Kiswahili epic poems composed of quatrains. In both, a mother teaches a daughter moral values and proper religious practices. Zaynab Himid Mohammed's poem is more explicitly autobiographical, the mother teaching through her own personal experience. The title of the full poem is redolent of a lullaby. The onion and the frankincense are two of the various herbs or spices used to cleanse and dry a new mother and her baby so that they heal faster.

The poet witnessed the onset of Western education and the gradual erosion of indigenous cultural values and norms. She opposed the idea that everything new and Western was superior, to be unquestioningly relished and embraced, and she wanted her daughter and other young women to value their own cultural heritage—dispelling the idea, for example, that rituals associated with pregnancy, birth, initiation, and marriage were to be discarded.

The extract below comes from the first ninety verses of "Hush, My Child, Hush," which portray the joys and tribulations of pregnancy and reflects the traditional Zanzibari practices for attending to a mother's good health, tending to the baby, and bringing blessings to the newborn. Most women had their children at home, with a local midwife attending and with other family members and even neighbors closely involved. The new mother remained in the tender care of the extended family both during her pregnancy and for the first forty days after the birth. The poet refers to such practices as massaging the stomach with oil to make it supple and capable of further expansion, and mentions many herbs and spices, some eaten and others thrown onto hot embers to provide continuous aromas from an incense burner. All are meant to be part of the healing process. In those days the grandmother, if alive, would be a constant visitor, being the most knowledgeable about herbs and other traditional healing practices. At birth the woman invariably moved to her mother's house, where she could receive the constant ministrations described in the poem. The text also hints at various defenses to ward off the "evil eye," such as drowning the labor screams with other shouts and noises. The pregnant woman is encouraged to seek solace in God, and reminded that her experience has been shared by the mothers of great religious figures— Maryam, mother of Jesus, and Amina, mother of Mohammed.

Abdulhakim S. Yahya and Saïda Yahya-Othman

✦

1. My child, let me explain.
Hearken to these words of mine.
Listen with care;
Hold them fast in your memory.

2. You are grown up now, dear;
That much you know.
You can distinguish
The good from the bad.

3. Keep away from trivialities,
From things of no consequence.
Observe sharply, oh daughter of mine,
The dangers you need to avoid.

4. Distinguish wisely
The good from the bad.
Do not let the world outwit you;
Do not let it drive you down.

5. Hold on to this advice;
Think it over.
You are a woman.
Modesty becomes a woman.

6. Think about your past
And now your present,
And thank God that you are alive today,
That you did not die in your mother's womb.

7. When I became pregnant
You grew in my womb.
Little did I know
What was going on.

8. In my womb you were
Installed as if a machine.
Your shape was invisible;
Nor did you see yourself.

9. From my back you grew,
A drop of seed.
With God's help
You penetrated the womb

10. In the womb you settled
With care and no impediment
So narrow was the passage
You would never have imagined

11. There in safety you stayed
While I did my daily chores.
A month passed of wondering,
What's this in me?

12. I became sick,
Throwing up every hour.
Pandemonium at home,
What throes!

13. This herb and that,
Herbs in basketfuls;
Parents wailing,
Our child is ailing

14. No doctor could
In those old times
Correctly tell
How far gone you were.

15. Grandma was your midwife,
Or it could be your neighbor.
Observe your granddaughter:
What's ailing her?

16. Thus did I find out
That I was pregnant.
From the dates I was given
My parents discovered it too.

17. I began counting the days;
Wished the months were screws
That I could turn
To hasten the womb.

18. And that is how it was:
The home helter skelter;
All night I cried;
Everyone in turmoil.

19. I was counting days and months
Like a coconut-climber;
Counting a coconut harvest
Into the gunny sack.

20. The first, the second,
And the third, the monstrous month—
No roaming during that month;
One must take it easy.

21. A difficult month it is:
Heavy duties one must forgo.
Miscarriage is dangerous;
It may bring dire consequences.

22. In those days, especially,
Those days of old,
Women did not have easy access
To doctors' home visits.

23. Pretty soon, the fourth month
Arrived on time,
And the fifth month came,
When something moved inside me.

24. When the sixth month came,
I began to feel
A scurrying in my belly.
What is this motion I feel?

25. Day and night I cried.
My parents admonished me:
Daughter of ours, they said,
You must calm down.

26. I cry out for mother,
Who is full of compassion:
There's something moving inside me, mother.
And what could she do?

27. She sought help from grandmother:
Go see my daughter.
Please conjure up something
To relieve her distress.

28. Into the room grandmother came,
A cup in her hand,
And she massaged my belly,
With what, I knew not.

29. I did not realize then
That was oil, not coconut but sesame.
She sat me in her lap
And looked into my eyes.

30. She massaged me with oil.
She dried my tears.
The baby is moving
Inside your belly.

31. This is how it is, dear one,
The state of pregnancy.
It is God's decree;
On Him we must rely for help

32. We all went through this,
Even Eve, the mother of us all,
Who was used to giving birth
Day in day out.

33. Except Lady Maryam
On whom, we understand,
God Almighty showered
His blessings.

34. She was a date,
Much like a toffee.
The baby moved and settled
Inside her.

35. She became confused
And filled with shame;
Hid herself indoors,
Not knowing what to do.

36. And so Jesus was born,
And she was dishonored,
Though she was innocent;
So God revealed.

37. He sent down a revelation
To inform the people
The child was a prophet
Sent by Him.

38. Amina, daughter of Wahabu,
Mother of the beloved;
She bore Mohammed,
The Prophet Esteemed.

39. The day he was born
His glow spread wide,
Filling the room
With divine light.

40. So do not feel, dear,
That you are alone.
Do not feel worried.
Believe my words.

41. This she would tell me
Whenever she came to me,
And many words of counseling
Did she pour on me.

42. Months soon go by,
So people say.
Often I donned my sandals
To go to the bathroom.

43. So passed the seventh month,
And the eighth.
And the ninth glorious month
Soon arrived.

44. So anxious was my mother:
"This is her month."
And so day and night
She prayed for me.

45. Bring the herbs to the boil;
Keep them ready in pots.
With asafoetida I was fumigated,
And with black cumin seeds.

46. I was confined to bed
And kept out of sight.
My grandmother was nearby,
Reciting from the Qur'an.

47. The sitting room overflowed
With concerned relations
And friendly neighbors galore;
Like a fête it was!

48. This gathering was on purpose,
And the purpose was
To muffle
A loud cry from inside.

49. The cry would be piercing
Of the mother-to-be
At the time of delivery.
May God help her.

50. She is inexperienced, they said,
Never gave birth before.
It won't be easy for her;
Believe me.

51. The time ordained for me came
To obey God's wishes.
The pain was not as dreadful
As I thought it would be.

52. When I screamed in pain,
All cried out in unison
To prevent my cries
From pervading the neighborhood.

53. These customs of old
Were full of wisdom,
Replete with value.
Give them deep thought.

54. And I gave birth to you.
You were safe and well.
The women were speechless
With happiness and joy.

Translated by Abdulhakim S. Yahya

Miria Obote
SPEECH ON INTERNATIONAL WOMEN'S DAY

Uganda 1984　English

Miria Obote lived a most private life in a public setting, as the wife of Apollo Milton Obote, the first prime minister of independent Uganda (1962–1966) and later its president (1966–1971 and 1980–1985). Born in a suburb of Kampala in 1936, she graduated from Gayaza High School and attended Makerere College, then took a secretarial course in London that eventually led to employment with the United Nations and the Ugandan Consulate in New York, where she met Milton Obote. She returned to Uganda to marry the young prime minister in 1963.

Miria Obote—known to supporters as "Mama" Obote—was one of the most soft spoken among Uganda's first ladies. She was a Muganda who had married a Lanjo, in a political climate of distrust between the Baganda and the Langi. The Obotes' much-celebrated marriage marked a period of cooperation between the two groups, which unraveled a few years later when Milton Obote abolished Uganda's traditional rulers, including the king of Buganda, and declared himself president. Women's participation in politics was still limited in the early years of independence, but Miria Obote is known to have advocated for local activism.

She was the first honorary president of the Uganda Association of Women's Organizations (UAWO), formed in 1966 as a rival to the Uganda National Council of Women (UNCW). She joined her husband in exile in Tanzania after he was deposed by Idi Amin, returning to Uganda during his brief and controversial second term as president, from 1980 to 1985, when this speech was made. In it, Miria Obote pays homage to Ugandan women's role in the independence movement and their long struggle for equality, and highlights issues familiar to women around the world, including day care, maternity leave, and equity in political representation.

After a second long period of exile, Miria Obote returned to Uganda after her husband's death in October 2005, when President Yoweri Museveni surprised many by holding a state funeral for his former bitter rival. She went on to assume leadership of Milton Obote's political party, the Uganda People's Congress (UPC), and in the election of February 2006, she became the first woman to run for president in Uganda.

Florence Ebila and Margaret Macpherson

✦

Your Excellency, The President of the Republic of Uganda, Cabinet Ministers, Your Excellencies, The Hon. Madam, Chairperson, National Council of Women, Invited Guests, My fellow Women,

It gives me great pleasure to welcome you all to this most important occasion. I am particularly happy that for the first time in the history of this country, Uganda has joined hands with the International Community in observing this occasion. This is also the most representative gathering of women in this country, since liberation and, indeed, in the history of Uganda. As a woman, I share the same concerns and problems that any woman faces in this country and the world over.

As you are aware, today we are here to celebrate International Women's Day (IWD). Some of you may well ask, What is International Women's Day? It is therefore fitting to remind us that IWD is a day born of the struggles by women to be taken as equal partners in all aspects of development. It [was] started in 1907 by an International Congress, which took place at Stuttgart in Germany, acknowledging that women had not been given a fair deal and therefore urging each country which [had] participated in the Congress to intensify their work to support women's struggle for socio-economic, socio-cultural, and political equality. In 1910 North American countries recognized Women's Day. In 1911 Germany and Austria recognized March 8th as International Women's Day. Since then many countries around the world have recognized IWD.

In 1913 International Women's day was fixed for March 8th, but for several years many countries celebrated Women's Day on different dates. In 1975, the United Nations, of which Uganda is a very active member, declared the International Women's Year. The U.N. further declared 1975–1985 to be the decade for women, and also that March 8th be a day on which all the member nations should recognize and honour women. Beyond this, it is also a day on which people all over the world stop to reflect on how far society has tapped the potential of woman in development.

Before today, Uganda had not done anything to recognize and honour woman on this day, because of the recent historical problems of this country. We are therefore grateful that IWD is today given that recognition. Under the circumstances it is fitting that the first celebration of International Women's Day, in Uganda, should begin at the State House.

While it is appreciated that the women of Uganda did not have to struggle to vote and to get equal pay for equal work, it is also a fact that there is still a lot Ugandan women have to achieve. It is statistically acknowledged that there are more women in Uganda than men. The question then is, why is it that women are not adequately represented at various government levels and other bodies? There is no negative aspect of the history of our country which has not touched women intimately. The women of this country supported their men in the struggle for independence. During the reign of terror, it was the women who were the comfort and backbone of the homes when men were imprisoned and murdered. Many women lost their husbands, sons, brothers, and relatives. Some even lost their lives. Ugandan women participated at various levels in the liberation of our country from the murderous regime of the seventies.

The Ugandan rural woman plays a most significant part in the economy of Uganda. She is the major producer of both food and cash crops. She is a food processor; she is a wife, mother, nurse, and comforter. She works more than fifteen hours each day. Yet if she wanted to improve her farm or business, she would have no access to a bank loan. This is because she is uneducated; and the land she farms belongs to the husband. Yet the bank insists on some form of security before it can give her a loan. She is often not recognized by the fieldworker as a vital recipient of modern farming methods. If the field officer meets her at all, in most cases he or she will talk to her about home economics only.

Let it be understood that the demand for more attention being given to women's issues is not out of selfishness on our part but rather out of an urgent need to achieve equality so that our country can leap ahead in development with two healthy legs rather than limp with one good male leg and one bad female leg. We believe that no meaningful development can be achieved without recognition, encouragement, and participation of more than half of the population.

One does not require many examples to show what we are trying to point out. There are no women in the Cabinet. There is only one woman Member of Parliament. The number of women on Boards of various other bodies is minimal. There are no women judges. At Makerere University, there is only one woman professor. There is only one woman permanent secretary and three undersecretaries. It is no wonder that the women of Uganda feel they have not been appreciated or taken seriously enough. The Ugandan community should try to address itself specifically to women as an important part of the population, especially during this time of rehabilitation and reconstruction of the country.

The women of this country recognize and appreciate the efforts government is putting in trying to raise the status of women through the Ministry of Culture and Community Development. We recommend the work the Ministry is doing through the National Council of Women. This working relationship has enabled the National Council of Women to set up a number of development projects particularly for rural areas. Good as it is, and although much has been achieved in this way, it may be in order for me to say that there are bottlenecks still slowing down the efforts of the society in trying to exploit more fully the potentials of women of this country. May I therefore say here that the consensus opinion of the womenfolk is that Government create a separate Ministry to deal exclusively with women's affairs. . . . This would initiate improved and more realistic focus on women's activities with an assured budget to enable implementation of programs and adequate liaison with women's organizations and groups. It would create a national machinery that would reach even the remotest rural woman who is not normally represented on National Planning Boards and whose economic contribution remains unacknowledged.

We are happy to note that the Government has always provided equal opportunities for both boys and girls in the field of education. However, we are disappointed by the high rate of school dropouts among girls. This is due to cultural attitudes, which force parents to withdraw girls from school when there is no money for fees. In the rural areas, a father would sell a bull to get a boy back to school but would rarely do so for a girl. We suggest that to remedy the situation, plans should commence towards the introduction of free primary school education for all. We recommend the establishment of village polytechnics and other vocational training institutions. We also support the revival of an all out adult literacy campaign by the Ministry of Culture and Community Development to stamp out illiteracy, of which the majority of victims are women, particularly in the rural areas.

We welcome the immunization program that the Government has introduced with international assistance. However, we know that many people still die from lack of medical facilities. Mothers die in childbirth due to lack of proper care. There is need for maternity hospitals, and the upgrading of the nursing profession to ensure greater efficiency. Better working conditions and higher pay would revive the morale of the nursing personnel and reduce incidents of negligence and unprofessional behaviour.

My fellow women, I would like us to address our minds to the family as a central unit in any society. There is no doubt that there has been a weakening in the ties that used to bind families together. There is a moral degeneration in our society, which has culminated into "Bayayeism" and loose morals which have pervaded every fibre of our nation. [*Bayaye* is a word used in East Africa to describe unemployed, often homeless young men who live on the fringes of urban society.] The holding of the family together is a joint responsibility of both parents—the man and the woman. To abscond from that responsibility is to contribute to the degeneration of our society. We all know, "Charity begins at home." Children are the responsibility of both parents and the family is the most important unit in the life of a child. It is up to the parents to bring up their children in an atmosphere of love and emotional security and this requires love, integrity, honesty and the presence of both parents if they are alive. It is said that: If there is righteousness in the heart; there will be beauty in character; If there is beauty in character; there will be harmony in the family home; If there is harmony in the home; there will be order in the Nation; When there is order in the Nation, there will be peace in the World. Every parent is aware of how difficult it is to bring up children in these turbulent times, but we must neither despair nor be complacent, because at all times we must have hope and think of the future generations.

The step taken by government to assist widows and orphans is greatly appreciated. However, there is still need for government, for religious institutions and other bodies to mount a campaign to protect even further the widows and orphans of this country. We know of incidents where relatives have turned widows out of their homes and on occasion deprived them access to their children. We know that there is a law of succession, which entitles a widow to stay in her house after her husband's death, but this law is either not known or not complied with.

The following four points among others also require serious attention and action by Government: Firstly, establishment of Day Care Centres at places of work is vital. Families, especially those of the working class, are experiencing problems in catering for the care of children of pre-nursery going age, and this has resulted in accidents in the home and improper up-bringing of our children. While there is positive action on the part of the NCW to establish Day Care Centres in every urban setting, this effort however is limited by lack of funds.

Secondly, while we are aware that maternity leave arrangements are extended to all women public employees, we are informed that in the teaching profession, unmarried women teachers are still denied this arrangement. We consider that this rather unfortunate policy calls for redress. Furthermore, women would appreciate longer maternity leave than the paid 45 days. Women are aware that maternity leave arrangements are made based on the consideration that the mother requires sufficient rest and also that the child at this delicate stage requires total care.

Thirdly, on the political field, we call upon all able-bodied women to opt for leadership position in politics and even to opt for candidature at general elections. Here we would like to call upon political parties to sponsor women candidates so that in this way we tap more women contributions in decision-making circles and at other levels.

Fourthly, the World Conference on Women is designed to mark the end of the Women's Decade in 1985. It is during this conference that meaningful stock-taking and, in particular, resolutions and programming that will lead to total elimination of all discrimination against women will take place. Women of Uganda therefore should send a big contingent of delegates to attend the Conference to accord them the opportunity of sharing ideas and experiences with their counterparts in other countries.

As we recognize the efforts of all the women of the world in the struggle for social justice and equality, we must resolve that this day in Uganda be a day on which the Uganda women's solidarity is born. Let us go out of here with a determination to have a united voice to articulate our aspirations for the good of our country regardless of our political, tribal or religious beliefs.

We resolve henceforth to be a part of the International Women's Movement. We need to put Uganda securely on the map of the world.

Queen Namunyala
THE LANGUAGE OF HEALERS

Uganda 1988   Lusamia

Queen Namunyala lives in a small village in Eastern Uganda, near the border with Kenya. At the time of recording this piece in 1988 she gave her age as fifty-two. A widow with no formal education, Namunyala is a funeral singer who leads and manages her own singing group. She performs with the group and composes all of its songs, many of which are recorded live at funerals. A female pioneer in a field dominated by male performers, Namunyala is a celebrity among her people because her songs are bold, challenging, and outspoken. They are meant to expose the problems faced by her people, especially in connection with underdevelopment and harmful cultural practices.

Singing at funerals is a widespread practice among the Baluhya community, of which the Basamia, Namunyala's people, are a subgroup, living on both sides of the Kenya-Uganda border. The singers perform not only dirges, but also topical songs about life and its many trials. The songs are original compositions, written in response to a specific death and referring to a particular individual, family, and community. The main intention of the performances is both to console the bereaved and other mourners and to help them pass the long hours of the communal wake, which is a necessary part of the funeral rites.

The song included here was performed at the funeral for the mother of Jackee Batanda, who recorded it. This satirical text spares neither traditional nor so-called modern medicine. The Ugandan medical services are organized in a kind of tiered system, ranging from village dispensaries through health centers to district and national hospitals. The staff running these different treatment centers have varying levels of qualifications and skills, and it is rare to find a full-time doctor at an institution lower than a hospital. To the ordinary person in the countryside, however, all personnel at these centers are *basawo*, or doctors. The diagnostic and treatment facilities are rarely satisfactory, even at the biggest hospitals. So the traditional healer remains popular as the last resort for people who have despaired of the inferior medical services. The problem with this, as Queen Namunyala suggests, is that traditional practice is itself infested with fast-talking quacks.

Austin Bukenya and Jackee Budesta Batanda

The disease that attacked my mother came like this;
The disease that attacked my mother came like this:
Fellow Basamia, the disease that came without warning
Attacked my mother in the head and the chest.

I took her to the health center at Buyinja,
And saw a doctor called Badru.
Badru examined her
And told me to take her to the health center
At Lutolo.

On arrival at the health center at Lutolo,
We saw a doctor called Ojiambo.
Ojiambo examined her
And he told us to take her to the health center
At Nambwere.

When we got to the health center at Nambwere,
A doctor called Syambi examined her
And told us that she had a bad infection in the chest.
Then he said we should take her to the health center
At Lumino.

When we got to the health center at Lumino,
A doctor called Nambogo examined her
And also told us that my mother's chest was badly infected.
And he also told us to take her to the health center
At Masafu.

When we arrived at the health center at Masafu,
We found there a doctor called Mulijo.
Mulijo examined her.
He told us that my mother's chest was in a sorry state.
He too advised us to take her to
Dabani Hospital.

When we got to Dabani Hospital,
The doctors examined her,
And they told us that my mother's ailment
Required traditional medicine.

On that advice I took my mother home,
And from home I picked up
Two thousand Uganda shillings
And gave them to the traditional healer.
The traditional healer told me
That it was evil spirits afflicting my mother.

So we had to slaughter a fowl for Were [God]
And another fowl for his friend.
But the sickness was getting worse.

While we were there,
More traditional healers came with bombo herbs.
Others came with other herbs, and banana leaves,
On which they made my mother sit.

Eeeeeee, eeeeeee, eeeeeee, sara sara.
Knock, knock, water.
We have chased them away.
Power, power.

Let me tell you about the tongues of diviners;
Let me tell you about the language of diviners:
We call them drug-addicted crooks.
They twist words around

They distort words in order to confuse us,
And take our money
While the disease spreads.
They do not cure any disease.

Translated by Jackee Budesta Batanda

Penina Muhando Mlama
CREATING IN THE MOTHER-TONGUE

Tanzania   1990   English

Playwright, performer, and educator Penina Mlama (known also through her writing as Penina Muhando or Penina Muhando Mlama) was born in 1948, the second oldest in a family of four boys and three girls. From early on, she developed strong family, ethnic, and national cultural identities, which became important in her later academic and creative work. Following her early education in the Morogoro and Dodoma regions of Tanzania, she received undergraduate, master's, and doctoral degrees from the University of Dar es Salaam, where she went on to hold a variety of academic and administrative positions, including professor and chair of the Department of Theatre Arts, dean of the Faculty of Arts and Social Sciences, and Chief Academic Officer of the university. She is now the executive director of the Forum for African Women Educationalists, a Nairobi-based, pan-African organization that advocates for the education of women and girls.

As a creative writer, Penina Mlama came to prominence with the successive publication of many plays, including *Hatia* (Guilt, 1972), *Tambueni Haki Zetu* (Recognize Our Rights, 1973), *Heshima Yangu* (My Honour, 1974), *Talaka Si Mke Wangu* (I Divorce You, 1974), *Nguzo Mama* (The Main Pillar, 1982), and *Lina Ubani* (There Is an Antidote, 1984). She also collaborated with two other women to produce *Harakati za Ukombozi* (Struggles for Liberation, 1982), and was one of the founders of the Paukwa Theatre Group, which produced the nationally acclaimed *Ayubu* (Job, 1984). She champions African orature by using it in various forms in her plays. The plays deal with issues of gender, women's rights, education, cultural tensions, and economic and political liberation struggles, and particularly highlight the inability of the postcolonial state to alleviate poverty and foster true development. She attacks cultural practices that victimize women, while endorsing those that support women's aspirations and expression. In addition to writing plays, Mlama has often performed with the Paukwa Theatre Group, and can be seen on film in *Mama Tumaini* (Tumaini's Mother), where she portrays a woman struggling to find economic and social independence.

Penina Mlama is a pioneer of the Theatre for Development Movement, which employs theater as a tool for community education and empowerment. In her 1983 thesis, *Tanzania Traditional Theatre as a Pedagogical Institution*, Mlama argued against the Eurocentric view that had long denied the existence and value of indigenous African theatrical forms and experiences. In her 1991 book, *Culture and Development: The Popular Theatre Approach in Africa*, she documented and analysed the early work of the Theatre for Development movement. During the early 1990s, she helped to found programs for young people, notably the TUSEME ("Let Us Speak Out") program and festival, seeking to empower girls to overcome gender-based obstacles to their education and personal development.

While Penina Mlama has written on culture and education in the English language, all of her plays are in Kiswahili, a choice she has identified as both aesthetic and political. In "Creating in the Mother-Tongue: The Challenges to the African Writer Today," Mlama deals with an issue that has been addressed by several other African writers, notably the distinguished Kenyan writer Ngugi wa Thiong'o, who chose to abandon English in favor of his native Gikuyu, and defended the choice in his 1986 book, *Decolonising the Mind*. In Penina Mlama's analysis, the choice to write in an African language is informed by a variety of historical and contemporary realities—including underdevelopment, poverty, loss of cultural identities, illiteracy, and neocolonialism—and has broad ramifications for both the writer and her audience.

Amandina Lihamba

I have chosen to speak on creating in the mother-tongue not because I myself write in Kiswahili and therefore want to preach to those who do not write in African indigenous languages to follow the example. Indeed, one may argue that my choice to write in Kiswahili has been greatly assisted by the historical fact that my country has Kiswahili as a national language. Neither am I going to dwell on my personal experiences in terms of the use of an African language in the actual process of creating my literary works.

Creating in the mother-tongue involves an issue that has been debated in African literature circles for several decades. Numerous viewpoints have been advanced by writers, critics, and linguists about whether or why African writers ought or ought not write in their mother-tongues (see Petersen). I will not bore you by repeating arguments which have been sufficiently aired elsewhere.

I speak of creating in the mother-tongue because the problem has not been resolved, and, therefore, the debate has not been concluded. We have not yet completed the task before us. Creating in an African language poses a number of challenges to the African writer today, and no serious African writer can ignore them.

From previous debate, we know that there is no questioning the right of African languages to serve as the media for communication and literary expression among African peoples. But we are also aware of the historical forces that have denied or suffocated that right and imposed English, French, or Portuguese, as well as the colonial and neocolonial conditions that have ensured the continual dominance of these foreign languages not only in African literature but in other types of communication.

We are familiar with the existing division among writers and critics on whether or not the African writer can write in his or her mother-tongue. Arguments against the choice of African languages and the consequent preference for foreign languages have included the clamor for an international audience. And indeed, the literary production infrastructures (including schools, publishers, book distributors, literary awards and prizes) make the international audience a coveted goal of the African writer and the foreign language an inevitable tool to reach that goal. A stronger explanation for the choice of the foreign language is the foreign-dependent, socio-economic structure in which the writer and the entire African continent are trapped. Within that structure are the class alliances which determine the writer's choice of audience and, with that, the choice of language as well. It has been argued that many African writers are writing for the elite rather than for the common men and women who form the majority of the African population. Thus, they choose English, French, or Portuguese, the languages of the elite, as opposed to African languages of the common populations (see Ngugi).

Many obstacles to writing in the mother-tongue for the writers who would genuinely wish to do so have also been cited. The existence of many African languages in one nation makes some writers' mother-tongues the languages of a very small minority. Ethnically-based political strife makes other writers' mother-tongues the languages of the oppressor. And indeed many African governments do not have the political courage to resolve the question of indigenous languages and instead promote the assumed neutrality of English, French, or Portuguese in the name of national unity, which often does not exist in any case. Forces of such governments have often been quick to brand writers who have written in their mother-tongues as "tribal" and "anti-national unity." (Some people have used that criterion to criticize Ngugi wa Thiong'o on his Kikuyu plays *Ngahika Ndeenda* and *Maitu Njugira*.) Such pressures have forced many African writers to follow the dictates of the status quo and to continue using foreign languages in their creative writings.

Others have argued that, due to brief or inexistent histories, many African indigenous languages are linguistically underdeveloped and, therefore, ill-equipped to express the scientific and technological concepts of contemporary African society. Considering the continual underdevelopment of Africa, one may ask what it is that is so scientifically and technologically developed that it can exhaust the expressive possibilities of languages. A reminder is also sounded that the same African languages regarded as inadequate have carried from one generation to another the great African civilizations, including their masterful literary creations such as epics, poetry, and songs (see Chu and Skinner). The same African languages were also good enough to translate the Hebrew folktales of the Bible in the early twentieth century, but they are now accused of being linguistically inadequate for African writers' literary creations. These same languages remain the communication media for the majority of Africans today. In the use of these African languages, these Africans are describing, analyzing, and interpreting the contemporary African society, whatever its complexities may be.

Some writers have pointed out that they have a handicap in using their mother-tongues, because they have become alienated from their own ethnic roots. Indeed, sometimes one comes across people who have grown up in environments, especially urban areas, which curtail their chances to master their mother-tongues. Sometimes, though, the mastery of an indigenous African language is an attitude of mind on the part of an individual or his/her parents. At times, writers themselves often have contradictory attitudes toward African languages.

The arguments are numerous, and African writers take different stands on the issues raised. Their choice to write in the mother-tongue or not is also determined by the different forces that each individual writer confronts. We know also that more African writers use the foreign languages than the indigenous ones. I am not arguing that contributions should be ignored just for the sake of pushing for African languages, although I would like to draw attention to the significant numbers of African writers who are writing in their mother-tongues today.

But the choice to create in the mother-tongue is, as it has been in the past, a difficult choice. It is difficult because the problems raised during the past three decades have not been resolved. Indeed, many of those problems have been intensified by the socio-economic realities of the African continent. For example, ethnic differences have intensified in many nations due to the realization that ethnicity has fostered the unfair distribution of political and economic power. Also, through the intensification of capitalism in Africa the control over the book production industry has fallen increasingly into the grips of multinational companies whose economic interest is served by the promotion of the international languages. Failing national economies have thwarted local book production ventures established, especially in the early 1970s, to encourage, among other things, writing in local languages. (The East African Literature Bureau which has now collapsed is one case in mind.) National language policies for most of our nations are still undefined.

The choice to write in an African language is often a choice for obscurity and a renunciation of the international limelight that writing in English, French, or Portuguese could offer a writer. As a writer in Kiswahili, for example, I have many times experienced how a foreigner's interest in my work has been switched off once I admit that I write in Kiswahili. Many good works in indigenous African languages remain unknown outside their national borders. In Tanzania, for example, over three hundred novels, plays, and short stories had been published by 1988 (see Bertoncini). The fact that the authors of these works are not much known outside Tanzania is not due to the poor quality of their writing because some of them are outstanding. It is because literature in Kiswahili is not given prominence internationally. The same is true for literature in Shona, Zulu, Yoruba, and other African languages.

For an African writer, the choice to write in the mother-tongue is not merely a whim. Those who choose to write in an African language belong to a class of writers who are willing to take a risk, writers who respond to the challenges posed by the realities of our African society today.

The challenge begins with a writer's re-examination of his or her role in the Africa of today. We know the role the writer has assumed in the past: in the struggle for political independence, in proving to the colonial master that Africa has her own Shakespeares, Shaws, Eliots, and Molières, in displaying the rich African cultural heritage and civilization whose existence the colonial master had attempted to deny in promoting literary talent, and so on (see Ngara). But what is the role of the writer in Africa today?

Here we need to remind ourselves that we are talking about an Africa that is ripped apart by an economic, social, and cultural crisis. An Africa where poverty has increased to frightening proportions, driving the majority of her people to the point of starvation. Ours is an Africa where many of our leaders have sold our countries wholesale to international capital, giving the control over our economies and consequently our welfare, indeed, our lives, to the IMF or the World Bank. We are talking about an Africa where the ruling classes are proud, instead of ashamed, of the blatant exploitation of the common people through international alliances and by use of means that defy description. It is an Africa where new problems arise before we have had time to understand how we got into the old ones. It is an Africa where all types of political systems—capitalist, socialist, feudalist, civilian, military—have produced the same results: poverty. The signs are clear in the setbacks we are suffering even in the small achievements of our previous efforts at development. We have built hospitals that now stand without drugs, factories that run below capacity for lack of raw materials or spare parts, schools that are increasingly unaffordable to many, service structures whose operational systems are determined by the changing tactics of the corrupt officials. Malnutrition, war, famine, and epidemics are becoming an African character trait. And in the midst of all this a very few people are amassing untold wealth, often without a drop of sweat.

What is the role of the writer in such a context? What does the writer create in relation to all this? A friend told me recently that it is time for African writers to describe flowers and clouds.

Many African writers now find it more difficult than ever before not to say something about the pathetic situation of African people. In his or her role as a communicator of ideas and feelings, the writer does not want to stand by and let this humiliating era continue. It is also extremely difficult for the writer not to take the side of the suffering majority. After all, many times, the writer himself or herself belongs to that category. The writer finds it difficult to suppress the urge to use the pen to communicate his or her people's anger and frustration. The writer often chooses to announce her or his position, or to conscientize and to mobilize his or her audience into understanding, analyzing their plight. Even though the situation seems to be so hopeless, the writer feels the need to tell the audience not to despair, and the bolder writer exhorts them to stand up and fight. But what chances does this writer have in reaching his or her audience?

If we take the book as the writer's communication medium, we know such media do not effectively reach the common population. Enough has been said to show that the mass media are not as effective as we are often made to believe. External control as well as financial and infrastructural problems have prevented radio, film, television, and the print media from reaching the majority of the population, especially in the rural areas (see Boafo). The cutbacks in the service sector adopted by the current IMF and World Bank controlled economies are worsening the situation.

African written literature has continued to be bogged down by the problems faced by the mass media in general. Limited and inadequate publishing and distribution systems have kept the audience of African writers very small. Many times the writer has to cling to the school audience, using all means to get his or her books into the school syllabus, for schools often represent the only sure market, although it is increasingly affected by cutbacks in government educational spending. Likewise, subsidized libraries and book distribution systems are forced to reduce their services and thus their audiences. Adult literacy circles have repeatedly lamented that it is difficult for graduates of literacy campaigns to maintain their literacy due to the non-availability of a literature that would allow them to keep up the reading skills.

The communication sector has already awoken to the inadequacy of the mass media, as manifested by the ongoing search for grassroots-based communication media. Efforts in this direction involve not only giving a grassroots character to radio, film, or the print media; there has also been an increasing recognition of the importance of indigenous communication media at the local level (see Moemeka). Interpersonal communication, the traditional arts such as dance, story-telling, song, and poetry are being accorded a communication role once denied them and often overshadowed by the externally controlled mass media. Many development programs in adult education, health, environment, women's projects, and so on now use the indigenous media, especially oral literary and performing art forms in communication for development. For example, the "Theatre for Development" movement has gained considerable significance in Africa during the last ten years because its utilization of indigenous African communication media has widened the opportunity to involve grassroots communities in communicating, analyzing, and solving their development problems (see Kamlongera and Mlama). Furthermore, village radio discussion groups, rural newspapers, educational pamphlets, and posters are encouraged in order to popularize, demystify, and democratize the process of communication.

These efforts have brought the indigenous languages to the fore because, by working at the grassroots level, one automatically works with local languages. People's participation is heightened by the use of the languages with which they are most familiar. For the majority of African rural populations, this means the indigenous languages. In recent years, development agents have adopted a more tolerant view toward African indigenous communication media, at the center of which are the indigenous languages.

African written literature, though, seems to lag behind these other media in the attempt to reach the grassroots. If African literature were to seriously address itself to the question of reaching the grassroots, then the question of African languages could not possibly be avoided. How can an African writer today address the African masses without using their African languages? We are all aware that, even though our countries have maintained English, French, or Portuguese as national languages for over twenty years, these are not the languages of the people. The majority of all African countries' populations still communicate in the indigenous languages which are their mother-tongues. The writer, in a way, seems to have no choice but to write in these languages. Writers who use languages foreign to their audiences also place themselves outside the community and operate as outsiders, as people who can reach their audiences only through translation.

Efforts to popularize African written literature, especially in the rural areas, have been few and far between. Theater is an exception because theatrical creations call for performances and thus have a better chance of reaching wider audiences, including the common people. In the theater, more use has been made of African languages than in novels or poetry. This is due to the proximity of the audience and the immediacy of the need to communicate effectively.

Indeed, there is a trend among contemporary communication and development agents toward paying more attention to oral literary and performing forms because such people recognize the immediate and wide impact these forms of communication can have in involving rural populations as communicators and as members of an audience. The current drive to ensure people's participation in development programs and projects has found an ally in the use of indigenous African oral literary and performing forms.

Because of my own involvement in theater for development, I have received many requests from various development agencies to conduct theater for development programs in rural areas. None of them have ever inquired about my written plays in relation to grassroots development work. And, apart from the schools, I have never found any of my published plays in the villages where I have worked or visited. During the last ten years, therefore, I have operated as an artist with two faces—one as a playwright for urban audiences and the other as an oral creator and performer for the rural audiences. Of course, urban audiences have the advantage of enjoying the oral creations as well, for orality is a characteristic of Tanzanian theater.

The increasing importance accorded to oral forms as a means of involving the masses in the development process defines a trend that may well be strengthened by the current culture and development decade that is promoting cultural identities. One wonders whether these initiatives will not soon overshadow the written literature, especially since the obstacles faced by written literature in reaching the African majority seem to be more and more insurmountable. We should also be aware of the fact that these oral literary and performative forms are still alive in Africa. Previous claims that modernity had killed them were exaggerated. In fact, they have continued to be the major communication media in large areas that have not been reached by the modern media. If oral literary forms are to be promoted in this way, African languages are certain to gain new significance in the African development process.

African writers may, therefore, find themselves being dragged into the African language issue without much choice, unless they want to restrict themselves to an elite or urban audience. More creative writers, however, may want to voluntarily face this challenge by addressing the African language question now.

If we regard the role of the writer in Africa today from a different angle and say that the African writer is the man or woman of culture, one who preserves, rejuvenates, and guides his or her society's perception of an acceptable way of life, its morals, values and attitudes, its integrity and identity, we raise another set of challenges and questions.

The first question is: what is African culture? It is not an exaggeration to say that most Africans cannot describe what represents culture in their own nations today. What is it that represents our way of perceiving and doing things, our identity as a people? Although the revival, promotion, and assertion of African culture represented rallying points for our political leaders during the struggle for independence, only lip service has been paid to the assertion of an African cultural identity during the first twenty or thirty years of independence. And there seems to be little concern over the added onslaught on African culture by contemporary capitalist and imperialist forces. The African way of life has been left to live, adapt, or die in proportion to its own ability to accommodate or fight incompatible foreign influences. At the same time, however, foreign culture necessary to the fostering of foreign-controlled socio-economic structures has been nurtured in Africa through such tools as television, films, the arts, education, and religion. While our governments have continued to give African culture an insignificant place in their development strategies, they have often aided the influx of foreign cultural influences and their negative impact on the African identity. Because of the increased entrenchment of capitalism in the last twenty years, Africa is increasingly becoming one culture with the rest of the capitalist world—a place where people's perceptions of the accepted way of life are guided by economic gain and the commoditization of everything, including people. Values based on humanity and the common good inherent in some indigenous African cultures are rapidly being replaced by values based on money and individual gain. Indeed, the way of life of the ordinary African man and woman is one basically of exploitation, oppression, and humiliation. It is a life where morals and values have often given way to tactics of mere survival.

We are talking of an Africa of lost, split, or confused identities. The confusion is obvious, even at national levels where governments have not yet reached a point of defining culture. It is common for African governments not to have cultural policies, and many limit their half-hearted attempts at promoting African culture to traditional dances, museums, antiquities, and, surprisingly, football, even though it is not a sport indigenous to Africa. Culture also seems to be the one domain that governments never know where to place in ministerial formations. A look at the African ministerial map sees culture placed together with other areas ranging from education, social welfare, labor, youth, women, community development, information, sports, and so on.

In Tanzania, for example, culture has been shifted to nine different ministries during the past twenty-eight years—an average of a new ministry every three years. No wonder there is not much to show in terms of an identifiable African culture today.

Writing for the African people today is writing for a people who have largely lost their perception of what constitutes "African," their ability to determine or influence their own way of life, their indigenous values and attitudes, and their identity as a people. One wonders whether there is much hope of changing this situation, even in light of current efforts by the United Nations and UNESCO to integrate culture into development, as the declaration of an international decade for Culture and Development (UNESCO: *The Cultural Dimension of Development*). Like the previous development strategies, this new wave (or development fad) of culture and development is controlled by forces external to Africa. The employment of European cultural anthropologists and sociologists as part of such development projects is already on the agenda of most so-called culture and development programs.

Of course, regaining the African identity calls for an all-encompassing struggle to change and influence both the internal and global factors, balances of power and control over markets as well as socio-economic structures. This struggle cannot be waged by the writer alone; neither can the writer claim to have all the answers. But if the writer has a genuine interest in saving the African cultural identity from this chaos (indeed, this humiliation), he or she will find many roles to play in the struggle.

In the many roles the writer may play, the indigenous African languages become important as carriers and tools of a people's culture. The 1987 Organisation of African Unity language plan of action for Africa states:

> Language is at the heart of a people's culture and . . . the cultural advancement of the African peoples and the acceleration of their economic and social development will not be possible without harnessing in a practical manner indigenous African languages in that advancement and development. (OAU)

It is difficult to imagine the African writer today making a significant contribution to asserting the African people's cultural identity without having recourse to African indigenous languages. In fact, language is the only feature that presently gives African societies their cultural identity.

However, writing in the mother-tongue alone is not enough. In order for the use of the mother-tongue to be meaningful, African writers must extend their interest to areas outside the realm of literary creations. These areas include the struggle to give indigenous African languages a respectable standing in national ideological systems such as education. The writer must see the struggle for the promotion of African languages, or for the institution of language policies favorable to African languages, as his or her own struggles. The writer must not shy away from the political sensitivity of such language struggles. The formation and implementation of language policies favorable to indigenous African languages should not be seen only as the business of the politician because language is, indeed, the writer's business as well. The writer also needs to assist in promoting efforts to provide literacy skills to the still illiterate masses of our countries. What use is it to write in Kiswahili, Bemba, Zulu, or Hausa when the majority of the audience the writer needs to address cannot read? As much as the adult educator and politician, the writer needs to be part of the literacy campaigns. At times, writers have been rightly accused of sitting on the periphery and of being concerned only with the production of their next book, as if these other struggles do not concern them.

Writing in the mother-tongue for the African writer may require not only writing in the writer's mother-tongue but also in the mother-tongue of one's audience. There are many cases where writers are actually fluent in other

African languages but refrain from using them on the grounds of political or ethnic prejudice. In situations where the writer is not competent in the audience's languages, the question of translation from the writer's mother-tongue to other African languages becomes important. We always talk of translating from African languages into English or French, but it is high time we emphasized the need for translations into the different languages of our linguistically diverse audiences. This throws out yet another challenge to the African writer who chooses to write in the mother-tongue.

Finally, I would like to point out that writing in the mother-tongue alone does not necessarily produce good or committed literary works. In confronting all these other challenges, good quality work in terms of both form and content is necessary because such writers have the responsibility to prove to the "doubting Thomases" that, when it comes to literary creations, African languages are just as good as any other language in the world.

There may not be many African writers writing in African languages at the present time. It is my belief, however, that many more African writers will soon be willing to face these challenges. Indeed, the realities of our continent may not allow the unwilling writers to sit on the periphery much longer. It is my hope that those who believe in the significance of these challenges to the future of African humanity will offer a hand of encouragement and support to these writers.

WORKS CITED

Bertoncini, E. *An Outline of Swahili Literature, Prose and Fiction*. Leiden: F.J. Brill, 1989

Boafo, K., ed. *Communication and Culture, African Perspectives*. Nairobi: African Church Information Service, 1989.

Chu, D., and E. Skinner. *A Glorious Age in Africa, the Story of Three Great African Empires*. Trenton, NJ: African World Press, 1990.

Kamlongera, C. *Theatre for Development in Africa with Case Studies from Malawi and Zambia*. Bonn: ZED, 1988.

Moemeka, A. *Local Radio—Community Education for Development*. Zaria: Ahmadu Bello University Press, 1981.

Mlama, P. *Culture and Development: The Popular Theatre Approach in Africa*. Uppsala: Scandinavian Institute of African Studies, 1991.

Ngara, E. "The Role of the African Writer in National Liberation and Social Reconstruction." *Criticism and Ideology*. Ed. K. Peterson. Uppsala: Scandinavian Institute of African Studies, 1988. 128–40.

Ngugi wa Thiong'o. "Writing against Neo-Colonialism." *Criticisms and Ideology*. Ed. K. Petersen. Uppsala: Scandinavian Institute of African Studies, 1988. 101.

OAU. *The Language Plan of Action for Africa*. Council of Ministers Forty-Sixth Ordinary Session, Res. CM/Pes 1123 (XLVI) Addis Ababa, 1987.

Petersen, K, ed. *Criticism and Ideology: Second African Writers Conference Stockholm 1986*. Uppsala: Scandinavian Institute of African Studies, 1988. 9–10.

UNESCO. *The Cultural Dimension of Development*. The Hague: The Netherlands National Commission for UNESCO, 1985.

Tsitsi V. Himunyanga-Phiri
FIGHTING FOR WHAT BELONGED TO ME

Zambia 1992   English

"Fighting for What Belonged to Me" is excerpted from Tsitsi V. Himunyanga-Phiri's 1992 book *The Legacy*, which portrays the struggles of a recently widowed Zambian woman named Mrs. Moya Mudenda. Under customary law, Mrs. Mudenda faces losing her home, and the small farm that has provided an income for herself and her children, to her late husband's younger brother. Opposing both her family and the dictates of her culture, she decides to hire a lawyer to appeal the decision of a local court, and fight for her property and her future. In this excerpt, she reflects upon her experience while awaiting the judge's decision in her case, and finds that, in merely taking up the fight, she has already achieved a victory over fear and passivity.

The piece reflects the dual legal system of statutory law and customary law that continues to govern the lives of many Africans. In Zambia, the laws of inheritance have become a flash point for the conflict between these two systems, as well as for battles over the rights of women, who are often disadvantaged by customary law. Despite legal reforms in the last two decades, both families and local courts at times disregard or interpret the law to deny widows their full share of their husband's property. In order to fight these decisions, women must be both aware of their legal rights and willing to break what Tsitsi V. Himunyanga-Phiri identifies as the code of silence that permeates women's lives and all domestic matters.

In *The Legacy* and in her subsequent book, *Celebrating the Law*, Himunyanga-Phiri tells stories of Zambian women using the law to demand their rights and to improve their own lives and the lives of their families and communities. She is currently working on the script for a television series entitled *The Legacy*, based on the issues and characters developed in her two books.

After graduating with a law degree from the University of Zambia in 1980, Himunyanga-Phiri was admitted to practice law before the High Court of Zambia. She went on to study social development and public policy, with an emphasis on women and development, at Pennsylvania State University, and has dedicated herself to projects that empower women legally, economically, or socially, including the provision of microcredit loans, civic education, and legal services. She founded the H-P Women's Development Company, which provides affordable housing to Zambian women, and has been actively involved with the Africa Legal Human and Civil Rights Organization, based in Washington D.C., dealing with the legal rights of African immigrants in the United States, as well as with issues of law and democracy in Africa.

Nalishebo N. Meebelo

✦

As I sat in the packed courtroom, waiting for my case to be called, I wondered how many other people here today felt like I did—lost, dejected and very lonely. I felt as if I was carrying the weight of the whole world on my shoulders, for the outcome of my case would affect many other women's lives. I was the guinea pig, so to speak. I had no control over what was to happen to me. That lay in the judge's hands. He would make the decision that would affect how my children and I would lead the rest of our lives.

I looked at Judge Chanda sitting solemnly on the Bench. He looked so distinguished in his red robe, white collar and wig. He did not look like an ordinary man, one who faced ordinary, everyday events. Did he know what it felt like to be in my shoes? A mother of six and a grandmother of four, a mother who had lost her husband less than a year ago, and now a mother who was about to lose her home and business—all she had worked for during the last fifteen years. Wasn't it enough that I had lost my husband?

Did the judge take into consideration all the work and effort that I had put into making life comfortable for my children, or was he like everyone else, who thought that a woman was a perpetual dependent—incapable of making important decisions and only able to survive under the care of "a man"?

Did he take into account the fact that even when my husband was alive, it was I and not my husband who listened to the daily problems? That it was I who decided how best to resolve them?

Did I really believe this judge was going to rule in my favour? Put the law first and society's rules and conventions last? Was I being overly optimistic or just plain naïve?

Maybe I should have accepted the Administrator-General's distribution of my late husband's property. Then I wouldn't have to go through all this pain and uncertainty. Perhaps I should have been satisfied with receiving one-quarter of my husband's pension; after all, the children had received half of it. At least between the seven of us we received three-quarters, while his parents, my *Ba mpongosi*, receive the remaining quarter and his brother, my *mulamu*, gets the house and the surrounding ten acres of land—the land that was my only means of livelihood.

Yes! His brother, who had not spent any time or money on the property, who had not shown any interest whatsoever in my late husband, the property, or my children until he had died. His brother who spends his salary on women and beer and is always borrowing money from me. Money that I have made growing vegetables on the land that the Administrator-General has handed over to him on a silver platter without regard for where my children and I would live. My *mulamu* made it abundantly clear that my children and I were not welcome on "his" property. He said that the K300 a month that we would be receiving from the pension would be enough for us to rent a house and to buy food. He generously said that he could find us a small house in one of the townships; after all, now that all the children except the last two had grown and were out of school, we didn't need a lot of space. I would be very comfortable, he assured me, and I could continue my business in the market if I so wished, only now I would have to buy the vegetables from him. If that idea didn't sound appealing I could move back to the village and stay with my *Ba mpongosi*. They would be very happy to have me. I could keep them company in their old age and help out with the household chores. My two youngest children could stay with their uncle during the school term and come to visit me in the holidays.

What my *mulamu* conveniently forgot was that for the last fifteen years I had worked long hours, up very early and going to sleep very late, so that my family could benefit. I transformed our property from a piece of land with a house on it, to a beautiful home with a well-kept lawn and a prosperous garden that had vegetables in it all year round. I had set up a thriving business through that vegetable garden and it was the profits of that same business that had paid for the household expenses and the children's schooling. We never even saw my husband's pay, which went to the mortgage for the property. I shuddered at the thought of all my labour and sweat going down the drain, buried together with my late husband.

Ba Mudenda, father of my children, why did you have to die? You used to say that you were the head of our house and as such you would always take care of everything.

Why aren't you taking care of things now? Why didn't you take the time to write a will?

A simple sentence would have ensured that your children would not suffer. That they would have the home they grew up in. You used to say that wills were only for old people, and, at 50 years of age, you were still a young man and didn't need one. As though there is a specific age that one has to be before one can die. Yes! You were only 50 years old on that fateful day when you left us, never to return.

When you said goodbye that evening, I didn't realize that you were not coming back. I said a non-committal goodbye to you, as I had long ago given up trying to find out where you would be going, or when you would be returning. I only found out that you had been attending a business reception when the police came to tell me that you had been killed in a car accident. You were gone and I had not said a proper goodbye. Gone, before you could secure your children's future. Perhaps I should have died first, then my children would never have been in danger of losing their home.

The whole situation seems so unfair and unjust: Should we have lost everything that we worked for for so long and so hard just because I am a woman and society decreed that I cannot take care of myself? It is just not fair!

"Life is not always fair, but this is not a matter of fairness, this is a matter of societal norms outweighing justice."

As I recalled those words, my gaze moved to where my lawyer, Miss Zulu, was sitting. She looked so poised in her white collar and black robe, with such courage and persuasiveness for one so young. She was the only one who had been willing to help me appeal against the Administrator-General's decision. I had taken my problem to two other lawyers who were not interested, as they thought that the Administrator-General was probably right. The upkeep of a big house and business would be too taxing for a woman on her own, they said.

I did not have salaried employment and my vegetable business could not be regarded as a means of providing a steady income to pay off the mortgage. Never mind the fact that it had been providing my family with a steady income for the last five years. Furthermore, for the same reasons I could not secure any other means of paying off the mortgage, as I could not obtain any form of loan. I had been on the point of giving up when I met Miss Zulu quite by accident and, ironically, I met her in the Administrator-General's office. I had gone there to tell him that I had decided not to appeal and that he could go ahead and distribute the property.

I was sitting in the reception area waiting to see the Administrator-General. His office door was slightly open and through it I could hear a young woman vehemently arguing with him, telling him that her client was entitled to receive her late husband's property. That it was the wife who had been responsible for the property's upkeep during her husband's lifetime, and why should all that change now that he was dead? As I listened, I marvelled at how familiar that case sounded, at the emotion in the young voice, as though she genuinely believed in what she was saying.

This is the person I need to argue my case, I thought excitedly. When she came out of the room, I jumped up and asked if I could speak to her. If she was surprised she didn't show it. She just sat down calmly in a chair, motioning me to do the same. She introduced herself and asked me what the matter was. I began to tell her about my husband's death and the Administrator-General's decision on how to distribute the property. I didn't need to say very much before she stopped me, saying she would try to help. She asked my name and asked me to see her in her office the next morning.

The next day when I went to her office, I was pleasantly surprised to find that she had a copy of my file from the Administrator-General's office. She was positive that the matter should be pursued, even if it meant going as far as the Supreme Court. She also pointed out the tough battle we had before us, as we were not just contesting the Administrator General's ruling. We were contesting our culture and its laws of inheritance and succession.

In the six months that followed, her positive attitude carried us through the injunction which restrained the Administrator-General from distributing the property, and through the hearing before Judge Chanda where I had stated my claim to the property. This morning our battle was coming to an end, for Judge Chanda would deliver his verdict.

Would I be able to keep my home and business or would I lose it all, just as I had lost my husband? Only the judge knew the answer to this question.

The judge.

I almost laughed as it dawned on me that it was yet another man who was going to decide my future. It seemed that all my life there had always been a man who decided what was good for me, and every time I had meekly accepted. But not this time. This time I was fighting for what belonged to me and my children. I had earned it and I wasn't going to give up without a fight, as I had done in the past.

Sister Mary John
WE WANT TO BE SISTERS

Uganda 1992   English

Sister Mary John is a Catholic nun of the Congregation of the Little Sisters of Saint Francis, founded in Uganda in 1923. Affectionately nicknamed "The Pillar" by her fellow nuns, she is the only surviving member of the first three women and five teenagers who joined the congregation at its inception. Sister Mary John was born Rachel Musoke in 1914 in Kibuye, a suburb of Kampala, the capital of Uganda. She asked to join the religious life at the age of fourteen, while she was studying under the legendary Mother Kevin at Nsambya Catholic Mission in Kampala. Her intentions were strongly opposed by her mother, but her father was wholeheartedly supportive. After her profession of religious vows, Sister Mary John trained as a teacher and taught with distinction between 1928 and 1978 at nearly all the major Catholic schools in what were then the Mill Hill Missionary dioceses of Kampala, Jinja, and Tororo.

A key figure in Sister Mary John's memoir, *Service in the Heart of Africa*, is the Founder of the Little Sisters of Saint Francis, Mother Kevin, for whom the author shows total love and admiration. Born Teresa Kearney in 1875 in Knockenrahan, Arklow, County Wicklow, Ireland, Mother Kevin came to Uganda in 1903 as one of a group of Franciscan Missionaries of Mary sent to help the evangelists in the newly founded Vicariate of the Upper Nile. Among her considerable achievements was the establishment, under a mango tree in 1903, of the medical treatment center that was to become Nsambya Hospital, mentioned in Sister Mary John's memoir. Now more than a century old, this institution is recognized as one of the best private referral and teaching hospitals in Uganda. It is interesting to note that many of the young women who went to study medicine at Nsambya ended up joining the Little Sisters of Saint Francis, as well. The congregation is undoubtedly the most impressive attainment of Mother Kevin's mission.

For Ugandan women, religious life represented an option with no precedent in their history or culture. A life and a career without marriage and family were almost unimaginable to most Ugandans in the 1920s, when the Little Sisters order was founded. To those who, like Sister Mary John, rose to the challenge, the rewards could be quite rich, especially for the Little Sisters, since their founder conceived of them not only as holy and devout religious women but also as highly educated and trained professionals. As Sister Mary John recalled, the Little Sisters' congregation was also designed to overcome ethnic, regional, and class differences that still divide much of East African society today.

Today, the Little Sisters of Saint Francis have spread from their headquarters, or Mother House, in Nkokonjeru, Uganda, throughout Uganda, Kenya, and Tanzania. Numbering over 550 today, the Little Sisters are to be found in high-profile professions all over the region. Some are administrators, others medical specialists, and yet others leading educators, including university professors.

With characteristic humility, Sister Mary John has not published her memoir; rather, it has circulated privately among her congregational sisters as an inspirational treatise.

Austin Bukenya and Ayeta Anne Wangusa

Late one evening, April 1923, as Mother Kevin was writing letters in her office, this elderly woman, Paulina Musenero, knocked sharply on the door. "Kodi," said Paulina. "Karibu," replied Mother Kevin. Mother, assuming it was a visitor, continued writing and said, "Yingira"—"Come in." She was however surprised to see a group of children lined up behind Paulina. They came in, knelt close to each other, and greeted Mother Kevin. Paulina spoke for the group, "Mama, we want to be Sisters." They all nodded, confirming what Paulina had said on their behalf. As it turned out later, this was the group out of which Mother Kevin was to found the family of the Little Sisters of St. Francis of Assisi.

This group consisted of Paulina Musenero, forty years old, Sera Cornelia, thirty years old and Emereciane, a Luo from Kenya. The latter, about eighteen years old, had been sent to Nsambya, here in Uganda, to study midwifery. Others in the group were: Maria Salome, Agnes, Theresa, Lucia and myself, Rachel. I later became Sr. M. John, the writer of this book. The last five were between the ages of twelve and fourteen and were students of St. Agnes' Boarding School then situated at Nsambya.

At first Mother Kevin was dumb-founded. She looked at the children with real disbelief. She took some time to answer. Finally, still greatly amazed, she asked the group questions. "Do you really want to be Sisters?" "Certainly we want to be Sisters," they replied. Their determination was deep and strong. They wanted to be Sisters like Mama Kevin and her Sisters.

Paulina, perhaps like St. Peter, kept on speaking for the group. She told Mother, "Many times I have discussed this matter with these children and in fact the rest of the girls take them to be your own group. Surely Mama, you do not doubt us," she continued, "we do not understand or realize the obligations of religious life, but we want to try it." At once, Mother Kevin told us what we had to know. "Being a Sister means leaving your family and clan; no visits home, no going for feasts and no wearing fashionable clothes." "We shall try," we answered emphatically. She then informed us of the daily programme, which included waking up at five in the morning, long hours of prayer while kneeling most of the time, silence, obedience, punctuality, no talking to outsiders, not even priests, nor our parents. We were not discouraged. We only insisted on being given a chance, a trial. Eventually, some would make it while others would fall by the wayside.

Marriage customs were different in each ethnic group. In some ethnic groups a dowry meant quite a lot. In those days, it was customary for parents, because they knew better, to choose suitors for their daughters. Girls had no say in the matter. All this Mother knew and respected. There was one more important thing for us to know about the life we wanted to embrace. She told us, "Sisters do not get married. This will be very hard for you." She went on to stress the point, "It will be hard for your parents too, who have to be consulted." Mother Kevin would not accept girls into the Convent without their parents' knowledge.

During her conversation with us she may have felt the spirit of God in our sincere request. She asked us to pray earnestly and to think seriously about our decision. We went away happily, for at least Mother had listened to us. We did not regret the interview. What about dear Mother Kevin? She had a venture to ponder about. Very soon doubts came to her and she began questioning herself, "What am I going to do with these young girls seeking to embrace a life they know very little about? What will the future be like?"

Although the girls were eager, this had to be seriously considered. They did not have the qualities necessary for religious life. They were not educated enough. Religious life and their traditional marriage customs were in contradiction. In short, they were too "raw" for the life they were longing to live. It was an adventure! It took her time. She had to look up many things. First the Bishop had to give his approval or refusal. Mother Kevin searched the laws of the Church of that time, which allowed people free from impediments "to drink the cup."

His Lordship Bishop Biermans was consecrated Bishop in 1912, after Bishop Hanlon had resigned from his office due to poor health. The new Bishop was very popular and was welcomed with great joy and love. He was full of zeal and courage. He had a population of nearly two million people in his Diocese of the Upper Nile. To evangelize all these people, he had thirteen priests and seven Franciscan Sisters as co-workers. Mother Kevin went to discuss the matter with him. At first Bishop Biermans thought Mother Kevin wanted to train helpers or women catechists like those of Bishop Streicher. But no, Mother Kevin wanted to train religious women. The bishop had doubts about the idea of making Sisters out of "the new material." He was aware of our traditional customs, some of them unChristian. However, he told Mother Kevin that he wanted to interview the girls. This was good news.

We went to his house, again led by Paulina. The Bishop looked at us, amazed at our ages. With the exception of the three older girls, five looked too young to understand what the talk was about. He talked about religious life, emphasizing celibacy unknown to the people here, obedience, and mortification. We assured him of our wish and determination to try. After the interview, the Bishop and Mother Kevin were pleased and more than ever convinced of our sincerity. He blessed us. After one week, Bishop Biermans said Mass in the Sisters' chapel and gave us khaki dresses. Despite lack of housing, Mother went ahead. So it was, that on May 1st, 1923, the Little Sisters' Congregation was founded by Mother Kevin O.S.F. after twenty years of her missionary work in Uganda.

The beginning was not easy. Mother Kevin was laughed at. "She is turning first communicants into Sisters," they said. Others criticized her for teaching us English. The gossip was, "She is making Europeans out of them." "How are they to know God in a foreign language?" Mother Foundress was always modern and up-to-date. She was the first to see the use of higher education for sisters and, as usual, always ahead of [her] time. She knew how education would help those who would come in contact with her Sisters, and she was right.

In the Sisters' compound there were four different groups, namely: the convent girls, workers for the sisters, the boarders, the nurses (usually called *Basawo*) and our new group called *Babeezi*, or helpers. We were very strange to the others. We were the girls whom Mother Kevin intended to carry on the same apostolates as the Franciscan Sisters. Mother Kevin converted three storerooms into the "helpers'" temporary accommodation. Our attire consisted of khaki dresses sewn out of simple fashion, a rosary hanging on the left hand side on a leather belt, and a medal of St. Francis on a big chain around the neck. We felt strange but happy, keeping all to ourselves. We went nowhere, except to Church and the gardens. We walked in silence usually in fours or threes and occasionally in twos, when going to the garden, but never alone. This new way of behaviour caused great curiosity among the three other groups in the Sisters' compound and in the villages. Some of those new formation rules were so painful and contrary to our culture that people got puzzled about us.

This was the beginning of the formation and we had to accept it from the start. Mother Kevin told us to have as our aim the glory of God and our own sanctification by the observance of the three vows: chastity, poverty, and obedience, not forgetting to pray for the Bishops and priests in the Diocese where we worked. She instilled in us the desire to teach women and children.

After May 1st, 1923, there were two occasions when more girls joined the young Congregation. On July 2nd, 1923, four girls entered. Magdalene Nabisoli, who had been teaching the children to read and write; Felistas from Naggalama, who had for a long time been with the Sisters; Magdalene Kafuko, from Budini Parish, the first Musoga girl in the Congregation; and Maria Bahirye, from St. Agnes' Boarding School. We now numbered twelve, the number of the Apostles. "I do not want any Judas," Mother would say. On September 17th, 1923, the feast of the Stigmata of our Father St. Francis, four more girls joined us. Maria Therese was a Mugishu from Nyondo Parish. She had come to Nsambya for nursing. She joined the *Babeezi* but did not stay long. Others were: Josephine Nankya . . . . Nakamya, a convent girl from Naggalama, and Philomena Zikusooka from Masaka, Kitovu Parish. These composed the original number of sixteen members in the Congregation. This was the first set of Sisters to be clothed and to be professed.

Unfortunately, some of the parents were furious with Mother Kevin because the group [was] comprised of many ethnic groups. The convent girls and the nurses had noticed what they called a mixture. The Luos, the Samyas, the Basoga, and Bagishu were sharing the same meal, using the same cups, plates, and cutlery. Everything was used in common. To the Baganda of that time, such a mixture of ethnic groups was a big insult. The parents felt offended. Nevertheless, this was exactly what Mother Foundress wanted and intended to foster: Unity in diversity, which has resulted in a rich Congregation of more than forty different ethnic groups among the African Congregations. Mother Kevin faced the challenge bravely. Slowly, it became easy to believe and live the fact that we are all Sisters, children of one Father.

During the early formation years, fresh aspirants found it very hard to wake up at five in the morning for meditation. For more than a month, the new aspirants would feel lost and extremely strained but "love knows no barrier."

Morning and night prayers were in the form of repeating words after Mother. "My God," My God, we would repeat. "Our Father," Our Father, "My God I love you" and so on. We learnt prayers mostly by repetition. After a while we got some simple prayer books. Those were of great help.

Sister Maria Camilla, O.S.F. taught us other prayers, including the mysteries of the rosary and the seven dolour rosary. It took us two months to memorize them. Mother Kevin loved prayer time and taught us the value of prayer. She lived a life of prayer. Her absolute belief in the Divine providence of her Heavenly Father was never shaky. Her devotion to Jesus, His birth, Passion and Resurrection was remarkable. She was dedicated to the sacred Passion, and said daily the way of the cross. In her prayer life Mother Kevin lived the liturgy of the church and taught us to love it too.

Marjorie Oludhe Macgoye
LEARNING THE SEX TRADE

Kenya 1993   English

Marjorie Oludhe Macgoye was born Marjorie Phyllis King in Southampton, England, on October 21, 1928. She developed a keen interest in reading and writing from an early age (a poem she wrote when she was only seven was published in the *Daily Mirror*). A dedicated and astute student, she earned a scholarship and successfully finished secondary school in 1945. She was then admitted to the Royal Holloway College of the University of London, where she studied English, graduating with a Bachelor of Arts degree in 1948. During the six years that followed, Macgoye worked in various bookshops and bookstores in London. It was also in the course of this time that she continued with postgraduate studies and obtained a Master of Arts degree from Birkbeck College, University of London.

In 1954 Macgoye came to Kenya to work as a bookseller for the Church Missionary Society (CMS). Six years later she married Daniel Oludhe Macgoye, a medical assistant, adopted his name, and gradually became fully integrated into the culture of her husband's people, the Luo. When Kenya attained independence in 1963, she chose to become a Kenyan citizen. Life in her adopted country turned out to be a long and tireless journey aimed at enhancing a literary culture in the East African region. This she has managed to achieve with remarkable success as manager of various bookstores, consultant with leading publishing firms, high school English teacher, and, most recently, as lecturer in creative writing at Egerton University, Kenya.

But it is above all as a creative writer that Macgoye has exerted a profound impact on East African literature. A writer across genres, her literary work has enriched and, to a large extent, given shape and direction to the tradition of women writing in East Africa, and Kenya in particular. In the corpus of her writing are to be found dynamic female characters: women who evolve new paradigms of living and visioning, and thus become active participants in Kenya's history as well as its insightful "writers."

Macgoye's novel *Coming to Birth* (1986) earned her worldwide renown by emerging winner of the 1986 international Sinclair Prize for fiction. The text was first published by Heinemann (London) and Heinemann Kenya (Nairobi) (now East African Educational Publishers). Another edition, by the London-based feminist publisher, Virago, is currently out of print. *Coming to Birth* is now available through East African Educational Publishers (Nairobi and Kampala) and The Feminist Press at the City University of New York, which issued it in 2000. The following year Macgoye's second novel, *The Present Moment* (1987), was published. It continues to be in print through East African Educational Publishers as well as The Feminist Press (2000). *Victoria and Murder in Majengo* (1993) was published by Macmillan (London and Nairobi) and is also in print. *Homing In* (1994), which won second place in the Jomo Kenyatta Prize for Literature, Kenya's highest literary award, in 1995, *Chira* (1997), and *A Farm Called Kishinev* (2005), have been published by East African Educational Publishers.

In its totality, Macgoye's writing constitutes an imaginative record of the multidimensional evolution of the Kenyan nation. The product of an artist of profound and unique talent, an intellectual and a moralist of the highest order, this record nurtures and elevates the mind, and ennobles the spirit.

Victoria, from which the following excerpt is selected, is the fascinating, soul-searching story of Victoria Abiero, who decides to run away from the confines and expectations of a largely patriarchal African traditional marriage in her rural Luo community in Western Kenya, and embark, after carefully considering all the available choices, "with complete deliberation," on the path of freedom and economic empowerment as an urban prostitute. As a sexual worker, Victoria not only opens up her worldview significantly; she also endeavors to make her life worthwhile by educating, at least to a reasonable level, the daughter she conceives in the course of her career; and by saving some of her earnings for the future. Hence when she "retires," a mature, elderly woman, she manages to organize her affairs in such a way that she eventually prospers as a "magnificent" businesswoman; and dies leaving behind a small legacy for her immediate relations. Victoria's thus becomes a life purposefully lived despite the invariably threatening socioeconomic circumstances.

In *Victoria*, the heroine and her house of sexual workers exemplify the view that with determination and hope, women can disengage themselves from the sociopolitical disparities that define them; and by forming communities, they may chart a value-laden future; which, however, still falls short of the realization of their full potential.

Emilia Ilieva and Lennox Odiemo-Munara

✦

The first time a man came for her she was surprised. It was like a mistake. But she had been married, after all. It was natural. Some of the girls, she found, had never been married, and this was hard to understand. She submitted dutifully, as she had been taught, but here was something she had not been taught, more like what she had experienced with the young fisherman, but different again, since it regarded her only indirectly. She soon got used to it. The provocation was not difficult for her, as she revolted from the whole humdrum experience of her marriage. To be wanted was a pleasure. To draw from Sara the cash for a new dress, a bottle of hair-oil, ear-rings, was a delight. She began to talk to the men, to ask them about their work, their schooling, for nearly all of them had been to school. They usually didn't mind her talking. If it got too much, Sara would warn her about it privately. Some of the men were from Uganda. There were even two Europeans who came quite often. They said they were not married, which she found hard to believe, judging their ages by their rolls of muscle and money. They said Kisumu was not the kind of place they would bring a wife to. She replied that it seemed very good to her and full of European things. They taught her to say in English "Have another drink" and "Come up and see me some time." Some of the black men found this very funny. Many were not Luos, and they tried to tell her that they all belonged to the same country, but she found this hard to understand. All the same she picked up a bit of Swahili.

All these weeks she did not hear any news from Gem or see anyone she had known before. She kept thinking about going home, but it was a girlhood picture of home, carrying the heavy water-pots and grinding, grinding away at the flour. One day she asked Sara, "How is it that you can stay here all the time without going back home? I must soon go to my mother's and then I will come back and see you."

Sara looked at her closely.

"In my country a *malaya* cannot go home."

"But I am not a *malaya*. I am married. My husband is old and unkind to me. Also he is not very much use as a husband. Therefore they must buy me back. But I was properly married. They received the cow of virginity for me."

"In that case your husband must have been of some use! Besides, before you came here you had a child."

"For that reason also I came away. But I am still married. When someone else wants me, he will bring the dowry to pay back."

"What will you tell them when you return?"

"That my husband is no good and they must buy me back."

"And what will you tell them about the time since you left Gem? It is two months now."

"That you were kind to me and I stayed until I felt better."

"And the child?"

"Did not the child die?"

"But not at home. Where is it buried?"

"Buried? At the mission."

"And do you belong to the mission?"

"No, not exactly. They wanted me to read, but I had not started. They were still asking me questions."

"And will they not say you are—spoiled? You have had other men, European men and circumcised men of other communities. You have got used to other ways of living. Will you go to one of your round villages and hoe and bring water with your hair all shaggy? Will you go as fourth wife to another old man, you who sit poring over a newspaper as though you can read it? Will you make do with millet porridge in a good season and pounded cassava in a dry season? And when your old man dies, will you be able to tear your clothes off and weep upon his body, showing that you have done him no wrong? Or if you cannot, what will they do to you?"

Victoria remembered falling silent. It was the first thing she remembered in her body as belonging to her present self, and her eyes pricked as they then did, but no tears came. The weeks in the house seemed unreal, as indeed they were at the time, an interlude in the life of digging and cooking which was the only kind she knew. She remembered the teaching the old women had given her as a girl, and the even closer segregation imposed on those of her friends who had been baptized. Perhaps indeed they would not welcome her, would not admire her fine clothes or share the meat she had meant to buy with the bit of money she had saved. She had just walked out of real life for a couple of months. Would it not be waiting for her when she came back? Would she be like the boy who had gone to boarding school and come home after a term to find fish swimming where his bedroom had been and his father away inquiring about tenant land elsewhere? She continued to stare at Sara Chelagat.

"The overseer took me away to the railway," said Chelagat, gazing past her. "He took several of my friends too. We did not find it too bad at first. But I never saw my father again. Even when he was dying he did not let them send for me. My mother came once or twice long afterwards, when I had started up in Kisumu here. She pretended to bring her gourds to sell in the market and I would meet her and give her some money. There was a time later on when I'd save a bit, and I used to get so lonely here among all foreign folks, that I thought I could get some poor man to marry me. I didn't need any dowry, you see, I had squared that by paying towards my brothers' marriages and all I would have needed was a bit of land to live on and have children. But I was sick by then—you know the white people brought diseases which a woman can get from a man or a man from a woman, and they said I would never have a baby then, though I was lucky to have been cured and not gone spotty. So no-one would look at me. You see. . . .Well, if they threaten to send me out of town, I pay them, that's all. You won't starve. You've got a good head, you know. Maybe you could even learn to read. They won't let you live like a whole woman but perhaps you learn to live half like a man. But don't say I made you. I gave you food and a place to rest, that's all. You did the rest yourself."

She shrugged her shoulders, ear-rings jangling, long skirts rustling, and left Victoria to think it over.

Field Marshal Muthoni-Kirima
WARRIOR WOMAN

Kenya 1993   English

The Mau Mau movement, or Land Freedom Army, operated both covertly, in urban and white-settled areas, and overtly, in the countryside and on the margins of colonial society. The movement, which is most closely associated with the "KEM" communities—Kikuyu (Gikuyu)-Embu-Meru—had roots in established organizations, the Kikuyu Central Association and the East African Trades Union Congress. It had been growing clandestinely for several years before 1952, when the British government in Kenya declared a state of emergency and arrested Jomo Kenyatta and other resistance leaders. The movement's ideology and strategy continues to be a subject of historical debate. Isolated groups often became fragmented through casualties; contacts with other fighters carried risks of betrayal; and the central task force providing supplies and information was increasingly hampered by the close scrutiny of the British government.

Muthoni-Kirima joined the Mau-Mau as a married woman. Though her parents worked on a European farm, after her marriage she moved to a village in the "reserve," the land set aside for Africans, close to Nyeri. Most women involved in liberation movements worked as carriers of information and supplies, as Muthoni herself did to begin with. However, she became one of the few women to claim active work as a fighter.

Muthoni describes much movement on foot, from Nyeri to the Aberdares, Thika (Chania), and Gilgil. Traveling was dangerous work, and individuals needed to be able to cover their tracks. It would have been highly unusual for fighters to move in a group of twenty, as in the plan Muthoni describes to obtain arms from Ethiopia.

Mau Mau leader Dedan Kimathi, who plays a central role in Muthoni's narrative, was captured and executed in 1956, a decisive step in the British progress toward winning the battle and losing the war. Muthoni asserts that her group learned of the release of Kenyatta and of forthcoming independence by observing changes in civilian behavior. Possibly these freedom fighters were so isolated that they had to fill in gaps of knowledge by conjecture or accept unreliable information. Muthoni joined other Mau Mau who laid down their weapons at the ceremony marking Kenya's full independence, at Ruringu Stadium in December 1963. After this point, her story clearly expresses the feelings of many of the thousands of freedom fighters who either surrendered their arms or were released from the brutal detention centers where they were kept between 1956 and 1963. Muthoni gives poignant voice to the disillusion they suffered because they were offered little recognition or reward by independent Kenya. The old landscape of scattered homesteads was never re-created, and in most cases the title-deeds issued while many claimants were shut away in detention camps were not reviewed. Muthoni was given permission to collect and sell "wild" ivory, until the trade was banned in 1976. She was nominated as councilor to Nyeri Counti Council in 1990.

Marjorie Oludhe Macgoye and Naomi L. Shitemi

✦

I grew up on a colonialist's farm. That is one of the reasons why I developed the need to fight for independence. My parents used to tell us that these people were foreigners and that was why they made us work like slaves.

I took my first Mau Mau oath in the African reserves and then introduced my husband, Mutungi, to the movement. In fact I looked for the goat used to administer the oath to my husband without his knowledge. By then I already knew that by doing so I was helping the movement.

Then, when I later learned that Field Marshal Dedan Kimathi was leading fighters in the Aberdare forest, I started supplying his troops with food and information. Such information included the movement of Home Guards and their patrols into the forest.

When my husband became fully aware of the importance of fighting for freedom he went into the forest and joined the fighters.

The Home Guards who monitored life in our village noticed that my husband was missing. They came and asked me where he was. I told them that he had taken some eggs to the market in Nyeri town.

On that night I had some money, Sh. 800, which I had to forward to the forest fighters. After the Home Guards had left me they went on their patrol into the forest but they came back at night. Their leader, Elijah, woke me up and demanded to know where Mutungi, my husband, was. I told them that he had not come back from the market. On hearing that they beat me up very badly.

One day before this incident I had learned that the British soldiers commonly known as Johnnies were going on a forest patrol towards where Dedan Kimathi was administering oaths. I ran ahead of the soldiers and warned Kimathi. The oathing stopped.

On my way home I met with the Johnnies. They roughed me up but later let me go. At the edge of the forest I put on a heavy coat that I had, in order to disguise my looks, and hide my bruises. To avoid being seen I crawled on my stomach towards our village. By the time I got home my stomach was so badly bruised that I had to use hot water with salt and liniment to treat the bruises. Village women and friends had to help me because by now my body was all swollen from beatings with military boots.

After three days the Home Guards came to my house and started beating me again mercilessly. Blood was oozing through my mouth and ears. All the house was blood stained. They ransacked the house looking for money. Luckily I never kept any money inside the house. I always hid it in the grass outside.

When my women friends saw the condition I was in they were filled with compassion. They took me from our home at Njoguni to Kihigaini, near where my sister-in-law, Wanjugu, lived. It was near the forest edge.

The village women there started treating me. When I felt a bit well I would go out to the forest edge collecting firewood, but I was actually spying on how I would escape into the forest.

After four days of planning I ran into the forest. I can't remember the date.

On my first day in the forest the only living thing I saw was an antelope. It coughed. Then I walked for about two kilometers into the forest and sat down to pray:

"God, you know why I have come into this forest. I pray to you to help me, for you know the reason best. Help us expel the foreigners from our land. God, you know how I have been mistreated. As I don't know where Kimathi is, help me to contact them, God."

I remained on the scene quietly until at about 4 P.M., when I started searching for Kimathi.

In those days there were very few people in the forest. Fighters would go into the forest and come out without much trouble. For many hours I would sit at a water fetching point, expecting to find people in search of water, but no one would come.

For two weeks I found no one. At night I would climb trees to avoid being trampled by elephants.

But in the village people were looking for me. When they failed to know where I was, they assumed that I must have gone into the forest.

One day, after two lonely weeks, I noticed ten people coming to the watering point. I noticed Kimathi's brother, Wagura Wambararia, and another called Gitungu. These are the ones who took me to Kimathi's camp.

My first assignment in Kimathi's army was in the group that went looking for food. We would raid European settler farms for cattle, goats and sheep. We once launched a raid from Rugoti bush [camp] into Karimurio farm, which was guarded by the colonial soldiers. We had a heavy battle in which we killed one white soldier and two African scouts. . . .

I had learned about the struggle for freedom when I was very young. I used to see fund raising meetings for somebody called Jomo Kenyatta. I would ask my mother, and she would tell me that the money was for a big man who would go overseas and then come back to free us. Sometimes I would be asked to keep the money . . . and I knew it was a secret to be hidden from the white settlers.

As the fighting continued in the forest there was hope that it would last only three months and then the country would be free.

Then came the aeroplanes. First it was the spotter planes, which produced sad sounds. These were followed by the bombers with slow and heavy sound, which created fear. This time we were up in the moorlands of the Aberdares.

Our camps were guarded a mile apart on each of the approach paths.

My experience of my first bombing is memorable. We saw the bottom of the bomber open and then something drop. Some of us said, well, so they also go to the toilet.

A man among us said it was a bomb and we should lie low, count to five and we would hear the explosion. Just as we counted to five the earth shook many miles around. Then shrapnel started flying past, above our heads. Some trees were falling like there was one big axe swinging past. Each bomber used to drop between five and ten bombs.

Just when we thought all was over they came again, spraying us with machine gun fire. We used to call it Bebeta. God is great, the greatest, because we survived all the strafing, which was like a tractor is ploughing the field. And we survived all these! . . .

Because of the situation we had found that it was a waste of time to slaughter an animal in the normal manner. One would only cut a chunk, together with the skin, and put it in the rucksack. This way we left no trails.

Mau Mau Parliament and Dedan Kimathi

Dedan Kimathi used to call meetings at Chania with people like Karari Njama taking notes.

Kimathi was a leader, very merciful and wise. The things he used to say, if people followed them, some of the bad things which have happened would not have happened. One of the things which was ignored was to reward freedom fighters. . . .

One time he asked: "What do you think should happen to Kamatimu (the Africans fighting on the side of colonialists) when we become free?"

Some said: "Execute them and their families." Others said: "Try them."

But Kimathi said: "Kamatimu have helped in some ways. We should not kill them. But something will be done like being made to work for us. If they are killed how shall they know what we are fighting for?"

But some people were very annoyed with him.

Kimathi would then say: "Kamatimu are producing children with our wives back in the reserves. Let them live and see that we were fighting for justice."

Kimathi's philosophy was proved right at Independence. He had prevailed upon the freedom fighters not to kill Chief Muhoya. It was Chief Muhoya who had signed the death warrant for Kimathi. But Muhoya lived to see Independence. (And because he had sworn that there would be no Independence, he was killed by one of his bulls immediately.)

Then there were people like Eliud Mahihu, who used to fly over the Nyandarua [Aberdares] broadcasting: "I am sure that no Independence will ever come. So surrender and come out holding green branches . . ."

Mahihu saw Independence and became a senior and prosperous civil servant. . . .

Split

One of the major splits among the Mau Mau fighting forces came not long after a Parliament was formed. It came during a trial.

The colonialists had suggested a truce, that the Mau Mau forces and the colonialists start exchanging letters before they could meet physically and negotiate a ceasefire.

Several letters had been exchanged through "dead letter drops" but Kimathi was not happy about it. So he called a meeting of all senior officials in the Aberdares. All camps in Nyandarua East and Muranga district were represented. The venue of the meeting was guarded in a ten mile radius. Kimathi's message was that those who had agreed to the exchange of letters did not understand the trick the colonialist was playing.

When the meeting assembled Kimathi explained the meaning of this letter game. He said the colonialist wanted to know the intelligence and the thinking of the Mau Mau. He said that at the proposed meeting the colonialist did not want to capture us nor kill us, but he would come with sweet talk, then we would be bitter and then tell all our secrets.

Kimathi ruled that from then on no one should cooperate with the colonialists. He said we should forget the dead letter drops.

He reasoned this way: how can two fighters separate themselves? It was only the politicians who could meet and talk.

He then ruled that anyone found contravening that ruling would be tried by the "big court" (Parliament).

I was a member of the Parliament and I had been elected by secret ballot.

General Mathenge Mirungi was also an elected member of the Parliament, and I was his junior.

Soon after this meeting, General Mathenge went ahead and met the colonialists. He was accompanied by one girl named Wangechi.

At the secret meeting with the colonialists Mathenge gave his gun to the enemy and the enemy gave him his. Mathenge's gun was the catapult version, which had become very effective. The colonial soldier studied the forest gun keenly before he returned it to Mathenge.

When Kimathi discovered that Mathenge had met the enemy against the ruling he had made, he summoned Parliament to meet at Chania. Mathenge was called and Parliament sat under a red flag. Mathenge was put on trial.

Kimathi: Mathenge, were you at the meeting which ruled against further meetings with the colonialists?
Mathenge: Yes.
Kimathi: Since you were there, then why did you go and meet them and disclose our secrets? Do you want us to be defeated? You, being a heroic fighter and everyone depends on you, do you know what your enemy is doing? Do you know that you are betraying yourself? What was on your mind? Are the colonialists your brothers?

Mathenge, do you want us to judge you for that action? Do you want to surrender? Tell us. If you want to surrender, go alone. Do not take us with you. Today this Parliament will judge you.

A member said: Mathenge should not be forgiven. He should be killed, for he went against the decision of this Parliament, so that no one else does like him.

Then all members of Parliament were asked their opinions.

I raised my hand before the group answered. I said I did not favour the death sentence. . . .

Other members of Parliament agreed with me. Then Mathenge and company [who had been tied to trees during the trial] were untied.

After one week we received reports that Mathenge continued to meet the colonialists. Kimathi was very annoyed. He ordered that Mathenge be sought and brought to him alive.

Since Mathenge knew what was happening he started hiding himself.

This incident happened towards the end of 1954. Just before it happened, Mathenge, myself, Karari Njama, Karuri wa Gakure—about 20 of us, had been selected to go to Ethiopia to seek help for ammunition. But before our journey could start was when Mathenge started meeting the colonialists secretly. His only companion on such missions was the girl Wangechi. Any time he was on secret meeting it was said he had gone to Nairobi.

We looked for Mathenge and did not find him. He had his own group. Then came the rumour that he had gone to Ethiopia.

Enthronement of Kimathi

Sometime in 1954 Dedan Kimathi had called an important meeting somewhere in Muranga. We from Kabage area had to go. Many were unable to attend because the security situation was very bad. On the way I felt like thousands of barrels of guns were pointed at me.

I had been told that we were attending a case. But it turned out to be a ceremony. I was one of those selected to attend the ceremony.

I met two old women from Muranga who dressed me in traditional regalia, all made of animal skin. They included "Nyathiba" (upper wear), "Muthuru" and "Mwehio" (for lower wear), and "hang'i" (earrings).

These two old women were accompanied by two old men of "Ndungu" age group. That means they were so old that they could not walk without support.

Before the ceremony took place we spent a week of prayers and feasting. We rarely slept.

On the 9th day Kimathi was dressed in a "githii" [cloak] and a colobus monkey headgear. I stood behind, dressed in my regalia. Then the old women brought some oil in a gourd. The oil was a mixture of sheep fat and castor oil. The oil was blessed with prayers in Kikuyu traditional style.

Then the old men took the oil and poured it on Kimathi's head. It dripped on his cloak. All this time there were chants of "Ngai Thaai." When the oil was poured on Kimathi's head I rendered some adulation. Then an old woman picked some of the remaining oil and smeared it on my face and back as she said: "Ngai Thaai."

After this solemn ceremony Kimathi said that we would go up to the Aberdares summit. There we hoisted flags with Kenya's national colours mounted on bamboo poles. There was a flag on each of the three peaks.

We were very tired after climbing. When the ceremony was over we went looking for camps where we could rest.

It was at this meeting of the ceremony that I was promoted to General. It was at the same meeting that Kimathi said that anyone who will fight to the end of the war will be called Field Marshal.

Before I was made a General people in our camp were in desperate state of hunger. They were afraid of going out and seeking for food. So I sacrificed myself by risking to go to the farm of one settler known as Lord Cole, who was growing crops by irrigation. His farm was tightly guarded.

That night I used my tactics and, avoiding security, dug under the fence, got into a maize plantation and noiselessly filled a sack with maize cobs. Then I crawled with my sack out of the farm, filled the hole under the fence, and returned to camp without leaving any trails.

When the people in the camp saw me back with maize, they carried me shoulder high. . . .

This year the air raids increased. We could not move from camp to camp. We did not see Kimathi. At one time he had sent a man to look for me, Nyina wa Thonje and my husband, Mutungi. At that time we were looking for him also.

People in the reserves did not give us food any more because they claimed we would be betraying them. This was so because they did not trust anyone any more due to the activities of the pseudo Mau Mau.

There were three types of pseudo gangs: those who persuaded one to leave the forest, others would run out of sight, and those who killed on sight.

We decided to avoid the villages. We could not trust any stranger. One had to answer the call of nature in sight of others.

When food was not available I lived on juices of tree fibres. At one time I was like the picture of Eve on being chased out of Garden of Eden. I used leaves to cover my breasts and genitals. . . .

It was around this time that we heard that Jomo Kenyatta had been released from detention. Then we started seeing members of the public coming close to the forest without fear like before. . . .

With the help of some friends I obtained a dress, shoes and a headscarf. Then I changed my skin dresses, which were made of hyrax skins.

People who were faithful to the Mau Mau movement arranged for my transport to Nairobi. They took me to an office near the Jevanjee Gardens where they tried to make an appointment for me to see Kenyatta. Kenyatta was busy with meetings but he directed that I be kept comfortable until he would see me.

After one week I met Jomo Kenyatta. This was in November, 1963. I told Kenyatta that I had come because of rumours that there would be freedom in Kenya. I told him that since you are the one who can tell the truth, tell me, because maybe people just wanted me to come out of the forest.

Kenyatta asked me with a lot of sadness, in a pensive mood and looking at me right in the eyes:

"Nyakinyua (Madam), is it not a joke that you have been in the forest all these years?"

"No, it is not a joke, Mzee (Elder). Are you doubting?"

Kenyatta did not say anything. He just stared at me and wept.

I told him: "Mzee, do you want me to prove to you? Just because you see new clothes . . .these were bought for me so that I could come to see you. I have come from the forest where I have been since 1952. If you want to believe . . ."

I removed my headdress and my hair came down. He extended his hand and touched my hair and asked: "How did you do it?"

I told him: "If you look carefully you will find lice eggs in the hair."

Kenyatta said: "I can see, and I believe. Now how many are you?" I told him: "We were many but now I know of only one who is with me. Some died and others surrendered."

He said: "And now with all that rain and sunshine you have lived there?"

I told him, yes, and that the weather could get worse.

He told me: "I will say nothing. And when you go say that Uhuru (freedom) is on December 12, and say it was Kenyatta who has told you. Go and announce to the others who might be there."

After asking him how we shall know that Uhuru was there truly without seeing the flag, Kenyatta told me that I would be picked from my forest hideout on the Uhuru day by his own vehicle. He also said that if there were more fighters in Mount Kenya forest they would be sent for, to meet at Ruringu on December 16, 1963. But for me I would be picked from Nyeri on December 12 for night ceremonies in Nairobi.

When I came out of the forest I could not look at the sun because the light was burning my eyes. At Ruringu is where I met people like Dr. Munyua Waiyaki [then Minister of Defence], who did a good job calming us.

I had thought that all those people who had left the forest first, those who had been in detention and other places, would have come to celebrate with us. But I was wrong because after one week I was brought some poisoned soda. That soda was intercepted by a young man called Nderitu.

That was when I found out that I was wrong when I thought I had lived with animals in the forest. It was now that I had come to animals.

Even when the ceremonies were over and we were told to go home I had to go to an uncle of my husband and build my own house. That was traditionally wrong. . . .

Elieshi Lema
TRYST WITH PERIL
Tanzania 1994   English

Elieshi Lema was born in 1948 in the Kilimanjaro region of Tanzania, and now lives in Dar es Salaam, where she works as a writer, publisher, and political activist. She has been an associate member of the Tanzania Gender Networking Program, a board member of the National Kiswahili Council, the educational reform organization Haki Elimu, and the African Publishers Network, and was one of the founding members and later chairperson of the Tanzania Culture Trust Fund. During the late 1980s and early 1990s she was the manager of the Tanzania Publishing House and in 1997 she and Demere Kitunga established E & D Publishing Company, the first and only publishing house in Tanzania owned and run by women.

Elieshi Lema nurtured her interest in literature and writing while pursuing a degree in English literature at the University of Dar es Salaam, and later at San Francisco State University, where she majored in creative writing. She also spent a year at Makerere University studying librarianship. Her first literary works were two poems published in 1980 in the anthology *Summons*. Books and short stories for children and young people followed, including *A Tear for Anna, A Stone for Mambo's House* (1986), *Safari ya Prosper* (Prosper's Journey, 1996) and *Mwendo* (1998).

In 2001, Lema published a novel in English, *Parched Earth*, which reflects her views on contemporary culture and politics as they affect the lives of Tanzanian women. Written from a woman's perspective, the novel portrays a woman's vigorous struggle against social and economic constraints, her obsessions, her joys, and her sensuality.

In "Tryst with Peril," Lema writes again about relationships between women and men—this time, about the common practice of older married men keeping younger women. The story references the prevalent belief in Africa that the younger the woman, the safer a man is from HIV/AIDS, and further, that a woman's willingness to forgo the use of condoms proves her concern for a man's pleasure. While the relationship in the story, between a young woman and a man old enough to be her father, appears in its own way to be mutually satisfying, Lema probes the grounds of that satisfaction. She questions not only the inequity inherent in a relationship based on sex for payment, but also the immanent dangers for young women exposed to unprotected sex and thus HIV/AIDS.

Amandina Lihamba

✦

The atmosphere in the room was comfortably warm. A single candle burned on the table furthest from the bed. The late afternoon sun through the drawn curtains into the room offered an extra gift of light. This was the fifth floor, away from the noise and eavesdroppers. Their short stay in the room had already made it seem familiar. No longer did they smell the room's cigarette smoke blended within a bouquet of older odors. Now the air was fragrant with the perfume of satiation. Their naked bodies beneath the sheets felt friendly as they descended gently from the wings of fantasy, feeling their weight on the bed. The man sighed, breathing out the used air in his lungs to make room for more play.

Everything was good: the sex, the young woman's body, the hard mattress, the crisp, clean sheets, and the light wind blowing through the window which they had opened, avoiding the air conditioner. Cold air tensed his muscles and made him irritable—experience had taught him that. He came here to relax, body and mind, so everything had to be perfect. And the high-class hotel was meant to make this possible.

After several bouts of hard breathing, which he did deliberately, he settled down to even more relaxation. The young woman lay quietly beside him, breathing easily, seemingly enjoying his satisfaction. That too relaxed him so that he could laugh and joke and tell her stories. It was possible to forget the pressure of work, the tension of competition that met his every move. Every time he earned money, big money, he pegged the next earning higher. He loved challenging himself like that. In the Party, he was constantly challenged to retain his position among the inner club, among men of substance who moved things, those who were themselves the law. Among his friends, rich and affluent, the struggle was to be best in the group by being one step ahead every time.

The disagreements with his wife inflicted different tensions. He resented this most of all because the problems with his wife never could be resolved without breaking the marriage, for they were grounded in the absence of freedom from each other's demands within an institution that had no space to spare for a woman. What he sometimes could not bear was the way she fought for that space, the way she demanded it from him so strongly that she broke the walls of his patience. On those occasions, he felt like leaving, to avoid the tension, to release the poison inside him that, he noticed, had aged so many of his colleagues. Often, the atmosphere of their home was rank with the foul breath of her unreleased anger.

Now, he toyed with expectations about the young woman. His thoughts moved in liquid time, recklessly forward into imagined possibilities. I could keep her somewhere in some nice house, he thought, where I could have her whenever I wanted. I could offer her a job, which would ease some of her money problems. I would like to be sure she'd be faithful. He had been captured by the mature body of the young woman, still carrying the delicacy of early youth. He did not want to guess her age, for this was no time for guilt, should she turn out to be too young. He suppressed that thought with comfort: She wasn't a virgin. He looked at her with gentle keenness, wanting to store a reel of images for retrieval later. He knew that these were dangerous times, with HIV creeping in on people just like that, with no particular rule, no formula to deal with this riotous, untamable virus. It irked him. He had been thinking lately of investing a bit more in relationships in order to keep himself free of the scourge. He imagined possibilities in full color, in landscapes full of magic and daredevil courage. I could even keep her as second wife, he thought, and there find care for her legitimately. Who will care about a constantly nagging Janice, who won't even notice that I've been away?

He laughed wryly at this thought, knowing well that Janice will notice his escapade immediately, and that on his return will pounce, asking those terrible questions as if he were an accused man she was cross-examining in court! It did not make any difference even, should she use the soft language. She was still the cat who had caught her prey and could take any number of days to kill it, her claws sharp as knives every time. He smiled at the metaphor and pulled the young woman to him as if to use her as shield.

She asked throatily, "What are you thinking about?"

"You and me," he lied, "how we seem to be perfect for each other."

"Perfect? How?" the young woman probed.

He did not want to get into that conversation, he did not want to be queried, so he pulled her closer to him and closed her mouth with kisses, touching her in those places which had earlier on aroused her to acceptance. The young woman responded by extricating herself from his embrace, still pressing, "Seriously, what makes us perfect for each other?"

He laughed. She sat up. She was serious, she wanted to place herself in his life, to know the weight of his desire for her body. He also sat and started to tickle her and her question was turned into a game where each explored the other's reservoirs of laughter.

Laughter brought other stories from him, nostalgic with the loss of his naivete. These stories moved backwards, to a childhood full of play and freedom. He had been a spoiled child, for sisters did the work while he cried crocodile tears to avoid beatings from a strict father, a teacher who believed in discipline by the rod as a way of life and particularly for his children, girls and boys. The man loved talking of those times, affirming his father's belief in success as a product of pain. That was an anecdote which explained his wealth and affluence but also justified his refusal to give to social causes because, as he usually put it, "people are too lazy to work hard."

The stories of the man's youth were laughter itself, punctuated with adventure and recklessness. His youth was a drunken spree that had made him dizzy with enjoyment. The enviable life he narrated touched a nerve in the young woman's feelings, since she was twenty-two and had never been as lucky as he. She had even forgotten that she had ever been young. Where she came from, children were aged by a life of abandonment to chance, a life that kept parents in the fields to earn a frugal meal at the end of the day.

She had completed primary schooling without expectations. Her life had no map of alternatives, no track to follow. Through a leap of courage, rebellion, and faith, she had come to the city to be a house maid. She was energetic and hardworking. The first job was not hard to get, since many working women were looking for her kind. It took no time for her to realize that to be a house maid was another dead end. She had left the village looking for a better life, a hope with a name. But what exactly was a better life? What was it exactly that she wanted, or needed?

On her way to the market every weekend, she had risked on a better life with a bus driver. He liked her. He told her that she was pretty, a woman as solid as steel, one to be made a wife. He indulged her with praises, and afforded her a new look. He enabled her to dress well in second hand clothes, and in them no one could tell she was a house maid! Then she became pregnant, after which she was summarily relieved of her job. "Get out! Get out of my house. Quickly before you bring AIDS into my house. Go."

She was young, a woman as solid as steel, one to be made a wife, so she went to live with the bus driver who had made her pregnant and the better life dissolved into a dark hole she could not define.

"Your times must have been better than ours," she commented without envy, knowing little of the forces that mark out people's lives without their knowledge. He did not care for those forces either, memory affording him memorable young adventures into blind experimentation, crimes without penalty or penance. He enjoyed narrating, and read appreciation in her comment, and was moved to brag a bit, unwittingly admitting his age: "The abundance of girlfriends made me popular, a young man to be envied. I always told my friends that I could never bite my nails at social evenings figuring out how to win a girl for a dance."

The young woman sighed. This time he read bitterness verging on sadness in her sigh and could not quite put his finger on its cause. He held her closer to his chest, for he did not want her to be sad. He wanted to please her. A fatherly feeling swept over him, but what he felt was not deep enough to question the girl about her sadness. Things had to be kept that way: no indulgences, no guilt, no commitment.

The man was forty-eight now, with two children in secondary school and a wife who was a corporate lawyer for an international business firm. She was too strong for his liking, but the right wife for his status. What man could claim any social weight and place among other men of substance without the right woman? He knew that, and he pegged the value of his marriage accordingly high. His wife was a busy woman who did her work well. It was difficult for her sometimes, having to care for the children, who were grown, and supervise house maids, when she was at work all day. But after more than fifteen years of marriage, he had learned that, with Janice, he could not escape being a father. She simply bartered fatherhood for any demand he made. That too irked him, that loss of total power over a wife.

He sighed. He did not want to talk about her to this young woman. This was their time, his and the girl's. Still he said, almost involuntarily, "Janice, my wife, was part of my growing up. I met her, fell in love, married her, and that was it."

She accepted his story in silence. She had acquired an instinct for sticking to dry ground by not competing with powerful foes. She did not know her, did not want to know her. Her silence was a weapon of the inarticulate, not chosen, but a survival instinct, since she could not articulate her own road to womanhood. Adeptly, she pushed the wife from her mind, she did not want her as guest in this room, neither in the man's mind or in hers. And he took her silence as his space unprobed. He talked to keep her interested in him. It was not his intention to brag about his success or sound arrogant or even patronizing. It was his way of being, with her, and so the stories he told pulled thin threads from the past to sew around their presence in candlelight.

The young woman listened. She chose to be taken in by the warmth of the moment. For once, she did not have to worry about caring for her little girl, whom she had left with a neighbor for this day. She did not have to think about what she would eat. The man had fed her well. She did not have to worry about whether she would earn enough for her other needs, the clothing and jewelry that she had come to consider necessary for success in securing love. She knew, with this man, she would earn. And for today, for him, she had the special imitation gold chain around her thin torso.

The room was soft with candlelight. This was his private pleasure, unspoiled by worry. Janice would never know. Who could tell her? She never entertained cheap gossip. She focused only on her man because she knew that that was where the truth of his life lay, in the man himself.

He concentrated on the woman with pleasure, his eye seeing only beauty. She smiled indulgently to contain the attention she was getting. Both trod softly on feelings too delicate to touch. Hours blended into hours and day into night as their bodies sought a language of union, building on each consonant and vowel to achieve the word.

They could open up and swallow each other were their bodies to obey the dictates of their minds dazed with fantasy. They could drink each other up, every drop of liquid, as a very thirsty person drinks water in gulps, seeking hasty relief, yet not finding it, and so drinking again and again.

They could partake of each other, cutting through tender skin to find things more tender further in. They could savor each other, like the fruit they ate, the apples and grapes which the man had bought from the supermarket. They chewed the fruit slowly, turning it around their tongues as though to discover new tastes: sugar, fresh natural juices, flesh texture different each time.

They did not hurry. The world of the hotel room, the time, thin as air, was theirs. They floated. Danger had no form, no smell, no texture. Danger lay only in their thirst, their desires, the illusions they sought to tame. So they found magic in simple things—in the words they uttered, ideas they tried to articulate, signs they shaped. And they looked for more magic in the curves of feet and toes, the finger tips, hair, eyes, ears, lips. They saw into their eyes, clear and bright, like reflections of stars in clear water under moonlight. They got drunk on brandy and the fruits providence had offered.

He wanted her to believe in the illusion he had desired to shape and so in the market he had also bought two roses to speak for him. The roses whispered into her ear the thoughts that had peopled his mind for days after she had agreed to meet him. The girl was impressed that this man cared for flowers and that he remembered to bring them for her. She inhaled the sweet smell deeply and said, "Thank you dear," with a voice untrained in the art of romance. He did not mind her inexperience. She would learn to rise to his tastes. For him, trysting was a hobby he enjoyed, his way of uncapping the pressure when his head felt heavy with fatigue. Trysting offered him another kind of power, the emotional catharsis that not even alcohol could achieve. He made his trysts private and perfect to serve his indulgences. For them, he entertained neither questions nor caution. He was tired of being cautious, of doing things right, of being safe. He used a condom with his wife because she forced him to and he was tired of it. He felt good that the girl did not object strongly. She did not say a condom was a non-negotiable condition for the tryst. Ah, this was like surfacing for air, and the harvest of her small body shook him, the elation settling gently into the pacified gut like pollen.

Yes, roses could say that which could not be said. She will hear the plea. She will take it without judgment. How simple the harvest of thorns!

The young woman was pleased; she had taken her chances and she had won. He loved her, she sensed, and was satisfied by her acquiescence. He was gentle; there were no unnecessary gymnastics that some young men demanded. And she was good. Was it not her aunt who had told her, with all seriousness, that she will keep her man only if she does it well? At that time, her aunt's piece of wisdom had settled into her brain as a shameful stain, but now she had come to appreciate it. She was surviving by it. Her little girl's father had called her a slut, especially after she had begun looking nice after odd jobs that led her to meeting people like her present lover. He had left her, the child's father. He had abandoned her in anger, without a cent to feed herself and her little girl, with no money even to pay rent, his hot jealousy fueled by second hand clothing. He left saying, "I will get others like I got you. There are plenty of girls I can get." He was bitter and resentful, and she became afraid and lonely. And now, look, she has met a gentle, educated, and rich lover. She has won.

The day passed and the night came upon them like an intruder they could not ignore. This was the moment the man hated, the fall of illusion. But he also had, through experience, acquired the skills of escape. He knew how to defy this last possible slide into chaos. It was instinctual. He became suddenly introspective and quiet. Silence walked in the room.

"Let us sleep here," the young woman suggested tentatively, feeling the new tension. She could not let him take her home; she could not show him where she lived. She did not want him to see her little girl. She was a sickly child, not bouncy like most little girls. She did not giggle when she played with other children. She whimpered all the time, wanting mother to carry her. She had never been without sickness since she was born. She sucked her thumb when she saw visitors.

The man remained introspective, looking at her. She left the bed and went to pour a drink. They shared it. He said, finally, "I will offer you a job somewhere, not in my office. I will ask my friends."

Her eyes filled with tears.

The man went to shower, urgency marking his actions. He dressed quickly, absent-mindedly. He said, when he was almost fully dressed, "Go and shower. It is getting late."

"I will stay here till morning. Please. I cannot go home now," she pleaded. It was early yet. The man looked at her. He seemed to be fighting something in himself, but that was brief because he said, "Okay," and kissed her on the lips. He poured more brandy and drank it in one gulp. "I will tell them to bring you dinner. Come to the office tomorrow."

She agreed with a shake of her head.

He opened the door and closed it gently behind him.

Grace Awach
LET US PRAISE PHOEBE, OUR MP

Kenya 1994   Dholuo

Grace Awach was born in 1942 in Nyanza Province, Kenya, an area inhabited primarily by the Luo, the ethnic community to which she belongs and in whose Dholuo language she sings. Awach is a leader of the Ramogi Singers, a women's singing group renowned in Kanjira Location for their rich repertoire. She sings mainly praise songs and poetry. She composed this song to herald the election of the first woman member of parliament for Karachuonyo constituency and the second female member of parliament in Kenya.

Phoebe Asiyo, in whose praise the song is composed, was born in 1936. She served as Kenya's National Girl Guide Commissioner and as an employee of Kenya Prisons, rising to be in charge of Langata Women's prison in 1963. In 1964, together with others, she founded the National Council of Women of Kenya (NCWK), and later became its chairperson. She ventured into politics in 1979, when she won elective office, only to see the results nullified following a successful court petition by her opponent. She recaptured the seat in the subsequent by-election in 1980, and went on to win the national parliamentary elections in 1984 and 1992. In 1997 she presented in parliament the affirmative action motion seeking to correct political discrimination against women. The motion was defeated, with nearly all the men voting against it. The same measure would again be introduced in parliament in 2000 by another female member, and this time it was approved. Phoebe Asiyo retired from politics in 1997 and founded the Kenya Women Political Caucus. In 2001 she was appointed a commissioner of the Constitution of Kenya Review Commission, which was charged by parliament to make recommendations for a new national constitution.

The song reflects the changing power relations in the political landscape of Kenya. The artist at first affects surprise and confusion at the fact that she is singing in praise of a woman rather than a man. (She compares herself to a follower of Legio Maria, the Christian-based Luo religious sect that reveres the Virgin Mary.) She nonetheless takes up the task with gusto, praising Phoebe lavishly. In doing so, she breaks taboos, describing Phoebe as waving of the flywhisk, a symbol of traditional authority for men. The artist concludes by reminding her listeners, "I have sung properly," fulfilling an artist's responsibility to tell the truth and reflect social change.

Milton Obote

I cannot understand this world;
I cannot understand it.
I am like a Legio Maria convert.
Alas, Okal, father of Mboya,
It is this world I cannot understand.
And my song, too:
Do I sing about our Land?
Do I praise Rabala, nephew of Magonya?
Do I praise the nephew of Mboya?
Son of Man from Rusinga,
Do I praise our auditor nephew of Mboya?

I hear something, that our people are determined;
People of Karachuonyo are determined.
We must praise Obisa, daughter of Opande
We must praise the daughter of the Nyamware people,
Daughter of Agoro, daughter of Gendia,
Daughter of the mother of Ojijo,
Phoebe the brown one.
Her teeth resemble the diviner's shells.
Send the message everywhere;
Send the message across the water:
Phoebe has arrived,
Mother of Agoro.

Alas, daughter of Obisa,
You have opened a school for disabled;
You have opened a school for orphans;
Maize flour is being distributed.
Oh, Phoebe the brown one,
I cannot understand this world.
Alas, daughter of Opande,
Now there is no more empty politics.
The land is determined;
People of Ndolo are saying that the land is determined.

I will sing my best once and for all;
I praise Phoebe, daughter of Opande.
The land is waiting.
A message goes to Seka; let us go to Seka.
We are going to see the daughter of Opande.
The daughter of Opande waved the flywhisk;

The daughter of Agoro waved the flywhisk;
We heard the message in the first meeting.

Our People of Karachuonyo,
Don't you remember the daughter of Gendia,
Her heart is as smooth as the pebble in the Ajua game.
Daughter of Karachuonyo, Phoebe is best;
Her heart is as white as cattle egrets.
Karachuonyo is determined;
The land is waiting to see.
I have sung properly.
I have praised Phoebe, daughter of Opande.

Translated by Milton Obote and Marjorie Oludhe Macgoye

Margaret A. Ogola
LIFE AND DEATH
Kenya 1994   English

Margaret Atieno Ogola was born in Asembo Bay, Kenya, on the shores of Lake Victoria, in 1958, the year *Penpoint*, the creative writing journal of East Africa was established and five years before Kenya gained independence from Britain. Invigorated by the new challenges of the postcolonial world she had entered, she went on a search for African cultural renewal that has led her on a successful two-career path as a pediatrician and a writer. An award-winning author, she is currently medical director of the Cottolenga Hospice for orphaned children with AIDS and the executive director of the Life Counseling Association in Kenya. Her Christian activism on issues related to women, health, family, and children has won her recognition at home and abroad.

Ogola's literary development began with the publication of *The River and the Source* (1994), a novel that chronicles the lives of four generations of women over a century of political and social upheaval in Kenya. A historical drama of suffering, courage, and heroism, it reenacts the evolution of Kenyan society from the perspective of a matriarchal Luo family swept up in an epic struggle for survival that culminates in a reaffirmation of the past and the spiritual bonds connecting individual characters to one another and to the nation. Akoko Obanda, matriarch and protagonist, is the locus of familial and social interactions, "the source" or fountainhead that nourishes an ancestral line, "the river," through the ebb and flow of events in Kenya, which range from precolonial times through independence and beyond. Her daughter, Nyabera, opens up new areas of experience with her conversion to Christianity, while she continues to build character and ensure the continuity of the family through her own daughter Elizabeth, a teacher and mother of seven children, who in turn forge various career paths in the modern world.

This narrative of irrepressible womanhood, recounted as oral history, is also a Christian tale of redemption told without a hint of anticolonial sentiment. In a significant departure from the conflict-shaped paradigm of African nationhood advanced by writers like Ngugi wa Thiong'o, Marjorie Oludhe Macgoye, and Chinua Achebe, Ogola reframes the nation-idea in terms of homemaking, drawing on women's enabling attributes to counteract social forces of disruption. The novel's view that "a home without a daughter is like a spring without a source" has appealed to many readers, and literary appreciation for the author came in 1995 when she won both the Commonwealth Writers Prize for Best First Book and the Jomo Kenyatta Prize for Literature. In addition, the book was adopted for four years as a required literature text in secondary school, selling 120,000 copies in one year alone. It has been translated into several languages. Ogola, married and mother of five children, has also written *I Swear by Apollo* (2002), a sequel to *The River and the Source*, focusing on the AIDS crisis; *Cardinal Otunga: A Gift of Grace* (1999), a biography of Maurice Michael Cardinal Otunga, Catholic archbishop of Nairobi from 1971 to 1997; and *Place of Destiny* (2005), her latest novel advancing her favorite theme about Kenya's future.

Chapters 5 and 6 of *The River and the Source* are included in this volume. They provide a snapshot of Elizabeth's family life and a representative sample of the interlocking relationships across generations.

Tuzyline Jita Allan

◆

Mark had the devoted love of his wife and the affection of all his children. He was not a hard man to love for he was fair and just; was firm but understanding and evidently loved them all; but between him and his youngest child grew the tenderest of attachments. This last one had come unexpectedly and had threatened miscarriage after miscarriage, needing frequent hospitalization of the mother and constant worry of the part of the father. The doctors said that she had high blood pressure and that the pregnancy might have to be terminated before time to prevent severe damage or death of the mother. Terminated! He was after all a man who valued human life; yet he loved his wife.

"We will try to hold back for as long as possible to give the baby a fighting chance; but you must realize this is a very serious condition and we might lose both mother and child." Mark just stared dumbly at the man.

"I suggest that you take her to the National Hospital where there are better facilities than we have here." The man waited for a while and getting no response, decided to go and write a referral note. At the time, the pregnancy was only six and a half months and the baby would have died if she had been born then—aborted the doctors called it; because according to them, it was only considered a miscarriage if the pregnancy was seven months or more with the possibility of a viable baby being salvaged. Viable meant that the chance of survival, in those days, was about twenty-five percent. Three out of four such babies died and the ones who survived had a high proportion of brain damage, mental retardation and blindness. Mark's head reeled under the onslaught. His wife would die for a baby who had practically no chances at all.

Elizabeth insisted on being told what was wrong. When she was sure that she had fully grasped what was being said, she took matters in her own hands. She was not the grand-daughter of Akoko for nothing.

"Of course we will go to that hospital. If they do admit me, Mark, you can go back to the children and only come to visit me over the weekends or whenever you can. Don't worry—my grandmother promised me that I would live a long life. And the baby will be quite all right. I will call her Nyabera—the good one—after my mother. You just wait and see."

"How do you know it is a girl?" asked the mystified Mark. Women were strange, but his wife was the strangest of them all.

"You think I have carried six children without learning a thing or two?" she asked smiling. He himself was only too glad to have the decision taken off his hands.

Elizabeth stayed in the hospital for another one and a half months, then it became imperative to induce labour to save both mother and child.

"If we leave it there any longer, the stress might kill it. We will give you an injection to start labour tomorrow."

"Would you call my husband please?" was all she said. Courage by any other name smells just as sweet. Anyone who has had induction of labor will tell you that natural labour is much easier. The pain is insistent and unremitting, building up to a crescendo of continuous agony; but Elizabeth survived it and so did the baby who was such a skinny, wizened little thing, that its mother took one look at it and asked for water. The puzzled nurses brought her a cupful in which she dipped her fingers, touched the baby's forehead and whispered:

"I baptise you, Mary, in the name of the Father, the Son and the Holy Spirit." Though there are other worlds, Mary, however, had no intention of leaving this one just yet. Once she was out of the stressful environment of the womb, she never looked back. After two weeks, she had gained a pound and a half and looked more like a human baby than a monkey. Her mother's blood pressure remained rock steady and Mark took his wife and his little daughter, held firmly in his arms, back home.

He could therefore not be blamed if he had a weak spot for this little one grabbed out of the jaws of death. He would come into the house and ask, "Where is Baby?" until the day his wife reminded him that there were six other children in the house as well as little Mary.

All his children had gone to public schools, but when it was Mary's turn, only a private school could do; and now that he had a car, and her little legs could not carry her to school, she had to be driven there. Only the fact that her mother kept her head prevented the young lady from being completely spoilt. Still she had to smile sometimes just watching father and daughter. However the other children grumbled a little.

"What does she have to do to be punished—commit murder?" asked Becky scathingly. She liked to be the centre of attention—and Mary threatened this.

"Go easy on her," said Vera who had an in-built sense of security that nothing could ruffle.

"But you know that he does anything she asks him to do. It's not fair."

"Grow up," replied Vera shortly. She was seventeen and so tired had she become of her sister's poutings and preenings and extreme selfishness that she made a promise to herself to go very far away from her as soon as she could. This would be very soon because the two were going to sit for their Ordinary Level examinations in a matter of two months. Vera had already applied for a place at the school she had missed out on four years ago when love for her sister had clouded her judgement.

That year, 1972, would also see young Tony sitting for his Certificate of Primary Education to try for a place at the school where Aoro was. He had worked incessantly hard and had his head buried in a book most of the time. He was short and stocky, with a driving determination that would take him far at whatever he chose to do. There was nothing errant or flighty about him. At thirteen he already knew what he wanted out of life and had accepted that hard work was the price.

Anyone who has had to live with someone faced with a major examination knows that the atmosphere is constantly charged and can be sparked off by literally anything. In 1972, the Sigus had three such candidates—Vera, Becky and Tony: it was lucky that Tony was a self-possessed fellow; but Vera, realizing by the minute the magnitude of the sacrifice she had made for her uncaring sister, was tense in her determination to recapture that lost chance. Becky, who was now well aware of the importance of doing well at school, not for her parents' sake, but for her own, was close to a nervous breakdown as she drove herself to work at a pace she was unaccustomed to; again, Vera had ceased to take her side automatically and now tended to bite her head off at the slightest provocation.

So it was that as Becky tried to take out her frustrations on her little sister Mary, Vera became more and more scathing until one night the whole thing blew up and the two started screaming accusations and counter-accusations.

"You hate me! You never liked me! You only came to my school to spy on me because you are jealous of me you ugly witch, you pretender!" This was too much for Vera.

"I sacrificed a golden chance to be with you, stupid girl, and you return it with nothing but insults!" Tears welled in her eyes and she dashed them away angrily with her fist; then she grabbed her sister just as their mother burst into the room. Elizabeth managed to cool down tempers somewhat and took Vera aside as the more reasonable one.

"Leave your sister alone! I expected better of you Vera, I really did." Vera sniffed angrily, madder now at the uncontrollable dams that were in her eyes. When would she ever learn not to take everything so to heart? A semblance of normality was restored, but the relationship between the twins had received a blow from which it would never fully recover.

Eventually the exam results were published. Vera got a first division pass with distinction in Mathematics, Biology, Physics, Geography and English and credits in Chemistry and Literature. She also managed a pass in Needlework, which pleased her immensely because she had feared that she would fail the confounded subject. She hated to fail and had therefore suffered the needle pricks gladly.

Becky managed a second division pass with which she was well pleased as were her parents. Tony whose calm assurance had began to show signs of cracking surpassed his wildest dreams by obtaining a perfect score of thirty-six points. He held himself tightly and then let out a lusty yell.

"Watch out guys, here I come!" he shouted. Elizabeth, who had a particularly soft spot for this son, smiled at him.

"You worked for it. I'm sure Aoro is dying to know. You must write and tell him."

"That's a great idea!" he ran on ahead. His joy simply could not be contained by a sedate pace.

Becky wanted to look for a job immediately. It would mean freedom and she craved freedom. Mark would not hear of it. His breathtaking eighteen-year-old daughter? Out in the streets full of predatory men, by herself? Never.

"That cannot be, young lady. You are going right back to your old school to study for your Advanced Level Certificate in History, Literature and Geography just like they have told you to."

"But Father! All I want to be is an air-hostess. Why should I go back to school? That's for Vera, who wants to be a professor."

"An air-hostess?" Mark could not believe his ears. "Over my dead body!"

Becky looked at his face and retreated to her room. She remembered the story of Aoro and his near starvation. She would bide her time; no use in antagonising the old geezer.

Vera enthusiastically took on Mathematics, Physics and Chemistry. This time she said good-bye to her sister and left without a backward glance. Tony left to join Aoro and his mother's heart went with him. Soon the house echoed with emptiness for even little Mary was away at school throughout the day. The children were growing up and the going away movement was becoming an exodus. Elizabeth wished that the twin boys were with her to fill the house with noise and good cheer.

One day a telegram arrived from Aluor. Now letters from that place were few and far between. They mainly consisted of notes from the twins asking for this, that or the other. A telegram rarely ever carried good news and Mark's hands shook a little as he tore it open.

"COME" it declared. "YOUR MOTHER IS VERY ILL." It must be Maria! He rushed out of his office and went to get his wife. She was in the middle of a lesson and one of the teachers had to call her out. One look at Mark's face was enough. He had never been much good at hiding things behind a blank mask and Elizabeth could read him like a book.

"What is wrong?" He said nothing, just quietly handed her the telegram.

"Mother ill! But she was so well when we went to see her last month! Oh my God! We must go at once!"

"Yes dear. I've already spoken to the headmaster—so just get into the car and we'll go right home." Firm, decisive Elizabeth was standing there looking confused and unsure of her next action. When they got home, she walked into the sitting room and again just stood there. She had the most oppressive premonition of doom pressing in on her from all sides and she simply could not make any sensible move. So Mark took over, packed a few things for her, made arrangements with the neighbours to collect little Mary, put his wife in the car and drove off.

Most children have a father and a mother and Elizabeth had been no exception apart from the fact that her father had been a woman—her grandmother Akoko. Now her mother was ill, probably dying, and she experienced a completely different pain from the one she had experienced at her grandmother's death. There is a bond that exists between mother and child that is completely primeval in nature and only comes to the surface of the conscious mind in all its primitive force when either mother or child is in some sort of peril—not surprising considering that as a child lies in its mother's womb, the first sound it hears is her heartbeat and the first human voice it recognises is hers. For the next many months, the child's most satisfying experience will be to lie next to her heart, nursing at the breast—so that the powerful connection is not severed with the cutting of the cord.

Maria Nyabera had been a good mother to Elizabeth and her cousin Peter and, in her own generous way, had given unstintingly of herself to them and to her own mother. Elizabeth remembered how tenderly she had looked after Akoko when she became old and ailing and she hoped with a sick despairing dread that she would get the same chance to show her mother how much she cared in spite of the distance between them.

"I have failed her." These were the first words she had spoken since their departure from Nakuru and now they were approaching the outskirts of Kericho town. Mark cautioned himself to tread carefully for he remembered only too clearly how she had almost broken off their engagement at her grandmother's death, blaming him for God alone knew what.

"How have you failed, dear?" he asked cautiously.

"Don't keep on calling me dear! You know very well I should visited her more frequently—instead of just staying with you, who are young and healthy and don't need me!"

Mark knew better than to point out that not more than two months had ever passed without Elizabeth dashing west to see her mother; or the great sacrifice that they had both made in giving up two of their children to her. He knew her well enough to know that she would only bite off his head and he liked it well enough where it was—firmly attached to his body. He was lucky for he had many brothers staying at home with his own mother so he didn't have to constantly worry on that score. He really understood her predicament.

"You don't understand anything at all!" the lady declared as if reading his mind. "You don't know how torn I've often felt, how I long to divide myself in two, so that I can be in both places at once!"

Mark said nothing but thought to himself that marriage was a very useful thing: there was always someone to vent one's fury on however and especially unjustifiably. Elizabeth kept on alternating between long silences and irrational self-accusatory statements until they were a few miles from Aluor. She then kept completely quiet. It was dark by then but when they approached the hut they found a crowd of people gathered there and both their hearts sank. She must be dead!

The twins rushed out into their parents arms, and the people surrounded them; but Elizabeth had no eyes for anyone—she just walked into the hut. She had to see that beloved face one last time.

"She is not here. Father Thomas took her to the hospital at Maseno." So she was not dead yet, thank God. It must have been eight o'clock, but she simply turned on her heels and went out to the car again despite the protests of the villagers. This night would not pass without her seeing her mother. Mark and the twins followed her out. They knew that argument was of no use.

When they finally reached Maseno at about nine o'clock, they had to plead to be allowed in. They found Maria, who had suffered a massive stroke, still in a coma. The clinical officer on duty held out no hope but suggested they return in the morning to confirm with the doctor. It was then decided that Elizabeth stay with her mother and Mark take the children home. He would return in the morning.

Elizabeth pulled up a stool and sat by her mother all that night listening to the changing patterns of her breathing; first it was stentorous but steady; then she went into periodic breathing with lapses so long that her daughter, afraid that she had stopped altogether, would squeeze her hand at which she would start breathing again. Once she actually opened her eyes and Elizabeth tried to talk to her but got no response. She would have bombarded the nurses with her questions but she was afraid they would throw her out.

At seven o'clock, just before the doctor came for his rounds, Maria Nyabera, daughter of Chief Owuor Kembo and Akoko Obanda, and wife to Okumu Angolo, breathed her last with her only daughter at her bed-side; but death is such a lonely and private matter that all others however loving, can only be observers. Elizabeth stood by that bed-side for a long time. It was a strange feeling to realize that one is an orphan even if one is forty-three and that the one person who has always loved one without question is no more.

Father Thomas, who had had a soft spot for this ever-smiling parishioner of his, was very helpful. He helped transport the body, and assisted His Lordship Bishop Peter Kembo with the requiem Mass, then the funeral procession, with altar boys leading, proceeded to the burial ground where Maria was laid to rest beside her mother. It was the end of an era. The year was nineteen hundred and seventy-three, almost a hundred seasons after the girl-child, Akoko Obanda had arrived wailing into the world—the first daughter of the great Chief Odero Gogni, by his second wife Akech. She it was who had been the source of this river which at one point had trickled to a mere rivulet in danger of petering out, but which once again in her grand-daughter Elizabeth, and in her seven children, was gathering momentum.

The dead have no use for the living who have eventually to tear themselves away so that the business of life might somehow continue. Elizabeth gathered her children and they left the fresh mound of red soil by itself in the hot afternoon sun. There were things to do—the hut had to be closed, a few cherished things taken, but most given away. The children had to go back to their various schools and she herself back to her house. There was nothing but memories to hold her to this place—her adoptive home to which she had come as a very little girl.

Ester Nakate
NAKAYIMA AND THE WONDER TREE

Uganda 1995   Luganda

The legend of Nakayima tells of a great medicine woman who once lived on Mubende Hill, in present-day Western Uganda. She is still widely thought to have had powers to disappear, and reappear, and to have eventually transformed herself into a tree that still grows on the hill today. The tree is quite gigantic, and continues to receive attention from worshipers, researchers, and tourists.

The practice of people-worshiping, or of assigning spiritual significance to unique natural phenomena, is not unusual in Uganda or elsewhere in Africa. In Uganda, several other sites, including caves, rivers, and rock formations, have also attracted attention, but few of them feature as forcefully as the Nakayima phenomenon in the lives of individuals in its area of origin, and of great interest as well beyond their localities.

The legend of Nakayima dominates the cultural, political, and religious lives of the people of Mubende. They take Nakayima as their guardian deity, and do many things in her name. A road and a hotel in Mubende town bear her name. Administrators freshly posted to the district are instructed in the particularities of the Nakayima cult, so that they can avoid offending the local people's sensibilities, and these same administrators learn to use Nakayima's name to admonish their citizens against doing things that "Nakayima would not approve of."

While a person called Nakayima lived in the remote past, the facts of her life are not clear, although they have been the subject of historical speculation and social myth-making. Her story has been told from several angles, and it has grown and adapted to the contemporary changes in the society around it.

While many versions of the story have been produced by male researchers, the version that follows is by a woman, Ester Nakate, the current custodian of the Nakayima shrine and tree. Nakate introduces herself as a close relative of Nakayima, and one who receives and interprets her will.

Nakate's version of the legend of Nakayima reveals aspects of the story that have not been emphasized by previous recorders of the legend. In particular, she depicts Nakayima as a woman who spent a substantial part of her time making peace between the warring kings of Bunyoro and Buganda, both of whom reside in Mubende.

Abasi Kiyimba

✦

My name is Ester Nakate. I belong to the Nte clan. My forefathers originated from the area now known as Fortportal, in Tooro, which was then part of Bunyoro. Our great great grandfather was a brother to Nakayima. We are the custodians of this site, and we inherit it from paternal aunt to niece. My ancestors came to this place years after Nakayima had disappeared, because they were called upon to take care of the site. I know the story of Nakayima very well because it has been told to me by my aunt, whom I replaced as custodian of this site.

Nakayima had a sister called Nyinamwiru, who was a great Munyoro princess. They came together from Bunyoro. Nyinamwiru settled at the bottom of Mubende Hill, and eventually turned into the river that passes near the army barracks. Her sister, Nakayima, settled on top of Mubende Hill, and became a great medicine woman who helped many people. However, she never gave medicine that was intended to hurt anyone, and did not entertain anyone with evil intentions at her shrine.

During her lifetime, Nakayima was a very important person, and was constantly consulted by great people like the kings of Buganda and Bunyoro. When they quarreled and fought, she made peace between them. It is because of her efforts at peace that the Banyoro and the Baganda did not kill themselves as much as they would have done. Also, in the area around Mubende, she was the ruler, and both the kings of Bunyoro and Buganda left her alone. In this area, the Banyoro and the Baganda lived in peace, and they still do so today.

Nakayima did not die. She simply disappeared because her time to disappear had come. When she disappeared, her people were so heartbroken that she decided to reappear to them again in form of a tree. So this tree that you see here is actually not a tree. It is the real Nakayima, and it always assures us that she is watching over us. The chambers in the tree are her shrine, and anyone can kneel there and pray for luck to get riches, women, and children. Also, when your marriage is not very stable or when you have failed to get a man, or when the man you have is very miserly, you can pray to Nakayima, and she gives you luck that will change the unhappy state of affairs. Students also come here to pray for luck to pass their examinations. People come from all over Buganda, Bunyoro, and even beyond to pray for Nakayima's protection, and they bring all kinds of gifts, especially chicken and goats.

When the white men came, they tried to cut down this tree, and to desecrate Nakayima in other ways, such as trying to drill a borehole on her sacred sites. But she resisted all these attempts. The tree refused to be cut; whenever they cut part of it and rested for the day, they would find it whole the next morning, until eventually they gave up. As for the borehole, the machinery that they were using simply got swallowed up in the ground by Nakayima's power.

Nakayima is always very close to her people and protects them from evil people. She communicates to me through dreams, and I tell the people what she wants. Also, some lucky people have seen her in her human form, because she sometimes appears to people she chooses. She has, for example, appeared to me twice, and on one of those occasions, she has given me local brew in a very beautiful *endeku* [small gourd]. Through dreams, Nakayima has told me that she is tired of being photographed, and that everyone who wants to photograph her must pay a fee.

Translated by Abasi Kiyimba

Janet Karim
EVERY WOMAN A CHILD OF GOD

Malawi 1995   English

Janet Karim was born Janet Mbekeani in 1954. She graduated from the University of Malawi, Chancellor College, in 1979 and has held a number of professional positions in teaching and journalism. Her writing on women's issues dates back to 1982, when she joined the *Daily Times* of Malawi; she was responsible for the "Women's Column," highlighting issues of women's rights, empowerment, and equity. In 1989 she began to publish a magazine, *Woman Now*, and from 1993 to 1999 she ran a newspaper, *The Independent.* Currently she is a regular contributor to a column entitled "These Freedoms," in which she discusses women's issues from a Christian perspective, which appears in the weekly *Malawi News.* She is currently working with the United Nations Development Program (UNDP) in development communications in Lilongwe, Malawi.

The inspiration for the following text dates back to December 1988, when the General Synod of the Church of Central Africa Presbyterian (CCAP) held a seminar called "Women in the 1990s" at Chilema, in Machinga District in southern Malawi. The seminar was the first of its kind, and the women who attended it offered strong resolutions concerning the participation and empowerment of women in the church, including a call for the ordination of women. These resolutions formed the basis for a women's protest that coincided with the World Council of Churches' declaration of 1988–1998 as the Decade of Churches in Solidarity with Women. The CCAP's General Synod empowered all synods to debate the issue of women's ordination within four years. But seven years later, in 1995, no policy had been made, and it was clear that the church was not willing to ordain its women and allow them to preach. A qualified female theologian, Gertrude Kapuma, had been denied ordination and instead assigned the running of a female training center at Chigodi in Blantyre.

Janet Karim's protest letter to Reverend Chitsulo, who was then the General Secretary of Blantyre Synod, supported an earlier petition presented by the Chigodi women. Published in her newspaper, *The Independent*, Karim's letter, which provides theological justification for women's ordination, served to draw wider attention to the longstanding issue. The Blantyre Synod of the CCAP ordained its first female clergy in 1999. In a conversation in August 2002, Karim again emphasized the need for the church to recognize women as full partners in evangelism.

Edrinnie Lora-Kayambazinthu

✦

Open Letter To Rev. Chitsulo
My Dear /Reverend Chitsulo
Every Woman A Child Of God; Saved By The Blood
I greet you in the precious name of our Lord and saviour Jesus Christ, in whose name I come to you today. . . . And it is my prayer that . . . this letter . . . does not become a dry theoretical or argumentative discourse, but one that is filled with the warm love of Jesus.

I refer you to the above subject in view of the women whose aborted march has, I am to understand led to the suspension of 11 of them who are in the employment of the Synod. . . .

I understand that one of the reasons given why women cannot take on positions of authority in your church hierarchy is because women are sinners. Their sins derive from the sin of Eve in the garden, so the reasoning goes. Subjecting women to the sin and burden of Eve, suggests that it is only men whom Jesus saved on the cross. But my Bible tells me in 1 Peter 1:18–19 that I have been purchased from my empty and sinful way of life with the precious and incorruptible blood of the lamb of God—there is no differentiation between male and female in the salvation program for God's people because God is not a respecter of persons, male and female. In 1 Peter 2:9–10 I am told that I am among the chosen people, a member of royal priesthood, a holy nation belonging to God, and that I, a woman, may declare the praises of Him who called me out of darkness into His wonderful light. . . .

Because I am a Christian, the curse bestowed on Eve in the Garden of Eden are no longer in my Record Book of Life—the blood of Jesus Christ wiped them out and my record is as white as snow. Therefore, I am no longer under any condemnation. God does not condemn me for Eve's sins.

What is the mind of Christ in relation to women, sin and the church? The good Lord himself demonstrated to the world on numerous occasions in the New Testament and they provide good reference for our everyday living.

On the human level, Jesus set an example on the gender equation. In the story of a woman caught in adultery, Jesus shows the Pharisees that it takes two to tangle! When she was brought to Jesus to be judged by Him, on the surface, the Lord questions whether there is any person in this world who can claim to be without sin, on the deeper level, He is telling the Pharisees that adultery cannot be committed by one person!—where is the woman's accomplice, Jesus quizzes the old guard of Judaism as he says, "If any one of you is without sin, let him be the first to throw a stone at her."

To the Christian men and the few women who support that women carry the Eve burden and therefore should not be given positions of authority, I ask: are you not guilty of throwing that stone? And if the stone you level at women is cast, are you therefore not saying that you are without sin?...

As noted earlier, Jesus—God made flesh—came to this world through a woman. God's perfect plan to use women in spreading His word completes the cycle when the resurrected Messiah appears first to a woman, and not a so-very-pure-and-holy woman—Mary Magdalene. To this woman, Jesus commissions to go and spread the Good News that Jesus Christ is risen! Jesus Himself gave women the authority to be His disciples. On the day of Pentecost, as the disciples (which we know also included women, among them Mary the mother of Jesus) were waiting in the upper room, the women also received the power from the Holy Spirit. Throughout history since the resurrection of Jesus there have been many examples of women, filled with the spirit of God, who have displayed this power and authority in their furtherance of spreading the Good News. And if women have both the authority and power from God to be His servants, does any mortal being possess any other greater authority and power to strip women of these God-given talents?

I think not, I pray not!

My good Reverend Sir, it is my prayer that you seek the Lord in this situation regarding women in the church. Choose to have the display of the mind of Christ in your future acts on the situation on hand and on any other situation where man-made dogma may appear to over-ride God given principles and commands.

> May God bless you
> Yours in His Service
> Janet Karim (Mrs.)

Zehra Peera
MEMORIES OF A ZANZIBAR WEDDING

Tanzania 1995   English

Traditionally, weddings in Zanzibar were communal affairs, carried out with the full participation of neighbors and friends and a rich element of street performance, both in the issuing of invitations and in the actual ceremony. Modern weddings are more clinically organized, with invitations issued by phone or through the mail, and celebrations themselves held in sequestered public halls and hotel restaurants. While many who live in Zanzibar are proud to take part in modern Western practices, Zanzibaris in diaspora, like the author, tend to dream of and yearn for what they left behind.

Zehra Peera is a second-generation Zanzibari who attended both Indian and Catholic-run schools before training to be a teacher. She then taught in primary and secondary schools, as well as in institutions of higher education in Zanzibar. Her first opportunity to travel outside Zanzibar came with a scholarship to Durham University in England, then another to Makerere University in Uganda. She left Zanzibar following her marriage in Dar es Salaam, and from 1980 forward she lived with her family in Australia, where she worked as an interpreter for immigrants and refugees. Sadly, she passed away in May 2006, as this volume was nearing completion.

Peera describes in detail the wedding rituals of the Khoja Shi'as, Zanzibari Muslims of Indian descent. She represents these rituals primarily as Indian, but aspects resemble the weddings of middle-class Africans and Arabs in Zanzibar at that time. The *nikah*, or marriage agreement, is an essential feature of any Muslim wedding. The seven days of ceremony, the bride's movement to and from her new home and her parents' home, her decorations with henna, the exchange of gifts, the astrologer picking an auspicious day—all these would have been common features in other weddings as well. Differences would have emerged in the costumes and the fare served at the wedding, although halwa and coffee are standard refreshments at the *nikah*. The expression of the developing relationship between the bride and her in-laws through the games and the exchange of gifts is particularly Indian.

Saïda Yahya-Othman

❖

Nostalgia overwhelms me as I look back upon my recollections of the weddings of the Khoja Shi'as, or Muslims of Indian origin in Zanzibar. The wedding rites which I remember as a child were authentically Indian in that they conformed to those practiced by the Indians in India. Over the years Western influence led to changes in the costumes worn by the bride and bridegroom, and other customs have been adopted, such as having a wedding cake and wedding rings. The ceremony is now a mixture of Eastern and Western traditions.

Because of our ethnic origin the wedding rites were an amalgam of ancient Hindu customs and Islamic requirements. In fact, the Islamic component consisted of only one, very practical, requirement: the *nikah*, meaning marriage or marrying. Islamic marriage is the product of an agreement between man and woman to take each other as husband and wife. To seal the agreement the man gives, or promises to give, *mahar* to the woman. This is a modest amount of money fixed by *sharia* or religious law, well within the capacity of any individual. In practice no money actually changes hands: the promise is given and accepted in order to satisfy the requirements. Though it is not necessary for a priest to officiate, a priest or a "Qadi" [judge] will represent the man or woman, and another male of repute will represent the other party. The two representatives read out the ritual words, in Arabic, that pronounce the agreement, and act as witnesses to the marriage.

On the other hand, the Hindu customs inherited from our forebears provided the romance and excitement of an authentic, classical Zanzibari wedding. These practices were observed without a true understanding of their origins in local Indian beliefs and superstitions. There were also influences arising from the association with the Swahilis, or native Africans of the coast, among whom the Khoja Shi'a had settled.

A wedding was preceded by an engagement ceremony. To seal the engagement a nose stud of seven diamonds was given to the girl by the boy's family, which she was then expected to wear in public. Changing times led to the replacement of the nose stud with a ring. On the engagement day the boy was invited to the girl's house, accompanied by his friends. On arrival the party was served with a specially prepared milk drink, enriched with Indian spices, nuts, and sugar and boiled until it condensed. Indian sweets were served with milk, followed by *paan*, a mixture of betel nuts, shredded coconut, fennel seeds and other spices, wrapped in a leaf to assist chewing. The girl's brother or near male relative then stepped forward and presented the boy with a ring and a suit. Other relatives of the girl presented gifts in the form of cash and handkerchiefs. After this the boy's party departed. Then there arrived a party of the young female members of the boy's family or friends. The boy's sister, or near female relative, placed the engagement ring upon the girl's finger, a sari on her lap, and a sweet in her mouth for good luck. After taking refreshments they left. Throughout the ceremony the girl sat in one place surrounded by her female friends—she did not see her prospective husband, nor was he allowed to see her.

The day of the wedding had to be propitious. It was therefore determined in advance by an astrologer. Once the date was fixed for the start of the ceremony, the ladies of the wedding party personally went to the homes of their friends and relatives to extend invitations. This emphasized the sincerity of the invitation, and was vital to ensure a person's attendance at the wedding—offence would be taken if the invitation arrived in any form other than a personal visit. Additionally, a town crier travelled through the streets calling everyone in the community to attend the wedding.

The entire ceremony spanned seven days, during which both the bride's and groom's households would be buzzing with activity. While the groom went out and about as usual, the bride began to receive special treatment. She was isolated from her family, confined to an exclusive position behind a curtain where she sat on a mattress spread on the floor. For the first three days she was visited by her bridesmaids who gave her home-made beauty treatments to soften and brighten her skin. She was also given a special diet. Lest she be visited and disturbed by some evil spirits, she wore a rosary, with a tiny golden penknife attached, on her wrist. The holy Qu'ran was kept beside her to provide additional protection from unfriendly spirits.

On the evening of the fourth day the colourful henna ceremony took place. The henna paste is made from the ground leaves of the henna tree, and is a colouring agent for the hair or body. Young girls from the groom's family arrived at the bride's house in procession, led by Swahili women bearing the henna on plates fringed with jasmine, the scent of which permeated the surrounding air. Candles, placed in the centre of the plates, cast light about the dark, narrow streets. The henna-bearers sang wedding songs accompanied by ululations and cries of merriment. The bride's friends, who had gathered at her house, then proceeded to use the henna to decorate the bride's feet and hands in intricate designs. They then applied henna designs to each other's hands. The same evening, the groom had henna applied to his own palms by his mother at their house, as did his female relatives.

The morning of the fifth day was the wedding day, and the community sent a representative to the bride's house. He took a position on the other side of the curtain behind which the bride sat, and enquired as to whether she was genuinely agreeable to the union. Having gained her verbal assent he then took her signature on the marriage certificate. He also informed her of the amount of *mahar* the groom had promised to give her for her hand in marriage. Later that day, the male members of both families accompanied the groom to the house of the priest where the recitation of *nikah* took place. The groom then signed the marriage certificate, with his guardian witnessing the signature. The bride's guardian attested to the bride's signature that had been obtained earlier. The elders of the community also put their signatures on the certificate. The ceremony ended with the sweet and sticky halwa, prepared by the Omani Arabs, served with strong Turkish coffee.

Later in the afternoon ladies from the groom's family called at the bride's house to deliver the jewellery and sari for the bride to wear that night. The bridal costume was then hung on a chair, above a small earthen pot. Sandalwood, cooked in sugar and the rich oriental perfumes of *ood* [a fragrant dried sap] were sprinkled over the burning charcoal in the pot, and had scented the fabric. The traditional color of bridal attire was aquamarine, now replaced by white saris. *Bahndri*, a drape rich in color and heavily embroidered with gold thread, formed part of the traditional costume, but is optional today.

The bridegroom's traditional attire consisted of white pants and shirt, over which he wore a knee-length coat, heavily embroidered with gold thread. A golden turban was placed upon his head, his face hidden by flowers dangling from the turban. A garland hung around his neck, and an ornamental sword in a golden sheath hung from his waist. Later, the Western suit and tie replaced the picturesque costume. As the groom grew ready to leave for the bride's house, his mother approached, holding money in her hand. She moved her hand in a circle over the groom's head and put the money in a tray in front of the groom, customarily held by the groom's barber. Other ladies, in order of seniority, followed suit. The groom then left the house for the bride's house, sometimes mounted on a horse. He was led in procession by a teacher of the

Qu'ran, reciting aloud the Arabic verses praising the Prophet Muhammed as the party wound its way through narrow streets.

At the bride's house, the groom and his party were entertained with soft drinks, sherbet, ice-cream, and *paan*. The groom was then presented with a suit and a watch. The best man then removed the groom's garland and sent it over on a tray to the bride. The bride donned this garland, and her family sent another garland over to the groom for him to wear. Finally, the groom circled the room, shaking and kissing the hands of the elders of the bride's family and the community. He then departed to await the bride's arrival at his home.

The women of the groom's family, and relatives and friends of the bridal party, arrived at the bride's house in their own procession, led again by singing Swahili women. While they were being entertained, the bridesmaids were making final touches to the bride's appearance. Wedding gifts, and the bride's dowry, were entrusted to the groom's mother, and the groom's mother and female relatives were given gifts by the bride's parents. Customarily these were shawls, ceremoniously draped over the recipient's heads, rather than handed to them as an ordinary gift.

An astrologer had previously determined the hour that it was most propitious for the bride to leave her parents' house. At the approach of this hour the groom's family were invited to the bride's room, the ladies bearing plates of sweets. There the bride sat, her head bowed, the top of her sari drawn down to cover her face. Her mother-in-law lifted her veil and placed a small piece of sweet in the bride's mouth, followed by the other ladies of the groom's family. It was regarded as auspicious for at least seven married women to take part in this ritual. The bride was now ready to leave. By way of farewell the bride's mother held to her daughter's lips a cup of milk from which she took a sip. In her hands the bride carried a small Qu'ran and a bundle of coconut and sugar, symbolising fertility. Then her father, brothers and uncles each placed their hand on her hand to bless her. It was customary to slaughter a sacrificial chicken at the threshold of the house, the bride stepping in the blood as she departed in a procession to the groom's house.

On reaching the groom's house another chicken was sacrificed at the entrance. Crossing the threshold, the bride stepped onto a low stool to stand beside the groom. The ladies of the groom's family showered the couple with flowers and rice. The groom's mother held up a cup of milk from which the couple drank in turn. Two earthenware bowls were placed on the floor in front of the stool, and were broken by the couple as they stepped off the stool. While the groom went to join his friends, the bride was taken into another room full of ladies sitting on the carpet. The bride sat on a mattress in their midst. Then her father-in-law entered the room carrying a bag full of silver coins. He emptied the coins into a tray placed in front of the bride. With the help of her bridesmaid the bride scooped up a quantity of coins which were counted. By the amount she was able to scoop, she was judged to be miserly or generous—all done in good humour! Her father-in-law then presented her with a gift of jewellery. After refreshments were served, bridesmaids escorted the bride to her bedroom, and the guests began to leave. Nowadays, a wedding cake is cut and distributed before the guests depart. After all the ceremonies were complete, it was well past midnight and the couple were finally alone together for the first time. Before dawn the couple were expected to pray for harmony and happiness.

Early in the morning, the bride was left alone in the room. Soon afterwards the bridesmaids arrived, to take the bride back to her parents' house to spend the day there. This day was known as *shinda*, meaning to spend the day at home. The bride would take leave of her mother-in-law by kissing her hand as a sign of respect. In the afternoon the groom, with his friends, went to the bride's house for lunch. On arrival they were seated in the lunch room after removing their shoes to sit on the carpet. It was customary, and part of the fun, for the bride's younger sister or brother to hide the groom's shoe—and to retrieve it he had to part with some money. The ladies of the groom's family were also invited. After lunch a game was engaged in between the bride and her mother-in-law, followed by other family members. A tray of grain was placed between the two participants. First the mother-in-law scooped up a quantity of grains, which she then poured into the cupped hands of the bride. The bride was supposed to hold the grains firmly and pour them back into her mother-in-law's hands. The exchange would continue, stop, and restart, with the bride initiating the process. At the end the bride was given a present in cash or jewellery by each participant. After lunch, the guests left and the bride was able to get some sleep before she was fetched by the groom to return to her matrimonial home in the evening.

Sattaro is the name given to the seventh and last day of the ceremony. On this day the groom invited his in-laws, relatives and friends to lunch. At this event the bride wore the clothing and jewellery she had been given as part of her dowry. After lunch the bride, accompanied by her friends and relatives, returned to her parents' home for the rest of the day. To commemorate the wedding a group photograph was taken in a public park, with the groom wearing his traditional wedding costume, sitting in the centre, flanked by the young male members of both family and friends. At night the groom called at his in-laws' house to take his bride back home. The bride would continue to visit her parents every Friday to spend the day with them, with her husband calling at night to bring her home.

A few weeks later there would be photographs taken at the studio of the couple, as well as group photographs of the female members of the groom's family with the bride. These were the only mementos of the occasion. Nowadays the entire wedding night ceremony is extensively photographed and videoed. As Indians in Zanzibar began to imitate their compatriots in the Westernized cities of India, former exotic and colorful ceremonies, mingling Indian, Islamic and Swahili traditions, have receded from the social landscape, leaving only memories deeply etched in my mind.

INTO THE TWENTY-FIRST CENTURY
(1996–2004)

Communal
ONE BLANKET
Uganda 1996   Lango

The song "One Blanket" was performed in the Lango language by eight women from Odokomit village in Lira, a province in northern Uganda. For decades, the region has been a site of violent conflict. In addition to brutal fighting between government forces and the rebel paramilitary forces, most notably the Lord's Resistance Army, people living in the eastern part of Lira had to contend with armed cattle raids by the neighboring Karimojong. Life in the area became so dangerous that most residents fled their homes. In 1996, when this song was recorded, five of the women singing had resettled in Odokomit, in the center of Lira.

The song dates back to an earlier period of turmoil in the 1970s, when Idi Amin was president of Uganda. Amin forced Asians, who had run Ugandan sugar factories and import-export businesses, to flee the country. He replaced them with his own people, whose inexperience led to shortages and then to rationing and then to still more serious shortages. It was common for families to lack such basic necessities as sugar, salt, and soap because of Amin's policies.

Among the Langi, communal songs are owned by everyone in the community, and anyone can revise songs to suit a particular situation. "One Blanket" is the kind of communal song sung at Langi beer parties and other social occasions that call for dancing. In Lango society, wealth is measured not only in cash but also in the number of children fathered by a single man. This is also a humorous song, in which the women ask—in response to their husbands' unspoken complaints— how they can possibly have more children when they have no privacy with their husbands.

Florence Ebila

✦

One blanket!
The children also included!
How can you say
That I have refused to deliver?

One blanket!
And for the children also included!
My husband,
How can you say
That I have refused to conceive?

Mr. The-Owner-of-Riches,
Curled inside his sack, really,
He quarreled till dawn.
How can you say that I refused to—
That I refused to conceive?

Mr. This-Man curled inside his sack,
Really,
He quarreled till dawn.
How can you say
That I refused to conceive?

My Boss!
One blanket!
The children also included!
The visitor is also around!
Now, how can you say
That I refused to conceive?

My Boss!
One blanket!
The children also included!
The visitor is also around!
Now, how do you say
That I refused to conceive?

Translated by Florence Ebila

SONGS COMPLAINING ABOUT HUSBANDS AND LOVERS

Complaints about husbands and lovers form the subject matter for many songs sung by women in East Africa. Often, women sing these on specific occasions, as is the case for the first five songs collected here. Other songs may be sung in various contexts, as is the case with the final two songs in this section.

"The Impotent One Climbed a Tree" is typical of the Langi songs sung by women at beer parties, where they may also feign drunkenness in order to express themselves without inhibition. The group of women of Odokomit village, in northern Uganda, who sang this song do not know the name of the original composer. The crested crane, an icon of honor and beauty, appears on the flag of Uganda; here it is used sarcastically in describing the husband. The repeated word *iya* in the song serves to give rhythmic emphasis to the singer's words.

"The Greedy Husband" was sung by S.C. Hara of Ekwendeni village in Mzimba, Malawi. This song is a *hlombe* song, sung during a dance performed by both men and women. Again, no one knows the name of the original composer. The repeated phrase in this song, *Siyayo hoyo mbelebele*, is a rhythmical repetition of syllables without specific meaning.

The three songs from women in the Rumphi District of Malawi were sung at a women's dance called *visekese*. The dance is part of a competition among various women's associations, called *boma*, held in the villages during September and October. As accompaniment, they use a *chisekese*, a square rattle made from straw. The first and second of these songs complain about a man who has migrated to Johannesburg for work, while the third is about the jealousy a woman feels when her husband is adulterous.

"Make Love and Not Babies" was sung in Kikamba by Louise Kalondu wa Maseki of Kitui, Kenya. The song is of a type sung by groups of Akamba women. In this song, the phase "this child" refers literally to a recently born child and metaphorically, especially in line five, to the man's penis. "The big machete" in the last line also refers to the man's circumcised penis.

"The Irresponsible Husband," sung by Njira Chenga, is a work song of Waduruma women, who create a common rhythm for their work. Women have typically sung such songs while cultivating and harvesting, as well as while doing household chores.

Ann Biersteker, Florence Ebila, Edrinnie Lora-Kayambazinthu,
and Sheila Ali Ryanga

♦

Langi Women of Odokomit
THE IMPOTENT ONE CLIMBED A TREE

Uganda 1996   Lango

The impotent one climbed up the tree.
When you see him, he appears like the crested crane.
The impotent one climbed up the tree, as if to shepherd me.
Iya, even if I am going to the well,
Iya, you follow me.
Iya, even on my way to pick vegetables
Iya, you follow me.
Iya, even on the way to collect firewood,
Iya, you follow me.
The impotent one, really, when one is useless!

Translated by Florence Ebila

S.C. Hara, THE GREEDY HUSBAND

Malawi 1997   Chingoni

Siyayo hoyo mbelebele.
Siyayo hoyo mbelebele.
Here is a gluttonous chief.
He eats anything.
He is a gluttonous chief.

She cooked okra.
Siyayo hoyo mbelebele.
Siyayo hoyo mbelebele.
Here is a gluttonous chief.
He eats anything.
He is a gluttonous chief.
He is a gluttonous chief.

She has cooked okra.
Siyayo hoyo mbelebele.
Siyayo hoyo mbelebele.
He is a gluttonous chief.

Translated by Boston J. Soko and Edrinnie Lora-Kayambazinthu

Women of Rumphi District, THREE *VISEKESE* SONGS

Malawi 2000   Chitumbuka

We Who Do Not Have Men
We who do not have men,
They have bought for us colorless clothes.
We who do not have men,
They have bought for us colorless clothes.
I cannot tolerate this.
Let's love each other, my relatives.
Let's love each other, my husband.
I cannot tolerate this.

You Who Go to Johannesburg
You who go to Johannesburg,
Please please tell him,
I am naked and so is his mother.
Leader: I am naked.
All: I am naked and so is his mother.
Leader: I am naked.
All: I am naked and so is his mother.
I am naked and so is his mother.

That Woman at Chombe
That woman at Chombe,
She has legs like a hedgehog.

That woman at Chombe,
She has legs like a hedgehog.
She is in agony; she is in agony.
Ah hi yo!
Ah hi yo!
She is in agony; she is in agony
She has been in agony all night; she is in agony.

Translated by Edrinnie Lora-Kayambazinthu

Loise Kalondu wa Maseki, MAKE LOVE AND NOT BABIES

Kenya 2000   Kikamba

Oh my, oh my, I have problems: why did you make me pregnant with this
child?
Oh me, oh me, many problems: why did you make me give birth to this
child?
I told you to take care of your child when you sleep because I was coming
to visit.
Why did you make me give birth to this child?
Oh my, oh my, I have problems: why did you make me pregnant with this
child?
Oh me, oh me, many problems: why did you make me give birth to this
child?
I told you we must not touch the child with the big machete.
Why did you make me give birth to this child?

Translated by Sheila Ali Ryanga and Mirenda Mutuvi

Njira Chenga, THE IRRESPONSIBLE HUSBAND

Kenya 2001   Kiduruma

Pound, my daughter, pound, and let the maize be clean.
The child is crying because she is sick.
When my husband goes for a drink, he does not come back home.
He says he is not yet through.
But when it is time for dowry negotiations, oh, my,
He dresses smartly in trousers and
He goes to count the cows and the money in hundreds.
When it is time to feast, he has no problems.
When I point this out,

I am accused of talking too much.
I do not talk too much, my friend,
I speak the truth about my old man.

Translated by Sheila Ali Ryanga

Communal
VIMBUZA SONGS

Malawi 1997   Chitumbuka

Vimbuza is a curative dance, danced primarily by women in the northern region of Malawi. Men sometimes dance *vimbuza*, but mainly for commercial purposes. For women, the dance is part of traditional treatment for illnesses of the mind and spirit, which are also called *vimbuza*. Women who seek cures through *vimbuza* may exhibit such symptoms as continuous headaches, fever, sensitivity to smells, belching, and trances, especially during the full moon or half moon. *Vimbuza* dancing, along with traditional medicines administered by a healer, are believed to either appease or exorcise the spirits and help to produce a cure.

The dance is performed at night near an afflicted woman's home. Both men and women form a circle, inside which an afflicted woman dances, accompanied by drumbeats and clapping. The dancer wears colorful beads and amulets, rattles on her arms and legs, and a short skirt made of animal skin. She smears her body with either ashes or flour paste. She is in total control of the proceedings, choosing the songs and drumbeats, since the spirits speak through her, and they must be obeyed and appeased. If the spirits have to be exorcised, exorcism specialists prepare herbs and sometimes a concoction of porridge made from uncooked maize flour and blood, which the woman drinks. The dance can last for one night or several nights, depending on the problem.

Legend has it that the *vimbuza* dance was brought to the Ngoni people of the Mzimba District by a Bisa woman from northeastern Zambia called Nyamvula, who had been taken captive. She danced, sang, and made utterances always in her Bisa language. The legend is supported by the fact that, up to the late 1940s, all *vimbuza* dancers in Mzimba, when in trance, made utterances in the Bisa language, in imitation of Nyamvula. In social and psychological terms, the *vimbuza* dance is an indirect way for a woman to inform the community that she is suffering. Songs often critique the patrilineal system followed by all northerners in Malawi. In the first song collected here, "Mr. Nyirongo with Syphillis" (*Anyirongo Gozoli*), a wife accuses her husband of infidelity, but also says she is glad that he has been punished—with syphilis—for his promiscuity. Although we assume that the song was first composed long before the coming of the HIV/AIDS scourge, it seems especially relevant today. The second song, "Mr. Nyirongo" (*Anyirongo*), complains about a man who has gone to work in the mines and no longer takes care of his wife and mother. The third song, "Mother-in-Law" (*Nyokovyara*), expresses the theme of a daughter-in-law's bad treatment by a mother-in-law and father-in-law.

Edrinnie Lora-Kayambazinthu, Boston J. Soko, and Desmond D. Phiri

✦

MR. NYIRONGO I

You don't know what has happened to Mr. Nyirongo.
Guess what has happened to Mr. Nyirongo.
    He has caught syphilis.
    The syphilis has made him sterile.

MR. NYIRONGO II

Mr. Nyirongo, I am suffering.
Please appeal to your son.
Your son has been gone so long
That I will have to remarry.

It is my father who gave me the basket.
It is my father who gave me the ladle.
It is my father who gave me the towel.
It is my father who gave me the cloth.
Everything in my house was given to me by my father,
So I am going to have to remarry.

Translated by Boston J. Soko

MOTHER-IN-LAW

When your mother-in-law abuses you,
You too must abuse her.
She has begun it;
Oh yes, oh yes, she has begun it;
She has begun it.

When your father-in-law abuses you,
You too must abuse him.
Oh yes, oh yes,
He has begun it;
He has begun it.

Translated by Desmond D. Phiri

Monde Sifuniso
BEIJING, BEIJING
Zambia 1997 English

For many Zambian women, the months leading up to the United Nations Fourth World Conference on Women, held in Beijing in September 1995, contained eye-opening experiences. Feminist activities in preparation for the conference raised some opposition from men, who viewed a call for equal opportunity and equal representation in both government and household decision-making as a threat. Some men fought an undeclared war against women during this period, trying to undermine women's preconference activities, deriding their goals, and proclaiming that women were lost without men to guide them. Feminists, on the other hand, viewed men as lost without women. To support this idea, women noted that while many divorced women never remarry, men marry within the first year of a divorce. Further, in Zambia there are more widows than widowers, since women, capable of lifelong emotional connections, mourn their partners for a longer time than men.

Monde Sifuniso was born in Barotseland in 1944, into a culture in which boys and girls were reared as equals. When Zambia attained independence in 1964, Barotseland was designated the Western Province of Zambia, and had to conform to the nation's dominant attitudes and practices, which relegated women to subservient status. When Sifuniso left Barotseland to attend secondary school and then college and university, she encountered both gender and race discrimination for the first time. She believes that this fact explains the high divorce rate among women of her generation in Zambia: because they were taught, in Barotseland, to expect equality, they could not easily conform to male domination.

Monde Sifuniso has had broad experience in educational broadcasting, scriptwriting, radio producing, and public relations She studied editing, book publishing, and marketing at Oxford Brookes University in Great Britain, returning to set up the University of Zambia Press. She served as publisher until 1997, when she retired to edit manuscripts and write fiction. Sifuniso has written several books, including one on the history of the women's movement in Zambia. In the story "Beijing, Beijing," she describes one conventionally sexist man moving through a world that is, momentarily, without women. The story suggests that once women realize their own power, they will be able to interact with men wisely enough to gain the respect normally denied them in a patriarchal society.

Nalishebo N. Meebelo

✦

Jack Zulu and his wife, Yvonne, had only one child, sixteen-year-old Richard. Richard was closer to his mother than he was to his father. Jack had used all sorts of tricks to lure Richard from his mother, but he had failed. Later, he tried to join them so that they could become a close-knit threesome but he soon found out that they would often be laughing at him, not with him. He gave up and helplessly watched his heir, product of his groin, being moulded by a woman.

Tonight Jack and Richard had just seen Yvonne off on the first leg of her trip to Beijing to attend the fourth Women's Conference. Jack looked at his son, sitting next to him in the car. As he drove up to their house he told himself that he was going to be alone with his son for two whole weeks and he was going to use that time constructively. He was going to talk to him about the Oedipus complex, about men being men and sticking together, about the evil influence women can have on men.

Richard jumped out of the car at the gate. While his father parked the car, he locked the gate and raced into the house. He felt uneasy in his father's presence. Jack followed his son into the house. He closed the front door gently, the way Yvonne wanted doors closed. He remembered then that Yvonne was away. Smiling, he opened the door again and banged it shut. He turned the key noisily in the lock then walked to his bedroom. He surveyed the room with dissatisfaction. He had felt more at home in hotel rooms than in this, his bedroom. Yvonne's presence was too strong. He had two weeks in which to stamp his own mark on the room.

He threw his jacket on his bed and decided to start working on his son that very night. When he knocked on Richard's door, he was met by silence. He turned the door handle but Richard had locked himself in. Did he always lock his door? Jack didn't know. Well, two weeks was a long time. He could start the following day which, after all, was Day One of his fourteen days of freedom.

Lying back in his bed later, Jack laid out plans for the coming fortnight. His relationship with his mistress, Milly, had soured. He had not been in touch with her for slightly over a month. This was partly because he had been under pressure for money from Yvonne. He had been in such a bad temper that he would have risked breaking up with Milly altogether had he attempted to contact her during that time. Now he had two weeks in which to use all his wiles to win her back. Released from all worry, he drifted off and slept the dreamless sleep of the contented.

When Jack woke up the following morning, there was total silence—no sound from the bathroom, no sound from the kitchen. He got up and had a shower. Normally, at this stage Yvonne would ask him what he was going to do that day. As he outlined his activities, she would decide what clothes would be suitable for the day and lay them out on his bed. He never argued; he simply went along with her choice. What was he going to wear today? He gave a short laugh. Surely he could choose his own clothes! What was wrong with him?

Dressed, he went to his son's bedroom, but found it empty. He walked to the kitchen and found a note from his son stuck on the fridge door with a strawberry-shaped magnet—his wife's favourite notice board. It read:

Dad, I had to go to school early.
Hope you can make your own breakfast.
See you later.

Jack looked at his watch—07:20. What time did Richard leave the house? Why did he have to go early? Jack was annoyed. Richard always knocked on their bedroom door and announced his departure, if they were still in their bedroom when he left. Why was he treating him differently? The boy certainly needed sorting out.

He couldn't face the prospect of making himself breakfast. He was tempted to drive to Milly's flat but he decided against it. He wanted to go there after work and spend a good part of the night with her. During the day he was tempted to ring her twice, but he fought down his desire again, choosing surprise as the best weapon to disarm her.

As the clock ticked towards the close of the working day, Jack's body came alive with anticipation. He stayed on for another thirty minutes after closing time to give Milly time to get back home. At 17:30 he left the office and drove to Milly's flat. Although the curtains were drawn, there was a light on in the sitting room. He was discomfited when a young man opened the door to his knock. He had allowed his expectations to play havoc with his feelings.

"Is Milly home?" Jack asked gruffly.

"No, she is not," the young man answered, blocking the doorway and offering no further explanation.

"I'd like to come in for a moment, if you don't mind."

Jack pushed past the young man who remained standing at the door. Displaying familiarity that he would never have dared show had Milly been around, Jack stopped the cassette player. He took out the cassette that was in the machine and inserted one of his choice. He walked to Milly's bedroom but found it locked. As he turned away from the door he saw the young man a distance away, watching him.

"Who are you?" Jack barked at the young man.

"I'm Milly's brother. Are you Mr. Zulu?"

"Yes. How do you know my name?"

"Milly said you might come. She left a note for you. I'm going to stay in her flat while she is away."

Jack walked back to the sitting room with the young man. The young man took a white envelope from a shelf and gave it to Jack. Jack ripped the envelope open and took out a small piece of paper.

Well, Jack, Yvonne is in Beijing and now you come running to me.
Sorry, mate, I've gone to Beijing, too.

What a sick joke! He felt tense as he walked out of Milly's flat. He suspected that Milly was hiding somewhere. He was going to catch her at her office the following day, or the day after. Two weeks was a long time. . . .

Jack drove aimlessly. He was drawn to a roadside bar that was belting out one of his favourite Tshala Muana songs. He parked his car but debated whether to join the revelling crowd or turn round and go home to his son. He decided to go in. Time enough for Richard. Tonight was his, no Yvonne, no Richard, no Milly.

As he walked into the bar he was met by bawdy laughter. Two men were dancing, with one gyrating suggestively. The rest of the group were leering and clapping their hands in time to the music. The barman shook his head and clacked his tongue as he handed Jack his beer. Jack found an empty seat and patronizingly looked at the pathetic scene before him. How could adult men behave like that?

Simon, one of his closest friends, walked in and joined Jack.

"I saw your car outside and decided to come in. What's going on here?"

"Just came in myself, Simon. I still haven't figured out what is going on."

"Two weeks without women. How is it all going to end?"

Jack noticed then that there wasn't a single woman in the bar.

"They couldn't have all gone to Beijing," he laughed.

"Well, Jack, my wife, your wife, Sally and Milly . . . those have certainly gone."

"How do you know Milly has gone too?"

"I gave her a lift to the airport because she couldn't dare ask you. She knew I was sneaking Sally to the airport before seeing Her Royal Highness off."

Sally was Simon's mistress. Jack looked around and wondered how many of the men there were truly monogamous. By now the tune had changed. There was a slow, romantic tune on. The men paired off and were dancing cheek to cheek with each other.

"This is sick," Jack said.

"You're right, Jack. Let's go home to our children and play fathers."

Outside they said their goodnights, each disgusted with the homoeroticism that the men in the bar were exhibiting. As Jack drove up to his house, he was startled to see a police car parked outside. He was convinced that his son had got on the wrong side of the law. He fumbled in his pocket for his key but the door opened before his hand came out of his pocket. The policeman holding the door open looked at him sternly.

"Are you Mr. Zulu?"

That question again. *Yes, I am. Who are you?* Jack silently replied. Aloud, he said,

"A policeman spells trouble. What has gone wrong here?"

Jack saw his son seated between two boys; one looked familiar but the other he had never seen before. Directly ahead of him sat Kennedy, Simon's son, and, next to Kennedy, stood another policeman. Richard kept his eyes down.

"Do you know these boys, Mr. Zulu?"

"Richard," he pointed at him, "is my son. Kennedy over there, I know. I don't know the other two."

"The two you don't know are Thomas and Stephen. We found them smoking dagga and causing a disturbance at Stephen's father's house. Your son jumped out of a window and thought he had escaped. We followed him here. A search in his room yielded no dagga. We'd like to search your bedroom."

"Do you have a search warrant?" Jack asked irrelevantly.

The policeman handed Jack the search warrant. He glanced at it briefly then led him to his bedroom. The other policeman remained behind, a fisherman gloating over his catch. Jack was unconcerned as the policeman rummaged around. Not even the mess the policeman was making seemed to affect him. He was quite relieved that the policeman had found nothing on his son or in his room. They could not arrest his son. Jack had escaped his wife's wrath.

"Well, Mr. Zulu, does your son get his dagga from you or does he have his own supplier?"

Jack looked at the dirty rag that the policeman was opening out on his bed. "Where did you find that?"

"In your drawer, Mr. Zulu, the one holding your underclothes and your ties."

"It doesn't belong to me. Let me talk to my son."

"I would advise you to talk to your lawyer, Mr. Zulu, not your son."

Jack remembered. The boy who looked familiar was his lawyer's son. He hurried to the living room and stood before the boy.

"Stephen, is your father at home?"

"No, sir," the boy said, his head bowed. "My mother and father left for Beijing yesterday."

"Your father, too?" Jack asked incredulously.

"My father is the chairperson of the Zambia Equal Rights Committee," Stephen explained.

Jack turned to the policeman.

"Officer, my lawyer is very smart. He is the smartest lawyer in the world. He went to Beijing with the women."

The policeman was glad that his wife had no idea what Beijing was. He himself had only come to know about the Beijing Conference the week before. He sighed and watched as the tenth man he was arresting that day broke down like the nine before him. They had committed different crimes, but they all had one thing in common: their wives had gone to Beijing. And this was only Day One!

Marjorie Oludhe Macgoye
THE WASTING DISEASE

Kenya 1997 English

Marjorie Oludhe Macgoye has used fiction to explore and illuminate social issues throughout her long literary career. (See the introduction to "Learning the Sex Trade" earlier in this volume.) Many of her readers, therefore, viewed the 1997 publication of her novel *Chira* as a deeply logical—almost an inevitable—occurrence. A writer of Macgoye's stature and social commitment could not have avoided addressing the plague that had cut a path of suffering and death through the core of her adopted country—HIV/AIDS.

In *Chira*, Macgoye provides a disturbingly vivid rendition of the HIV/AIDS scourge in Kenyan society. Ignorant of the facts about *chira* (the Luo term for a "wasting disease," which is today applied to AIDS), people in this society—young and old, men and women, urban and rural—offer little resistance to the spread of the disease that threatens to wipe out huge portions of their population. This ignorance is compounded by dangerous customary beliefs and practices, social shame, women's disempowerment, misguided and inadequate public health programs, and lack of access to the antiretroviral drugs that were, even at the time of the novel's publication in 1997, rapidly becoming available in the West.

Focusing on two women—one of them fighting for her life against AIDS, the other fighting to find the courage to admit that she is HIV-positive—Macgoye shows how these various forces work together, with devastating results. But she also offers tenuous hope that her country may learn how to resist *chira*. This hope lies in the character of Theodore, the enlightened evangelist, who works with the afflicted and advocates both honesty and virtue as means to combating the disease.

The word *chira*, in the novel, clearly refers both to the physical illness and the moral, ethical, and social diseases that threaten to annihilate Kenyan society. In the two passages that follow, the realistic and metaphorical levels of narration coexist, culminating in the haunting and terrifying image of the intangible but lethal "carrier" of disease and death.

Emilia Ilieva and Lennox Odiemo-Munara

✦

"I brought Njoki," said Esther at last. "She used to come and see me in the office sometimes. We happened to meet at the bus stop and she said she was very ill and unhappy. So I brought her."

"We will pray for you, Njoki," said Theodore. "What is the nature of your sickness? You look well." He truly thought so. But Elizabeth could see the dry skin, the passive hair, the blouse hanging loose, the desperation in the eyes.

"I am not feeling very ill," whispered Njoki, "but the doctor has warned me and I am getting thin. You see I had, I had . . ." The kindest did not strain themselves to hear her. "I had a sugar daddy. She knows—Esther knows. She did not reproach me. I thought I was well off. I left the boyfriend I had been intending to marry. The man was generous and usually polite as well. I thought it would last a bit longer. Then when he went overseas I met my old friend again. And then the doctor told me, told me . . ."

Esther caught her arm. She had not heard this before.

"How long ago was this?" asked Theodore.

"Six months ago—a bit more than six."

"So it was not a baby. And he did not send you to the Special Clinic?"

"No, not the Special Clinic."

"And you are not so very thin. You can eat well, sleep?"

"Yes, I can eat when I remember to. I do not sleep well. But you see, I cannot be cleansed. I carry the sickness within me . . ."

You might have thought Theodore was the sick one. Shadows lurked under his cheekbones. It was more the passion of redemption than its joy that burned through him. He was gaunt not from deliberate fasting but from preoccupation with other needs. His voice might be worn down not with rhetoric but by arguing cases with petty officials.

In contrast, many of the young men he tried to counsel did not look like AIDS victims at all. Jeans clad, strikingly barbered, some of them, indeed, went in for long, loose jackets, concealing the thin ribs within. You did not always notice as their cheeks grew more impressively hollow, their refusal of food apparently an economy measure, not escape from the dreadful diarrhoea that followed eating. A time would come when they were too weary to scrub the jackets or tuck lifeless hair back into the crochet caps. They would fade from memory and others crowd to take their places. Theodore prayed, grieved, bullied, and pleaded. But if you are sleeping mixed, eight to a room, the air is dank with human smells, mats are rustling, old people are muttering and someone's sister is trying to dig money out of you to photocopy her certificates and get a new second hand blouse for the interview—what other joy is there? The future does not, in any case, bear thinking about.

Some of them are carriers: this you will never know for sure. They remain the same when others vanish from sight around them. Or if they get thinner it is because funerals of mates and school-friends drain them, because the pop group or the *jua kali* team is decimated by death and no longer brings in a living, because the house where they sewed or cobbled is avoided as being of ill omen. Some even grow fat as a greater share of the business falls to them. Also they procreate abundantly. But the children, somehow, wither and often die. It is because the mother is too sickly to look after them, or because the father has faded away and does not support them, or because the neighbour has put the evil eye on them, or because the little girl *ayah* has pricked them with a pin and. . . .

And in society at large the carriers flourish too. Close to them funds drain away into privy channels or trickle into malodorous corners. Schemes that looked smooth and tender erupt in blotches and blackheads, drawing offensive matter tight and throbbing just below the surface. Organisations that were pregnant with promise abort, leaving smears of blood and frustrated waters behind them. And still the facilitator smiles and deprecates, planning great things, fluent in excuses, golden-tongued, wide open to ecstatic embrace, fertile in ideas, fatal in execution. . . .

Susan N. Kiguli
I AM TIRED OF TALKING IN METAPHORS

Uganda   1998   English

Susan Kiguli was born on 24 June 1969 in the Luweero District of central Uganda. Her childhood was made particularly difficult by two sad developments: She lost her father at a very early age, and her mother, Joyce, was left to raise her on her own. Then, when she was eleven, a brutal five-year civil war broke out, with Luweero its epicenter. These events significantly affected Kiguli, and they are reflected in her verse.

Young Susan Kiguli distinguished herself early as a scholar and was admitted to the famous Gayaza High School for her secondary education. She earned bachelor's and master's degrees from Makerere University, as well as a master's of literature from Strathclyde University in Glasgow, Scotland, and a doctorate in literature from the University of Leeds in England. She is currently a tenured lecturer in literature at Makerere University.

A respected poet in her own right, Susan Kiguli has also written and published extensively on Ugandan poetry and oral performance. Several of her short stories have appeared in local journals and anthologies. She was nominated for the Keith Memorial Poetry award at Strathclyde University in 1996, and her first volume of poetry, *The African Saga*, won the National Book Trust of Uganda (NABOTU) Poetry Award in 1999. She writes poetry in both English and Luganda, her mother tongue, and often performs her verse live at various functions.

Susan Kiguli's poetry is characterized by a combination of reflective and assertive responses to the social and political experiences of her Ugandan community. Her style is strongly influenced by Ugandan orature. In the poem included here, Kiguli focuses on the rampant cases of violence against women frequently reported in the Ugandan media, including some particularly brutal cases of wife battering over political differences during the 1996 presidential elections. Allusions to Baganda customs and beliefs in the poem include the hooting of an owl as an omen of impending bereavement, the negotiation of a bride-price by suitors and the male relatives of the bride, and the slaughtering of roosters to feed important guests.

Austin Bukenya

✦

I will talk plainly
Because I am moved to abandon riddles.
I will tell you of how we held our heads
In our hands
Because the owl hooted all night
And the dogs howled as if in mourning:
We awaited bad news.
We received it.
Our mother blinded in one eye,

Crippled in the right leg,
Because she did not vote
Her husband's candidate.

I will remind you
Of the time the peeled plantains
Stood upright in the cooking pot.
We slaughtered a cock
Anticipating an important visitor.
We got her:
Our daughter—pieces of flesh in a sack—
Our present from her husband.
No, I will not use images.
I will just talk to you:
I do not fight to take your place
Or constantly wave my fist in your face.

I refuse to argue about
Your "manly pact"
With my father—
Buying me for a bag of potatoes and pepper.

All I want
Is to stop denying Me.
My presence needs no metaphors.
I am here
Just as you are.
I am not a machine
For you to dismantle whenever you wish.
I demand my human dignity.

Winnie Munyarugerero
INDEPENDENCE, 1962

Uganda   1998   English

Winnie Munyarugerero was born Winfred Gashumba in the Kisoro region of southwestern Uganda. She attended the prestigious Gayaza Girls High School just outside Kampala before taking an honors degree in English and French at Makerere University. She also studied at the University of Madagascar in Tananarive, and she worked for several years as an educator before turning to nongovernmental organization activities. She is a member of Action for Development (ACFODE), an advocacy and action organization for the improvement of education and the alleviation of poverty among Ugandan women. She was also for many years the vice-chair of the Uganda Women Writers Association (FEM-RITE). She contributes to several of their publications as both writer and editor.

"Independence, 1962" is an impressionistic narrative of Uganda's first Independence Day, on 9 October 1962. Looking back on the experience across a distance of thirty-six years, the author ponders, rather gloomily, the meanings of that important event for Ugandans, both then and in 1998. Her pessimism stems from what she concludes is the dismal performance of Uganda, since independence, as a viable nation state. Despite the optimism of 1962, Uganda became an arena for mismanagement, misrule, and dictatorships, as well as civil wars. The author seems to suggest that the "independence baby" was stillborn, probably because the original participants in the event, both the Ugandans and their British colonizers, failed to define and understand properly the meaning of independence.

It was widely believed at the time of independence that, of the three East African countries of Kenya, Tanganyika (later Tanzania), and Uganda, Uganda was the best-favored both by nature and history. Endowed with extremely fertile land and a mild climate, it was easily the most productive of the three, in agricultural output at least. Politically, the "protectorate" form of colonialism obtaining there was more benevolent than the settler colonialism of Kenya. Uganda was given its independence without much of a fight, avoiding the kind of bitter and violent struggle that took place in Kenya. Many of the best development projects targeting Africans were set up in Uganda, and many East Africans who wanted a good education, for example, went to Uganda to attend high school and university. Yet, nearly four decades down the road, Uganda seems still to lag far behind its regional counterparts.

The author ends her piece with a simple but devastating question: "What went wrong?" One of many answers is clearly found in the very terms of its creation as an independent country. While all colonial states were artificial creations, Uganda was even more tragically so. The label *Uganda* itself referred only to one region of the new nation, and it was precisely with the natives of this region that the British had negotiated all the terms of their colonial enterprise, which were then imposed on the rest of the people in the "country." Even the much-vaunted developments were largely confined to the "Uganda" area, while the other regions were used as sources of cheap labor and low-ranking security personnel. To make matters worse, the British had trained no viable cadres to take over their responsibilities when they left. Gayaza High School, where the staff at independence was 99 percent British, was symptomatic of the nation. In brief, independence was granted, in 1962, to a country that lacked unity or equity among its many peoples, and was ill-prepared, after years of colonialism, to bear the burdens of nationhood—an obvious prelude to the tragedies that were to befall the country.

Kampala, the commercial capital of Uganda, became at independence the political capital as well, replacing Entebbe, on the shores of Lake Victoria. The airstrip where the independence ceremonies were held is on the southeastern slopes of Kololo, one of the legendary "seven hills" on which Kampala is built. The airstrip has since become a prominent venue for all kinds of national celebrations, and a corner of it has been turned into a "Heroes' Acre," where eminent nationalists are buried.

Austin Bukenya and Ayeta Anne Wangusa

I was one in that mass of humanity at Kololo Airstrip on that historical day of 9th October 1962. To be more precise, it was from 8th October to 9th October, for it was at midnight of 8th October that the crowd held its breath as the Union Jack came down. Then the unison shout of joy as the new Ugandan flag went up for the first time.

It may have been my young and impressionable mind, perhaps, but I don't remember any other occasion when there was excitement to equal the rock solid excitement of that occasion. Everyone in that crowd breathed excitement. (I hesitate to call that gathering of people "a crowd." For that word "crowd" suggests some lack of order or organization.) In actual fact, the huge gathering of people at the airstrip that night were very orderly and well organized. Each group or category of people had its section to sit. The schoolchildren had their section, and if I remember correctly, schoolchildren were allocated the Nyonyi Gardens or Wampewo Avenue side. We sat facing the Acacia Avenue direction, slightly to the right as the rostrum and main VIP shed was erected, not where the present one is, but closer to the Upper Kololo Avenue embankment. I remember we sat on the ground—I suppose there was more grass than dust then—so, the neatly cut grass was adequate for the sitting arrangement.

What characterized the occasion, however, was the excitement that permeated the atmosphere. The excitement was so heavy and real that you could almost touch it, you felt it in your bloodstream, right through your entire body. The person sitting next to you, on your right and on your left, the one behind you and in front of you, felt the same. The total sum of the excitement from the thousands of people, was something I have never felt since. It was not an individual excitement; it was a collective excitement, a national excitement.

I was a young adolescent at Gayaza High School. The staff at the school those days, was more than 99% white—British, to be more accurate. A few porters on the kitchen and the farm were the only African staff. Even the cateress and the farm manager were British. Our British teachers did not do much to prepare us for Independence. They may have discussed it with the older students, but those in senior one and two were not told much. The teachers themselves may have been a little bewildered and may not have understood the issues well. But young as we were, we were vaguely aware of the significance of the Independence event. In spite of the lack of much political awareness, the excitement about Independence swept across the school, and, I have no doubt, across the whole population. Everybody, young and old, illiterate and literate, felt that Independence was significant for Uganda, the infant nation, but also for every Ugandan individual.

The excitement for us at school was a combination of several excitements. The idea of getting out of school, of an outing, was a big thing in itself. The idea of an outing at night was poetic and romantic. Then later at the airstrip, the fireworks, the large mass of people—all these added to a huge excitement for us schoolchildren.

The evening of 8th October, we got ready to leave for Kampala. I am sure there were no classes that day, and if there were, everyone would have been too excited to be attentive. Those girls who could be picked [up] to go home had left, but the majority of the student body, which by the present standard was very small, probably not more than 250 in all, prepared for the night out. We were dashing here and there, propelled by the hurricane of excitement in the air. That day, as there was to be no supper, we were served high tea; that term alone, "high tea," added to our feeling of, and it increased, our anticipation. The high tea comprised of bread, eggs, cheese, even possibly tinned beef, accompanied by tea. It was a rich meal that was intended to carry us through the evening and night. I can't remember well but I have this feeling that we must have packed something to eat later, for our teachers were very mindful of our health and young appetites. We then got into the fleet of waiting UTC buses and, feeling as important and special as brides to their grooms, we were driven to Kampala. The city—I don't think it was called a city then for it was a much smaller out-fit—was ablaze with excitement. I think we were driven around to see the dec-orated city before we headed for Kololo airstrip. The weather those days knew how to behave; it was respectful of the great event because it did not rain. As we sat under the clear night sky, it was difficult not to feel or imagine the divine presence of God to bless the occasion.

I can't remember much of what was said in the speeches by the dignitaries. What I remember is the trim looking, youthful Prime Minister Obote. He seemed to have and to inspire confidence. The older people may have had their doubts but for the fourteen- and fifteen-year-olds present, Obote appeared capable of steering the new-born state.

After the function at Kololo that night—rather morning—we boarded the buses and returned to school, tired and sleepy but filled with a sense of being part of history in the making, of being actors, however small the role, in the making of the history of our country.

The next morning, the 9th October, we were taken to Kampala for more cel-ebrations. What I remembered most vividly were the floats—moving vehicles displaying the products and services, in the most imaginative impressions, of each industry and government department. To a young girl from a rural back-ground this was most captivating.

As we took in the full importance of the Independence event, we saw stretched before us development and prosperity. We saw a future offering new opportunities, a nation rising to the heights. Perhaps in our young minds we understood freedom naively, as young people do. We did not understand the responsibility that accompanies freedom. It would appear that even the adults did not know better; otherwise why did things go wrong!

As it turned out later, my generation of Ugandans—those in secondary school at the time—became the most disillusioned and the hardest hit. We expected so much as we witnessed and participated in the birth of a nation. And what did we get? The harsh realities of Amin's rule in the economic war period.

The older people may have been cushioned from the full impact by the cynicism that comes with age and experience.

Those who came later—in secondary schools in the late sixties and early seventies—had not witnessed the birth. They had not drunk in the mouthfuls of excitement and expectations that heralded Independence. I suppose it is not by accident that people who led the fight to restore Uganda's dignity are essentially those of my generation.

Kololo airstrip hosts many celebrations each year. Independence Day, 9th October, attracts the smallest crowds. It is an event that few Ugandans seem to understand the significance of.

Independence Day means very little to many Ugandans. This is very sad indeed for those of us who were at Kololo on 9th October 1962. What went wrong?

Vuyo Ophelia Wagi
TWO POEMS
Tanzania 1999   English

Vuyo Wagi was born in Johannesburg, South Africa, to a South African mother and a Tanzanian father. The family lived in Britain in the 1950s before settling permanently in Dar es Salaam in the 1960s. Vuyo Wagi attended secondary school in Tanzania before leaving to study at Indiana University in Bloomington, where she earned a bachelor's degree in social psychology, cultural anthropology, and microbiology in 1986. Upon her return to Tanzania, she worked as a freelance writer and consultant, and as an editor for the Dar es Salaam University Press. A collection of her poetry, *Safe Crossing*, was published in 1999, and before her untimely death in 2001, she was in the process of compiling another collection, entitled *Conversations*.

Vuyo Wagi was one of the very few Tanzanians who wrote in English. She wrote sad and contemplative poetry, often grappling with life's intangibles—the meaning of life, death, time, the hereafter—as well as the social predicament of the destitute, the powerless, and women in general in Africa.

A tragic streak runs through her poems—a realization of the presence, necessity, and indeed, imminence, of death. This is in part explained by the poet's own tragic experience: Her Ugandan husband died in Yoweri Museveni's "bush war" in Uganda, and her only sister died at an early age as well, leaving her alone and unemployed to take care of her aging mother and her two small children.

Underlying the two poems that follow are the harsh realities of HIV/AIDS and economic underdevelopment. Since 1983, when AIDS was first discovered, Tanzania has suffered devastatingly from the pandemic. It is believed that more than 10 percent of Tanzania's 33 million people are infected with HIV. Thousands have already died from the disease, leaving behind numerous orphans in need of assistance. But assistance is not always forthcoming, even from near relatives, let alone the government and the public at large. "AIDS Orphan" mourns the young left motherless and fatherless, and derided and shunned by everybody, including those who pretend to be religious.

The economic problems of Tanzania and other developing countries have led to an increase in the numbers of jobless and homeless youths. This has in turn encouraged child labor, with young girls from the countryside being the greatest victims of this system. "Slave Girl 2000" looks at the plight of the housemaid, who comes to town from the rural areas in search of life and success, only to end up as a virtual slave—despised, discarded, forced to do backbreaking menial labor, and often physically and sexually abused. When such girls become pregnant, they are thrown onto these streets. In these circumstances, some end up abandoning their babies because they are unable to care for them.

M.M. Mulokozi

✦

AIDS ORPHAN

Shockquake has passed.
The dust has settled on life's ruins.
Man, woman, child, home,
From school to a cold hearth
And stove and no lighting
Mama's voice, calling, badgering,
Yes, it is true,
Oh, to hear even the sound
of her nagging.

No light shining and lost
In the dim of grieving.
How do men, women like these, cry?
They become adult
Between the passings,
Another rite of passage,
To where?
Child to child, child to adult.

Uniform politely tattered,
No more money for food, fees,
One more year to go
And how to get there?
No more, never any more,
"Love thy neighbor as thyself."
Standing down is out as the
Sun shines on the hazy trail . . .

SLAVE GIRL 2000

Village fetched, wide eyed,
Clinging wood smoke smell,
Nil knowledge of city life,
Lured by promises of "education,"
A "better life," still a child,
Childlike in her belief,
Intimidation invocation by "civilized" people.
Strong enough to taste,
Swift casualness of life,
Shining lights blinding, not street wise,
She found the city has its wisdom.

The work!
Buy me for free an ox or plough horse,
Cook, clean, wash, babysit, and the boss
Wants more besides.
More, sir?
Skincrawl groping hard breathing
And furtive looks, suggestions, plans:
"I will be at the chicken shed at dawn."
He gathers eggs too?

Unwillingly taken, unwillingly giving.
Ete noire!! No protests here!
Depending on the silence
Of the powerless.
Discovered! By madam no less.
Shrieks of protest, profanities, accusations:
"You w——— ungrateful, sneaking . . ."
Words water falling too fluent for words.

"But Madam I . . ."
"Shut up!
You encouraged him, you will pay!"
With my dignity, self respect?
They forget, she's somebody's daughter.
Now the belly is swelling,
Glances askance, whispers,
She cheapened herself,
Be careful of them, they are sly
And conniving.
Family meetings:

What should be done?
Only blame and nobody
Thinks to ask her,
Alone with the curses
And insults ringing in her ears.

Nine months later, a child to be born.
Will it be poison for her?
And the unborn child or dumping?
Dumping is chosen, life though bitter,
Can be sweet, irony doesn't care.
Now she's homeless
From slave girl to street girl.

Street life, more pain, it's not fun here,
With the competition, drugs and policemen
Taking their liberties.
Another kind of slavery;
How will it end?

Mary Penelope Mfune
THE SINGING DRUM

Zambia 1999   Chiyanja

Raised by a family of storytellers, Mary Penelope Mfune was born in 1938 at Chief Mukutuma's village in Ndola Rural District in Zambia's copper belt. Her mother, Kasapato, who passed on this folktale, hailed from Congo Kinshasa, bordering western Zambia, and had married a Malawian, Jeremiah Kamanga Mfune, who came to Zambia in search of employment in the copper mines. The story was originally told to young Mary Mfune and her two sisters in the local Lamba language in the 1940s. Mfune later translated it into Chinyanja, a language commomly spoken in Zambia's Eastern Province, and performed a contemporary version for her granddaughter in 1999.

Mary Penelope Mfune obtained her primary school certificate at Mindolo Primary School and later attended Chipembi Girls' Secondary School, a Protestant mission school in the Central Province in the 1950s. She is a retired registered nurse, a widow, and a grandmother, currently living in Lusaka.

"The Singing Drum" and many other African folktales provide lessons on proper conduct, as well as warnings against dangers. The stories are creatively designed to make instruction more interesting and easy to grasp. They are normally told in the evening, often around a fire after dinner, before the family is ready to retire to bed. These tales have traversed many African lands and generations. Zambian folktales, for example, show marked similarities to many tales found elsewhere in eastern and southern Africa, due to cross-cultural contacts and exchanges, intermarriage, trade, and migration. Stories were regularly transferred to new terrain. Labor-driven migrations in the twentieth century also ushered new folktales into Zambia.

This short folktale carries a simple lesson: Young girls should always return home before dark. The word *dzimwe*, which is used as the name of the villain in the story, refers to a "beast" in most Bantu languages.

Nalishebo N. Meebelo

◆

Once upon a time, there was a young girl popularly known as Mwachangale. Mwachangale lived with her parents in the village of Mulundu in the east. She was greatly loved by her parents and many in the community. She had a beautiful voice whenever she sang various tunes. Mwachangale enjoyed bathing in the river with her friends every day on her way from school. When this young girl was born, her maternal grandmother gave her the name Mwachangale, and put a traditional necklace around her neck. She wore this necklace at all times.

One day, while returning from school with her friends, Mwachangale went to the river to bathe with them, just as she always did. At the river, she removed her clothes and her necklace, and her friends followed suit. They bathed all afternoon until sunset. When it was time to return to the village, Mwachangale and her friends put on their clothes and began their walk back to the village. Before she reached the village, Mwachangale remembered her necklace. She had left it at the river! She told her friends that she was going back to look for it. The friends begged her not to go back after dark because there was a bad man called Dzimwe to look out for.

Mwachangale went back to the river to look for her necklace. She met Dzimwe on the way. Dzimwe asked her, "What are you doing here child?" Mwachangale answered, "I left my necklace at the river when I was bathing with my friends." Dzimwe then lifted Mwachangale and threw her into his big drum, together with her necklace.

Mwachangale begun to sing:

I am not a drum I am Mwachangale,
Mwachangale. I forgot my necklace at the river,
Necklace at the river. I found Dzimwe had picked it up.
Dzimwe had picked up and put it in his drum,
Put it in his drum, which goes, "lingo lingo liziya wa jimwa buka aye!"

Mwachangale's parents began to look for her because she had not arrived home. Her friends said that she had returned to the river to look for her necklace. Everyone in the village was concerned because they loved the young girl very much. The whole village was worried and did not find her for many days.

At that time people in the village of Mulundu heard that there was news of a drum that could sing. Dzimwe went to this village to show off his singing drum. The people were amazed but did not pay attention to the words of the drum's song. When Dzimwe reached the home of Mwachangle's parents, he played his drum again and the drum sang:

> I am not a drum, I am Mwachangale,
> Mwachangale. I forgot my necklace at the river,
> Necklace at the river. I found Dzimwe had picked it up.
> Dzimwe had picked up and put it in his drum,
> Put it in his drum, which goes, "lingo lingo liziya wa jimwa buka aye!"

Mwachangale's parents heard the song and were surprised. They recognized the voice of their child. They asked Dzimwe to play his drum again. The drum sang loudly:

> I am not a drum, I am Mwachangale,
> Mwachangale. I forgot my necklace at the river,
> Necklace at the river. I found Dzimwe had picked it up.
> Dzimwe had picked up and put it in his drum,
> Put it in his drum, which goes, "lingo lingo liziya wa jimwa buka aye!"

Everyone in the village heard this song and realized that Mwachangale was in the drum. They all rose and beat Dzimwe and removed the girl from the drum. Chief Mulundu banished Dzimwe from the village and warned him never to return.

Translated by Nalishebo N. Meebelo

Neera Kapur-Dromson
SEEKING MY HUSBAND IN KENYA

Kenya 1999   English

A fourth-generation Kenyan of Indian descent, Neera Kapur was born in Nairobi during the Emergency, and attended school and college there. From the beginning, she was an avid reader and eagerly absorbed stories of the "old days," which were current in her home. Later, she studied the art of Indian classical dance with gurus in India. She continues to perform and to give lecture demonstrations and workshops in Orissi, a form of classical dance from the northeastern Indian state of Orissa. Married to a former director of the French Cultural Center, she spends part of each year in France.

"Seeking My Husband in Kenya" is part of the opening chapter of a novel, *From Jhelum to Tana*. The novel traces the experience of three generations of

Punjabi ancestors in Africa, especially the women of the family, who are torn among three different cultures. The first chapter contains the journey and arrival of Hardei, the great-grandmother, who travels with a small son through turbulent seas and violent storms to the shores of East Africa in 1904. She is searching for the husband who never returned from a business trip while she was still pregnant. When she finds him, later in the novel, she asserts herself to an extent that astonishes the community. The novel depicts actual physical and psychological conditions, which have led to the rooting and intertwining of many threads in Kenyan lives. Kapur is especially interested in the lives of mixed African/Indian families. The *solar topee* is a white colonial hat worn by all the administrative staff working in the African Public Works Departments, especially the railways.

Marjorie Oludhe Macgoye

✦

Kucci tutt gai jina di yari, patannan the rohn khadiyan.
When fickle lovers leave the beloved and go away, the beloved can do nothing but weep by the riverside.

Hardei had been standing at the station for a very long time. Her six-year-old son was getting agitated. He was hungry, so was she, but they had very little money left. Moreover, they had never seen so many strange faces before. They did see some black slaves being brought in at the port when they had arrived in Karachi, but she had not expected to see so many of them in this new country she had just stepped into. "Habashi!" she exclaimed in total amazement without thinking, and held on to the white *dupatta* as if to protect herself from unseen forces.

She was a little afraid. "Am I going to live among them?" she thought momentarily, but was quickly distracted by her son who had just then pulled the *dupatta* off her head, revealing her bosom and the slightly graying hair. "O, *Habshiya*," she smacked him lovingly and quickly covered her head again. Despite her embarrassment and those of the onlookers, she smiled at her son and held on to him. Stories from childhood appeared before her: "A *Habashan* will take you away if you don't drink your milk quickly," that was how mothers would scare their children. To the likes of Hardei, all people with black skins and frizzy hair were *Habashis*. How or why *Habashis* had acquired the air of apparent ferocity, Hardei could not for the world have told you, but the name evoked terror, and this she had passed on to her child.

Abash, Havash, Habashi, Habeshi—all were common terms for Abyssinians. A Semitic tribe of mixed Arab descent, these strangers were to be found in the north of East Africa, in what is now Ethiopia. With a recorded history extending back two thousand years over almost unbroken lines of kings to Menelik I, the reputed son of King Solomon and Queen Sheba, the Abyssinian Christians of the highlands considered themselves superior and highly cultured with numerous rigorous religious festivals and austere fasts.

"So many sahibs and memsahibs!" Here she came across all of them, it seemed. Her father had talked about them—the *firenghis*. Hardei tried to recall why. "Perhaps it had to do with some business deals," she continued mumbling to herself. "Memory fails me. I must be very tired." She closed her eyes for a minute and then looked around again. Back in her town, people were wheatish—some more than others—in complexion. She could not understand it all very well. A chill ran down her spine. In spite of the hot December afternoon, she shivered. Surely, she was tired, or was it the sudden panic—the strange place, new faces and sounds—all that she was not familiar with.

She suddenly cursed herself: "Why have I come? Why did I leave the familiar world behind? Do I even expect to find him here? What if he refuses to recognize me?" Question piled upon question, and her heart sank a little. Biting hard into her nails, her anxiety deepened. "What if there is already another woman in my place. Seven years is a very long time." Hardei knew that no man could do without a woman for that long. A thousand thoughts crossed her mind all at the same time. She felt a little dizzy and thoroughly confused. It was unusual for her to feel so unsure of herself. A Punjabi woman was known for her confidence, for strength of character, and for her physique. Perhaps even for a touch of aggressiveness—for after all, had they not had to fight centuries of invasions. Endless battles had left their scars, but more important, had deeply influenced a will to face new conditions with courage, fortitude, and a sense of adventure.

The sun had just risen. The clouds that had settled were streaked yellow and blue. Was it going to rain? She couldn't say for sure; even the vast sky and the cumulus clouds appeared different here. Hardei took a deep breath and looked at her son. He had fallen asleep on the hard bench. She smiled and took him into her lap. She was used to sitting cross-legged—on the rough floor, or on the *charpai*, the thin ropes of the cot cutting into her soft bottom; it didn't matter—the position was just so much more comfortable.

Ever since Kirparam's parents had passed away, Hardei and her husband had had to share a house with his father's younger brother and his wife, his Chacha and Chachi. Chachi especially had been hard on Hardei. Still very young and naïve to the ways of the world, Hardei thought to herself, "How difficult they had made my life, especially when there was no news about my husband." Curses and abuses she could manage for herself. It was when she realized that she was pregnant that she decided to run away, back to what was once her home. She sought refuge with her brother, but there too she had to deal with her stepmother.

Her son shifted in his sleep. Hardei patted him and lulled him back to sleep. "*Soja mere rajkumar* . . . sleep, my prince," her heavy voice had a drowsy effect on him. Her left hand patted his head, her right hand his small bottom, her lap moved up and down—all rocking his head and body rhythmically. With her whole body swaying to the lullaby, the child went to sleep at once. Chunilal was six, but had yet to see his father. "Will he recognize his own son?" she wondered. She studied his face closely. "Was there any resemblance? The same big forehead." She shook her head and smiled.

Time dragged. She was nervous waiting for the train that was supposed to arrive in forty minutes, according to the big clock in the railway station. It seemed ages ago that she had left Miani, a little town on the Jhelum, in northwest Punjab. There too she had waited with her son for the train. Her brother had not come to the station to see them off. He did not want to spend two whole rupees on the return journey. She had been hurt but she knew him by now.

No one had come to see Hardei and her son off at Miani railway station, though it seemed that every other passenger was accompanied by a dazzling fanfare of colorful, noisy ceremonies. Relatives and friends had come to the station with flower garlands—invariably the marigold, saffron-colored flowers, which left a very distinct fragrance reminiscent of temples and *puja* rooms. Others carried *mithais* and shoved boxes of sweets at their friends. Some waved a rupee note or two around the departee's head as *sagan*, auspicious money for the journey, and then thrust the note into their friend's hands. All kinds of advice filled the air: "Promise that you will write . . . that you will not eat beef . . ." A few wept; others waved their right hands. Hardei felt a little sorry for herself. Here she stood alone, with her little son. People with wet handkerchiefs drying tear-filled eyes embraced each other. Perhaps they would never meet again. Miani Station was a place for goodbyes. At that moment for Hardei, it spelled no-man's-land.

A distant hoot announced the train's arrival, a major event in an East African station. The platform came to life. The station became a market place. Hardei woke out of her trance-like state and regained some of her resilient composure. She was in an altogether different world here. "*Chungwa! Ndizi! Chungwa!*" African men in red blankets and bare-headed, beaded women were thrusting bananas, oranges, and even live fowl from the platform up at passengers staring at them from open train windows, their right hands outstretched to the goodies.

The Indian station master gave a signal—nearly all station masters so far in East Africa were Indians. Packed high with acacia branches used as fuel, the engine made a preparatory start. Enormous Garrett engines, the biggest and most powerful, had to be wood-fired. Passengers hung around outside, talking until the last minute. Then suddenly, as if shot from a gun, they rushed about looking for their baggage, their children, their carriage . . .

The train began to climb, slowly and laboriously, through the forest of palms to the high hills overlooking Mombasa. Especially suited to growing coconuts, Changamwe, the first stop, abounded with fertility. Huge fruit orchards of oranges, bananas, pineapples, and limes fed the eyes. Soon the coconut palms gave way to a semi-desert, dense with thorn trees right up to Tsavo where suddenly the sun bared its ultimate ferocity. It was like being in a pan of smoldering iron . . . Meriakani, Maji ya Chumvi, Samburu, MacKinon Road, the train seemed to stop at every station for at least ten minutes. Each time, a new Indian station master walked along the platform with his kerosene lamp and then disappeared quickly. "One night the station master lingered on the platform after the train had left and was taken away by a lion," a nearby passenger said to Hardei. She stared at him in disbelief.

Steam had to be kept up all the time to drive the engine. At stations sometimes the driver drew off a pot full of boiling water from the boiler. Other times, when he came within easy reach of wood, he stopped the train. Passengers were requested to ascend: "Would you please help cut up some *kuni*?" They were quite happy to oblige. The wood and a dose of paraffin soon started burning merrily, and the steam dial began to register. It gobbled up tons of wood fuel. The wood-fed engine hooted a lot, then stopped at yet another station, where no house, apart from the station building, was visible anywhere. The driver opened the regulator to let off the steam . . . oof oof oof chook . . . and the music changed.

The train vibrated a lot as the metal lines expanded under the hot tropical sun. The train puffed and blew. One hundred miles away from Mombasa, the train finally arrived at Voi for the night halt. A change of guard—always Indian—and a shift of drivers. Voi was the first landmark on the line. The dak bungalow at Voi was reserved for European passengers; here they ate and slept. Behind the good shed little fires sprang up. Natives made their meals of maize and bananas. Indians relieved themselves in the bazaar just behind. In the best of British tradition, trains were compartmentalized into three separate classes. Moreover first-class trains had first-class drivers; others had second-class drivers.

"Amma, amma, look, look," Chunilal screamed in great excitement at his first discovery of large wild animals—his body half-hanging out of the huge window. Hardei held on to his legs. With his feet banging hard against her thighs, and his small body dancing up and down, she feared that he might fall out, but she could also feel some of the same excitement coursing through her as well. Apart from squirrels and the endless monkeys, back home in Miani, Hardei was a witness to this grand spectacle for the first time, something she was to see again and again: herds of zebra, giraffe, Thomson's gazelle, kudu, dik dik—they all looked more or less the same to her right now, and her initial fear turned to enthusiasm.

The sun had risen since the last quarter of an hour. Its first rays struck the fields of snow in splendor. Another gift of their journey was a glimpse of the snow-capped Mt. Kilimanjaro far in the distance. With her eyes raised toward the summit, Hardei paused in silent admiration for a long moment before she could find words to express her admiration: "Proud and royal, how like the Himalayas, the abode of gods. Perhaps Shiva meditated here too," she told her son, and bowed in salutation with her hands joined together. "Here some god must also live," she continued, feeling like a child in front of an image of the eternal. Who was not inspired by a view of a snow-capped mountain? Kilimanjaro—she did not know its name then—stood with greatness and dignity, a monument to aspiration.

The heavy and mysterious mists rose slowly, reaching the snow peaks, each rivaled in its whiteness. A few seconds later, the snows disappeared, the mists had encircled the area. The white mists covering the arrogant summit finally seemed to triumph. Kilimanjaro was usually visible until ten in the morning, the rest of the day enveloped in clouds.

The few intense moments had diverted her low spirits. But as the train approached the town called Nairobi, Hardei grew nervous again. What awaited her here? She wondered in panic whether she remembered what he looked like. She didn't have a photograph—they had not taken one at their wedding. "Come to think of it," Hardei thought to herself, "I had my first glimpse of the man only long after the marriage ceremony, and even then I had dared only to take a quick peek through my long veil, while his *sehra* was being removed. We were both so young," she continued half aloud. "He did not even have a proper beard, and I was still flat-chested. Who told us what to do? It was so awkward." She closed her eyes, sighing deeply within her soul, remembering.

Very soon, even before the color of henna had drained off her palms, Hardei was put to work in her new house. She felt sorry for herself: "At least they could have waited for the usual bridal period before they asked me to help in the bake shop." It was hard work. Up very early in the morning, she lit the charcoal fire and helped to make all kinds of pastries—halwa, jalebis, purees, pakoras. From time to time Chacha sent his nephew to Karachi to buy spices. "Better and cheaper there," he had said.

The last time Kirparam had not returned from Karachi. Hardei could still recall his goodbye. He had not lingered over it. Typical. A Punjabi man never looked back to wave in nonchalant sentimentality. A quick "*acha*" and he was gone. She had wanted to shout after him, "*Mein kya*, you have forgotten your umbrella," but had restrained herself. The words had frozen in her throat: "Bad omen to call someone back." She thought instead, "He will buy one in Karachi, a better one," and she had smiled to herself then.

Karachi was a port full of beautiful things from faraway places—silks, spices, sugar, rice, and cereals; indigo, wool, and European goods, and more. In her daydreams, Hardei often saw herself in the port of Karachi running from one shop to another, admiring the beads, feeling the softness of the silks. "Even if I could not buy anything, just looking would have been so much fun," she sighed. "*Hai rabba, hai rabba*," she called out to her god not once but many times, until she could not bear it any longer. The dream lay shattered before her and tears poured forth. "Perhaps he will take me with him the next time that he goes to buy spices for the shop," she tried to console herself. Such was not her kismet, for eventually, when she did cross Karachi all by herself, it was in a hurried and panicky state, without the leisure she had hoped for.

Alone in Miani, day after day she had gazed through the small iron barred window for his familiar shadow, for the sound of his quick footsteps. At times she caught herself speaking to him, "*Mein kya*, I say. . . ." She did not use his name, of course. "Kirparam," no, no, she could not have called him thus: it was just not done. No wife addressed her husband by his first name, or any other name. At other times, to draw his attention, she would say, "Have you heard . . ." Kirparam himself did not often use her name either. Usually, each drew the other's attention in an indirect way—a cough, a clearing of the throat, sometimes only a sound sufficed.

Nothing seemed to alert him this time. Not her cries, nor her fervent prayers. Hardei pleaded with the gods. The family searched all over the village, spoke with his friends—to no avail. Kirparam did not return from his journey to Karachi. She wandered about feeling fetid and forlorn. At such moments she felt the loss of her mother. She longed for the assurance of some steady love; perhaps a biological need gripped her.

Now on the train she awoke with a start, nearly frozen. Clouds had thickened over the sky. Tall trees darkened the forest they were passing through. Chunilal drew closer to his mother. It seemed to be his turn to feel frightened. She clung to him, held him close to her, hoping to draw some courage herself from his human contact. The train advanced toward its destination—the tin city of Nairobi . . .

Many people hurried to the station to enjoy the exciting atmosphere. . . . The guard, feeling very smart in his *solar topee*, a mark of colonial power, blew the whistle. The train came to a halt. Hardei's heart leaped. She bent forward to look through the window: "Perhaps by some chance miracle he has come to meet us," she thought for a moment, and then immediately chided herself, "How could he know of our arrival?" Her body sagged with the realization that they had not communicated for years.

Slowly she went back to her seat. Kirparam had never written. Hardei would never have known of his whereabouts had she not heard some stories from people in her town who had returned from "Afrika." He had not even been aware that his wife had been pregnant when he left. Taking a deep breath, she sat at the edge of her seat, ready to rise.

On long low benches the Indians sat, rising like crows in a field to greet the train and storm the coaches reserved for Asians. Bundle-clutching, dhoti-clad Indians hastened to descend from the train. Others with black steel trunks on their heads, their once elegant kurta-pyjamas now limp and crushed. Perspiring profusely, they heaved and pushed their way through the crowd. For every traveler there were perhaps a dozen greeters. Driven in rickshaws pulled by Kikuyus covered in sweat; in *gharries*; in bullock tongas, in two-wheel carts drawn by mules, driven by a turbaned Sikh. The hustle and bustle of people talking at the top of their voices, the rickshaw men grabbing the luggage and making off with it. Everybody seemed to be in a hurry. Except Hardei.

So great was the congestion at the Nairobi station, it seemed as though everyone in the capital had converged there. Intensity. Excitement. Commotion. Hardei looked around her—for a familiar face perhaps? Turbaned men— Sikhs, Pathans, Arabs, African families carrying bulging cloth-wrapped bundles on their heads, babies strapped with a colorful piece of cloth behind their backs. At the far end of the train were the reserved carriages for Europeans only, into which no native or Indian would dare to step.

New settlers had arrived: civil servants in starched khaki uniforms and white *topees*, others in felt hats. Women in their long flowing gowns, large straw hats and white parasols covering their heads, full white gloves enveloping their hands and arms. Hardei stared at them for a long while and wondered why they were so covered. Much later she learned that they regarded the sun as a dangerous animal that would strike them down like a cobra. "What would the memsahibs do in our hometown in Miani, where summer temperatures could really scorch? With their white faces going blood red, they would probably quiver under the blazing sun."

Hardei's arm automatically surrounded her son, as if trying to retrieve some comfort, to relocate a necessary security. And then she burst out laughing. Beside her, he stood all red. She touched his face and said "*Gullal*," for he looked like little Krishna during the festival of *holi*, all covered with *gullal*. Was it not like the first day of spring when one had the joy of painting each other with brightly colored powders, red being the most popular? The sudden strong rays of the sun accentuated the red colors and gave her visual delight. In spite of her anxiety, she laughed and cried at the same time.

But then everybody else—all the fellow travelers—seemed to have changed complexion. She wiped her own face with the edge of her white *dupatta*, and it came off red. She looked down at herself—her clothes were covered in red. The ochre-red dust had penetrated everything, filling the eyes, nostrils, hair, and pores of the skin. All the disembarking passengers were united in one common color. This time it was not the sun, but the fine dust of the African plains. Red ochre was the color of the Maasai, the color used by the Samburu, the color of Africa. It enveloped each one. It welcomed every new arrival into the heart of the land. It stamped and marked every disembarking passenger from the train. For a day or two afterward, traces of the Taru desert appeared as red streaks on the wiping cloth.

She waited. People started leaving. Newly arrived coolies carried beds made of lemon wood and crisscross hemp on their heads. Slowly the station began to empty. Hardei clutched her son's hand tightly, held the little black trunk in her other hand, and began to walk out. A three-yard-long, one-and-a-half-yard-wide white veil thrown over her head fell in graceful folds nearly to her feet. A loose bodice concealed her bosom, a pair of slippers covered her feet, its soles clearly cracked. She wore no makeup. After a life spent almost always in the open air, she looked forlorn, solitary, and tired. She hesitated before joining the group of Indians as they left the station and walked down the main road toward the Indian bazaar.

Sarah Nyendwoha Ntiro
FIGHTING FOR WOMEN'S RIGHTS

Uganda   1999   English

Sarah Nyendwoha Ntiro was the first female university graduate in East Africa. Born near Hoima town in the Bunyoro-Kitara Kingdom of western Uganda in 1926, she attended some of the best schools in the country, including King's College Budo, where she excelled in mathematics. She was among the first six women admitted to Makerere College, now Makerere University, in 1945. She enrolled as the only woman in a class of thirty-two mathematics majors, but the mathematics tutor refused to have her in his class. She was forced to change her courses to history, geography, and English. After studying Latin and obtaining the classics qualifications necessary for her admission, she attended and graduated from St. Anne's College, Oxford. She went on to teach at the prestigious Gayaza High School. At Gayaza Sara Ntiro staged a firm protest against unequal pay between male and female teachers. She refused to accept her salary until the wife of the colonial Governor of Uganda intervened to ensure that equal pay was effected.

Between 1958 and 1961, Sarah Ntiro was one of the first two women members of the Legislative Council, Uganda's lawmaking organ during the colonial period. She was also a member of several Ugandan delegations to the United Nations General Assembly in the period just before independence. Between 1961 and 1964, she lived in London with her late husband, Professor Sam Joseph Ntiro, then Tanganyika High Commissioner to Britain. Returning to Uganda, she established the Uganda Teachers' Service Commission, now the Educational Service Commission, while working at the Ministry of Education, and was a senior administrator in the Vice-Chancellor's Office at Makerere University. The excesses of the Idi Amin regime forced her to flee into exile in Kenya, where she remained for nearly a decade, running a higher education consultancy for African refugees. Ntiro is a member of numerous scholarly, advocacy, and developmental organizations, many of which she helped to establish in Uganda. Among these are the Uganda Society, the Uganda Council of Women, the Young Women's Christian Association of Uganda, the Family Planning Association, the Development Network of Indigenous Voluntary Associations, and the Uganda Association of University Women.

In 2001, the Uganda chapter of the Forum for African Women Educationists (FAWE) established an annual public lecture and award in honor of Sarah Ntiro, given to women scholars or researchers who have distinguished themselves in their fields. FAWE also chose Ntiro to spearhead a campaign to encourage Ugandan girls' participation in the sciences. In 2003, Spelman College in Atlanta, Georgia, awarded Sarah Ntiro an honorary doctorate.

Sarah Ntiro's discourse here covers a period of particular excitement in Uganda, witnessing the growth of educational and political institutions in the two decades preceding Uganda's independence. Among the schools she mentioned are some of the best-known in Uganda, several of them girls' schools, like Gayaza High School, just outside Kampala; Kyebambe Girls' High School, near the legendary Mountains of the Moon in Western Uganda; and Tororo Girls High School in Eastern Uganda, which was one of the first major projects to be funded by the United States in Uganda. Nyakasura School, also in Western Uganda, is a boys' institution started by a Scotsman, who for a long time insisted on his students wearing kilts as part of their uniform. King's College Budo, the best-known school in the country, was founded by Anglican missionaries and was the first major coeducational secondary school in Uganda.

Ntiro also provides some interesting details about Makerere College, now Makerere University, East Africa's most prestigious institution of higher learning in East Africa, where most of the region's leaders, including Julius Nyerere, Milton Obote, Mwai Kibaki, and Benjamin Mkapa, were educated. The first women students at Makerere were housed in a wing of what is now the Makerere Guest House, which was built of wood. This led to its being nicknamed "The Box"— which is still used as a nickname for the women's main residence at Makerere. Female students are often referred to as "Boxers," a term that, over time, has come to suggest the tough, no-nonsense character associated with classic Makerere women students. The origin of the name appears to be more factual than attitudinal, as suggested by Sarah Ntiro.

Wandegeya is a rather down-market suburb of Kampala, just outside the University walls, much loved and patronized by undergraduates because of its modestly priced shops and recreational facilities.

The notable personalities mentioned in Ntiro's narrative include Lady Damali Kisosonkole, the dowager queen of Buganda. She was the *nabagereka*—queen and wife—of the late *kabaka* of Buganda and first president of Uganda, Sir Edward Frederick Muteesa II, popularly known as "King Freddie." She attended Sherbone School for Girls in England, and exhibits the growing tendency of the Buganda aristocracy of the time to identify closely with the British colonials but also a belief in quality education for their daughters.

Sarah Ntiro narrated this early phase of her life—from her birth in 1926 to the early 1960s—in an interview she granted to Susan Kiguli in 1999.

Austin Bukenya and Florence Ebila

✦

I was born in Hoima, in the Kingdom of Bunyoro-Kitara. Both my parents were teachers in a missionary-founded school. I was born on a Sunday morning in Hoima Hospital. My mother was taken to hospital in a hammock. In those days there were no ambulances and my parents did not have a vehicle. She was taken to hospital at the time when people were going to church. The services then used to be very long, taking about three or more hours. My mother was taken to hospital, had me, and my birth was announced in the church service— the arrival of the first child of these two teachers. This was in 1926. My parents went on teaching in other missionary-founded schools in other parts of Bunyoro-Kitara. I went to Duhaga Girls' Boarding School in the kindergarten class in 1932. Duhaga Boarding School was for the girls who could afford to pay the school fees. I do not know if my parents could, but the headmistress, who was my godmother, a British missionary called Miss Edith Ainley, was instrumental in finding ways of promoting my education. She knew about the King George Bursary, which was being given by the government of the day to some children to go to prestigious schools, which were expensive and were out of reach for ordinary people, like King's College Budo.

That was how I went to primary five at King's College Budo, a co-educational school in the sense that there was a sprinkling of girls and hundreds of boys. But it suited me perfectly, since all my siblings and cousins were males, although Budo was far away from home [in Kampala]. But the school nurse, who was also the matron for the girls, was a princess of Toro kingdom— Princess A. Nyamutoka—and she and my mother had been schoolmates at Toro Girls School. She took it upon herself to see to it that I would not feel homesick and uncomfortable. I did not know Luganda, which was the language spoken in the neighborhood of the school. But Budo had the tradition of speaking English. Children had to speak English during the day. I do not know whether this was because the government had declared English as a medium of instruction and administration in Uganda in 1931 or because it was perceived to be an effective leveling strategy in the school.

At that time Budo's students came from all the tribes in the country and even beyond Uganda, from Kenya, Tanganyika, Nyasaland [Malawi]. Whatever the reason, the use of English was a good idea for learning to communicate beyond tribal borders. My father had been at Budo as a student and the children of old Budonians were given priority for entry into the school. In Budo I completed the primary part of the school and continued to the Junior Secondary School, then went on to Makerere College about 1946.

I was the first girl to go straight from school into the mainstream of the arts course at Makerere College, as it was called then. There was some affirmative action for people who did not fulfill the required academic standard of entry but who were deemed to have the potential for further studies. Such people were given a second opportunity by offering them entrance to Makerere in the preliminary year and a second chance to take the entry examination. If they were successful in the entry examination then they would join the formal First Year. When I went to Makerere, we were about a dozen girls, and I stayed in what is now part of the Makerere University Guest House. The male students rudely called it "The Box" because there were very strict rules for the women students, especially about when to go out and with whom to go out. Every time we went out we had to sign the warden's book, even when it was just going to Wandegeya. If one had to go out and miss a meal, one had to say whom one was going out with and where and state the reason for going out. It was in order if it was a known boyfriend, as long as his name was written down in the Warden's Book. At that time there wasn't this business of just disappearing from the Women's Hostel without telling the warden.

Although there was strict discipline, this is something which I really do not regret, because I have seen so many girls who did not have that kind of discipline fall by the wayside. They are now unrecognizable: They have been eaten up by the world because they did not take discipline seriously. While I was at Makerere the warden, together with an education officer, Miss Helen Neatby, thought that my time at Makerere had not stretched me academically and that I ought to try and go to a well-established university for further academic studies, because Makerere was still a college loosely affiliated to London University and only giving certificates and diplomas at the completion of courses. So Miss Margaret Graham, who was the women's first warden, got in touch with people in Oxford University and made enquiries about the possibility of entering that university. Oxford said that I would be considered if I had Latin.

When I left Makerere, I went to teach at Kyebambe Girls' School while making preparations to go to Oxford. That was a lovely experience for me because my mother had been to that school when it was called Toro Girls' School, and we used to tease her that she had gone abroad for higher education. Toro women who had been at school with her were delighted to see Jane's daughter come to teach at their former school. Also, one of the former Makerere women students, Majorie Kamuhigi Kabuzi, was married and was living at Nyakasura School, where her husband was teaching. That meant I could go to Nyakasura School for weekends. Boating on the volcanic lakes was one of the weekend's delights. In addition, two of my King's College Budo friends also went to Nyakasura School for teaching practice: the late Erisa Kironde, whom I had been with from primary five at Budo; and Nelson Mugerwa, who until recently was with the Teaching Service Commission.

While I was at Kyebambe, there were some expatriate staff who knew Latin well and were willing to teach Latin. After passing my Latin examinations I was admitted to Oxford University, where I went to read a history honours degree. It was an exciting time, a learning experience as well as an opportunity for interacting with all sorts of people from various parts of the world. The students of East Africa formed the East African Association. This comprised students who came from East Africa regardless of their ethnicity or background. There were two students who were the sons of the governor of Tanganyika; others were children of British nationals who were working or had worked in East Africa; others were children of Kenya, Uganda, and Tanganyika. Somehow we all felt that we had a common destiny.

I also had a "home" in Oxford because one of the rectors in the neighbouring villages had been in Hoima as a priest and at Budo as a teacher doing missionary work. This meant that when other students broke off at the end of a term and went to their homes, I also went to my "home." Since it was a rectory, it had a huge house and I had a room to myself where I could relax and keep my belongings that I did not need at the university, and I could be a member of a family.

When I was at Oxford, I made friends with some young Englishwomen who are still my friends. One of them travelled with me, when we finished our courses and were waiting for our examinations results, throughout Europe. In those days we could hitchhike, and one of our stopping places was in Rome.

Susan, my friend—she is now Lady Susan Briggs—had been to a convent school where we could stay. It was in one of the convents just outside the Vatican. The nuns fed us extremely well and were so generous to us. The nuns were very hospitable to us and very protective. They helped us choose the places of touristic interest which we could visit for our enlightenment and enjoyment. They also drew out attention to the dangerous spots for girls in such a huge international city.

After Oxford I went to Bristol University to do a course in teaching. I did not have to study for a whole year because I had already done a year at Makerere. I was at Bristol for one term and got my diploma in teaching. I was very lucky that a friend of mine who was an engineering student at the time in another part of England had a car, which he lent me so I could use it to do my teaching practice.

Miss Margaret Graham had also retired from Makerere and lived in Bristol, where she was head of a teacher training college. It was wonderful for me to have a friend from my Makerere days near at hand, and many things worked out beautifully for me, like selecting schools for my teaching practice. One of the schools where I went to do my teaching practice was Sherborne School for Girls. It is a famous school for society girls and was twinning with Gayaza High School. The second Nabagereka of Buganda, Damali Kisosonkole, had gone to school there. I made some friends there too.

When it was time for me to come back, I decided to bring with me the bicycle I had used in Oxford as a student. This offered me an opportunity to see parts of the world I had never dreamt of visiting. I asked the Colonial Office if I could come by sea since that way I could safely transport my bicycle. I sailed from Britain around Spain into the Mediterranean Sea, into the Suez Canal and the Red Sea, then into the Indian Ocean and up to Mombasa. I travelled by train from Mombasa to Kampala. In Kampala, I found my father and many Banyoro family friends, who excitedly waited for my arrival. The train was very late, but they still waited for me. There was great excitement. We stayed in Kampala for the night, and the next day I went to Gayaza High School to see the Headmistress, Miss Joan C. Cox.

Miss Cox had found me in Oxford Street on the last Saturday of shopping before Christmas, after I had left Bristol. In the Christmas season Oxford Street is very crowded, and in this crowd (a sea of white faces), someone screamed at me, "*Katonda yeebazibwe! Nkusanze*" [Thanks be to God! I met you]. It was Miss Cox. Apparently she had been trying to get in touch with me and had failed to do so. She wanted to recruit me to teach at Gayaza High School. Previously I had been asked to go to Budo to teach some courses or undertake other responsibilities. I was asked to be the assistant warden of the girls, a post which meant my working under a European, looking after African girls. This was unacceptable to me. I envisaged a situation where I would be blamed for the girls' behaviour and the European would be commended for the girls' good behaviour and successful performance. I turned down that offer and was going to return home without securing any employment opportunity. Well, Miss Cox had invited me to go and teach at Gayaza, so on my first morning in Uganda I went and formalized the contract. Then I went home to see my parents, father, mother, relatives, and friends. When we got home I had a wonderful reception. One of the missionaries working in Hoima and his wife, who had encouraged me to go and study abroad, had a huge reception for me, which was attended by the whole community—chiefs and their wives, religious leaders, schoolchildren, passersby—for my home area people were very excited. There I was, at home with my luggage from England, including my bicycle. When I had settled down, my mother called me aside and asked me to do her one big favour.

She requested me not to ride my bicycle, for only the girls in town who were perceived to be loose did that. So that was the end of my dream of riding my bicycle, which had made me sail home through the Suez Canal, spending about a month on the way. I used to watch that bicycle being ridden by a male servant going to the market, or even my brother, but not I, its owner. Well, after about a fortnight I left Hoima and went to Gayaza, and apart from the domestic science teacher, I was the only African member of the teaching staff. All the other teachers were British missionaries. We worked very well together.

One of the problems that came up quite early on during the time I was at Gayaza was the salary I was going to be paid (I do not remember the exact amount) but it was three-quarters less than what the male counterparts were going to be paid. I discussed this matter with Miss Cox and told her that I would go on teaching but I would not like to be paid. I did not want to accept that which I regarded as an insult. It wasn't the amount of money, but it was the principle: that a man—there was one who had been at Oxford with me and had got a lower grade than myself—would earn more than I by virtue of his gender. So I decided that I would teach for six months without being paid and then call it a day. I knew I had some obligation to do some work within a government-sponsored school as a way of showing my appreciation for having been given a scholarship to study abroad.

Before long the story reached Government House at Entebbe as it was called then. In Government House the lady of the house was an Oxford graduate like myself. She was outraged that I could even consider leaving the noble profession of teaching, but I told her that I could not fight a battle by myself. At that time I found out that there was not a single African woman graduate in the whole of East and Central Africa. Well, the people in power thought it would be very embarrassing that an Oxford graduate could not be contained in her home area and practice the profession for which she had been trained. They feared this could be sending out wrong signals to people who were encouraging girls to go on with higher education. So it was decided that, since I was the only one, I should be given what I wanted: "After all, she might even get married before long."

From that incident the Ugandan government started paying graduate women like graduate men. Later this spread to the whole civil service. Thus the principle of equal pay for equal work was launched and established.

While teaching at Gayaza I was very happy there, and it is only my students who might make comments on how they perceived me and how I appeared to them. In my second year of teaching, two people who were teaching in my home area where I grew up—that is, in Hoima—went to England for further studies and were not replaced. So I decided, out of loyalty to my home area, to go and teach there and assist the students during the school's third term, when the students were sitting for national examinations. So I taught at Duhaga Junior Secondary School from September 1957 to December 1958 and saw them through the examinations. But I stayed there for about two years until I got married. It was an interesting period also because wherever I went I was a new phenomenon. People did not know how to treat me and they never knew how I was going to react. About the late 1950s, I became the acting head of Duhaga Junior Secondary School.

In Y.W.C.A, we were the pioneers of the family planning association. I lived at Makerere as a housewife; my husband was teaching at the Makerere Art School. We lived there until my husband was offered a job in London. One of the things that happened while I was at Hoima in November 1958 was that I was appointed a member of the Legislative Council. Around this time, some Americans wanted to put up a school for girls in Uganda. Most of the schools then were missionary-based, but the American constitution did not allow American funds to be invested in schools with a religious base. So we found a way of going around this. The school hall was built with alcoves instead of a chapel and each religious group had its own alcove.

The other question was whether the school would have enough girls to fill a full-blown secondary school. Two of my friends and I convinced the Americans that there were more than enough girls to fill such a school. I promised them that I would move all over the north of Uganda to sensitize people about the need of educating girls and there would be enough girls to fill a secondary school. Unconvinced, the Americans decided to put the school near the border so that if Ugandan girls could not fill it, they would find Kenyans to fill it.

At that time I was heavily pregnant. They were amused and quite rightly at my promise to mobilize people too, because we had our last meeting on Saturday morning and I had my second son on that Saturday night. When my second son was born, my husband had been given a job in London and we moved on. Then I lived the life of a housewife, which I enjoyed because I wanted to be near my sons during the formative years. While at Makerere as a student, I had done educational psychology and we had learned how parents were crucial to a child's growth and development. I had grown up with parents who cared for me and I did not see why I could not give the same treatment to my children. There were also stories about child abuse, which I really did not want to happen to my own children.

When I was in Uganda, I had a fair amount of exposure by being in the Legislative Council, where some members were elected but others were appointed like myself. I was reminded recently that I was the first legislator to talk about environmental protection. The other concerns I took an interest in were girls' and women's education, as well as their welfare and well-being. Some Indian women lawyers told me that there wasn't a law bringing together all the marriage systems. The Hindu and Moslem marriages were not in our statute books. So if there was child abuse or domestic violence in those marriages there was no way of taking the culprits to court, because legally such marriages did not exist. Young Indian girls would be brought in from India for arranged marriages and the girls who did not know English, Luganda, or Swahilli were completely under the thumb of the mother-in-law, and if they had not brought enough dowry, they were harassed and mistreated, and many of them committed suicide, but there was no provision to take the people responsible to court. So I brought a Private Members' Bill motion because African men did not want to be involved in other people's marriage problems. Even though there were Indian ministers, they did not want to be labeled people who exposed the goings on in the Indian community. So we were the only people who dared to point out what was going wrong. Once we had tabled the bill, then all the information came in and there was debate and the bill was eventually passed as an Act of the Legislative Council and it became law. This is why I am interested in the case that is going to be the first case in which a Hindu marital problem is going to be subjected to courts of law. Before I brought in the Private Members' Bill, this would have not been possible.

To tell you about the environment: One would know that an African had entered a house at Makerere when all the trees and hedges were being cut down. Even the Uganda Electricity Board would come and cut down trees to install their wires and poles. This was really damaging the environment, so I went and raised my concern and asked that there should be a law to make sure that people simply should not cut down trees. That was nearly forty years ago. Once we had tabled the bill, then all the information came in and there was debate and the bill was eventually passed as an Act of the Legislative Council and it became law.

Loise Kalondu wa Maseki
A COURAGEOUS WOMAN

Kenya 2000   Kikamba

Mama Loise Kalondu wa Maseki was born in 1914 in the Kitui District of the Eastern Province of Kenya. No longer very physically mobile due to her old age, she is still energetic and very cheerful, actively involved in her current women's groups and farming activities, which she manages from her chair on the verandah of her house. On the day she provided this interview, she had grown tired, but refused to stop for the evening, saying: "Let's talk my child. What do you want to know? I have thrown sleep out of the window." She happily narrated her story, from the colonial period through the Mau Mau struggles for independence to the post-independence era.

Mama Kalondu's independent mind and strong spirit are revealed in such episodes as her confrontation with the white missionaries in her area, whom she defied in allowing her daughter to marry a white man. While raising twelve children, educating them all, and starting a business that would provide them a financial legacy, she became a model farmer and a leader of other farmers. During the transition period between the late 1950s and 1964, as Kenyans were fighting for political freedom, Mama Kalondu joined other women all over the country in an association called Maendeleo ya Wanawake. This nongovernmental organization, which remains active today, was created to bring development to women at the grassroots level, and to empower women financially so that they might independently manage their affairs.

In her late eighties at the time of this interview, Mama Kalondu remains an outstanding, formidable leader, known in Kitui as a role model in modern farming techniques, and as a woman who supported education for girls and encouraged other women in self-development.

Sheila Ali Ryanga

◆

When we were young, families or friends used to work together helping each other's families. We called this *mwethya*. I used to go with another girl, and we would cultivate one time on our farm, and the next time on their farm. We used to do the same during harvesting and we would sing good songs as we worked. I was a big girl when we went for *mwethya*.

Then I met people of God who told me the good news of God. Then I became a Christian and went to Mulango Missionary School [at the Africa Inland Mission], where I met the man I married. His name is Timotheo Maveki. At the Africa Inland Mission we were taken care of by a missionary family by the name of Aveck. Miseveki [Miss Aveck] was a nurse I used to assist. I joined that family when my mother put me in school in Mulango. I stayed with Miseveki and my mother paid school fees of fifty cents until the missionaries discovered that my mother was a widow. Then Miseveki took over the school fees and also bought me clothes. She did that for me while I assisted her with her household chores.

I went to school from 1934 to 1937. I was married on a Saturday at 2 P.M. in 1935. My first child was born in 1936. How could I be so foolish as to forget such a happy day? I met my husband in Mulango. He was a primary school teacher. Now I can read the Bible in Kikamba. It is Kiswahili that I don't know well. I was in school while I was married because my mother-in-law generously allowed me to go to school until standard five. In Mulango we were taught how to march and I used to be caned for missing steps. But I learned very well later and was awarded a marching prize for the area. I sang and danced in *wathi*, the peer dance for young women and men, until I married. I danced in *wathi* before I became a Christian and afterwards.

In 1954 my daughter was to marry a white man who was a teacher, but the missionaries said that it was not God's will that a black person should marry a white person. The white man was then transferred from Kitui to a high school in Kakamega in an effort to separate him from my daughter. Bibi Davis, one of the missionaries, did not like the idea of my daughter marrying a white man. She became annoyed and one day, when I passed near her, she kicked me from behind. I was enraged. I turned back to her and told her, "I will kick you till you learn never to kick another Mukamba woman." Then I kicked her so hard she fell down.

Other Akamba women asked me why I had kicked a white woman and if I was not afraid. I replied that I had done to the white woman what she had done to me. Many days later that white woman apologized, saying that we were both Christians and should ask forgiveness of each other. So in 1959, when the marriage of my daughter to the white man took place, I told Bibi Davis that she should not interfere with my daughter's marriage because when her daughter decided to get married she would not see me interfering.

When the Maendeleo ya Wanawake movement began in the mid 1950s I joined it. One time we went to the Kaloleni section of Nairobi and we were well received by the Honorable Ronald Ngala and President Daniel Toroitich Arap Moi, who was then vice president. We had a meeting of all Maendeleo ya Wanawake groups in Kenya. Our leaders were Mrs. Jael Mbogo, the national leader, and Mrs. Nzioka, who was our leader from Kitui. Also there was Masaa wa Nzia. The coastal leader was Meggy Gona. This was during the early 1960s.

We had requests to put forward to the government ministers. We told them that women were tired of staying alone at home while their men went to work in Nairobi. The ministers laughed. We then told them that we were tired of trying to reach remote villages by walking on foot. We needed vehicles to enable us to help others benefit from Maendeleo ya Wanawake. We were promised vehicles and soon after that we got them. Our Land Rover in Kitui is still running.

My husband, the teacher, and I became farm leaders long ago. I used to travel sponsored by the Ministry of Agriculture to see what other farmers were doing in the 1960s. In 1959 and 1960 I attended a training program in agriculture at the Better Living Institute in Kitui. This was during the colonial era. Because my husband was busy teaching he allowed me to go to various places and do the training. I used to go to Meru, Nyeri, and Isiolo to be shown how other farmers worked. The Ministry of Agriculture took me and a few others around as farm leaders from our area.

In the 1960s and 1970s, the D.C. [district commissioner] of Kitui used to come with the district agricultural officer, elders, and groups of farmers from other areas to see my farm. I raised laying chickens. I bought my chicks from Kigwaru Farm and I sold eggs. After selling these chickens, I bought other chicks from Langata Farm. I stopped chicken farming after my husband died in 1977. Then I prayed to God to give me money to build shops because my husband and I had planned during the 1960s to do this. God gave me the money to build three shops. Then I said to myself that a person should leave an inheritance for her children. I have six daughters and six sons. Therefore I shared the shops. One shop is for the six daughters and two shops are each for the two sons. They will inherit them when I die. I built the shops with the money that came from my farming. Are you hearing me, my mother?. . .

During the time of Mau Mau we were living in a certain way. When the government announced that all Mau Mau would be arrested, my husband told me to hide all of the letters from the Kenya African Union [KAU]. Even if you are a government agent, I'm still going to tell you. I hid the letters in the bush so that the imperialists would not find them. I hid them by covering them with stones in one place. Then I removed them and hid them somewhere else, for fear that they would be found. I did this repeatedly until sunset. We were neither helping the Mau Mau fighters nor fighting for them. We sympathized with them when Jomo Kenyatta was imprisoned by the colonial government. When Kenyatta became president, the colonialists said, "The monkey has come down from the trees," meaning the Mau Mau fighters came out to take over the government.

The colonial government burned the houses of Mau Mau fighters and those who supported them. Therefore, when I went to arrange for my son's marriage in 1970 in Gatundu, my Gikuyu in-laws asked me if we really had supported the Mau Mau fighters. They asked about the songs that we had sung. I sang the following song about Mbeti, a member of the Legislative Assembly before independence:

> Mbeti, you should tell the colonialists
> When Kenyatta takes over the government
> They should pack their belongings
> And go back to London.

The Gikuyu in-laws allowed the marriage to proceed happily. My daughter in-law's father, Kirori Kirite, showed me the houses where the Mau Mau had killed those who refused to help them, and also the houses of those killed by the colonial government for being Mau Mau.

I become surprised these days when I hear Kenyans talking about President Moi. I remember that, during the colonial days, I was caught and forced to pay tax for a cow that I owned. But since Kenyatta's time we have never paid tax on cows. Our independence is good. I wish that they would speak properly to each other as leaders and succeed each other in a positive way. It is bad, even before God. God hates their quarreling.

We educated all our children, both boys and girls, because, when we became Christians, we learned about education and also learned that every child comes from God and that they are equal. We took no dowry for our girls because their father said that he would not sell children who had been given to him freely by

God. I asked if I could not even get one goat from the girls' dowries and he told me that he would buy the goats for me if I wanted goats. We educated the girls with difficulty because of limited financial resources and with ridicule from our neighbors for being Christians. My husband never beat me. He loved me very much and I loved him too. [Sings:]

> When you hear ku ku ku, it is a chicken laying eggs.
> And so a boy is born into that family and teachers are increased.
> You are crying because of love,
> You are crying because of love,
> You are crying because of love.
> When you hear va va va, it is a chicken laying eggs.
> And so a girl is born into that family and teachers are increased.
> You are crying because of love,
> You are crying because of love,
> You are crying because of love.

Many people did not educate their daughters in those days because they wanted to marry them off early so as to gain cows. Now they regret it. They wish they had educated them like Maseki and Munuve, the two families that educated all their children. They have realized that there is wealth in education. At eighty-seven, I am still involved in the Maendeleo ya Wanawake movement. Women come to me for advice, and we drink tea together. Even now they also come here for the mutual love we have for one another. Currently we have twenty-four members in our local women's group. Maendeleo ya Wanawake has helped us to open schools. We have formed a widows', widowers', and orphans' cooperative bank in which each member has eighteen shares. One can get a loan according to how many shares she or he has invested.

Early in 1990 I helped to start our bank in Kakiani. Even now, I'm still its leader. These days we have *mukilye*, that means "lift her up." Each person contributes twenty shillings. I contribute under my three different names: Kalondu twenty shillings, Loise twenty shillings, Ng'a Ngwili [the wife of Ngwili] twenty shillings. This way I gain more shares. When it's my turn, I get three times the contributions of the group instead of only one. This is allowed if one can afford it. Those who contribute less get less money. I also still help women who are mistreated by family members. They come here and stay with me while resolving their problems. Sometimes they help me with some work on the farm and I pay them for it.

Translated by Mwende Mutuvi and Sheila Ali Ryanga

Pelagia Aloyse Katunzi
TWO RIDDLE POEMS

Tanzania 2000   Kiswahili

Born in 1954, Pelagia Aloyse Katunzi completed primary education, married, and had four children before her husband died of AIDS. She then embarked on an anti-AIDS crusade through counseling, educational campaigns, activism, and poetry. She has publicly declared herself to be HIV-positive, and decided to devote the rest of her life to fighting the epidemic. Her poems are an integral part of her AIDS counseling activities.

The two poems included here fall within the Swahili dialogue verse tradition. In this tradition, one poet poses a question or riddle, and other poets are expected to unravel it. In the past this was done orally and publicly; these days such dialogue is usually carried on in newspapers and on the radio.

"What Load Is This Without a Reliever?" laments the depth of suffering and loss that so many must bear, often alone and unaided, when a beloved person dies. The author explains the circumstances of the composition of the poem as follows:

> I composed this poem when I saw a woman who had lost her three children [to AIDS]. Now her fourth child was also very ill, exhibiting the HIV symptoms of the deceased siblings. As the mother watched her child, whose soul wanted to depart and yet lingered on, the mother exhibited deep sorrow and lamented loudly. I observed her with sadness. Later that child died. It was then that I realized that DEATH is a load that has no reliever. If it were possible to relieve one of impending death, the mother would have volunteered to die in the place of her child.

"What Sugar Is This That Contains Poison?" poses another riddle, in which the "sugar" is supposed to be sexual love and the poison is HIV/AIDS (UKIMWI in Swahili). Such poems, often recited in public, are a very effective way of passing on the message regarding HIV/AIDS.

M.M. Mulokozi

✦

WHAT LOAD IS THIS WITHOUT A RELIEVER?

1. Editor, I salute you, allow me into your office.
Receive this work of mine and print it.
I am helpless and anxious:
What load is this without a reliever?

2. I ask the bards of the Mainland and the Islands.
The big load is too much for me, indeed.
Dispel my ignorance, inform me:
What load is this without a reliever?

3. This load, friends, I do not know what it is.
That's why I ask you to enlighten me.
I ask for your blessings so I may rejoice:
What load is this without a reliever?

4. This is no load but a hassle. You cannot carry it on the head,
Hold it upright, grasp it by the hand,
Or hang it dangling in the air:
What load is this without a reliever?

5. The load is hard to grasp and hard to shoulder.
Indeed, it cannot be shaken even by monsoons,
And it is hard to guess what it contains:
What load is this without a reliever?

6. The load is unmistakable, it cannot be weighed,
And it is in no hurry when your heart yearns for it.
You can get it instantly for it is close by:
What load is this without a reliever?

7. All you poets of Kagera, in towns and in the countryside,
Those of Arusha and Mtwara, and over there in Dar es Salaam,
And you, my joking relations of Mara, unravel this riddle:
What load is this without a reliever?

8. Finally, here I rest, I won't go further.
Past and present do not match.
Ladies and gentlemen, decipher this riddle of the load:
What load is this without a reliever?

WHAT SUGAR IS THIS THAT CONTAINS POISON?

1. Allow me, editor, to enter your office.
I bring some news through this poem.
I want to ask about sugar—clear my doubts for me:
What sugar is this that contains poison?

2. Snow-white is the sugar;
It drives users to crave for it;
In the end it kills, alas, this sugar!
What sugar is this that contains poison?

3. Its poison amazes me, for it is tasteless
Even when you swallow it; it does not tear your entrails apart,
But later it starts working inside your body:
What sugar is this that contains poison?

4. It is drunk gracefully by both rich and poor.
Its taste in the mouth is pleasing,
Yet in the end it causes distress by turning into poison:
What sugar is this that contains poison?

5. The sugar is very mischievous and yet sweet.
It kills officers resplendent in their neck-ties,
Yet we cannot do without it, for it is essential to life:
What sugar is this that contains poison?

6. It has devoured intellectuals of all disciplines.
Even great economists have been overcome.
How can you and I escape?
What sugar is this that contains poison?

7. American specialists have been brought in
To examine the bodies of the dead,
And they established that sugar was the cause:
What sugar is this that contains poison?

8. I think whoever dislikes sugar must be deficient;
Whoever does not taste this worldly sweetness
Must be physically inadequate:
What sugar is this that contains poison?

9. We all love sugar—who disagrees?
We drink it willingly although it contains poison.
Let's drink it and face the consequences:
What sugar is this that contains poison?

10. Now I put down my pen, for I have to rush to work.
I hope you will respond and decipher this riddle of sugar.
And if you come to abstain you should tell me seriously:
What sugar is this that contains poison?

Translated by M.M. Mulokozi

Loise Kalondu wa Maseki
PROTEST AGAINST POLYGAMY

Kenya 2000   Kikamba

Polygamy has long been a part of many African cultures. Even in communities where it is standard custom and accepted by both men and women, problems often arise when a husband shows preference for a newer, younger wife, and the first wife feels neglected. Traditionally, first wives have approved and even taken part in selecting second and third wives, but in practice this custom has not always been observed.

    This version of a communal song from the Akamba community was narrated by Mama Loise Kalondu wa Maseki, and transcribed and translated by her daughter. In it, a woman laments and protests the fact that her husband has abandoned her in favor of a young wife. She lets her husband know that she is still sexually alive and desirable, and can offer as much as this new girl, "who came with her mother"—suggesting that she is an inexperienced baby. In fact, it is the husband who does not measure up. She also lets him know that her parents have sent a vehicle for her to go back to her home, showing how they still value her.

Sheila Ali Ryanga

✦

Take me in a vehicle.
Take me in a vehicle.
I have been sent for from my home.
I have been sent for from my home.
This one who came with her mother,
What does she have that I don't have?
I want a man who is eight feet.
The one who came with her mother,
What does she have that I don't have?
I want a man who is eight feet.

Translated by Mwende Mutuvi

Goretti Kyomuhendo
RWANDA: IN THE SHADOW OF GOD

Uganda 2000   English

Goretti Kyomuhendo was born in 1965 in Hoima, Western Uganda, where she received her early schooling before moving to Kampala to study marketing at the Uganda College of Commerce (now the Makerere University Business School). She then earned a master's degree in creative writing from the University of Natal in South Africa, and became the first Ugandan woman to be awarded a visiting fellowship to the famous University of Iowa Writers' Workshop. She is a founding member of FEMRITE, the Uganda Women Writers' Association, and as its coordinator she oversaw the establishment of its publishing enterprise, which put out more than a dozen titles by Ugandan women writers between 1999 and 2002.

Kyomuhendo, whose name means "precious object" in her Runyoro mother tongue, is a prolific writer whose texts have, not without controversy, come to represent the new Ugandan woman's voice: well-informed, articulate, concerned, assertive, and challenging or provocative, depending on where one stands on the issue of female empowerment. Her first novel, *The First Daughter* (1996), was an instant success, and her second, *Secrets No More* (1999) won the Best Novel of the Year Award from the National Book Trust of Uganda. Her third novel, *Whispers From Vera* (2002), was serialized in 2003 in Uganda's leading independent daily *The Monitor*. Both *Whispers from Vera* and *Secrets No More* generated heated debate over their frankness about female sexuality. Kyomuhendo has also published several short stories.

"In the Shadow of God" was written in June 2000 while Kyomuhendo was attending a writers' conference called "Women and Violence," held in Kigali, the capital of Rwanda. She had been invited to the conference in recognition of her novel *Secrets No More*, which deals extensively with the effects of political violence on women and girls.

Rwanda became internationally notorious because of the 1994 genocide in which nearly a million people were massacred in ethnic conflicts. Rwandese society, like many others in the Great Lakes region (which also includes Burundi, Congo Kinshasa, Kenya, Tanzania, and Uganda), was for centuries characterized by conflicts and rivalries among different classes, especially between the pastoral Tutsi and the agricultural Hutu. Belgian colonialism in Rwanda (1918–1960), which codified perceived racial differences and favored the minority Tutsi over the majority Hutu, hardened the differences between the two antagonistic castes that came eventually to be regarded as ethnicities, despite their common language, Kinyarwanda, and religion, the largely Catholic Christianity introduced by the missionaries. The pogroms began just before independence in 1962, when a Hutu revolt overthrew the Tutsi *umwami*, or king, of Rwanda and his representatives, attacking and killing large numbers of Tutsi in the process. Many Tutsi who survived the conflict fled into exile in neighboring countries, especially Uganda. Because of the close linguistic and cultural similarities between them and the people of southwestern Uganda, the exiles quickly adapted to their new environment; many became naturalized Ugandans, although a significant number retained their desire to return to Rwanda. Meanwhile the then-ruling Hutu systematically oppressed the Tutsi who had remained at home, and resisted all suggestions of peaceful repatriation of the exiles.

In October 1990, a group of armed Tutsi exiles calling themselves the Rwandese Patriotic Front (RPF), invaded Rwanda from Uganda. Many of the invaders were well-trained and battle-hardened fighters who had participated in the Ugandan guerrilla struggles that eventually overthrew Idi Amin and the succession of dictators after him. They advanced with lightning speed, gaining control of most of Northern Rwanda within the first few months of their campaign. The Hutu establishment in Kigali reacted with panic to these developments. Unable to deal the invaders a decisive military blow and stop their advance, the Rwandese Hutu government resorted to a systematic hate campaign against all Tutsi, including those inside Rwanda. The Hutu-controlled media, including the newsletter *Kangura* and the station Radio des Milles Collines (named for the numerous green hills of Rwanda, mentioned in Kyomuhendo's text), started advocating the "elimination" of all Tutsi from Rwandese society. The hate-machine described the Tutsi as foreigners and as "cockroaches" infesting the land, and referred to them as "long noses"—a reference to the stereotype of the more Ethiopian-type features of the Tutsi as contrasted with the more Negroid features of the Hutu. Meanwhile, the Rwandese government, probably with some help from some European countries, embarked on a plan to strengthen their defense forces and also set up militias, called the Interahamwe (Those Who Strike Together), ostensibly to act as village vigilante groups. These groups turned out to be the deadliest destroyers during the "ethnic cleansing" that was to come.

The crunch came in April 1994 when, after signing an ineffectual agreement with the invaders, the Rwandese president Juvenal Habyarimana was killed in a plane crash near Kigali Airport, rumored to have been caused by a missile, possibly fired by the RPF invaders. The killings of the Tutsi began immediately, starting with Interim Prime Minister Agathe Uwilingiyimana, a presumed RPF sympathizer, who was gunned down by her own Hutu bodyguards. The few UN military observers on the ground hastily pulled out, and the world looked on as one of the largest and most savage massacres of the twentieth century unfolded. During the next three and a half months, nearly a million Rwandese, mostly Tutsi but also including all the Hutu who tried to preach or exercise moderation, were massacred: dynamited inside public buildings where they had sought refuge, shot and, most commonly, hacked to pieces with machetes, or *pangas*. Many of the killing orgies were preceded by gang rapes and defilement of the Tutsi victims. Crucial in these grisly operations were the Interahamwe vigilantes, who identified their Tutsi neighbors and then proceeded to wipe them out.

Eventually the RPF managed to overrun Rwanda and oust the Hutu regime. Many of the murderous soldiers and Interahamwe fled into exile, most of them in Congo Kinshasa; others were arrested in Rwanda, where they were arraigned on charges of genocide. An international court was set up in Arusha, Tanzania, to deal with the cases of those who had organized and supervised the massacres; most of them were charged with crimes against humanity. The trials are likely to run through the first decade of the twenty-first century.

The Rwanda genocide shocked and traumatized the entire world, and especially the people of the region. Even in Kyomuhendo's Uganda, which had suffered all sorts of disasters since independence, including Idi Amin's dictatorship and a succession of civil wars, nothing equaled the scale and savagery of what had happened in Rwanda, which overrode all human and humanitarian codes, including religion: Several church people were tried, and so far two nuns have been convicted in Belgium for participating in the genocide. Several major sites of massacres, including churches, remain preserved as "museums" or "souvenirs" of the genocide.

One positive development since the advent of the RPF government in 1994 has been the increasing visibility and empowerment of Rwandese women in both the public and private spheres. Rwanda has one of the continent's highest number of women representatives in parliament and in the cabinet. There is also greater equity than in most African countries in the allocation of administrative responsibilities, and women, both Hutu and Tutsi, are the undisputed leaders of the healing and reconciliation process in the country.

Austin Bukenya, Florence Ebila, and Jackee Batanda

◆

For Veronique Tadjo—with love and respect

There is a church. There is a group of houses made of red bricks, standing close to the church. There are eucalyptus trees standing in two rows, lining the road to the church. And outside the church, there is a group of women and children singing. Singing songs of praise to the Lord. Sad songs. Sad tones. Their bodies answer to the slow, rhythmic drumbeats with gentle, skillfully executed gyrations.

Beyond the singing and dancing women, there stand the sprawling, spectacular green hills wrapped in fertile volcanic soils; nurturing gardens of potatoes and plantations of bananas.

Inside the church, skulls and bones recline. Smiling skulls and sleeping bones. Heads, arms, legs . . . crudely severed from their owners with Iron Age weaponry with Stone Age savagery, whispering silent messages to their spectators. The Virgin Mary stands in the corner, solitary and resolute. Her outstretched hands beckoning to her sinned children to come for salvation. Her eyes seemingly affirm: "I saw it all."

Inside the church, the walls bear evidence of the bullets, the butchery, the brutality of the killers. Of a race gone berserk, ballistic, with hatred, malevolence, madness. . . .

Outside the church, emblems of death litter the weeping grounds. Some are marked. Some are not. Otherwise peace and tranquility reign both in the weeping grounds and the green hills yonder.

Who killed them? Why were they killed?

They were sinners. They sinned at birth. They sinned to be born under a different star. Different from that of the powers that be. They were born with cockroach legs and tanned skins. They were born with pointed noses.

They had come to the temple for safekeeping.

And they were cleansed of their sin—for good.

Hannah Tsumah
MEKATILILI, THE MIJIKENDA WARRIOR

Kenya 2000   Kiduruma

Mekatilili wa Menza is a historical figure who has achieved legendary status among her people, the Giryama, who belong to the Mijikenda cluster of nine ethnic groups situated along the coastal strip of Kenya. (Others are the Duruma, Digo, Jibana, Kambe, Chonyi, Rabai, Ribe, and Kauma). She led a localized but significant resistance movement against colonialism that came to a head in 1913 and 1914, into the early months of World War I. This resistance arose in response to moves by the British to impose taxes, seize lands, and recruit Giryama for forced labor and then to fight in the war; it included efforts to eradicate traditional culture by destroying *kayas*, the sacred shrines and places of worship for the Mijikenda people.

After escaping and returning from exile, Mekatilili did lead the Giryama to win some concessions from the British, who could not afford an indigenous rebellion as World War I took hold. Her success ensured her a heroic place in the history of her people. There are almost as many versions of the story of Mekatilili wa Menza as there are communities of the Mijikenda and other coastal peoples. Some see the leadership of Mekatilili wa Menza as a prophecy fulfilled; such a prophecy would indeed be a rarity in a patriarchal community.

Hannah Tsumah, who lives in Maandani, near Kaloleni Township in the Kilifi District, here tells her version of Mekatilili's life and achievements. Perhaps because she lives close to Mekatilili's original home, her version closely resembles recorded information. After her standard-eight education, Hannah Tsumah trained as a teacher and taught for many years in both rural and Mombasa city schools. Later she enrolled in adult education courses and passed an examination that qualified her for superior teaching positions. Widowed since the late 1970s, she raised six children, and retired from teaching in 1994 to live on her farm in Maandani.

Kayas are sacred shrines and places of worship for the Mijikenda people, and each tribe had its own *kaya*. These shrines were usually secluded and situated in forests. Traditionally the council of elders lived there. It was said that when a foreigner came to one, he could not see the way in. However, if one found the way into the *kaya*, he would not see the people within, though those inside would see him. For this reason, whenever wars erupted, women and children would hide there for protection. Ordinarily no one would be allowed in except those designated. Nowadays, *kayas* still exist, but only a few are being maintained.

Sheila Ali Ryanga

✦

Mekatilili wa Menza was a Giryama woman and her home was Kaloleni. She lived at the time of the First World War. She was then already a mature person. Since childhood, she was very active and alert. When she was growing up, people used to live the *kaya* way of life in which the *kaya* elders were highly respected. When the white men came and started their master-servant relationship, Mekatilili was not very happy about it. It made her think of ways to help her people. The white man used to come and take their husbands and sons to work in the European farms without any payment. Medicine men were no longer respected; neither were their powers recognized. The *kayas* and the council of the elders were destroyed by the white men and in their place they instituted chiefs and headmen as leaders. This leadership previously was the domain of the *kaya* elders.

The chiefs and headmen were stooges of the colonialists. They did not try to help their people. Mekatilili hated the white men because they had destroyed the *kayas* and made slaves of their husbands and sons. One day a governor went to a certain chief and Mekatilili was there. The governor told the chief to give him young men who would go and fight in the war. It was during the preparations for the First World War. Mekatilili told the chief to tell the white man that, if he wanted African children to go and fight in the war, to try and pick one chick and see what the mother hen would do to him. Mekatilili was telling the white man a riddle, that if he indeed picked a chick, the hen would attack and inflict scratches on him, so as to protect its chicks. The white man did pick the chick and the hen attacked and scratched him. The white man then took a gun and shot the hen and killed it. He was returning a message: that any person who would bring resistance would be killed in a similar way.

The bitterness that Mekatilili felt caused her to take her campaign to women in various villages, encouraging them not to allow their sons to be enslaved and sent to war. She told them that the war was between Europeans and did not involve Africans. People listened to her and followed her instructions. Some men refused to offer free labor, some people refused to pay taxes, and others refused to attend the chiefs' meetings. People began agitating for the rebuilding of their *kayas*. The Europeans saw Mekatilili as one who was creating problems for them, so they caught her and brought her to court, accusing her of being a medicine woman and convening women's gatherings. When Mekatilili responded to the accusations, she said she was not a medicine woman. She acknowledged calling the meetings, but said that those meetings could have been called by any other woman who gave birth, because of the pain they felt about their children. It did not need a medicine woman to call them.

Mekatilili was an orator with a strong commanding voice that the people listened to. Men followed her because of her fearlessness and her courage in responding to white men. She fought for people to go back to the *kaya*, saying that most calamities came about because people did not adhere to the taboos and instructions of either the medicine men or the *kaya* elders. Also the Europeans had made their land unclean and they needed to go back to the *kayas* to cleanse it.

The Giryama people, led by medicine men, followed her, both men and women. They all started their journey back to the *kaya* in Giryama. Mekatilili announced that any woman who would not come with her would pay a fine.

There were some who did actually pay the fine. When they arrived at the *kaya*, Mekatilili narrated before them all the grievances they had—paying tax by force, the destruction of the *kayas*, slavery, forcing young men to fight in the war, and the establishment of chiefs who were stooges for the Europeans in place of the council of elders. People were moved by her words and agreed with her. Medicine men were called upon to cleanse the land. These, together with the *kaya* elders, administered some oaths for unity.

They administered three types of oaths: the oath of Mwanza, the oath of Fisi, and the oath of Mukushekushe. Whoever broke these oaths would get a mother's curse, or one would simply die. After taking each oath, the herbs used for cleansing the *kaya* were put into water pots which were carried by women. These women sprinkled the herbal water in every place where there was water, including rivers and lakes.

Based on the powers of the oaths, people refused to attend chiefs' meetings. Local cases were presented to *kaya* elders as in the past, and no one paid taxes. The chiefs who were stooges were told to stop giving away Giryama children as bribes or reporting where the youngsters were hiding. The chiefs feared the people because the community believed in Mekatilili.

Clashes began between the Giryama and the European colonialists. The Giryama could no longer be governed and they were not afraid of guns. Mekatilili urged people not to be afraid of the white men. She went to many places, including Marafa and Galana, urging the people to be united, with the intention of fighting for their rights as citizens. Commands by the white rulers were neither accepted nor implemented. Some medicine men and a man called Wanje supported Mekatilili. These urged other people to support her as well.

When clashes increased, Mekatilili and Wanje were caught by the white men through the help of the chiefs. To make sure that they would no longer incite their people, they were sentenced and banished to a prison in Kisii [a town in Nyanza Province, in western Kenya], very far from their home. They did not stay in jail long. They ran away and travelled back home, walking all the way from Kisii to the coast. They reached home and had many months of working with the people quietly, without being seen by the white men who by now were looking for them. The white men gave orders, offering a reward for anyone who could report the whereabouts of Mekatilili. Four months later she was caught at her home, at a time when she had already prepared her people for a resistance. . . . Finally the white men saw that they could not contain her nor influence what she was doing. They decided to make her a leader of her people. She told the white men that, if they wanted peace, they had to agree to the re-establishment of the *kayas* and the council of elders. The white governors agreed to her conditions. The Giryama people were victorious because of Mekatilili. In her old age she settled down at Kaloleni, her home.

Her death was miraculous. She was pounding [grain] in the village, and then the earth opened up slowly as she sank with her mortar, pounding until she disappeared under the ground. To this day in the village, there is a medicine man who claims to be possessed by Mekatilili's spirit whenever he is healing a sick person. When possessed, the spirit tells him which herbs would heal the sickness. Her grave is at the place where she sank with her mortar. To this day, there is a bush at the grave, which is never cleared. Instead it is used as a shrine. The village, however, has moved slightly away from the area.

Translated by Sheila Ali Ryanga

Esther Mwachombo
I WANT SCHOOL, NOT MARRIAGE

Kenya 2001   Kiswahili

Esther Mwachombo is from Maandani in Jibana, Kilifi District. Her home was close to Ribe, a former Methodist church mission center for freed slaves, and her father was one of the first local people to become an elder in the Methodist church. Married with several children, she now lives in Kambe, near Kaloleni, Giryama.

Whereas in the highlands and the Central Province of Kenya, education for Africans started as early as the late 1890s, among the Mijikenda on the coast, formal education was slow to come for boys and girls alike. Often education was viewed as something for the former slaves, who were said to be lazy and had nothing else to do. Through the advocacy of the church missionaries, the Mijikenda community began sending boys to school in the morning, while they continued to herd cattle in the evening. Girls, for the most part, continued to be prepared for marriage from their childhood. Mwachombo's experience is therefore quite remarkable, made possible only by her relationship with the missionaries and by her own strength of spirit and determination to receive an education.

Beginning in the 1940s, Mwachombo was a pioneer in education for girls in Jibana. She became a teacher, a social worker, and a school matron, and worked with several church and national women's groups. She also won renown in her community as an expert on progressive farming practices and an authority on raising chickens for eggs (layers) and meat (broilers), and she continues to receive groups of people who come to consult with her on these subjects. Like other women in this volume, she was pleased to be interviewed. Her life story has become a model for other families considering the value of education for girls.

Sheila Ali Ryanga

✦

When I first went to school, I made up my mind that I would not get married until I completed school. I desired to learn so much that I did not want anyone to stand in my way. It is after I completed school that boys came to propose to me. I told them that I was considering their requests. There was one boy whom I had asked to wait a while, but instead he did the contrary. He took his family to meet my parents and asked them for my hand in marriage. When they told my father their intentions, he called and asked me in front of all of them if I loved that boy. I told them that I did not want to be married at all. My father insisted that I should marry. He arranged the marriage with the boy's family and took part of the dowry to be paid for me. My father preferred that I marry that boy.

I refused and said that I could not stand in church to say "I do," confessing love which I did not have for the boy. My father refused to listen to me. He said that the dowry had already been taken and he could not pay it back. Therefore I had to get married. My mother supported my father, and insisted that I get married, because in those days, a woman could not express views different from those of her husband.

I decided to go back to the missionaries, to ask them to lend me enough money to enable me to pay back the boy so that he would not have to marry me. That was in 1948. A missionary called George Martlew and one African pastor, upon hearing about my case, told me not to worry but to go on with my teaching at the school, and that they would find out what could be done. George Martlew the missionary gave me a message to give my father: "Tell your father that Mr. Kombo and I will visit him at home."

When they came, father was not happy with their suggestions. He asked them why they made girls go to school when they needed to be given in marriage. The missionaries answered, saying that refusing to educate girls was something of the past. They told my father to name the amount of money that was paid for my dowry. Then they gave my father money so that he could go and repay the boy who wanted to marry me. The boy got his money back, but my father was furious because he felt humiliated by my disobedience. It was not easy for me, to have my mother blaming me and my father quarrelling with me. I had disregarded the traditions and had brought shame to my parents. That was the year that I was transferred from Maandani School, to go and work at Ribe secondary school as a matron. . . . I encountered problems because it was not usual for girls to go to school in those days. In addition, the idea of refusing to be given in marriage was not only seen as abnormal; it was unheard of in my community.

In those days more than now, a girl's life moved toward marriage. Customarily, boys were more valued than girls, a view that made the education of girls difficult. When a girl attained the age of about ten years, her parents were already preparing her for marriage. When a suitor came to a girl's parents, it all depended on the father. If the father liked the boy and accepted him, then the girl would have to marry the boy whether she liked him or not. She had no choice. Therefore, my refusing to marry a boy who had already paid dowry, and returning the boy's dowry to him, were both shocking to many. My mother was more difficult and gave me more problems than my father. My mother quarrelled a lot about my going to school because, when I was in school, she did not have someone to help her take care of my younger siblings. She feared that she would not be able to teach me housekeeping and cooking in preparation for living in my husband's home. But later, when I was working, my mother saw the benefits of educating a girl. When there was the great famine called Njaa ya Nganu [wheat famine], my parents and my siblings did not suffer. They ate the food that I bought and provided for them. I was able to buy clothes for them and to educate my young brothers. She saw how a girl was able to do many things, which many boys in the community were not able to do. My mother came and asked for forgiveness from me. She confessed that she had not understood the concept of education when she disapproved of my going to school. The provisions I could supply during the famine period made her realize that this same daughter who was able to take care of her was the same person who had resisted early marriage.

I started going to school in 1943 at Ribe School. In standard four, I sat for the Common Entrance Examination and passed. I could not go on with school because my father could not pay the intermediate school fees for me. In 1947 the missionaries at Ribe employed me to teach a standard one class for a year. During this time, Mrs. Martlew, the missionary's wife, taught me how to teach small children. In 1948, I was transferred to go and teach at Maandani for one year. In 1949, I stopped teaching and was taken to college to train as a matron. On completion, I became the matron of Ribe Secondary School for four years. Later I was called upon to work as a woman social worker for the church. Through this job, I was taken to Kabete College, where I trained for one year as a woman social worker, after which I was employed as a worker for Maendeleo ya Wanawake, a national association for Kenyan women, in Kwale District. I got married in 1959. I left employment when I began having my children, because of ill health, but I went on assisting groups of churchwomen.

I was a leader of women's groups when I worked in the church. I organized courses for women to learn about cleanliness, cookery, keeping chickens, and general farming techniques. I learned all these skills from the missionaries and the different places I had visited. I had a small farm for vegetables and tomatoes that was used by the agricultural officers as a model farm, to teach other people better farming techniques. I was a model farmer in my home area. Already, in those days, I was keeping laying chickens for eggs. This was used as a model for other women in my home community, as well as in other areas of the Coast Province. There were very few African women then who understood such progressive activities. When I became a teacher at Ribe, I was the first African woman to teach in my home area. Equally, I was the first African woman to be a secondary school matron. Meggy Gona and others came long after me. In 1960 I left the leadership of women's groups and concentrated on general farming and the keeping of laying chickens for eggs. This is because my health had deteriorated and I could not manage activities that involved lots of movement.

Translated by Sheila Ali Ryanga

Charlotte Poda
FROM SLAVERY TO SCHOOL

Kenya 2001   Kiswahili

Charlotte Poda's ancestors were slaves. Like many people descended from slavery, she prefers not to talk about her family's history in detail. She lives in Rabai, on the Kenyan coast, which became one of the centers for freed slaves after the abolition of slavery was declared in Europe and the United States. Rabai and other freed slave centers along the coast—Ribe, Kaloleni, Mazeras, and Frere Town in Mombasa—were also missionary centers. (Ribe and Mazeras were Methodist, Rabai and Kaloleni Anglican.) Most slaves who came to Kenya were from Nyasaland, now Malawi. Indigenous Kenyans who were enslaved were usually taken across the Indian Ocean to India, Oman, and other Asian countries.

Charlotte Poda was educated in a mission school in Mombasa in the late 1940s. Very often, former slaves and their children were employed as teachers and clerks because of their education and their close association with whites. Poda became known not only to local missionaries and colonial officials, but also to influential Africans who would become leaders of an independent Kenya; as her story demonstrates, she could hold her own in both the black and the white communities.

In this selection, Charlotte Poda talks about her founding of an independent black school, which she successfully maintained, with the help of local women, against the objections of both the local tribal chief and white missionaries and colonial administrators. In the 1950s, the curriculum in British-run schools included only what Europeans thought Africans should know, whereas in independent schools such politically charged topics as land ownership could be freely taught. The mushrooming of independent African schools like Charlotte Poda's, which met with considerable resistance, was an important facet of the movement toward independence.

Sheila Ali Ryanga and Ali Wasi

✦

My name is Charlotte Poda Mwatsama. I was born right here in Rabai, but I never lived here during my childhood. First of all, my mother passed away when I was a child and I grew up with only my father at home. My grandmother lived with us but in her own house. In those days it was the custom to live with your grandmother, but I really did not feel like staying with her. At one time my grandmother took me to her ex-slave friend who was a Banyoro by tribe. Her name was Binti Juma. These two were such close friends that they could be mistaken for sisters or close relatives. Binti Juma lived in Mombasa, in an area called Majengo. Binti Juma lived with her husband, Akilimali Bin Omari, who was from the Zaramo tribe in Tanzania. Binti Juma had no child of her own, so she asked my grandmother to let me go and live with her. She was to bring me up as she would her own child, a practice that was common in those days. Binti Juma, however, was a Muslim, and there was the fear that I would be forced to convert to Islam. My father's fears were allayed when they assured my father that I would remain a Christian.

I am grateful to Binti Juma and Akilimali Bin Omari, because I lived with them happily and my father's requests were fulfilled. Every Sunday I was encouraged to attend Sunday school. I was given thirty cents, twenty cents of which was my return bus fare between Majengo and the Cathedral. The remaining ten cents was for me to give as alms. I stayed with this family until I started going to school in Mombasa. The only missionary school in those days was at Manyimbo, and the European teachers were Ms. Lloyd and Ms. Valerie. I later moved from the home of Binti Juma and Akilimali Bin Omari to live with these teachers.

At the Mombasa Cathedral there was a stone building called Ladies' House. I lived in this building with these European teachers. They took over paying my school fees, since my father's relatives opposed further schooling for me. They could not understand why a girl had to continue with schooling instead of getting married. The subjects I studied included home science and methods of assisting the European women in translating and interpretation. You know, in those days everything was done by and for Europeans. In 1940 I began to see a young man in Mombasa, after which I returned home to Rabai, where I stayed until my wedding day on 13 June 1941.

The Struggle to Start a School

Before 1960, Madam Maria and I got the idea of starting a nursery school. We asked why not, since in other regions women had started their schools under trees as they waited to build classrooms. We thought we could start a nursery school for African children without informing the governing authorities. But we took the proposal to the primary school committee in the area. The committee was not opposed to our proposal, but they did not pass it on for approval to the relevant hierarchies. In 1960, the women's group invited the Honorable Ronald Ngala, who was then a Kenyan activist advocating for independence. We informed him of our intention to register a mother's union at Rabai. In order for the union to be registered, the group had to stipulate the aims and objectives of its operation. Ngala intervened and told the authorities that our union should be registered because the mothers wanted an organization that would spearhead the founding of a nursery school and entertainment for young people. The union was registered with his help.

After the union was registered, the next problem was getting the land where the school could be built. We tried to acquire a church building that had been put up by Ludwig Krapf, the missionary and founder of the mission center at Rabai. The church elders initially accepted the idea, but later on changed their minds and said the building belonged to the church and was for church use only. My husband took the matter to the European district commissioner, Mr. Kelly, who accepted the mothers' union proposal. He also proposed to give his own cash donation toward the nursery school because, since that building had been abandoned by the Europeans, he saw no reason why the women could not use it as a nursery school. But the church elders continued to object to the idea.

When I decided to start the nursery school under a mango tree, I began with six children of African political leaders in the area. The next opposition came from Ms. Chilson, a European social worker. She joined the colonial chief in opposing me, and started another nursery school nearby. Her school building was put up quickly compared to our school, whose support came only from the parents of the few children. The local women said that I should continue with the school even if it had a thatched roof instead of iron sheets. We all agreed that we did not want our children to go to Shikadabu nursery school, which was in the same compound as the colonial court.

Ms. Chilson's school offered toys to attract children, but the African mothers said they were not interested in those toys, since our children were used to playing with coconut shells. Ms. Chilson offered milk to the children in her school, but the African mothers said that their children did not need milk. They instead offered to provide our children with porridge. Every mother brought some flour and they prepared the porridge on the school premises. So our children drank porridge instead of milk.

The business community was on our side. One day the Honorable Ronald Ngala brought us a visitor, Mr. Francis Khamis, a journalist who sought to know why we were putting up our own school, when there was one already in the surrounding area. Before I could answer him, the women said, "This has nothing to do with you. It's our business." But there were also two women, one from Kisauni in Mombasa, and the other from Tsunza, near Mariakani, who thought we were disobeying the government by not taking our children to Chilson's school. Still, other mothers and some of my teachers brought us chairs and even clothes for the nursery children.

Mr. Bengo, an elderly man who had land in Rabai, offered us a place to put up the school. We built the school ourselves, using our own hands. The chief, who paid homage to the Europeans, came and ordered us to stop, since we had not sought for his permission before putting up the school building. He sent the village elders to stop us, but we did not listen to them. We just continued with our building work. The chief tried to intimidate me by bringing the colonial police, the district commissioner, and the education officer, who were all Europeans, in a Land Rover to our school. The police asked why I had defied the chief's orders. The district commissioner did not understand why his colleagues were opposed to the school.

After this incident, Ms. Chilson later offered me 800 shillings—which was a lot of money in those days—but I refused her offer. She wondered what tribe I came from, saying that a Rabai woman would not have refused such an inducement. The local women stood by me, and when the chief threatened to arrest me, they volunteered to be arrested instead of me, claiming that they were the ones who had brought their children to me to teach them: "Arrest us together with the children, for we are the ones who gave her the children." Some Europeans brought more donations to support the school, but we were suspicious of them. The women refused to accept the donations, thinking that it was part of the conspiracy to close their school. So the school went on and the children increased in numbers. Some of the women who originally came from Nyasaland [Malawi] used to assist whenever my child was ill or hospitalized in Kaloleni Mission hospital, so that I could attend to the school's needs. As they looked after the children, they would sing in their mother tongue, Kinyasa, as follows:

> Push hard as you give birth.
> The child is not due yet.
> Let's wait, the child is not yet due.
> It's not yet due, let's wait.

In those days, mothers used to give birth at home and other women used to sing to keep the mother who was in labor company. Such songs too were used as lullabies.

Translated by Sheila Ali Ryanga and Ali Wasi

Katherine Wanjiru Getao
TWO POEMS
Kenya 2001 English

Katherine Wanjiru Getao was born in 1960. Her paternal grandfather was a distinguished clergyman from Kiambu with a special concern for women's education, and her father was a publisher and civil servant. Two of her aunts had been pioneer students at Makerere College. She attended Kenya High School and then continued her education in England, eventually earning a master's degree at the University of Essex and a doctorate at the University of Lancaster. She now directs the Institute of Computer Science at the University of Nairobi. However, she is most widely known as the author of the "Flakes" column in the Saturday magazine section of the *Daily Nation*, a Kenyan newspaper.

Getao has been writing poems ever since she was a schoolgirl. She says she writes poems instead of keeping a diary, so as to re-create and remember feelings and experiences. While only a few of her poems have been published, her voice is individual and unmistakable. She can occasionally be persuaded to read a poem at a poetry festival or memorial program. The poems included here deal with a woman's domestic life. In "Homework," a recitation of daily chores reveals powerful feelings of rebellion; we are left wondering what might happen next. In "Woman," a much darker poem, the water the woman carries becomes emblematic of her own predicament—denied freedom and burning with longing for another kind of life.

Marjorie Oludhe Macgoye

HOMEWORK

I bend at the hearth
And bow at the pot
To stir my sullen stews.

I crouch at the basin
And submerge my fingers in water
To soothe the soil from my clothes.

I kneel by the armchair
And lie down on the mat
To gather my rebellious dust.

I stand to attention by the door
And raise my arms for the children
To welcome my rowdy souls home.

I lie on my bed
And surrender my body to my oaths
To conquer my omnipresent husband.

WOMAN

Here in the shadow of the mountain my
callused feet beat paths into the red
slopes as I carry water from the stream where
it longed to run helter-skelter to the
ocean, and I captured it and took it,
sloshing and screaming, to pots, where I
burned it with fire. This is what I
have become. Woman. A bent head, silent,
voiceless as a dream. It screams and screams.

Qabale Kosi, Shane Halake, and Darmi Dida
ALLISOO IS AN INSULT

Kenya 2001   Borana

The Borana are a pastoral community living in the northern part of Kenya and southern Ethiopia. Like many nomadic peoples, their way of life is increasingly threatened by urbanization and changing patterns of land use, as well as drought. Borana women have traditionally occupied a subservient position in their society, widely perceived as beasts of burden who are virtually owned by men. They do not attend public meetings, which are the preserves of men. Even if they are litigants or witnesses in cases, women offer their pleas as remarks while facing away from the gathering, with heads covered, and are required to leave immediately afterward.

Allisoo are humorous, satirical songs in which Borana women ridicule men and masculinity. The songs are not directed toward a particular person, but rather describe typical situations. The singers recount the follies of men in their daily experiences, undercutting their social standing. Their songs attempt to demolish grandiose male self-images, and invite men to consider their own flaws.

Performed during the *jilla*, or naming ceremony, which allows some transgressions to be tolerated, women sing *allisoo* within the conventions of *qoosa*. *Qoosa* is an amorphous term that refers to a generic category of satirical songs and verbal art performed about men by women, about women by men, and clans and age sets among themselves. The *qoosa* sung by groups of women challenges the traditional social order by recounting the follies of men in their daily experiences. Women's *qoosa* serves as a verbal weapon for women who have been relegated to subservient positions by a male-dominated culture. As is often the case, female humor has a subversive function, allowing women to criticize men and manhood freely, and to resist male power by making fun of it.

This kind of song is passed from one generation to the next with creative additions. Although *allisoo* is known in some form by all women in Borana, and thus has been collectively written, this particular version was performed in June 2001 by three women of Madho Adhi village, in the Sololo Division of Moyale District in Kenya. The occasion was the *jilla* of Wario Huqa's child. The singers, the song, and the occasion were all common to villages in Sololo and among the Borana in general. For the most part, three soloists led the satirical song in turn while other women made up the chorus. Throughout the song, the three soloists, Qabale Kosi, Shane Halake, and Darmi Dida, articulated in multiple voices the feelings of the group.

Famous for her sharp tongue, Qabale is in her mid-thirties, married, with four children. Whenever the village engages in verbal performances specific to women, she is called upon. Consequently, she and the others have become known as village singers. None have education or formal skills from which they could earn their living. Neither is their group formal in any sense of the word. They sing because they know how to, because they enjoy singing, and also because the occasion is a communal one to which everyone contributes talents. When women are requested to come and "open their mouths for the people of the *jilla*," as the locals would say, they oblige gladly because each of them may be in need of such service one day.

In this song they emphasize the enduring spirit of the women seething under a male culture that subordinates them. This kind of song is passed from one generation to the next with creative additions, in which the central theme of resenting male power marks it and gives it its resilient identity.

Fugich Wako

✦

Allisoo allisoo, I say to you,
Allisoo is an insult, listen to me.
He walks in the village and asks about the market day.
The market is tomorrow; he sells his cattle;
He receives the money; he asks for the beer hall.
One liter of alcohol is one sip for you.
The price of one bull is one day's expense for you.
The money is not shared with his wife and son—this is shameful
He slaughters the blue bull and turns his back on cattle.
He prepares and stores the meat by himself.
He turns his back on cattle and faces the meat.
He comes home wobbling and quarrels about a fan.
After getting the fan, he quarrels about everything.
In the center of the cattle pen, he quarrels for enclosure.
In the center of the house, he quarrels for food.
I am going to market, give me food, he says.
I do not want it soft, make it hard, he says.
The hard one is unpalatable; make it soft, he says.
He slaughters a calf; he claims it is an ox.
An old cow dies; he says it is a mature heifer.
A dog snatches the lung; he says it is the breastbone.

Did you hear the case of the mean one?
I haven't; tell me.
He roasted the raw hide, did you hear?
He tied together the string meat, did you hear?
Did you hear the case of the owner of millet?
He counted the millet grains, did you hear?
He counted the entrails, did you hear?
He asked me for the small intestines, did you hear?
As he is untying the food container, did you hear?
His mother-in-law caught him, did you hear?
She asked what was happening, did you hear?
It is the norm of drought he said, did you hear?
As he licked the container, did you hear?

The bracelet got stuck, did you hear?
The bracelet cannot be broken, did you hear?
The container cannot be smashed, did you hear?
His hand cannot be cut, did you hear?
As he melts the fat, did you hear?
The dog snatched his member, did you hear?

Consumer, my consumer,
He consumes cups of porridge,
He consumes yellow maize with its coat,
He consumes fruit with their peels,
He consumes tubers with a knife,
He consumes kudu with the horns,
He consumes giraffe with hooves,
He consumes chewing gum with its wrappers,
He consumes *miraa* with sugar,
He consumes alcohol with bottles,
He consumes and squeezes out a fart.

Oh, oh, father of whoever,
We are meant for each other.
We understand each other in speech.
Oh, oh, my runner,
He is mine who has no back; he must lie down.
He is mine who takes little food.
Oh, oh, he has the nose of a milk container.
He drips mucus in the cold season.
He has a dry face in the hot season.
I will leave a word for you in death, will remember you in sleep.
Oh, oh, the one whose tuft of hair is cut,
The foolish one with mucus in the nostril,
Oh, oh, the one whose knee is like a pipe,
He is a glutton with veins on the belly,
People hate to see him.

Translated by Fugich Wako

Mbuyu Nalumango
POUNDING SONGS

Used to grind food grain, such as maize, peanuts, sorghum, finger millet, and cassava, for easy consumption, the mortar and pestle is a common apparatus in most parts of rural Zambia, as it is in much of Africa. Maize forms the staple food for the majority of the Zambian population and is either eaten whole or ground into a fine powder, which is used to prepare porridge for breakfast or to make a thick mush usually consumed at dinnertime, accompanied by stew and vegetables. Women in Zambia's communal societies typically prepare food in large quantities, in order to feed an extended family.

The process of pounding is an art, which requires precision in order to avoid spillage of food or damage to hands. In most cases two people carry out the pounding process using two pestles and one mortar, hence the importance of accurate timing during the act. The women alternate their movements up and down with the pestle in the mortar and rely on communal pounding songs to direct their motions and intervals. Because the process is lengthy and may prove monotonous and tiring, women also enjoy singing as a form of entertainment and an aid to endurance.

Some songs call attention to important issues in society, such as gender biases and traditional norms. Other songs bemoan a woman's heavy burden and express anger at men, who appear to live easy lives at the expense of women. In some cases women will rest from the singing and simply share jokes. Performed by Mbuyu Nalumango in 2001, the following communal songs were sung in Kikaonde, a language of northwestern Zambia; Chinyanja and Chitumbuka from the east; and Silozi from the Western Province. Nalumango is a member of the Zambia Women Writers Association and has edited several literary works. She is currently the head of a national publishing company in Lusaka, Zambia.

Nalishebo N. Meebelo

✦

LET ME TRY WHETHER I CAN POUND

Zambia   2001   Kikaonde

Let me try whether I can pound.
Let me try whether I can pound harder.
Let me try to pound, pay attention.
Let me try the way I used to in the past.
Let me try harder, the way I used to in the past.
Let me try the way I used to in the past, pay attention.
There are bananas in our village.
There are plenty of bananas in our village.
There are bananas in our village, pay attention.
When my breasts were still firm,
Young men used to come

to see how young women pound.
My mother sent them away.
My child is still young.
She does not remember to boil water.
She only knows how to pound.
I am old and forgotten
And my husband is gone,
But I know he will come back tomorrow.
My husband is divorcing me.
He loves those who wear makeup.
I want to return to my home.

LET US POUND, LET US POUND

Zambia 2001   Chiyanja

Let us pound, let us pound.
Oh, let us pound with our feet apart.
When the chief's wife enters the shop,
She actually has her feet apart,
With a fly whisk and walking stick in her hands.
Oh, let us pound with our feet apart.

OH, GRANDMA

Zambia 2001   Chitumbuka

Pounding is painful.
If only one could just eat.
Oh, Grandma.
When your friend's child has grown bigger,
Take the child and put it on your back.
Oh, Grandma,
Where will you find a white customer?
Oh, Grandma.

I AM POUNDING FOR MR. JOHN

Zambia 2001   Silozi

I am pounding for Mr. John.
He is lying there in idleness, Mr. John,
With his big stomach, Mr. John,
Like a toad, Mr. John.
Look at the chunks he takes off, Mr. John.
Look at the way he swallows, Mr. John.

His throat is like a bottle, Mr. John.
Ci ci ci ci, Mr. John.
Ci ci ci, Mr. John.

OH, MY VISITORS

Zambia 2001 Silozi

Oh, my visitors,
Oh, my visitors,
What are they going to eat?
No, sir or madam, I have a bit of maize meal for myself,
In a bowl with a cover.
I only ask that a young boy
Should prepare some porridge for me.

Translated by Nalishebo N. Meebelo and Mbuyu Nalumango

SIX RURAL PROTEST SONGS

These songs address several interrelated aspects of Ugandan reality today: internal war, the HIV/AIDS pandemic, the position of women, and the need for unity. The performers, Santa Apoto, Sarah Atoo, Beta Aida, Lalweny Fanta, and Christine Lamwaka, are residents or former residents of rural Acoliland, in Northern Uganda, a region seriously neglected throughout the colonial period. While providing educational and economic opportunities to the Bantu areas south of the River Nile, the British colonists relegated the Nilotic peoples of the north, bordering the Sudan, to near oblivion, recruiting them only into menial and unskilled occupations, especially the lesser ranks of the army and the police.

The early years of independence held hope for the Acoli, as Milton Obote, a member of the closely related Lango community, became Uganda's first prime minister in 1962. This, coupled with the numerical strength of the north in the security forces, seemed to promise a move toward a fairer sharing of power and economic resources between the north and the south. But in 1971 Idi Amin, then army commander, colluded with another clique within the army and overthrew Obote in a bloody coup. Fearing a backlash from the Acoli and Lango soldiers, Amin and his supporters organized a series of "cleansing" massacres that left a mass of widows and orphans in its wake. Some Acoli officers and other soldiers fled into exile, to return for the struggle that eventually ousted Idi Amin in 1979. With the return of Obote to power in 1980, the north-south hostilities continued until 1985, when the Acoli faction within the army staged a successful coup against Obote, only to be overrun in turn by Yoweri Museveni's guerrillas, who seized power in 1986.

The ousting of the Acoli-led military junta by Museveni's mainly Bantu southern and western forces seemed to convince the Acoli community that they were facing extermination. Large numbers of Acoli armed fighters fled into southern Sudan or remote areas of Acoliland. The first wave of resistance, under the name of the Holy Spirit Movement, was nominally led by Alice Lakwena, who inspired her fighters with promises of invincibility and supernatural protection against all forms of attack. Lakwena's forces advanced to within sixty-odd miles of Kampala before Museveni's government troops stopped and scattered them. She fled to Kenya in 1987, but remnants of her fighters launched the Lord's Resistance Army (LRA), under Joseph Kony, to continue the struggle.

The LRA insurgency, which has been raging over large areas of northern Uganda since 1987, is the subject of Santa Apoto's song, "I Am Sitting Down to Write a Letter." Like the husband of the persona in the song, many Acoli men left their homes and "went to the bush" to join the insurgency. As in the song, however, people have become increasingly disillusioned about the prolonged conflict, for contrary to its claims, LRA has turned into a monstrous terror gang preying mainly on the Acoli people themselves, plundering, raping, maiming, and killing helpless civilians, and abducting young boys and girls to use as child soldiers and sex slaves for Kony and his commanders.

In response to the LRA raids, the government has relocated villagers into camps, away from their fields, their sources of food and work. The camps themselves have been described as environmental and sanitary disasters. Equally disastrous has been the total destruction of the fabric of Acoli cultural and social structures. As many knowledgeable observers have pointed out, it is impossible to ensure standards of moral or social decency in the crazed war situation that has created the topsy-turvy world of the camps. Although the singer in Beta Aida's "Apoto the Girl" seems to blame the fate of the young victim of AIDS—or as it is widely called in Africa, "Slim"—on her promiscuity, an unspoken subtext is the impossibility of healthy or decent survival in such conditions.

Lalweny Fanta's "When We Say" uses the age-old wisdom of the proverb with beguiling simplicity, to identify the basic problem in Acoliland's and Uganda's situation as a whole: a lack of unity and cooperation, and the stubborn rejection of reconciliation by every side. Ethnic, religious, and political differences have escalated so that force and violence appear the only alternatives. Is it too much to ask Ugandans, the poet sings, to put their five fingers together and "hold the mingling ladle"?

Sarah Atoo's "Without Women" asks its question—"Where would the world be without women?"—with some irony, since without women there would be no world at all. Ultimately, the song describes the work of women as their "drink," using the image of sustenance to remind listeners that the nourishment provided by women is what ensures "that this world may remain very firm." In "The Monstrous Disease," Atoo sings of "Slim"—HIV/AIDS—describing the disease's decimation of homes, even whole village populations, and then urging listeners to take measures that might diminish its power.

Christine Lamwaka's "We Are Now Equal" is addressed to Joseph Kony, leader of the Lord's Resistance Army. Lamwaka refers to Kony as a "boy," and tells him that he is defeated. Women, she says, are his equals: He is not gaining from the war and neither are they.

Austin Bukenya and Florence Ebila

✦

Santa Apoto, I AM SITTING DOWN TO WRITE THIS LETTER

Uganda 2001   Acoli

I am sitting down to write this letter,
This letter to my husband,
My husband who left his home.
He left to join the rebels,
The rebels his brother died fighting for,
His brother who turned a deaf ear,
A deaf ear to his mother,
His mother who begged him to stay at home.

I am sitting down to write a letter,
A letter with words I can't put on paper,
Paper that my friend over there gave me.
She gave it so I might pour my heart out,
My heart, which is weary and tired,
So tired worrying about my husband,
My husband who left me with seven children,
Seven children who need food, clothing, school, and medicine.

I am sitting down to write this letter,
My friend who gave me the paper will write the words for me,
My words, which my husband must hear.
He should hear because I am his wife,
His wife who bore his daughters and sons,
His sons who ask for their father every day,
Every day which I live in agony,
Agony because my husband is married to this senseless war.

I am sitting down to write this letter.
I am not sure it will reach him.
If it reaches him, I pray my sorrow wears his heart down,
A heart threaded with revenge and hate,
Hate which is digging a grave for him,
A grave his body must never lie in,
Because he will die and rot in the grasses afar,
Because he will leave me in our marital bed.

I will sit and write another letter,
Another letter to this war.

I will write to war like this:
War, give me back my husband.
Untangle your hands from his legs.
Let him come home to his family.
Let his spirit be of peace.
Let my husband be free of war.
War, you have stolen all our men away.
Let them come back to their families.
Let crops sprout with joy.
Let children roll in soil with happiness.
Let wives' beds fill with warmth at night.
War, let us be, let us be.

Beta Aida, APOTO THE GIRL

Uganda 2001   Acoli

Apoto, Apoto, Apoto,
Who didn't know Apoto, the girl?
That small girl, sturdy as a mortar,
Dark and smooth-skinned
As if shea butter
Covered her body.

Apoto, Apoto, Apoto,
Who doesn't know this girl?
Now she lies in her father's hut
Over in the hills,
This once striking girl now wasted.
Have you seen Apoto today?

Apoto, Apoto, Apoto,
All your looks will go with you
To the lonely grave you looked for.
Oh, little girl,
Your breasts came out only yesterday;
We all saw them.
We, the women and men of this land, saw you grow;
Now we watch you die.

Apoto, Apoto, Apoto,
You are a heap of bones in the hut.
Why did you have to open your legs

To anyone, any man who whistled after you?
Now Slim, the thinning disease, has caught you.
No one can blame Slim.
We all know it was you, my child.
You roamed every bachelor's house.
You squeezed every woman's husband behind her hut.
We all weep for you, Apoto.
No one can look at you now.
Only those who gnash their teeth can bear your sight.
Why did you, Apoto, beauty of this land?
Why Apoto, why Apoto, why Apoto?
Why did you have to end this way?
Like this, like this, like this!

Apoto, Apoto, Apoto,
You laughed at us when we told you
To wait for your beloved,
The one God has chosen for you,
That man whose children you would bear.
But look at you now:
You are wasted
Because you opened your legs
To all the men on God's earth.
Didn't you know your times
Are times of bloody war?
Didn't you know Mr. Slim?
This gentleman would catch up with you?

I don't laugh at you, Apoto,
But I have to say,
You sought your fate alone.
Tomorrow when you die
We shall bury you,
But I will wait patiently
For any girl who dares be like you,
Any girl who saw you then and now,
Any girl who dares seek death,
Dares greet those in the land of the dead.
Tell them in that land they are not
Getting any more from our side,
Not anyone who will seek
Their fate as you did,
Not anyone who will look
For death even whether or not he wants her then.

Apoto, Apoto, Apoto,
We see you waste away before us.
What can we do? Nothing,
Or perhaps something:
We shall tell everyone,
Even those who put cotton in their ears,
Watch out!
Or you will meet a fate like Apoto's,
This dreaded illness
That everyone in every land fears and calls
Slim, Slim, Slim.

Lalweny Fanta, WHEN WE SAY

Uganda 2001 Acoli

When we say
One rat alone
Does not dig a hole,
We mean
Two heads are better than one.

When we say
A person who heeds not
Goes with feces into her mother-in-law's hut,
We mean
You need to hear others and they need to hear you.

When we say
Being near the anthill
Made the fox turn brown,
We mean
You reap what you sow.

When we say
A monkey that remains behind
Laughs at the other monkeys' tails,
We mean
When you laugh hard you might be laughing at yourself.

When we say
A hare's cunning is better
than an elephant's strength,

We mean
Think with your head, not your hand.

When we pass all these sayings on, from generation to generation,
We pass on our knowledge, we pass on our knowledge,
Our ways, our ways,
Our learning, our learning,
For a better us, for a better us.

Put your five fingers together
And you can lift a pot,
You can grip firewood,
You can hold a mingling ladle.
Two is better than one;
Three is better than two.
Let us all put our heads together,
Work together,
For a better us,
For a better tomorrow,
For a better community.

Sarah Atoo, WITHOUT WOMEN

Uganda 2001 Acoli

Soloist: Without women really,
Which direction would the world take to develop?
Which direction would the world take to develop?
Which direction would the world take to develop?
Which direction would the world take to develop?

All: Without women really,
Which direction would the world take to develop?
Which direction would the world take to develop?
Which direction would the world take to develop?
Which direction would the world take to develop?

Soloist: It is true what women do
cannot be counted.

All: Without women, really,
Which direction would the world take to develop?

Soloist: It is true that only a foolish man
Despises a woman.

All: Surely what women do
cannot be counted.

Soloist: You people, really, without women,
Which direction would the world take to develop?
Which direction would the world take to develop?

All: You people, really, without women,
Which direction would the world take to develop?
Which direction would the world take to develop?

Soloist: All of us women, let us join hands.

All: To develop this world so that our homes are strong.

Soloist: Aai, development is truly in the hands of women.

All: Truly, the strong gourd should not crack.

Soloist: Clansmen, see my drink.
Clansmen, see my drink.

All: What is that drink of yours?

Soloist: My drink is my homestead.
My drink is building that school.
My drink is casting a vote.
My drink is . . .

All: Seeing that the homestead is not dead,
That the chief's court is not overgrown with grass,
That the roads are clean,
That the children have uniforms,
So that this world may remain very firm!

Sarah Atoo, THE MONSTROUS DISEASE

Uganda 2001 Acoli

My people, see,
This monster disease has finished us in this world.
You see, Slim has finished the world.
It has finished us, the young and the old.
You see, Slim has wiped out the women.

It has wiped women off this world.
You see, Slim has emptied the homestead.
It has emptied the whole homestead, really.
You see, graves surround the homestead, really.
Graves surround us, really, on all sides.
Shortly I will go to the village chief, eh, eh.
He will be down with this disease.
You see the vicar has dried up, really.
People, he has dried up completely.
My people, we are confused.
This disease, where did it come from and where is it taking us?
I drink the herbs in vain, really.
This disease has refused, really refused to go.
Clansmen, hear my fading voice.
Open your ears to these words.
I am only a woman beseeching you.
Because of this disease which has killed the home,
Even if you look down on women,
First, open your ears wide,
Listen to my fading voice.
Let's all put our hands together.
Let's chase this disease, chase this disease.
Really, how about you?
What will you do? What will you do to rally against this disease?
Really, you women, men, and elders,
Put your hands together for the sake of this disease.
Have relations only with those you are married to.
If you act like goats in the dry season,
This disease will wipe away all of us.

Christine Lamwaka, WE ARE NOW EQUAL

Uganda 2001 Acoli

We are now equal.
My brother, come back home.
My brother, come back home.
The world has already defeated Kony.
Kony, come back home.
The world has defeated the boy.
Kony, come back home.
The world has defeated the boy.

We are now equal.
Kony, come back home.
Kony, come back home.
We are now equal.
Kony, come back home.
Kony, come home.
The world has defeated the boy.
Kony, come home.
The world has defeated the boy.

Translated by Beatrice Lamwaka and Monica Arac de Nyeko

Esther Shadrack Mwachiru
MY MOTHER, MY HERO
Kenya 2001   Kiduruma

The narrator of this text, Esther Shadrack Mwachiru, was born in Kinango, the firstborn of the seven children of Mama Lois Kamwelele Mazera. She is a retired midwife who worked first with the government, and later with the Municipal Council of Mombasa. She saw that all ten of her children were educated. Mwachiru is now a farmer in a township called Pingilikani, in Kilifi District. She is in her late sixties, but still cheerfully attending to expectant mothers in the village while also managing her farm. She told her mother's story with enthusiasm, reliving those times when her mother was alive.

Mama Lois Kamwelele Mazera's achievements, over her short life, were quite remarkable for her time and place. In the 1950s and 1960s, she advocated for women's marital rights and spoke out against early marriages for girls. By the early 1960s, through her efforts, early marriages had declined, and later they were outlawed in Kinango. Mama Kamwelele was involved in the local Kinango primary school board, and by the late 1950s, girls had begun going to school, most of them completing the elementary level. She helped to establish Maendeleo ya Wanawake groups and churchwomen's groups, and later she became a sergeant major of the Salvation Army Church at Kinango. She was adventurous enough to take on responsibilities usually reserved for men, exercising them with confidence and winning admiration from the community. She died in an accident at an early age, but more than forty years later her name is still fresh in the memories of the Duruma people in Kinango, as one who initiated and brought awareness about many programs on development.

Sheila Ali Ryanga

✦

My mother, Lois Kamwelele Mazera, was a woman who was blest from birth. When the First World War began, she was about ten years of age. Father and mother settled at Kingango. They were initially Moslems. There was famine soon after in Duruma, so father and mother went to her uncle's place in Msambweni. After the famine ended, my father, Mazera, went back to Kinango, and worked as a cleaning person in the Kinango dispensary. He attended literacy classes with the missionaries, and when he could read and write, they gave him the job of collecting medicines from Msambweni district hospital, for the dispensary at Kinango. The Church Missionary Society missionaries began preaching to him, without much response. But when the missionaries from Salvation Army Church came and preached to him, he soon converted and became a Christian.

My father began to talk to my mother about Christianity, but she refused to be converted from Islam until later, when my young brother became sick. He was treated traditionally by medicine men with all the expertise, and yet he died. He was accorded a Christian burial and not the traditional funeral because his father was now a Christian. Mother was impressed by the preciseness of the burial, and she came to believe that Christianity was the better religion. The Christian funeral given to her son did not force her to go through the traditional rigorous rituals of a bereaved mother. This convinced her, and she converted from Islam to Christianity in the Salvation Army Church.

She studied the catechism until she qualified and was baptized. Then she joined her husband in the literacy classes, to learn how to read and write, and to attend Bible classes taught by the missionaries. My parents were the first in Kinango to know how to read and write. Other men joined the literacy classes, but mother remained the only woman within the group. She continued until she could write her own name and read the Bible. My father was rarely home when we were growing up. After retiring from the dispensary, he went to live in Utange, the outskirts of Mombasa, where he had another farm. He only came once in a while to Kinango. So mother brought us up for the most part single-handedly. My father died in 1981.

She joined church activities, and began to teach other women cleanliness, cookery, and sewing, as she had been taught by the missionaries. Her progress was good and her enthusiasm was felt in the community. By the 1920s, she began to represent the Salvation Army Church in national congresses at Mombasa because she was the only African woman from Kinango who knew how to read and write. She could find hymn numbers in the hymn books; she could sign documents and read the Bible by herself and during church services.

God blessed her with the gift of natural midwifery. If someone was pregnant she could examine her to ascertain if the baby was fine. If the baby was a breech, she knew how to turn it to the right position in the womb, so that the baby would have a normal birth. She attended to any woman of any race who came to her with pregnancy problems. The Indian community in Kinango benefited from her midwifery skills. This was evident at her burial when many Indians came and testified about the assistance and friendship she had extended to them. She helped many women in this regard because, though she was strong in character and a no-nonsense person, her heart went to the people.

She was blessed. She was sent as a coastal representative of the Salvation Army Church to major church congresses in Kisii. This was the first meeting that took her far from her home area. There she was shown many different things and was eager to learn as much as she could from other churchwomen. Because she became knowledgeable, she taught others what she had learned. When she came back to Kinango she started women's church groups so that she could teach them what she had so far learned. This was through her own initiative, in an attempt to improve the living standards of other women.

Mother was the first woman to be advanced in Duruma. The government noticed her progressive attitude and aptitude. Chiefs and district officers started involving her in development programs. Mother was never a chief nor employed as one, but her progress in church activities and her own efforts in assisting people made her well known to many people beyond Kinango. The district commissioner and district officers in Kwale, the district headquarters, admired her work. In Kinango, chiefs and district officers called upon her to organize receptions for official government guests visiting the location. She had many household items and dishes for such duties. She used to hold a reception for them in her own house, emulating what she had seen in the Kisii church meetings and elsewhere. The meetings would take place, and then guests would come to eat lunch at mother's house. The churchwomen's group she had started often assisted her. She was the first to start a Maendeleo ya Wanawake branch at Kinango, and to organize the building of a social hall for the Maendeleo group, where women could learn to read and write, sew, and cook dishes, ranging from local delicacies to cakes and cookies.

Soon after his conversion to Christianity, father enrolled his children in school. My late brother died while in standard three; at the time I was in standard two. Mama did not like the idea of her daughter being in school at first, since she was still a Moslem. This schooling also angered her mother, who said that if her granddaughter remained in school, she would no longer be respectful or shy and would be spoilt. She also asked my mother to whom she would give all her ornaments and gold items when she died, since her granddaughter would no longer be the good, respectful girl who would benefit from the items.

But mother later changed her mind after her conversion to Christianity, and especially after learning to read and write herself. She saw to our education on her own because father was often away from home.

In 1939 when I, her firstborn child, was in standard two, I was the only girl in school. Other girls joined and left soon after. Mother encouraged me to go on with school and today I am a retired trained midwife, well known in Mombasa. My parents insisted that I go to school, even against the wishes of grandmother.

Mother was fortunate. Because of both her local activities and social service, the government recognized her efforts. She began being called to the Court Council meetings to talk about women and development. Since becoming Christian and learning the Bible, she had begun fighting for women's rights in marriage. She talked against polygamy as being against God's laws. She talked against early marriages in which girls were married off at a very early age without their consent. She had been such a victim herself, since at the age of between ten and fourteen, she was betrothed to my father. My father had seen mother, liked her behavior, and asked his parents to ask for her hand in marriage. Mother accepted this arrangement, and her father took a number of cows for the dowry. However, before she was to go to her husband, her father died.

Soon after that her uncle, the brother of her father, secretly arranged a marriage with another suitor elsewhere, who gave him more cows than my father had given her father. When the uncle announced his intentions to nullify the first suitor, mother was home alone with her mother. When mother refused to be married off to another man, the uncle literally dragged mother from the village. My grandmother and mother shouted, protesting her abduction. As she was dragged along the path, sharp sticks pierced her, leaving marks on her body that are still there. Another uncle and neighbors who heard the cries rescued mother and brought her back home. She was soon after that sent to her husband's home—that is, my father's.

Her vigilance as a self-made advocate for women was recognized by the authorities. Ultimately the government appointed her to be a councillor in Kwale. She was the first woman to be appointed a councillor there. She never sought to be elected; she was appointed to the position. This was towards the end of the 1950s and the beginning of the1960s, before independence.

When mother became a councillor, she bought a farm at Shimba-Hills settlement. That farm was divided into two parts. On one side, she planted her own food crops. On the other side, the farm was used for giving instructions and demonstrations by government agricultural officers. These officers gave my mother graded cows for demonstration. Hers was to be the model farm for other farmers in the area to learn from. The agricultural officers used to come with groups of farmers to teach them there. They also gave her beans and other cereals for planting in the model farm.

During all these activities with the women's church groups, Maendeleo ya Wanawake, being a councillor, and her progress in educating her children, five girls and two boys, singlehandedly, men feared her. They nicknamed her Muche Mulume [literally, "the She-man"], because of her courage and hard work. They feared and at the same time respected her, because, despite all her public involvement, she cared for her family.

By this time father had long since left Kinango. In fact it was mother who educated us singlehandedly. Father had put us in school, but mother was the one who took care of us and educated us, as well as the children of other relatives. Her home had endless visitors. The home was near a hospital, so many people stayed there while visiting the hospital until they were well. Families who lived far away from Kinango brought their children to stay and to go to school from our home. All important visitors passed through our home. Teachers in the Kinango primary school visited her for advice, and to seek guidance in some local issues. She had become a beacon of light.

Soon after Kenya got its independence, the Salvation Army missionaries left Kinango. Father and mother took over the church leadership. They built the church at Kinango and later other church branches were built in rural areas, though Kinango remained the center of all branches. Within the Salvation Army Church ranks, mother rose to the rank of Sergeant Major, the first African woman with that rank in Kwale, organizing and leading the church programs. In her days the Salvation Army Church at Kinango was famous, and its branches flourished all over Duruma area.

She fought for the education of girls in Duruma, and for them not to be given in early marriages. She educated her children as an example. At the district officers' and chiefs' meetings, she urged people to send both boys and girls to school. She fought for women's rights, for girls and women not to be forced into marriage. Just before her death, she came home one day celebrating the news that forced early marriages had been abolished in the area. She died in the prime of her life, because of a bus accident while on the way to her model farm at Shimba-Hills settlement. Until her death, she served as a church leader, social worker, and councillor for Kwale County Council. Her legacy in the area has not been equalled by another woman.

Translated by Sheila Ali Ryanga

LULLABIES

Women have sung lullabies to babies all over the world from time immemorial. African women rock babies to sleep while they are strapped to their backs or held on their laps, providing them with a complete sense of security.

The Kiswahili lullabies included here are from Zanzibar, but are similar to lullabies recorded in Tanga in northeast Tanzania. Though they have different themes, all are sung to the same tune and with the same refrain. They indicate either explicitly or implicitly a bond between the singer, usually the mother, and the baby, with references to the singer's own mother, and to the sadness that the child's crying engenders in the mother.

Lullabies, formed into rhymed stanzas of varying lengths, often seem melancholy, harkening back to the pain and suffering of childbirth and perhaps to the difficulties of life. Swahili mothers may wish for the child's rapid growth to maturity, as well as for the child's extreme grief when the mother dies. Children are expected to be acutely, even violently grieved should a parent die. The Swahili word *kukuwa*, from which the second selection takes its name, means "grow." It is said not only when a child sneezes, but when they do something positive, even an errand. Numerous references to both political and cultural happenings of the time—royalty and slavery, seagoing vessels and spices—fix the cultural location of these lullabies.

Most Ugandan lullabies, constructed around experiences of the mothers and child-minders, offer insights into economic activities, women's and men's work, and the interests of the mothers and other caretakers. These lullabies come from the Baganda of central Uganda, the Bagisu in the east, and the Acoli and Langi in the north.

Characterized by a uniform tempo, which allows the singer to rock the baby slowly to sleep in direct rhythm with the lullaby, most of the songs sung in Zambia's seventy-three languages have a marked similarity in tune and meaning. The focus is mainly on the baby's desire for food and sleep. These are brief songs, the stanzas repeated until the baby falls asleep. Words such as *"iyee"* and *"ayiye"* have no specific meaning other than to soothe and hypnotize. The following lullabies from Zambia, transferred through generations, come from the Nyanja in the east, the Bemba in the north, and the Mbunda in the west

Saïda Yahya-Othman, Nalishebo N. Meebelo, and Florence Ebila

✦

Communal, Nine Lullabies from Zanzibar

Tanzania 2002   Kiswahili

Don't Cry
Don't cry, don't cry, you will make me cry too.
Reserve your tears for when I die,
When you will bang yourself against walls, and be restrained,
When you will throw yourself against trees, and be under watch.
Ooh, my child, ooh.
Ooh, my child, ooh.

When My Mother
When my mother brought me into the world, she called me Kukuwa.
All the Prophet's people recognize me as such.
He who is not my creator cannot uncreate me.
Ooh, my child, ooh.
Ooh, my child, ooh.

Grow, My Child
Grow, my child, grow, grow big.
Grow like the banana tree, the coconut is too slow.
Grow like the coconut tree, the banana withers away.
Ooh, my child, ooh.
Ooh, my child, ooh.

Grow, my child, grow, grow big,
So I can give you a cattle herd, and a goat herd,
So you can drink milk.
Ooh, my child, ooh.
Ooh, my child, ooh.

Chale's Mother Inquired

Chale's mother inquired, what do you want with Chale?
He has not gone with a begging basket, to Darajani [the marketplace].
He has not gone with a basket, to beg at Forodhani [the seafront].
Chale took poison and left this world
To become a cow, feeding on grass.
Ooh, my child, ooh.
Ooh, my child, ooh.

That Canoe Approaching

That canoe approaching, no doubt has something for me.
It has beads for me to string, the size of my neck.
I will not string them, nor give them to my mate.
I will give them to my mother, who shares my secrets.
Ooh, my child, ooh.
Ooh, my child, ooh.

Slave Girl

Slave girl, let me send you on an errand, to King Hassan,
Who wears a voile tunic, and carries a cane.
The mistake I made, who will intercede for me?
Only the stars, and the king's son.
Ooh, my child, ooh.
Ooh, my child, ooh.

Hush, Child, Hush

Hush, child, hush, onion and frankincense.
A snake lies on the path, let's crush its head
To let by hewers of wood, and fetchers of water.
Ooh, my child, ooh.
Ooh, my child, ooh.

My Beautiful Child

My beautiful child, may God let her grow.
When she grows up, I'll send her to school.
Ooh, my child, ooh.
Ooh, my child, ooh.

My Bad Child

My bad child, she cries shamelessly.
If she stops crying, I'll send her to Europe.
Ooh, my child, ooh.
Ooh, my child, ooh.

Translated by Saïda Yahya-Othman

Communal, FOUR LULLABIES FROM UGANDA

Uganda 2002   Luganda, Lango, Acoli, Lugisu

Hush Hush (Luganda)

Hush, hush,
My baby.
Hush, hush,
My baby.
Hush, hush,
A little baby
Does not refuse to sleep.
Baa
The little lamb smoked tobacco.
Baa
The little lamb smoked tobacco.

My mother's baby,
Hush and sleep.
When your mother comes back
I will tell her.
Baa
The little lamb smoked tobacco.
Baa
The little lamb smoked tobacco.

My baby,
Hush, hush.
My child
Hush, hush.
My father's baby,
Hush and sleep.
A little baby
Does not refuse to sleep.
Baa
The little lamb smoked tobacco.

Hush, Baby (Lango)

Hush, baby,
Mother has gone to the well.
The babysitters' meal
Is in the earthware container.

This Mother, Oh (Acoli)

This mother, oh,
She cooks at night.
This mother, oh,
She cooks at night.
She says when the meal is cooked:
Bring me my baby, you might break my baby's back
When she sees the meal is not yet ready
She says, "Take the child out to play."

Olele, Olele, Baby Sister (Lugisu)

Olele, olele, baby sister, I sing for you.
Child, your mother will return.
Then you will breastfeed.
Then you will breastfeed.
Olele, baby sister, I sing for you.

Translated by Florence Ebila and Ayeta Anne Wangusa

Communal, FOUR LULLABIES FROM ZAMBIA

Zambia 2002   Chinyanja, Chibemba, Chimbunda

When the Baby Cries (Chinyanja)

When the baby cries, it is hungry.
When the baby cries, it is sleepy.
When the baby cries, it is hungry.
When the baby cries, it is sleepy.
Iyee Iyee.
Iyee Iyee.
The baby is crying.
The baby is crying in Dinase's backyard .

The Baby Cries for Milk (Chinyanja)

Ayiye,
The baby cries.
Ayiye,
The baby cries.

The baby cries for what?
The baby cries for milk,
Milk from the cow.

The Baby Cries for Comfort (Chibemba)

Ayiye,
The baby cries.
Ayiye,
The baby cries.
"Let them put me on their back
In my cloth."
"Bought by whom?"
"Bought by my Father,
"Father Matunda."

The Baby Cries for Sleep (Chimbunda)

Aaaiyeeee
The baby cries.
The baby cries for milk,
Milk of the cow.
Aaaiyeeee
The baby cries.
It cries for sleep.
It wants to sleep,
To sleep on the back,
On the back of its mother.

Translated by Nalishebo N. Meebelo

Miria Matembe
I MUST CALL MYSELF A FEMINIST

Uganda   2002   English

Miria Matembe was born in 1953 in Rutooma village in western Uganda. She was educated at Bweranyangi Girls School, Namasagali College, and Makerere University, from which she graduated with honors in 1976. She also holds a law degree from the University of Warwick in England. She has worked in the Ministry of Justice, the Uganda College of Commerce, and the Bank of Uganda, and is the mother of four sons.

Matembe became instrumental in the founding of the Uganda Association of Women Lawyers (FIDA) and Action for Development (ACFODE), a women's advocacy organization that grew to become a significant part of the Ugandan women's movement. In 1995, Matembe became a member of the National Resistance Council and the Constituent Assembly. She has been a member of parliament since 1989, and in 1998, she was appointed Minister for Ethics and Integrity She was also one of the only two female commissioners on the twenty-one-member Constitutional Commission, elected in 1998. Among Matembe's notable achievements in parliament was her work on the controversial Domestic Relations Bill, aimed at giving women and girls greater equality in matters relating to marriage, divorce, and family property, then in the process of being rewritten by the Uganda Law Reform Commission.

During the National Executive Committee meeting in 2003, she was one of the few politicians who stood up and openly opposed President Yoweri Museveni over the issue of running for a third term as president, a move that required amending the constitution. She argued that it was better for him to leave power when he was "still loved." She lost her ministerial post in the 2003 cabinet reshuffle, but remained a member of parliament, and in the same year she was elected to the Pan-African Parliament, an initiative of the African Union.

Jackee Budesta Batanda and Florence Ebila

✦

Up to the time when I went to the UK to get my Master's degree at the University of Warwick, I had refused to be called a feminist. The reason was basically that the word *feminist* did not augur well in Uganda at the time. According to public perceptions of the period, "a feminist" was dangerous, a terrible woman. If you mentioned that word, people would distance themselves from you. "She's on the wrong track," they would say, and they wouldn't listen. Part of the reason the term was really looked upon as dangerous was that it came from the Western world.

It is interesting to note that, in Uganda, men and people in general are encouraged to take up new ideas and innovations from the West. Many things from the Western world are promoted as progressive. However, patriarchal society, fearing its downfall, designates new (progressive) ideas about gender relations as "foreign" and "not suitable" for Africans. While the latest ideas about quantum physics, astrology, computer technology, etc., are welcomed, the idea of gender equality is most likely to be condemned.

Under the circumstances, I didn't want to be called a feminist. Many of us who were women activists knew that identifying ourselves as feminists was counterproductive. To do this would hurt our cause. Besides, I had my own way of defining myself. For some time, I had been very clear that I was fighting for women, so I would say, "Me, I'm not a feminist. I'm a self-styled advocate for women's rights." That's what I called myself. But when I went to Britain for my master's programme, I came to understand that a feminist is a person who is struggling to uplift women, someone who is challenging systems and structures that oppress women. There in Britain I decided, if that is the proper designation, then I must call myself a feminist.

There is another reason that I have now accepted this designation. These days women in Uganda have reached a certain stage in public life so that we are able to say that we are feminists, and it doesn't get us into trouble as it did a decade ago. In the beginning of our struggle, it was a good strategy to vehemently deny you were a feminist and call your activism something else. If you can imagine, in those early days we didn't even use the word *equality*. Even that word, *equality*, sometimes caused us problems. So we would say something like, when women are doing many things for the family, for the community, for the country, surely let them be entitled to certain rights.

When our point of view started to be accepted, the foundation was laid. These days we are in a different position. Yes, we can now say we are feminists without doing damage to our cause. Using that term now is not auguring badly because people have seen that, although we are feminists, we are doing certain things that need to be done and talking about things that need to be talked about. Don't you see? This change indicates that we have broken through and that many people now accept what we are saying and what we are doing. Most people are no longer scared of the word. So now I can say, easily, openly without fear, "Yes, I'm a feminist."

There is another issue closely related to the one I have just described. When I went to do my Master's programme, I had a reluctance to take up feminist theory. I was aware that theory, any theory, is not some kind of truth that provides answers to life's most difficult questions, but rather that theory serves as a framework within which to investigate something and then analyse your findings. Yes, I knew that. However, I remember being concerned that I might get confused by someone's line of reasoning, and that the result might be that I would be disassociated from my rural women. I was not willing to go in that direction.

Instinctively I knew what I wanted, in a straightforward manner, in some form. When a class I took began to take up some theoretical questions, about for example, how to define exactly what a "woman" is, I was not willing to follow that line of inquiry. I knew which women I was talking about. I was talking about the rural women of Uganda, my mother, my rural aunt, my rural women who were suffering. I wanted these women to enjoy rights over land. I wanted them to inherit property. I wanted them to have rights to education, training and jobs. I wanted them to assert themselves and to follow their dreams as I had followed mine. I felt those kinds of things were what they wanted also, but that they might not be enlightened and empowered enough to speak about these things for themselves. I felt that they had paid fees for me through their suffering. Therefore I felt I must take up the work of articulating for them.

At some point I told one professor that I didn't want to be confused by theory devised by others which might or might not fit our circumstances in Uganda. I told her that I came there to take a Master's in law and development, specifically because I wanted to do research about how law could be used as an instrument for the development and liberation of women, and I wanted to maintain my particular focus. I had certain questions that begged for answers, such as the following: How can we use law to liberate women from all this bondage that denies them the chance to fulfil their potential? What kinds of laws are needed to enable women to empower themselves? How can law protect women from the worst abuses of patriarchal society?

Ruth Meena
THE FEMALE HUSBAND

Tanzania 2003 English

Ruth Meena was born in 1946 and received her early education near Moshi, in the Kilimanjaro region. After she completed her studies at the Ashira Middle Girls Boarding School, her father wanted her to take a teacher training course, while she aspired to higher education. Financial assistance for needy children was available from the local government council, but only fathers could present requests for assistance for their children. Lacking her father's support, Ruth Meena confronted the council and pleaded her own case. She thus learned early to fight for individual and collective rights. She was given assistance to attend secondary school and attended the H. H. Aga Khan High School in Dar es Salaam, and then the University of Dar es Salaam, where she successfully pursued three degrees.

Ruth Meena has been a feminist political scientist and professor in the Department of Political Science and Public Administration of the University of Dar es Salaam, from which she has recently retired. She is an articulate and committed activist on human rights, environmental, and gender issues not only in Tanzania but throughout the eastern and southern regions of Africa. In 1991 she joined the Southern Africa Political Trust (SAPE) as coordinator of its gender unit, her work there culminating in the 1992 book *Gender in Southern Africa: Theoretical Issues*. The book set out to contrast the nature of feminism in Africa with that conceived by European and American scholars. She has been instrumental in mobilizing for gender mainstreaming at the institutions of higher learning in Tanzania and especially at the University of Dar es Salaam, where she has also introduced the first course in gender and politics.

In 1995, Meena founded and became chair of the Environmental, Human Rights, and Gender Organization (Envirocare), whose objectives include enabling people, especially women, youth, and children, to access information critical to fighting poverty and illiteracy, to closing the gender gap, and reducing environmental degradation. Besides her work with community organizations in Dar es Salaam, Kilimanjaro, Mara, and other parts of the country, she has worked closely with such national organizations as the Tanzania Media Women Association, Tanzania Women Lawyers Association, and the Gender Dimensions Task Force. Collaborating with the Tanzania Gender Networking Program, she also worked on the Gender Budget Initiative, which analyzes the impact of public spending priorities on men, women, and children, and encourages public participation in the national budget process. The initiative has become a model for other countries on the continent.

Among the Kurya people in the Mara region of northwestern Tanzania, where Ruth Meena has worked, there is a traditional practice called *nyumba ntobo* that allows women to marry other women. In many cases, women who have no children of their own and have also acquired some status and wealth—mostly in the form of cows—may marry other women, who are usually younger, upon the payment of dowry. The female husband, whose status is transformed into that of a male, controls the pair's resources and assumes male responsibilities and privileges, while the other woman's status is that of a conventional wife. The inequities between the two partners mimic those of traditional male-female unions. The female husband chooses sexual partners for the wife, and the children from such unions belong to the female husband, who has usually entered into the marriage in order to have sons, who provide both heirs and security in old age. More often than not, such marriages are organized between the father of the bride and the female husband-to-be. It is not unusual to see young girls forced out of school to be married, and early marriages reportedly contribute to the Mara region's low enrollment of girls in primary schools and high dropout rates. The many sexual partners that the young women are forced to submit to make them vulnerable to HIV/AIDS. For the few who have managed to escape, their lot is the street far away from home.

In Meena's short story "The Female Husband," the speaker is a mother who laments the plight of her daughter, destined to be trapped as a wife of a female husband. She castigates not only the society that allows such practices to be sustained by a culture of silence, but also chastises herself for her role in perpetuating the practice. Meena, however, is not interested in portraying a woman who is merely a victim; rather, she focuses on the conscious need to stop those cultural practices that undermine women's rights. At the end of the piece, the voices of the fictionalized character and the writer merge in a call to action.

Amandina Lihamba

✦

I am black and beautiful but bruised and battered.

I hail from Mara region, a land that produced the first president of this Republic. I am proud of this origin, which associates me with the liberation of my country and the continent. Black and beautiful, yes! Proud of a fighting culture that liberated this chained, bruised, and pained me. Yes, I am also forced to pretend that I love to be brutalized since it is supposed to be an expression of affection.

I was worth a couple of cows, which this man had to part with, the price of which I am paying heavily! Daily battered, insulted and deprived of choices, this is what I have had to pay for those cows, which my father added to his own stock! Do not advise me to walk out of this battered relationship!! AHAA! Where will I go? Who will be my host? Definitely not my father nor my brothers, since they are not about to part with a single cow that came as part of my dowry. I have a feeling I shall continue to pay this price! For how long? Do not ask me, as I do not see a flicker of light on this in the near future.

But I am also a custodian of a culture which often forces me or my daughters to cohabit with another woman, whose social status has been transformed by wealth. She plays a male role! Yes, she can pay the "dowry" and this is the price for my freedom. Yes, my husband colluded with a headmaster, whose name I am not going to mention, to indicate in the school register that my daughter had died, since there was a woman who was able to pay the dowry. As my daughter was walking out of my home, I was saying to myself, it is the end of her sweet laughter, the end of her beautiful skin, the end of her elegance!

But I am not supposed to express this pain. I have to be hard; if she comes back beaten and brutalized I have to force her back to the "prison." This is our way of life, and who is she to defile "this culture"! Yes, I am not about to admit that I did not socialize her into this role! Even if she comes back bleeding, hurt, and humiliated, I have to demonstrate hardness and I am not going to let my emotions betray me. As I bleed inside with pain, I shall have to assume the iron lady character when it comes to dealing with my battered daughter! Yes, she will understand why I am as cold as a stone, expressionless, and yet full of love and affection. My daughter will understand when she grows to have her own daughters!

Yes, *Nyumba Ntobo* is a culture which gives her no freedom to choose whom to father her children. She will dare not say no to the suspected HIV positive guy who has been the choice of her supposedly female husband. And yet, she will be expected to be proud of her culture. Yes, it's cultural and it's African. And who dare say that what is African and cultural is wrong! Not me, as I shall be accused of being a "Western stooge" copy cat, petite bourgeoisie, sell out, or Western feminist! I fear labels. I have to pretend that my schooling did not transform my mind set, the constructed Africanness and femaleness!! I have to pretend that I am not what I am; I also need acceptance, recognition and identity. But what a price am I paying!

I know I have no choice but to endure the daily beatings, the daily insults, the hard work in the fields and in the home. Call me "*Ma Endurance.*" That is my culture. How long is it going to be sustained, do not ask. But somehow, I have a dream that this culture will one day be questioned, if not by my children, by my grandchildren, or great-grandchildren. Yes, one day they are going to redefine it from their own viewpoint, they are going to say no more beating, no more insults, no more sexual slavery, no more *Nyumba Ntobo* and no more dowry. This is the time when those who enslaved us, who continued to chain us will have to pay the price which I am paying. Yes, proud, beautiful and black! Call me Ma endurance, that is my culture!

Hello, fellow women, how long are we going to protect the brutalities in our diverse cultures, in their diverse forms? Brutality is not part of the African way of life, and there is no beauty in being battered or mutilated, or sexually exploited! We could pick a voice from every cultural context with more or less the same message. Rise up and say NO! ENOUGH is ENOUGH.

Culture is a dynamic force; let us use it to challenge the culture of oppression which reduces women into sexual objects, into beasts of burden and into second-class citizens. The advantage which we have is the very fact that we are and we shall remain custodians of our cultural heritage. We remain the main socializers of boys and girls into adulthood. Let us use the influence we have on our children to impart upon them values and norms that challenge oppressive norms and values, particularly those which position women and girls into low social status.

There is a lot we can do to impart an alternative culture. Let's call a spade a spade! Human rights language is now a politically correct language accepted by a very masculine internationally defined standard. Let's make the most out of this space to demand protection from torture and to demand accountability from the duty bearers for abuses against our fundamental rights as human beings. Let's search for a culture that has peace, love, and equality; a culture that defines civility from our point of view. After all, we women constitute the majority of world citizens.

Martha Qorro
LANGUAGE IN TANZANIA

Tanzania 2003   Kiswahili

Martha Qorro is a prominent lobbyist for the movement to change the medium of instruction in Tanzania from English to Kiswahili. Born in 1952, Qorro is a lecturer in English at the University of Dar es Salaam, and former head of the Department of Foreign Languages and Linguistics. She has campaigned tirelessly for both improvement in the teaching of English, and the use of Kiswahili, the language best understood by the nation's children, as a medium in secondary and higher education. Because of her work, she has recently been appointed to the National Kiswahili Council, a body that oversees the creation of new Kiswahili terminology and generally provides support for the advancement of Kiswahili.

In 1997, Qorro collaborated with Zaline M. Roy-Campbell on *The Language Crisis in Tanzania: The Myth of English Versus Education*, which reports on research into reading failures in Tanzanian secondary schools. Her doctoral work focused on writing problems of secondary school students. Recently, Qorro has been involved in the LOITASA (Languages of Instruction in Tanzania and South Africa) project, which conducts research on introducing African languages into teaching.

A debate on the appropriate language of instruction has been raging in Tanzania for the last three decades. A few years after independence, in 1967, the Tanzanian government took the then-revolutionary step of declaring Kiswahili the language of primary school education, and successive governments have considered instituting Kiswahili as the medium for the entire educational system. In spite of the evidence provided by Qorro and other scholars and activists, the movement toward change has encountered opposing pressures from the West, including the policies of the

World Bank and International Monetary Fund and such organized efforts as the English Language Teaching Support Project, funded by the British government. To date, English continues to perform a gate-keeping function, which excludes the majority of Tanzanians from educational and employment opportunities.

The text below is a translation of a talk Qorro delivered to members of the Chama cha Mapinduzi (CCM), the ruling party in Tanzania since independence, on the importance of the language issue to national development, particularly agriculture and industrialization.

Saïda Yahya-Othman

✦

It has been remarked that the standard of education in Tanzania is low and needs to be uplifted, for good-quality education results in an improved economy, better standards of agriculture, and more productive industries. The important question is: How can we attain better education, or how can we transform the low quality of education now prevalent? In other words, wherein lie the problems that result in poor education? One can point to numerous problems, including shortages of properly trained teachers and educational equipment, inadequate classrooms, and an inadequate medium of instruction. Since I am a language teacher, I will talk about the last problem, first noted in 1967 and still unsolved. Further, if we were to succeed in solving all the other problems but this one, the standards of education in the country would continue to remain low.

I will begin by reviewing numerous pieces of research on the medium of instruction in secondary schools in Tanzania, and the findings and recommendations emanating from that research. Later, I will offer suggestions about what can be done to raise the standards of education and thus improve the economy and revolutionize livestock-rearing and crop-farming.

How is it that we go on complaining about low levels of education while we ourselves set up the policies, and are reluctant to adapt them to fit with the times?

The teaching environment in schools is deplorable. For instance, at a seminar in April 2002, a head teacher of one of the secondary schools pointed out that out of fifty teachers in his school only three were proficient in English. This is tantamount to saying that the other forty-seven taught in bad English. That is, mathematics, civics, history, and other subjects, as well as English, will be taught in bad English. What kind of English would the pupils have learned at the end of the day—good English taught by the teacher of English, or bad English spoken by the other nine teachers? With this in mind, can we really say that our children are being educated? Will children really learn English in such circumstances? We have continued the same language policy for twenty-seven years, although the first research findings laid open the language problem. Still, we are surprised that educational standards are low! We are surprised that pupils have no command of the English language, nor do they know Kiswahili! Where and from whom are they supposed to learn under such deplorable circumstances? Are such circumstances conducive to better education and better economic conditions for the majority of Tanzanians? Are we likely to revolutionize crop farming and livestock rearing under such circumstances? Why do we go on with this self-deception?

We were earlier given food for thought when the question was posed: Why do Tanzanians, or educated Tanzanians, speak with such meekness? I do not have a definitive response to that question, but it could be that we, the educated, are not confident of the real meaning of what we are talking about simply because we have gained our education through a language that we have not properly grasped.

Someone has remarked that our children do not know their history. I entirely agree with him. But we need to ask, How can they learn the subject if it is taught in a language they do not comprehend? How can they learn science if it is taught in a language they do not understand?

One of the announced aims of secondary school education in Tanzania is to enable pupils to learn both Kiswahili and English. Theoretically, bilingual education should not use two languages at once, but should use each of the languages in separate domains. A recognized pedagogic principle holds that one should teach pupils in the language most familiar to them, and at the same time, teach a second or foreign language as a subject rather than a medium of instruction. This pedagogical principle is the one applied for teaching a second or foreign language in all the developed countries. I have said "developed countries," because these countries "developed" through the use of their own languages as media of instruction, resulting in the majority of their people having access to education and thus contributing to national development. We are erring in thinking that developed countries have managed to use their own languages as media of instruction because they were already developed! Why can't we see the logic in the fact that no nation can attain development through educating its people in a language they do not understand?

Translated by Abdulhakim Yahya and Saïda Yahya-Othman

Monica Arac de Nyeko
IN THE STARS

Uganda 2003 English

Born in 1979, Monica Arac de Nyeko comes from the Kitgum District in northern Uganda, which has been affected by war since 1986. For twenty years, residents have been trapped between the rebels of the Lord's Resistance Army and the government forces, many of whom had once been guerrillas themselves and were often equally brutal. The fourth child in a family of five, she studied at Shimoni Demonstration School in Kampala and at Gulu High School in northern Uganda. At the peak of the war she was forced to study in Luwero, in the south of the country, where she completed her secondary education. She later attended Makerere University, earning a bachelor's degree with honors in education with a specialization in teaching literature and English language.

Her growing concern about the war and the suffering and death among her people, the Acoli, inspired her to go to the University of Groningen in the Netherlands to study for a master's degree in humanitarian assistance. She believes that her studies will enable her to work with women and children in war zones like that of her homeland. Since completing her master's degree, Arac has worked for international humanitarian organizations in Italy and Sudan, and now in Kenya.

Monica Arac began publishing stories and poems while still in her twenties. The Ugandan Women's publishing house selected several of Arac's stories and poems for anthologies. A collection of her poems will be published by Poetry International, and a novella, *The Last Dance*, by Fountain Publishers in Kampala.

In 2003, "In the Stars" won the Women's World contest, "Women's Voices in War Zones," cosponsored by The Nation Institute with support from the Puffin Foundation. Women's World—Women's Organization for Rights, Literature, and Development—is a global free speech and advocacy network of feminist writers, based in New York. The contest was designed to bring forward voices not being heard in the current discussion of war and terrorism, particularly those of ordinary women trapped in military, political, economic, and domestic war zones. "In the Stars" was first published on the Women's World Web site.

Beatrice Lamwaka and Florence Ebila

✦

Where does your hope or security lie?
In the stars.

My mother used to talk about him; my Uncle Oryema. How she begged him not to become a soldier. "He didn't listen," she always said and swallowed hard like she never forgave him for disappearing from our grasp like *raa* smoke. He was so far away from home, somewhere in the jungles, holding his rifle when death beckoned. A man brought the news to my grandma. Said the gunfire had been heavy. Her son had been shot in the stomach. That he had tied an old green army uniform to hold his bowels together and fled for his life. The man offered to go back to search for our Uncle Oryema with another uncle who later joined the army, to fight the demons that haunted him of his brother's death. They combed *Kituba* trees where they say spirits live, the long grasses of the blazing Kitgum wilderness with scorpions and snakes. Uncle Oryema would now remain a memory in our hearts. On his "grave" grandma laid four large stones to show where we should have laid his body.

Of the many things I remember of him, it's the toffee sweets he brought me when he returned from college, and told Ma he was going to fight. That day he took me to the cinema. My first time ever to see motion picture with images the size of our city council house.

I went to the family cemetery yesterday. There was Ma lying beside Uncle Oryema; she had joined him seven years later. At least she had not been struck on the head with an axe or set ablaze in a hut. Meningitis took her.

Sitting there and staring at their graves, it was hard to think of Ma and Uncle Oryema as ancestors. Worry had drained Ma's spirit. She carried memories. She suffered the pain of knowing the past and future. Tears never stopped. When she followed Uncle Oryema into death, I wished that perhaps she would learn to forgive him. She would learn not to worry about this war. But she had died knowing we would never go to school because it was always bullets and bombs. Our virginity would fall prey to wicked savagery. We would be abducted and forced to fight. Our bodies would rot in the wild.

The 1986 war against The Lord's Resistance Army (LRA) in Northern Uganda started as only as a joke, but it has eaten away Acoli. It's like an imaginary-tale. Children are trained to be lethal massacre weapons. Sometimes they flee back home to seek what was taken from them, but they discover they cannot stay because their minds think of blood and killing only. They tell of the urine they drank from the unbearable thirst. The young girls, our former schoolmates, have been sex-slaves and loathe male company. Many, we will never know what happened to them.

We are a generation of thorns. Memories of nights in rain and gripping fear creep into our dreams. Sleep should be the only place where there is no worry. It should be dreamland, hope land. But our sleep knows not the vague images of paradise created from longing; there are images of ghosts of dead friends and relatives. The ones we watched *pangas* hack. Those we heard from our hiding places flogged to death. Those we see headless, limbless, noseless, lipless when we blink.

It's sad that the situation is hopeless and there is nothing much that we without power can do. Our government has been fighting futilely for sixteen years but they will not talk serious peace. Our president Y.K. Museveni calls Joseph Kony the rebel leader a jigger that can be dealt with in an instant. But numbers of Acoli civilians dwindle in cheap talk. They say in every news bulletin, "the war will end real soon." Soon has become sixteen years.

We have learned to survive and say our prayers before trying to sleep. In case we wake up in another world it has got to be Heaven, vague as it might seem to atheists.

We have learned to seal our lips and pretend we know nothing of what goes on. We cannot trust anyone. The rebels do not care whether we live or die. We do not know why they fight. We know nothing of treaties signed by important men. We know not what words like *terrorists*, *victims* and *universal declarations of human rights* mean. But we know that we are going to die, from bullets, hunger, or hopelessness.

The low-ranked government soldiers, who are sent to protect us, run and hide in their brick-walled barracks to protect themselves when the rebels come. They return when it's calm to rape our grandmothers, light our huts for pure pleasure and in the evening we hear the radios say, "Look what the bloody rebels did again, take heart brothers and sisters in the north, and try to understand; that the government is liberating you." But we cannot try to understand; there is nothing to be understood.

For the army majors, as long as the war goes on, there will always be countries willing to donate large monies. Then they can buy banks, government property, and own the entire nation. Their wives can own massage parlors and designer boutiques to serve foreign diplomats in Sheraton, Equatorial or Grand Imperial Hotels; their children can go to international schools and play Barbie doll.

When heaven seems so far off sometimes, we dream and wait for miracles and look at the stars. The twinkling of stars far off in the sky and the lone silence of the night's presence remind us that one day we shall smile, because the stars will twinkle only for us.

The immortal stars whisper that they watch over us as we await fate. So we place our hopes, not in the rebels or our government or the United Nations, but in the night sky, where the stars twinkle bright.

Margaret Wangui Mwema
THE STORY OF WACU

Kenya 2004   Gikuyu

In this version of the tale of Wacu, an ill-treated wife receives the providential gift of meat. In other versions of the story, Wacu is a child privileged by her rich father, the owner of many animals, who allows her to eat meat. In that version, she is, through her youth, a shunned tomboy, for she herds the animals as her father does, and spends time with him listening to his advice and stories. She grows as strong and capable as the boys in the village. When she comes of age for marriage, she is not popular, but eventually she meets and marries a man from another village before he hears of her reputation. She seems to conform to village custom, but she continues to eat meat secretly. She has many children, all boys, and when she feels comfortable about her life, she openly eats meat as part of a protest. Healers cannot cure her, though they advise her husband to prevent her from eating his meat. Nevertheless, she either buys meat secretly or she curses her husband when he refuses to give her any of his. In the story's conclusion, a feast of Gikuyu elders—all male, of course—is the occasion for the eagle's appearance. The bird steals the elder's meat and drops it into the arms of Wacu. Young men find Wacu and the meat and report back to the elders, who then "resolve to give their women the right to eat meat in their homesteads." One version of the tale ends with this sentence: "'*Ciakorire Wacu mugunda*' [meat found Wacu in the field] is a common joke when one meets some luck without much effort."

Margaret Wangui Mwema lives in Thika, Kenya. She learned the story of Wacu, along with other tales, from her mother and grandmother, who told stories to Wangui and her siblings at night before the children went to sleep. In turn, after she married, Mwema was a nursery school teacher for twenty years and often told stories to the children she taught, as well as to her own six children. Margaret Mwema is married to Lawrence Mwema, who transcribed and translated the story of Wacu for this volume.

Ann Biersteker and Marjorie Oludhe Macgoye

✦

Once upon a time there lived a woman by the name of Wacu. Wacu was married. Her husband had two wives, of whom Wacu was one. Unfortunately, Wacu was not the favorite wife. The other woman was much loved and she too disliked Wacu. So Wacu lived the life of a humiliated wife.

One day Wacu's husband invited his friends to come and eat a roasted goat at his home. He brewed beer and slaughtered a fat he-goat for them. They had a big feast.

Just as the slaughtering of the goat started, Wacu quietly took her farming knife and a basket and she walked away to her garden of sweet potatoes. The sky was heavy with rain clouds as Wacu was busy working in her sweet potato garden. She took her time in the garden cultivating and picking some sweet potatoes for her dinner.

Back at her home, the men were drinking and anxiously awaiting the appetizing meat roasting on the grill. Wacu, who was famished, found shelter under a dry fig tree as the rain continued to pour down.

All of a sudden an eagle carrying a burden landed on the fig tree. The eagle dropped a huge goat sausage. Wacu did not hesitate when she sensed what had just happened at her home. The carousing men had waited, expecting to share the huge goat sausage, but the hungry eagle had snatched the juicy chunk of meat. As the eagle had landed on the tree, it had dropped the meat as it tried to bite it.

Wacu picked up the meat at once and sat down to eat all of it. Hence the popular proverb, "Wacu's lucky find." Wacu ate and ate until she was satisfied. She wrapped what remained in a banana leaf and placed the parcel of meat in her potato basket.

Wacu was happy thinking of how lucky she was that day. She thought, "They did not remember me, but God has. I've eaten to my satisfaction. Thank you, God."

When she reached home, Wacu finished eating the sausage. She did not tell her husband anything about what had happened that day.

This reminds us that our God loves even those who are held in contempt by others.

My tale ends there.

Translated by Lawrence Mwema

Wangari Maathai
NOBEL PEACE PRIZE LECTURE

Kenya 2004   English

Wangari Maathai is the first feminist, the first environmentalist, and the first African woman to be awarded the Nobel Peace Prize. As a scholar, an activist, and a teacher, she is an advocate for the environment, for women's rights, and for social and political justice. Since 2002 she has been Kenya's Assistant Minister for the Environment and Natural Resources and a Member of Parliament for Tetu District, in central Kenya. In 2004 she was declared by Kenya's parliament to be Kenya's envoy to the world for the environment, human rights, and democracy. She was elected the first president of the Economic, Social, and Cultural Council of the African union in 2005.

Wangari Maathai was the first woman in Eastern and Central Africa to earn a PhD and was the first woman to chair a department, Veterinary Anatomy, at the University of Nairobi. She did her undergraduate work and earned an MA in the United States. She did her PhD work at the University of Nairobi. Wangari Maathai established the Green Belt Movement in 1977 while active in the National Council of Women of Kenya. The Green Belt Movement plants trees to prevent soil erosion and to provide wood used in making charcoal, the primary cooking fuel in rural Kenya. Central to the movement's goals has been the involvement of rural women in sustaining the environment that provides their livelihood. The movement has established 6,000 local nurseries and has planted over 30 million trees in Kenya. It has also been successful in encouraging community mobilization and environmental activism. Wangari Maathai led the Green Belt Movement in struggles to secure public spaces and forests in Kenya. The movement was successful in preventing the construction of a skyscraper in Nairobi's Uhuru Park and in preventing private takeover of the state-owned Karuna Forest. The Green Belt Movement also holds seminars to encourage international reforestation efforts.

In addition to the 2004 Nobel Peace Prize Wangari Maathai has been awarded the French Legion d'Honneur, the Goldman Environmental prize, the UN's Africa Prize for Leadership, the Edinburgh Medal, the Jane Addams Conference Leadership Award, and the Golden Ark Award. Williams College, the University of Norway, Hobart and William Smith Colleges, and Yale University have awarded her honorary degrees.

Wangari Maathai's publications include two editions of *The Green Belt Movement: Sharing the Approach and the Experience* and her 2006 autobiography *Unbowed*. She has also published articles in a wide range of international publications including *The Christian Science Monitor, The International Herald Tribune, The Nation, The New York Times*, and *WSQ: Women's Studies Quarterly*. In addition, she often contributes articles on environmental, social justice, and feminist issues to *The Nation* and East African newspapers in Kenya.

Ann Biersteker

✦

Your Majesties
Your Royal Highnessess
Honorable Members of the Norwegian Nobel Committee
Excellencies
Ladies and gentlemen,
I stand before you and the world humbled by this recognition and uplifted by the honour of being the 2004 Nobel Peace Laureate.

As the first African woman to receive this prize, I accept it on behalf of the people of Kenya and Africa, and indeed the world.

I am especially mindful of women and the girl-child. I hope it will encourage them to raise their voices and take more space for leadership. I know the honour also gives a deep sense of pride to our men, both old and young. As a mother, I appreciate the inspiration this brings to the youth and urge them to use it to pursue their dreams.

Although this prize comes to me, it acknowledges the work of countless individuals and groups across the globe. They work quietly and often without recognition to protect the environment, promote democracy, defend human rights and ensure equality between women and men. By so doing, they plant seeds of peace. I know they, too, are proud today. To all who feel represented by this prize I say use it to advance your mission and meet the high expectations the world will place on us.

This honour is also for my family, friends, partners and supporters throughout the world. All of them helped shape the vision and sustain our work, which was often accomplished under hostile conditions. I am also grateful to the people of Kenya—who remained stubbornly hopeful that democracy could be realized and their environment managed sustainably. Because of this support, I am here today to accept this great honour.

I am immensely privileged to join my fellow African Peace laureates, Presidents Nelson Mandela and F.W. de Klerk, Archbishop Desmond Tutu, the late Chief Albert Luthuli, the late Anwar el-Sadat and the UN Secretary General Kofi Annan.

I know that African people everywhere are encouraged by this news. My fellow Africans, as we embrace this recognition, let us use it to intensify our commitment to our people, to reduce conflicts and poverty and thereby improve their quality of life. Let us embrace democratic governance, protect human rights and protect our environment. I am confident that we shall rise to the occasion. I have always believed that solutions to most of our problems must come from us.

In this year's prize, the Norwegian Nobel Committee has placed the critical issue of environment and its linkage to democracy and peace before the world. For their visionary action, I am profoundly grateful. Recognising that sustainable development, democracy and peace are indivisible is an idea whose time has come. Our work over the past 30 years had always appreciated and engaged these linkages.

My inspiration partly comes from my childhood experiences and observations of Nature in rural Kenya. It has been influenced and nurtured by the formal education I was privileged to receive in Kenya, the United States and Germany. As I was growing up, I witnessed forests being cleared and replaced by commercial plantations, which destroyed local biodiversity and the capacity of the forests to conserve water.

Excellencies, ladies and gentlemen,

In 1977, when we started the Green Belt Movement, I was partly responding to needs identified by rural women, namely lack of firewood, clean drinking water, balanced diets, shelter and income.

Throughout Africa, women are the primary caretakers, holding significant responsibility for tilling the land and feeding their families. As a result, they are often the first to become aware of environmental damage as resources become scarce and incapable of sustaining their families.

The women we worked with recounted that unlike in the past, they were unable to meet their basic needs. This was due to the degradation of their immediate environment as well as the introduction of commercial farming, which replaced the growing of household food crops. But international trade controlled the price of the exports from these small-scale farmers and a reasonable and just income could not be guaranteed. I came to understand that when the environment is destroyed, plundered or mismanaged, we undermine our quality of life and that of future generations.

Tree planting became a natural choice to address some of the initial basic needs identified by women. Also, tree planting is simple, attainable and guarantees quick, successful results within a reasonable amount of time. This sustains interest and commitment.

So, together, we have planted over 30 million trees that provide fuel, food, shelter, and income to support their children's education and household needs. The activity also creates employment and improves soils and watersheds. Through their involvement, women gain some degree of power over their lives, especially their social and economic position and relevance in the family. This work continues.

Initially, the work was difficult because historically our people have been persuaded to believe that, because they are poor, they lack not only capital, but also knowledge and skills to address their challenges. Instead they are conditioned to believe that solutions to their problems must come from "outside." Further, women did not realise that meeting their needs depended on their environment being healthy and well managed. They were also unaware that a degraded environment leads to a scramble for scarce resources and may culminate in poverty and even conflict. They were also unaware of the injustices of international economic arrangements.

In order to assist communities to understand these linkages, we developed a citizen education program, during which people identify their problems, the causes and possible solutions. They then make connections between their own personal actions and the problems they witness in the environment and in society. They learn that our world is confronted with a litany of woes: corruption, violence against women and children, disruption and breakdown of families, and disintegration of cultures and communities. They also identify the abuse of drugs and chemical substances, especially among young people. There are also devastating diseases that are defying cures or occurring in epidemic proportions. Of particular concern are HIV/AIDS, malaria and diseases associated with malnutrition.

On the environmental front, they are exposed to many human activities that are devastating to the environment and societies. These include widespread destruction of ecosystems, especially through deforestation, climatic instability, and contamination in the soils and waters that all contribute to excruciating poverty.

In the process, the participants discover that they must be part of the solutions. They realize their hidden potential and are empowered to overcome inertia and take action. They come to recognize that they are the primary custodians and beneficiaries of the environment that sustains them.

Entire communities also come to understand that while it is necessary to hold their governments accountable, it is equally important that in their own relationships with each other, they exemplify the leadership values they wish to see in their own leaders, namely justice, integrity, and trust.

Although initially the Green Belt Movement's tree planting activities did not address issues of democracy and peace, it soon became clear that responsible governance of the environment was impossible without democratic space. Therefore, the tree became a symbol for the democratic struggle in Kenya. Citizens were mobilised to challenge widespread abuses of power, corruption and environmental mismanagement. In Nairobi's Uhuru Park, and Freedom Corner, and in many parts of the country, trees of peace were planted to demand the release of prisoners of conscience and a peaceful transition to democracy.

Through the Green Belt Movement, thousands of ordinary citizens were mobilised and empowered to take action and effect change. They learned to overcome fear and a sense of helplessness and moved to defend democratic rights.

In time, the tree also became a symbol for peace and conflict resolution, especially during ethnic conflicts in Kenya when the Green Belt Movement used peace trees to reconcile disputing communities. During the ongoing re-writing of the Kenyan constitution, similar trees of peace were planted in many parts of the country to promote a culture of peace. Using trees as a symbol of peace is in keeping with a widespread African tradition. For example, the elders of the Kikuyu carried a staff from the *thigi* tree that, when placed between two disputing sides, caused them to stop fighting and seek reconciliation. Many communities in Africa have these traditions.

Such practises are part of an extensive cultural heritage, which contributes both to the conservation of habitats and to cultures of peace. With the destruction of these cultures and the introduction of these new values, local biodiversity is no longer valued or protected and as a result, it is quickly degraded and disappears. For this reason, the Green Belt Movement explores the concept of cultural biodiversity, especially with respect to indigenous seeds and medicinal plants.

As we progressively understood the causes of environmental degradation, we saw the need for good governance. Indeed, the state of any country's environment is a reflection of the kind of governance in place, and without good governance there can be no peace. Many countries, which have poor governance systems, are also likely to have conflicts and poor laws protecting the environment.

In 2002, the courage, resilience, patience and commitment of members of the Green Belt Movement, other civil society organizations, and the Kenyan public culminated in the peaceful transition to a democratic government and laid the foundation for a more stable society.

Excellencies, friends, ladies and gentlemen,

It is thirty years since we started this work. Activities that devastate the environment and societies continue unabated. Today we are faced with a challenge that calls for a shift in our thinking, so that humanity stops threatening its life-support system. We are called to assist the Earth to heal her wounds and in the process heal our own—indeed, to embrace the whole creation in all its diversity, beauty and wonder. This will happen if we see the need to revive our sense of belonging to a larger family of life, with which we have shared our evolutionary process.

In the course of history, there comes a time when humanity is called to shift to a new level of consciousness, to reach a higher moral ground. A time when we have to shed our fear and give hope to each other.

That time is now.

The Norwegian Nobel Committee has challenged the world to broaden the understanding of peace: there can be no peace without equitable development; and there can be no development without sustainable management of the environment in a democratic and peaceful space. This shift is an idea whose time has come.

I call on leaders, especially from Africa, to expand democratic space and build fair and just societies that allow the creativity and energy of their citizens to flourish.

Those of us who have been privileged to receive education, skills, and experiences and even power must be role models for the next generation of leadership. In this regard, I would also like to appeal for the freedom of my fellow laureate Aung San Suu Kyi so she can continue her work for peace and democracy for the people of Burma and the world at large.

Culture plays a central role in the political, economic and social life of communities. Indeed, culture may be the missing link in the development of Africa. Culture is dynamic and evolves over time, consciously discarding retrogressive traditions, like female genital mutilation (FGM), and embracing aspects that are good and useful.

Africans, especially, should re-discover positive aspects of their culture. In accepting them, they would give themselves a sense of belonging, identity and self-confidence.

Ladies and gentlemen,

There is also need to galvanize civil society and grassroots movements to catalyse change. I call upon governments to recognize the role of these social movements in building a critical mass of responsible citizens, who help maintain checks and balances in society. On their part, civil society should embrace not only their rights but also their responsibilities.

Further, industry and global institutions must appreciate that ensuring economic justice, equity and ecological integrity are of greater value than profits at any cost.

The extreme global inequities and prevailing consumption patterns continue at the expense of the environment and peaceful co-existence. The choice is ours.

I would like to call on young people to commit themselves to activities that contribute toward achieving their long-term dreams. They have the energy and creativity to shape a sustainable future. To the young people I say, you are a gift to your communities and indeed the world. You are our hope and our future.

The holistic approach to development, as exemplified by the Green Belt Movement, could be embraced and replicated in more parts of Africa and beyond. It is for this reason that I have established the Wangari Maathai Foundation to ensure the continuation and expansion of these activities. Although a lot has been achieved, much remains to be done.

Excellencies, ladies and gentlemen,

As I conclude, I reflect on my childhood experience when I would visit a stream next to our home to fetch water for my mother. I would drink water straight from the stream. Playing among the arrowroot leaves, I tried in vain to pick up the strands of frogs' eggs, believing they were beads. But every time I put my little fingers under them they would break. Later, I saw thousands of tadpoles: black, energetic and wriggling through the clear water against the background of the brown earth. This is the world I inherited from my parents.

Today, over fifty years later, the stream has dried up, women walk long distances for water, which is not always clean, and children will never know what they have lost. The challenge is to restore the home of the tadpoles and give back to our children a world of beauty and wonder.

Thank you very much.

CONTRIBUTORS

EDITORS

Amandina Lihamba is a performer and a director for stage and screen productions. She has published plays and many articles on theatre, culture and politics, and gender and communication. She is a professor in the department of fine and performing arts at the University of Dar es Salaam, where she teaches theatre practice and art for social mobilization. She is a cofounder of the national children theatre project and festival as well as the Tuseme program, which agitates for education for girls. She has chaired national and regional organisations including The Tanzania Cultural Trust Fund, The East African Theatre Institute, and the National Museums of Tanzania. She has been head of department, associate dean, dean, and member of the university council.

Fulata L. Moyo is a systematic theologian; church historian; and gender and HIV and AIDS activist. Her interests lie in the area of women's sexuality and their interconnectedness to ecology (as Mother Earth).

M.M. Mulokozi is a Kiswahili poet and writer of fiction and plays. He has published 15 books (two of them in English) and many scholarly papers on language, literature, culture and publishing. He is also a recipient of several literary awards. Professionally he has worked as an editor in a publishing company, and is currently a research professor in literature in the Institute of Kiswahili Research at the University of Dar es Salaam. He has taught Kiswahili poetry, African literature, oral literature, comparative literature, and Kiswahili for foreigners at the University of Dar es Salaam and in the United Kingdom and the United States. He has also served as the secretary general of the Tanzania Writers Association, Chairperson of the Childrens' Book Project for Tanzania, and Director of the Institute of Kiswahili Research at the University of Dar es Salaam.

Naomi L. Shitemi is an associate professor of Kiswahili. She teaches theory and practice of translation and language use. She has been involved in various language-related researches with a focus on Kiswahili. She has been dean of the School of Arts and Social Sciences; head of the Department of Kiswahili and Other African Languages, and acting deputy vice chancellor for Research and Extension at Moi University. She is coordinator of the Departmental Graduate Program. She has served as secretary to the Commission on Higher Education's Committee on Reforms in Higher Education. She has published in the areas of Kiswahili language and literature; language planning and policy; translation; gender and women's issues.

Saïda Yahya-Othman is an associate professor in the Department of Foreign Languages and Linguistics, where she teaches pragmatics and critical discourse analysis. She has been involved in various projects to do with religion, democracy, and philanthropy in Tanzania. She chairs the Research and Publications Committee of the Research and Education for Democracy in Tanzania (REDET) program, and is currently the vice chair of the University of Dar es Salaam's academic staff assembly. She has been head of department, associate dean, and director of postgraduate studies and has monitored all the Tanzania multi-party elections so far. Her main publications have been in pragmatics and language politics.

ASSOCIATE EDITORS

Austin Bukenya was born in Masaka, Uganda, in 1944. He studied and taught at universities in Uganda, Tanzania, Madagascar, the United Kingdom, and Kenya. He has been working in "Orature" (the term he and his late teacher, Pio Zirimu, coined for "oral literature") since 1968 and he was responsible for establishing this discipline at Makerere University in 1969. He has published numerous articles and books on oral literature, language, and language teaching and literary theory. He has also published fiction, verse, and drama. He teaches at the Kigali Institute of Education in Rwanda, after retiring from Makerere University in Uganda.

Florence Ebila is a lecturer in the Department of Women and Gender Studies at Makerere University, Kampala where she also studied for her BA (Hons) and MA (women's studies). She is currently on a doctoral program at the University of Wisconsin, Madison. She has published a short story and an essay on the women's movement in Uganda. She was one of the editors of *The Focus*, a quarterly magazine of the Gender Mainstreaming Division of Makerere University.

Susan Kiguli is a Ugandan poet and academic. She recently completed her PhD in English at The University of Leeds under the prestigious Commonwealth Scholarship Scheme. She is a lecturer in the Department of Literature, Makerere University, Uganda, and is currently the chairperson of FEMRITE, Uganda Women Writers' Association. Her first volume of poetry, *The African Saga* (1998) won the National Book Trust of Uganda Poetry Award. She has also written criticism on Ugandan poetry, oral performance, and the position of women writers in African literature. She served on the panel of judges for the Commonwealth Writers' Prize (African Region, 1999).

Edrinnie Lora-Kayambazinthu is an associate professor in English at Chancellor College, University of Malawi, specializing in sociolinguistics and language planning. Her consultancy and research work have been in the areas of language use, translation, governance and human rights, information, education and communication, gender and political communication. She has served as head of department, dean of faculty, University of Malawi Senator and a senate representative on the University Council. She has edited a book and published a monograph and journal articles in the areas of linguistics, human rights, and political communication.

Marjorie Oludhe Macgoye (See page 312.)

Nalishebo N. Meebelo is a PhD candidate in the faculty of Business and Law at Edith Cowan University, Perth. In 2000, she steered the collection and analysis of objective data on Zambia's structural adjustment program (for the decade 1991 to 2000), for book publication, as a research assistant under the Press and Public Relations Department of State House in Zambia. She is a founding member of the Karibu project, which looks at issues relating to the settlement of African students at Edith Cowan University and the Perth Institute of Business and Technology. She is also a founder and active member of the Organisation of all Zambians Living in Western Australia.

Sheila Ali Ryanga is a lecturer in the Department of Kiswahili and African Languages at Kenyatta University, Kenya. She has published a play, and children's books. She has also co-authored several high school class readers. She is a co-editor of the *Methodist Digest* in Kenya, and she has published several articles in international language journals.

Contributing Editors

Tuzyline Jita Allan teaches African American and postcolonial literatures at Baruch College, City University of New York. She is author of the award-winning book *Womanist and Feminist Aesthetics: A Comparative Review*; co-editor of *Literature Around the Globe*; and editor of *Teaching African Literatures in Global Economy*, a special edition of *WSQ: Women's Studies Quarterly*. Allan has published widely on the writings of African and African American women writers. Her latest articles include "Feminist Scholarship in Africa" and "Modernism, Gender, and Africa." She is currently co-director and series editor of *Women Writing Africa*.

Ann Biersteker teaches African languages and literatures at Yale University. She is the author of two books on Swahili poetry and of numerous articles on African literatures and languages.

Text Editor

Florence Howe is emerita professor of English at The Graduate Center, City University of New York. In April 2005, she left retirement to become interim executive director of The Feminist Press at the City University of New York, founded in 1970, which is responsible for the rediscovery of scores of "lost" women writers in the United States and in many countries of the world. She is currently the publisher of The Feminist Press. Since 1994, she has been co-director of Women Writing Africa. She has written or edited more than a dozen books and more than a hundred essays. Her books include *No More Masks! An Anthology of Twentieth-Century Poetry by American Women* (1973 and 1993), *Myths of Co-Education: Selected Essays, 1965–1983* (1984), and *The Politics of Women's Studies: Testimony from 30 Founding Mothers* (2000). She is writing a memoir.

TRANSLATORS AND HEADNOTE WRITERS

Matle Akonaay has been teaching Kiswahili and English in various secondary schools for more than 30 years. He now teaches in a village school in Karatu, Northern Tanzania.

Monica Arac de Nyeko is from Uganda and in 2004 was short-listed for the Caine Prize for Africa Writing for her short story "Strange Fruit." Her fiction and poetry has appeared in several anthologies and magazines including: *Memories of Sun* (Greeenwillow Books), *Fountain Junior HIV Series* (Fountain Publishers), *Word from a Granary*, *Tears of Hope*, *New Era*, and *Wordrite* (FEMRITE Publications). Her recent fiction has appeared in *African Love Stories*—an anthology edited by Ama Ata Aidoo, and is forthcoming in *Miracles, Dreams, and Jazz* the anthology of new fiction from Africa edited by Helon Habila and Khadija George.

Jackee Budesta Batanda is enrolled in the Forced Migration Studies MA program at the University of the Witwatersrand, South Africa. She has been Peace Writer at the Joan B. Kroc Institute for Peace and Justice, University of San Diego, California. A member of the Uganda Women Writers Association (FEMRITE), she has been Writer-in-Residence at Lancaster University where she worked on *The Big Picture*, a collaborative book with three writers from the north west. She was regional winner of the 2003 Commonwealth Short Story Competition. She has published a children's book, *The Blue Marble*. Her stories have been published in various journals and short story anthologies.

Emilia Ilieva is an associate professor in Literature at Egerton University, Kenya. Her publications are in the areas of African literary history, the sociology of African literature and its aesthetics. She has contributed to the *Encyclopedia of Post-Colonial Literatures in English* (1994), *The Encyclopedia of World Literature in the 20th Century* (1999), *The Companion to African Literatures* (2000), *Encyclopedia of Life Writing* (2000), *The Historical Companion to Postcolonial Literatures in English* (2005). She has also translated African fiction into Bulgarian.

Ng'wanza Kamata is a lecturer in political science at the University of Dar es Salaam. He wrote his PhD thesis for the University of Dar es Salaam on environmental change and the politics of control and marginalization in Tanzania. He has published on popular struggles for land rights and democracy in Tanzania.

Jane Kawalya is a librarian at Makerere University. She is also a doctoral student in library and information science at the University of Gothenburg, the Swedish School of Library and Information Science, Boras, Sweden.

Saifu D. Kiango was formerly a senior research fellow at the Institute of Kiswahili Research at the University of Dar es Salaam. He currently freelances as a translator, book reviewer, and evaluator of manuscripts.

Abasi Kiyimba is the deputy dean in charge of administration and finance in the Faculty of Arts at Makerere University. He is also a senior lecturer in the literature department. He has written extensively on the images of women in Ugandan literature and on Ugandan literature in general.

Yusuf Lawi is senior lecturer in history at the University of Dar es Salaam. He teaches African history with a focus on environmental, social, and cultural-historical issues. He has co-published a book and a number of journal articles and book chapters covering themes ranging from local ecological perceptions and their implications for the environment to the ideology of school history in postcolonial Tanzania.

Joshua S. Madumulla is an associate professor in the Department of Kiswahili, teaching Kiswahili literature. He has worked with associations such as the East Africa Book Development Association as deputy chairperson; The National Book Development Council of Tanzania as its first chairperson; The Writers' Association of Tanzania as treasurer; Reading Association of Tanzania as its chairperson; Children's Book Project as chairperson of the Children's Book Committee and as its first training and monitoring coordinator of the reading program. He had published four books.

Bright Molande is lecturer in English Literature, specializing in literary and cultural theory at the University of Malawi. He headed the Department of English between 2003 and 2005 after reading for an MA in Postcolonial Studies (Literature) at the University of Essex, United Kingdom. He is an emerging African postcolonial authority on the theory of "re-writing and power." He also has his first volume of poetry in press.

Hendrine Msosa is a lecturer in African history, specializing in feminist theory and women's history. She holds a PhD from Dalhouise, Halifax and currently heads the history department at Chancellor College, University of Malawi. She has published a number of articles in *The Journal of African History* and *The Journal of Religion in Africa*. Her current area of interest is adaptation of indigenous institutions to change.

Hilda Ntege Mukisa works as an assistant registrar in the Academic Registrar's Department of Makerere University.

Beverley Nambozo is a Ugandan writer born in 1976. She has been a member of the Uganda Women Writers' Association (FEMRITE) since 2000. She has published more than a dozen stories and essays. She is currently working on a collection of erotic poetry and a novel, *Two Lives*. She has also written a few academic papers on gender, media, and literature.

Rehema Nchimbi teaches in the history department of the University of Dar es Salaam. She recently completed her PhD on "Women's Beauty in the History of Tanzania" with the University of Cape Town, South Africa. She has published four scholarly articles, including "Gender, Labor, Capital and Forms of Market Struggles among the Mbugwe Women in Tanzania, 1960s to 2002" and "From *Unyago* to Kitchen Party: Changing Forms and Patterns for Women's Social Adjustment Mechanism in Tanzania."

Milton Obote is a lecturer in literature at Egerton University, Kenya. His teaching and research interests are in the areas of literary theory, and literature and gender. He is currently pursuing PhD studies in the Department of Comparative Literature at the University of Massachusetts.

Lennox Odiemo-Munara is a graduate assistant in literature at Egerton University, Kenya. His academic interests are in postcolonial studies and gender criticism. He writes for Kenya's weeklies, *Sunday Nation* and *The Sunday Standard*, and has contributed to *A Historical Companion to Postcolonial Literatures in English* (2005). He is also a creative writer.

Desmond D. Phiri is a graduate of University of London. He worked as a civil servant in Tanzania and Malawi until 1976 when he founded a private distance education institution called Agrrey Memorial School which he still manages. He has written seventeen books and is a regular columnist in The Nation, one of Malawi's leading newspapers. He holds an honorary degree of PhD from the University of Malawi and is a fellow of the Royal Economics Society.

Martha Qorro is a senior lecturer in the Department of Foreign Languages and Linguistics at the University of Dar es Salaam, Tanzania. She has conducted research and published papers on the specific issue of language of instruction. She has co-authored, with Prof. Zaline Roy-Campbell, *Language Crisis in Tanzania: The Myth of English Versus Education*, recently published.

Stanley Sabuni is a former arts student at the University of Dar es Salaam.

Monde Sifuniso (see page 358.)

Boston Soko obtained his PhD in France in ethno-linguistics. Retired from the University of Malawi in 2001, he is now professor of French at Mzuzu University, Malawi, and the head of Languages and Literature. Soko has written a number of articles and books on African oral literature, including: "Translating Oral Literature into European Languages: The Folklore," "Labour Migration in Vimbuza Songs," and "The Vestiges of Ngoni Oral Literature."

Kapepwa I. Tambila is an associate professor in the history department. He was head of the department in the 1980s, was for a number of years between 1984 and 1995 chairman of the University of Dar es Salaam's Academic Staff Assembly and in 1991 and 1992 a Commissioner in the Presidential Commission on One or Many Parties in Tanzania (the Nyalali Commission). He has been associated with Tanzania Election Monitoring Committee activities since the 1995 elections and the REDET program since 1997 as a principal researcher in Pemba, Zanzibar.

Fugich Wako obtained his PhD in Literature from the University of the Witwatersrand, South Africa. He teaches at Egerton University, Kenya, and is currently chair of the Department of Literature, Languages and Linguistics. He has published a number of articles on gender issues, and is working on a book about the oral literature of the Borana.

Ayeta Anne Wangusa is a Ugandan writer currently based in Tanzania where she works as a Civil Society Strengthening Advisor for the Netherlands Development Organization. She is a founding member of the Uganda Women Writers Association FEMRITE, which published her first novel *Memoirs of a Mother* in 1998. That same year she attended the prestigious Iowa Writers Program in the United States. She was a judge for the Commonwealth Writers Prize (African Region) in April 2003.

Marcia Wright has been an advisor to the Women Writing Africa project from its beginning. She is professor of history at Columbia University, her specialities Eastern and Southern African history.

Abdulhakim S. Yahya, a long-time teacher and retired publisher, is now a writer of educational books in Kiswahili.

Permissions Acknowledgments and Sources

For previously published texts not in the public domain, sources and rights-holders, to the extent possible, are indicated below. Original texts published with permission for the first time in this volume are copyrighted in the names of their authors. Unless otherwise noted, English-language translations commissioned for this volume are copyrighted in the names of their translators. Headnotes contained in this volume were commissioned for this edition and are copyrighted in the name of the Feminist Press. Archives and libraries that provided access to rare texts, or gave permission to reproduce them, are acknowledged below.

In the case of oral materials such as interviews and songs, every effort has been made to locate and gain permission from the original speaker(s). In the case of written materials, every effort has similarly been made to contact the rights-holders. Anyone who can provide information about rights-holders who have not been previously located is urged to contact the Feminist Press. *Those seeking permission to reprint or quote from any part of this book should also contact the Feminist Press at the following address:* Rights and Permissions, The Feminist Press at the City University of New York, Suite 5406, 365 Fifth Avenue, New York, NY 10016.

Sultan Fatima binti Muhammad Mkubwa, Peace and Security
Text from the Archives Museum of Goa, Panaji, India. Translation copyright © 2007 by Ann Bierstecker.

Mwana Kupona binti Msham, FROM A Mother's Advice and Prayer: An Epic Poem
Translation copyright © 2007 by Ann Biersteker and Naomi L. Shitemi. J.W.T. Allen's edition of the poem provided the basis for our translation: *Tendi: Six Examples of a Classical Verse Form with Translation and Notes* (New York: Africana Publishing House, 1971).

Emily Reute, aka Princess Salma of Zanzibar, A Royal Childhood in Zanzibar
Translation copyright © 1993 from Sayyida Salme/Emily Reute 1993. *An Arabian Princess Between Two Worlds.* Ed. and trans. by E. van Donzel. Leiden. The Netherlands: Brill Academic Publishers. Published by permission of Brill Academic Publishers.

Martha Thabi, My God, Why Have You Forsaken Me?
Text from the National Archives of Malawi, Zomba. Translation copyright © 2007 by Desmond D. Phiri.

Jessie Nyagondwe, LET NOT YOUR HEART BE TROUBLED
Text from the National Archives of Malawi, Zomba.

Bwanikwa, TEN TIMES A SLAVE
Translation by Dugald Wright, from Marcia Wright, ed. 1993. *Strategies of Slaves and Women: Life Stories from East/Central Africa*. New York: Lilian Barber Press. Published by permission of Marcia Wright.

E. May Crawford, FACE TO FACE WITH WANGU WA MAKERI
Text from Emily May Crawford. 1913. *By the Equator's Snowy Peak*. London: Church Missionary Society.

Anonymous, BINTI ALI THE CLEVER
Translation from Captain and Mrs. C. H. Stigand. 1914. *Black Tales for White Children*. London: Constable & Company.

Jane Elizabeth Chadwick and Eva Chadwick, MY STUDENTS
Text from the Papers of Miss Jane Elizabeth Chadwick, in the Church Missionary Society Unofficial Papers, University of Birmingham, Information Services, Special Collections Department, Birmingham, UK.

Siti binti Saad, FOUR SONGS
Texts transcribed in Issa Magna. 1991. *Jukwaa la Taarab Zanzibar*. Helsinki: MediAfrica. Translation copyright © 2007 by Saïda Yahya-Othman.

Communal, SONG OF THE COFFEE GIRLS
Translation by Dr. J. W. Arthur.

Luiza, I WANT A DIVORCE
Text from Civil Cases, Feira, 1920–1929, in the National Archives of Zambia, Lusaka.

Zeina binti Mwinyipembe Sekinyaga, CIVILIZED MOTHERHOOD
Text from *Mambo Leo* 1926, in the Institute of Kiswahili Research Archive, University of Dar es Salaam, Tanzania. Translation copyright © 2007 by M.M. Mulokozi.

Mwana Hashima binti Sheikh, A PETITION
Translation copyright © 2007 by Anonymous.

Nyambura wa Kihurani, Raheli Wariga wa Johanna, and Alice Murigo wa Meshak, LETTER OPPOSING FEMALE CIRCUMCISION
Text from the Presbyterian Church of East Africa Archives. Translation copyright © 2007 by Joseph Karauki Murithi.

Miriam Wandai, WHEN OGRES LIVED
Text from Miriam Wandai.1946, *Mundaalo Tsia Amanani*. Nairobi: Highway Press. Translation copyright © 1997 from Barak O. Muluka. 1997. *When Ogres Lived*. Nairobi: East African Educational Publishers. Published by permission of East African Educational Publishers.

C. M. binti Hassan, AN AFRICAN MARRIES A WHITE THROUGH MERE WORLDLY DESIRES
Text from *Mambo Leo* 1946, Institute of Kiswahili Research Archive, University of Dar es Salaam, Tanzania. Translation copyright © 2007 by Martha Qorro.

Nyense Namwandu, FIGHTING FOR A WIDOWS' PROPERTY AND THE RIGHT TO REFUSE MARRIAGE
Text copyright © 2007 from the unpublished papers of Nyense Namwandu. Translation copyright © 2007 by Abasi Kiyimba.

Z and G, WOMEN ARE HUMAN BEINGS
Translation copyright © 1991 by Brigitta Larsson. 1991. *Conversion to Greater Freedom? Women, Church and Social Change in Northwestern Tanzania Under Colonial Rule*. Acta Universitatis Upsaliensis. Stockholm: Almqsuist & Wiksell International.

Bibi Pirira Athumani, TWO POEMS
Texts copyright © 1991 by Bibi Pirira Athumani, from recordings in the Institute of Kiswahili Research Archive, University of Dar es Salaam, Tanzania. Translation copyright © 2007 by M. M. Mulokozi.

Communal, Gidmay: FAREWELL TO A BRIDE
Text collected by Matle Akonaay. Translation copyright © 2007 by Martha Qorro and Yusuf Lawi.

Mama Meli, FROM SLAVERY TO FREEDOM
Text copyright © 1954 by H. E. Silanda, from *Uzya wakwe mama meli*, Lusaka and Blantyre: Publications Bureau. Translation by M. Sichilongo and Barbara Lea, copyright © 1993, from Marcia Wright, ed. 1993. *Strategies of Slaves and Women: Life Stories from East/Central Africa*. New York: Lilian Barber Press. Published by permission of Marcia Wright.

L. B., THE IMPORTANCE OF READING
Text from *Mthenga*, 1951, National Archives of Malawi, Zomba. Translation copyright © 2007 by Bright Molande and Fulata L. Moyo.

Ng'washi ng'wana Nzuluge, AND BIRDS WILL MOURN HER
Text copyright © 1999 by Ng'washi ng'wana Nzuluge, recorded by Stanley Sabuni, Ilumba, Kwimba District, Mwanza Region, Malawi, December 1999. Translation copyright © 2007 by Stanley Sabuni and Amandina Lihamba.

Zaynab Himid Muhamed, LETTER ON OWNING LAND
Text copyright © 2007 by Saïda Yahya-Othman. Published by permission of Saïda Yahya-Othman.

Florence Lubega, DEBATE ON HIGHER EDUCATION
Text copyright © 1959, from the Hansard of the Parliament of Uganda, Proceedings of the Legislative Council's 39th Session, Part II, 1959.

Joyce Masembe Mpanga, SPEECH TO THE LEGISLATIVE COUNCIL
Text copyright © 1961, from the Hansard of the Parliament of Uganda, Proceedings of the Legislative Council, June 6, 1961.

Joyce Masembe Mpanga, GAYAZA HIGH SCHOOL AT THE DAWN OF MODERN TIMES 1947–1952
Text copyright © 1989 by Joyce Masembe Mpanga, from the Gayaza High School's *Golden Jubilee* magazine, Kampala, Uganda, 1989.

Anonymous, PRAISED BE JESUS CHRIST
Translation copyright © 2007 by Kapepwa Tambila.

Princess Nakatindi, BLESSING THE JOURNEY OF KENNETH KAUNDA
Text copyright © 1963. Published in E. Dahlschen. 1970. *Women in Zambia*. Lusaka: Educational Company of Zambia.

Princess Nakatindi, PRINCESS OF POLITICS
Text copyright © 1971, from the *Sunday Times of Zambia* 1:31, May 30, 1971, in the National Archives of Zambia, Lusaka.

S. Nyakire, LETTER ON SECLUSION
Text copyright © 1964 from *Kiongozi*, July 1, 1964. Translation copyright © 2007 by Kapepwa Tambila.

Genda Mislay Lohi, AN UNUSUAL GIRLHOOD
Text © copyright 1964, 2007 by Martha Qorro, recorded by Martha Qorro in Tanzania, 1964. Published by permission of Martha Qorro. Translation copyright © 2007 by Martha Qorro.

Rose Chibambo, THE TRUTH WILL ALWAYS SPEAK
Text copyright © 1964, published in *The Lamp*, Malawi, 2000.

Susan Buxton Wood, WHAT WE HAVE IN COMMON
Text copyright © 1964, from Susan Buxton Wood. 1964. *A Fly in Amber*. London: Collins-Harville.

Babro Johansson, THE ADVANCEMENT OF WOMEN
Texts copyright © 1964, 1965, from the Hansard of the Parliament of Tanzania, February 20, 1964, and June 29, 1965. Published by permission of the Speaker of the National Assembly. Translation copyright © 2007 by Saïda Yahya-Othman and M.M. Mulokozi.

Lucy Lameck, AFRICANS ARE NOT POOR
Text copyright © 1965, from the Hansard of the Parliament of Tanzania, June 15, 1965. Published by permission of the Speaker of the National Assembly. Translation copyright © 2007 by Saifu Kiango and M.M. Mulokozi.

Bibi Titi Mohamed, SACRIFICES FOR CHANGE
Text copyright © 1965, 1967, from the Hansard of the Parliament of Tanzania, June 14, 1965, and July 1, 1967. Published by permission of the Speaker of the National Assembly. Translation copyright © 2007 by Saifu Kiango, Saïda Yahya-Othman, and Amandina Lihamba.

Hannah Kahiga, A MODEL DAY DURING THE EMERGENCY
Text copyright © 1966, recorded and broadcast on "In Black and White, Radio Uganda, 1966; published in David Cook, ed. 1976. "In Black and White." Nairobi: East African Literature Bureau. Published by permission of the Kenya Literature Bureau.

Grace Akinyi Ogot, ELIZABETH
Text copyright © 1968, from Grace Akinyi Ogot. 1968. *Land Without Thunder*. Nairobi: East African Educational Publishers. Published by permission of East African Educational Publishers.

Hamida Mohamedali, THE RETREAT
Text copyright © 1967, from Leonard Okola, ed. 1967. *Down Beat: East African Poems*. Nairobi: East African Educational Publishers. Published by permission of East African Educational Publishers.

Rose Mbowa, RUIN and THAT GAME
Text copyright © 1971, from David Cook and David Rubadiri, eds. 1971. *Poems from East Africa*. Nairobi: East African Educational Publishers. Published by permission of East African Educational Publishers.

Rose Mbowa, LIGHT
Text copyright © 1967, from *East Africa Journal*, January 1967.

Mwajjuma Nalwadda, A WIDOW'S LAND INHERITANCE
Text copyright © 2007 by Mwajjuma Nalwadda, from unpublished personal papers of Mwajjima Nalwadda. Translation © copyright 2007 by Abasi Kiyimba.

Grace Akello, PRAY, NO REVENGE
Text copyright © 1979 by Grace Akello, from Grace Akello. 1979. *The Barred Entry*. Nairobi. Published by permission of Grace Akello.

Miriam K. Were, THE MISCHIEVOUS COW
Text copyright © 1980, from Miriam K. Were. 1980. *Your Heart Is My Altar*. Nairobi: East African Educational Publishers. Published by permission of East African Educational Publishers.

Anna Chipaka, A BAR-MAID'S LIFE
Text copyright © 1980, from Magdalena K. Ngaiza and Bertha Koda, eds. 1980. *The Unsung Heroines: Women's Life Histories from Tanzania*. Dar es Salaam: Women's Research and Documentation Project. Published by permission of the Women's Research and Documentation Project. Translation by copyright © 1980 by Alice Nkhoma-Wamunza.

Fatma binti Athuman, MY HUSBAND WENT TO PATE
Text copyright © 2007 by Fatma binti Athuman. Translation © copyright 2007 by Ann Biersteker.

Fatma binti Athuman, THE DAUGHTER, THE MOTHER, AND THE HUSBAND
Text copyright © 1996, from Ann Bierstecker. 1996. *Kujibizana: Questions of Language and Power in Nineteenth- and Twentieth-Century Poetry in Kiswahili*. East Lansing: Michigan State University Press. Translation copyright © 1996 by Ann Biersteker and Salma Hussein.

Zaynab Himid Mohammed, From HUSH, MY CHILD: OF ONIONS AND FRANKINCENSE
Text copyright © 1983, from *Kiswahili Journal* 50 (September 2, 1983), Institute of Kiswahili Research, University of Dar es Salaam, Tanzania. Published by permission of the Institute of Swahili Research. Translation copyright © 2007 by Abdulhakim Yahya.

Miria Obote, SPEECH ON INTERNATIONAL WOMEN'S DAY
Text copyright © 1984, published by permission of Miria Obote.

Queen Namunyala, THE LANGUAGE OF HEALERS
Text copyright © 1998 by Queen Namunyala, recorded by Jackee Budesta Batanda, Uganda, 1998. Translation copyright © 2007 by Jackee Budesta Batanda.

Communal, ONE BLANKET
Text copyright © 1996, 2007, recorded by Florence Ebila, Odokomit, Lira, Uganda, 1996; published in Florence Ebila. *The Portal of Gender Relations in Lango Oral Poetry and Its Part in the Socialisation Process*. M. A. thesis, Makerere University, 1997. Translation copyright © 1997 by Florence Ebila.

Langi Women of Odokomit, THE IMPOTENT ONE CLIMBED A TREE
Text copyright © 1996, 2007, recorded in Odokomit, Lira, Uganda, 1996. Translation copyright © 2007 by Florence Ebila.

S. C. Hara, THE GREEDY HUSBAND
Text copyright © 1997, 2007 by S. C. Hara, recorded in Ekwendeni, Mzimba, Malawi, 1997. Translation copyright © 2007 by Boston J. Soko and Edrinnie Lora-Kayambazinthu.

Women of Rumphi District, THREE *VISEKESE* SONGS
Text copyright © 2000, 2007 recorded in Rumphi, Malawi, 2000. Translation copyright © 2007 by Boston J. Soko and Edrinnie Lora-Kayambazinthu.

Loise Kalondu wa Maseki, MAKE LOVE NOT BABIES
Text copyright © 2000, 2007 by Loise Kalondu wa Maseki, recorded in Katui Kenya, 2000. Translation copyright © 2007 by Sheila Ali Ryanga.

Njira Chenga, THE IRRESPONSIBLE HUSBAND
Text copyright © 2001, 2007, recorded in Kenya, 2001. Translation copyright © 2007 by Boston J. Soko and Edrinnie Lora-Kayambazinthu.

Communal, MR. NYIRONGO I and MR. NYIRONGO II
Text copyright © 1997, 2007, recorded in Mzimba, Malawi, 1997. Translation copyright © 2007 by Boston J. Soko.

Communal, MOTHER-IN-LAW
Text copyright © 1997, 2007, recorded in Mzimba, Malawi, 1997. Translation copyright © 2007 by Desmond D. Phiri.

Monde Sifuniso, BEIJING, BEIJING
Text copyright © 1997 by Monde Sifuniso, from Norah Mumba and Monde Sifunsio, eds. 1997. *The Heart of a Woman: Short Stories from Zambia*. Lusaka: Zambia Women Writers Association. Published by permission of Monde Sifuniso.

Marjorie Oludhe Macgoye, THE WASTING DISEASE
Text copyright © 1997 by Marjorie Oludhe Macgoye, from Marjorie Oludhe Macgoye. 1997. *Chira*. East Lansing: Michigan State University Press and Nairobi: East African Educational Publishers. Published by permission of the author.

Esther Mwachiru, My Mother, My Hero
Text copyright © 2001, 2007, by Esther Shadrack Mwachiru, recorded by
Sheila Ali Ryanga, Pingilikani, Kilifi, Kenya, 2001. Translation copyright ©
2007 Sheila Ali Ryanga.

Communal, Nine Lullabies from Zanzibar
Texts copyright © 2002, 2007, recorded in Zanzibar, Tanzania, 2002. Translation copyright © 2007 by Saïda Yahya-Othman.

Communal, Four Lullabies from Uganda
Text copyright © 2002, 2007, recorded in Uganda, 2002. Translation copyright
© 2007 by Florence Ebila.

Communal, Four Lullabies from Zambia
Text copyright © 2002, 2007, recorded in Zambia, 2002. Translation copyright
© 2007 by Nalishebo N. Meebelo.

Miria Matembe, I Must Call Myself a Feminist
Text copyright © 2002, 2007 by Miria Matembe, from Miria R. K. Matembe
with Nancy R. Dorsey. 2002. Miria Matembe: *Gender, Politics and Constitution
Making in Uganda*. Kampala: Fountain Publishers. Published by permission of
Fountain Publishers.

Ruth Meena, The Female Husband
Text copyright © 2007 by Ruth Meena.

Martha Qorro, Language in Tanzania
Text copyright © 2003 by Martha Qorro, from talk delivered to National Executive Committee, Chama cha Mapinduzi, July 2003. Published by permission
of Martha Qorro. Translation copyright © 2007 by Abdulhakim Yahya and
Saïda Yahya-Othman.

Monica Arac de Nyeko, In the Stars
Text copyright © 2003 by Monica Arac de Nyeko, first prize winner in
"Women's Voices in War Zones," sponsored by Women's WORLD (Women's
Organization for Rights, Literature and Development: www.wworld.org) with
The Nation Institute.

Margaret Wangui Mwema, Wacu and the Eagle
Text copyright © 2007 by Margaret Wangui Mwema. Translation copyright ©
2007 by Lawrence Mwema.

Wangari Maathai, Nobel Peace Prize Lecture
Text copyright © 2004 by the Nobel Foundation. Published by permission of
the Nobel Foundation.

AUTHORS LISTED BY COUNTRY

KENYA

Alice Murigo wa Meshak, Anonymous, Grace Awach, Eva Chadwick, Jane Elizabeth Chadwick, Njira Chenga, Communal, E. May Crawford, Fatma binti Athman, Katherine Wanjiru Getao, Nellie Grant, Elspeth Huzley, Hannah Kahiga, Neera Kapur-Dromson, Wangari Maathai, Marjorie Oludhe Macgoye, Loise Kalondu wa Maseki, Hamida Mohamedali, Field Marshal Muthoni-Kirima, Esther Shadrack Mwachiru, Esther Mwachombo, Mwana Hashima binti Sheikh, Mwana Kupona binti Msham, Margaret Wangui Mwema, Nyambura wa Kihurani, Margaret A. Ogola, Grace Akinyi Ogot, Margery Perham, Charlotte Poda, Qabale Kosi, Raheli Wariga wa Johanna, Hannah Tsumah, Miriam Wandai, Miriam K. Were, Susan Buxton Wood

MALAWI

Chauwa Banda, Rose Chibambo, Communal, S.C. Hara, Janet Karim, L.B., Emily Mkandawire, Jessie Nyagondwe, Martha Thabi, Women of Rumphi District

TANZANIA

Anonymous, Bibi Pirira Athumani, Bibi Titi Mohamed, Anna Chipaka, C.M. binti Hassan, Communal, Genda Mislay Lohi, Barbro Johansson, Pelagia Aloyse Katunzi, Lucy Lameck, Eliesha Lema, Sultan Fatima binti Muhammad Mkubwe, Ng'washi ng'wana Nzuluge, S. Nyakire, Zehra Peera, Penina Muhando Mlama, Martha Qorro, Emily Ruete, Siti binti Saad, Vuyo Ophelia Wagi, Z and G, Zaynab Himid Muhamed, Zeina binti Mwinyipembe Sekinyaga, Zeyana Ali Muh'd

UGANDA

Grace Akello, Sarah Atoo, Beta Aida, Communal, Monica Arac de Nyeko, Erusa Kibanda, Susan Kiguli, Lusi Kyebakutika, Goretti Kyomuhendo, Lalweny Fanta, Christine Lamwaku, Langi Women of Odokomit, Florence Lubega, Joyce Masembe Mpanga, Miria Matembe, Rose Mbowa, Mothers Union Members, Winnie Munyarugerero, Ester Nakate, Mwajjuma Nalwadda, Nyense Namwandu, Sarah Nyendwoha Ntiro, Miria Obote, Queen Namunyala, Santa Apoto, Sister Mary John

ZAMBIA

Bwanikwa, Communal, Tsitsi V. Himunyanga-Phiri, Mrs. E. Akapelwa Inambwae, Martha Kapanga, Luiza, Mbuyu Nalumango, Mama Meli, Mary Penelope Mfune, Princess Kaiko Nambayo, Princess Nakatindi, Monde Sifuniso

INDEX